Discrete Event Simulations

edited by
Aitor Goti

Discrete Event Simulations
Edited by Aitor Goti

Published by InTech
Janeza Trdine 9, 51000 Rijeka, Croatia

Publishing Process Manager Ana Nikolic

Technical Editor Teodora Smiljanic

Cover Designer InTech Design Team

Additional hard copies can be obtained from orders@intechopen.com

Discrete Event Simulations, Edited by Aitor Goti
p. cm.
ISBN 978-953-307-115-2

For EU product safety concerns:
IN TECH d.o.o., Prolaz Marije Krucifikse Kozulić 3, 51000 Rijeka, Croatia,
info@intechopen.com or visit our website at intechopen.com.

Meet the editor

Aitor Goti Elordi is Engineer in Industrial Management from Mondragon University and Ph.D. from Politechnic University of Valencia. He is currently lecturer at the University of Deusto, where he teaches in the Bilbao campus. His teaching focuses on the degrees of the department of Industrial Technologies and the double degree in Business administration plus Engineering. Specifically, he teaches Business Administration (Basque and Spanish), Management of processes via ERP information systems, Industrial Organization, Economics and Technical Office (English and Spanish). His publications are focused mainly with Industrial Organization. He belongs to the Industrial Management and Logistics research group, recognized as group by the University since 2002. Other interest areas of research are: Maintenance, Operations, Discrete Event Simulation, ERP, BIG DATA.

Contents

Preface IX

Chapter 1 **Discrete Event Simulation** 1
Professor Eduard Babulak and Dr Ming Wang

Chapter 2 **A dynamically configurable discrete event simulation framework for many-core chip multiprocessors** 11
Christopher Barnes and Jaehwan John Lee

Chapter 3 **Modelling methods based on discrete algebraic systems** 35
Hiroyuki Goto

Chapter 4 **Supply chain design: guidelines from a simulation approach** 63
Eleonora Bottani and Roberto Montanari

Chapter 5 **A simulation technology for supply-chain integration** 79
Shigeki Umeda

Chapter 6 **Optimisation of reordering points considering purchasing, storing and service breakdown costs** 105
Aitor Goti and Miguel Ortega

Chapter 7 **Reverse logistics: end-of-life recovery pledge** 115
R.C. Michelini and R.P. Razzoli

Chapter 8 **Simulating service systems** 141
Raid Al-Aomar

Chapter 9 **Evaluation of methods for scheduling clinic appointments in surgical service: a statecharts-based simulation study** 165
Boris G. Sobolev, PhD, Victor Sanchez, MSc and Lisa Kuramoto, MSc

Chapter 10 **Condition based maintenance optimization of multi-equipment manufacturing systems by combining discrete event simulation and multiobjective evolutionary algorithms** 187
Aitor Goti and Alvaro Garcia

Chapter 11 **Advanced discrete event simulation methods with application to importance measure estimation in reliability** 205
Arne Huseby, Bent Natvig, Jørund Gåsemyr, Kristina Skutlaberg and Stefan Isaksen

Chapter 12 **Agent-based modelling and simulation of network cyber-attacks and cooperative defence mechanisms** 223
Igor Kotenko

Chapter 13 **Wireless sensor networks: modeling and simulation** 247
Sajjad A. Madani, Jawad Kazmi and Stefan Mahlknecht

Chapter 14 **Discrete event simulation of wireless cellular networks** 263
Enrica Zola, Israel Martín-Escalona and Francisco Barceló-Arroyo

Chapter 15 **Discrete-event supervisory control for under-load tap-changing transformers (ULTC): from synthesis to PLC implementation** 285
Ali A. Afzalian, S. M. Noorbakhsh and W. M. Wonham

Chapter 16 **Stability analysis of 2-d linear discrete feedback control systems with state delays on the basis of lagrange solutions** 311
Guido Izuta

Preface

This book is an initiative encouraged by Sciyo to promote the Discrete Event Simulation (DES) technique. Considered by many authors as a technique for modelling stochastic, dynamic and discretely evolving systems, this evolution of Monte Carlo stochastic but static technique has gained widespread acceptance among the practitioners who want to represent and improve complex systems. Since DES is a technique applied in incredibly different areas, this book entitled Discrete Event Simulations reflects many different points of view about DES, thus, all authors describe how DES is understood and applied within their context of work, providing an extensive understanding of what DES is. It can be said that the name of the book itself, Discrete Event Simulations, reflects the plurality that these points of view represented.

The manuscript embraces a number of topics covering theory, methods and applications to a wide range of sectors and problem areas that have been categorised into the following five groups:

The first group presents some of the latest evolutions in the technologies of DES. Thus, it begins with the work by Babulak & Wang, who present the state of the art in the DES technologies. Secondly, the manuscript developed by Barnes & Lee discusses the design and construction of a dynamically configurable DES framework for many-core chip multiprocessors. Third, Goto goes deep into the modelling methods, presenting a choice based on discrete algebraic systems.

The second set of chapters introduces elements related to the design and management of supply chains: Bottani & Montanari start this set of chapters by describing some important guidelines for the design of supply chains, and this work is followed by Umeda, who demonstrated the modelling capabilities of a simulation framework proposed. After that, Goti & Ortega introduce a DES based optimizer of reordering points they have developed and applied within the context of a research project. Lastly, Michelini & Razzoli present a software tool for consultation aid for the management of reverse end-of-life logistics.

The third group deals with the management of simulation of system services in general. Al-Aomar begins this section by presenting the simulation basics of service systems with application case studies. After that Sobolev, Sanchez & Kuramoto summarise a simulation study based on state charts for the evaluation of methods for scheduling clinic appointments in surgical services. Finally, Goti & Garcia present a maintenance optimisation case where DES and multi-objective evolutionary algorithms are applied.

The fourth arrangement analyses issues related to dependability, the dependability being a system property that integrates such attributes as reliability, availability, safety, security, and maintainability. In this area Huseby, Natvig, Gasemyr, Skutlaberg&Isaksen, use the advantage that DES provides in the modelling of multi-component systems for its application to the area of reliability estimation. After that and embracing the whole concept of vulnerability, the work of Kotenko represents the conceptual framework for modelling and simulation, the implementation peculiarities of the simulation environment as well as the experiments aimed on the investigation of distributed network attacks and defence mechanisms.

The last series of chapters is closely related to information technologies and electric-electronic hardware and software: within this group, Madani, Kazmi & Mahlknecht present their latest developments in the modelling and simulation of wireless sensor networks by using DES. Zola, Martin-Escalona & Barcelo-Arroyo work in the same direction, but they centre on the simulation of wireless cellular networks, analysing layout and mobility issues, concerns related to the radio channel used, technology dependent restrictions and simulation elements. After that, Afzalian, Noorbakhsh & Wonham describe the procedure they have followed to implement in Programmable-Logic-Controllers or otherwise known PLCs, a discrete-event supervisory control for under-load tap-changing transformers. This series ends by presenting a stability analysis for a class of 2-d feedback control systems, this being a work non-limited to but mainly applied in the world of electronics.

As well as the previously explained variety of points of view concerning DES, there is one additional thing to remark about this book: its richness when talking about actual data or actual data based analysis. When most academic areas are lacking application cases, roughly the half part of the chapters included in this book deal with actual problems or at least are based on actual data. Thus, the editor firmly believes that this book will be interesting for both beginners and practitioners in the area of DES.

Editor

Aitor Goti
University of Mondragon – Mondragon Unibertsitatea, Spain

1

Discrete Event Simulation

Professor Eduard Babulak and Dr Ming Wang
University of the South Pacific, Suva, Fiji and Air Industry
babulak@ieee.org, ming604@telus.net

Abstract

Discrete-event simulation represents modeling, simulating, and analyzing systems utilizing the computational and mathematical techniques, while creating a model construct of a conceptual framework that describes a system. The system is father simulates by performing experiment(s) using computer implementation of the model and analyzed to draw conclusions from output that assist in decision making process. Discrete event simulation technologies have been extensively used by industry and academia to deal with various industrial problems. By late 1990s, the discrete event simulation was in doldrums as global manufacturing industries went through radical changes. The simulation software industry also went through consolidation. The changes have created new problems, challenges and opportunities to the discrete event simulation. This chapter reviews the discrete event simulation technologies; discusses challenges and opportunities presented by both global manufacturing and the knowledge economy. The authors believe that discrete event simulation remains one of the most effective decision support tools but much need to be done in order to address new challenges. To this end, the chapter calls for development of a new generation of discrete event simulation software.

Keywords: Discrete and interactive simulations, hybrid manufacturing systems, what-if-analysis, systems modeling.

1. Overview of Discrete Event Simulation Technologies

Discrete event simulation quantitatively represents the real world, simulates its dynamics on an event-by-event basis, and generates detailed performance report. It has long become one of the mainstream computer-aided decision-making tools due to availability of powerful computer [1]. Figure 1 illustrates the ways of study a system. Most often system is studied via experiment with actual model, or experiment with a model of actual system.

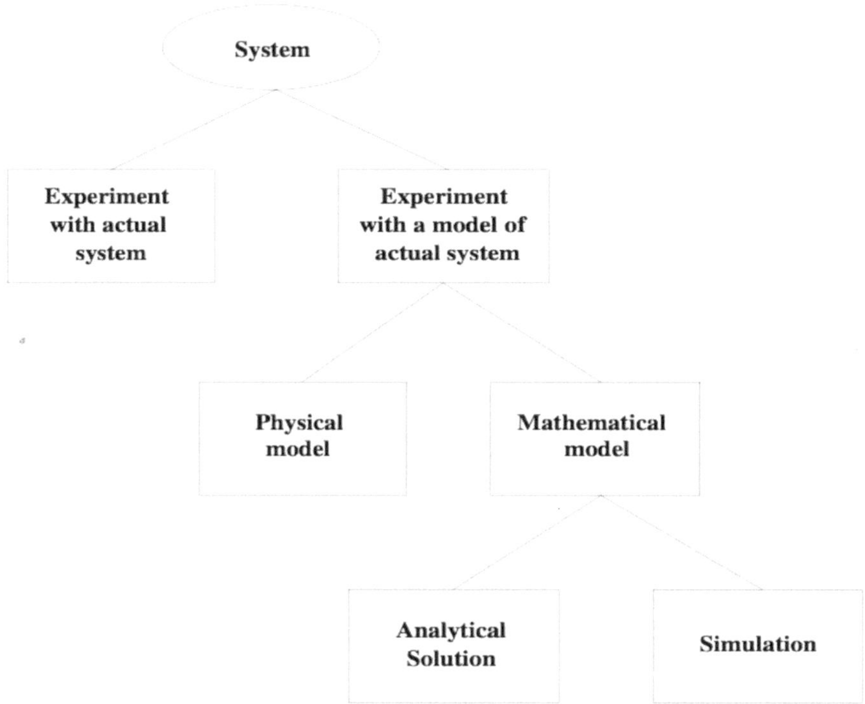

Fig. 1. Ways to study a system [15].

Figure 2, illustrates the model taxonomy used in the simulation process utilizing either deterministic or stochastic models.

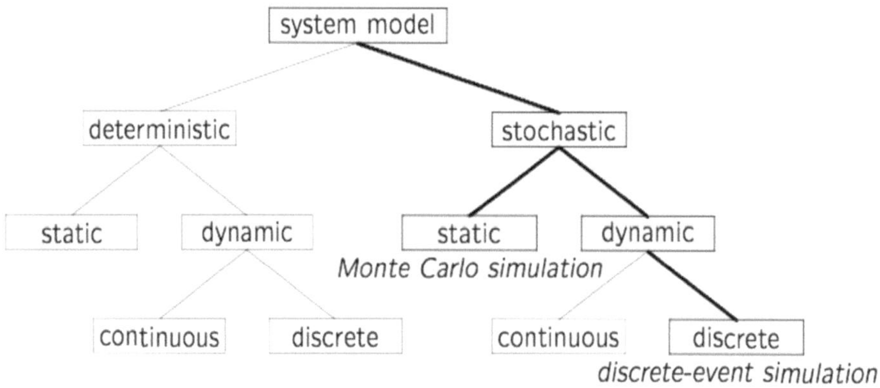

Fig. 2. Model Taxonomy [15]

The development of the discrete event simulation software has been evolved progressively since 1960s, and many systems have been developed by industry and academia to deal with various industrial problems. In brief, four generation of simulation software products have evolved [2], these being:

- ***1st Generation (late 1960s)*** - Programming in high level languages (H.L.L) such as FORTRAN. The modeler was obliged to program both the model logic and the code to control the events and activities, or 'simulation engine', in the model.
- ***2nd Generation (late 1970s)*** - Simulation languages that have commands like event control "engine", statistical distribution generation, reporting, etc. A model in the simulation language was compiled and then linked with the supplied subroutines to produce an executable model. Examples are GPSS (IBM), See Why (AT&T), AutoMod(ASI).
- ***3rd Generation (early 1980s)*** - Simulation language generators that are front-end packages that generate the code in a simulation language. The generated code is complied and then linked to produce an executable model. It reduced the model development time, but still required the modeler to master all aspects of the simulation mechanism. Examples are SIMAN (Systems Modeling), EXPRESS (AT&T).
- ***4th Generation (late 1980s)*** - Interactive simulation packages that enable "what you see is what you get", allow models to be modified at any time, speed up 'what-if' analysis. The simulation models can be built very quickly by industrial managers and engineers, thus encouraging those people with knowledge and first hand experience of the problem to build the model themselves. The example is WITNESS (AT&T), ARENA (Systems Modeling).

By mid 1990s, the virtual reality technology had created a new excitement among the simulation community. A significant amount of effort was made in developing an integrated simulation environment by which engineers can simulate product design and manufacture without going through different simulation packages. The two leading simulation software vendors at that time, Lanner Group and Deneb Inc., announced a plan to jointly develop a new generation of simulation software to support both process and detailed simulation with superior modeling and graphic capabilities. However, the excitement was soon overshadowed by unprecedented changes in manufacturing industries as a result of globalization. The simulation software vendors went through the industrial consolidation. AutoSimulation, System Modeling, Simple++, Deneb, are now part of large corporations. There are new breed of vendors with different business models and using internet for online product sales and support, noticeably Simul8 Inc.

Overall, there is no significant development in the discrete event simulation technologies and software since the 4th generation. On the other hand, tremendous changes in business environment have presented new challenges and opportunities to the discrete event simulation as discussed below.

The paper presents in first section the review of discrete event simulation technologies. The second section discusses the applications of discrete event simulations in manufacturing sector and in the third section in education sector. In last two sections four and five, authors discuss future opportunities and conclusions.

2. Applications of Discrete Event Simulation in Manufacturing Sector

Discrete event simulation is traditionally used for industrial applications. In the 1980s and 1990s, there had been a rapid development of advanced manufacturing technology in industrialized countries: CAD (Computer-aided Design), CAM (Computer-aided Manufacture), AGV (Automatic Guided Vehicle), Robotics, FMS (Flexible Manufacturing System) and CIM (computer integrated manufacturing) in industrialized countries. The same can be said about the discrete event simulation technologies. Many companies had invested heavily in new technologies in order to make their manufacturing operations flexible. The discrete event computer simulation software was the tool to help managers make right decisions. Every production manager wanted to improve productivity in terms of higher throughput, shorter lead time, low work-in-process and high resource utilization. Through simulation, they could evaluate behavior of a manufacturing process under different sets of conditions; carry out 'what-if' scenario analysis in order to identify better physical configuration and operational policies. Overall the discrete event simulation software has been used in the following areas [3]:

1) Design and evaluation of new manufacturing processes.
2) Performance improvement of existing manufacturing processes, for example, feasibility study of an automated material handling system.
3) Establishment of optimum operational policies, for example, studying how many Kanban cards should be introduced on production shop floor in order to reduce work-in-progress.
4) An algorithm (or engine) to support production planning and scheduling.

A survey sponsored by the Department of Trade and Industry of the UK showed that the simulation modeling is used at all levels of management in the 500 largest corporations in the United States. It also found that where simulation has been used, capital costs were saved between 5% and 10% [4]. Manufacturing sector was the main market for the discrete event simulation software.

Changing business environment and new challenges: By late 1990s, the manufacturing landscape started to change rapidly, with China emerged as the "world manufacturing base". Many corporations have either outsourced their productions to third party or relocated their production lines to low-wager countries. One example is Motorola Inc. In the 1990s Motorola run 6 plants in Singapore, Malaysia and Philippines. The managers and engineers had used the discrete event simulation software for productivity improvement. Since early 2000s, Motorola went through several rounds of restructure. Now most of the plants are owned and run by two corporations spin-off from Motorola, On Semiconductors Corp and Freescale Semiconductors Corp. For those that remain in Motorola, some production lines have been relocated to China and some have been outsourced to sub-contract manufactures. Essentially Motorola does not run any manufacturing operations in Singapore, Malaysia and Philippines. The company has set up Global Supply Chain Control Office in Singapore to manage "its global third party component procurement activities"[5].

When a company is going through transformation, applications of discrete event simulation are always in doldrums. The large scale of "industrial transformation" has led to new problems to managers and new challenges to discrete event simulation technologies, as described below:

1). **Virtual corporation:** Global manufacturing and supply chain simply means multiple locations and multiple parties involved in global supply-chain. It also means complicated relationships among all parties, so called "virtual corporation". With zero inventory and just-in-time practice, all parties work under pressure. It would be ideal if all parties to understand behavior of the entire supply chain and impacts from their individual operations on the supply chain. It requires each of the parties to model an individual operation and to share the model and data with the others. It is no longer an isolated model but the *distributed modeling and simulation*. There are research works in the distributed modeling and simulation, noticeably, High Level Architecture (HLA), "the standard architecture for defense programs in the United States" [6]. Recently efforts have been made in applying HLA to industrial applications [7, 8].

2). **Hybrid manufacturing systems:** Many corporations have shut down highly automated plants in industrials countries and shifted production to low-wage countries where operations are primitive with limited managerial and engineering skills. What has emerged in low-cost countries is a mixture of advanced machinery and abundant of labors, a hybrid manufacturing system. Typically, advanced machines are used to carry out certain processes where quality consistency or high precision is critical, whilst all auxiliary processes and material transfer are done manually. The hybrid manufacturing system proves to have much higher responsive flexibility than an automatic manufacturing system, that is, the ability to increase or reduce production capacity rapidly and significantly.

Historically the discrete event simulation software was developed to model and simulate automate manufacturing processes. In a hybrid manufacturing system, human factors play a prominent role and are more important than advanced machines in influencing the system performance. Therefore it is critical to model human performance with different level of skills and under various working conditions.

There are many studies on human performance modelling, for example, the work by the human performance modelling technical group of the Human Factors and Ergonomics Society, by the International Society for Performance Improvement. However, the discrete event simulation software has not taken the findings into account and it remains problematic to model the human performance. At present, commercial discrete event simulation software are not able to handle these issues both effectively and efficiently. Much more work need to be done to make the discrete event simulation software capable of modeling *all* manufacturing activities in ear of globalization.

3. Applications of Discrete Event Simulation in Service Sector

Whilst manufacturing sector is on the decline, service sector in industrialized countries has been expanding fast. The scale of operation has been increased significantly and the nature of operation has become very complicated. Managers have tried to balance excellent customer service with operational efficiency (meaning shorter processing time, less waiting time for customers and higher resource utilization). Many of them have found that discrete event simulation can help them make right decision. In the way similar to manufacturing applications, they use the discrete event simulation software to model their business processes and evaluate behavior of the service system under different sets of conditions;

carry out 'what-if' scenario analysis in order to identify better way to deliver their services [9, 10]. Some examples are:

- Banking and finance services: call center modeling & simulation, bank branch modeling & simulation, simulation of vehicle routing (cash carriage services) and number of cash carriage services per routing, simulation study of cash management of ATM such as minimum re-order point, optimum budget and so on.
- Healthcare and hospitals: in-patient and out-patient waiting list modeling, bed planning, new/existing facility modeling, hospital and service expansion/merger, operation theatre scheduling etc.
- Logistic and transportation: shipping strategy analysis, design of sorting centers and/or material handling system, manpower and facility planning etc.
- Public sector: modeling of police emergency response, optimization of armed response vehicle deployment, re-engineering criminal investigation process etc.

Modeling of service operations is different from that of manufacturing operations, as described below:

1) **Process flow**: A manufacturing process is always associated with physical flows of materials/components and therefore can be easily identified. It may not be the case for many service applications where business activities are information-based and triggered by an external or internal event such as a written or oral request. The current solution is to use a business process mapping tool to capture the business process and then convert the process model to the discrete event simulation model [KBSI, Lanner].

2) **Process related data such as processing time:** In a manufacturing company, industrial engineers are responsible for time study, setting processing time and balancing flow. Most of service companies do not hire industrial engineers or have equivalent position within organizations. As a result, much of the process related data are not readily available.

3) **Knowledge workers:** In many service companies, employees work primarily with information or develop and use knowledge. They are *knowledge workers,* a term coined by Peter Drucker. A knowledge worker tends to be self-motivated, work interactively and make decisions constantly. How to represent knowledge workers and human-decision making process in discrete event simulation remains a subject under study [10].

In the postindustrial economy, the service sector makes up more than half of the American economy. Since mid 1990s, the sector has generated almost all of the US economy increases in employment. Knowledge workers are now estimated to outnumber all other workers in North America by at least a four to one margin [11]. Thus, there is a great potential for discrete event simulation technologies in service sector. However, new approach and techniques are required to model and simulate knowledge workers and their decision-making processes.

4. New Opportunities for Discrete Event Simulation

The changing business environment and technological developments have created other opportunities for discrete event simulation technologies. In particular, we would highlight following two areas::

1) **Business Intelligence (BI) systems:** Throughout 1990s ERP systems had taken the centre stage in the electronic enterprise. Corporations have spent a great amount of resources and effort in implementing ERP systems. Now many corporations have a solid IT infrastructure

in place with a high degree of information integration. From the discrete event simulation viewpoint, it is much easier to get the data to drive a simulation model than before as the data is readily available from the ERP system. The management focus has shifted from getting information to making intelligent use of information for improving business performance. Business Intelligence (BI) software helps companies have a more comprehensive knowledge of the factors affecting their business, such as metrics on sales, production and internal operations. However, to make better business decision, one has to consider how to deploy resources to the opportunities being identified, or *process capability*. The discrete event simulation is an ideal platform to support managers to make decisions on the resource deployment or process capability. Therefore a complete Business Intelligence (BI) system should include both the data analysis capability and a predictive technology. The data analysis capability gathers and analyzes large quantities of unstructured data such as production metrics, sales statistics, attendance reports and customer attrition figures with emphasis of having a comprehensive knowledge of the factors affecting business. The predictive technology enables managers to evaluate different options in order to make right business decisions.

2) **Simulation-based Education:** When a corporation has decided to outsource production to third party, a major implication is how to sustain the in-house engineering knowledge and expertise in the long term, provided that the corporation still wants to design and develop their own products. Erosion of engineering knowledge and expertise is the challenge not only to corporations but also to educational establishments in industrialized countries. One possible solution is to create a simulated manufacturing environment for executives, managers, engineers and students to experience and learn how to manage manufacturing and logistical operations. Discrete event simulation is an ideal platform for such an application. Moreover, there is abundance of simulation cases and models which can be adopted for the engineering and business education. Given current advances in Internet and Telecommunications Technologies, the future of logistics and manufacturing process will become fully automated [12, 13].

5. Conclusions

Discrete event simulation technologies have been up and down as global manufacturing industries went through radical changes. The changes have created new problems, challenges and opportunities to the discrete event simulation. On manufacturing applications, it is no longer an isolated model but the distributed modeling and simulation along the supply-chain. In order to study the hybrid manufacturing systems, it is critical to have capability to model human performance with different level of skills and under various working conditions. On service applications, the most critical part is to model knowledge workers and their decision making process.

The authors believe that discrete event simulation continue to be one of the most effective decision support tools both in global manufacturing and knowledge economy. There are new opportunities for discrete event simulation such as business intelligence systems and simulation-based education. At the same time, there is a strong need to develop a new generation of discrete event simulation software by taking account of changes in application environments.

Acknowledgment

Author wishes to express his sincere gratitude to colleagues in the industry and academia for the support provided during this work.

6. References

[1] Law, A. M. and Kelton, W.D. (2000) "Simulation Modeling & Analysis" 3rd Ed. McGraw-Hill.
[2] Wang, M. and Sun, G. (1993). "Manufacturing Simulation: An Effective Tool for Productivity Improvement". In *Proceedings of 3rd International Microelectronics & Systems '93 Conference.* August 1993 Malaysia.
[3] Wang, M., Sun, G. and Nooh, M. (1995). "Application of Simulation to Reduce Manufacturing Cycle Time" In *Proceedings of 4th International Microelectronics Systems'95 Conference.* May 1995 Malaysia
[4] "Manufacturing Simulation in the UK" (1992). by UK Ministry of Trade and Industry.
[5] "Motorola launches $60 million supply chain center in Singapore" (2006) *Logistics Today* July 2006, Published by Penton Media, Inc New York
[6] Fujimoto, R. M.(2000) "Parallel and Distributed Simulation Systems" John Wiley & Sons, Inc.
[7] Chen, D.; Turner, S.J.; Boon Ping Gan; Wentong Cai (2004) "HLA-Based Distributed Simulation Cloning" Distributed Simulation and Real-Time Applications, 2004. DS-RT2004. Eighth IEEE International Symposium on Volume, Issue, 21-23 Oct. 2004 Page(s): 244 - 247.
[8] Lendermann, P. et al. (2003) "Distributed Supply Chain Simulation as a Decision Support Tool for the Semiconductor...Journal of Simulation 2003; 79: pp126-138, Published by Sage Publications.
[9] "Transforming the way: Delivering a better and quicker way for organizations to improve service delivery and process performance". A white paper by Lanner Group
[10] Swank, C.K. (2003) "The Lean Service Machine" Harvard Business Review October 2003, pp123-139.
[11] Robinson, S. et al (2007). "Modeling Human Interaction in Organizational Systems". from Fishwick, P.A "Handbook of Dynamic System Modeling". Publisher: Chapman & Hall/CRC (June 1, 2007), pp113-122
[12] Haag, S et al (2006) Management Information Systems For the Information Age (3rd Canadian Ed.). Canada: McGraw Hill Ryerson, p3.
[13] Babulak, E: "*Quality of Service Provision for the Modern Telecommunications Infrastructures in Transport and Industrial Logistics Solutions*", **invited and presented Keynote Addres,** the International Conference on Logistics LOGI 2005, February 15-16, 2005, Czech Republic
[14] Babulak, E: "*E-Manufacturing for 21st Century, State-of-the-Art and Future Directions*" **invited and presented Keynote Address,** the First International Conference on Management of Manufacturing Systems presentation, Presov, Slovakia, November 18th - 19th, 2004.
[15] Fishman, G: *Discrete-Event Simulation: Modeling, Programming, and Analysis*, 2001

Web sources

[1] Simul8 Corporation: www.simul8.com
[2] The human performance modelling technical group, The Human Factors and Ergonomics Society: www.cogsci.rpi.edu/cogworks/hpmsite/
[3] The International Society for Performance Improvement (ISPI): www.ispi.org
[4] Lanner Group: www.lanner.com
[5] KBSI Inc: www.kbsi.com

Authors

Professor Eduard Babulak is Director of Japan Pacific ICT Center, Chair of PacCERT and Head of School of Computing, Information and Mathematical Sciences at University of South Pacific in Suva, Fiji.

Dr. Ming Wang is industry consultant in Vancouver, BC, Canada.

2

A dynamically configurable discrete event simulation framework for many-core chip multiprocessors

Christopher Barnes and Jaehwan John Lee
Indiana University Purdue University Indianapolis
U.S.A.

1. Introduction

1.1 Background

Processor simulation is often a cornerstone in the research of new processor concepts and the education of computer architecture students. Simulators are used by researchers to validate architecture designs and explore new concepts before actual implementation. Educators use simulators to elucidate concepts in computer architecture through hands-on exercises and demonstrations. To be useful for both researchers and educators, simulators must be flexible, easy to use, easy to understand, and fast.

Simulation speed and configurability are two important aspects in the design of processor simulators. In the past, fast simulations were typically made with a monolithic design and were written to simulate a particular architecture. However, this approach required a complete understanding of the source code before the user could deviate from the original design. To overcome this drawback, some simulators embraced a more modular design, while others attempted to provide some customizability in the simulator by integrating and using Architecture Description Languages (ADLs) to describe its functionality. This approach is easier but still requires the user to undergo a lengthy learning curve to begin generating useful results.

As the industry moves toward merging many different, highly specialized processor resources on one physical chip, there is a need for a highly configurable discrete event simulation environment for the study of heterogeneous processor designs. Introduced in this chapter is Mhetero, a novel simulation framework that enables users to easily construct and perform discrete event simulations that meet this need.

Our simulation framework addresses the need for fast as well as configurable simulations by taking advantage of the dynamic compilation capabilities of the Microsoft's .NET development library in two ways. First, we use dynamic compilation to produce simulations based on configuration information gathered through an easy-to-use GUI. The entire process is a seamless and user-friendly experience, meaning that the user does not leave the framework to execute external compilers, write source code, or edit configuration files. Second, the simulations produced by the framework are compiled to an intermediate language (Compiling to MSIL, 2010), resulting in quick compilation time as well as execution speeds matching that of other compiled .NET programs. While the overall performance of C# does not match that of C++, there are numerous advantages of utilizing C# for scientific computing (Gilani, 2004), which are leveraged in our framework. Moreover, the framework's design is open and modular, allowing simulation designers to produce any sort of simulator that they may desire, even simulations extending beyond the tasks associated with a typical processor simulator. Although here we describe the techniques used in the design of Mhetero, the techniques are also applicable to other types of discrete event simulators.

Mhetero's simulation infrastructure is similar to other discrete event/time simulators with a few notable differences that facilitate processor simulation. First, instead of using a single, global event queue, Mhetero maintains several, separate event queues each modeling a communication channel between any two entities/modules of simulation. Second, instead of activating modules when certain events occur, entities/modules are activated during each cycle and these modules can then choose to process corresponding events immediately or after a specified number of cycles ensuring causality and synchronism between events in the simulation (Lee & Vincentelli, 1998). Hence, Mhetero's simulation infrastructure can be categorized as a synchronous, discrete time-simulation infrastructure which by definition itself is a discrete event simulation infrastructure (Lee & Vincentelli, 1998). As a result, the framework is not only an interesting and powerful alternative to other discrete event simulators but also a useful tool for computer architecture researchers, educators, and students.

In this chapter, we will discuss the design and construction of our simulation framework. We will begin by reviewing some of the previous work in the area of computer architecture simulation. We then discuss our configuration interface (Sections 2 and 4), dynamic compilation technique (Section 3), and intra-resource communication (Section 4). Finally, we will discuss several experiments that were conducted to verify the framework's design (Section 5).

1.2 Previous Work

Over the past several decades a considerable amount of research has been done in the area of computer architecture simulation. SimpleScalar (SimpleScalar LLC., 2010) and its variations have been used mostly for single processor simulation and research while the SimpleScalar multiprocessor version (Univ. of Minnesota, 2010), GEMS (Martin, et al, 2005), RSIM (Pai, et al, 1997), VASA (Wallin, et al, 2005), and WWT-II (Mukherjee, et al, 1997) (as well as its earlier versions) have been used mainly for multicore or chip-multiprocessor (CMP) simulation. While these simulators are very fast, they are not intended to produce retargetable simulations; i.e., these simulators are monolithic and cannot simulate other architectures beyond the originally intended architecture. Other simulators such as Simics (Magnusson, et al., 2002), Bochs (Bochs, 2010), and GxEmul (GXEmul, 2010) are full-system simulators for both single and multiprocessor simulation. These simulators are typically used for the development and testing of software on various platforms, and are also not designed to be easily retargetable.

A previous approach to retargetable simulators is investigated through the use of computer Architecture Description Languages (ADLs) such as Expression (Halambi, et al, 1999), LISA (Zivojnovic, et al, 1996), nML (Freericks, 1991), and RCPN (Reshadi & Dutt, 2005). These tools have been proposed primarily for automatic generation of computer architecture simulators. Although these tools produce retargetable simulators, their respective ADLs can often be difficult for new users to learn. Additionally, the generation of simulators is typically a disjointed and error-prone process that depends on external compilers and programs to function.

Asim (Emer, et al., 2002), a framework for modeling the performance of a processor (e.g., timing delays and signal propagation delays), most closely resembles Mhetero as it is a retargetable simulation framework that segments functional units into modules and includes two graphical tools for generating and viewing configuration files. However, Asim includes a seperate controller program used to execute simulations. On the contrary, Mhetero builds on the concept of using a single unified GUI for both configuration and simulation, creating a seamless environment. This approach, enabled by the techniques described in this chapter, allows the user to focus on developing their simulations without being burdened by the inner workings of the simulator's configuration.

Our simulation framework is built to minimize the difficulties associated with retargetable simulators by providing an easy-to-use GUI intended to offer a minimal learning curve. Additionally, simulators built by our framework are compiled using a technique that is completely concealed from the user, avoiding any compiler configuration concerns. Finally, simulators generated by our framework are capable of being competitive with other major simulators in terms of instructions per second. The performance of the resulting simulations is addressed in Sections 3.7 and 5.5.

1.3 Definitions

Before we proceed with the explanation of our simulation framework, we will take a moment to explain some of the terminology used throughout this chapter.

Resources represent any high level component in a simulated system such as a processor core, I/O, or memory. Resources can perform any sort of behavior that the simulation designer wishes. Note that the network is treated separately from a resource by the framework, and is explained in detail in Section 4.

Modules represent functional units within a resource, such as processor stages, branch predictors, and forwarding units.

Simulation designer is the user who is using the simulation framework for the purpose of producing or revising a processor simulator.

Configurability refers to the process of creating or customizing a new simulator by changing the settings (e.g., cache configuration) and source code of modules, resources, and routers in the simulation configuration.

2. Resource Configuration Interface

2.1 Overview

Option-based or text-based configuration of processor simulators can often be a confusing and difficult task for novice and expert users. This process typically requires the user to learn a new programming language or data format, and can require external, third party tools. To improve the configuration process, our framework allows users to completely configure their simulator in a Microsoft Windows GUI, making the learning curve minimal to non-existent. Discussed in this section are the various editors that can be used by the simulation designer to configure their simulations. Figure 1 depicts the organization of the editors for the design and configuration of simulations.

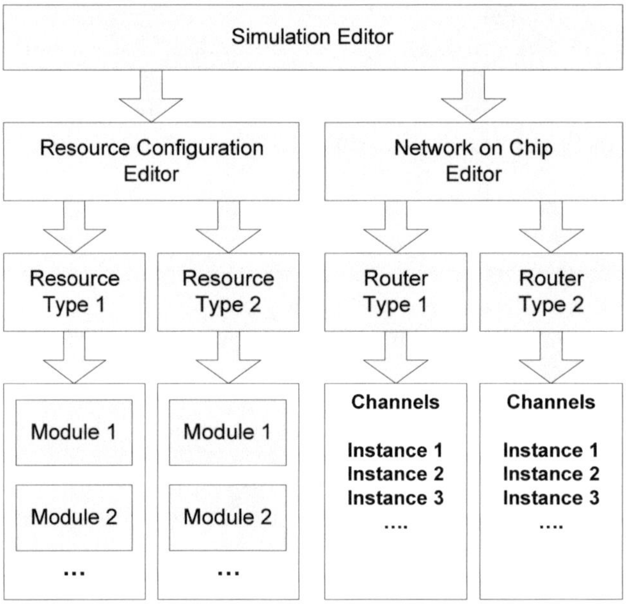

Fig. 1. Organization of editors within the simulation framework.

2.2 Simulation Editor

The *Simulation Editor*, the first editor that users encounter, acts as a gateway to the Resource and Network-on-Chip (NoC) Configuration Editors. Simulation configurations are composed of multiple types of resources and networks; therefore, this layer is necessary to allow users to choose either editing existing resources and networks, or defining new ones. Once the user selects a resource or network, its respective editor is initiated for the user to modify its functionality. The remainder of Section 2 details the Resource Configuration Editor, and the NoC Configuration Editor is discussed in Section 4.

2.3 Resource Configuration Editor (RCE)

The *Resource Configuration Editor (RCE)* is the central location for editing the function or structure of a resource type. Within the RCE, there are many tabs that enable users to modify every aspect of the resource type, including instructions, registers, memory, cache, data flow, and behavioral logic. Figure 2 shows the RCE interface. Several of the more simple tabs are discussed in this subsection, and the remaining tabs are described in Sections 2.4 - 2.7.

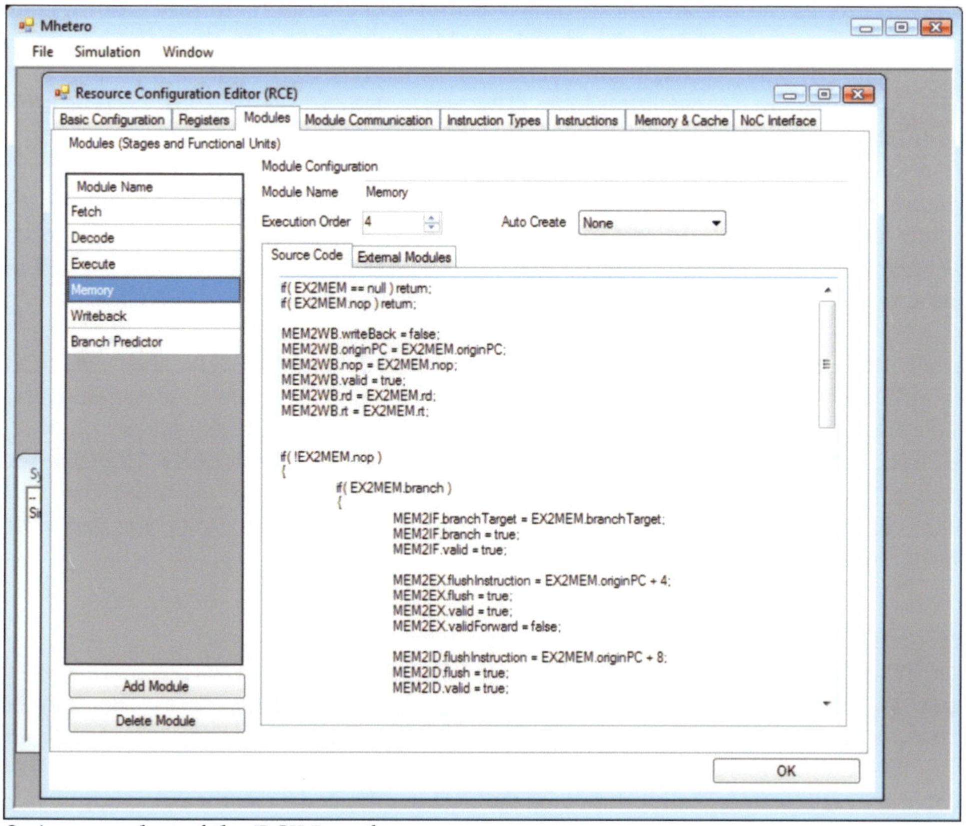

Fig. 2. A screenshot of the RCE Interface.

The *Basic Configuration* tab contains fields for the name of the resource type, the number of instances, and the applications to execute on each instance of the resource. Users are able to choose a default program that will run on all instances, and/or choose particular programs to run on specific instances. For example, to implement a master/slave distributed processing application, two programs could be used. The master program, executing on one resource instance, would be used to aggregate the results of the slave resources, running a different program.

The *Registers* tab provides an interface for the user to specify the register names, number of registers, and data types. The *Instruction Types* tab allows the user to specify the instruction format which is used to disassemble the resource's program for debugging purposes. The

NoC Interface allows the user to specify the input and output queues, queue size, and data type for the resource's network interface.

2.4 Module Editor

Modules are a core concept to the extendibility and configurability of the framework. A set of modules forms a resource. Modules can represent stages or components such as branch predictors, data forwarding units, hazard detection units, or any sort of experimental unit. The modularity of the framework facilitates completely configurable simulations, enabling users to conceive of any sort of chip resource. Moreover, modules allow the user to easily extend the functionality of their simulations by defining a new module and assigning it a position in the resource's execution loop. The newly defined module will become a part of the simulation in its next execution.

The module editor (shown in Figure 2) allows the user to input the module's name, execution precedence (i.e., order), and a section of C# source code describing the module's behavior into the framework. The module's behavioral source code has access to all of the inputs and outputs to the module, as well as the resource's memory and registers.

External modules can also be linked to the resource in this tab. The user can choose a precompiled Dynamic-Link-Library (DLL) file, the name of the class to instantiate, and the variable name of the instantiated class (which may be referenced by other behavioral source code). External modules give the user complete control over the modules' implementation, including the ability to define additional functions, classes, and variables that will be available to other modules in the resource. Details on how external modules are linked to the resource are given in Section 3.5.

2.5 Module Communication

Under the *Module Communication* tab, the user can describe data channels that connect one module to another as the resource is executed. The user must specify the source and destination modules, channel name, and variables to be included in the data channel. During the compilation process, these channels are combined into data structures that are available as variables to the module's behavioral source code. A module should read its available inputs and act upon them, as well as produce valid outputs, if necessary. The management of communication data between modules is handled by the framework through the use of *Queues* (MSVC Dev. Center, 2010).

Module communication combined with the module's execution precedence allows the user to design versatile resources such as a pipelined execution unit. The open architecture of our framework allows users to specify arbitrary pipeline designs as shown in Figure 3.

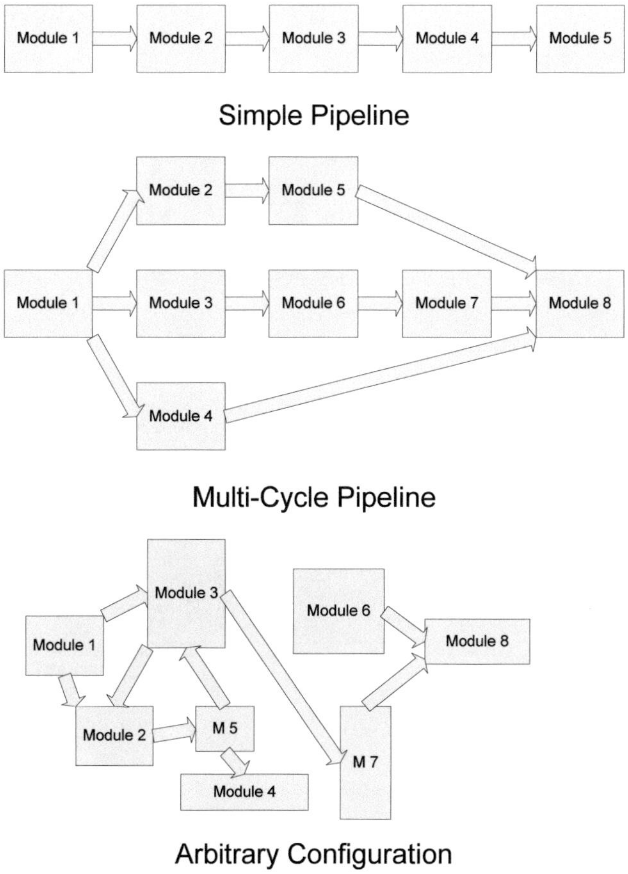

Fig. 3. Potential pipeline configurations.

2.6 Instructions

The *Instructions* tab provides access to the instructions that are implemented in the resource. Here, users can add, delete, or edit instructions. Instructions have an associated name, op code, and instruction format type (which are specified in the *Instruction Types* tab). The C# source code that describes the behavior of the instruction is also entered here. If desired, the instruction source code may be used to automatically generate execution stage source code during compilation (detailed in Section 3.3).

2.7 Memory and Cache

The *Memory & Cache* tab enables the user to specify the size and type of the data and instruction memory as shown in Figure 4. The user may specify single or multi-level cache systems with various configurations. The framework supports Direct Mapped, Set Associative, and Fully Associative cache types, as well as Least Recently Used (LRU) and random replacement schemes. The user may also specify the cache size and latencies of each cache level.

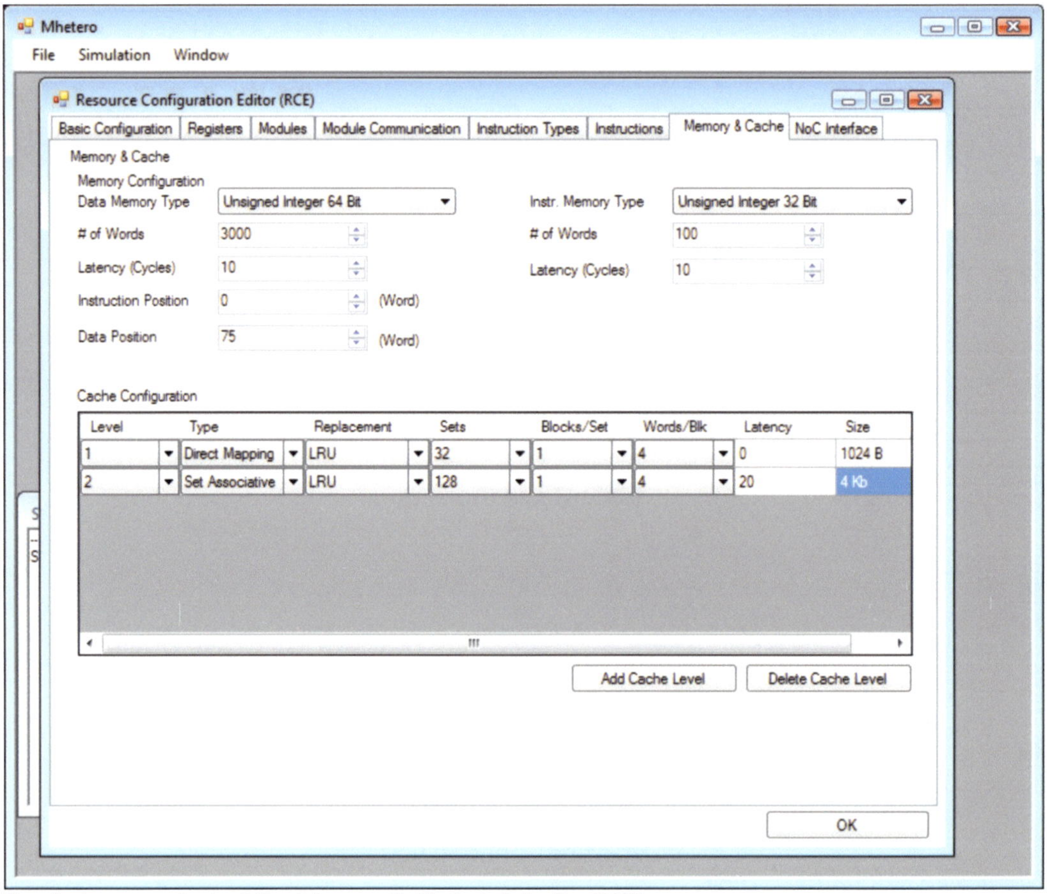

Fig. 4. A screenshot of the *Memory & Cache* tab in the RCE.

The cache and memory systems are built into the framework and are optional for the simulation designer to use. If the cache system is used, information regarding the cache's performance is reported at the end of the simulation. Each core has direct access to the memory system; however, it may be desirable for memory to be accessed over an intra-core network. For example, this would be useful for emulating a shared cache/memory. In this case, the simulation designer must implement a network and its protocol to access a resource modeling a memory module. Details about intra-core networks are explained in Section 4.

2.8 Simulator Configuration Data File

Information regarding the simulator's configuration is loaded and saved in an XML format utilizing the .NET Document Object Model (DOM) XML classes *XmlDocument*, *XmlNode*, and *XmlTextWriter* (MSVC Dev. Center, 2010). The process of saving a configuration starts with creating an empty XML configuration file. Another class, *ResourceConfig*, was implemented to store resource settings and handle the saving and loading of configuration data for resource types. Similarly, a *NetworkConfig* class was created that performs the same functions for networks. Once the output file has been created, the *Simulator* class loops through each resource and network (stored in a list as *ResourceConfig* and *NetworkConfig* classes, respectively) and invokes their individual *SaveConfiguration()* functions. The *SaveConfiguration()* function creates a new node in the XML file, and inserts its settings.

To load a configuration, the *Simulator* class must load the XML file, and examine the XML tree to determine the number of types of resources and networks that must be instantiated and loaded. *Simulator* instantiates the appropriate number of resources and networks, and then invokes the *LoadConfiguration()* function. The *LoadConfiguration()* function is sent a reference to the appropriate portion of the XML tree to load as an *XmlNode*, which it uses to read settings from.

The behavioral source code of modules, instructions, and routers, entered by the user through their respective editors, is also stored in the configuration XML file. The behavioral source code must be encoded so that characters such as greater-than and less-than signs do not interfere with the XML format. We solve this problem by using another Microsoft .NET class, *HttpUtility* (MSVC Dev. Center, 2010) typically used for Internet communication. This class contains two functions which encode and decode text to and from a format that will not interfere with the XML file's formatting. This organization of configuration data allows the framework to store and load entire simulation configurations, including multiple heterogeneous cores and networks, into a single file.

3. Dynamic Compilation

3.1 Overview

One of the primary benefits of our framework is its ability to dynamically compile source code into executable code quickly and seamlessly. Dynamic compilation refers to the framework's ability to take configuration and behavioral data, and produce an executable library at run-time. Without leaving the framework's interface, the user can make large and small modifications to a simulator's configuration and test those modifications immediately. The framework does not generate any external executable files that the user would need to run as a separate process. Instead, the framework takes the simulation configuration that is entered into the framework's GUI and assembles a complete simulator which is loaded into memory and executed as part of the main framework.

Simulator compilation generally takes less than a second as the source code is compiled to an intermediate language called MSIL (Compiling to MSIL, 2010). The behavioral source code of a module, instruction, or router can be modified through their respective editors. If there are any errors present in the behavioral source code, the framework provides detailed error reports similar to those provided in Microsoft Visual Studio. Thus, errors can be quickly and easily corrected inside the framework's GUI, and a new simulator can be built. Since the .NET framework includes all of the necessary functionality, the entire process has no external dependencies that are required for the user to download and install.

Integrating the C# compiler into the framework provides users with a very convenient and excellent development experience specialized for computer architecture simulation without any of the pitfalls associated with relying on third party compilers or development tools. This technique also enables the framework to compile and link processor simulators to memory leaving no left-over files in the file system for cleanup.

In this section, we discuss how we structure the framework to support this behavior, how the dynamic compilation is implemented, and how the framework communicates with the newly generated simulator executed inside the framework.

3.2 Framework Structure

Two classes, *Simulator* and *Network,* make up the core of the dynamic compilation implementation. Figure 5 shows the organization of these two classes within the framework. The simulation executes in a different thread (referred to as "Simulation Thread" in Figure 5) from a thread of the framework and its GUI (together referred to as "Framework Thread"). The *Simulator* class was constructed to interface the simulation framework to the chip's resources and networks. *Simulator* handles the compilation, initialization, and instantiation of the various resources within the simulator. The *Network* class provides an interface from the *Simulator* class to the individual routers and is treated similar to other resources. The primary difference between the *Network* class and other resources is the compilation process. *Network* handles the router compilation process, which is initiated after *Simulator* has compiled all of the resources. Since *Network* must execute during the simulation, it is executed in the simulation thread, similar to other resources, instead of the framework thread (details about the simulation execution are provided in Section 3.6).

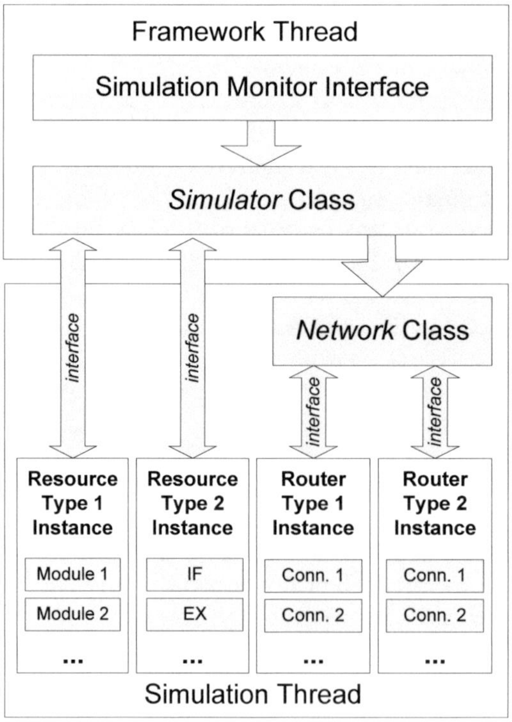

Fig. 5. Organization of the framework structure and communication interface.

The framework allows the user to create multiple types of resources and routers in the simulated system. Each resource and network type can be instantiated an arbitrary number of times, according to the simulation's configuration. Creating multiple types of resources thus leads to a heterogeneous simulation. Multiple types of networks are desirable for transferring different types of information. For example, one network may transmit data streams, while another may transmit small packets. Additionally, some NoC implementations may include a memory system modeled as a chip resource, so networks for accessing memory may also be necessary.

3.3 Implementation of Dynamic Compilation

Before the compilation process can begin, the source code of the simulator must be gathered by the framework. Figure 6 shows the flow of how the source code is combined to produce an executable simulator. A generalized parent class, *Resource,* is included in the framework that contains only the basic structure and functionality needed to interface with the framework. The configuration data gathered in the RCE for each resource is combined into the *Resource* class to construct a new class that implements the behavior of the resource. The source code of the modules within each resource is gathered and inserted into the *Resource* class at the appropriate locations based on each module's execution precedence (defined in the RCE). The network routers undergo a similar process as the resources; their configuration data is combined with a generalized *Router* class and they are then instantiated and managed by the *Network* class. The remaining resource configuration and simulation settings are also analyzed and interpreted by the framework to generate the remainder of the source code.

In addition, the framework can automatically generate source code for an execution stage during compilation. This is necessary to make use of the instruction source code that is entered by the simulation designer in the *Instructions* tab of the RCE. In the *Module Editor,* the user can specify a module for the framework to insert the automatically generated execution stage source code. If this option is chosen, the framework will assemble every instruction's source code into a *switch* statement during the compilation process. The *case* statements in the *switch* correspond to the instructions entered by the user. The instruction's behavioral source code is then inserted into the body of the *case*. During the simulation, a decoded instruction's op-code is used to select the appropriate instruction source code to execute.

Once the simulator source code has been pieced together, the program is compiled. The compilation utilizes the C# Compiler (CSC.exe) included in the .NET framework distribution, assuring wide availability with no additional configuration or installation. The C# compiler produces the same error messages along with their line numbers as the Microsoft Visual Studio development environment does. If errors are found, they are displayed in a status window for users to examine and make corrections to their module, instruction, or router source code.

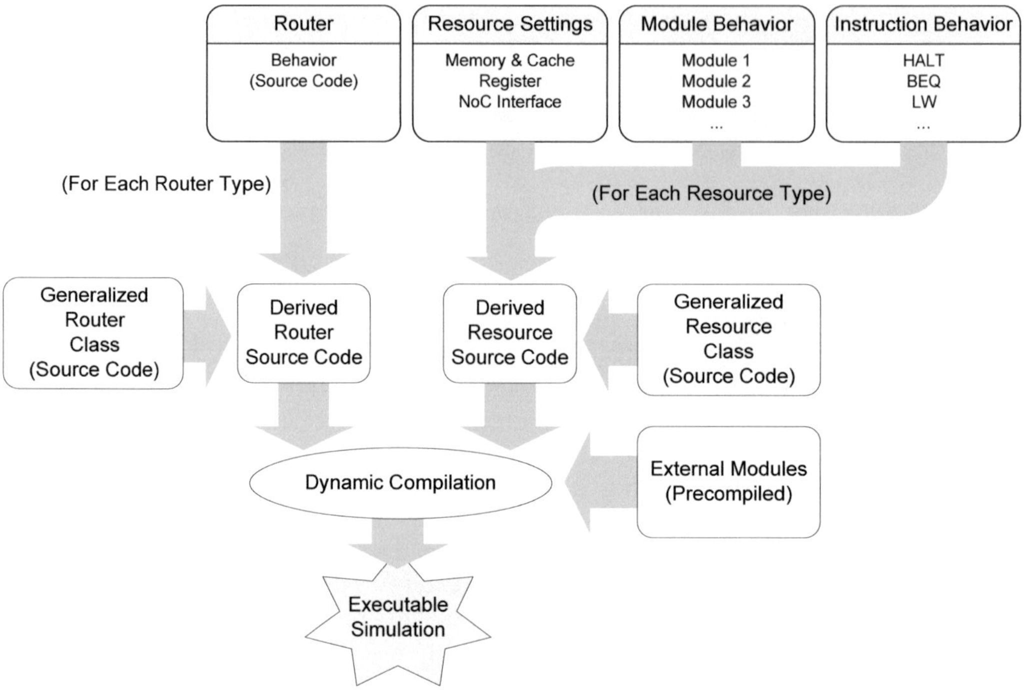

Fig. 6. Flow chart of the dynamic compilation process.

The execution of the C# compiler is managed by the *CSharpCodeProvider* class (MSVC Dev. Center, 2010). We use the *CompileAssemblyFromSource()* function included in the *CSharpCodeProvider* class to produce an *Assembly* (MSVC Dev. Center, 2010) which represents the compiled code. *CompileAssemblyFromSource()* takes two parameters, the source code and *CompilerParameters*. *CompilerParameters* contains many of the compiler settings available to developers in the Microsoft Visual Studio, such as setting warning levels and including debug information. We make use of the *ReferencedAssemblies* property to include external modules, as well as *System.dll*. *CompileAssemblyFromSource()* returns compilation results which provide a reference to a compiled *Asssembly* if the compilation was successful or a list of error messages (i.e., module or router source code compilation errors). The compiled *Assembly* data structures are stored in a *List* and used for instantiating the new resource and router classes.

3.4 Communication Between the Framework and Simulator Components

Communication between the framework and the resources and routers is facilitated by the *interface* capability which is provided in C#, as well as other object oriented languages. *Interface* enables developers to generalize the signature of function calls which may be included into a compiled *Assembly*, the result of the dynamic compilation process (discussed in Section 3.3). That is, *interface* provides a method to initiate function calls between the framework and the classes of the dynamically compiled simulator. The generalized resource and router classes (shown in Figure 6) implement standard calls that allow the framework to communicate with the compiled and instantiated code. The communication is primarily used for transmitting statistical information, as well as starting and stopping the simulation. Communication between resources and routers is discussed in Section 4.

3.5 External Modules

External modules are precompiled Dynamic-Link Library (DLL) files containing a class that implements the functionality of a module. During the compilation process (described in Section 3.3), any external modules specified in a resource are loaded and linked into the compiled code. This is accomplished by referencing the external module in the *ReferencedAssemblies* property of the *CompilerParameters* class, which is prepared before compilation is initiated. When the resource is instantiated, the external module is available to the resource and executed as if it were an internal module.

External modules provide several benefits that may make them desirable to some users. First, external modules make it easier to swap modules into and out of the framework, and transmit them with other users. Second, external modules give users complete control over the programming of the module, as long as it implements the *Init()* and *Run()* functions. For example, the user can declare new classes, additional variables, and/or additional functions, which regular modules do not provide since they must only implement the behavioral source code. Third, the functions declared in external modules are available for other modules (in the same resource) to call, which may be desirable in some circumstances. For example, if the user chose to implement a power consumption external module, the module could implement a function that would be called from other modules to tally power consumption. Finally, the module can be implemented using any .NET-compatible language whereas internal modules must be written in C#.

Although regular (internal) modules provide less flexibility than external modules, they require less expertise to implement since the simulation designer is primarily tasked with developing the module's behavioral source code. Thus, external modules should be considered as a more advanced configuration option.

An external module must be compiled with a reference to the framework's executable (i.e., in the Visual Studio project settings). The reference enables the external module class to implement the appropriate *interface*, *IModule*, which ensures that the DLL file will be compatible with the framework. Additional functions may also be implemented and used within the module, or to be called from other modules.

Figure 7 illustrates how two external modules could be integrated into a resource's execution loop.

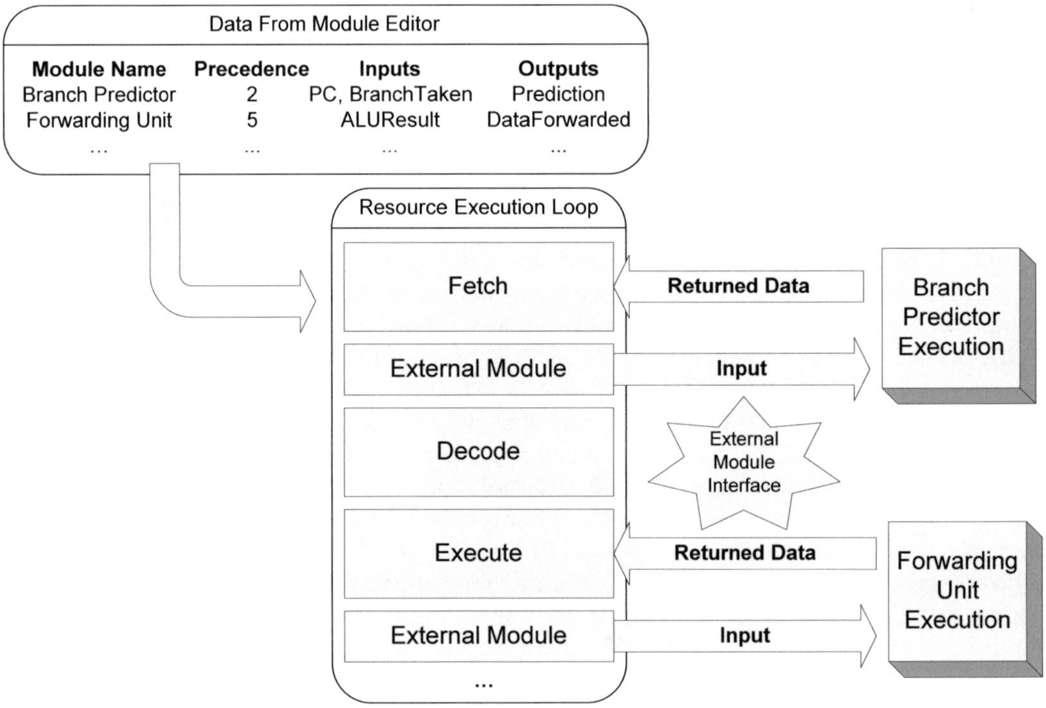

Fig. 7. Two external modules integrated into a resource's execution loop.

3.6 Execution

The compilation of the resources and routers is initiated when the user builds the simulator, which is a process that must be completed before the user can initiate the Simulation Monitor. The Simulation Monitor is an interface that monitors the execution of the simulation. A screen shot of the Simulation Monitor is shown in Figure 8. Executing the Simulation Monitor instantiates the classes and prepares the execution of the simulation thread. The user must press the "Start Sim" button to begin the simulation.

Once the simulation is started, the simulation thread is initiated and every instance of the resources and networks is executed. They are executed one cycle at a time, repeatedly, until each resource has completed executing their assigned program (i.e., the program that the simulated resource is running). During a resource's cycle, all of its modules are executed within a try-catch block which protects the framework thread from exceptions. During a network's cycle, each connection is examined for data waiting to be transmitted and then each router's routing function is executed to process the data.

The Simulation Monitor periodically checks on the status of each resource to see if execution has completed. Once the resource has completed its simulated program, its status is changed to "Done", and performance and statistical information regarding the resource's performance are presented to the user. Runtime exceptions are also reported to the user in an information text box that is located in the Simulation Monitor window.

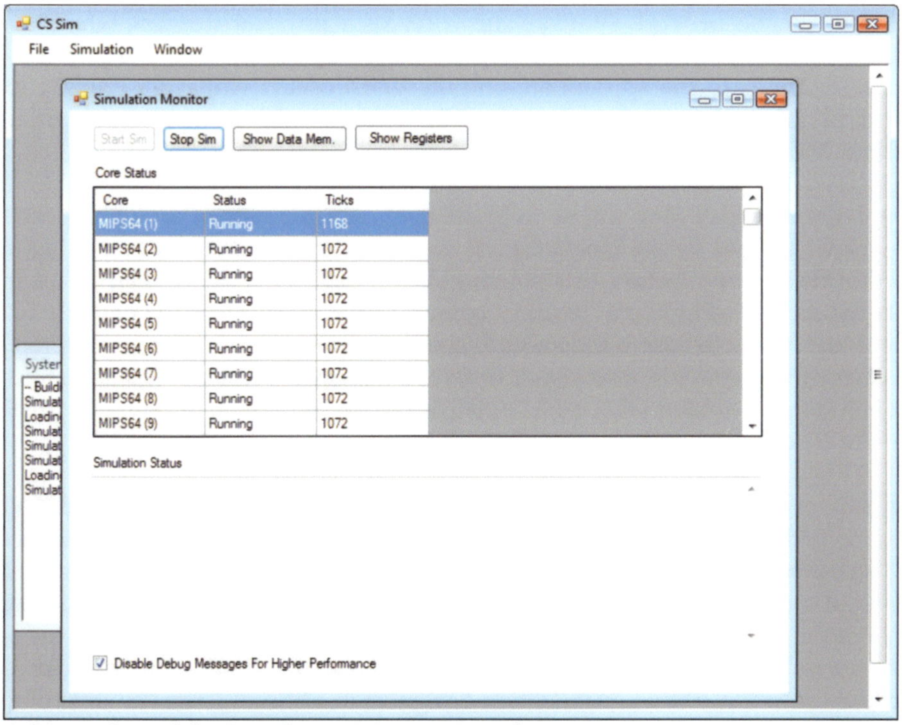

Fig. 8. A Screenshot of the Simulation Monitor Interface.

3.7 Performance Concerns

Due to the nature of the framework, the performance of the resulting simulation can vary greatly depending upon the simulation configuration and modeling detail. During the development of the framework, every effort was made to keep the simulation overhead to a minimum. In Section 5.5, we show that simulators generated using our framework can be competitive with other major simulators.

4. Network-on-Chip

4.1 Overview

Network-on-Chip (NoC) has become one of the leading methods for intra-core communication in current and emerging processor designs. NoCs are widely viewed as fast, power efficient, and scalable to hundreds of cores. Additionally, NoCs can support multiple voltage domains, clock frequencies, and heterogeneous designs. Thus, NoC support is a critical part of our support for heterogeneous many-core simulations. In this section, we discuss our NoC implementation, the NoC Configuration Editor, and explain how the NoC executes within the simulation framework.

4.2 Network-on-Chip Structure and Execution

Routers and resources interface with the network using inputs and outputs, which are implemented using the FIFO queue .NET class, *Queue.* Connections (described in more detail below) in the network simulate the wires of a physical network which make the connection from an output to an input. Routers are responsible for managing the flow of data from its inputs to the appropriate output, which occurs within the routing function. The *Network* class (described in Section 3.2) manages the flow of data through the connections and executes the routing functions for each *Router* instance.

The simulation designer may choose to implement multiple networks. This is common in modern NoC designs, as each network is used for a specific purpose such as memory requests, cache synchronization, or streaming data. Each network type can define multiple router types, as well as multiple instances of each router type. Since the network interfaces of routers and resources are standardized, connections can span between different router type and even router types existing in different networks. This results in an extremely flexible NoC implementation that can simulate arbitrary network topologies. Figure 9 shows an example 2D mesh network.

During each cycle while the simulator is executing, each network will process all of its connections and initiate the routing functions of each router instance. The *Network* class stores the connection configuration data in a list that it iterates through to move data packets from outputs to their corresponding inputs assigned to the other end. The size and data type of the data packet depend on the output and input types, specified by the network interface in either the NoC Configuration Editor or the RCE. Packets can also be represented by arrays, enabling simulation designers to transmit large amounts of data per cycle (this functionality is provided to maximize configurability, and may not be realistic in a physical implementation).

Resources and routers communicate through the network by manipulating their input and output queues, which are available to their behavioral source code. Resources can expose the network interface to the simulated program any number of ways and it is left up to the simulation designer to specify how this should work. For example, network transmissions can be implemented by either register mapping for I/O, or memory mapping, or instruction mapping (creating and using user-defined instructions for I/O).

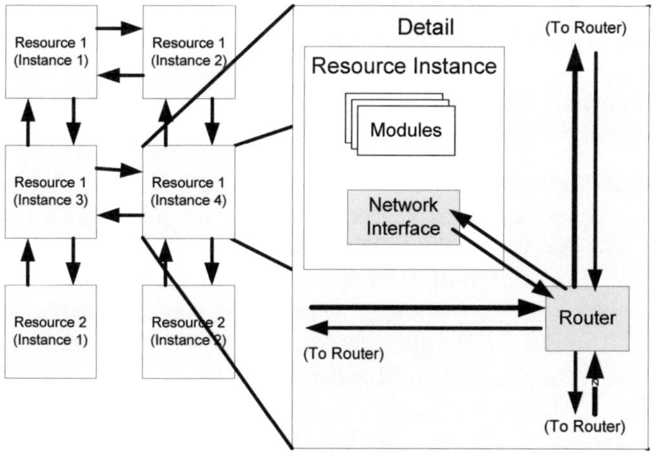

Fig. 9. An example of a 2D mesh network topology.

This NoC implementation is extremely open, allowing the simulation designer to produce virtually any kind of network topology imaginable. Moreover, the simulation configuration is also not limited to any particular routing function or router placement.

4.3 Network-on-Chip Configuration Editor

The NoC Configuration Editor (similar to the RCE shown in Figure 2) allows users to define the router types and connections between the routers and resources. Router types have a name, the number of instances, source code, and input and output queues. The source code describes the routing function of the router, i.e., which inputs connect to which outputs. The input and output queues are assigned a name, size, and data type. The queues are accessible by the routing function, along with the router's instance number (ID). The instance number can be used to determine the router's location within the network.

Connections must specify which type of resource or router it is connecting to, and which input and output queues to read from or write to. The user must also specify which instance number that the connection is operating on. Connections can also have a delay (in cycles), which enables users to simulate the transmission of a packet of data over the connection in multiple pieces, known as flits, a common occurrence in current NoC designs.

5. Experimentation

5.1 Overview

The goal of these experiments was to demonstrate and verify the configurability of our framework, as well as its ability to produce cycle-accurate discrete event simulators. Four experiments were conducted, each exploring different areas of the framework's functionality. In each experiment, several different simulators were constructed by varying settings within the framework. Then each simulation was executed, and the results of the new settings were observed.

The experiments were conducted on a computer equipped with a 2.4 GHz Intel Core 2 Quad CPU and 4GB of RAM, running the 64-bit version of Windows Vista. Similar experiments have been conducted on different machines, and the results of the experiments are reproducible across various hardware platforms.

5.2 Cache Simulation Experiment

The purpose of this experiment was to demonstrate the framework's cache system. One level of 1KB cache was used with three different mapping schemes: direct, set associative, and fully associative. Three different block sizes were used for each test: 2, 4, and 8 words per block. Set associative and fully associative mapping schemes also tested with the Least Recently Used (LRU) and random replacement methods. The small cache size is used because we used a micro-benchmark for this experiment.

This experiment was conducted using a single-processor configuration based on the MIPS64 instruction set architecture. An insertion sort algorithm was performed on 1600 64-bit values, which executed 106,740 instructions that took between 118,620 and 255,060 cycles to complete. The cache accuracy results (shown in Figure 10) demonstrate that the cache's performance varies with different configurations and the accuracy responds in a manner that is in line with expectations.

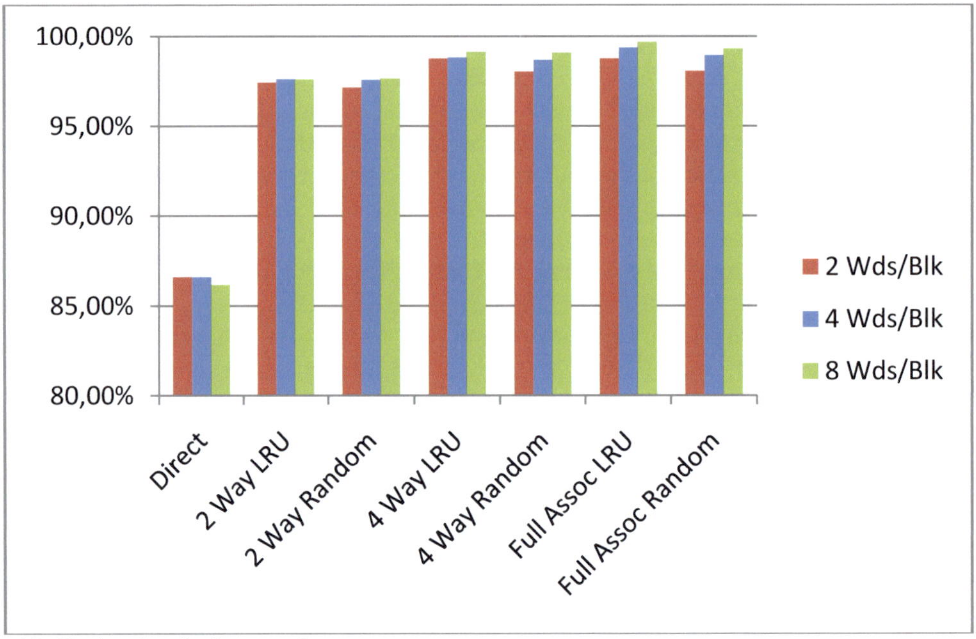

Fig. 10. Cache simulation results.

5.3 Branch Prediction Algorithm Comparison Experiment

This experiment was conducted to demonstrate the capability of using external modules with the framework. The framework along with a preconfigured MIPS64 simulation was given to a group of graduate computer architecture students to produce external branch predictor modules. Each student was provided with the source code for a simple two-bit branch predictor and was tasked with creating a two-level correlating predictor and a tournament predictor. The students produced DLL files which were loaded by the framework as the simulator was constructed as described in Section 3.5. The program that tested the branch prediction modules was comprised of many loops and conditional statements in an attempt to emulate program flow that is commonly observed in typical programs, but does not perform any specific function.

Results across all of the students were similar. The branch prediction results from one project are shown in Figure 11(a) and Figure 11(b). Figure 11(a) shows the branch prediction accuracy across each branch prediction scheme. As the branch prediction accuracy improves, the number of cycles used to complete the program is reduced, as shown in Figure 11(b) . The results demonstrate that the external modules are a viable method of integrating functional units into a simulation. Additionally, the nature of the external modules allowed the students to focus only on their portion of the simulation. This method provides an easy-to-use and standardized environment for testing and comparison.

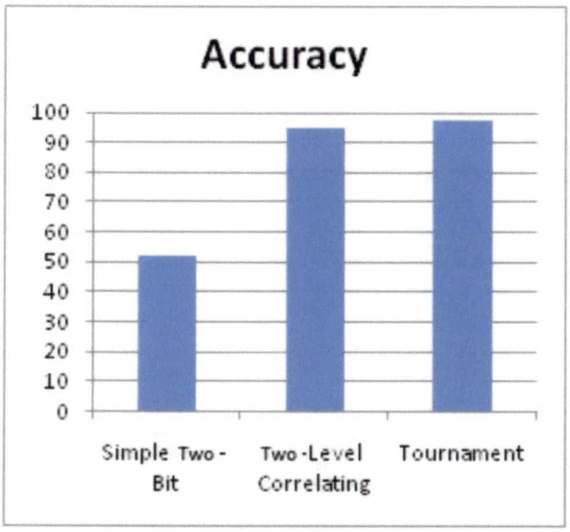

(a) Branch Prediction Accuracy

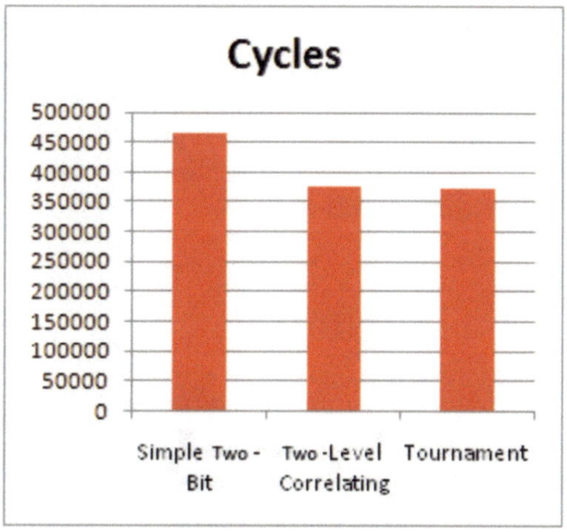

(b) Number of Cycles

Fig. 11. Branch Prediction accuracy and number of cycles required by each scheme.

5.4 Network-on-Chip Experiment

This experiment is a brief demonstration of the NoC capabilities of the framework. The simulation has one master core (resource) that is used to distribute data and aggregate the results of calculations performed on a varying amount of slave cores. At the beginning of the simulation, when ready, each slave core sends a request for data to perform calculations with. The master core responds by sending a packet of data to the slave core, and the master core moves on to the next portion of data. Once the slave core receives the packet, the calculations are performed and the results are transmitted back to the master core. This process repeats until all of the calculations have been completed. This is similar to how MPI (A. Gabriel, et al, 2004) or PVM (Sunderam, 1990) processes.

To demonstrate the capabilities of the NoC, we implemented a 2D mesh network topology (similar to the one shown in Figure 9) and then varied the number of slave cores performing the calculations and observed the number of cycles needed to aggregate all of the results. In this experiment, 600 pairs of 64-bit values were used to perform a dot product calculation on each slave core. The cores interacted with the network through registers mapped to network inputs and outputs.

The number of cycles required to perform the calculation was varied to produce large and small workloads. The large workload required twice the number of cycles to complete the calculation as the small workload. The purpose of collecting the two different sets of results was to observe how the total number of cycles required to produce a result was affected by increasing the runtime of the simulated programs running on the slave cores.

The results (shown in Figure 12) demonstrate that as additional slave cores are added, the number of cycles required by the application to complete the calculation is reduced. However, in both data sets, the speedup is diminished as the number of cores increases, due to the network overhead approaching the workload required to perform the calculation. In other words, as the number of cores increases, the number of routers that each packet must traverse increases, reducing the benefit of additional cores. As can be seen in the figure, an especially large speedup occurs after increasing the processing cores from 4 to 16 with a large workload due to the high ratio of slave core processing time to communication overhead. With 512 cores, the total execution times for the small and large workloads became nearly identical.

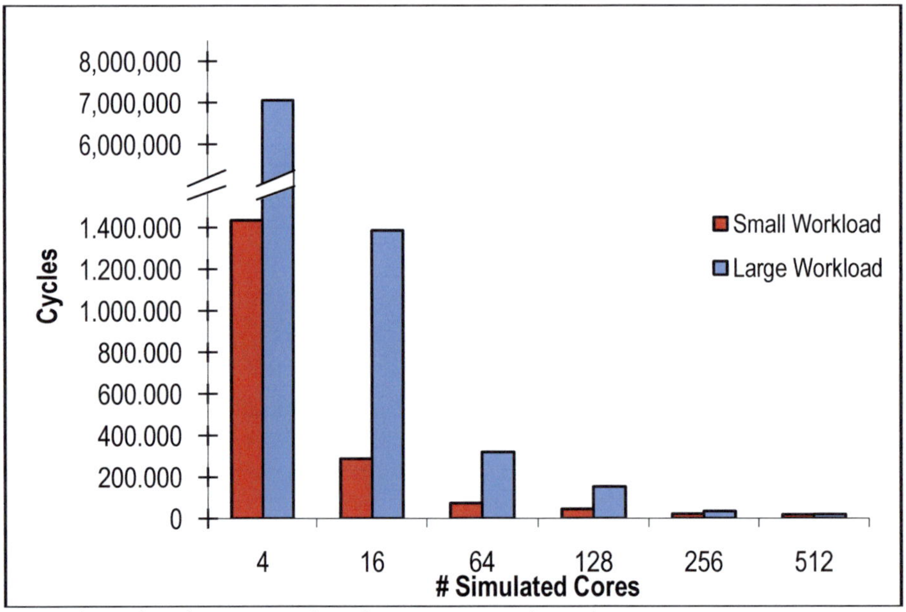

Fig. 12. Number of cycles required with varying number of cores.

5.5 Simulation Performance Experiment

The purpose of our last experiment was to examine the performance of a simulator generated by the framework. A MIPS64 configuration was executed several times with a varying number of cores, each executing an insertion sort application. There was no network executing during this experiment.

The results of the experiment are illustrated in Figure 13, which shows that as the number of cores increases, the total Instructions-Per-Second (IPS) degrades only slightly, while the IPS per core degrades proportionally to the number of cores. Additionally, the simulation performance for a single-core simulation is competitive with other major simulators.

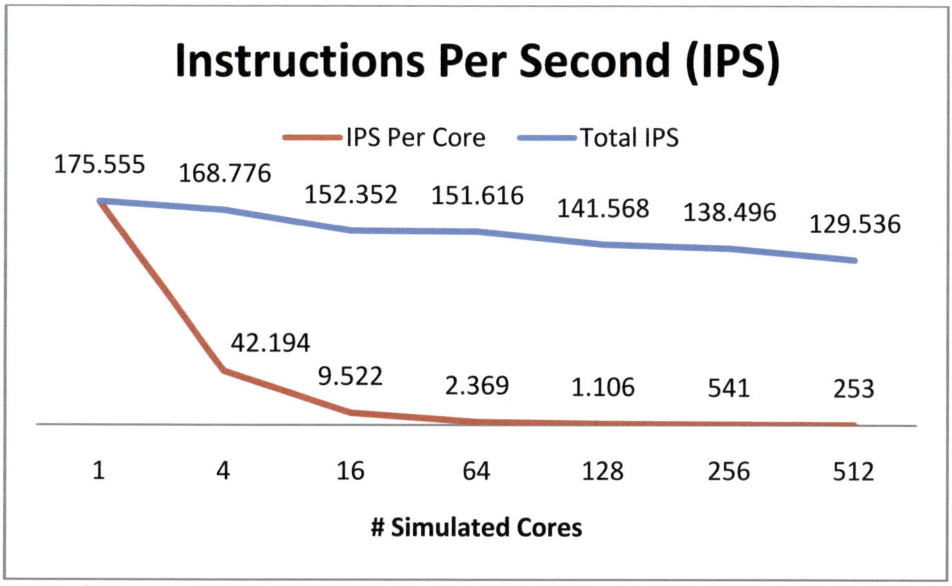

Fig. 13. Performance results with increasing number of cores executing concurrently.

6. Summary and Conclusion

6.1 Summary

In this chapter, we have discussed a simulation framework for dynamically configurable discrete event simulators for many-core chip-multiprocessors. In particular, we have discussed how users can use the framework to configure, construct, and execute simulations, and the details behind the framework's implementation. We also discussed how we applied our configurability approach to a NoC implementation in the framework. Finally, we performed several experiments to verify our framework, and showed how it can be used to further computer architecture research and education.

6.2 Conclusion

The simulation framework discussed in this chapter provides several contributions in an effort to improve discrete event and processor simulation for the purpose of research and education. The dynamic compilation technique produces fast simulations and quick compilation with nearly unlimited configurability. The techniques that we described here allow the framework to maintain the easy-to-use and capable interface for simulation configuration and execution, producing a cohesive and seamless experience that is approachable by novice and expert users alike. The framework's modular design allows users to easily test new implementations and extend a simulator's functionality. Additionally, the network-on-chip infrastructure builds on the framework's configurability and compilation capabilities to provide a structured environment for intra-chip communications. Combined, these features create an interesting and powerful simulation platform that provides an exciting computer architecture research and education experience.

The framework can be accessed from:
http://www.ece.iupui.edu/~johnlee/index.php?section=tools

7. References

A. Gabriel, A. F. (2004). Open MPI: Goals, concept, and design of a next generation MPI implementation. *Proceedings, 11th European PVM/MPI Users*, 97-104.

Bochs: The open source IA-32 emulation project. (2010). Retrieved from SourceForge: http://bochs.sourceforge.net/

Emer, J., Ahuja, P., Borch, E., Klauser, A., Luk, C., Manne, S., et al. (2002). Asim: A Performance Model Framework. *Computer, 2*, 68-76.

Freericks, M. (1991). The nML machine description formalism. *Fachbereich Informatik.*

Gilani, F. (2004). *Harness the Features of C# to Power Your Scientific Computing Projects.* Retrieved 2010, from MSDN: http://msdn.microsoft.com/en-us/magazine/cc163995.aspx

GXEmul. (2010). Retrieved from SourceForge: http://gxemul.sourceforge.net/

Halambi, A., Grun, P., Ganesh, V., Khare, A., Dutt, N., & Nicolau, A. (1999). EXPRESSION: a language for architecture exploration through compiler/simulator retargetability. *Design, Automation and Test in Europe Conference and Exhibition 1999*, 485-490.

Lee, A. and Vinentelli, A. (1998). A framework for comparing models of computation. *IEEE Trans. on Computer-Aided Design of Integrated Circuit and Systems*, 1217-1223.

Magnusson, P., Christensson, M., Eskilson, J., Forsgren, D., Hallberg, G., Larsson, F., et al. (2002). Simics: A full system simulation platform. *Computer, 35*, 50-58.

Martin, M. (2005). Multifacet's General Execution-driven Multiprocessor Simulator (GEMS) Toolset. *Computer Architecture News*, 92-99.

Microsoft Corporation. (2010). *Compiling to MSIL.* Retrieved from MSDN: http://msdn.microsoft.com/en-us/library/c5tkafs1

Microsoft Corportation. (2010). *MSVC Dev. Center.* Retrieved from Microsoft Developer Network: http://msdn.microsoft.com/en-us/vcsharp/default.aspx

Pai, V., Ranganathan, P., & Adve, S. (1997). RSIM: An execution-driven simulator for ILP-based shared-memory multiprocessors and uniprocessors. *Third Workshop on Computer Architecture Education.*

Reshadi, M., & Dutt, N. (2005). Generic pipelined processor modeling and high performance cycle-accurate simulator generation. *Design, Automation and Test in Europe, 2*, 786-791.

S. Mukherjee, S. R. (1997). Wisconsin Wind Tunnel II: A Fast and Portable Architecture Simulator. *Workshop on Performance Analysis and Its Impact on Design.*

SimpleScalar LLC. (2010). *SimpleScalar Overview*. Retrieved from http://www.simplescalar.com/

Sunderam, V. (1990). PVM: A framework for parallel distributed computing. *Concurrency: Practice and Experience*, 315-339.

Univ. of Minnesota. (2010). *SIMCA, the Simulator for Superthreaded Architecture.* Retrieved from ARCTiC Labs: http://www.arctic.umn.edu/SIMCA/index.shtml

Wallin, D., Zeffer, H., M.Karlson, & Hagersten, E. (2005). Vasa: A simulator infrastructure with adjustable fidelity. *Parallel and Distributed Computing and Systems.*

Zivojnovic, V., Pees, S., & Meyr, H. (1996). Lisa machine description language and generic machine model for hw/sw co-design. *Proceedings of the IEEE Workshop on VLSI Signal Processing.*

3

Modelling methods based on discrete algebraic systems

Hiroyuki Goto
Nagaoka University of Technology
Japan

1. Introduction

A typical and significant feature of discrete event systems is that the behaviour is non-continuous; that is to say, events occur at discrete time instants and the values of internal states change non-continuously. A simple and well-known example of a discrete event system is a traffic signal network. Each signal has a current status of three possible states: green, yellow and red. Moreover, the status changes by predetermined time intervals, which are usually determined by inspecting past traffic conditions relevant to the site. A more complicated example is an air traffic control system at an airport. Clearances for take-off and landing issued by controllers can be understood as a sort of signal. However, the controller must take into account no-concurrency issues of the runway and the necessary time intervals for take-off or landing, as well as scheduled times. Thus, this system is more complex than the previous.

If we model and analyse such discrete event systems using the conventional formalism, we often have to incur specific constraints on the internal variables and parameters. For example, there are often cases whereby the explanatory variables have only Boolean (0/1) logical or integer values. This tends to make the formulation more complex and more difficult to solve. In view of this, several specific methods suited for discrete event systems, automaton (Kelarev, 2003) and Petri net (Girault & Valk, 2002) for instance, have been developed. These are modelling tools for simply representing the target systems, and are beneficial for analysing the behaviour of these; for example, so that critical sections such as so-called dead-lock or infinite-loops can be detected. The essence of these methods, however, is a kind of symbolisation, rather than formalisation. Thus, they are not suitable for taking into account varying parameters or structures.

Now let us go back to the essence of discrete event systems. What is the obstacle in using the conventional formalism? A primary point would be its non-linearity. In the above case of air traffic control, before clearance for take-off can be given to a pilot of an aircraft, the controller must check whether the runway is available, that no other aircraft is on or about to cross the same runway, and moreover is not in a take-off or landing phase. Several constraints of these are non-linear, but the non-linearity is weak. For instance, the status of whether multiple conditions are satisfied simultaneously is equivalent to the result of an 'and' operation. In terms of a time axis, clearance is given after the 'maximum' time of which all necessary conditions are satisfied. Moreover, the phrase 'about to' can be interpreted as the result of considering a margin time, equivalent to time offset. As the above issues imply, several classes of discrete event systems may be formulated by combinations of simple non-linear functions. Accordingly, if we use algebraic systems suited for representing logical operations, 'and', 'or', 'max' and 'min' for instance, constraints may be formulated simply.

A most famous algebraic system would be the Boolean algebra (Harrison, 2009), which is popular in the field of electrical engineering and plays an essential role in designing logical circuits. In the Boolean algebra, the 'or' and 'and' operations are defined as logical addition and multiplication, respectively. Under these definitions, the essential properties in conventional algebra such as the laws of commutativity, associativity and distributivity are invoked in this algebraic system. With the help of this structure, several types of basic circuits can be modelled simply.

Another well-known structure is referred to as the Dioid algebraic system (Baccelli et al., 1992). This system requires defining two operators for addition and multiplication that satisfy the above laws. If we can determine a set of operators by which the constraints of the target system can be represented, the behaviour of the system would be formulated by simple equations. For instance, the max-plus algebra (Heidergott et al., 2006), a subclass of Dioid algebra, defines the 'max' and '+' operations as addition and multiplication, respectively. This algebraic system is suited for describing synchronisation of multiple events and time margins. This algebra is also referred to as the schedule algebra, and plays an essential role in this chapter. As this name implies, the max-plus algebra can be beneficially used in solving several classes of scheduling problems.

Let us now take a glance at the approach based on the max-plus algebra. In representing the behaviour of a target system, a set of linear equations is used. A simple and typical form is: $\boldsymbol{x}(k) = \boldsymbol{A} \otimes \boldsymbol{x}(k-1) \oplus \boldsymbol{B} \otimes \boldsymbol{u}(k)$, $\boldsymbol{y}(k) = \boldsymbol{C} \otimes \boldsymbol{x}(k)$, where $\oplus$ and $\otimes$ represent the operators for addition and multiplication in the max-plus algebra, respectively. The reader familiar with control theory may already have noticed that the form is similar to the state-space representation in modern control theory. Hence, this approach is also compatible with concepts in control theory, and several research accomplishments in control theory have been applied to this field, typical research reports of which will be referred later. In addition to these, the max-plus algebraic system itself has a number of interesting features because of its specific definition. Thus, there is also a number of reports devoted to these pure mathematical aspects. Typical examples include the existence of solutions of simultaneous or polynomial equations, and eigenvalue problems.

As these issues indicate, for modelling and analysis methods for a class of discrete event systems, much attention has been paid to the approach based on the max-plus algebra. It seems though that there is less concerted research effort on extending the range of application and improving its practicability. For instance, the above state space representation has been sufficiently generalised and well-studied in past research. However, there is still little research on how to formulate systematically the behaviour of practical systems, which would be paramount when needed in applications to complex systems.

In view of this, we aim to improve the practicability of the state-space representation in Dioid and max-plus algebras. The basic concept and framework are explained in the subsequent section. Several recent developments are then introduced in the latter sections.

2. Preliminaries

This section first clarifies the research scope using simple illustrative examples, and then confirms the necessity of Dioid and max-plus algebras.

2.1 Simple example

The primary concern of this chapter is to provide a systematic framework for deriving the state-space representation for practical systems. Target applications include scheduling problems for a class of manufacturing systems.

Let us now consider the behaviour of a simple manufacturing system depicted in Fig. 1. The system has two external inputs, three facilities and one external output. Facility 1 receives raw material from input 1, processes it, and sends the resulting part to facility 3. The behaviour of facility 2 is the same as facility 1. Facility 3 receives the processed parts from facilities 1 and 2, processes them, and sends the resulting output to the external output. Assuming that this process is carried out repeatedly, let us derive the earliest process start times.

Facilities 1 and 2 can start processing after the processing of the previous part is completed and the required resource materials are fed. Moreover, facility 3 can start processing after the processing of the previous part is completed and the processed parts are received from facilities 1 and 2. For the k-th part, let us denote the earliest process start and processing time in facility i by $x_i(k)$ and d_i, respectively. Moreover, we denote the material feeding times from external input i by $u_i(k)$ and the earliest output time to the external output by $y(k)$. Then, the earliest process start and output times can be expressed in the following manner.

$$x_1(k) = \max\{x_1(k-1)+d_1, u_1(k)\},\ x_2(k) = \max\{x_2(k-1)+d_2, u_2(k)\} \tag{1}$$

$$x_3(k) = \max\{x_3(k-1)+d_3, x_1(k)+d_1, x_2(k)+d_2\} \tag{2}$$

$$y(k) = x_3(k)+d_3 \tag{3}$$

As is easily seen, all calculations consist of only two types of operations, max and +. Since the max operation is non-linear, the above equations are also non-linear in nature. However, if we use a specific discrete algebraic system, such types of equations can be represented by a set of linear equations. This can be accomplished by using Dioid algebra.

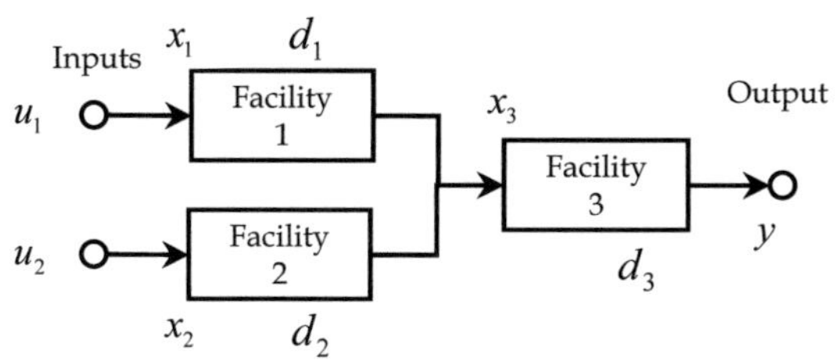

Fig. 1. A system with two inputs, one output and three facilities

2.2 Dioid and max-plus algebras

The basic concepts underlying Dioid and max-plus algebras are explained. Dioid algebra is defined in the field D and endowed with a set $\{\oplus, \otimes, \varepsilon, e\}$ consisting of two operators for addition and multiplication, and two unit elements, respectively. For arbitrary elements x, y, $z \in \mathsf{D}$, the following axioms, all of which are well-known in conventional algebra, are enforced:

$$\text{Commutative law: } x \oplus y = y \oplus x \tag{4}$$

$$\text{Associative law: } (x \oplus y) \oplus z = x \oplus (y \oplus z)\,,\ (x \otimes y) \otimes z = x \otimes (y \otimes z) \tag{5}$$

$$\text{Distributive law: } (x \oplus y) \otimes z = (x \otimes z) \oplus (y \otimes z)\,,\ z \otimes (x \oplus y) = (z \otimes x) \oplus (z \otimes y) \tag{6}$$

For the unit elements ε and e, referred to as the zero and identity elements, we enforce the following properties:

$$x \oplus \varepsilon = x\,,\ x \otimes \varepsilon = \varepsilon \otimes x = \varepsilon\,,\ x \otimes e = e \otimes x = x\,,\ x \oplus x = x \tag{7}$$

We observe that only the last property is different from that in conventional algebra, and gives Dioid algebra its distinguishing and remarkable feature. Note that the Dioid is a collection of algebraic systems, and does not assume more specific operation rules.

As a subclass of Dioid algebra, max-plus algebra is endowed with a set $\{\oplus, \otimes, \varepsilon, e\} \equiv \{\max, +, -\infty, 0\}$ defined in $\mathsf{D} \equiv \boldsymbol{R}_{\max} = \boldsymbol{R} \cup \{-\infty\}$, where $\boldsymbol{R}$ represents the real field. As we can easily confirm, this set satisfies the above axioms (4)—(7), as follows:

$$x \oplus y = \max(x, y) = y \oplus x$$

$$(x \oplus y) \oplus z = \max(x, y, z) = x \oplus (y \oplus z)\,,\ (x \otimes y) \otimes z = x + y + z = x \otimes (y \otimes z)$$

$$(x \oplus y) \otimes z = \max(x, y) + z = \max(x + z, y + z) = (x \otimes z) \oplus (y \otimes z)$$

$$x \otimes (y \oplus z) = x + \max(y, z) = \max(x + y, x + z) = (x \otimes y) \oplus (x \otimes z)$$

$$\max(x, -\infty) = x\,,\ x + (-\infty) = (-\infty) + x = -\infty\,,\ x + 0 = 0 + x = x\,,\ \max(x, x) = x$$

Max-plus algebraic system is a subclass of Dioid algebra, but it is not unique. For example, the following sets also satisfy the axioms (4)—(7).

$$\{\oplus, \otimes, e, \varepsilon\} \equiv \{\min, +, +\infty, 0\} \text{ defined in } \mathsf{D} \equiv \boldsymbol{R} \cup \{+\infty\}$$

$$\{\oplus, \otimes, e, \varepsilon\} \equiv \{\max, \times, +0, 1\} \text{ defined in } \mathsf{D} \equiv \boldsymbol{R}^{+} \text{ (positive read field)}$$

$$\{\oplus, \otimes, e, \varepsilon\} \equiv \{\max, \min, -\infty, +\infty\} \text{ defined in } \mathsf{D} \equiv \boldsymbol{R} \cup \{-\infty\} \cup \{+\infty\}$$

We leave as an exercise for the reader to confirm that these sets also satisfy the axioms of the Dioid algebra.

Moreover, we adopt the notational rules for addition, multiplication and exponent in conventional algebra to this algebraic system. That is, we simply denote:

$$\bigoplus_{k=1}^{l} x_k \equiv x_1 \oplus x_2 \oplus \cdots \oplus x_l\,,\ xy \equiv x \otimes y\,,\ x^l \equiv \underbrace{x \otimes x \otimes \cdots \otimes x}_{l}$$

when no confusion is likely to arise.

Next, let us extend the max-plus algebraic system for scalars to matrices. For $\boldsymbol{X} \in \boldsymbol{R}_{\max}^{m\times n}$, $\boldsymbol{Y} \in \boldsymbol{R}_{\max}^{m\times n}$, $\boldsymbol{V} \in \boldsymbol{R}_{\max}^{n\times l}$, we define the operational rules for addition and multiplication and unit elements in the following manner.

$$[\boldsymbol{X} \oplus \boldsymbol{Y}]_{ij} = \max([\boldsymbol{X}]_{ij}, [\boldsymbol{Y}]_{ij}),\ [\boldsymbol{X} \otimes \boldsymbol{V}]_{ij} = \bigoplus_{k=1}^{l}([\boldsymbol{X}]_{ik} \otimes [\boldsymbol{V}]_{kj}) = \max_{k=1,\cdots,l}([\boldsymbol{X}]_{ik} + [\boldsymbol{V}]_{kj})$$

$\boldsymbol{\varepsilon}$: all elements are ε

$\boldsymbol{e}$: only diagonal elements are e and all off-diagonal elements are ε

Under these definitions, for arbitrary matrices $\boldsymbol{X} \in \boldsymbol{R}_{\max}^{m\times n}$, $\boldsymbol{Y} \in \boldsymbol{R}_{\max}^{m\times n}$, $\boldsymbol{Z} \in \boldsymbol{R}_{\max}^{m\times n}$, $\boldsymbol{V} \in \boldsymbol{R}_{\max}^{n\times l}$ and $\boldsymbol{W} \in \boldsymbol{R}_{\max}^{l\times m}$, the following properties, essentially correspond to (4)–(7), hold true.

$$\boldsymbol{X} \oplus \boldsymbol{Y} = \boldsymbol{Y} \oplus \boldsymbol{X},\ (\boldsymbol{X} \oplus \boldsymbol{Y}) \oplus \boldsymbol{Z} = \boldsymbol{X} \oplus (\boldsymbol{Y} \oplus \boldsymbol{Z}),\ (\boldsymbol{X} \otimes \boldsymbol{V}) \otimes \boldsymbol{W} = \boldsymbol{X} \otimes (\boldsymbol{V} \otimes \boldsymbol{W})$$
$$(\boldsymbol{X} \oplus \boldsymbol{Y}) \otimes \boldsymbol{V} = (\boldsymbol{X} \otimes \boldsymbol{V}) \oplus (\boldsymbol{Y} \otimes \boldsymbol{V}),\ \boldsymbol{W} \otimes (\boldsymbol{X} \oplus \boldsymbol{Y}) = (\boldsymbol{W} \otimes \boldsymbol{X}) \oplus (\boldsymbol{W} \otimes \boldsymbol{Y})$$
$$\boldsymbol{X} \oplus \boldsymbol{\varepsilon} = \boldsymbol{X},\ \boldsymbol{X} \otimes \boldsymbol{\varepsilon} = \boldsymbol{\varepsilon} \otimes \boldsymbol{X} = \boldsymbol{\varepsilon},\ \boldsymbol{X} \otimes \boldsymbol{e} = \boldsymbol{e} \otimes \boldsymbol{X} = \boldsymbol{X},\ \boldsymbol{X} \oplus \boldsymbol{X} = \boldsymbol{X}$$

We should note here that care is required with respect to the second and third relationships in (7). The sizes of the unit matrices $\boldsymbol{\varepsilon}$ and $\boldsymbol{e}$ must be adjusted in advance so that multiplication can be defined.

2.3 State space representation

We now simplify (1)–(3) using max-plus algebra. By replacing the max and + operations with $\oplus$ and $\otimes$, respectively, the equations can be expressed as:

$$x_1(k) = x_1(k-1) \otimes d_1 \oplus u_1(k),\ x_2(k) = x_2(k-1) \otimes d_2 \oplus u_2(k) \tag{8}$$
$$x_3(k) = x_3(k-1) \otimes d_3 \oplus x_1(k) \otimes d_1 \oplus x_2(k) \otimes d_2 \tag{9}$$
$$y(k) = x_3(k) \otimes d_3 \tag{10}$$

By substituting (8) into (9), we obtain:

$$x_3(k) = x_1(k-1) \otimes d_1^2 \oplus x_2(k-1) \otimes d_2^2 \oplus x_3(k-1) \otimes d_3 \oplus u_1(k) \otimes d_1 \oplus u_2(k) \otimes d_2 \tag{11}$$

We now notice that $x_i(k)$ and $y(k)$ are represented by linear functions of $x_i(k-1)$ and $u_i(k)$ in a max-plus algebraic system, and it seems that these can be simply expressed if we use a matrix representation. In fact, (8), (10), and (11) are summarised as follows.

$$\boldsymbol{x}(k) = \boldsymbol{A} \otimes \boldsymbol{x}(k-1) \oplus \boldsymbol{B} \otimes \boldsymbol{u}(k) \tag{12}$$
$$\boldsymbol{y}(k) = \boldsymbol{C} \otimes \boldsymbol{x}(k) \tag{13}$$

where:

$$\boldsymbol{x}(k)=\begin{bmatrix} x_1(k) \\ x_2(k) \\ x_3(k) \end{bmatrix},\ \boldsymbol{u}(k)=\begin{bmatrix} u_1(k) \\ u_2(k) \end{bmatrix},\ \boldsymbol{y}(k)=[y(k)],\ \boldsymbol{A}=\begin{bmatrix} d_1 & \varepsilon & \varepsilon \\ \varepsilon & d_2 & \varepsilon \\ d_1^2 & d_2^2 & d_3 \end{bmatrix},\ \boldsymbol{B}=\begin{bmatrix} e & \varepsilon \\ \varepsilon & e \\ d_1 & d_2 \end{bmatrix},\ \boldsymbol{C}=\begin{bmatrix} \varepsilon \\ \varepsilon \\ d_3 \end{bmatrix}^T$$

Equations (12) and (13) are referred to as the state and output equations, respectively. Moreover, the set of these equations is called the state-space representation. Variables $\boldsymbol{x}(k)$, $\boldsymbol{u}(k)$ and $\boldsymbol{y}(k)$ are referred to as the state, input and output variables, respectively. Matrices $\boldsymbol{A}$, $\boldsymbol{B}$ and $\boldsymbol{C}$ are referred to as the system, input and output matrices, respectively. A system whose behaviour can be described by the set of linear equations (12) and (13) is referred to as the max-plus linear system.
As the reader may have noticed, the equations are similar to the state-space representation in modern control theory in conventional algebra.

$$\dot{\boldsymbol{x}}(t)=\boldsymbol{A}\cdot\boldsymbol{x}(t)+\boldsymbol{B}\cdot\boldsymbol{u}(t)$$
$$\boldsymbol{y}(t)=\boldsymbol{C}\cdot\boldsymbol{x}(t)$$

With this similarity, several research developments in modern control theory have been applied to max-plus algebraic systems, the details of which will be explained in the following section.

3. Literature Review

We introduce several typical research accomplishments with respect to the state-space representation approach in max-plus and Dioid algebras. Roughly speaking, the relevant research may be classified into two types: methodologies and applications. After briefly outlining several research areas, we explain our own research motivation and objectives.

3.1 Methodologies

As mentioned above, the state-space representation in Dioid algebra is similar to the representation in modern control theory in conventional algebra. Thus, several research developments in modern control theory have been applied to Dioid or max-plus algebraic systems, and they now provide several useful and powerful tools for a class of discrete event systems. Typical examples include supervisory control, IMC (Internal Model Control), MPC (Model Predictive Control), and adaptive control and fully described in the current literature.
For instance, the concept of supervisory control is applied in Ramadge & Wonham (1987) and Cofer & Garg (1996). In particular, the latter takes the framework of supervisory control for a timed event graph into account in max-plus algebra. If the specification for a system is given by a set of firing times for transitions, the control specification can be accomplished by delaying the firing times of controllable transitions. This is caused by control signals from the supervisor.
In Boimond & Ferrier (1996), the concept of IMC, often utilised in controller designs for chemical plants, is applied. With these developments, a controller installed in a target

system adjusts completion times to desired times. A general result of this study is that the control inputs for perturbed systems can be made robust.
In Schutter & Boom (2001) and Boom et al. (2007), the concept of MPC has been utilised. MPC determines the control inputs by solving an optimisation problem in which the performance of the system for a finite step is formulated. In addition to MPC, a theory of adaptive control is applied in Schullerus et al. (2006) and Boom et al. (2003). In particular, Boom et al. (2003) realises on-line control by combining a method for system identification and MPC, which they call adaptive MPC. This controller can adjust the states on-line even when the properties of a system are changed unexpectedly.
We can also find other research studies on controller designs for hybrid systems (Heemels et al., 2001) and parameter estimation problems of state-space representations (Schutter et al., 2002).

3.2 Applications

Several application fields for practical systems are introduced. A typical field of application is manufacturing systems, as illustrated in the previous section. In modelling these types of systems, feeding times of resource materials and completion times of manufactured parts correspond to input and output variables for the system, respectively. Each process's start and processing times are assigned to internal states and system parameters, respectively.
Similar examples include diagnosis and fault detection for batch-processing lines (Sampath et al., 1996; Schullerus & Krebs, 2001). In such systems, the input times correspond to start times for injection of a substance or solvent, and the output times are equal to completion times for the outflow of the resulting substance. The system parameters are equal to the reaction times, which include the injection and the outflow times. The internal states are start times for the injection or completion times for the outflow.
Several problems in transportation planning using max-plus algebra are reported (Heidergott & Veries, 2001; Moh et al., 2005; Goverde, 2007). These problems can be formulated by setting the system variables in the following manner: For instance, in railway networks, the respective inputs and outputs correspond to departure times from stations of origin, and arrival times at terminals. The system parameters are equivalent to travel times between stations, and the internal states correspond to the departure or arrival times at intermediate stations.
In addition to the studies described above, we can also find developments in TCP flow-control problems arising in the field of communication networks (Baccelli & Hong, 2000).

3.3 Problems to be resolved

As introduced above, much attention has been paid to modelling and analysis methods based on Dioid and max-plus algebras. However, there are currently obstacles in this approach to their practical use. In actual systems, there are usually constraints regarding the maximum in-process jobs that can exist within single and between facilities. These are interpreted as capacity constraints. Moreover, occupation times in facilities, processing times for instance, differ for each job in several systems. This situation requires considering additional constraints to disallow overtaking of a previous job or jobs. In Krivulin (1996), a queuing model which can consider the capacity constraints in single facilities was proposed. However, the paper assumes that occupation times are fixed and independent of job numbers, and no capacity constraint between facilities can be taken into account. Furthermore, based on current methods, deriving the state-space representation is performed manually and ad-hoc, as no systematic and unified method is available. In the light of these difficulties, the following sections propose a systematic framework for deriving the state-space representation. The target systems are allowed to have capacity constraints within single and between facilities, and moreover have varying processing times for each job.

4. Considering the Capacity Constraints

We extend the conventional state-space representation in Dioid algebra, and derive a systematic framework for modelling a class of repetitive systems with capacity constraints. Prior to the extension of the state-space representation, we first introduce several operators.

4.1 Additional operators

For use in later discussions, we define additional operators and elements. First, we denote the field $\boldsymbol{R} \cup \{-\infty\} \cup \{+\infty\}$ by $\overline{\boldsymbol{R}}_{\max}$. For scalar variables $x, y \in \overline{\boldsymbol{R}}_{\max}$, we define the following operators.

$$x \wedge y = \min(x, y)\,, \quad x \setminus y = -x + y$$

The first definition satisfies the commutative law: $x \wedge y = y \wedge x$; in contrast, the second is non-commutative. For the zero element of $\wedge$, we define $\mathsf{T}\,(=+\infty)$. This yields $x \wedge \mathsf{T} = \mathsf{T} \wedge x = x$ and $x \setminus \mathsf{T} = \mathsf{T}$. In addition, we enforce the following properties for operator $\otimes$:

$$\varepsilon \otimes \mathsf{T} = \mathsf{T} \otimes \varepsilon = \varepsilon \tag{14}$$

based on the axiomatic rules in (7). For operator $\setminus$, we define the following operation rules for mathematical convenience:

$$\varepsilon \setminus \varepsilon = \mathsf{T} \setminus \mathsf{T} = \mathsf{T} \tag{15}$$

In conventional algebra, (14) is tantamount to defining the rule: $(-\infty)+(+\infty)=(+\infty)+(-\infty)=-\infty$. In contradistinction, (15) corresponds to the rule $-(-\infty)+(-\infty)=-(+\infty)+(+\infty)=+\infty$. Both seem to be contradictory in terms of conventional algebraic systems. However, we should note here that these rules are defined exclusively for operators $\otimes$ and $\setminus$, not for + and -.

For multiple numbers, if $x_i \in \overline{\boldsymbol{R}}_{\max}$, we simply denote:

$$\bigwedge_{k=1}^{l} x_k \equiv x_1 \wedge x_2 \wedge \cdots \wedge x_l$$

For matrices $\boldsymbol{X}, \boldsymbol{Y} \in \overline{\boldsymbol{R}}_{\max}^{m \times n}$ and $\boldsymbol{Z} \in \overline{\boldsymbol{R}}_{\max}^{n \times l}$, we define the following two operations in analogy to the $\oplus$ and $\otimes$ operations.

$$[X \wedge Y]_{ij} = \min([X]_{ij}, [Y]_{ij}),\ [X \odot Z]_{ij} = \bigwedge_{k=1}^{l}([X]_{ik} \backslash [Z]_{kj}) = \min_{k=1,\cdots,l}(-[X]_{ik} + [Z]_{kj})$$

For simplicity, several references adopt a different definition for operator $\odot$, where $X \odot Z$ gives the same result as $X^T \odot Z$ based on the above definition. Nevertheless, we have defined the above rule in an analogous manner to operator $\otimes$. In referencing the relevant papers, we recommend verifying its definition first.
For $X, Y \in \overline{R}_{\max}^{m\times n}$, $Z \in \overline{R}_{\max}^{n\times m}$, $v, w \in \overline{R}_{\max}^{n}$, the following properties hold:

$$\begin{gathered}(X \oplus Y) \odot v = (X \odot v) \wedge (Y \odot v),\ X \odot (v \wedge w) = (X \odot v) \wedge (X \odot w),\\ Y^T \odot (Z^T \odot v) = (Z \otimes Y)^T \odot v\end{gathered} \tag{16}$$

The operators $\wedge$ and $\backslash$ also have other interesting and attractive properties that are not used in this chapter. The interested reader is referred to Heidergott et al. (2006) or Baccelli et al. (1992) for details.

4.2 Assumptions and notations

Assumptions and notations for the target systems are clarified here. Although we use terms adapted from manufacturing systems, the same concepts can also be applied to other classes of discrete event systems such as transportation systems.
Assume the system has a fork-join structure with n facilities, m external inputs, and p external outputs. Transit times between facilities are initially ignored although they are considered in a later subsection. With respect to order constraints, assume the following are imposed:

- Each job uses all facilities and each is used only once. Thus, the system has an acyclic structure.
- Facilities with predecessors cannot start processing until the process in the preceding facility is finished.
- Facilities that have external inputs cannot start processing until all required resource materials are supplied.
- Facilities that have capacity constraints cannot start processing until the number of in-process jobs in the corresponding region is equal to, or less than, the predetermined value.
- Process start and completion occur sequentially according to job number order in all facilities. In other words, the jobs are processed based on a FIFO (First-In, First-Out) policy.

For the k -th job in facility i $(1 \le i \le n)$, denote the processing time, process start and completion times by $d_i(k)(\ge 0)$, $[x^s(k)]_i$ and $[x^c(k)]_i$, respectively. For external input i $(1 \le i \le m)$, $[u(k)]_i$ represents the material feeding time. For external output i $(1 \le i \le p)$, $[y(k)]_i$ denotes the output time for the product. Subscript suffixes E and L are used to express the earliest and latest times.

4.3 Forward type representation

We extend the state-space representation (12) and (13). We refer to this type of representation as forward type, by which the earliest start and completion times of the various processes are calculated. The essence of the extension is to take into account constraints with respect to buffer capacities in single and between facilities.

To represent several parameters and constraints such as processing times, precedence relationships, and locations of external input and outputs, we introduce the following matrix parameters $\boldsymbol{P}_k$, $\boldsymbol{F}$, $\boldsymbol{H}^{(h)} \in \boldsymbol{R}_{\max}^{n\times n}$, $\boldsymbol{B} \in \boldsymbol{R}_{\max}^{n\times m}$ and $\boldsymbol{C} \in \boldsymbol{R}_{\max}^{p\times n}$:

$$[\boldsymbol{P}_k]_{ij} = \begin{cases} d_i(k) : \text{if } i = j \\ \varepsilon \quad : \text{if } i \neq j \end{cases}$$

$$[\boldsymbol{F}]_{ij} = \begin{cases} e : \text{Facility } i \text{ has a preceding facility } j \\ \varepsilon : \text{Facility } i \text{ does not have a preceding facility } j \end{cases}$$

$$[\mathbf{H}^{(h)}]_{ij} = \begin{cases} e : \text{The maximum number of jobs that can exist between facility } i \text{ and its} \\ \quad\ \text{downstream facility } j \text{ is } h \\ \varepsilon : \text{The number of jobs between facilities } i \text{ and } j \text{ is not constrained} \end{cases}$$

$$[\mathbf{B}]_{ij} = \begin{cases} e : \text{Facility } i \text{ has an external input } j \\ \varepsilon : \text{Facility } i \text{ does not have an external input } j \end{cases}$$

$$[\boldsymbol{C}]_{ij} = \begin{cases} e : \text{External output } i \text{ has a preceding facility } j \\ \varepsilon : \text{External output } i \text{ does not have a preceding facility } j \end{cases}$$

We refer to these matrices as the weight, adjacency, capacity, input and output matrices, respectively. Moreover, for facility i, denote the list of preceding facilities, external inputs, and downstream facilities with maximum capacity $h\,(\geq 1)$ by R_i, Q_i and M_{ih}, respectively. Fig. 2 depicts an image of these symbols.

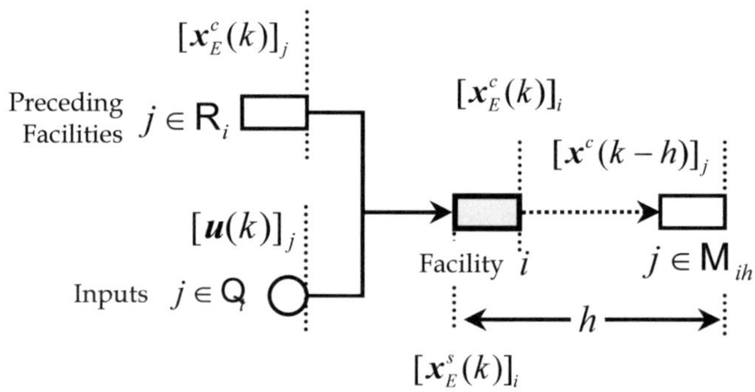

Fig. 2. External inputs and facilities following the *i*-th facility

Let us now obtain the earliest process start and completion times in facility i $(1 \le i \le n)$. With regard to process completion times, we stipulate that each must be equal or greater than the following two time instants:

- The time at which the processing time $d_i(k)$ has elapsed from the earliest process start time $[\boldsymbol{x}_E^s(k)]_i$.
- The process completion time of the previous job $[\boldsymbol{x}^c(k-1)]_i$.

The second condition is established by the FIFO policy. Thus, the earliest process completion time, denoted by $[\boldsymbol{x}_E^c(k)]_i$, is formulated using the weight matrix $\boldsymbol{P}_k$ as follows:

$$\begin{aligned}[\boldsymbol{x}_E^c(k)]_i &= \left([\boldsymbol{x}_E^s(k)]_i + d_i(k)\right) \oplus [\boldsymbol{x}^c(k-1)]_i = \bigoplus_{j=1}^{n}\left([\boldsymbol{P}_k]_{ij} \otimes [\boldsymbol{x}_E^s(k)]_j\right) \oplus [\boldsymbol{x}^c(k-1)]_i \\ &= [\boldsymbol{P}_k \boldsymbol{x}_E^s(k)]_i \oplus [\boldsymbol{x}^c(k-1)]_i\end{aligned} \tag{17}$$

Next, we consider the earliest process start time. To begin the process in facility i, all conditions below must be satisfied.

- All processes in the preceding facilities R_i are completed.
- All required materials from the external inputs Q_i are supplied.
- The number of on-going jobs between facilities i and $j \in \mathsf{M}_{ih}$ is equal or smaller than h.
- Processing of the previous job $k-1$ has begun.

The third condition corresponds to capacity constraints, and the last invokes the FIFO policy. Accordingly, the earliest process start time, denoted by $[\boldsymbol{x}_E^s(k)]_i$, is formulated in the following manner.

$$\begin{aligned}[\boldsymbol{x}_E^s(k)]_i &= \left(\bigoplus_{j \in \mathsf{R}_i} [\boldsymbol{x}_E^c(k)]_j\right) \oplus \left(\bigoplus_{j \in \mathsf{Q}_i} [\boldsymbol{u}(k)]_j\right) \oplus \left(\bigoplus_{h=1}^{H} \bigoplus_{j \in \mathsf{M}_{ih}} [\boldsymbol{x}^c(k-h)]_j\right) \oplus [\boldsymbol{x}^s(k-1)]_i \\ &= \left(\bigoplus_{j=1}^{n} [\boldsymbol{F}]_{ij} \otimes [\boldsymbol{x}_E^c(k)]_j\right) \oplus \left(\bigoplus_{j=1}^{m} [\boldsymbol{B}]_{ij} \otimes [\boldsymbol{u}(k)]_j\right) \\ &\qquad \oplus \left(\bigoplus_{h=1}^{H} \bigoplus_{j=1}^{n} [\boldsymbol{H}^{(h)}]_{ij} \otimes [\boldsymbol{x}^c(k-h)]_j\right) \oplus [\boldsymbol{x}^s(k-1)]_i \\ &= [\boldsymbol{F}\boldsymbol{x}_E^c(k)]_i \oplus [\boldsymbol{B}\boldsymbol{u}(k)]_i \oplus \bigoplus_{h=1}^{H} [\boldsymbol{H}^{(h)} \boldsymbol{x}^c(k-h)]_i \oplus [\boldsymbol{x}^s(k-1)]_i\end{aligned} \tag{18}$$

H is the maximum buffer size imposed on the system. Noting that (17) and (18) hold true for all i $(1 \le i \le n)$, they can be summarised in matrix form as follows:

$$\begin{bmatrix} \boldsymbol{x}_E^s(k) \\ \boldsymbol{x}_E^c(k) \end{bmatrix} = \begin{bmatrix} \varepsilon & \boldsymbol{F} \\ \boldsymbol{P}_k & \varepsilon \end{bmatrix} \otimes \begin{bmatrix} \boldsymbol{x}_E^s(k) \\ \boldsymbol{x}_E^c(k) \end{bmatrix} \oplus \begin{bmatrix} \boldsymbol{B} \\ \varepsilon \end{bmatrix} \otimes \boldsymbol{u}(k)$$
$$\oplus \bigoplus_{h=1}^{H} \begin{bmatrix} \varepsilon & \boldsymbol{H}^{(h)} \\ \varepsilon & \varepsilon \end{bmatrix} \otimes \begin{bmatrix} \boldsymbol{x}_E^s(k-h) \\ \boldsymbol{x}_E^c(k-h) \end{bmatrix} \oplus \begin{bmatrix} \boldsymbol{e} & \varepsilon \\ \varepsilon & \boldsymbol{e} \end{bmatrix} \otimes \begin{bmatrix} \boldsymbol{x}^s(k-1) \\ \boldsymbol{x}^c(k-1) \end{bmatrix}$$

This can be simply represented as follows:

$$\boldsymbol{x}_E(k) = \overline{\boldsymbol{F}}_k \boldsymbol{x}_E(k) \oplus \bigoplus_{h=1}^{H} \overline{\boldsymbol{H}}^{(h)} \boldsymbol{x}(k-h) \oplus \overline{\boldsymbol{B}} \boldsymbol{u}(k) \tag{19}$$

where:

$$\boldsymbol{x}(k) = \begin{bmatrix} \boldsymbol{x}^s(k) \\ \boldsymbol{x}^c(k) \end{bmatrix},\ \overline{\boldsymbol{F}}_k = \begin{bmatrix} \varepsilon & \boldsymbol{F} \\ \boldsymbol{P}_k & \varepsilon \end{bmatrix},\ \overline{\boldsymbol{B}} = \begin{bmatrix} \boldsymbol{B} \\ \varepsilon \end{bmatrix},\ \overline{\boldsymbol{H}}^{(1)} = \begin{bmatrix} \boldsymbol{e} & \boldsymbol{H}^{(1)} \\ \varepsilon & \boldsymbol{e} \end{bmatrix},\ \overline{\boldsymbol{H}}^{(h)} = \begin{bmatrix} \varepsilon & \boldsymbol{H}^{(h)} \\ \varepsilon & \varepsilon \end{bmatrix}\ h \geq 2 \tag{20}$$

We note here that (19) is an implicit expression for $\boldsymbol{x}_E(k)$. Thus, by substituting the entire right-hand-side of (19) with $\boldsymbol{x}_E(k)$ in the first term of the right-hand-side, we obtain the following relationship:

$$\boldsymbol{x}_E(k) = \overline{\boldsymbol{F}}_k \left(\overline{\boldsymbol{F}}_k \boldsymbol{x}_E(k) \oplus \bigoplus_{h=1}^{H} \overline{\boldsymbol{H}}^{(h)} \boldsymbol{x}(k-h) \oplus \overline{\boldsymbol{B}} \boldsymbol{u}(k) \right) \oplus \bigoplus_{h=1}^{H} \overline{\boldsymbol{H}}^{(h)} \boldsymbol{x}(k-h) \oplus \overline{\boldsymbol{B}} \boldsymbol{u}(k)$$
$$= \overline{\boldsymbol{F}}_k^2 \boldsymbol{x}_E(k) \oplus (\boldsymbol{e} \oplus \overline{\boldsymbol{F}}_k) \left[\bigoplus_{h=1}^{H} \overline{\boldsymbol{H}}^{(h)} \boldsymbol{x}(k-h) \oplus \overline{\boldsymbol{B}} \boldsymbol{u}(k) \right]$$

Furthermore, by repeating this transformation, we obtain:

$$\begin{aligned} \boldsymbol{x}_E(k) &= \boldsymbol{F}_k^3 \boldsymbol{x}_E(k) \oplus (\boldsymbol{e} \oplus \overline{\boldsymbol{F}}_k \oplus \overline{\boldsymbol{F}}_k^2) \left[\bigoplus_{h=1}^{H} \overline{\boldsymbol{H}}^{(h)} \boldsymbol{x}(k-h) \oplus \overline{\boldsymbol{B}} \boldsymbol{u}(k) \right] \\ \cdots &= \overline{\boldsymbol{F}}_k^l \boldsymbol{x}_E(k) \oplus (\boldsymbol{e} \oplus \overline{\boldsymbol{F}}_k \oplus \overline{\boldsymbol{F}}_k^2 \oplus \cdots \oplus \overline{\boldsymbol{F}}_k^{l-1}) \left[\bigoplus_{h=1}^{H} \overline{\boldsymbol{H}}^{(h)} \boldsymbol{x}(k-h) \oplus \overline{\boldsymbol{B}} \boldsymbol{u}(k) \right] \end{aligned} \tag{21}$$

With regard to $\overline{\boldsymbol{F}}_k$, the following relationship holds:

$$\overline{\boldsymbol{F}}_k^2 = \begin{bmatrix} \boldsymbol{F}\boldsymbol{P}_k & \varepsilon \\ \varepsilon & \boldsymbol{P}_k\boldsymbol{F} \end{bmatrix},\quad \overline{\boldsymbol{F}}_k^3 = \begin{bmatrix} \varepsilon & (\boldsymbol{F}\boldsymbol{P}_k)\boldsymbol{F} \\ (\boldsymbol{P}_k\boldsymbol{F})\boldsymbol{P}_k & \varepsilon \end{bmatrix},\quad \overline{\boldsymbol{F}}_k^4 = \begin{bmatrix} (\boldsymbol{F}\boldsymbol{P}_k)^2 & \varepsilon \\ \varepsilon & (\boldsymbol{P}_k\boldsymbol{F})^2 \end{bmatrix},\quad \cdots,$$
$$\overline{\boldsymbol{F}}_k^{2\cdot l-1} = \begin{bmatrix} \varepsilon & (\boldsymbol{F}\boldsymbol{P}_k)^l \boldsymbol{F} \\ (\boldsymbol{P}_k\boldsymbol{F})^l \boldsymbol{P}_k & \varepsilon \end{bmatrix},\ \overline{\boldsymbol{F}}_k^{2\cdot l} = \begin{bmatrix} (\boldsymbol{F}\boldsymbol{P}_k)^l & \varepsilon \\ \varepsilon & (\boldsymbol{P}_k\boldsymbol{F})^l \end{bmatrix}$$

In addition, there is an instance s $(2 \le s \le n)$ that satisfies:

$$(\boldsymbol{FP}_k)^{s-1} \neq \varepsilon\,,\ (\boldsymbol{P}_k\boldsymbol{F})^{s-1} \neq \varepsilon\,,\ (\boldsymbol{FP}_k)^{s} = (\boldsymbol{P}_k\boldsymbol{F})^{s} = \varepsilon$$

which is dependent on the precedence relation of the system. With the help of this property, (21) is finally transformed into:

$$\boldsymbol{x}_E(k) = \overline{\boldsymbol{F}}_k^{*}\left[\bigoplus_{h=1}^{H} \overline{\boldsymbol{H}}^{(h)}\boldsymbol{x}(k-h) \oplus \overline{\boldsymbol{B}}\boldsymbol{u}(k)\right] \tag{22}$$

where:

$$\overline{\boldsymbol{F}}_k^{*} = \boldsymbol{e} \oplus \overline{\boldsymbol{F}} \oplus \cdots \oplus \overline{\boldsymbol{F}}^{2\cdot s-1} = \begin{bmatrix} (\boldsymbol{FP}_k)^{*} & (\boldsymbol{FP}_k)^{*}\boldsymbol{F} \\ (\boldsymbol{P}_k\boldsymbol{F})^{*}\boldsymbol{P}_k & (\boldsymbol{P}_k\boldsymbol{F})^{*} \end{bmatrix},$$
$$(\boldsymbol{FP}_k)^{*} = \boldsymbol{e} \oplus (\boldsymbol{FP}_k) \oplus \cdots \oplus (\boldsymbol{FP}_k)^{s-1},\ (\boldsymbol{P}_k\boldsymbol{F})^{*} = \boldsymbol{e} \oplus (\boldsymbol{P}_k\boldsymbol{F}) \oplus \cdots \oplus (\boldsymbol{P}_k\boldsymbol{F})^{s-1}$$

Superscript * refers to the Kleene star (Heidergott et al., 2006), a well-known concept in the field of information theory. The original definition assumes the infinite summation over sequential powers of a given matrix:

$$\boldsymbol{X}^{*} = \bigoplus_{l=0}^{\infty} \boldsymbol{X}^{l} = \boldsymbol{e} \oplus \boldsymbol{X} \oplus \boldsymbol{X}^{2} \oplus \cdots$$

If there is an instance s such that $\boldsymbol{X}^{s-1} \neq \varepsilon$ and $\boldsymbol{X}^{s} = \varepsilon$, $\boldsymbol{X}$ is said to be nilpotent and the above operation reduces to a finite sum of powers of $\boldsymbol{X}$. The adjacency matrix of target systems is a case in point. Several efficient computation methods for the Kleene star have been proposed. See Goto & Takahashi (2009) for details.

Moreover, we note here that $\boldsymbol{P}_k(\boldsymbol{FP}_k)^{*} = (\boldsymbol{P}_k\boldsymbol{F})^{*}\boldsymbol{P}_k$ holds. This means that $(\boldsymbol{FP}_k)^{*}$ and $(\boldsymbol{P}_k\boldsymbol{F})^{*}$ are related as follows:

$$[(\boldsymbol{FP}_k)^{*}]_{ij} + d_i(k) = [(\boldsymbol{P}_k\boldsymbol{F})^{*}]_{ij} + d_j(k) \tag{23}$$

Thus, once either $(\boldsymbol{FP}_k)^{*}$ or $(\boldsymbol{P}_k\boldsymbol{F})^{*}$ has been calculated, the other can be calculated with low computation load.

Next, we consider the earliest output time. For external output i, let us denote the list of preceding facilities by T_i. Then, the output time must be equal or greater than the maximisation of the process completion times in these facilities. Thus, the earliest output time in external output i $(1 \le i \le p)$ can be expressed as:

$$[\boldsymbol{y}_E(k)]_i = \left(\bigoplus_{j \in \mathsf{T}_i} [\boldsymbol{x}^{c}(k)]_j\right) = \left(\bigoplus_{j=1}^{p} [\boldsymbol{C}]_{ij} \otimes [\boldsymbol{x}^{c}(k)]_j\right) = [\boldsymbol{C}\boldsymbol{x}^{c}(k)]_i$$

Since this holds true for all i $(1 \le i \le p)$, $\boldsymbol{y}_E(k) = \boldsymbol{C}\boldsymbol{x}^c(k)$ is obtained. Moreover, this can also be represented as the following using the same state variable as appears in (22):

$$\boldsymbol{y}_E(k) = \overline{\boldsymbol{C}}\boldsymbol{x}(k) \tag{24}$$

where:

$$\overline{\boldsymbol{C}} = [\varepsilon \ \ \boldsymbol{C}] \tag{25}$$

Equations (22) and (24) are extended versions of the state and output equations, respectively.

4.4 Backward type State-space representation

We derive a backward state-space representation taking capacity constraints into account. The same matrix parameters, $\boldsymbol{P}_k$, $\boldsymbol{F}$, $\boldsymbol{H}^{(h)} \in \boldsymbol{R}_{\max}^{n \times n}$, $\boldsymbol{B} \in \boldsymbol{R}_{\max}^{n \times m}$ and $\boldsymbol{C} \in \boldsymbol{R}_{\max}^{p \times n}$, are used as in the previous subsection. Fig. 3 depicts the relevant constraints regarding facility i $(1 \le i \le n)$. With respect to facility i, S_i and P_i represent the number of succeeding facilities and attached external outputs, respectively. Suppose there is a constraint for the maximum number of jobs between the process completion point in facility i and the process starting point in upstream facility j, and denote the collection of facilities j by N_{ih} if its corresponding number is h. For the k-th job in facility i, represent the latest process starting and completion times as $[\boldsymbol{x}_L^s(k)]_i$ and $[\boldsymbol{x}_L^c(k)]_i$, respectively.

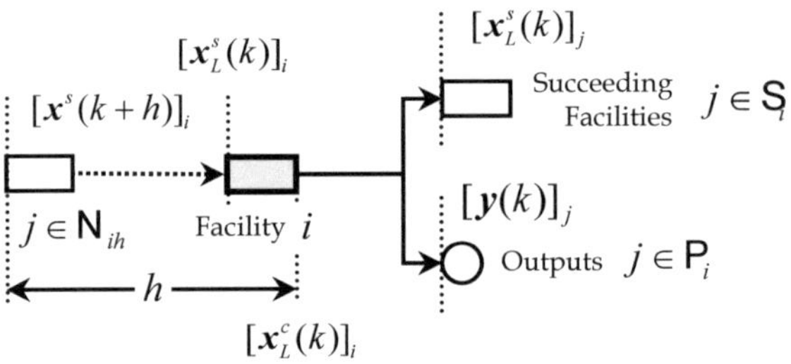

Fig. 3. External output and facilities following the i-th facility

The completion time of the k-th job in facility i is equal to, or earlier than, the following four times:

- The latest start time $[\boldsymbol{x}_L^s(k)]_j$ in succeeding facilities $j \in \mathsf{S}_i$
- Output time $[\boldsymbol{y}(k)]_j$ to external output $j \in \mathsf{P}_i$
- The start time $[\boldsymbol{x}^s(k+h)]_j$ of the ($k+h$)-th job in upstream facilities $j \in \mathsf{N}_{ih}$
- The completion time $[\boldsymbol{x}^c(k+1)]_i$ of the subsequent job

Accordingly, the latest completion time in facility i can be formulated as follows:

$$\begin{aligned}[\boldsymbol{x}_L^c(k)]_i &= \left(\bigwedge_{j\in S_i}[\boldsymbol{x}_L^s(k)]_j\right)\wedge\left(\bigwedge_{j\in P_i}[\boldsymbol{y}(k)]_j\right)\wedge\left(\bigwedge_{h=1}^{H}\bigwedge_{j\in N_{ih}}[\boldsymbol{x}^s(k+h)]_j\right)\wedge[\boldsymbol{x}^c(k+1)]_i \\ &= \left(\bigwedge_{j=1}^{n}[\boldsymbol{F}^T]_{ij}\setminus[\boldsymbol{x}_L^s(k)]_j\right)\wedge\left(\bigwedge_{j=1}^{p}[\boldsymbol{C}^T]_{ij}\setminus[\boldsymbol{y}(k)]_j\right) \\ &\qquad \wedge\left(\bigwedge_{h=1}^{H}\bigwedge_{j=1}^{n}[\boldsymbol{H}^{(h)T}]_{ij}\setminus[\boldsymbol{x}^s(k+h)]_j\right)\wedge[\boldsymbol{x}^c(k+1)]_i \\ &= [\boldsymbol{F}^T\odot\boldsymbol{x}_L^s(k)]_i\wedge[\boldsymbol{C}^T\odot\boldsymbol{y}(k)]_i\wedge\bigwedge_{h=1}^{H}[\boldsymbol{H}^{(h)T}\odot\boldsymbol{x}^s(k+h)]_i\wedge[\boldsymbol{x}^c(k+1)]_i\end{aligned} \tag{26}$$

Moreover, the process starting time of the k -th job in facility i is equal to, or earlier than:

- The time at which $d_i(k)$ is subtracted from the latest completion time in the corresponding facility.
- The start time of the next job $[\boldsymbol{x}^s(k+1)]_i$.

Thus, the latest start time for processing can be formulated as follows:

$$\begin{aligned}[\boldsymbol{x}_L^s(k)]_i &= \left([\boldsymbol{x}_L^c(k)]_i - d_i(k)\right)\wedge[\boldsymbol{x}^s(k+1)]_i \\ &= \bigwedge_{j=1}^{n}[\boldsymbol{P}_k^T]_{ij}\setminus[\boldsymbol{x}_L^c(k)]_j\wedge[\boldsymbol{x}^s(k+1)] = [\boldsymbol{P}_k^T\odot\boldsymbol{x}_L^c(k)]_i\wedge[\boldsymbol{x}^s(k+1)]_i\end{aligned} \tag{27}$$

Equations (26) and (27) hold true for all i $(1\le i\le n)$, and can be summarised in matrix form as follows:

$$\begin{aligned}\begin{bmatrix}\boldsymbol{x}_L^s(k)\\ \boldsymbol{x}_L^c(k)\end{bmatrix} &= \begin{bmatrix}\varepsilon & \boldsymbol{P}_k^T\\ \boldsymbol{F}^T & \varepsilon\end{bmatrix}\odot\begin{bmatrix}\boldsymbol{x}_L^s(k)\\ \boldsymbol{x}_L^c(k)\end{bmatrix}\wedge\begin{bmatrix}\varepsilon\\ \boldsymbol{C}_0^T\end{bmatrix}\odot\boldsymbol{y}(k) \\ &\quad\wedge\bigwedge_{h=1}^{Q}\begin{bmatrix}\varepsilon & \varepsilon\\ \boldsymbol{H}^{(h)T} & \varepsilon\end{bmatrix}\odot\begin{bmatrix}\boldsymbol{x}_L^s(k+h)\\ \boldsymbol{x}_L^c(k+h)\end{bmatrix}\wedge\begin{bmatrix}e & \varepsilon\\ \varepsilon & e\end{bmatrix}\odot\begin{bmatrix}\boldsymbol{x}^s(k+1)\\ \boldsymbol{x}^c(k+1)\end{bmatrix}\end{aligned}$$

Moreover, using the augmented matrices in (20) and (25), the following simplified expression is obtained:

$$\boldsymbol{x}_L(k) = \overline{\boldsymbol{F}}_k^T\odot\boldsymbol{x}_L(k)\wedge\bigwedge_{h=1}^{H}\overline{\boldsymbol{H}}_0^{(h)^T}\odot\boldsymbol{x}(k+h)\wedge\overline{\boldsymbol{C}}_0^T\odot\boldsymbol{y}(k) \tag{28}$$

Equation (28) is an implicit form of $\boldsymbol{x}_L(k)$. Iteratively substituting the entire right side of (28) with the first term and using the relational expressions in (16), equation (28) is transformed into the following explicit form:

$$\begin{aligned} \boldsymbol{x}_L(k) &= \overline{\boldsymbol{F}}_k^{2T} \odot \boldsymbol{x}_L(k) \wedge (\boldsymbol{e} \oplus \overline{\boldsymbol{F}}_k)^T \odot \left[\bigwedge_{h=1}^{H} \overline{\boldsymbol{H}}^{(h)T} \odot \boldsymbol{x}(k+h) \wedge \overline{\boldsymbol{C}}^T \odot \boldsymbol{y}(k) \right] \\ &= \cdots = \overline{\boldsymbol{F}}_k^{*T} \odot \left[\bigwedge_{h=1}^{H} \overline{\boldsymbol{H}}^{(h)T} \odot \boldsymbol{x}(k+h) \wedge \overline{\boldsymbol{C}}^T \odot \boldsymbol{y}(k) \right] \end{aligned} \tag{29}$$

Fig. 4 depicts the relationships regarding external input i relevant to calculating the latest input time. W_i is a collection of succeeding facilities attached to external input i. Since the start time for the k-th job in succeeding facility $j \in W_i$ is $[\boldsymbol{x}^s(k)]_j$, the latest feed time for the corresponding job $[\boldsymbol{u}_L(k)]_i$ can be determined as follows:

$$[\boldsymbol{u}_L(k)]_i = \bigwedge_{j \in W_i} ([\boldsymbol{x}^s(k)]_j) = \bigwedge_{j=1}^{n} ([\boldsymbol{B}^T]_{ij} \setminus [\boldsymbol{x}^s(k)]_j) = [\boldsymbol{B}^T \odot \boldsymbol{x}^s(k)]_i$$

This holds true for all i $(1 \le i \le m)$, and can also be expressed using the same state vector as (22), thus:

$$\boldsymbol{u}_L(k) = \overline{\boldsymbol{B}}^T \odot \boldsymbol{x}(k) \tag{30}$$

From the above we obtain the state equation (29) and output equation (30) which represents the latest possible times for the k-th job.

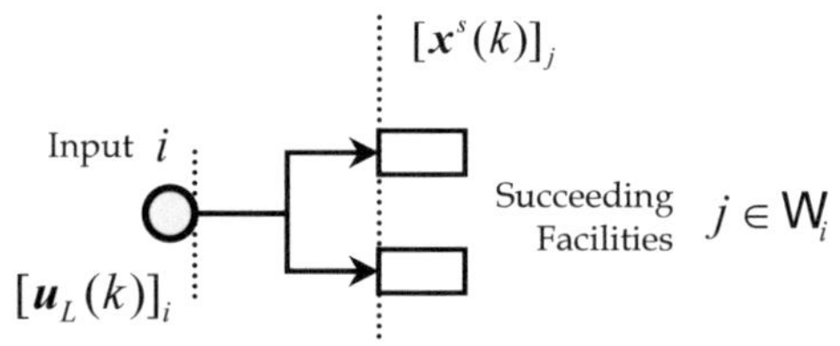

Fig. 4. Facilities following the i-th external input

4.5 The parameter matrix of the capacity constraint

This subsection concentrates on a method for generating matrices $\boldsymbol{H}^{(h)}$ that specify buffer capacities between facilities. Such a method is required to provide H matrices for deriving state equations, that may be complicated if they are specified individually. Hence, we provide a single matrix $\boldsymbol{G}$ to represent all capacity constraints.

$$[\mathbf{G}]_{ij} = \begin{cases} e: \text{The maximum number of jobs that can exist between facility } i \text{ and its downstream facility } j \text{ is } h \\ \varepsilon: \text{There is no constraint on the number of jobs from } i \text{ to } j \end{cases}$$

The downstream facility j may include facility i itself, namely $i = j$. For this definition, the following relation holds true:

$$\bigoplus_{j=1}^{n}\bigoplus_{i=1}^{n}[\boldsymbol{G}]_{ij} = H$$

Matrices $\boldsymbol{H}^{(h)}$ can be generated by applying the following rule for all h $(1 \le h \le Q)$.

$$[\boldsymbol{H}^{(h)}]_{ij} = \begin{cases} e : \text{if } [\boldsymbol{G}]_{ij} = h \\ \varepsilon : \text{otherwise} \end{cases}$$

For systems in which the maximum buffer is one for a single facility and infinite between adjacent facilities, the parameter matrix is $\boldsymbol{G} = \boldsymbol{e}$. Moreover, the definition of $\boldsymbol{G}$ yields:

$$\text{If } [\boldsymbol{G}]_{ij} \ne \varepsilon,\ [\boldsymbol{G}]_{ji} = \varepsilon$$

for all i and j $(i \ne j)$.

4.6 Consideration of transit times

From here on the transit times between adjacent facilities that were ignored to this point are taken into account. First, let us consider a case where transit time is constant and does not depend on the job number k. Since jobs do not overtake each other during transits here, no additional order constraints need be considered. To take transit times into account, we need only set the (i, j) -th element of the adjacent matrix that holds $[\boldsymbol{F}]_{ij} = e$ for the corresponding transit time.
Alternatively, if the transit times between facilities depend on the job number, k, additional order constraints should be considered. In this case, we can install an imaginary facility between adjacent facilities. Consider the case presented in Fig. 5 as an example. Assume the transit time from facility b to a is dependent on the job number, k, and let this time be represented by $\tau_{ab}(k)$. Here the order constraint is forced to disallow overtaking between successive jobs. Thus, we can install an imaginary facility s between facilities b and a, whose occupation time for the k -th job is $\tau_{ab}(k)(\equiv d_s(k))$. In addition to the installation of the imaginary facility, we can update the adjacency matrix $\boldsymbol{F}$. The original matrix follows the next relationship:

$$[\boldsymbol{F}]_{ab} = e\,(\equiv [\boldsymbol{F}^{(0)}]_{ab} \in \boldsymbol{R}_{\max}^{n\times n})$$

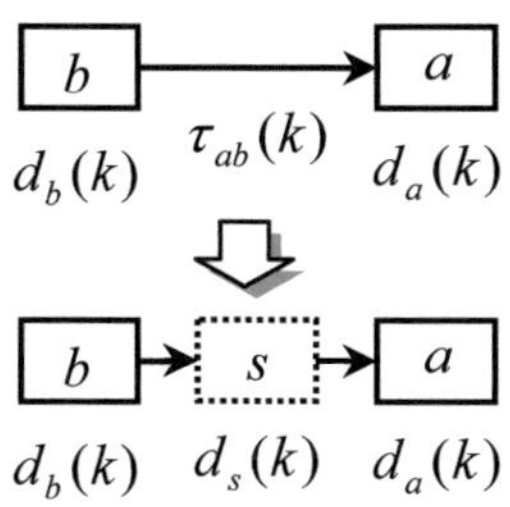

Fig. 5. Installation of an imaginary facility

Through the installation of facility s, the modified adjacency matrix $\hat{F}^{(1)} \in R_{\max}^{(n+1)\times(n+1)}$ satisfies the following properties:

$$\hat{F}^{(1)} = \begin{bmatrix} F^{(1)} & v_a^{(1)} \\ v_b^{(1)T} & \varepsilon \end{bmatrix},\ [F^{(1)}]_{ij} = \begin{cases} \varepsilon : \text{if } i = a \text{ and } j = b \\ [F^{(0)}]_{ij} : \text{otherwise} \end{cases}$$

where

$$[v_a^{(1)}]_b = \begin{cases} e : \text{if } a = b \\ \varepsilon : \text{ if } a \neq b \end{cases},\ v_a^{(1)} \in R_{\max}^{n\times n}$$

Moreover, the matrix parameter P_k is modified in the following manner:

$$\hat{P}_k^{(1)} = \begin{bmatrix} P_k^{(1)} & \varepsilon \\ \varepsilon & d_s(k) \end{bmatrix}$$

A new adjacency matrix can be generated using this procedure for all paths on which the transit time is dependent on the job number k. Let the number of installed imaginary facilities be g, and the modified adjacency matrix be denoted by $\hat{F}$. Then, the remaining representation matrices are modified as follows:

$$\hat{H}^{(1)} = \begin{bmatrix} H^{(h)} & \varepsilon \\ \varepsilon & e \end{bmatrix},\ \hat{H}^{(h)} = \begin{bmatrix} H^{(h)} & \varepsilon \\ \varepsilon & \varepsilon \end{bmatrix} (h \geq 2),\ \hat{B} = \begin{bmatrix} B \\ \varepsilon \end{bmatrix},\ \hat{C} = \begin{bmatrix} C & \varepsilon \end{bmatrix}$$

4.7 Duality of state-space representation

This subsection examines the duality of the derived state-space representations. This duality is understood in a stricter manner than simply similarity of representation, as has been discussed in the previous research.

Goto *et al.* (2007) has focused on systems in which buffer capacities are one in a single facility and infinite between adjacent facilities, which is a narrower class than this chapter handles. This class does not require consideration of order constraints since jobs cannot overtake each other even for event-varying systems. This means either $[x^{\{s,c\}}(k-1)]_i$ does not appear in (17) and (18) and $[x^{\{s,c\}}(k+1)]_i$ does not appear in (26) and (27), and they form sets of closed equations regarding $x_E^c(k)$ and $x_L^s(k)$, respectively. These equations can be represented in a form whose relationship is similar to dual systems in modern control theory. A primary advantage of this duality is that the same system matrices can be used for both forward and backward types, and the calculation time can be reduced accordingly. This reduction is effective for on-line operation especially for large-scale systems.

It is important, at this point, to remember the main concern of this chapter. Since buffer sizes must be considered flexibly, order constraints should be taken into account to disallow overtaking between jobs. This yields a closed equation for $x_E^c(k)$ or $x_L^s(k)$ that cannot be formulated as a forward type. The same situation holds true for the representation of backward type state equation. However, if we compose the augmented state-vector $x_E(k)$, equations (17), (18), (29) and (30) can be represented as dual form. This means that all required schedules can be calculated using only four representation matrices, $\overline{F}_k^*$, $\overline{H}^{(h)}$, $\overline{B}$ and $\overline{C}$. Among these matrices, only $\overline{F}_k^*$ depends on the job number. Thus, the question of how to calculate this matrix efficiently especially in event-varying systems becomes central. Due to the composition of the augmented state-space representations, the number of elements in the system matrix is quadrupled. However, as mentioned in (23), once $(P_k F_0)^*$ is calculated, the remaining three blocks of $\overline{F}_k^*$ can be calculated by simple algebraic operations. Accordingly, we know that the derived augmented state-space representations are effective, especially in on-line scheduling problems that require calculation of both earliest and latest times.

5. Rescheduling

When job parameters are changed after a job has commenced it becomes very important to be able to predict scheduling for remaining jobs in an on-line scheduling system. Typical examples of such changes in parameters are a delay in processing or tardiness in material feeding. Thus, this section considers a rescheduling method for the extended state-space representation.

5.1 Forward type

Assume that the system parameters or state variables in previous jobs changed after job commencement, and let the updated values be denoted by appending a tilde symbol [$\tilde{\cdot}$] in the following manner:

$$\tilde{P}_k,\ \tilde{u}(k),\ \tilde{x}(k-h)\ \ (1 \le h \le Q)$$

Moreover, suppose the i-th element of the state vector for job number k has changed as follows:

$$[\tilde{x}^{(+0)}(k)]_i$$

It is possible that the number of changed elements i is greater than one. Set ε for elements whose corresponding times are to be recalculated. The superscript $(+0)$ stands for the initial value for the iterative calculation. Equations (17) and (18) are formulated to model the propagation of the earliest starting time downstream. By tracking (22), the earliest start time one-step downstream can be determined as follows:

$$\tilde{x}_E^{(1)}(k) = \tilde{F}_k \tilde{x}^{(+0)}(k) \oplus \bigoplus_{h=1}^{H} \overline{H}^{(h)} \tilde{x}(k-h) \oplus \overline{B}\tilde{u}(k) \quad (31)$$

where:

$$\widetilde{F}_k = \begin{bmatrix} \varepsilon & F \\ \widetilde{P}_k & \varepsilon \end{bmatrix} \tag{32}$$

Note that the element number for (31) is abbreviated for simplicity, it holds true only for elements one-step downstream from the altered facility. Repeating the same procedure downstream, the updated earliest time j -steps downstream can be obtained thus:

$$\begin{aligned}
\widetilde{x}_E^{(j)}(k) &= \widetilde{F}_k \widetilde{x}^{(j-1)}(k) \oplus \bigoplus_{h=1}^{H} \overline{H}^{(h)} \widetilde{x}(k-h) \oplus \overline{B}\widetilde{u}(k) \\
&= \widetilde{F}_k^2 \widetilde{x}^{(j-2)}(k) \oplus (e \oplus \widetilde{F}_k) \left[\bigoplus_{h=1}^{H} \overline{H}^{(h)} \widetilde{x}(k-h) \oplus \overline{B}\widetilde{u}(k) \right] \\
\cdots &= \widetilde{F}_k^j \widetilde{x}^{(+0)}(k) \oplus (e \oplus \cdots \oplus \widetilde{F}_k^{j-1}) \left[\bigoplus_{h=1}^{H} \overline{H}^{(h)} \widetilde{x}(k-h) \oplus \overline{B}\widetilde{u}(k) \right]
\end{aligned}$$

Calculate this for all j $(1 \le j \le 2 \cdot s)$, and use the next trivial relationship:

$$\widetilde{x}_E^{(+0)}(k) = \widetilde{x}^{(+0)}(k)$$

By using the $\oplus$ operation for these equations, the following expression can be obtained:

$$\widetilde{x}_E(k) \equiv \widetilde{x}_E^{(+0)}(k) \oplus \widetilde{x}_E^{(1)}(k) \oplus \cdots \oplus \widetilde{x}_E^{(2 \cdot s)}(k) = \widetilde{F}_k^* \left[\widetilde{x}^{(+0)}(k) \oplus \bigoplus_{h=1}^{H} \overline{H}^{(h)} \widetilde{x}(k-h) \oplus \overline{B}\widetilde{u}(k) \right] \tag{33}$$

Equation (33) is a general form of forward state equation that is applicable even when the states are changed after the commencement of job k. If all elements of the state variables require recalculating, the following relation holds:

$$[\widetilde{x}^{(+0)}(k)]_i = \varepsilon \text{ for all } (1 \le i \le 2 \cdot n)$$

In this case, equation (33) is equivalent to (22).
Furthermore, consider a particular case that only contains delays in the initial schedule that occur between facilities For initial values of the state vector, set the latest values for elements in which delays occurred and keep the initial values for other elements. Using these settings, the following relationship holds:

$$\widetilde{x}^{(+0)}(k) \ge x_E(k)$$

Hence, equation (33) can be simplified as follows:

$$\tilde{\boldsymbol{x}}_E(k) = \tilde{\boldsymbol{F}}_k^* \left[\tilde{\boldsymbol{x}}^{(+0)}(k) \oplus \bigoplus_{h=1}^{H} \overline{\boldsymbol{H}}^{(h)} \tilde{\boldsymbol{x}}(k-h) \oplus \overline{\boldsymbol{B}} \tilde{\boldsymbol{u}}(k) \right] = \tilde{\boldsymbol{F}}_k^* [\tilde{\boldsymbol{x}}^{(+0)}(k) \oplus \boldsymbol{x}_E(k)] = \tilde{\boldsymbol{F}}_k^* \tilde{\boldsymbol{x}}^{(+0)}(k) \tag{34}$$

Equation (34) indicates that we can reschedule by performing only the $\tilde{\boldsymbol{F}}_k^* \otimes$ operation on the updated state vector $\tilde{\boldsymbol{x}}^{(+0)}(k)$, in cases where only delays from the initial schedule occurred. This expression is much simpler than (33), and provides an easy-to-use method in on-line scheduling, for instance, real-time progress management.

5.2 Backward type

Backward states can be handled using a method analogous to that discussed in the previous section. Assume that the system parameters and state variables are changed after the commencement of the k -th job in the following way:

$$\tilde{\boldsymbol{P}}_k,\ \tilde{\boldsymbol{y}}(k),\ \tilde{\boldsymbol{x}}(k+h)\ \ (1 \le h \le Q)$$

For both the start and completion of the k -th job, suppose the i -th element of the state vector is changed as follows:

$$[\tilde{\boldsymbol{x}}^{(-0)}(k)]_i$$

There may be multiple corresponding elements for i, and set T for elements whose values are to be recalculated. The superscript (–0) represents the initial value for an iterative calculation. Equations (26) and (27) are formulated to characterise the upstream propagation of the latest times. In a similar way to (28), the latest time one-step upstream can be formulated in the following manner:

$$\tilde{\boldsymbol{x}}_L^{(1)}(k) = \tilde{\boldsymbol{F}}_k^T \odot \tilde{\boldsymbol{x}}^{(-0)}(k) \wedge \bigwedge_{h=1}^{H} \overline{\boldsymbol{H}}^{(h)^T} \odot \tilde{\boldsymbol{x}}(k+h) \wedge \overline{\boldsymbol{C}}^T \odot \tilde{\boldsymbol{y}}(k) \tag{35}$$

where $\tilde{\boldsymbol{F}}_k$ is the same as (32). Equation (35) holds true only for elements one-step upstream from the altered facility. Repeat the same procedure moving upstream, to obtain the latest time for j -steps upstream. An iterative substitution obtains the following:

$$\tilde{\boldsymbol{x}}_L^{(j)}(k) = (\tilde{\boldsymbol{F}}_k^2)^T \odot \tilde{\boldsymbol{x}}^{(j-1)}(k) \wedge (\boldsymbol{e} \oplus \tilde{\boldsymbol{F}}_k)^T \odot \left[\bigwedge_{h=1}^{H} \overline{\boldsymbol{H}}^{(h)^T} \odot \tilde{\boldsymbol{x}}(k+h) \wedge \overline{\boldsymbol{C}}^T \odot \tilde{\boldsymbol{y}}(k) \right]$$

$$\cdots = (\tilde{\boldsymbol{F}}_k^j)^T \odot \tilde{\boldsymbol{x}}^{(-0)}(k) \wedge (\boldsymbol{e} \oplus \cdots \oplus \tilde{\boldsymbol{F}}_k^{j-1})^T \odot \left[\bigwedge_{h=1}^{H} \overline{\boldsymbol{H}}^{(h)^T} \odot \tilde{\boldsymbol{x}}(k+h) \wedge \overline{\boldsymbol{C}}^T \odot \tilde{\boldsymbol{y}}(k) \right]$$

Calculate this for all j $(1 \le j \le 2 \cdot s)$, and use the next trivial relationship:

$$\tilde{x}_L^{(-0)}(k) = \tilde{x}^{(-0)}(k)$$

The following expression is obtained by performing the $\wedge$ operation on all the resulting equations:

$$\begin{aligned} \tilde{x}_L(k) &\equiv \tilde{x}_L^{(-0)}(k) \wedge \tilde{x}_L^{(1)}(k) \wedge \cdots \wedge \tilde{x}_L^{(2 \cdot s)}(k) \\ &= (\tilde{F}_k^*)^T \odot \left[\tilde{x}^{(-0)}(k) \wedge \bigwedge_{h=1}^{H} \overline{H}^{(h)^T} \odot \tilde{x}(k+h) \wedge \overline{C}^T \odot \tilde{y}(k) \right] \end{aligned} \tag{36}$$

Equation (36) is a general backward type state equation that is applicable even if states are changed after commencement of the k -th job. If all elements are to be calculated, it follows that:

$$[\tilde{x}^{(-0)}(k)]_i = \mathsf{T} \;\text{ for all }\; (1 \le i \le 2 \cdot n)$$

and (36) is equivalent to (29).
Moreover, consider a particular case where the initial schedule is moved forward after job commencement. For the initial values of the state vector, set the updated values for elements whose schedules have been put forward, and keep the original values for the other elements. These settings lead to:

$$\tilde{x}^{(-0)}(k) \le x_L(k)$$

Thus, equation (36) can be simplified to:

$$\begin{aligned} \tilde{x}_L(k) &= (\tilde{F}_k^*)^T \odot \left[\tilde{x}^{(-0)}(k) \wedge \bigwedge_{h=1}^{H} \overline{H}^{(h)^T} \odot \tilde{x}(k+h) \wedge \overline{C}^T \odot \tilde{y}(k) \right] \\ &= (\tilde{F}_k^*)^T \odot [\tilde{x}^{(-0)}(k) \wedge x_L(k)] = (\tilde{F}_k^*)^T \odot \tilde{x}^{(-0)}(k) \end{aligned} \tag{37}$$

Equation (37) indicates that if the schedule is moved up from the original only the $(\tilde{F}_k^*)^T \odot$ operation is required on the updated state vector $\tilde{x}^{(-0)}(k)$ for rescheduling. This relationship provides a simpler method than (36).
We now have two state-space representations for event-varying systems with capacity constraints for both forward and backward state spaces.

6. Numerical Experiment

We present an applied example of the proposed method for a simple system. Fig. 6 shows a manufacturing system with two-inputs, one-output and four-facilities. F1-F4 represents the facilities 1-4 respectively, numbers in parentheses ( ) above facilities are the processing times. Numbers in square brackets [ ] below or between facilities represent buffer capacities. For instance, facilities 2 and 3 can process a maximum of two jobs simultaneously. Considering these structures, the relevant representation matrices are set as follows:

$$\boldsymbol{P}_k = \mathrm{diag}[1\ 2\ 4\ 3],\ \boldsymbol{F} = \begin{bmatrix} \varepsilon & \varepsilon & \varepsilon & \varepsilon \\ \varepsilon & \varepsilon & \varepsilon & \varepsilon \\ e & e & \varepsilon & \varepsilon \\ \varepsilon & \varepsilon & e & \varepsilon \end{bmatrix},\ \boldsymbol{B} = \begin{bmatrix} e & \varepsilon \\ \varepsilon & e \\ \varepsilon & \varepsilon \\ \varepsilon & \varepsilon \end{bmatrix},\ \boldsymbol{C} = \begin{bmatrix} \varepsilon \\ \varepsilon \\ \varepsilon \\ e \end{bmatrix}^T,\ \boldsymbol{Q} = \begin{bmatrix} 1 & \varepsilon & \varepsilon & 6 \\ \varepsilon & 2 & 4 & \varepsilon \\ e & e & 2 & \varepsilon \\ \varepsilon & \varepsilon & e & 1 \end{bmatrix}$$

The transit time from facility 1 to 3 is positive and finite, and fluctuates periodically as:

$$\tau_{31}(k) = \{0.5, 1, 0.5, 1, \cdots\}$$

which is dependent on the job number. Recalling sect. 4.6, install a new imaginary facility 5 between facilities 1 and 3, and modify the relevant representation matrices. The number of jobs to process is $k = 16$, and let all required materials be ready at time $t = 0$. This indicates $\boldsymbol{u}(k) = [0\ \ 0]^T$ $(1 \le k \le 16)$. Moreover, assuming the initial condition is empty, yields $\boldsymbol{x}(0) = \varepsilon \in \boldsymbol{R}_{\max}^{10\times 1}$.

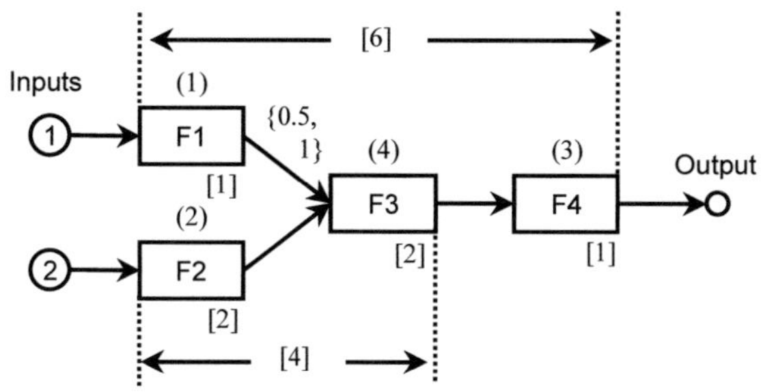

Fig. 6. A Simple manufacturing system

Fig. 7 shows the earliest process start time in facilities 1-4. The horizontal axis represents job number k. Looking at the system as a whole, the facility with the highest processing ability is 1, and the lowest is 4. In facility 1, the earliest time depends on its processing ability for $1 \le k \le 6$, but for $k \ge 7$, it comes to depend on the process completion times in facility 4 due to the capacity constraint between them. Facility 2 can process two jobs at maximum simultaneously, the facility processes jobs in accordance with its own ability in $1 \le k \le 4$. However, for $k \ge 5$, it is limited by the capacity constraint of facility 3. Facility 3 can also process two jobs at the same time, which implies that its effective throughput is greater than facility 4. Thus, as the job number k grows and the system approaches a stationary state, the entire throughput becomes dependent on facility 4 which has the lowest processing ability.

Next, let us consider a system reschedule. Suppose facility 3 breaks down for a period during processing with $k=3$, delaying completion for 10 time units. The results for recalculating the schedule using (34) for $k=3$, and (22) for $k \geq 4$ are shown in Fig. 8. The first effect of this change on the succeeding facility 4 for $k \geq 3$, followed by facility 2 that has its capacity constrained by facility 3 when $k \geq 7$. Moreover, facility 1's capacity is constrained by facility 4 when in $k \geq 9$. The relative values between facilities for $k=10$ are similar to those for $k=2$ in Fig. 7, which implies that the through-puts in facilities 1-3 may become subordinated to facility 4.

Let us now consider an example of on-line monitoring that uses both forward and backward state-space representations. Fig. 9 shows the float times in facilities 1-4 when the required output times are equal to those in Fig. 8. Float times are derived from the difference between the latest and earliest starting times; a negative value means that there is no float in the corresponding facility. Facility 4, which is located furthest downstream, is affected by the delay in $k=3$ immediately. This delay affects facilities 1-3, upstream, only after several jobs have been processed. As the processing proceeds, facilities 1-3 regain float times, with facility 2 holding the largest as it can process two jobs simultaneously. Although the effective throughput of facility 1 is equal to facility 2, it can process only one job at a time. Thus, its float time is comparable to facility 3.

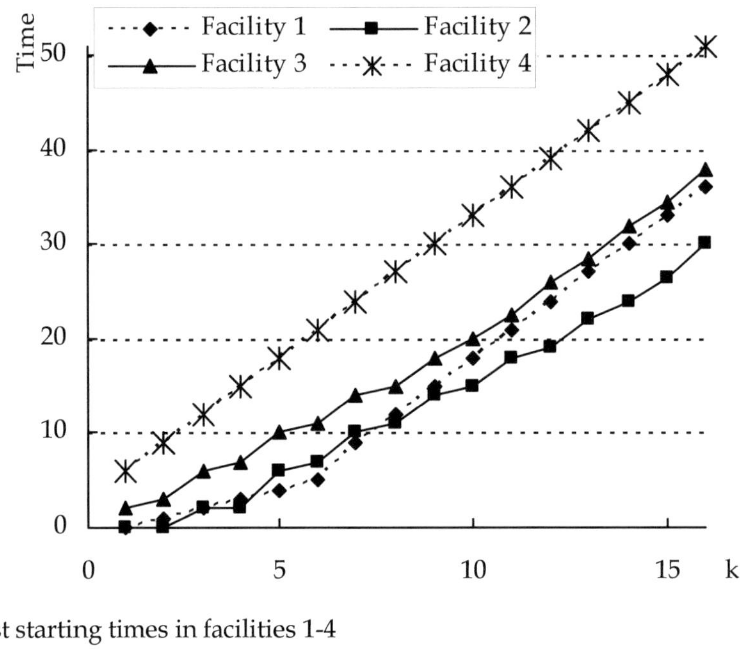

Fig. 7. Earliest starting times in facilities 1-4

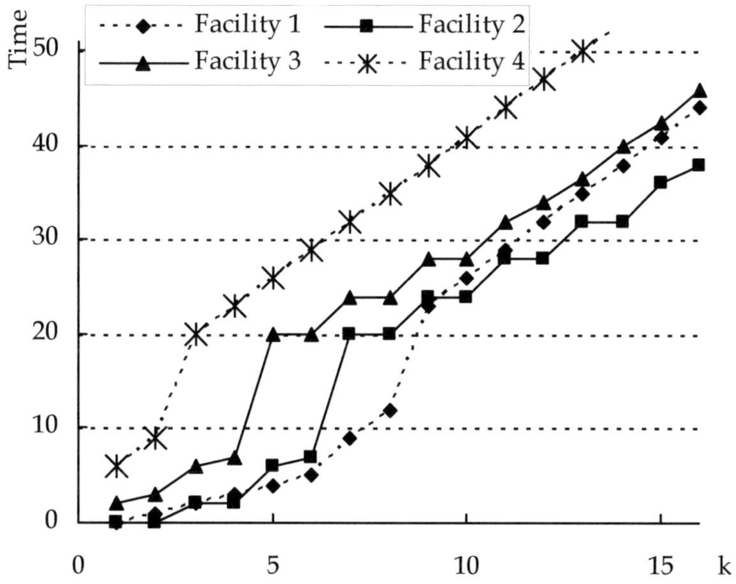

Fig. 8. Results of rescheduling

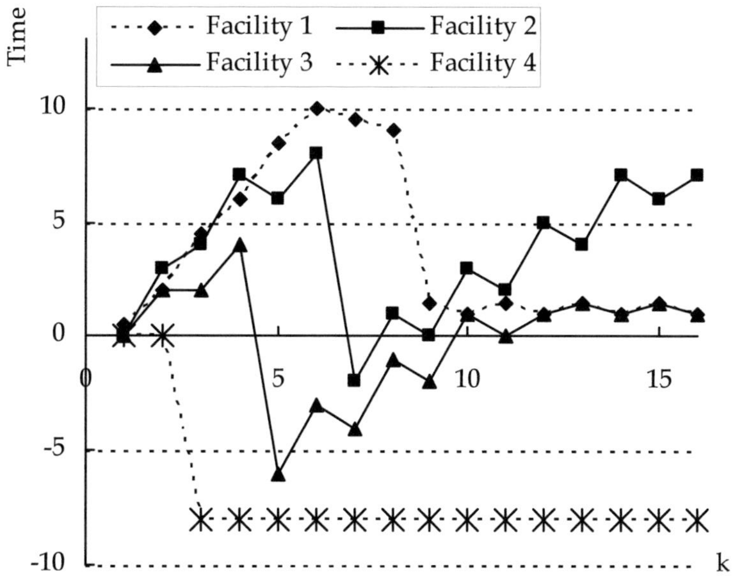

Fig. 9. Float times in facilities 1-4

7. Conclusion and future insights

This chapter has introduced modelling methods for a class of discrete event systems. Specifically, we have focused on and extended the state-space representation in Dioid and max-plus algebras. The simplest representation can only describe the behaviour of systems in which the buffer capacities are one in single facilities, and infinite between two adjacent facilities. This constraint is restrictive when applying the representation to practical systems. To resolve this, we have intensively worked on developing a systematic framework to derive state-space representations for systems where the capacity constraints for a single or between two arbitrary facilities can be taken into account. Two types of representations called forward and backward, were derived, by which the earliest and latest process start and completion times can be calculated. By using both, the float times of internal facilities can be calculated. In addition, we considered a rescheduling method that can be used for cases where the process start or completion times, or processing times are changed after the corresponding job has commenced. Using the derived formula, we can accomplish an on-line scheduling where the internal parameters change frequently.

Finally, we mention insights that point to future directions in this research field. First, the state-space representation should be extended to be able to consider the set of engaged facilities. This research assumed that all jobs use all facilities. However, in several systems, railway systems for instance, the set of facilities engaged for a particular job may differ. Moreover, capacity constraints in single facilities and between facilities are usually invoked. In existing methods, one or other constraint is taken into account, but no method that considers both of these simultaneously has been proposed. Such developments would be very important for practical applications. Second, efficient computation methods for the state equation should be developed. In terms of computation time, the time for computing the state equation increases rapidly as the system's size increases. Thus, developing efficient algorithms is essential for on-line operations. These issues should be of primary concern in future work with the potential to offer greater scope in applications.

8. References

Baccelli, F. & Hong, D. (2000). TCP is max-plus linear: and what tells us on its throughput, *Proceedings of ACM-SIGCOMM*, pp.219–230, Stockholm, August 2000

Baccelli, F.; Cohen, G., Olsder, G.J. & Quadrat, J.P. (1992). *Synchronization and Linearity: An Algebra for Discrete Event Systems*, John Wiley & Sons, North River Press, ISBN: 047193609X, New York. http://maxplus.org

Boimond, J.L. & Ferrier, J.L. (1996). Internal model control and max-algebra: controller design. *IEEE Transactions on Automatic Control*, Vol. AC-41, No. 3, 457–461, ISSN: 0018-9286

Boom, T.; Heidergott, B. & De Shutter, B. (2007). Complexity reduction in MPC for stochastic max-plus linear discrete event systems by variability expansion. *Automatica*, Vol.43, No.6, 1058–1063, ISSN: 0005-1098

Boom, T.; De. Schutter, B., Schullerus, G. & Krebs, V. (2003). Adaptive model predictive control using max-plus-linear input-output models, *Proceedings of the American Control Conference*, pp.933–938, Denver, June 2003

Girault, C. & Valk, R. (2002). *Petri Nets for Systems Engineering: A Guide to Modeling, Verification, and Applications*, Springer , ISBN: 3540412174, Berlin

Cofer, D.D. & Garg, V.K. (1996). Supervisory control of real-time discrete event systems using lattice theory. *IEEE Transactions on Automatic Control*, Vol.41, No.12, 1751-1778, ISSN: 0018-9286

Goto, H. & Takahashi, H. (2009). Fast computation methods for the Kleene star in max-plus linear systems with a DAG structure. *IEICE Transactions on Fundamentals*, Vol.E92-A, No.11, 2794-2799, ISSN: 0916-8508

Goto, H. (2007). Dual representation of event-varying max-plus linear systems. *International Journal of Computational Science*, Vol. 1, No.3, 225-242, ISSN: 1992-6669

Goverde, R. (2007). Railway timetable stability analysis using max-plus system theory. *Transportation Research Part B*, Vol. 41, No.2, 179-201, ISSN: 0191-2615

Heemels, W.P.M.H.; De Schutter B. & Bemporad, A. (2001). Equivalence of hybrid dynamical models. *Automatica*, Vol.37, No.7, 1085–1091, ISSN: 0005-1098

Harrison, J. (2009). *Handbook of Practical Logic and Automated Reasoning*, Cambridge University Press, ISBN: 0521899575, New York

Heidergott, B.; Olsder, G.J. & Woude, J. (2006). *Max Plus at Work: Modeling and Analysis of Synchronized Systems*, Princeton University Press, ISBN: 0691117632, New Jersey

Heidergott, B. & De Vries, R. (2001). Towards a (max,+) control theory for public transportation networks. *Discrete Event Dynamical Systems: Theory and Applications*, Vol.11, No.4, 371–398, ISSN: 0924-6703

Kelarev, A. (2003). *Graph Algebras and Automata*, Marcel Dekker, ISBN: 0824747089, New York

Krivulin, N. (1996). Max-plus algebra models of queuing networks, *Proceedings of International Workshop on Discrete Event Systems*, pp.76–81, London, August 1996

Moh, A.; Manier, M., Manier H. & Moudni, A. (2005). A max-plus algebra modeling for a public transport system. *Cybernetics and Systems*, vol. 36, 1-16, ISSN: 0196-9722

Ramadge, P.J. & Wonham, W.M. (1987). Supervisory control of a class of discrete event processes. *SIAM Journal on Control and Optimization*, Vol.25, No.1, 206–230 ISSN: 0363-0129

Sampath, M.; Sengupta, R., Lafortune, S., Sinnamohidden K. & Teneketzis, D. (1996). Failure diagnosis using discrete event models, *IEEE Transactions on Control System Technology*, Vol.4, No.2, 105–124, ISSN: 1063-6536

Schullerus, G.; Krebs, V., De Schutter, B. & Boom, T. (2006). Input signal design for identification of max-plus-linear-systems. *Automatica*, Vol.42, No.6, 937–943, ISSN: 0005-1098

Schullerus, G. & Krebs, V. (2001). Diagnosis of batch processes based on parameter estimation of discrete event models, *Proceedings of the European Control Conference*, pp.1612–1617, Porto, September 2001

De Schutter, B.; Boom, T. & Verdult, V. (2002). State space identification of max-plus-linear discrete event systems from input-output data, *Proceedings of the 41st IEEE Conference on Decision and Control*, pp.4024-4029, Las Vegas, December 2002

De Schutter, B. & Boom, T. (2001). Model predictive control for max-plus-linear systems. *Automatica*, Vol.37, No.7, 1049–1056, ISSN: 0005-1098

4

Supply chain design: guidelines from a simulation approach

Eleonora Bottani and Roberto Montanari
Department of Industrial Engineering, University of Parma
Parma (ITALY)

1. Introduction

Supply chain management (SCM) is the process of integrating suppliers, manufacturers, warehouses, and retailers in the supply chain, so that goods are produced and delivered in the right quantities, and at the right time, while minimizing costs as well as satisfying customer's requirements (Cooper et al., 1997).

Managing the entire supply chain is a key factor for a successful business. World-class organizations now realize that non-integrated manufacturing processes, non-integrated distribution processes and poor relationships with suppliers and customers are inadequate for their success (Chang & Makatsoris, 2001).

A typical supply chain consists of a number of organizations; it starts with suppliers, who provide raw materials to manufacturers, which manufacture products and keep the manufactured goods in the warehouses. Then, products are sent to distribution centres and shipped to retailers. Due to the complexities of supply chain and to the numerous players involved in the product flow, supply chain design is a relevant topic for developing an optimal platform for an effective SCM (Yan et al., 2003). The proper design of a supply chain encompasses a set of decisions, embracing both strategic and tactical levels. Examples of such decisions concern number of echelons required and number of facilities per echelon, reorder policy to be adopted by echelons, assignment of each market region to one or more locations, selection of suppliers for sub-assemblies, components and materials (Chopra & Meindl, 2004; Hammami et al., 2008).

At the same time, there are several expected benefits from a proper supply chain configuration, which include better coordination of material and capacity, reduced order cycle time, decrease in inventory cost and bullwhip effect (Lee et al., 2004), transport optimization, and increased customer responsiveness (Chang & Makatsoris, 2001).

An analysis of the recent literature shows that the problem of optimizing supply chain design is approached by researchers either with linear programming (operational research) models or through simulation models. Linear programming models are exploited with several aims, which encompass determining the number, location, and capacity of DCs, minimizing the total cost, or maximizing the profit of the supply chain (e.g., Yan et al., 2003; Tiwari et al., 2010; Bashiri & Tabrizi, 2010). Furthermore, problems such as supplier

selection or technology management can be included in the model (e.g., Hammami et al., 2009).
As an alternative to operational research models, simulation is recognized as a powerful tool to observe the behaviour of supply chains, assess their efficiency level, evaluate new management solutions, identify the most suitable configuration and optimize the distribution channel (Iannone et al., 2007). Among its advantages, simulation allows evaluating the operating performance of a system prior to its implementation or in conditions different from its current status; moreover, it enables the examination of the sensitivity of a system to its design parameters and initial conditions. Finally, results of a simulation may suggest a better mode of operation or method of organizing (Harrison et al., 2007). By using simulation models, researchers often quantify the benefits resulting from SCM, in order to support decision making either at:

- strategic level, including redesigning the structure of a supply chain; or
- operational level, including setting the values of control policies (Kleijnen, 2003).

Simulation is also useful when complex supply chain configurations (e.g., supply networks) should be examined and investigated in detail. The analysis of the literature, however, shows that the existing studies are often limited to the analysis of simple supply chain configurations, usually referring to two-echelon systems, with one or few players per echelon. However, due to the increased complexity of real systems, the contribution of such studies to the optimization of supply chain design is quite limited. Conversely, there are only few studies which either investigate multi-echelon supply chains or supply networks. Among those works, Hwarng et al. (2005) modelled a complex supply chain and investigate the effects of several parameters, including demand and lead time distribution, and postponement strategies, on the resulting performance. Shang et al. (2004) applied simulation, Taguchi method and response surface methodology to identify the 'best' operating conditions for a supply chain. These authors examined the following supply chain parameters: information sharing, postponement, capacity, reorder policy, lead time and supplier's reliability. By exploiting a discrete-event simulation model, Bottani & Montanari (2010) investigate the behaviour of a fast moving consumer goods (FMCG) supply chain under 30 different configurations, stemming from the combination of several supply chain design parameters. Specifically, among the design parameters, the authors consider two planning decisions (i.e., number of echelons and reorder policy), one exogenous variable (i.e., demand behaviour), as well as some operational elements (i.e., demand information sharing mechanisms and responsiveness of supply chain players). The authors quantitatively assess the effects of different configurations on the resulting costs and bullwhip effect of the supply chain; their findings are summarised in 11 key results, supported by statistical evidence, which can be useful to optimise supply chain design. In another publication (Bottani & Montanari, 2009), the same authors have analysed four network configurations, stemming from the combination of two parameters, namely: (i) number of echelons; and (ii) number of facilities per echelon. As further decision variables, the authors consider the reorder policy (Economic Order Quantity vs. Economic Order Interval) adopted by each player and the service level delivered to customers (low vs. high). Moreover, demand behaviour (seasonal vs. non seasonal demand trend), demand stochasticity (low vs. high demand standard deviation) and procurement lead time (stochastic vs. deterministic) are examined as exogenous variables. Overall, the authors consider 128 scenarios, for which they compute four main performance parameters, namely the total costs of the network (and the related cost components), the bullwhip effect, the throughput time of items along the chain and the waiting time of customers at the retail store due to out-of-stocks.

Pero et al. (2010) investigate the relationships between some supply chain design parameters and the resulting performance of the supply chain. Design parameters considered by the authors are: (i) number of supply chain levels; (ii) number of players at each level; (iii) number of sources for each node; and (iv) distance between nodes. As a relevant performance parameter, the authors investigate the occurrence and entity of stock-outs at retail stores. In the work by Pero et al. (2010), simulation and statistical analyses of outcomes are exploited to identify statistically significant effects of design parameters on the observed outcomes.

In line with our previous studies on the topic, in this chapter our main goal is to assess the effects of different supply chain configurations on the resulting costs and bullwhip effect. We consider quite complex supply chain configurations, both in terms of number of echelons and number of players per echelon. The configurations we examine are also referred to as supply networks, and aim at being representative of realistic scenarios, so that our analysis can provide effective insights for supply chain optimization. The design parameters considered in this study are:

- number of echelons composing the supply chain;
- number of facilities per echelon;
- reorder policy adopted by each echelon.

As far as the latter point is concerned, in this study we suppose that supply chain echelons operate under an Economic Order Interval (EOI) policy. In a previous publication (Bottani & Montanari, 2008), we have dealt with supply chain design and optimization through simulation, under an Economic Order Quantity (EOQ) policy. This study thus completes our previous work by examining the EOI policy. Moreover, we provide a detailed comparison of the results obtained under EOI and EOQ inventory management policies. To make the comparison effective, in this study we consider the same supply chain configurations examined in our previous work. The analysis performed is based on a discrete-event simulation model, reproducing a FMCG supply chain, and on the computation of the resulting supply chain costs and of the demand variance amplification for each configuration examined. The chapter is organized as follows. Section 2 describes the supply chain simulation model, the supply chain configurations examined, and the corresponding software implementation. The key results of the simulation runs are detailed in section 3. Concluding remarks and future research directions are finally proposed.

2. The supply chain simulation model

2.1 The supply chain configurations examined

The typical structure of a FMCG supply chain may encompass three (i.e., manufacturer, distribution center, retail store) to five (i.e., manufacturer, first-tier distribution center,

second-tier distribution center, third-tier distribution center, retail store) echelons (Bottani and Montanari, 2010), while the number of players per echelon can substantially vary depending on the complexity of the supply and distribution networks.
To be consonant with Bottani & Montanari, (2008), three supply network configurations are examined, referring to 3-, 4- and 5-echelon systems. The supply networks are described on the basis of products and orders flow (Shapiro, 2001), and their structure is proposed in the schemes in Figure 1. As can be seen from Figure 1, the number of retail stores (RSs) is the same (i.e., 500) for all configurations investigated. In addition to RSs, the 3-echelon supply chain is composed of a manufacturer and 25 distribution centers (DCs). The 4-echelon system encompasses a manufacturer, 3 first-tier DCs and 50 second-tier DCs, while the 5-echelon supply chain is composed of a manufacturer, 3 first-tier DCs, 25 second-tier DCs, and 100 third-tier DCs. RSs directly face the final customer's demand, which is modeled as a stochastic variable with normal distribution $N(\mu;\sigma)$.

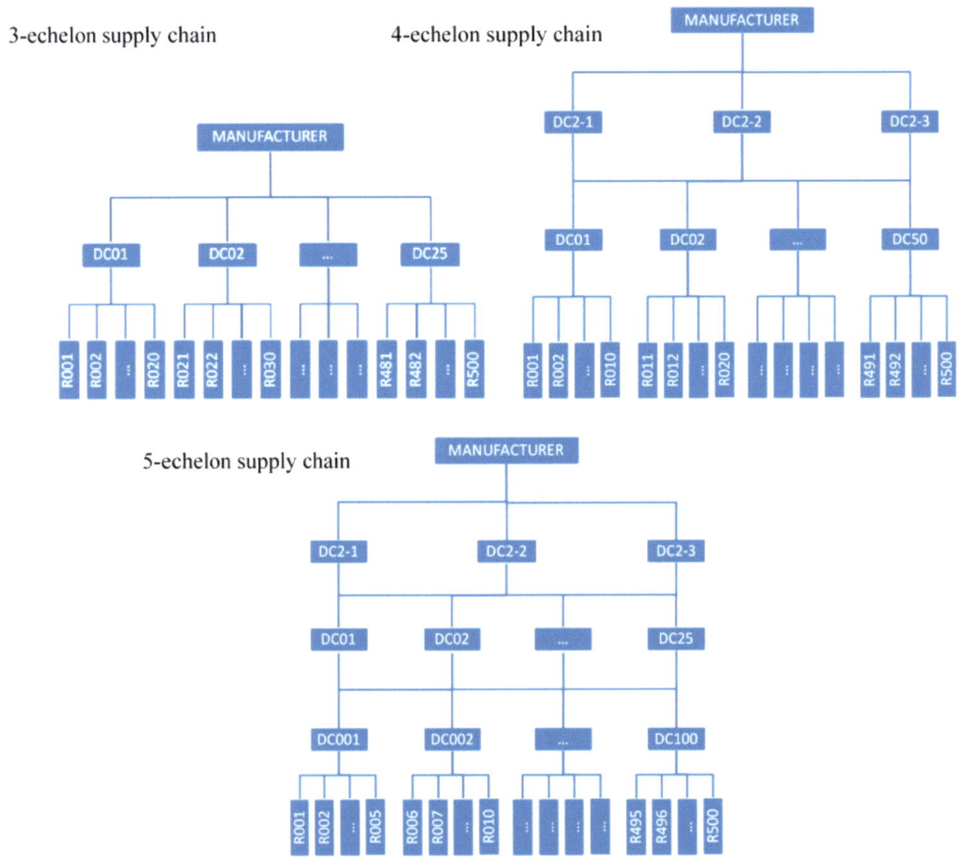

Fig. 1. The network configurations examined (DC=distribution centre; RS=retail store).

2.2 The reorder process

The reorder process of the generic *i*-th echelon is proposed in Figure 2. The following notation is used to describe the product and order flow:

t simulated day (t=1,...N_{days})
i supply chain echelon (i=1,...N)
$d_{t,i}$ demand value faced by echelon i at time t [pallets/day]. Depending on the supply chain echelon considered, this parameter can reflect the final customer's demand or the order received by the previous echelon
μ mean of the final customer's demand [pallets/day]
σ standard deviation of the final customer's demand [pallets/day]
$I_{t,i}$ inventory position of echelon i at time t [pallets]
$Q_{t,i}$ quantity ordered by echelon i at time t [pallets/day]
$Q_{s\text{-}o,t,i}$ quantity supplied by the external player for echelon i, at time t [pallets/day]
$\mu_{t,i}$ estimated demand mean at time t for echelon i [pallets/day]
$\sigma_{t,i}$ estimated demand standard deviation at time t for echelon i [pallets/day]
m moving average interval [days]
$OUL_{t,i}$ order-up-to level for echelon i at time t [pallets]
EOI_i economic order interval for echelon i [days]
$\mu_{LT,i}$ lead time mean for echelon i [days]
$\sigma_{LT,i}$ lead time standard deviation for echelon i [days]
k safety stock coefficient
$c_{o,i}$ unitary order cost for echelon i [€/order]. This also includes the transportation activities required to deliver the product to echelon i
$c_{s\text{-}o}$ unitary cost of stock-out [€/pallet/day]
h unitary cost of holding stocks [€/pallet/day]

According to Figure 2, at each day t (t=1,...N_{days}) the reorder process of the generic i-th echelon consists of several steps, ranging from the time an order is received from echelon i-1 up to the time an order is placed to echelon i+1. More precisely, each supply chain echelon receives products from the following one, in response to an order from the previous one, or, alternatively, to the daily customer's demand ("*order from echelon i-1*").
Anytime an order is received, echelon i should verify whether the available stock allows fulfilling it ("*can the order be fulfilled with the available inventory?*"). In the case the available stock is insufficient (i.e., $d_{t,i}>I_{t-1,i}$), the order is fulfilled by an "*external player*", which is modeled as a warehouse with infinite stock availability. Product supplied by the external player ($Q_{s\text{-}o,t,i}$) is used to compute the cost of out-of-stock for the echelon considered. Conversely, if the available stock is sufficient to fulfill the order (i.e., $d_{t,i} \leq I_{t-1,i}$), echelon i sends the product to echelon i-1 ("*order fulfillment*").
As a further step, on the basis of the demand faced at each day t, echelon i estimates the demand mean $\mu_{t,i}$ and standard deviation $\sigma_{t,i}$ according to a moving average model with m observations ("*estimation of demand mean and standard deviation*"). The following formulae are used for the computation:

$$\mu_{t,i} = \frac{1}{m} \sum_{k=t-m}^{t} d_{k,i}$$
$$\sigma_{t,i}^2 = \frac{1}{m-1} \sum_{k=t-m}^{t} \left(d_{k,i} - \mu_{t,i}\right)^2 \tag{1}$$

Echelon i should now decide whether or not to an order should be placed. As the echelon operates according to an EOI policy, orders are placed at fixed time intervals, which are computed for the generic i-th echelon on the basis of the following formula:

$$EOI_i = (2c_{o,i}/(h_i\mu))^{1/2} \tag{2}$$

The resulting values of EOI_i, computed by exploiting eq.2 and the input data described later in this chapter, are proposed in Table 1. The estimated values of $\mu_{t,i}$ and $\sigma_{t,i}$ are used to compute the parameters of the inventory management policy (*"computation of parameters of the reorder policy"*) and in particular the order-up-to level ($OUL_{t,i}$) at time t, according to the following formula (cf. Bottani et al., 2007):

$$OUL_{t,i} = (EOI + \mu_{LT,i})\mu_{t,i} + k\sqrt{(EOI + \mu_{LT,i})\sigma_{t,i}^{\;2} + \mu_{t,i}^2\sigma_{LT,i}^2} \tag{3}$$

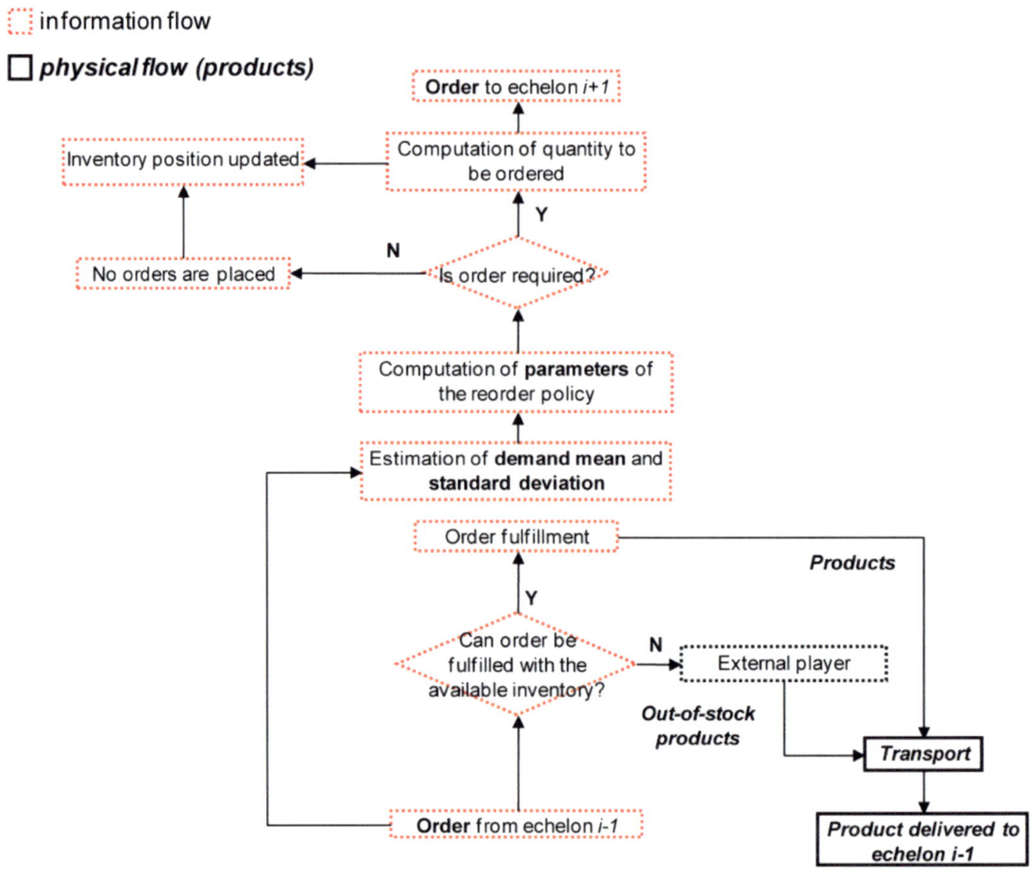

Fig. 2. The reorder process for the i-th supply chain player.

In the case an order is placed, the corresponding quantity will be available after a defined lead time (LT) has elapsed. The quantity to be ordered $Q_{t,i}$ results from the comparison between the $OUL_{t,i}$ and the inventory available $I_{t-1,i}$ for the supply chain player considered, i.e.:

$$Q_{t,i} = OUL_{t,i} - I_{t-1,i} \quad (4)$$

Echelon i will not place an order in the case the available inventory exceeds the required $OUL_{t,i}$. Regardless of the order placement, echelon i finally updates the inventory position accordingly ("*inventory position updated*"). The following formula is used to determine the stock level at time t:

$$I_{t,i} = Q_{t,i} + I_{t-1,i} - d_{t,i} \quad (5)$$

In the case the order has not been placed, we have $Q_{t,i}=0$ in the equation above.

The decision process described above is valid for all supply chain players modeled, except the manufacturer. In fact, as per the case of the external player, the manufacturer is modeled as a warehouse with infinite stock availability. Hence, it can always fulfill orders from DCs, and consequently, there is no need for the manufacturer to forecast the demand based on the orders received. For the same reason, we do not compute the total logistics cost of this player.

To make the results comparable to those of our previous study, further assumptions are also made in developing the model. More precisely, we suppose that μ_{LT}, σ_{LT}, c_o, h, k and m are known parameters, whose numerical values are partially deduced from a previous study performed by the authors in the field of FMCG (Bottani & Rizzi, 2008). According to this previous study, numerical values for the above input data could vary depending on the supply chain echelon considered. For instance, it is reasonable that the order cost changes depending on the number of echelons composing the supply chain, and to the echelon considered; in particular, order cost is probably higher when 5-echelon supply chains are considered. In fact, in 5-echelon systems, an increase in the quantity ordered by upstream supply chain players is often observed; hence, transportation activities, whose cost is included in the order cost, are significantly enhanced in those scenarios.

A similar consideration holds for the procurement lead time. We assume that the lead time is higher when considering upstream supply chain players, while it should slightly decrease when considering downstream players. The rationale behind this assumption is that the downstream supply chain players (e.g., RSs or end-tier DCs) should be served regularly, in a short time, to ensure the availability of product at the store shelves and to enhance the efficiency of the whole supply chain. LT is modeled as a stochastic variable, characterized by μ_{LT} and σ_{LT}; we assume a uniform distribution of LT, between two boundaries, which are progressively lower as downstream players are considered. μ_{LT} and σ_{LT} can be easily obtained from the boundaries on the basis of the uniform distribution. The full list of input data is proposed in Table 1 for each supply chain configuration considered.

Finally, according to Bottani & Rizzi, (2008), stock-out costs and costs of holding stock are estimated to account for 0.8 [€/pallet/day] and 0.384 [€/pallet/day] respectively for all echelons, regardless of the configurations considered. The final customer's demand is characterized by an average (μ) of 0.25 [pallet/day] with 0.0625 [pallet/day] standard deviation (σ). Those numerical values reflect the demand of a single product.

3-echelon	4-echelon	5-echelon
DC Lead time: random variable with uniform distribution between 5 and 10 days order cost: 300 €/order EOI : 17 days	$DC_{1\text{-}3}$ Lead time: random variable with uniform distribution between 5 and 10 days order cost: 3000 €/order EOI : 22 days	$DC_{1\text{-}3}$ Lead time: random variable with uniform distribution between 5 and 10 days order cost: 6000 €/order EOI : 29 days
RS Lead time: random variable with uniform distribution between 3 and 7 days order cost: 75 €/order EOI : 40 days	$DC_{1\text{-}50}$ Lead time: random variable with uniform distribution between 5 and 8 days order cost: 225 €/order EOI : 24 days	$DC_{1\text{-}25}$ Lead time: random variable with uniform distribution between 5 and 8 days order cost: 825 €/order EOI : 29 days
	RS Lead time: random variable with uniform distribution between 3 and 7 days order cost: 75 €/order EOI : 40 days	$DC_{1\text{-}100}$ Lead time: random variable with uniform distribution between 4 and 8 days order cost: 150 €/order EOI : 25 days
		RS Lead time: random variable with uniform distribution between 3 and 7 days order cost: 75 €/order EOI : 40 days

Table 1. Input data of the model.

2.3 Software implementation

The decision process described in the previous sections was implemented in a proper simulation model, developed under Microsoft Excel™. In particular, for each supply chain configuration considered, an *ad hoc* spreadsheet is used to reproduce the decision process of each supply chain echelon, as shown in Figure 3. We thus programmed several different Microsoft Excel™ files, corresponding to the supply chain configurations proposed in Figure 1.

According to the orders' flow, a Microsoft Excel™ file starts by reproducing the decision process of RSs, on the basis of a random generation of final customer's demand data. In this file, we thus have 500 spreadsheets corresponding to the RSs composing the supply networks. As the number of RSs is the same in all configurations considered, the spreadsheets reproducing the RSs have been exploited for all subsequent Microsoft Excel™ files. As a result of the implementation of the decision process under Microsoft Excel™, each spreadsheet reproducing a RS provides, as output, the flow of orders from this RS to end-tier DCs.

The orders of RSs should be aggregated to get the demand "seen" by a DC. We note from Figure 1 that the number of DCs is different depending on the supply chain configuration examined, and specifically it accounts for 25, 50 and 100 respectively when considering 3-, 4- or 5-echelon systems. Hence, each DC serves a different number of RSs in the three network configurations examined. For instance, in the case of 5-echelon supply chains (as proposed in Figure 3), the network is composed of 100 DCs; consequently, it can be assumed that each DC approximately serves 5 RSs. Under this scenario, we thus gathered the order flow of 5 RSs and used the aggregate flow as the demand "seen" by a DC; this value has been used as the input in a further Microsoft Excel™ file reproducing the decision process of DCs. As a result of this step, we obtain the flow of orders from end-tier DCs to the upper-tier DCs.
The same procedure is followed to derive the flow of orders for upper-tier DCs, and, in general, it is repeated for all echelons composing the supply chains investigated. Figure 3 graphically shows the full procedure in the case of a 5-echelon supply chain.

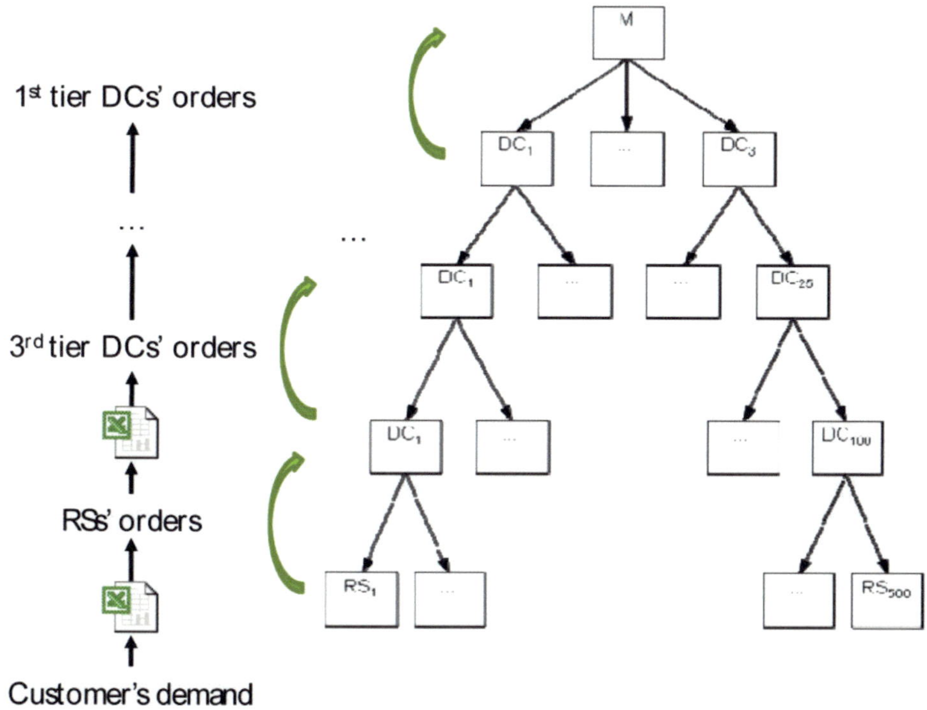

Fig.3. Software implementation of the simulation model for a 5-echelon network.

2.4 Computation of outputs

The simulation duration was set at N_{days}=1000 days, corresponding to approx 4 years operating period of the supply network, having hypothesised 5 working days/week.
For each supply network considered, we assessed several outputs, on the basis of the numerical values proposed in Table 1 and on the simulation outcomes. The output computed for the supply networks are described in the list below.

- Bullwhip effect. We assessed the bullwhip effect as the ratio between variance of orders received by echelon N (i.e., the manufacturer) and the variance of the final customer's demand, i.e. σ_N^2/σ^2. σ_N^2 is computed on the basis of the flow of orders received by the manufacturer;
- Cost of holding stocks (C_{stocks}). For the i-th player, it is computed starting from unitary cost of stocks and amount of stock available at the warehouse, i.e.:

$$C_{stocks,i} = h\sum_{t=1}^{N_{days}} I_{t,i} \tag{6}$$

The total cost of holding stocks C_{stock} is obtained by adding up the contributions of each supply chain echelon, except the manufacturer, which is excluded from the computation due to infinite stock availability. As an outcome of the computation, we report the daily average value of C_{stock} for each supply chain echelon, which is obtained by adding up the contribution of each echelon (e.g., the RSs) and dividing by the number of players composing the echelon (i.e., the number of RSs) and the simulation duration N_{days}. The average value is thus expressed in [€/echelon/day]. Moreover, we also computed the overall average of C_{stocks} for the network examined, which is again expressed in [€/echelon/day]. The overall average results from dividing the total cost of holding stocks by the total number of players composing the network and the simulation duration.

- Stock-out cost ($C_{s\text{-}o}$). For the i-th player, the cost of stock-out is computed starting from the unitary cost of out-of-stock and from the quantity supplied by the external player $Q_{s\text{-}o,t,i}$, according to the following formula:

$$C_{stock-out,i} = c_i\sum_{t=1}^{N_{days}} Q_{s-o,t,i} \tag{7}$$

The total cost of stock-out is obtained by adding up the contributions of each supply chain echelon, except the manufacturer, for which stock-out cannot occur. As outcome, we report the daily average value of $C_{s\text{-}o}$ for each supply chain echelon and the overall average of $C_{s\text{-}o}$. Both values are expressed in [€/day/echelon], according to the computational procedure described for the previous outcome.

- Order cost (C_{order}). For the i-th player, it is computed on the basis of the unitary cost of orders $c_{o,i}$ and of the number of orders placed by the supply chain player $N_{orders,i}$, i.e.:

$$C_{order,i} = c_{o,i}N_{orders,i} \tag{8}$$

The number of orders is a direct outcome of the simulation model. We thus obtain the total order cost of the supply chain configuration examined by adding up the contributions of the different echelons, except the manufacturer. As outcome, we report the daily average value of C_{order} for each supply chain echelon and the overall average of C_{order}. Again, such values are expressed in [€/day/echelon], according to the same computational procedure described for the previous outcomes.

- Total supply chain cost [€/day]. This is computed for the whole supply chain, by adding up the cost components previously described and dividing by N_{days}.

3. Results and discussion

In this section, we report the relevant results of the study, in terms of order cost, cost of holding stocks, and stock-out cost, for each supply chain echelon. As mentioned, we provide the daily average values of such costs for each echelon composing the supply chain. We also report the total cost and the variance ratio for the whole supply chain. Such outcomes are proposed in Table 2. In the same table, in italic we provide the outcomes resulting in the case the EOQ policy is considered (cf. Bottani & Montanari, 2008).

	Network configuration		
Outcomes	**3-echelon**	**4-echelon**	**5-echelon**
Average stock-out cost [€/player/day]	overall average: 0.09 (*0.01*) $DC_{1\text{-}25}$: 1.48 (*0.29*) RS: 0.02 (*0.00*)	overall average: 0.20 (*0.05*) $DC_{1\text{-}3}$: 19.02 (*1.01*) $DC_{1\text{-}50}$: 1.12 (*0.45*) RS: 0.02 (*0.00*)	overall average: 1.19 (*0.32*) $DC_{1\text{-}3}$: 126.35 (*7.16*) $DC_{1\text{-}25}$: 9.69 (*5.51*) $DC_{1\text{-}100}$: 0.72 (*0.66*) RS: 0.02 (*0.00*)
Average order cost [€/player/day]	overall average: 2.49 (*3.01*) $DC_{1\text{-}25}$: 15.67 (*19.24*) RS: 1.83 (*2.20*)	overall average: 3.96 (*3.96*) $DC_{1\text{-}3}$: 145.00 (*174.00*) $DC_{1\text{-}50}$: 9.79 (*11.41*) RS: 1.83 (*2.20*)	overall average: 4.50 (*4.10*) $DC_{1\text{-}3}$: 220.00 (*256.00*) $DC_{1\text{-}25}$: 27.39 (*33.99*) $DC_{1\text{-}100}$: 5.71 (*6.23*) RS: 1.83 (*2.20*)
Average inventory cost [€/player/day]	overall average: 4.48 (*3.52*) $DC_{1\text{-}25}$: 43.58 (*31.49*) RS: 2.53 (*2.13*)	overall average: 5.42 (*5.41*) $DC_{1\text{-}3}$: 477.15 (*289.73*) $DC_{1\text{-}50}$: 31.50 (*21.20*) RS: 2.53 (*2.13*)	overall average: 21.63 (*6.95*) $DC_{1\text{-}3}$: 1680.79 (*482.62*) $DC_{1\text{-}25}$: 194.33 (*68.25*) $DC_{1\text{-}100}$: 24.18 (*15.97*) RS: 2.53 (*2.13*)
Total costs of the network [€/day]	3,708.50 (*3,438.60*)	6,225.95 (*5,210.47*)	17,118.60 (*7,142.82*)
Bullwhip effect σ_N^2/σ^2	323.73 (*190.19*)	40,115.90 (*15,224.77*)	142,123.70 (*28,006.42*)

Table 2. Results of the simulation runs. Note: *italic* = results under EOQ policy (from Bottani & Montanari, 2008).

The outcomes in Table 2 allow drawing some conclusions and guidelines for supply chain design. They are proposed in the following subsections.

3.1 Stock-out costs

As a first outcome, we note that, no matter the reorder policy considered, the average stock-out cost substantially increases when moving from 3-echelon to 5-echelon systems, suggesting that the occurrence of stock-outs is higher when considering complex scenarios.
A significant increase in stock-out costs is observed in terms of the overall average, which ranges from 0.09 [€/player/day] for 3-echelon systems to 1.19 [€/player/day] for 5-echelon systems, under EOI policy, and from 0.01 [€/player/day] to 0.32 [€/player/day] under EOQ policy. From outcomes in Table 2, it can also be noted that stock-out occurrence is always negligible for retail stores, accounting for 0.02 and 0.00 [€/player/day] respectively under EOI and EOQ policy. Hence, the increase in stock-out cost in complex systems can be ascribed to a corresponding increase in stock-out occurrence for upstream supply chain players. In other words, with the increase of the number of echelons and number of players per echelon, stock-out situations at the upstream echelons are more likely to occur. This is confirmed by the increase in the average stock-out cost for the specific supply chain echelon when moving from 3-echelon to 5-echelon systems. In turn, the occurrence of stock-out situations for 5-echelon systems is a possible consequence of the exacerbated demand variance amplification observed in such scenarios, which leads to irregular orders.
By comparing the results of EOI and EOQ policies, it can also be appreciated that stock-out costs are systematically higher under EOI policy. This is probably due to the fact that EOQ policy requires continuously monitoring the stock level and frequent reordering, thus preventing stock-out occurrence. Nonetheless, this point would probably benefit from a deeper investigation, as other studies provide different outcomes (e.g., Bottani & Montanari, 2009).

3.2 Cost of stocks

The trend of inventory costs is similar to that observed for stock-out costs. In particular, no matter the reorder policy considered, inventory costs tend to increase when moving upstream in the supply chain (i.e., from RSs to DCs). Specifically, in the case of 5-echelon supply networks, such costs account for 2.53 and 2.13 [€/player/day] for RSs, while they reach 1680.79 and 482.62 [€/player/day] when examining first-tier DCs, respectively under EOI and EOQ inventory management policy. This result can be explained based on the increase in safety stocks involved by the bullwhip effect. A direct comparison between EOI and EOQ leads to the conclusion that inventory costs are systematically lower when the supply chain players operate under EOQ policy. Again, this could be justified based on the fact that EOQ policy allows better monitoring the stock level compared with EOI. Bottani and Montanari (2009) found that the reorder policy significantly impacts on the cost of holding stocks, and, in particular, that such cost is higher under EOI than EOQ policy. The main reason for such outcome is that EOI policy causes a higher average stock level, as a consequence of the lower number of orders, with wider quantities. This also explains why the increase in the average stock level is more relevant when the supply network is composed by numerous echelons and numerous players per echelon (i.e., 5-echelon systems).

3.3 Cost of order

Compared with the other cost components, the cost of order shows a slightly different trend. More precisely, we always observe an increase of order cost when moving upstream in the supply chain. Such an increase is particularly evident when considering complex systems, i.e., 5-echelon supply chains. In this scenario, the order cost ranges from 1.83 and 2.20 [€/player/day] for RSs to 220.00 and 256.00 [€/player/day] for first-tier DCs, respectively under EOI and EOQ policies. A corresponding increase is also observed for the overall average of order cost when moving from 3-echelon to 5-echelon systems (2.49 and 3.01 vs. 4.50 and 4.10 [€/day], respectively under EOI and EOQ policies).
However, although the order cost increases when examining upper-tier echelons and 5-echelon systems, it is systematically lower under EOI than EOQ policy, unlike the other cost components. A similar result has been observed by Bottani & Montanari (2009). More precisely, the authors found that the use of EOI policy provides a slight decrease of the order cost, and that the effect is supported by statistical evidence. This result can be justified based on the fact that EOI policy involves periodical ordering, and hence the number of orders in a given time period is almost defined. Consequently, the number of orders is lower compared to EOQ, where, conversely, supply chain echelons should place an order anytime the inventory level is lower than a defined threshold. Such effect is amplified when the supply chain is composed of numerous echelons or numerous players per echelon (Bottani & Montanari, 2009).

3.4 Total cost of the supply network

It is reasonable that the total cost of the supply network experiences an increase when moving from 3- to 5-echelon systems, indicating that complex networks are affected by relevant total costs. As a matter of fact, the increase in the number of supply chain echelons or in players per echelon involves an increase in all cost components previously considered, due to the need of adding the cost contributions of each player. We also note that the total costs are lower under an EOQ policy. This is a known result (cf. Bottani & Montanari, 2009; 2010), which can be explained on the basis of the consideration that the total supply chain cost is mainly determined by the cost of stocks, and that the EOI policy significantly increases such cost component, as already explained. The increase in the average stock level is also expected to be more relevant when considering complex supply networks, composed of numerous echelons and numerous players per echelon. This consideration is supported by this study; in fact, looking at the total cost proposed in Table 2, one can see that the difference between EOI and EOQ policies is significant when considering 5-echelon systems (17,118.60 vs. 7,142.82 [€/day]), while it is substantially lower for 3-echelon systems (3,708.50 vs. 3,438.60 [€/day]).

3.5 Bullwhip effect

From Table 2, one can see that the bullwhip effect substantially increases when moving from 3-echelon to 5-echelon systems. This is an obvious result, directly stemming from the definition of bullwhip effect available in literature (e.g., Chen et al., 2000). Moreover, the bullwhip effect is significantly amplified when the network is composed of numerous players per echelon, as per the case of 5-echelon systems modeled in this study. There are very few studies in literature which address the topic of quantifying the bullwhip effect in a supply network. Among them, we found the work by Ouyang and Li (2010). This study suggests that a high number of players per echelon has potential to affect the resulting bullwhip effect of the network, and, in particular, it exacerbates the demand variance amplification. In turn, this is a possible consequence of the fact that the bullwhip effect is caused by independent rational decisions in demand signal processing and order batching (Lee et al., 2004; Lee, 2003); with numerous players per echelon, the effect of non-coordinated demand can be amplified.

In addition, EOI policy usually involves a higher bullwhip effect than EOQ. Most studies available in literature (e.g., Jakšič and Rusjan, 2008) suggest that the bullwhip effect is higher when the supply chain operates under an EOI policy, because, in general, "order-up-to" policies have the potential to increase the demand variance. The reason for this outcome, which is also confirmed by our study, is that, under the EOI policy, orders are placed at a defined time interval. This leads to several null orders, and to orders with very wide quantities; thus, an amplification of the demand variance is seen by the upper-tier echelon.

4. Conclusions

The problem of optimizing the design of a supply chain has a direct impact on both strategic objectives of supply chain management and on the costs of the system. This chapter has analyzed the topic of supply network design, with a particular attention to the identification of the optimal configuration of the network to minimize total cost. The topic has been approached through a simulation model, developed under Microsoft Excel™. The model reproduces a FMCG supply chain, whose input data have been partially deduced from previous studies of the authors in that field.

As outputs of the simulation runs, we computed the total logistics cost, including its cost components, and the demand variance amplification, which allows providing an estimate of how the different configurations react to the bullwhip effect. The simulation outcomes can be summarized in the following key points. First, we note that all design parameters investigated (i.e., number of echelons, number of players/echelon and reorder policy) have a direct impact on the observed cost and bullwhip effect. Moreover, both the number of echelons and the number of players/echelon tend to increase the total cost of the network and the bullwhip effect. Conversely, the reorder policy has a different impact on the cost components examined. Specifically, stock-out cost and inventory cost increase when EOI policy is adopted by supply chain echelons, while the order cost tends to decrease under such policy. The above outcomes provide useful guidelines to optimize supply chain design and to identify the optimal supply chain configuration as a function of the total costs.

The present study can be extended in several ways. Specifically, to derive more general results, it would be appropriate to extend the simulation model to include the flow of different products, with different characteristics. Moreover, order crossover phenomena (Riezebos, 2006) and their occurrence in supply networks can be investigated in greater detail.

5. References

Bashiri, M. & Tabrizi, M.M., (2010). Supply chain design: A holistic approach. *Expert Systems with Applications*, Vol.37, No.1, 688–693

Bottani, E. & Montanari, R., (2008). A simulation tool for supply chain design and optimization. *Proceedings of TCN CAE 2008 - International Conference on Simulation Based Engineering and Sciences*, October 16-17, Venice (Italy)

Bottani, E. & Montanari, R., (2009). Design and performance evaluation of supply networks: a simulation study. Internal report of the Department of Industrial Engineering, University of Parma (Italy). Submitted for publication to the International Journal of Production Economics

Bottani, E. & Montanari, R., (2010). Supply chain design and cost analysis through simulation. *International Journal of Production Research*, Vol.48, No.10, 2859–2886

Bottani, E. & Rizzi, A., (2008). Economical assessment of the impact of RFID technology and EPC system on the Fast Moving Consumer Goods supply chain. *International Journal of Production Economics*, Vol.112, No.2, 548–569

Bottani, E., Montanari, R. & Volpi, A. (2007). Quantifying the Bullwhip Effect in inventory management policies. *Proceedings of the 12th International Symposium in Logistics*, pp.455-461, ISBN: 978-0-85358-218-2, Budapest (Hungary), July 8-10, 2007

Chang, Y. & Makatsoris, H. (2001). Supply chain modeling using simulation. *International Journal of Simulation: Systems, Science and Technology*, Vol.2, No.1, 24-30

Chen, F., Drezner, Z., Ryan, J.K. & Simchi-Levi, D., (2000). Quantifying the Bullwhip Effect in a Simple Supply Chain: The Impact of Forecasting, Lead Times, and Information. *Management Science*, Vol.46, No.3, 436-443

Chopra, S. & Meindl, P., (2004). *Supply chain management: Strategy, planning and operations – 2nd edition*. Prentice Hall, Upper Saddle River (USA)

Cooper, M.C., Lambert, D.M. & Pagh, J.D., (1997). Supply chain management: More than just a new name for logistics. *The International Journal of Logistics Management*, Vol.8, No.1, 1–13

Hammami, R., Frein, Y. & Hadj-Alouan, A.B., (2008). Supply chain design in the delocalization context: Relevant features and new modeling tendencies. *Journal of Production Economics*, Vol.113, No.2, 641-656

Hammami, R., Frein, Y. & Hadj-Alouane, A.B., (2009). A strategic-tactical model for the supply chain design in the delocalization context: Mathematical formulation and a case study. *International Journal of Production Economics*, Vol.122, No.1, 351–365

Harrison, J.R., Lin, Z., Carroll, G.R. & Carley, K.M., (2007). Simulation modeling in organizational and management research. *Academy of Management Review*, Vol.32, No.4, 1229–1245

Hwarng, H.B., Chong, C.S.P., Xie, N. & Burgess, T.F., (2005). Modelling a complex supply chain: understanding the effect of simplified assumptions. *International Journal of Production Research*, Vol.43, No.13, 2829–2872

Iannone, R., Miranda, S. & Riemma, S., (2007). Supply chain distributed simulation: An efficient architecture for multi-model synchronisation. *Simulation Modelling Practice and Theory*, Vol.15, No.3, 221–236.

Jaksic, M. & Rusjan, B., (2008). The effect of replenishment policies on the bullwhip effect: A transfer function approach. *European Journal of Operational Research*, Vol.184, No.3, 946–961

Kleijnen, J.P.C., (2003). *Supply chain simulation: a survey*. Tilburg University, Center for Economic Research, discussion paper n.103. Available at http://ideas.repec.org/p/dgr/kubcen/2003103.html (accessed February 2009)

Lee, C.B., (2003). *Multi-Echelon Inventory Optimization - Evant White Paper Series*. Available at http://www.stanford.edu (accessed November 2009)

Lee, H.L., Padmanabhan, V. & Whang, S., (2004). Information distortion in the supply chain: the bullwhip effect. *Management Science*, 50, supplement 12, 1875-1886

Ouyang, Y. & Li, X., (2010). The bullwhip effect in supply chain networks. *European Journal of Operational Research*, Vol.201, No.3, 799–810

Riezebos, J., (2006). Inventory order crossover. *International Journal of Production Economics*, Vol.104, No.2, 666–675.

Shang, J.S., Li, S. & Tadikamalla, P., (2004). Operational design of a supply chain system using the Taguchi method, response surface methodology, simulation, and optimisation. *International Journal of Production Research*, Vol.42, No.18, 3823–3849

Shapiro, J., (2001). *Modelling the supply chain*. Duxbury Thomson Learning, Pacific Groove (USA).

Tiwari, M.K., Raghavendra, N. Agrawal, S. & Goyal, S.K., (2010). A Hybrid Taguchi–Immune approach to optimize an integrated supply chain design problem with multiple shipping. *European Journal of Operational Research*, Vol.203, No.1, 95-106

Yan, H., Yu, Z. & Cheng, T.C.E., (2003). A strategic model for supply chain design with logical constraints: formulation and solution. *Computers & Operations Research*, Vol.30, No.14, 2135–2155

5

A simulation technology for supply-chain integration

Shigeki Umeda
Musashi University
Japan

1. Introduction

Modern companies in industrially advanced countries face to low-growth of world scale economy. Every enterprise makes various efforts to survive in such severe management environment. Mass production style has gone away, and manufacturer must provide goods which customer favours, when the customers hope to get them.

Organizations today cannot do it alone. Most of modern enterprises depend on the collective efforts of a group of trading partners to stretch a supply-chain from the raw material supplier to the end customer. A trading partner in this context means any external organization that plays an integral role in the enterprise and whose business fortune depends all or in part on the success of the enterprise. This includes factories, contract manufacturers, sub-assembly plants, distribution centres, wholesalers, retailers, carriers, freight forwarder services, customer broker services, international procurement organization (IPO), and value-added-network (VAN) services.

A supply chain system is a chain of processes from the initial raw materials to the ultimate consumption of the finished product spanning across multiple supplier-customer links. It provides functions within and outside a company that enable the value chain to make products and provide services to the customers. The objectives competitive supply-chain design is to weave each of the trading partners into a seamless fabric of information flow, physical distribution flow, cash flow for the benefit of the end customer. The trading partners achieve their profit, or loss, through their ability to work within the context of a supply-chain where each organization is dependent on the other. Each trading partner benefits by gaining the profits of access to a larger market share than might be possible going it alone.

The supply chain system terminology originated in the "Quick Response" initiative in the '80s. In 1985, Kurt Salmon Associates were commissioned to conduct a supply chain analysis for the apparel industry. The result of this study showed the delivery time for apparel supply chain, from raw material to consumer, was 66 weeks long, 40 weeks of which were spent in warehouses or in transit (Kurt Salmon Associates, Inc. (1993)). This study led to the development of the "Quick Response" (QR) strategy. QR is a partnership in which retailers and suppliers work together to respond more quickly to consumer needs by sharing information.

A group of grocery industry leaders succeeded to this work. They created a joint industry task force called the "Efficient Consumer Response" (ECR) working group in 1992 (Kurt Salmon Associates, Inc. (1993)). The most remarkable result of this study has been an identification of a set of best practices, which, if implemented, could improve overall performance of the supply chain substantially. The successful adoption of ECR for a manufacturer depends on the manufacturing flexibility, which enables matching supply with demand.

ECR was further succeeded by the concept of "Continuous Replenishment" (CR) (ECR Performance Measures Operating Committee (1994)). The CR concept is, in a sense, similar to the Japanese Just-In-Time system concept, which is based on a pull system based on consumer demand. Point-of-Sales (POS) system was introduced to forward sales transactions directly to manufacturers by computers to keep retailers replenished and balanced just-in-time.

More recently, a Supply Chain Operations Reference (SCOR) model has been defined as a generic process model (Supply Chain council). The SCOR model can be used to describe supply chain systems using a common framework and terminology. It defines five process types: PLAN, SOURCE, MAKE, DELIVER, and RETURN, that can be used to describe a supply chain. Levels of detail can be successively added to understand the processes involved. Best practices are being defined at the detailed levels to help industry implement them and measure their own performance.

Modern information and communication technologies have enabled high-speed and low-cost communications. These have accelerated commercial use of the Internet, as is seen in e-marketplaces by increasing use of broadband communications. Such e-marketplaces are currently used not only in consumers' purchase but also for business-to-business (B2B) purchases among worldwide suppliers. Enterprises must integrate all their business processes to compete and participate in the global business community.

A supply-chain system is hard to be modified, once the system has been built. This is because processes in various organizations are tightly coupled with each other, and its business systems are relative to their business communication rules. System design of a supply-chain needs to estimate its performances and behaviours at assessment stages.

Simulation is a powerful tool to optimize designs and operations of such manufacturing and logistics systems. Especially terminated simulation provides predictions of system's behaviours potential status by "what-if scenario" (Banks, 1998). Thus, simulations have been used as a powerful solution tool for operational management problems, such as capacity planning, resource planning, lead-time planning, supplier selection, and outsourcing planning.

This chapter describes a new approach to support life-cycle management of supply-chain system. First, section.2 categorizes planning problems, which are often discussed in supply-chain management. Second, section.3 proposes an original supply-chain simulation models and a framework to evaluate system performance. And, section.4 describes results of simulation experiments by using an actual supply-chain system. Section.5, finally proposes a novel framework for supply-chain life-cycle management.

2. Supply-chain problems and simulation technologies

2.1 Supply-chain management problems

This section presents common supply chain planning problems. The problems described here are faced by many system designers and managers during design, planning and operation of a supply chain system (Umeda & Jain, 2004). The problems are interlinked, as will be clear in the discussion.

(1) Capacity planning problems

Capacity planning is a process that determines the amount of capacity required to produce in the future. This function includes establishing, measuring, and adjusting limits or levels of capacity. In general, this planning includes the process of determining in detail the amount of labour and machine resources required to accomplish the tasks of production.

In traditional MRP systems (a planning support system for a single factory), there are two stages to plan the system capacity: Rough-cut capacity planning (RCCP), and Capacity Requirement Planning (CRP).

The RCCP is the process of converting the master production schedule into requirements for key resources, often including labour, machinery, warehouse space, suppliers' capabilities, and, in some cases, money. The master-schedule items and quantities are multiplied by the total time required to build each item to provide the total number of hours to produce the schedule. Historical work centre percentages are then applied to the total number of hours to provide an estimate of the hours per work centre to support the master schedule.

Similar to RCCP, the CRP module estimates workload on each work centre in factories but at a more detailed level. In this case, open shop orders and planned orders in the MRP system are input to CRP. It uses parts routings and time standards to translate into hours at work centres by time period. Even though the RCCP may indicate that sufficient capacity exists to execute the MPS, CRP may show that capacity is insufficient during specific time periods.

These methodologies are also applicable to supply chain systems. These are, so to speak, Rough-cut Supply chain Capacity Planning (RSCP) and Supply chain Capacity Requirement Planning (SCRP). The problem examples for the former are:

- How much capacity individual suppliers should provide to meet the long-range demand mean? These are, for example, number and types of supplier plants, the location of the suppliers, manufacturing capacity of suppliers, the location and capacity of warehouses for transportations, type of manufacturing plants and warehouses, and so on.
- What workload each supplier should handle?
- How much of the raw materials and products should be prepared to ship among suppliers, plants, warehouses, and customers?

The examples for the latter are:

- Which suppliers would be the bottlenecks, when a particular shipment plan is given?
- When and how much production capacity does each supplier need, when the market demand reaches its peak point during a certain time period?
- How much of demand should be supplied from inventory and from production in a certain time period, when a particular demand variation is given?

(2) Resource planning

Resource planning is capacity planning conducted at the business plan level. It is the process of establishing, measuring, and adjusting limits or levels of long-range capacity. Resource planning is normally based on long-term production plans but may be driven by higher level plans beyond the time horizon for the production plan, e.g., the business plan. It addresses those resources that take long periods of time to acquire. Resource planning decisions always require top management approval.

(3) Lead-time planning problems

The term "Lead-time" has basically two meanings: a span of time required to perform a process (or series of operations), and the time between recognition of the need for an order and the receipt of goods. The second one is often used in a logistics context. Individual components of lead-time can include order preparation time, queuing time, processing time, move or transportation time, and receiving and inspection time. We use this term in this paper with its second meaning. This problem directly impacts the inventory planning problems through the Lead-time inventory, the inventory that is carried to cover demand during the lead-time.

The examples of this class of problems are:

- When and what suppliers should produce, and associated due dates?
- When and how much volume of products or component parts should be transported?
- Which transportation channels should be used?
- Suppose that all of the factories in the chain use a common database for purchase ordering process, what impacts occur on total lead-time in the chain?

(4) Production planning problems

There are two phases of production planning: the first phase is an aggregate production planning and the second phase is an operational production planning.

An "Aggregate production plan" implies budgeted levels of finished products, inventory, production backlogs, and plans and changes in the work force to support the production strategy. Aggregate planning usually includes total sales, total production, targeted inventory, and targeted customer backlog on families of products. One of the primary purposes of this plan is to estimate the production rates, when the system works according to the given plan. The production rate is an important decision parameter since it determines whether the system is meeting its' management's objective of satisfying customer demand while keeping the work force relatively stable. As the production plan affects many company functions, so it is normally prepared with information from marketing, and coordinated with the functions of manufacturing, engineering, finance, materials, etc.

It is the function of setting the overall level of manufacturing output (production plan) and other activities to best satisfy the current planned levels of sales (sales plan or forecasts), while meeting general business objectives as expressed in the overall business plan such as profitability, productivity, competitive customer lead times, and so on.

Operational production plan is a more detailed set of planned production targets that meet the goal of the higher level manufacturing output plan. It is based on an agreed-upon plan that comes from the aggregate (production) planning function. It is usually stated as a monthly rate for each product family. Measurement units depend on the plan and the products, such as units, tonnage, standard hours, and number of workers. The production plan is management's authorization for the master scheduler to convert it into a more detailed plan, that is, the master production schedule.

2.2 Simulation technologies for supply-chain management

Simulation software tools have been on the market for at least 40 years. Simulation software comes in two flavours: languages and packages. Simulation languages, which first appeared in 1960's, deal with the flow of entities through the system. Examples of material entities in manufacturing line simulation include parts, operators, tools, and machines. There are three different views of that flow: activity, event and process. Simulation packages support many features including graphical model building tools, tabular data entity, automated debugging, and wide range of animation utilities. Graphical mode building tools simplify, but not eliminate, the need to use underlying language.

Several industrial companies have developed supply-chain simulation systems. These companies own by themselves huge supply-chain systems that include their own and vendors factories. These are originally used as internal tools rather than software products. IBM developed a Client/Server/Web-based system tool to support supply-chain management (Chen, et al.). CSCAT (Compaq Supply Chain Analysis Tool) by Compaq Corporation owns simulation elements of supply-chain systems, and it supports performance evaluation. They further make additional functions such as animation facilities and business-score boards. (Ingalls & Kasales, 1999)

Umeda and Zhang developed generic simulation models for supply-chain system analysis, and applied them to several types of supply-chain systems. (Umeda & Zhang, 2006) The scopes of their works are a Push-system, a Pull-system, and a Hybrid-push-pull system. Their analysis covers inventory management problems, lead-time planning problems, and system performance analysis in supply-chain systems.

2.3 Simulation technologies appeared in Winter Simulation Conference

Society of Computer Simulation (SCS) organizes Winter Simulation Conference (WSC) every year. This conference is the biggest one related to discrete event simulation in the world. This conference covers the topics of every areas of discrete event simulation: theory, architecture, application, tools, and so on.

This section summarizes a states-of-the-art in supply-chain simulation and its relative fields from a point of applications views by academic and industrial papers mainly using recent winter simulation conference proceedings.

(1) Supply-chain system simulation

There are several characteristics in supply-chain system simulations. These are (1) Consideration of information-flow, (2) Consideration of business process flows, (3) Pull system concept, (4) Simulation modelling, (5) Huge system simulation, and et al.

First, the scopes of supply-chain simulation often include information-flow in addition to materials-flow in comparison with manufacturing system simulation, which had been very popular. This is because one of the principle of designs for supply-chain systems to introduce information sharing mechanisms. Sarac et al. reported the impacts of introducing of RFID in supply-chain systems (Sarac et al, 2008). Liu et al. showed simulation results for supply-chain configuration based on information sharing (Liu et al., 2006). Gavirneni evaluated supply-chain performance in the case that the system performed fully centralization of information (Gavirneni, 2005). Its information-flows often include scheduling information.

Second, business process-flows are often scope in design supply-chain systems. Business process simulation includes such transformation of organizations (Ding at al., 2006). Cui et al. presented a case study of using the BPS tool to demonstrate the effects of BPR on restraining stocking-up and overdue payments in the distribution management of a supply chain (Cui et al., 2008). Consideration of Small-and-Medium-sized Enterprise (SMEs) is one essential items of supply-chain management. Byrne and Heavy summarized useful methods to analyzing SME industrial supply-chains (Byrne & Heavey, 2004).

Third, Supply-chain system needs implementation of "Pull" system. Bagdia and Pasek proposed an analytical method enables projection of the end-customer demand information to upstream of the supply chain and estimate demand forecast at the individual tier levels (Bagdia & Pasek, 2005). Bhaskaran proposed a simulation methodology for supply-chain systems, and applied it to a supply-chain of General Motors Co. (Bhaskaran, 1998). His scope is systems' stability through inventory management. His analysis covers an opportunity of practice of continuous improvement of systems. His reports also include comparisons between MRP and Kanban system.

Fourth, modelling methodologies are often discussed in supply-chain simulation. As supply-chain systems are generally huge, so modelling workload, needless to say, becomes heavy. Vieira and Junior developed conceptual models, which are useful to creation of certain types of supply-chain simulation projects (Vieira & César, 2005). Song et al. applied a methodology of simulation meta-model to a multi-echelon supply chain problem and make statistically analysis of the parameters (Song et al., 2008). Cope et al. proposed an approach that provides a simulation solution that is affordable at the same time can be quickly implemented (Cope et al., 2007). Umeda et al. developed generic simulation models for supply-chain system analysis, and applied them to several types of supply-chain systems (Umeda & Lee, 2004b). The scopes of their works are a Push-system, a Pull-system, and a Hybrid-push-pull system. Their analysis covers inventory management problems, lead-time planning problems, and system performance analysis in supply-chain systems. Jain focuses on issues in building a generic simulation capability for supply chains. His work discussed approaches for building generic supply chain simulation capability. Such approaches include data-driven simulators, interactive simulators, and sub-models for supply chain components (Jain, 2008).

Fifth, the scale of supply-chain system is often very huge. Examples are semiconductor and chemical industries. Arons et al. presented an application of a supply-chain simulation for bulk chemicals by using system dynamics methods (Arons et al., 2004). As other scopes, there are many discussions on performance evaluation and simulation optimizations problems (Jain & Leong, 2005)(Yoshizumi & Okano, 2007). Chong et al. proposed a semiconductor supply-chain distributed simulation by using HLA (High Level Architecture)(Chong, 2004).

(2) Manufacturing (including semi-conductor)

Manufacturing applications had been on the top position in discrete-event simulation areas. It still keeps many discussions, today. Benedettini proposed a method to integrate resource

allocation methods and simulation for Engineering-To-Order (ETO) type supply-chain system (Benedettini et al, 2001). This method has been applied to an aerospace manufacturing supply-chain system. Krishnamurthy and Claudio discussed a pull system simulation (Krishnamurthy & Claudio, 2005). A group of Lendermann reported a case study of an integrated manufacturing and service network in Singapore (Lendermann, 2005). MacDonald and Gunn applied simulations to analysis and design of a production control system (MacDonald & Gunn, 2008). Enns analyzed a model for total inventory and delivery performance by mathematical formation, and compared with simulation results by using experimental design methods (Enns, 2007).
One of current major application is semiconductor manufacturing system. Jarugumilli et al. discussed assembly-test facilities using integrated optimization-simulation models for semiconductor manufacturing system (Jarugumilli, 2008). Recently, these discussions are expanded from single manufacturing system to areas of supply-chain simulation. Similar examples are semiconductor supply-chain simulation based WIP management (Miyashita et al., 2004), and semiconductor supply-chain systems (Morrice et al., 2005) (Chang, 2005)).

(3) Logistics and transportation
There are also a lot of reports of applications to logistics system and transportation system. The targets system in this area generally owns large scales. Examples are a proposal of a flexible modelling method for a large-scale transportation-inventory system (Miwa & Takakuwa, 2005), a shipment delivery supply-chain (Oh, 2005), warehouse operations (Gagliardi et al., 2007), a simulation-based optimization retailer network (Subramaniam & Gosavi, 2004).
Object-oriented modelling is a just fit approach for logistics simulation. This is because transporters (a truck, a train, a ship, et al.) and stock facilities (warehouses, shipping facilities) have common specifications, individually. Object-oriented methods provide reduction of workload for simulation modelling and for reuse of models. Rossetti and Nangia presented an object-oriented framework for simulating full truckload transportation (Rossetti & Nangia, 2007).

(4) Risk management
Discussions introduced here belong to different types of discrete-event simulation. Deleris and Elkins presented a supply chain risk analysis that is based on a Monte Carlo simulation of a Generalized Semi-Markov Process (G.S.M.P.) model. Specifically, they estimated the probability distribution of supply chain losses caused by disruptions (Deleris & Elkins, 2004). Deleris and Erhun used similar approaches for supply-chain risk management (Deleris & Erhun, 2005)

(5) SD and its applications
Rebelo et al. introduced a methodology for detecting and predicting supply-chain behaviour changes based on dynamics of the supply-chain business environment (Rebelo et al.,2004). Dulac et al. used system dynamics to analyze risks of management in complex systems (Dulac et al., 2005). An and Jeng developed system dynamics models based on a given business process models along with associated reference contexts, and further, and analyzed a case of supply-chain (An & Jeng, 2005). Venkateswaran analyzed effectiveness of effect on stability of supply-chain (Venkateswaran & Son, 2005). Alvarez analyzed impacts of traffic status in Panama canal to make political decision support. The common item among

these examples is to utilized a merit of System-Dynamics' merit that is good at analyzing feedback mechanisms in a system.

(6) Theory and methodologies
Mazzuchi and Wallace discussed to use discrete-event simulation and experimental design method together (Mazzuchi & Wallace, 2004). The discussion a relation between simulation and experimental design is very important, however, discussions of this kind are not so many.
Benjamin et al. discussed solution concepts for the use of ontology for simulation model integration (Benjamin et al., 2007). A group of Fayez proposed an ontology-based approach to integrate several supply chain views and models which capture the required distributed knowledge to build simulation models. The core of the ontology core is based on the SCOR model (Fayez, 2005). A group of people of IBM discusses similar topics on ontology for supply-chain simulations (Fordyce et al, 2008).
Many of discussions of simulation methodology cover simulation modelling areas. This would be because modelling process is the most important and it also needs workload. Muler gave an overview of a framework for automatically generating large-scale simulation models in a domain of semiconductor manufacturing (Mueller et al, 2007). Adams et al. propose a teaching method of supply-chain management by usages of spreadsheet and discrete event simulation (Adams, 2005). Yang discussed possibilities of data-driven simulations through inventory simulation model. He also compared with the case using discrete event simulations (Yang, 2008).

(7) Tools and package development
Simulation packages include graphical user interfaces, window-based utilities, and multi-purpose simulation languages. These packages support many features including graphical model building tools, tabular data entity, automated debugging, and wide range of animation utilities. Graphical mode building tools simplify, but not eliminate, the need to use underlying language.
Several industrial companies have developed supply-chain simulation systems. These companies own by themselves huge supply-chain systems that include their own and vendors factories. These are originally used as internal tools rather than software products. IBM developed a Client/Server/Web-based system tool to support supply-chain management (Chen et al., 1999). Gensym Corporation developed a supply-chain simulator that is based on SCOR model (Barnett & Miller, 2000). This system provides performance evaluation functions with graphical visualization facilities. This system is available not only to estimations of business model at introduction stage but to estimations for performance improvement.
CSCAT (Compaq Supply Chain Analysis Tool) by Compaq Corporation owns simulation elements of supply-chain systems (Ingalls & Kasales, 1999), and it supports performance evaluation. They further make additional functions such as animation facilities and business-score boards.

(8) Gaming and simulation
Gaming is one of the effective methods to train business practitioners, and supply-chain planner is the same. However, implementation of such training game needs very high programming skills. Verbraeck and Houten developed an object-based module library to

implement supply-chain training games (Verbraek & Houseten, 2005). They also implemented a distributor game, and analyzed it by using in a MBA courses (Houten et al, 2005). A group of Zhou et al. implemented an internet-based supply-chain business game (Zhou et al., 2008). The major objectives of the proposed game are to increase players' SC awareness, facilitate understanding on various SC strategies, and to foster collaboration between partners, and to improve problem solving skills. Further, A group of Ingalls reported on-going work of integrating supply-chain research into the graduate curriculum in the form of a Supply Chain Modelling course (Ingalls et al., 2008).

(9) Others
The works in other application categories are quality controlled logistics (van der Vorst, J. G.A.J. et al.), a call center communication (Takakuwa & Okada, 2005), economic policy analysis (Barnes et al., 2005).

3. Simulation modelling framework

3.1 A hierarchical modeling framework

Simulation modelling is to describe visible target systems by using abstracted simulation modelling notations. A hierarchical framework often clarifies such simulation modelling structure (Fig. 1).

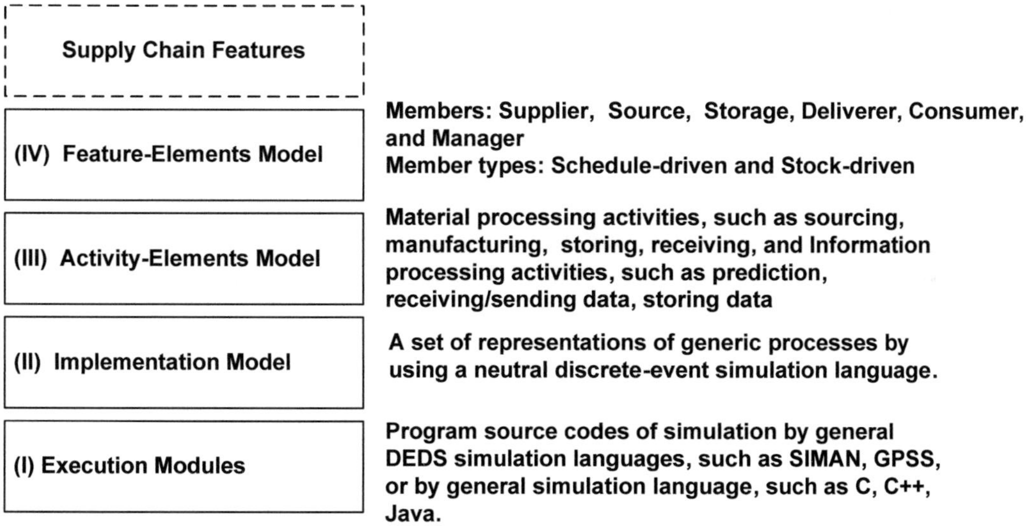

Fig. 1. A hierarchical simulation modelling framework

3.2 Feature-Elements model

There are many supply-chain systems; meanwhile, the types of chain member are countable. Feature-Elements model (LEVEL IV) is such a set of models representing chain members. The members in supply chain systems are categorized into six types by way of organization view: These are "Supplier", "Source", "Storage", "Deliverer", "Consumer", and "Manager". Some of these are further classified into two types by way of control view: stock-driven and schedule-driven. Stock-driven member autonomously work to replenish its relevant inventory stock. Its inventory stock level is often defined as its replenishment point. While, a schedule-driven member basically work to operational orders given by the manager. The details of these control views are described later.

(1) Element: Supplier; An organization that provides materials in the chain. There are two types of Stock-driven and Schedule-driven. Stock-driven supplier observes material stocks of an item in a particular supplier. The observation target is usually a stock of input materials at an immediate downstream supplier. When the stock volume is below the replenishment point, supplier autonomously starts to work to replenish the target part / product inventories. Schedule-driven Supplier receives production orders from Planner, which generates a Master Production Schedule (MPS). It executes the order, when it receives production orders from the Planner. Examples are Parts manufacturers, material manufacturers; parts assemble manufacturers, and final products plants.

(2) Element: Source; An organization that starts the material-flows in the chain. There are two types of Stock-driven and Schedule-driven. Stock-driven Source observes material stocks of an item in a particular supplier. The observation target is usually a stock of input materials at an immediate downstream supplier. When the stock volume is below the replenishment point, source autonomously starts to work to replenish the target part / product inventories. Schedule-driven Source receives material orders from the Planner, which generates a Master Production Schedule (MPS). It executes the procurement orders per the schedule received from the Planner. Examples are Material manufacturers, and Parts manufacturers.

(3) Element: Storage; An organization that holds materials, parts, or products. There are two types of Stock-driven and Schedule-driven. Stock-driven Storage receives materials from other chain members to hold them, and it autonomously ships materials to replenish stock inventories at particular suppliers. Schedule-driven Storage receives materials from other chain members to hold them, and it ships materials when it receives delivery orders from a planner. Examples are Warehouses, transportation bases, store- houses, wholesalers, and plant warehouses.

(4) Element: Manager; An organization that controls material-flows and information-flows in the chain. Manager receives orders from Consumers, and sends delivery orders to deliverer. The Manager stores the order as a demand-log. It predicts products demand in next phase and generates Master Production Schedule (MPS). This MPS is updated by orders that are given by the Consumer. The functions of this organization include: master scheduling, receiving orders from Consumer, forecasting demands, making commitments on replenishment with stock-driven members and sending orders to chain members. For stock-driven stages in the supply-chain, the role of the manager is to set the replenishment points and change them as required over time due to changes in market and demand. Examples are a headquarters of a final products manufacturer, and a supply chain control centre.

(5) Element Deliverer; An organization that transports products, parts, and/or materials between members. It receives delivery order from other chain members, and it works according to the delivery order. The sender of this order is the upstream supplier of this deliverer. Examples are 3rd party logistics companies, UPS, and post office.

(6) Element Consumer; An organization or individual who acquires products. It gives products purchase orders to manager. Also inspects the incoming products for quality and tracking. Examples are Buyers, consumers, and trading companies

3.3 Function-Elements model, Implementation model, and Execution modules

Function-Elements Model (LEVEL III) is a set of representations of fundamental business activities in supply chain operations. These activities are classified into material processing operations or information processing operations. The former includes "Material sourcing", "Manufacturing", "Storing", Receiving", "Delivering", and the later includes miscellaneous information/data processing, such as "Demand prediction", "Sending/Receiving data", "Storing/Updating data", and others. Individual is transferable to micro-scale modeling provided in Level II.

Implementation Model (LEVEL II) is a set of representations of activities by using a neutral DEDS simulation language, which provides generic activities, such as Enter_queue, Exit_queue, Size_resource, Release_resource, Set_attribute, Get_attribute, Reset_Attribute, Delay, and others. Individual is transferable to language descriptions provided in level I.

An Execution modules (LEVEL I) is a set of simulation object codes Programming source codes of simulation by using DEDS simulation language (SIMAN, GPSS, etc.) or general programming languages, such as C, C++, Java, and etc.

3.4 Supply-chain Control model

The previous section described that particular feature element models are controlled by two types of methods: Schedule-driven and Stock-driven. These features are useful to model supply-chain simulation. (Umeda & Jain, 2004) (Umeda & Lee, 2004a). The details of these are described here.

(1) Schedule-driven control

Schedule-driven control uses a production schedule, the so-called "Master Production Schedule" (MPS), which the supply-chain manager generates. The manager receives purchase orders from marketing channels in a periodic cycle time, and it saves the orders as demand data. It also periodically updates the MPS by using the accumulated demand prediction data. MPS is a schedule about which finished-goods items are delivered to consumers. To generate MPS, the manager is generally based on demands forecast, production plan, availability of materials, and availability of capacity.

The main function of the chain manager is to give periodical operational orders to supply-chain members by using MPS and Bills Of Materials (BOMs). The schedule-driven suppliers regularly work according as orders from manager. As shown in Fig. 2, the manager uses schedule-driven control to repeat the above activities cycle. The activities of "Manager" are summarized as follows:

1. It receives purchase orders from consumers.
2. It accumulates this purchase data.
3. It generates future demand predictions by using the accumulated demand data.
4. It updates MPS by using the predicted demand and feedback data from supply chain members.
5. It gives orders (sourcing, manufacturing, and shipping) to corresponding chain members.

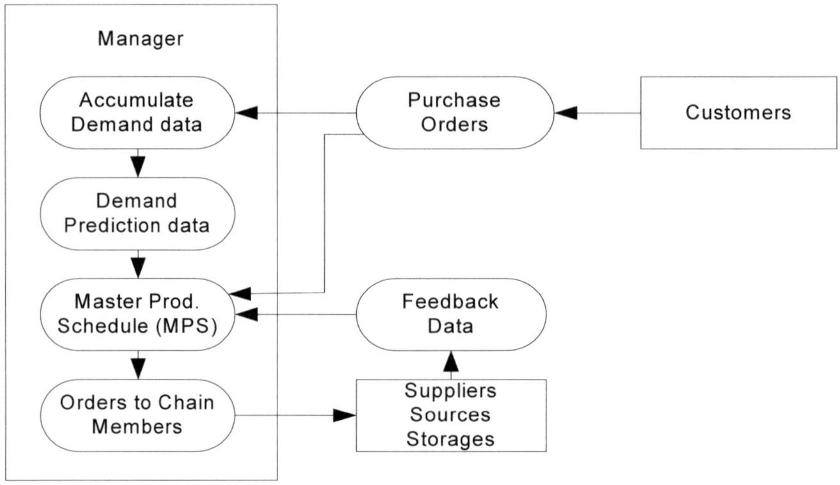

Fig. 2. Schedule-driven Supply Chain Control

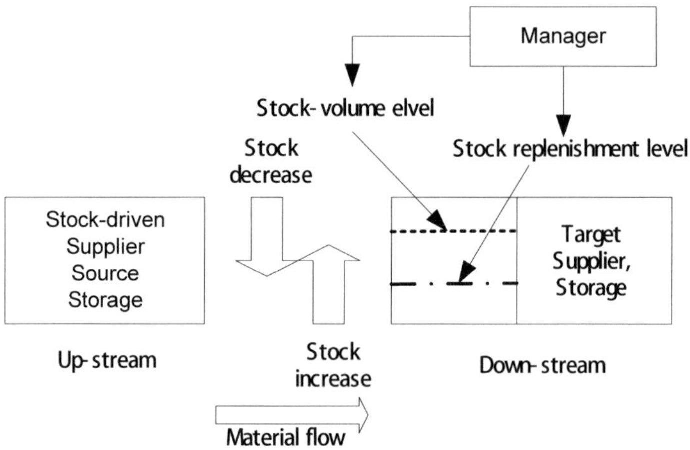

Fig. 3. Stock-driven Supply Chain Control

3.5 Supply-chain configurations by using schedule- and stock-driven control

Combinations of the Feature-Elements models enable to define the configuration of supply-chain systems. This section demonstrates some of typical supply-chain system configuration using Feature-Elements models (Umeda & Jain, 2004).

Fig. 4 represents a configuration example of schedule-driven supply-chain system. In this system, the chain manager receives purchase orders from consumers and it gives production orders to each chain member. Every supplier produces products according to orders given by the supply chain planner. A particular member might receive orders directly from other chain members as is shown in the deliverer in this case.

Connection of schedule-driven members results in a supply chain operating as a push system. The manager plays a very important role in this system. The manager receives purchase orders from consumers and accumulates past order data to predict demands in

future. It further generates production orders and sends them to each chain member. The manager needs to collect various kinds of data from the chain members so as to give proper orders to each member. This configuration results in concentration of data and information with the planner, and the success of the supply chain is dependent on decision making capability of the manager.
A particular supplier might operate using stock-driven control. When the system includes such members, commitment would be needed between the supplier and the manager. An example illustrated in Fig. 5 includes a stock-driven source that autonomously provides materials to the parts supplier.
Fig. 6 illustrates a configuration example of purely stock-driven supply-chain system. In this system, manager receives commitment from the suppliers to provide materials and parts. Every supplier works autonomously to provide materials to individual downstream suppliers. The data and information are distributed to individual supplier, and manager's direct control on suppliers is minimized in this system.
Connection of stock-driven members makes a pull system. The role of the manager is less important here than in the case of push system. Individual stock-driven supplier autonomously works according to the predefined operational commitments with the planner. The manager plays a role of communicator between consumers and final product plant. Another role of the manager is to define the replenishment points and receive operational commitments from suppliers for maintaining the stock.
The role of manager is more of a data communication enabler rather than a controller of suppliers.

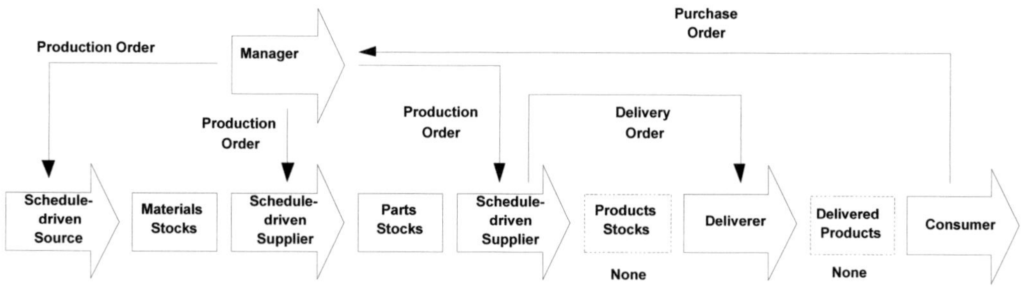

Fig. 4. A configuration example of schedule-driven supply chain

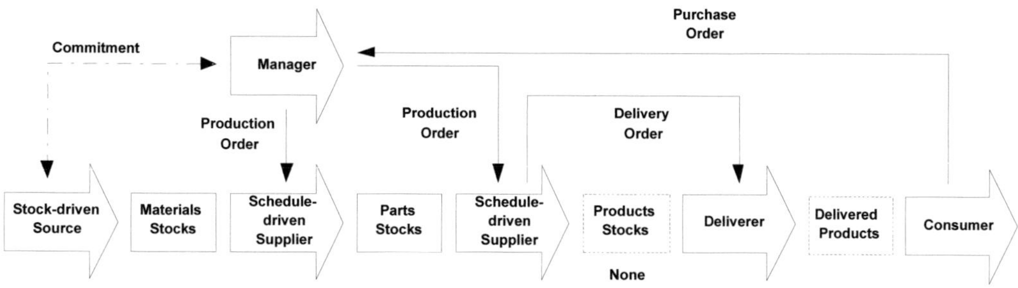

Fig. 5. A configuration example of hybrid schedule and stock-driven supply chain

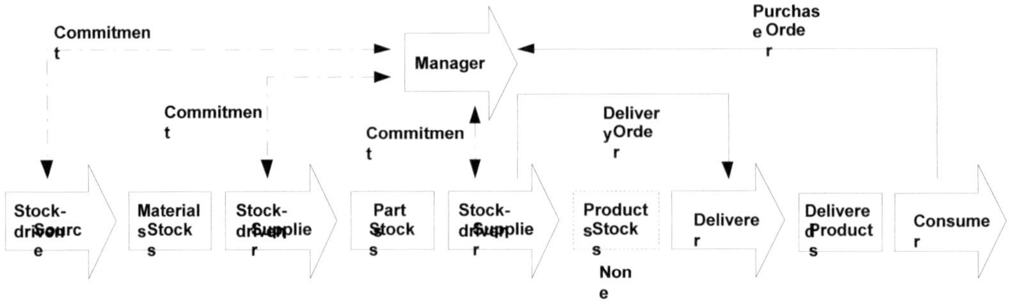

Fig. 6. A configuration example of stock-driven supply chain

3.6 Management environment model

Supply-chain activities have relevance to its business environment. Suppose that a supply-chain system realizes a high performance and it shorten the consumers' purchase lead-time. In this case, the demand volume in market would increase because of the shortened purchase lead-time; the system would be busier by the increased demands. These activities give favourable or harmful influences to its external world, and their feedbacks can also give similar influences to the supply-chain.

Similar scenarios would be applicable to relations between other supply-chain systems' activities and their feedbacks. They are, for examples, quality improvement programs in factories, manufacturing process automation programs, and operational improvement in parts/products transportation between suppliers.

System dynamics has been defined as "A method of analyzing problems in which time is an important factor, and which involve the study of how the system can be defended against, or made benefit from, the shocks which fall upon it from outside world" (Sterman, 2000). There are many SD applications to manufacturing systems, such as relations between demand-supply operations and manufacturing system performance, cause-and–effect relations among equipment maintenance, productivity, manufacturing cost, and others (Riddalls et al., 2000).

This approach is useful to capture complex real-world situations, which include delays and feedback mechanisms. Practical applications include understanding market environments and assessing possible future scenarios. Dynamics complexity is not related to number of nodes or actors concerned, but the behaviour they create when acting together.

One of the advantages of SD is to describe complex systems including uncertainty and cause-and-effect relations in a system. The SD models represent interdependency in a system by using elements, such as "Stock", "Flow", and the relative variables. SD evaluates both systems' effect on a particular element and its feedback effects on the system in itself.

We tried to implement a model that describes product supply capability, market demands, and their mutual feedback mechanisms. Fig. 7 illustrates a conceptual mechanism that the consumers in market react to supply-chain performance and it gives feedbacks to the chain as order volumes. This figure represents a cause-and- effect mechanism between supply-chain performance and market order volumes by system dynamics notations.

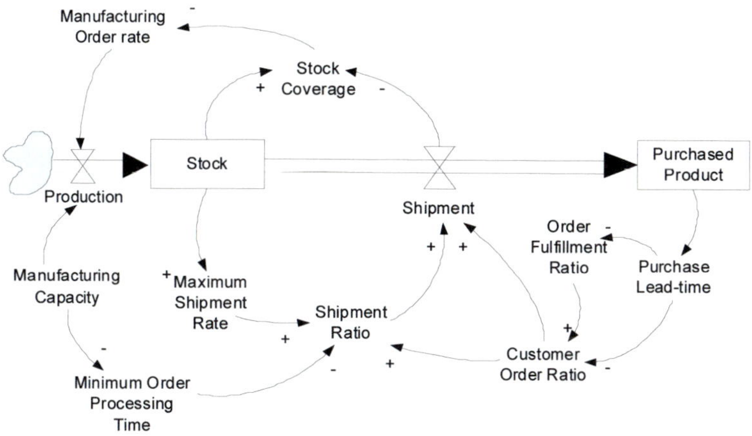

Fig. 7. Causes and effects relation by using System dynamics modelling

3.7 Hybrid modeling framework for supply-chain system

Based on the above discussions, this paper proposes a generic hybrid-modelling framework for supply-chain simulation. Fig. 8 represents a conceptual chart of this modelling framework. Framed rectangles represent supply-chain members' model, which is discrete-event-based, and rounded rectangles represent dynamics of supply-chain management environment (Umeda & Zhang, 2009) (Umeda & Zhang, 2010).

Supply-chain feature model represents abstracted supply-chain members, which described in 3.2. The manager get purchase orders from consumers, and it gives orders to suppliers and transporters.

Market dynamics model represents reaction mechanisms of consumers to supply-chain system performance. If serviceability of supply chain would be measurable in market, the consumers' satisfactions to its serviceability would be influential with their future purchase preference. Plant dynamics model represents influences of process performance improvement in supplier's plants on the system performance. And further, traffic dynamics model represents changes in outside transportation systems

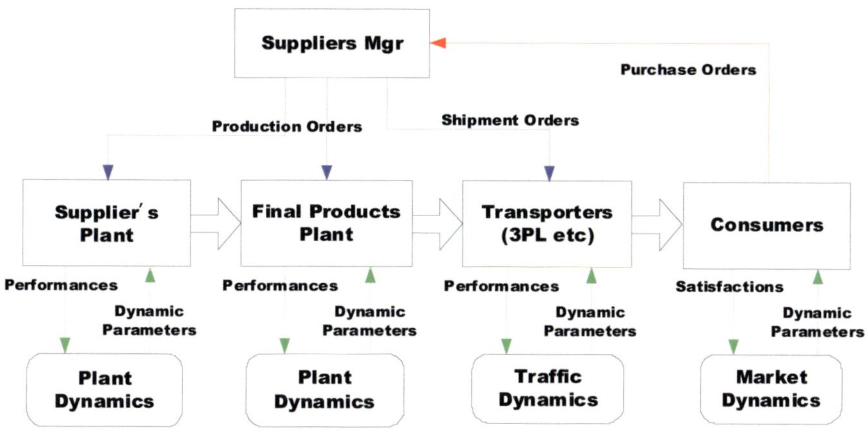

Fig. 8. A hybrid-modelling framework for supply-chain simulation

4. Simulation experiments

4.1 Supply-chain system

The supply-chain system discussed here is originally a very huge system. It possesses more than ten first-tier suppliers. Several of them own subordinate second-tier suppliers. It includes eight parts suppliers and a final product plant. The distinctive features of them are described as the following items.

- This supply-chain system belongs to a schedule-driven type. The manager builds a master schedule based on a demand prediction mechanism.
- The final product is manufactured in a product factory that posses an assembly line.
- The final product plant works according as daily production orders from the manager.
- The final product plant controls the manufacturing line so that a variance of daily-going-rate keeps a small range.

There is a variance of every order from consumers; however, the demand trend does not change in the long term. Majority of first-tier and second-tier suppliers works according as a periodic ordering method. The period is almost a week and the order volume is variable.
The particular first-tier suppliers work according as the daily-based manufacturing orders as well as the final product plant. A particular second-tier supplier owns a long order lead-time. A particular first-tier supplier works according to stock-driven operations.
Third party logistics companies deliver between suppliers; accordingly, every delivery time is a constant regardless of volumes. A configuration of the target system is shown in Fig. 9.

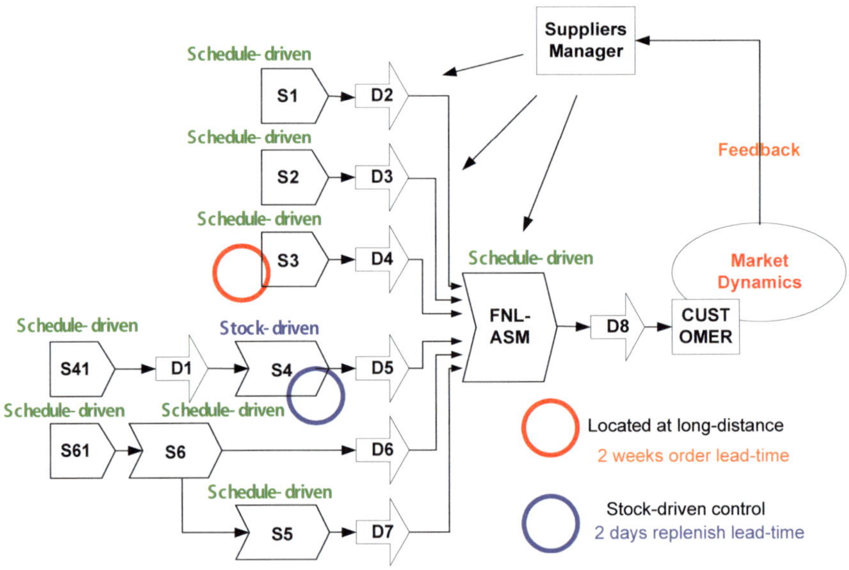

Fig. 9. A configuration of the target supply-chain system

Supplier S4 is an only supplier that is controlled by "Stock-driven" method. The manager decides both stock replenishment level and stock volume level. S4 autonomously provides parts to the final assembly parts by using this stock volume information.

The outlines of activities and controls of every chain member (agent) are based on the description in the previous section. Every chain member owns its processing capacity. When it receives an order that is over its capacity, the overflowed one is transferred to the next one. The feedback mechanism works by using a monitoring data of supply-chain performance in an observation phase and decisions mechanism for demand volume in the next phase. A summary of this mechanism is as follows.

Purchase orders from market occur every day. When products are moved to consumers, system observes order lead-time in all of these orders. At that time, the system also calculates its moving average and variance. When the moving average and its variance is large, system restrains purchase order volume in next term. System then uses smaller random variables on orders' generation. Meanwhile, when the moving average and its variance is small, system releases purchase order volume in next term. System then uses larger random variables on orders' generation.

System uses a system-dynamics (SD) model at that time. In this model, the mainstream data flow starts "source" (data generation), and go through "flow" (data modification that make a decision of demand volume), and finally reaches "stock" (data store). In these processes, system uses the past observation data and their variance data.

4.2 System performance evaluation by using test case models

We, at first, compared two patterns of demand distributions in this system. These are Normal distribution and Uniform distribution. The difference of these does not give any influences on performance of the supply-chain system. System performance is measured by parts inventory volumes at supplier S4 and S5, parts inventory volumes at the final assembly plant, and order lead-time of consumers.

When the demand mean is set on low level, the difference of its variances does not give any influences on system performances. However, when the demand mean is set on middle and high level, even so keeping demand variance at low level, the differences of its variance are increased. Performances are, for examples, measurable by observations of the following items.

(1) Parts inventories at the final assembly plant

(2) Purchase order lead-time observed by consumers

(3) Parts inventory at supplier-5 (Schedule-driven supplier)

(4) Parts inventory at supplier-4 (Stock-driven supplier)

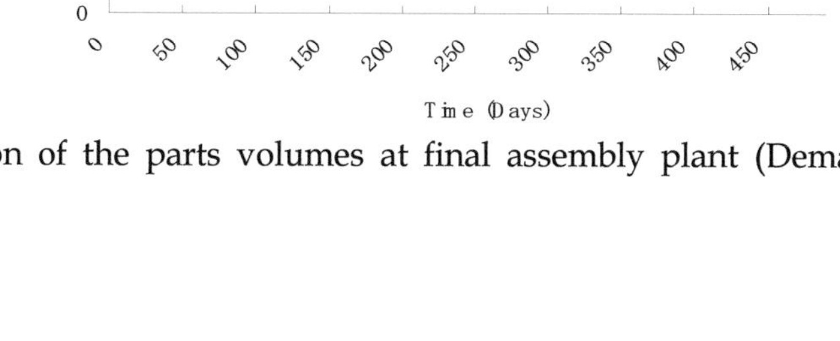

Fig. 10. Transition of the parts volumes at final assembly plant (Demand distribution = N(40,6))

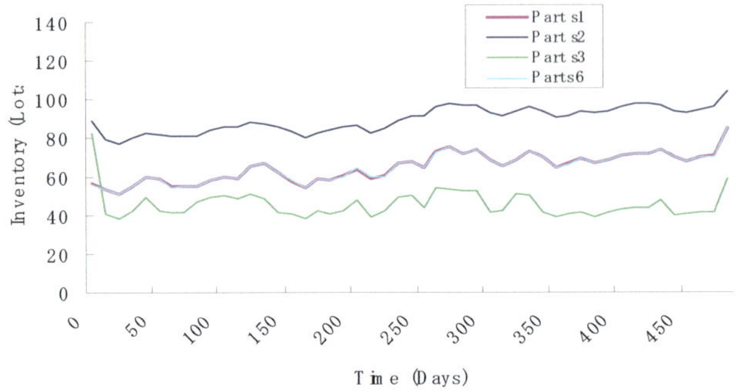

Fig. 11. Transition of the parts volumes at final assembly plant (Demand distribution = N(60,6))

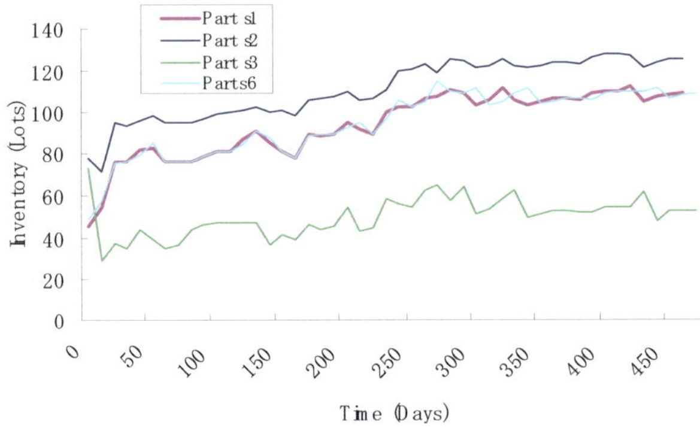

Fig. 12. Transition of the parts volumes at final assembly plant (Demand distribution = N(80,6))

Transition curves of inventories at the final assembly factory are shown in Fig, 10, 11, and 12. The differences of inventories of each part are enlarged, according as increase of the demand mean. The transitions of order lead-time are shown in Fig. 13, 14, and 15. When demand mean is in high level, lead-time transition raises up immediately after the simulation starts, and it keeps in high level through the simulation. This phenomenon explains that the delay of orders has passed into a chronic state. Transitions of parts volume at final assembly plant are shown in Figure7, 8, and 9. The part volumes stocked there are proportion to the average of demand distribution that is given as the parameters.

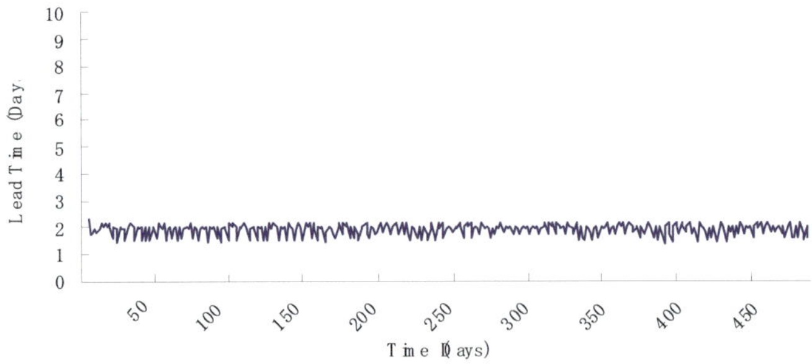

Fig. 13. Transition of the purchase lead-time (Demand distribution = N(40,6))

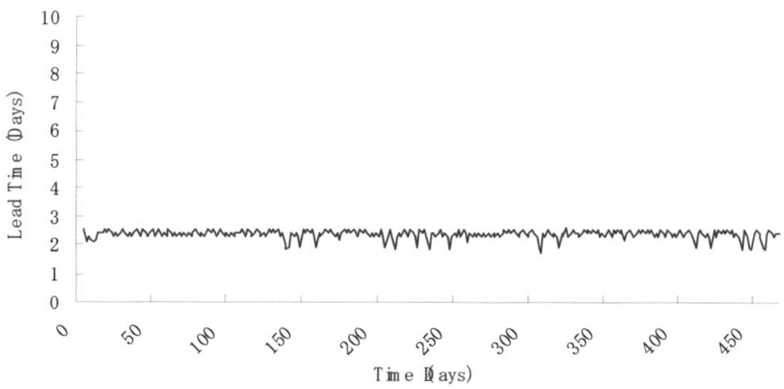

Fig. 14. Transition of the purchase lead-time (Demand distribution = N(60,6))

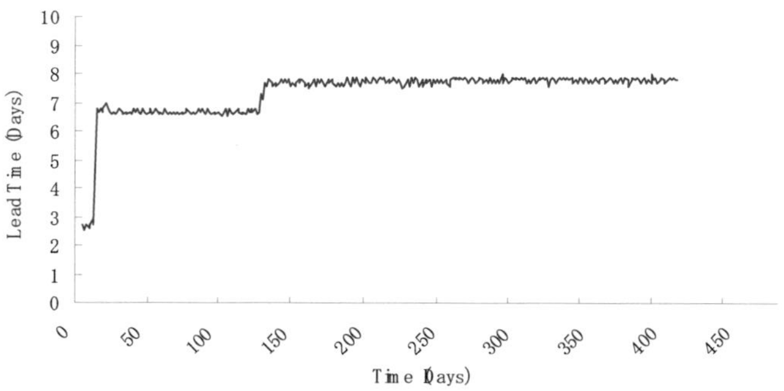

Fig. 15. Transition of the purchase lead-time (Demand distribution = N(80,6))

4.3 Hybrid simulation considering management environment

Supply-chain activities have relevance to its business environment. We consider here this issue according as the scenario discussed in 2.4. The principal cause is the observed purchase lead-time in every purchase activity. The rule defined here is, in a word, summarized as follows.

Short purchase lead-time gives favourable impression to customers, and the order volume increases. Accordingly, the chain system becomes busy; order processing at every task in the chain becomes tight. While, long purchase lead-time gives unfavourable impression to customers, and the order volume decreases. Accordingly, the chain system becomes calm; order processing at every task in the chain becomes loose.

Fig. 16 represents the transition curves of purchase order volume by customers and demand prediction by the manager. The value draws a cyclical curve in initial duration of simulation, and it becomes stable later. This phenomenon is based on the fact that a chronic order delay occurs. The curve of purchase lead-time also shows the same patterns as this transition. And further, there is no case that parts become shortage. This is the reason why the purchase order volume becomes stable.

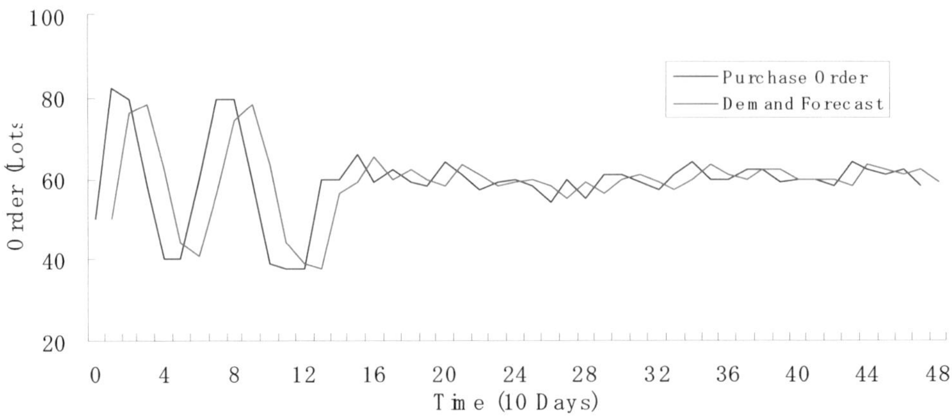

Fig. 16. Transitions of purchase order volume by customers

5. A life-cycle system management framework for supply-chain system using hybrid system simulation

Considering above discussions, this section proposes a novel framework life-cycle management of supply-chain. Fig. 17 illustrates a diagram of this framework. This framework derives from a waterfall model that is well-known as a software development process model. "Constraints Management" corresponds to a "Requirement specification". Supply-chain system owns various constraints in its designs and operations. The examples are, for examples, 'Contracts between a prime contractor and suppliers', 'Common business rules', 'Information exchange methods', and others. Many of them are deeply relative to 'Capacity planning', 'Resource planning', and 'lead-time planning' problems discussed in section 2.

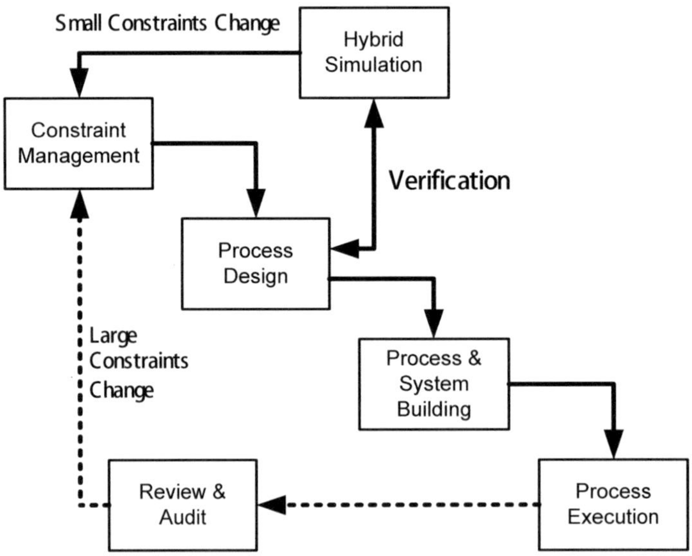

Fig. 17. A life-cycle system management framework

"Process Design" is a designing stage of supply-chain processes. A supply-chain builder plans and designs supply-chain business processes. Many existing processes should be re-constructed in many cases. A reference business model, like SCOR model, would be very useful in this stage.
"Hybrid Simulation" stage verifies the designed process by using the supply-chain simulator which section 3 described in detail. Simulation can evaluate supply-chain behaviours in tactical phase using the discrete-event simulator alone. The simulation output would helps to solve supply-chain problems such as discussed in section 2
"Hybrid simulation" accompanied with system-dynamics models, would provide solutions of the supply-chain problems. Hybrid simulation can evaluate system behaviours considering the business environment of the chain. It would provide solutions in a comparably long term. Most of strategic problems described in section 2 would find management solutions by considering transitions in a long term. Particular simulation results can be feed-backed to "Constraints Management" to rebuild major constraints of the chain.
The relationship among these stages is similar to the case of Water-fall model accompanying with prototypes. The prototypes help to find faults in external design phase, and to prevent design bugs from sending to next stage. The role of the "Hybrid Simulation" corresponds to such prototypes. "Process & System Building" is an implementation phase. After that, practice phase would start. This is a stage named as Process Execution".
After continuing practices in several years, the supply-chain system would be faced to the stage of "Review & Audit". This stage discusses not apparent modifications but drastic changes. Large-level constraints would be discussed for the next cycle in management.

6. Conclusions and future researches

This chapter has described a new approach to support life-cycle management of supply-chain system. The core technology of the proposed framework is a hybrid modelling method, which combines discrete-event modelling and system-dynamic modelling.
The proposed framework and models would be effective in supply-chain system evaluation for a long duration. Similar scenarios would be appropriate to other supply-chain systems' activities such as quality improvement programs, manufacturing processes automation programs, and efficient transportations operational programs.
The proposed approach will be the first step to a simulation & gaming methodology to support supply-chain operations. More case studies would be needed. The scale of this kind of simulation is complex and very large. Accordingly, it includes lots of simulation parameters. Efficient ways for simulation experiments design would be needed. "Taguchi method" would be the best solution to apply supply-chain simulation experiment design. This method uses orthogonal matrices to assign simulation parameters. The merit of this way is that parameters are assigned by a fixed form. In addition, experiment numbers are extremely reduced in comparison with traditional design methods.

7. References

Adams, J.; Flatto, J., Gardner, L. (2005). Combining hand-on spreadsheet and discrete event simulation to teach supply chain management, Proceedings of the 2005 Winter Simulation Conference, pp.2329-2337, 2005

Alvarez A. H. R.; Solis, D., Cano S. A. R., Sala-Diakanda, S. (2006). System dynamics simulation of expansion of the Panama canal, Proceedings of the 2006 Winter Simulation Conference, pp.660-666, 2006

An, L. & Jeng, J. (2005). On developing system dynamics models for business process simulation, Proceedings of the 2005 Winter Simulation Conference, pp.2068-2077, 2005

Arons, H. S.; Asperen, E., Dekker, R., Polman, M. (2004). Coordination in a supply chain for bulk chemicals, Proceedings of the 2004 Winter Simulation Conference, pp.1365-1372, 2004

Bagdia, R. R. & Pasek, Z. J. (2005). Upstream demand projection and performance mapping in supply chains, Proceedings of the 2005 Winter Simulation Conference, pp.1633-1642, 2005

Barnes, J. N.; Kalaitzandonakes, N. G. & Crowe, T. J. (2005). Using simulation for economic policy analysis in the global agricultural supply chain, Proceedings of the 2005 Winter Simulation Conference, pp.2034-2041, 2005

Banks, J. (eds.) (1998). Handbook of Simulation: Principles, Methodology, Advances, Applications, and Practice, John Wiley & Sons, New York.

Barnett, M. W. & Miller, C. J. (2000). Analysis of the virtual enterprise using distributed supply chain modelling and simulation: An application of e-SCOR, Proceedings of the 2000 Winter Simulation Conference, pp.352-355, 2000

Benedettini, O.; Iavagnilio, R., Mossa, G., Mummolo, G., & Ranieri, L. (2001). Integrating Resource Allocation and Simulation in Project-type Production Planning and Control of Supply Chains: A Case from the Aeronautics Industry, Proceedings of Int. Working Conference on Strategic Manufacturing, pp.26-29 Aug. 2001

Benjamin, P.; Akella, K., Verma, A. (2007). Using ontologies for simulation integration, Proceedings of the 2007 Winter Simulation Conference, pp.1081-1088, 2007

Bhaskaran, S. (1998). Simulation Analysis of a Manufacturing Supply Chain, Decision Sciences Vol. 29 No.3, pp633-657, Summer 1998

Byrne, P. J. & Heavey, C. (2004). Simulation, A framework for analysing SME supply chain, Proceedings of the 2004 Winter Simulation Conference, pp.1167-1175, 2004, Society for Computer Simulation

Chang, S.; Su, S. & Chen, K. (2008). Priority mix planning for cycle time-differentiated semiconductor manufacturing services, Proceedings of the 2008 Winter Simulation Conference, pp.2251-2259, 2008

Chen, H.; Bimber, B. Chhatre, O. Poole, C. E. & Buckley, S. J. (1999). eSCA: A Thin-Client/Server/Web-Enabled System for Distributed Supply Chain Simulation, Proceedings of the 1999 Winter Simulation Conference, pp.1371-1377, Society of Computer Simulation, 1999 Dec.

Cheng, F.; Lee, Y. M., Ding, H. W., Wang, W., Stephens, S. (2008). Simulating order fulfillment and supply planning for a vertically aligned industry solution business, Proceedings of the 2008 Winter Simulation Conference, pp.2609-2615, 2008

Chong, C. S.; Lendermann, P., Gan, B. P., Duarte, B. M., Fowler, J. W., Callarman, T. E., (2004). Analysis of a customer demand driven semiconductor supply chain in a distributed simulation test bed, Proceedings of the 2004 Winter Simulation Conference, pp.1902-1909, 2004

Cope, D.; Fayez, M. S., Mollaghasemi, M., & Kaylani, A. (2007). Supply Chain simulation modeling made easy: an innovative approach, Proceedings of the 2007 Winter Simulation Conference, pp.1887-1896, 2007

Ding, H.; Wang, W. Dong, J. Qiu, M., Ren, C. (2007). IBM supply-chain network optimization workbench: An integrated optimization and simulation tool for supply chain design, Proceedings of the 2007 Winter Simulation Conference, pp.1940-1946, 2007

Dong, J.; Ding, H., Ren, C., Wang, W. (2006). IBM SmartSCOR - A SCOR based supply chain transformation platform through simulation and optimization techniques, Proceedings of the 2006 Winter Simulation Conference, pp.653-659, 2006

Dulac, N.; Leveson, N., Zipkin, D., Friedenthal, S., Cutcher-Gershenfeld, J., Carroll, J., Barr, B. (2005). Using system dynamics for safety and risk management in complex engineering systems, Proceedings of the 2005 Winter Simulation Conference, pp.1311-1320, 2005

Deleris, L. A. & Elkins, D. (2004). Analyzing losses from hazard exprosure: A conservative probabilistic estimate using supply chain risk simulation, Proceedings of the 2004 Winter Simulation Conference, pp.1384-1391, 2004

Deleris, L. A. & Erhun, F. (2005). Risk management in supply networks using Monte-Carlo simulation, Proceedings of the 2005 Winter Simulation Conference, pp.1643-1649, 2005

ECR Performance Measures Operating Committee (1994). Performance Measurement, Applying Value Chain Analysis to the Grocery Industry, Joint Industry Project on Efficient Consumer Response

Enns, S. T. (2007). "Pull" Replenishment performance as a function of demand rates and setup times under optimal settings, Proceedings of the 2007 Winter Simulation Conference, pp.1624-1632, 2007

Fayez, M.; Rabelo, L., Mollaghasemi, M. (2005). Ontologies for supply chain simulation modeling, Proceedings of the 2005 Winter Simulation Conference, pp.2364-2370, 2005

Fordyce, K.; Degbotse, A., Milne, J., Orzell, R., Wang, C. (2008). The ongoing challenge - An accurate assessment of supply linked to demand to create an enterprise-wide end to end detailed central supply chain plan, Proceedings of the 2008 Winter Simulation Conference, pp.2267-2270, 2008

Gagliardi, J.P.; Renaud, J. & Ruiz, A. (2007). A Simulation model to improve warehouse operations, Proceedings of the 2007 Winter Simulation Conference, pp.2012-2018, 2007

Gavirneni, S. (2005). Simulation based evaluation of information-centric supply chains, Proceedings of the 2005 Winter Simulation Conference, pp.1677-1683, 2005

Houten, S. A.; Verbraeck, A., Boyson, S., Corsi, T. (2005). Training for today's supply chain: an introduction to the distributor game, Proceedings of the 2005 Winter Simulation Conference, pp.2338-2345, 2005

Ingalls, R. G. & Kasales, C. (1999). CSCAT: The Compaq Supply Chain Analysis Tool, Proceedings of the 1999 Winter Simulation Conference, pp.1201-1206, Society of Computer Simulation, 1999 Dec.

Ingalls, R. G.; Cornejo, M., Methapatara, C., Sittivijan, P. (2008). Integrating simulation and optimization research into a graduate supply chain modeling course, Proceedings of the 2008 Winter Simulation Conference, pp.2527-2533, 2008

Jain, S. & Leong, S. (2005). Stress testing a supply chain using simulation, Proceedings of the 2005 Winter Simulation Conference, pp.1650-1657, 2005

Jain, S. (2008). Tradeoff in building a generic chain simulation capability, Proceedings of the 2008 Winter Simulation Conference, pp.1873-1881, 2008

Jarugumilli, S.; Keng, N., Askin, R., Fu, M., DeJong, C., Fowler, J. (2008). Framework for execution level capacity allocation decisions for assembly - test facilities using integrated optimization - simulation models, Proceedings of the 2008 Winter Simulation Conference, pp.2292-2297, 2008

Koelling, P. & Schwand, M. J. (2005). Health systems: A dynamic system —Benefits from System dynamics, Proceedings of the 2005 Winter Simulation Conference, pp.1321-1327, 2005

Krishnamurthy, A. & Claudio, D. (2005). Pull systems with advance demand information, Proceedings of the 2005 Winter Simulation Conference, pp.1733-1744, 2005

Kurt Salmon Associates, Inc. (1993). Efficient Consumer Response: Enhancing Consumer Value in Grocery Industry, Food Market Institute

Lee, H.; Cho, K. Kim, J., & Kim, B. (2002). Supply chain simulation with discrete- continuous combined modeling, Computers & Industrial Engineering Vol.43, pp.375-392,

Lendermann, P.; Turner, S. J, Lee, L. H., Hung, T., Simon J.E. Taylor, S. J. E., McGinnis, L. F., Buckley, S. (2005). An Integrated and adaptive decision-support framework for high-tech manufacturing and service network, Proceedings of the 2005 Winter Simulation Conference, pp.2052-2062, 2005

Liu, J.; Wang, W., Chai, Y., Liu, Y. (2004). Easy-SC: A supply chain simulation tool, Proceedings of the 2004 Winter Simulation Conference, pp.1373-1378, 2004

Liu, R. ; Kumar, A. & Stenger, A. J. (2006). Simulation results for supply chain configurations based on information sharing, Proceedings of the 2006 Winter Simulation Conference, pp.627-635, 2006

MacDonald, C. & Gunn, E. (2008). A simulation based system for analysis and design of production control systems, Proceedings of the 2008 Winter Simulation Conference, pp.1882-1890, 2008

Mazzuchi, T. A. & Wallace, R. B. (2004). Analyzing skill-based routing CALL centers using discrete-event simulation and design experiment, Proceedings of the 2004 Winter Simulation Conference, pp.1812-1820, 2004

Miyashita, K.; Okazaki, T. & Matsuo, H. (2004). Simulation-based advanced WIP management and control in semiconductor manufacturing, Proceedings of the 2004 Winter Simulation Conference, pp.1943-1950, 2004

Miwa, K. & Takakuwa, S. (2005). Flexible module-based modeling and analysis for large-scale transportation-inventory systems, Proceedings of the 2005 Winter Simulation Conference, pp.1749-1758, 2005

Morrice, D. J.; Valdez, R. A., Chida, Jr. J. P., Eido, M. (2005). Discrete event simulation in supply chain planning and inventory control at Freescale semiconductor, inc., Proceedings of the 2005 Winter Simulation Conference, pp.1718-1724, 2005
Oh, S.; Kumara, S. R. T., Yee, S., Tew, J.D. (2005). A family of market-based shipment methodologies for delivery supply chain, Proceedings of the 2005 Winter Simulation Conference, pp.1759-1765, 2005
Rabelo, L.; Helal, M. & Lertpattarapong, C. (2004). Analysis of supply chains using system dynamics, neural nets, and eigenvalues, Proceedings of the 2004 Winter Simulation Conference, pp.1136-1144, 2004
Ralph Mueller, Christos Alexopoulos, Leon F. McGinnis, (2007). Automatic Generation of Simulation Models for Semiconductor Manufacturing, Proceedings of the 2007 Winter Simulation Conference, 648-657, 2007
Riddalls, C. ; Bennett, E.S. & Tipi, N. S. (2000). Modeling the dynamics of supply-chains, Int. J. of System Science, 31, 8, pp.969-976
Rossetti, M. D. & Nangia, S. (2007). An object-oriented framework for simulating full truckload transportation networks, Proceedings of the 2007 Winter Simulation Conference, pp.1869-1877, 2007
Sarac, A.; Absi, N. & Dauz`ere-P´er`es, S. (2008). A simulation approach to evaluate the impact of introducing RFID technologies in three-level supply-chain, Proceedings of the 2008 Winter Simulation Conference, pp.2741-2749
Song, L.; Li, X. & Garcia-Diaz, A. (2008). A. multi-echelon supply chain simulation using metamodel, Proceedings of the 2008 Winter Simulation Conference, pp.2691-2699, 2008
Sterman, J. D. (2000). Business Dynamics - System Thinking and Modeling for a complex World, Irwin McGraw-Hill, Boston
Subramaniam, G. & Gosavi, A. (2004). Simulation-based optimization for material dispatching in a retailer network, Proceedings of the 2004 Winter Simulation Conference, pp.1412-1417, 2004
Supply Chain council. Supply Chain Operations Reference Model: Overview of SCOR Version 6.0, Available online at http://www.supply-chain.org/.
Takakuwa, S. & Okada, T. (2005). Simulation analysis of inbound CALL center of a city-gas company, Proceedings of the 2005 Winter Simulation Conference, pp.2026-2033, 2005
Umeda, S. & Jain, S. (2004). Integrated Supply Chain Simulation System (ISSS) - Modeling Requirements and Design Issues, NISTIR 7180, National Institutes of Standards and Technology, US Dept. of Commerce.
Umeda, S. & Lee, Y. T. (2004a). Integrated Supply Chain Simulation System --A Design Specification for A Generic Supply Chain Simulator, NISTIR 7146 National Institute of Standards and Technology, US Dept. of Commerce, Maryland
Umeda, S. & Lee, Y. T. (2004b). Design specifications of a generic supply chain simulator, Proceedings of the 2004 Winter Simulation Conference, pp.1158-1166, 2004
Umeda, S. & Zhang, F. (2003). System Simulation for Integrated Supply Chain, Proceedings of the IFIP WG5.7 Working Conference on Human Aspects in Production Management Vol. 2, Conference Vol. 6-2003, pp.41-48, October, 2003

Umeda, S. & Zhang, F. (2004). Supply Chain Simulation: A Technological Approach For System Performance Evaluation to Supply Chain, Proceedings of World Automation Congress Ninth International Symposium on Manufacturing with Applications (WAC/ISOMA2004) Conference, Jun. 2004, Seville, Spain

Umeda, S. & Zhang, F. (2006). Supply chain simulation: generic models and application examples, Production Planning & Control, Vol.17, No.2, pp.155-166

Umeda, S. & Zhang, F. (2009). A life-cycle system management framework for supply-chain by using hybrid system simulation, Proceedings of Promac2009, SPM, Bangkok

Umeda, S. & Zhang, F. (2010). A simulation modeling framework for supply-chain system analysis (submitted to 2010 Winter Simulation Conference) .

Venkateswaran, J. & Son, Y. (2005). Information synchronization effects on the stability of collaborative supply chain, Proceedings of the 2005 Winter Simulation Conference, pp.1668-1676, 2005

Verbraeck, A. & Houten, S. A. (2005). From simulation to gaming: An object-oriented supply chain training library, Proceedings of the 2005 Winter Simulation Conference, pp.2346-2354, 2005

Vieira, C. E. & César, O. Jr, (2005). A conceptual model for the creation of supply chain simulation models, Proceedings of the 2005 Winter Simulation Conference, pp.2619-2627, 2005

van der Vorst, J. G.A.J.; Tromp, S. & van der Zee, D. (2005). A simulation environment for the redesign of food supply chain networks: modeling quality controlled logistics, Proceedings of the 2005 Winter Simulation Conference, pp.1658-1667, 2005

Yoshizumi, T. & Okano, H. (2007). A simulation-based algorithm for supply chain optimization, Proceedings of the 2007 Winter Simulation Conference, pp.1924-1931, 2007

Yang, M. (2008). Using data driven simulation to build inventory model, Proceedings of the 2008 Winter Simulation Conference, pp.2595-2599, 2008

Zhou, L.; Xie, Y., Wild, N. Hunt, C. (2008). Learning and practicing supply chain management strategies from a business simulation game: A comprehensive supply chain simulation, Proceedings of the 2008 Winter Simulation Conference, pp.2534-2542, 2008

Optimisation of reordering points considering purchasing, storing and service breakdown costs

Aitor Goti[1] and Miguel Ortega[2]
[1]University of Mondragon – Mondragon Unibertsitatea
[2]Polytechnic University of Madrid
[1,2]Spain

Abstract

This paper focuses on the problem of the optimisation of reordering points through the usage of an educational version of a commercial Discrete Event Simulation software. A product for the optimisation of reordering points has been developed and successfully tested. After that, it has been used to optimise the reordering points of a plastic manufacturing company. The satisfactory results obtained have been useful not only to reduce the storage and backorder costs, but to train the purchasers of different plants.

Most companies implement lean production principles. These are related to the minimisation of waste due to unneeded and inefficient operations, such as excessive buffering operations to serve the client or backorders (Narasimhan, Swink, & Wook Kim 2006). These two inefficiency types can be faced by defining a proper reordering point, as too low reordering points may worsen service rates whereas excessively high reordering points increase the storage costs.

The optimisation of the reordering point of raw materials and maintenance spare parts is a problem extensively studied in the academic field, but poorly solved in the context of plant management. Thus, several authors (i.e. Namit & Chen 2007;Namit & Chen 2005;Taskin Gumus & Fuat Guneria 2009) study the problem of determining optimal reordering points. As a result, several tools for the development of reordering policies have been launched to the market; i.e. NSI developed a freeware tool (NSI 2004) for the optimisation of the reordering point of a single reference: to do that it is necessary to bring the monthly consumption of the reference during the last year, its lead time and the items per order of the element. As a result it offers different options of reordering points, each one with a determined expected service and confidence levels. Concerning the non freeware utilities, for example, Lokad (2008) offer its safety stock calculator, capable of interacting with the database of the company to determine proper safety stock levels. Nevertheless, practitioners state that most academical solutions developed do not reach SMEs. Tools as Lokad's must deal with the severe resource restrictions SMEs deal with, whereas freeware tools are normally close-source utilities that may not respond properly to the needs of the companies.

Previous experiences of the research team involved in the project have been useful to detect abnormal situations in the implementation of reordering policies; for example, the company where the tool has been tested, Tajo S. Coop. (Tajo), has six productive plants spread around the world, but did not have defined reordering point policies until this project was launched. Thus, each of the six purchasers of the six plants had determined a particular policy, so that there were two moderately risky, two moderately conservative, two risky and one very conservative purchase. This situation was too expensive to be afforded: in some cases the storage costs were excessive, whereas in others the lack of raw material delayed the products to be delivered to the clients.

Having tested that this problem is relatively common within the companies the research team works with, this works aims at presenting the results of the design, development and implementation of a tool that calculates optimal reordering points considering purchasing, holding and backorder costs. Specifically, the software tool can jointly optimise the reordering point levels and transportation types of elements, by combining Discrete Event Simulation with optimisation algorithms. The tool has been successfully used for a preliminary study in Tajo, a plastic component manufacturer who serves products to the automotive auxiliary and domestic appliance sectors.

Specifically, the software tool jointly optimises the reordering point levels and transportation types of elements, by combining the educational version of commercial Discrete Event Simulation software with a pseudo brute-force algorithm. Thus, a product for the optimisation of reordering points has been developed and successfully tested. After that, it has been used to optimise the reordering points of a plastic manufacturing company. The satisfactory results obtained have been useful not only to reduce the storage and breakdown costs, but to train the purchasers of different plants.

It is worth noting that the development presented herein has been considered as a case of success in the European Manunet platform (see the following link for further information (The Manunet platform 2010)). The Manunet platform is a joint effort for the promotion of research and development in manufacturing; the platform comprises 22 contractor partners, representing 13 regions and 5 countries, plus 10 extra associated partners, based on a shared view for Europe.

1. Optimisation problem

The optimisation problem studied herein consider several input variables, constant variables, assumptions and output objectives, whose overall context is described in Fig. 1 (input and output data) and 2 (representation of the model), and described below.

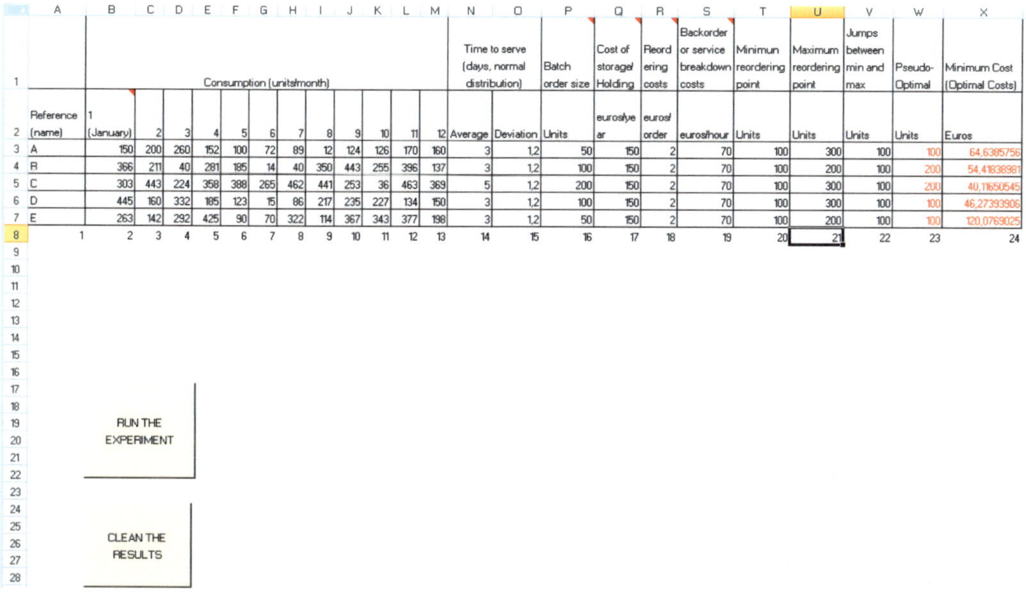

Reference (name)	Consumption (units/month) 1 (January)	2	3	4	5	6	7	8	9	10	11	12
A	150	200	260	152	100	72	89	12	124	126	170	160
R	366	211	40	281	185	14	40	350	443	255	396	137
C	303	443	224	358	388	265	462	441	253	36	463	369
D	445	160	332	185	123	15	86	217	235	227	134	150
E	263	142	292	425	90	70	322	114	367	343	377	198
1	2	3	4	5	6	7	8	9	10	11	12	13

Reference (name)	Time to serve (days, normal distribution) Average	Deviation	Batch order size Units	Cost of storage/ Holding euros/year	Reordering costs euros/ order	Backorder or service breakdown costs euros/hour	Minimun reordering point Units	Maximum reordering point Units	Jumps between min and max Units	Pseudo-Optimal Units	Minimum Cost (Optimal Costs) Euros
A	3	1,2	50	150	2	70	100	300	100	100	64,6385756
R	3	1,2	100	150	2	70	100	200	100	200	54,41838981
C	5	1,2	200	150	2	70	100	300	100	200	40,11650545
D	3	1,2	100	150	2	70	100	300	100	100	46,27393906
E	3	1,2	50	150	2	70	100	200	100	100	120,0769025
1	14	15	16	17	18	19	20	21	22	23	24

Fig. 1. Input (in black) and output (in red) data of the problem to be solved in the optimisation interface

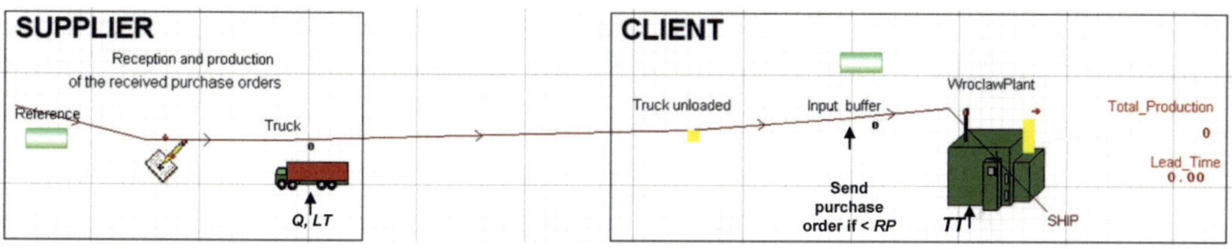

Fig. 2. Graphical description of the problem to be solved

The problem deals jointly with 5 references for the following two input variables (of each of these references):

- The product comes in *Q* size batches.
- The reordering point (*RP*).

Concerning the constant values and assumptions to be modeled it is supposed that;

- The logistic lead-time (*LT*), the time taken from a purchase order is submitted to the arrival of the products related to that order, is variable but known (historical data is available, so that information can be fitted to a known distribution).
- The customer demand rate of client *TT*, thus is, the speed the client consumes buffered products is known (historical data is available, so that information can be fitted to a known distribution).
- The buffer containing the arriving products has an infinite capacity.
- Each batch of products jointly bought has a fixed purchasing order cost (C_e).

- Each product has a fixed cost per unit of time for being stored in a buffer (C_s).
- A fixed backorder cost (C_b) is assigned each time a client needs to take a product from the buffer and does not find any products within.

Finally, the outcomes to be optimised may consider the joint optimisation of the following costs:

- The minimisation of the total cost spent on submitting purchase orders (C_{et}).
- The minimisation of the total holding cost for elements in the buffer (C_{st}).
- The minimisation of the total cost of not serving the client because the buffer is empty (C_{bt}).

Each one of these cost will be calculated by multiplying the times an event related to the above mentioned costs happen by its concept of cost. So, being n_e and n_b respectively the amount of purchasing orders submitted and the amount of non-served products in the studied period, C_{bt} and C_{et} are calculated as follows:

$$C_{bt} = n_b \,.\, C_b \tag{1}$$

$$C_{et} = n_e \,.\, C_e \tag{2}$$

While for the calculation of C_{st} is performed taking into account C_s and the amount of time each of the m products is stored in the buffer (t_s), as it is shown in Equation (3):

$$C_{st} = C_s \,.\, \sum_{i=1}^{m} t_{s_i} \tag{3}$$

2. Problem formulation

Optimisation of Q and RP variables considering C_{bt}, C_{st} and C_{et} criteria can be formulated as Single-Objective Problem (SOP) or a Multi-objective Optimisation Problem (MOP). A SOP could be presented summing all purchasing, buffering and backorder costs, while MOP would be formulated to optimise a vector of functions of the form (Martorell et al. 2004):

$$f = \left(f_1, f_2, \ldots, f_n\right) \tag{4}$$

where f are functions which depend on the decision variables, Q and RP. The optimisation proposed in this paper considers the total costs detailed in Equation (5) as a SOP problem:

$$f(Q,RP) = C_{st} + C_{et} + C_{bt} \tag{5}$$

Additionally, and although the software application is prepared to deal with different values of Q, the application cases tested with the collaboration of Tajo considered only RP as decision variable, so that for the case the function shown in Equation (5) is modified as follows:

$$f(RP) = C_{st} + C_{et} + C_{bt} \tag{6}$$

3. Modeling and optimisation techniques:

3.1 System DES model

DES concerns the modeling of a system as it evolves over time by a representation in which variable states change suddenly at separate points in time. These changes happened in the system are considered events. Systems do not change between events, so DES considers that it is not necessary to analyse what happens in a system in periods taken place between two events.

A single traffic light is an example of the concept of 'variable time between consecutive events' (Fig. 2). In the example shown below, the states of a traffic light are shown based on the DES technique. As can be appreciated in the figure, consecutive events do not occur after the same periods of time. While Δt=15s when changing the state of the traffic light from red to green, it varies to Δt=50s and Δt=100s when changing the state from red to green and green to yellow, respectively.

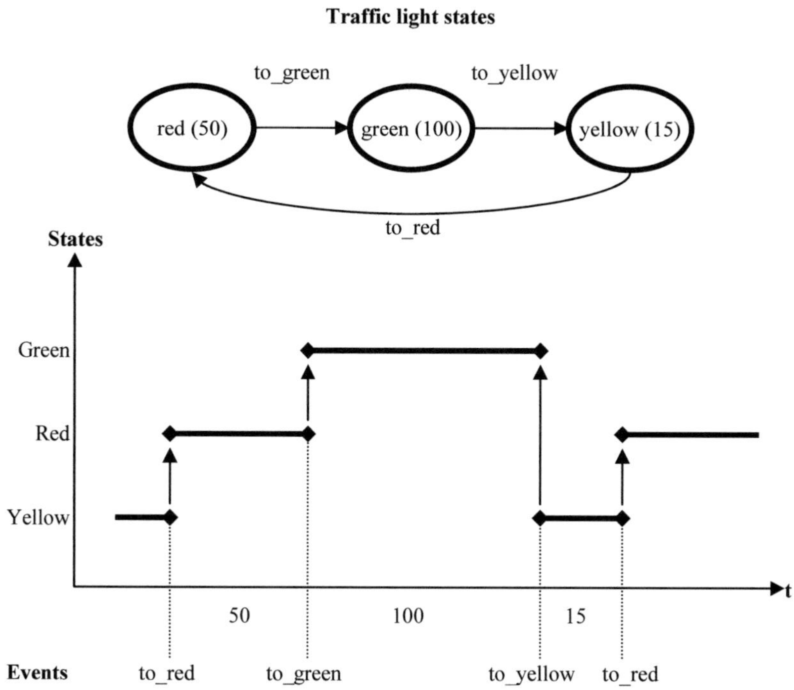

Fig. 3. States and events graph in a traffic light using DES (Oyarbide-Zubillaga 2003)

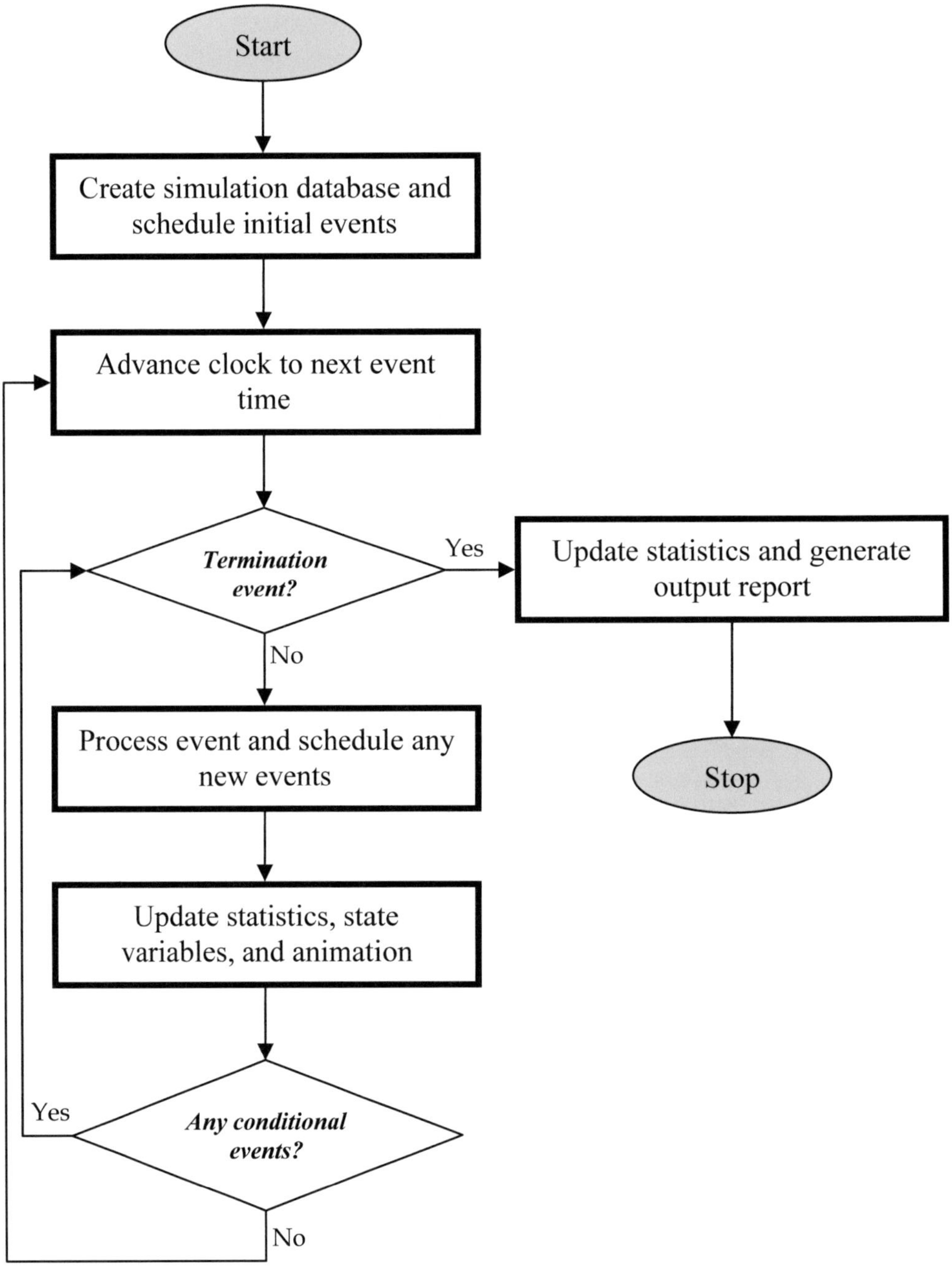

Fig. 4. Diagram of Discrete Event Simulation process (Harrell et al., 2000)

The main advantages of DES are two (Goti, Oyarbide-Zubillaga, & Sánchez 2007;Law & Kelton 1991;Oyarbide-Zubillaga, Goti, & Sánchez 2008): i) standard DES-based tools provide capabilities of modeling or modifying complex system models easily, and ii) DES is closely related to stochastic systems so they are appropriate when simulating real-world phenomena, since there are few situations where the actions of the entities within the system under study can be completely predicted in advance. In order to generate stochastic events, simulation packages generate pseudo-random numbers to select a particular value for a given distribution. Thus, using pseudo-random numbers it is possible to implement the stochastic nature of real models in DES models. Therefore, DES was used as modeling technique for the modeling tool to be developed. The running mechanism of DES, extracted from Ref. (Harrell, Ghosh, & Bowden 2000) is shown in Fig. 3.

Specifically, the development of the model was performed using en educational version of Witness (Lanner 2008). This was a collaboration between the authors and Tajo, so that they could experience the potencial benefits of a DES approach for addressing real-world situation, which are to quiet some extent different from those that can be found in text books. The study focused on some references using the data available at that moment in time. Indeed, Tajo was very satisfied with the proposed approach and stated that values obtained from the study were very reliable and would be implemented.

The authors are very confident that Tajo will rely on the future in DES approaches for both this type of analysis and for other ones. As to reordering point studies they may end up acquiring some software to recalculate values (as data change overtime) and to extend the analysis to other references and, even more, carry on analysis when setting policies for references in combination (for example, it may be interesting to launch a reordering order for a product although for a particular reference the reordering point has not been reached if for other reference it has, and simultaneous ordering saves some money).

3.2 Brute-force as a pseudo optimisation algorithm

Depending on the complexity and the characteristics of the optimisation problem different techniques can be used. For instance, if the problem is faced as a MOP a Multiobjective Evolutionary Algorithm (MOEA) (i.e. the Non-Dominated Sorting Genetic Algorithm NSGA-II, by Deb et al. 2002) can be used. In case as a SOP (minimisation of overall cost as the unique objective) is presented, a single objective optimisation algorithm is enough to solve the problem. In this case, as the exploratory space of many of the references was not wide in many cases, these cases were optimised using the brute force (test of all the range of choices) technique.

More specifically, the brute force technique was applied, but not testing all the reordering point choices of all references. For each case, a minimum and a maximum reordering point and a 'jump' step scale were defined (see Fig. 1, columns T, U and V): Thus, the optimisation process will start by analysing the minimum reordering point (100 in file 3 of Fig. 1), to then try the minimum plus the jump value (Fig. 1, minimum 100, jump value of 100, 200), increase again the tested amount with the step value (300), until the maximum value is achieved (300 in file 3 of Fig. 1).

4. Implementation case

As it was previously stated, the set of modeling plus optimisation techniques was applied to optimise the reordering points of several references of Tajo. Tajo is part of the Mondragon

Group (known until last year as "Mondragon Corporación Cooperativa", the seventh largest corporation in Spain). Tajo has produced and supplied plastic sub-assembles and components since 1963 for the automotive auxiliary and domestic appliance sectors, consisting of six manufacturing plants, two in Spain, two in Poland and one in the Czech Republic.

There are some elements of special interest to be optimised, as they are sub-products supplied to the six plants by Spanish dealers. Additionally, these references are not stocked in the dealer's warehouse, and the total LT value can round the 21 days. This means that, for these cases, the reordering point must consider not only the amount of elements within the client plant buffer (the storage location at the beginning of the client plant of Poland or the Czech Republic), but also the already ordered elements which have not arrived the client plant.

The implementation case uses the data shown in Fig. 1, who are referred to 5 raw material and consumable references. Finally, it is need to be said that the warm-up period and the simulation period values are of 5 and 229 days respectively, and have been calculated considering the suggestions provided by the theory of the simulation, compiled in Ref. (Goti 2007)

5. Results

The overall results obtained after the optimisation process using the previously shown values are specified in Fig. 1. For each one of the references, the optimisator presents the input and output values for each simulation; the results of one reference are shown in Fig. 4:

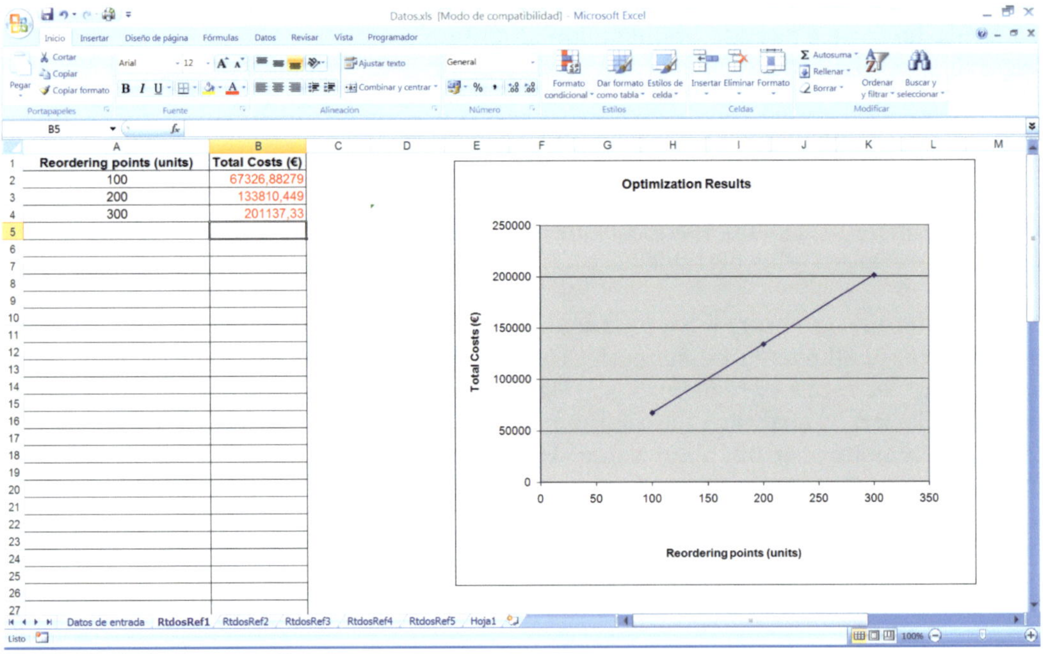

Fig. 4. Optimisation results

The consolidation of the results obtained has been considered successful, and as a consequence, several plants within the Mondragon Group are testing the initiative to optimise production raw materials and maintenance spare parts, but considering both *RP* and *Q* values.

6. Acknowledgements

We would like to thank the help and support provided by Lanner, developer of Witness, and OptTek, Implementer of OptQuest.

This project has been funded by the following funding programs:

DEMAGILE TOOLS: Development of decision making tools for the implementation of principles related to the 'Leagile production'. Project funded by the Basque Gobernment (Basic and Applied Research Project, PI2009-24 code).

SERVISTOCK: Development of a tool for the joint optimisation of logistic safety stock levels and transportation types (European transnational project MANUNET-2008-BC-001).

AVAILAFACTURING: Development of a tool for the management of technical assistance service networks for the availability maximization of Manufacturing equipment and/or products (European transnational project MANUNET-2009-BC-006).

7. References

Deb, K., Pratap, A., Agarwal, S., & Meyarivan, T. 2002, "A fast and elitist multiobjective genetic algorithm: NSGA-II", *IEEE Transactions on Evolutionary Computation*, vol. 6, no. 2, pp. 182-197.

Goti, A. 2007, *Optimisation of preventive maintenance policies in productive systems using genetic algorithms*, PhD, Polytechnic University of Valencia.

Goti, A., Oyarbide-Zubillaga, A., & Sánchez , A. 2007, "Optimising preventive maintenance by combining discrete event simulation and genetic algorithms", *Hydrocarbon Processing*, vol. 86, no. 10, pp. 115-122.

Harrell, C., Ghosh, B. K., & Bowden, R. 2000, *Simulation using ProModel* McGraw Hill, New York, USA.

Lanner. *Witness* [CD-ROM], ver. 2008, [Computer programme]. Available distributor: Lanner Group Limited, The Oaks, Clews road, Redditch, Worcestershire, B98 7ST, UK. 2008. Ref Type: Unpublished Work

Law, A. M. & Kelton, W. D. 1991, *Simulation modelling and analysis*, 2 edn, McGraw-Hill, New York.

Lokad. Lokad safety stock calculator, version 1.8.1404.1. Lokad . 2008. Ref Type: Electronic Citation

Martorell, S., Sánchez , A., Carlos, S., & Serradell, V. 2004, "Alternatives and challenges in optimising industrial safety using genetic algorithms", *Reliability Engineering and System Safety*, vol. 86, no. 1, pp. 25-38.

Namit, K. & Chen, J. 2005, "An excel spreadsheet application for the calculation of reorder point of an ARMA lead-time demand with discrete stochastic lead time", *Journal of the Academy of Business and Economics* no. March.

Namit, K. & Chen, J. 2007, "Determining reorder point in the presence of stochastic lead time and Box-Jenkins time series demand", *Journal of the Academy of Business and Economics* no. Feb.

Narasimhan, R., Swink, M., & Wook Kim, S. 2006, "Disentangling leanness and agility: An empirical investigation", *Journal of Operations Management*, vol. 24, no. 5, pp. 440-457.

NSI. Reordering point calculator. New Standard Institute . 2004. Ref Type: Electronic Citation

Oyarbide-Zubillaga, A. 2003, *Manufacturing systems simulation using the principles of System Dynamics,* PhD thesis, Cranfield University.

Oyarbide-Zubillaga, A., Goti, A., & Sánchez , A. 2008, "Preventive maintenance optimisation of multi-equipment manufacturing systems by combining discrete event simulation and multiobjective evolutionary algorithms", *Production Planning & Control*, vol. 19, no. 4, Special Issue on Maintenance and Facility Management, pp. 342-355.

Taskin Gumus, A. & Fuat Guneria, A. 2009, "A multi-echelon inventory management framework for stochastic and fuzzy supply chains", *Expert Systems with Applications*, vol. 36, no. 3(1), pp. 5565-5575.

The Manunet platform. Case of success in Manunet SERVISTOCK: Development of a tool for the joint optimisation of logistic safety stock levels and transportation types (European transnational project MANUNET-2008-BC-001), link http://www.manunet.net/index.php?option=com_content&view=article&id=72:development-of-a-tool-for-the-joint-optimisation-of-logistic-safety-stock-levels-and-transportation-types&catid=5:success-stories&Itemid=30. 2010. Bilbao, Innobasque. Ref Type: Generic

7

Reverse logistics: end-of-life recovery pledge

R.C. Michelini and R.P. Razzoli
DIMEC - University of Genova
Italy

1. Introduction

The growth requires wealth creation with less eco-impact. For the wellbeing expansion, the underlying organisations and technologies present shared features, with unifying tools in refit engineering, deployments in products-services and support in extended enterprises. The EU already enacted economic instruments aims at: voluntary agreements, for the on-duty conformance management; compulsory regulations, for the recovery targets. The ICT aids play main roles in their support. Moving to lifecycle concern, the knowledge-driven frames are necessary, to make possible assessing the items impact and the natural resources decay. The frames establish on three facts (Michelini & Razzoli, 2000), (Michelini & Razzoli, 2004a), (Sakao & Lindhal, 2009):

- to market products-services, with collaborative aids for clients' support;
- to establish extended enterprises, for point-of-service conformance guarantees;
- to monitor the tangibles yield per unit service, by third-parties certifying bodies.

The frame develops with hierarchical topology (Michelini, 2010), (Michelini & Razzoli, 2005), (Michelini & Razzoli, 2008):

- the inner cluster, to link the extended enterprise partners, for product-service delivery;
- the specialised links, to support the point-of-service communication with the buyers;
- the outer selective data channels, for the overseeing bodies, under security protocols.

The common, varying-topology, information set-up is unifying context, sliced into layers, (Aggeri, 1999), (Blumberg, 2004), (Popov & DeSimone, 1997), (Weizsäcker et al., 1997), with:

- lowest levels (product ideation/ construction), at the extended enterprise inner cluster;
- intermediate levels (product lifecycle), for data management at the clients' satisfaction;
- upper levels (eco-consistency and charges collection), controlled by accredited bodies.

The picture is coherent with a controlled collaborative net, linking extended enterprise to individual clients, so that the supply chain (i.e., the delivered product-service) is monitored by an accredited certifying body, for on-duty conformance assessment, undyingly accessed by governmental agencies (Michelini, 2010), (Michelini & Razzoli, 2004b).
The outlined agenda is considered by the chapter, chiefly addressing the EU environmental policy in the automotive domain, and suggesting end-of-life vehicle recovery/reclamation duty models, properly adapted to the enacted sustainability targets. The issues are tackled summarising topics, as it follows:

- the knowledge-driven organisation consistent with the EU enacted recovery reclamation targets, assigned to manufacturers' responsibility under the free-take-back scheme;
- the reverse logistic information flow (exemplified by PMAR**RL**ELV simulator), supporting data management by virtual net-organisation with the provider-user-controller links;
- the sample analysis of innovation typical features, to help evaluating the backward-streams effectiveness by focusing critical aspects for recovery-driven sustainability;
- the example study of basic treatment facilities, where the end-of-life item disassembly is accomplished and the recovery and reclamation data are monitored and certified.

The concluding comments address the links between ecological constraints and economic instruments, and stress on the fundamental role played by the ICT aids, both, as off-process and as on-process enabling tools.

2. The EU recovery and reclamation goals

The growth, by ceaselessly replacing tangible goods, built transforming natural resources into waste and pollution, grants benefits to the directly involved consumers, with penalty to third parties and future generations. The consumers side covers the all supply chain: manufacturer and user. The former establishes the product functional properties, choosing materials, specifying operation properties and eco-impact, and providing the construction files for maintenance and dismissal. The latter needs comply the technical and legal regulations, to be allowed to enjoy the purchased items. The industrial revolution has highly widened the manufacture market, by increased process productivity, but has, as well, speeded up the resource decay and the environment downgrading, so that the growth becomes critical. We are, apparently, approaching a bottleneck. Voluntary provisions and mandatory restrictions shall urgently apply, to alleviate or slowing down the world decay. The EU has set ambitious goals and sketched severe policies, based on the manufacturer's responsibility, considering three phases, (EC, 2006):

- within the production: antipollution regulations are issued at manufacturing, and design is promoted by series of advices and warnings (e.g., Eco-design of End-use Equipment, draft proposal directive);
- along the supply chain: the eco-consistency figures, included in the construction file, need to be followed, for conformance-to-use, and the service engineering comes out as valuable opportunity;
- at the product disposal: (mainly) the durables (in future, consumables) fall within the suppliers' responsibility, under the free-take-back scheme, aiming at reverse logistic flow for resource recovery, consistent reclamation and dump avoidance.

The regulation acts look after establishing eco-costs, to be included in all the (tangible) goods, brought to the market. These costs need to cover cleaning up, reclamation and consumption quotas, and correspond to explicit tax (collected through producers/dealers), to refund the supply chain burden.

Recovery is fostered as antidote, having the inherent task of educating the consumers to conservative behaviours. Example mass-produced goods are chosen, such as end-of-life vehicles, ELV, and waste electrical and electronic equipment, WEEE, burdening the replacement market, with high environmental impact. The eco-consistency is ruled through producers' responsibility, by enforceable targets regulations. The ELV case gives clarifying hints to this trend. The 2000/53/EC Directive, enacted the 18.09.2000 (with Member States acknowledgement before April 2002), defines the rules to be followed by national acts for vehicles disposal, urging the carmakers for selling cars respectful of legal requests. The Commission integrates the rules by notes, e.g., the 2003/138/EC, to explain standards for materials and parts. Basic aspects are summarised in the Fig. 1. The EU is concerned by end targets, not about how they are fixed. A Guidance Document collects harmonisation hints, to avoid misinterpretation.

- collecting systems for exhausted vehicles and parts need to be established at authorised sites, for treatments, to grant safety and security fitting out, by removing potentially dangerous components;
- withdrawal needs to be performed without charge on the final owners (prescription to be fully enabled from 01.01.2007), but recovery visible-fees are included, as attribute of the product-service delivery;
- manufacturers (and dealers) have technical responsibility of the product lifecycle, end-of-life recovery included, being liable of environment impact and resource consumption, due to design choices;
- users co-responsibility is sanctioned, for voluntary non-conservative behaviours, when critical pieces are damaged, removed or modified, altering the original setting of the supply;
- recovery and reclamation duties ought to be acknowledged, with visibility of reused parts, recycled materials, thermo-exploitation and residuals dumping, to be notified to the European Commission.

Fig. 1. Basic aspects of the EU Directive for ELV recovery

The EU goals are differently transferred into national acts; still, the role of manufacturers is fundamental, to support reverse logistics by product-data management. The governmental authorities ought to analyse the whole supply chain, to distinguish one producer from another, on the forward and backward chain, and to define proper taxing rule, with costs ascribed to consumers, by visible fees collection at the point-of-sale. On these facts, the EU environmental policy is promoting relevant changes, (Dyckhoff et al., 2004), (Larson, 2009), (Schmidt et al., 2005), at least with twofold issues:

- to require lifecycle visibility of forward and backward supply chains, so that product data management and service engineering are inherent parts of actual deliveries, with full transparency of the on-duty and disposal impacts, assessed through certified monitoring and reporting;
- to promote urgent restructuring of the manufacture industry, with competitiveness driven by lifelong product responsibility and joined service/recovery duties, so that the lifecycle design aids become main request, enjoying virtual prototype testing and behaviour simulation.

The relevance of the ICT tools clearly emerges, directly, promoting knowledge-driven industry, indirectly, due to the role played by service engineering along the goods lifecycle and from disposal on. The information intensity offers several facets, (Abe et al., 1999), (Meijer & DeJong, 2009), (Michelini, 2009), (Michelini & Razzoli, 2008), (Pertsova, 2008):

- with focus on externalities, stress is in the eco-impact, to acknowledge actual effects of on-duty, for allowed use, after conformance-to-use checks, and of end-of-life goods, for recover (reuse/recycle) and dump lawful operation;
- with focus on internalities, stress is in the enterprise capability to preset the on-duty and dismissal data, with extensive resort to off-process simulation aids and virtual prototype testing.

The complexity and vastness of the information frames are immediately evident. The all supply chains need to be monitored and recorded, explicitly joining suppliers and clients.

Results shall be reported to national agencies (and notified to European Council officers, which verify their compliance), using proper data handling and vaulting caution, granting citizens privacy and security. For the eco-consistency, the information system, (Dekker et al., 2004), (Freedman & Jaggi, 2006), (Loeffe, 2009), (Sperling, 2009), should be conceived with two goals:

- to cover the lifelong product-service supply, say, the (tangible and intangible) delivery to a client, granting enjoyment of specified functions, by life-cycle indentures, warranted by deliverers, with return on investment, by factual resort to the scope economy;
- to accomplish monitoring and control of the environmental impact, with result reporting by overseeing third party certified bodies (independent on dealers and purchasers) with access to the supply chain, in view to assess and to record the products lifecycle data.

The two goals are deeply connected, since the users are the beneficiaries, to keep on-duty reliability and eco-conformance, but manufacturers have, in both cases, the responsibility of the overall technicalities, and, if something does not properly fit, the all supply chain becomes defective, and out-of-law the items' use (Schmidt, 2004).

To guarantee the eco-consistency, the information framework lumps together purveyor and buyer, both monitored by independent (accredited) supervisors. The three parties rule is good compromise to enhance competition, to grant privacy and to balance commitment, by fair-trade set-ups. The environment footprint transparency is achieved by recording the actual running conditions of the forward and backward flow , (CEN, 1999), (Kahraman & Baig, 2009), (Veleva & Ellenbecker, 1996). Such scheme includes:

- purveyors, covering the all supply-chain data: materials provision, items manufacture, lifecycle up-keeping, backward recovery; the ecological responsibility is dealt with by clustering several firms within a factual alliance of co-operating stakeholders;
- users, purchasing products-services to profit of the delivered functions with reliability figure close to one; the payments include point-of-service conformance certification and the end-of-life take-back, the after tax collection against tangibles' depletion;
- supervisors, assuring third party duties for the today and tomorrow environment and society protection; the certifying bodies report to authorities and follow legal metrology standards, having access to the delivery lifecycle data-bases.

Once the changes of the EU environmental policy are on full effect, the manufacturers responsibility will lead to deeply different entrepreneurial organisations, due to knowledge-driven patterns and linked to computer-based instrumental aids. Recovery is fostered as antidote of the affluent society, with the inherent task of educating consumers, towards more conservative behaviours, (Leavis & Thompson 1993), (Michelini & Razzoli, 2004), (Michelini, 2010), (Muñoz, 2009), (O'Neill, 2001), (Uchitelle, 2006).

Broadband actions are chosen, such as the ones dealing with the end-of-life vehicles, ELV, mass-produced goods, typically, feeding the replacement market, with high eco-impact. Conservativeness is achieved through the carmakers' responsibility, setting out regulations with enforceable targets and visible fees, easy to run and control. The mentioned ELV regulation provides explanatory hints. The 2000/53/EC Directive defines the rules to be followed by national organisations for vehicles dismissal, and by automotive producers for trading cars respectful of legal requests. The Commission further modified and integrated the rules by special specifications, e.g. the 2003/138/EC, to establish standard codes for parts and materials. It needs to be mentioned that the EU is concerned by final issues, not about how these achievements are obtained by Member States. This creates drawbacks to carmakers, which ought to comply with uneven interpretations; the Guidance Document is, thus, added, to collect harmonisation hints. The fast growing documentation, (Michelini & Coiffet, 2010), (Michelini & Kovàcs, 2002), (Paul, 2006), (Sperling, 2009), leads to a few remarks, such as:

- regulation addresses environment protection, conferring responsibility to the producers;
- design for disassembly, for recovery, for recycle, etc. practices shall become standard job;
- extensive resort to re-manufacturing, to re-use of parts, materials, etc. is rewarded;
- fit aids (modularity, identifying codes, etc.) are given to make dismantling easier, etc.;
- lifecycle monitoring and reporting certify on-duty conformance-to-specification issues;
- not-justified high-impact and non-consistent behaviours are taxed or totally forbidden.

The remarks show that business paradigms changes are fostered, based on new design patterns, with concern on enhanced point-of-service performance and full commitment for withdrawal. The focus on growth sustainability is basic driver. Obviously, it leads to reverse logistics entrepreneurship, with larger role for competitiveness played by actors in the backward cycle. The present study deals with the recovery, reuse and recycle duties, and it specifically addresses topics in end-of-life vehicles, ELV.

Eco-consistency by reverse logistics entrepreneurship does not develop by itself, as the backward chain outcomes do not have explicit purchasers, lacking links of actual needs to them. Then, to separate backward, from forward chain leads to deviating issues, keeping benefit within a set of individuals, but damaging third (and future) ones. The cost/profit ratio is to be assessed balancing the profit of the consumers side (producers and users), against the protection of all people not involved by the specific value chain. In that sense, regulation for the eco-consistency is peremptory task that governments need to undertake, enacting rules to charge the consumers side for environmental impact linked to the whole supply chain, disposal and recovery (EC, 2006) included. The automotive field is of note, with widely spread market of registered items: the falls-off affect large amount of users; the end-of-life vehicles are individually recognised and recorded. Thereafter, the EU approach specifies mandatory charges, by specified bylaws, notably:

- member states shall establish collecting systems for the exhausted vehicles and parts, at authorised sites, where preliminary treatments will grant safety and security fitting out, by removing noxious and harmful parts;
- withdrawal needs to be assured without charge on the final owners (prescription to be fully enabled from 01.01.2007), but included in the product-service delivery, as inherent attribute, to bring out every new car;
- users co-responsibility could be invoked for special non-conservative behaviours: critical pieces are damaged, removed or modified, altering the original setting of the supply;
- the dismantling and destruction course shall be certified, with assessment of recovery parts, re-cycled materials, thermo-recovery and residuals dumping, to be notified to the European Council.

Those scenarios outlined by the EU directives are, chiefly, enacted for pollution remediation. The mandatory targets distinguish: recovery (up to 90-95%, by contrast with dump residues, e.g., as low as 10-5% in weigh), from reuse (second-hand market, possibly, up to meaningful fractions) and from recycle (secondary materials, replacing raw provisions). The recovery, which establishes on such targets, favours the expansion of materials, rather than energy, market, due to severe limits on landfill dumping (Michelini & Razzoli, 2004), (Naess, 1989). Anyhow, the EU eco-policy rouses economic and ecologic effects. In the affluent society, the ceaseless replacing of goods was optimal choice, in front of high labour costs; in the thrifty society, the conservativeness of recycling is restricted by the energy using up. However, these targets are consistent with minimising the eco-impacts, once linked with regulating harmful/noxious refuses and polluting wastes. The approach, then, highlights the critical nature of the ELV's disassembly process, for removal of dangerous liquids and parts and safety fitting of the whole material flows. As a result, the recovery characterises by, Fig. 2:

- the need of logistic nets, with collecting and transportation aids, storage points, handling and processing stands, and joint information flow, for acquisition and recording;
- the establishment of proper dismantling shops for safe parts withdrawal, and of suitably located shredding facilities, to grind the left-out hulks to tiny pieces;
- the resort to specialised sorting plants, to separate the different metals (ferrous alloys, stainless steels, brass, aluminium alloys, etc.), from glass, plastics, etc.;
- the expansion of used-parts and recycled-materials tracks, once enhanced the design, manufacture and maintenance based on second-hand provisioning practices.

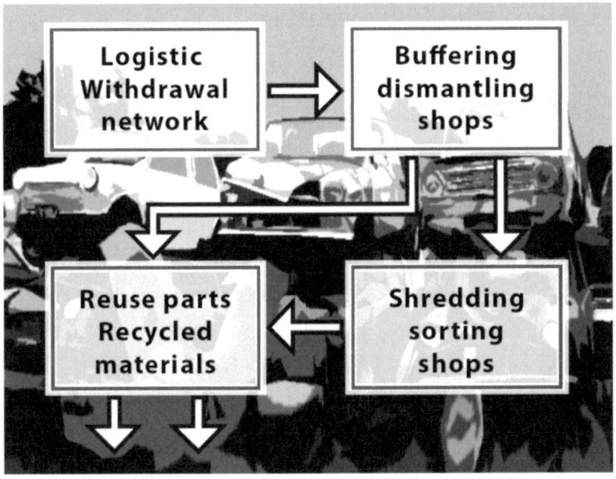

Fig. 2. Reverse logistics material flow

The four processes lead to innovative set-ups: the Authorised Treatment Facilities, ATFs. These work under proper supervision, with full visibility of the achieved issues. From a technical viewpoint, the second and third processes deserve particular interest, with robot aids to be conceived and exploited for irksome and dangerous tasks, today, accomplished by front-end personnel. Besides, the material flow deals with a stream of poor, but large and heavy parts; the handling and dispatching costs could be serious drawback, with high energy consumption. Then, effectiveness would look at distributed processing units and new rigs. Last, but not least, in the backward cycle, the joint information flow bears great relevance, distinguishing (Blumberg, 2004), (Michelini & Razzoli, 2008):

- the reference knowledge, to make efficient the dismantling, recycling, etc. duties, according to the product data (by means of International Dismantling Information System, etc.), compulsorily provided by the manufacturers;
- the operation flow, with data acquisition, handling, processing and vaulting, to issue the requested records and certificates and to give account of the process compliance;
- the framework assessment, to evaluate competing arrangements and to develop high yield, availability and safety reverse logistics facilities, for enhanced business efficiency.

All in all, the reverse logistics business is deemed to require effective work-organisations, not less than the traditional forward flow, and the role of disassembly will be central as the one of earlier assembly, unless that, now, the technicalities depend on enforced targets and return on investment is driven by the enacted legal regulations.

3. The computer simulation tool

Hereafter, the PMAR**RL**ELV code, for reverse logistics simulation, is recalled as investigation tool on the ELV case, to provide introductory explanations. The reverse logistics is the process to design, plan and control the recovery and reuse of worn-out products, in view to preserve natural resources and protect the eco-system. The considered simulation aids develop, exploiting occurrence-driven architectures, to aim at real-time, description of the backward flows, by duplicating the effects of every forcing (and disturbing) inputs, as they take place in the reality. At the same time, alternatives of physical resources and/or logical plans are modelled, making un-expensive virtual tests, without actually building pilot plants. The basic options offered by this kind of simulation aids are well known, and we do not enter into details, (Mihailovich & Lalic, 2009), (Michelini & Razzoli, 2009), (Scarpa & Alberini, 2005), (Wackernagel & Rees, 1995).

The PMAR**RL**ELV code has featuring property to be based on standard packages, Fig. 3, (Acaccia et al., 2006a), (Acaccia et al., 2006b):

- WITNESS tool, version logistics, for the collection-dispatching modules, and version manufacture, for the dismantling-shredding-sorting modules, with virtual reality aids, leading to self-sufficient and friendly modelling.
- MS ACCESS software, standard relational database, released as MS office suite.
- VISUALBASIC.NET, based on the .NET-platform, powerful and flexible, but reasonably friendly also for web applications, assuring management aids to create and to run interfaces with other languages, procedures and databases; to define interactions of blocks; to start/stop concurrent processes; to enable web applications; to establish masks and graphic displays.
- CRYSTAL REPORT XL, as standard to reporting.

That environment aims at providing parametric assessments (Mihailovich & Lalic, 2009), together showing the causal progress of the physical processes and the heuristic chaining of the decision logic (Michelini et al., 1997), (Michelini et al., 2001), (Michelini et al., 2002). In the present case, the net-frame is further detailed, Fig. 3, to allow reaching further scopes, such as:

- creation of digital mock-ups of actual operation shops, involved in reverse logistics duties, suitably identifying the authorised treatment facilities (ATF) functions;
- provision of personalised access to web-clients (authorities, operators, certifiers, etc.), interested to investigate special outcomes and opportunities;
- build-up of qualified knowledge data-bases, by systematic ranking set of architectures and schedules, permitting comparative appraisals.

The involved physical resources distinguish different operation areas: transportation and dispatching, dismantling and recovering, and, furthermore, shredding and sorting, with local buffers and materials handling rigs. From computer engineering viewpoint, the open network architecture is important feature, due to the multiplicity of involved stakeholders: carmakers, end-users, service providers, certification bodies, etc., all of which have different operation styles and interests. The knowledge build-up bears multiple fruits, directly, to acknowledge the behavioural properties of the piece or process under investigation, and indirectly, to re-engineer the whole supply chain (Lapide, 2005), (Michelini, 2010), (Scarpa & Alberini, 2005), (Stark, 2005).

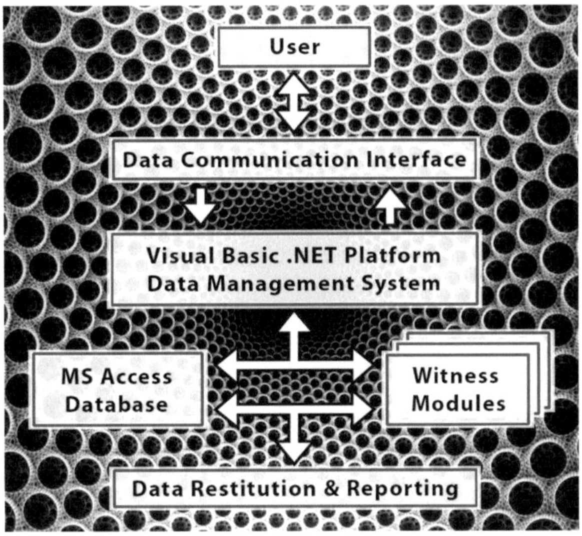

Fig. 3. Block schema of the PMARRLelv code

The shared access to web-clients provides ubiquitous computing and communication, to deal with lifecycle interactivity between stakeholders at different levels of integration, and with multi-task assignments at several involvement requirements and responsibilities. Through the purveyor/user/supervisor scheme, the enterprise boundary blurs into virtual organisation or net concern, linking autonomous (co-operating, conflicting or overseeing) legal entities, to combine core competencies and assemble eco-comprehensive delivery. The virtual organisation leads to dynamic structured partnership, which aims at quick business alignment, when the market changes to deal with externalities (by contrast with earlier car-making vertical flow-shops) in the environment protection and recycling.

Further sets of involved PMAR**RL**ELV web-clients come from government/local authorities, in view to establish the overseeing/control set-ups. Virtuality is assumed to exploit a twin interface, above and under each node, which interposes a broker, hiding the client and/or the server; the operation unit or partner, does not see the real structure: it sees its virtual image, supported by the manager of the interposed relational database. In this way, the (real) knowledge units (in the PMAR**RL**ELV) exist, but the web-client works in the virtual space, without interfering with the real units (or blocks of WITNESS architecture). The code needs careful programming, as the .NET-platform specialisation is done (based on standard instructions), to give personal access to the web-clients (by twin-layer interfacing), and to allow agility/flexibility to the dynamic partnerships, as worthy eco-transparency means.

Based on the shortly expounded PMAR**RL**ELV structure, the ELV treatment analysis includes four domains (Acaccia et al., 2005) :

- a logistic net, for items collecting and transfer, storage spots, handling and inspection devices, and the joint information flows for data acquisition and recording;

- adequate dismantling shops for safe parts recovery and storing, with forwarding of the residual hulks to suitably located shredding facilities, for grinding to tiny pieces;
- detailed parts-reuse and materials-recycle tracks, with feedback on maintenance-service aids and on design/manufacture practices with second material provisioning;
- efficient sorting plants, to pull out metals (ferrous alloy, stainless steel, aluminium alloy, brass, etc.), different plastics, glass, etc., and safe incineration plants.

The four domains bore, up today, little overlapping with traditional automotive fields. Only recent EU regulations foster design-for-recovery and enforce end-of-life take-back, so each carmaker can modulate his engagements by voluntary agreements for the lifecycle service, and by explicit obligations for the end-of-life recovery. The three parties scheme binds the producers/sellers, with the clients/users and, both, with the overseeing/certifying agencies. The existing ICT aids make possible apt net concerns, with varying topology lay-outs, so that each partner (an activity-node in the net) is allowed full visibility (through twin-layer interfacing) of every details, as specified by the enacted compulsory eco-rules. The resulting virtual organisation does not correspond to a single industrial company. The simulation needs to duplicate peculiarities and facets of the net concerns, based on factual job-agendas.

4. Recovery/reclamation information flow

The PMAR**RL**ELV code, as said, aims at assessing the ELV treatments, leading to a set of modules, in order to grant:

- the take-back and gathering of end-of-life vehicles, for lawful disposal treatments;
- the ELV dismantling, with parting of reuse-parts and recycle-materials, from residuals;
- the material recycling processes, after shredding/sorting, and safe landfill dumping;
- the backward-to-forward chain data-flow to exploit conditioning economic instruments.

The code includes the EU enacted mandatory targets, namely:

- from 01.01.2006: 90% by weigh of the vehicle ought to be recovered or recycled, and only 10% can be dumped (suitably neutralised) to landfill; in any case, materials recycling should be as high as 85%, since only 5% can be used as auxiliary fuel;
- from 01.01.2015: the figures are modified, allowing 10% for fuel use, but only 5% to landfills (aiming at the recovery figure of 95% by weigh).

The enforced figures are input set-points, and could be object of revision. Today, the ELV metallic content is consistent with 85% recycling target, since, generally over than 15 years old car are withdrawn. The plastics content of recent cars is quite higher, and this target becomes difficult. Moreover, the landfill limitation (10% today, and 5% from 2015) is quite restrictive, being mainly driven by anti-pollution summons, with no concern on and energy consumption. The eco-soundness should dress overall balances, measuring the results in terms of natural resources decay and modifying the enacted targets, whether the recovery figures bring to higher consumption (and pollution). Of course, these balances highly depend on available technologies. The product (vehicle different design) or process (new forward/backward chains) innovation will open more effective tracks. Setting enforceable targets, together with fixing up the manufacturers' responsibility, will, most likely, promote competition and, thereafter, innovation. At least, this is hoped by the EU, aiming at common market, along fair trade tracks. The PMAR**RL**ELV code results help to such purpose.

The knowledge flow transparency is prerequisite of fairness. At the moment, the backward streams bear quite loose operation styles: ELV are fetched at random times and scattered locations and dropped to off-hand wrecking shops; disassembly and reuse duties are often done by extempore operators, as case arises; only, shredding and sorting tasks have resort to mechanised plants, still requiring human-intensive attendance. The economic and ecologic efficiencies of the whole are, both, very low, with no interest of the car-makers to bring forth enhanced resource recovery, as this might pull down the sale of new items, till when the free take-back are avoided by unscrupulous manufacturers (and incompetent controllers). The producers responsibility will foster more conservative behaviours, on condition to achieve transparent management of the economic instruments, so that drawbacks and benefits are distributed with objective fairness. This condition, however, is still to come, with involved actors often operating with low visibility.

The PMAR**RL**ELV code is especially conceived to carry out analyses on the backward chain, acknowledging the critical steps, so that complete visibility of actually fulfilled processes is quantitatively achieved. The enabling role of the ICT ought to be emphasised, as it assures technology up-grading and systemic innovation for a class of policies based on:

- the resort to manufacturers' responsibility, linked with economic instruments drivers;
- the involvement of stakeholders, with dissimilar technological profile and capability, uneven market position and power, and unlike interest towards sustainability;
- the planning of the mandatory targets achievement, by business paradigm shifts, where the products-services and the extended enterprises (or net-concerns) play critical role.

These three policies apply when the recovery-reuse-recycle targets lead to fixed figures, and compulsory regulations are ratified, with sanctions and fines to infringers. The enacted targets are quite rigorous, but the transparency of the actually obtained results is, by today, largely neglected by most of the EU member states. Noteworthy exception is, perhaps only the Netherlands, within which a steering Foundation grants effective co-operating between, partners, showing that the recovery/reclamation obligations are actually accomplished at comparable low (and decreasing) costs (ARN, 2008).

Elsewhere, the lack of reliable data is impressive. The PMAR**RL**ELV code is, thus proposed to help stimulating the consciousness of the problems.

Indeed, the knowledge build-up by simulation is powerful way to assess drawbacks and benefits, and their sharing by the involved stakeholders. Actually, the waste items (from cars, domestic appliances, etc.) quickly reach negative value, in face of all-inclusive recovery (reuse/recycle) targets, due to dismantling and dumping costs higher than the sale prices of reused parts and recycled materials. Then, the pace-wise up-grading, based on voluntary agreements between private partners, is unable to economically achieve the mandatory EU targets with return on investment, thus inter-dependent value-chains shall be pursued (BMW, 2004), (Mayer & Cohen, 2003). On these facts, the induced off-springs addresses:

- the creation of networks of transporters, collectors, dismantlers, shredders, sorters, etc., with the related links, upwards, to manufacturers and dealers, and downwards, to parts re-users and materials recyclers;
- the analysis of sets of certified bodies, registered by the national authorities and notified to the EU, to accomplish overseeing duties, to record achievements, to draw eco-fees, and, whether the case arises, to inflict the punishments;
- the review of product-service deliveries, with high recovery figures (avoiding dangerous substances or parts, good dismantling properties, modular sub-items, etc.), supported by virtual/extended enterprises, with lifecycle responsibility.

Liguria (2004):	
total de-registration:	1 578
collected ELV:	34 052
District of Genova (2004):	
total de-registration:	21 982
collected ELV:	18 284

Table 1. Arrival rate

Separately, the induced off-springs do not have the potential to reach economical profit together with eco-sound targets. Important up-grading might exploit special adjustments (e.g., cascade recycling, say, the resort to secondary materials to increase the tangibles yield per unit service, etc.), but only integrating the options leads to method innovation, say, the industrial setting based on knowledge-driven entrepreneurship.

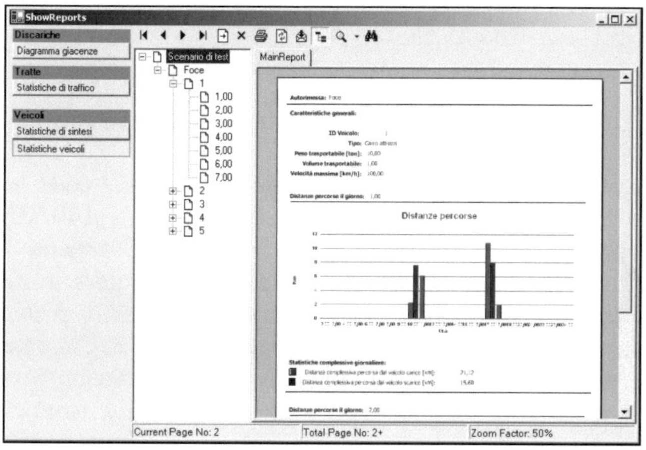

Fig. 4. The PMAR**RL**ELV environment example output

As example application, the PMAR**RL**ELV environment is used as reference tool for the local authorities of Genova, to establish an effective withdrawal policy for dropped out end-of-life vehicles, whose lawful recovery is not easily traceable. The reclamation tasks are let out to a set of wreckers, required to fetch and bring the left-out vehicles to given store-shops in the town near-outskirts. The problem deals with local issues, Table 1, detailed by:

- the map covered by the withdrawal service;
- the travelled road lay-out, with traffic-periods weigh;
- the duty-service of the selected wreckers;
- the capacity of the temporary store-shops.

The analysis considers several competing lay-outs, changing the wreckers allocation, the duty-cycles, the job priorities, etc.; then, typical performance charts are generated, providing synthetic indices (Fig. 4) to show the wreckers utilisation ratio, the average figures of the considered tasks, with specification of the total amount of removed vehicles and nominal properties of each service. The considered issue is direct outcome of the burdensomeness in Italy of de-registration practices, so that the owners of old crocks profit by dropping off their ELV, to by-pass bureaucracy and costs. The local boroughs need to fulfil reclamation duties, with the further constraints to find-out the law infringers and to satisfy the enacted eco-rules. The local biasing conditions are, however, a relevant aspect to understand the actual effects risen by applying the EU directives.

Set-in-safeness stand:	**ELVs per loading capacity**
drained fluids:	231
electrical batteries:	1448
tyres:	74
Dismantling/shredding stand:	**ELVs per loading capacity**
glasses:	746
plastics:	217
ferrous metals:	30
non-ferrous metals:	202

Note. The transported materials are considered shredded.

Table 2. Number of ELV necessary to fulfil the loading capacity of a lorry

In the existing surroundings, the application of the PMAR**RL**ELV code in the Genova (and Liguria) case, has to deal yearly, see the Tab. 1, with some 20 000 (and 40 000) ELV, 20% of them coming from dropped-off vehicles (more or less, at known locations, Fig. 3). The study considered different competing solutions. The EU directives require to single out the set of Authorised Treatment Facilities, ATFs, which guarantee process monitoring and targets achievements. These are, mainly, storing and dismantling stands, in charge of the safe materials separation for the recovery (reuse, recycle) jobs and the remediation functions. Preliminary assessments show that suited efficacy could be reached with yearly treatment of around 10 000 ELV. The figure balances the fetch/transport costs, with the dismantle fees: the higher efficiency of mass-dismantling vanishes due to the higher handling/transport costs of the scattered old crocks. This gives a preliminary guess to chose the number and the location of sound ATFs.
In fact, on the said regional basis, the backward flow fittingly organises, distinguishing the needed transportation, buffering and processing resources. An example arrangement could include temporary buffers, separately: - for the dropped-off ELV, six collection stands: 3 in Genova, 3 in the district (with comparatively long demurrage, for the law requests); - for the ELV withdrawn by the car dealers, twenty collection stands: 10 in Genova, 10 in the district; followed by four ATFs (2 nearby Genova, each one treating around 9 150 ELV per year). In order to acknowledge the overall lay-out, the monthly productivity is devised.
Then, with simulation runs of four weeks, some 1 524 ELVs need to be treated, and, parcelling out the yearly arrivals over the 48 working weeks (established on 5 work-days and single 8 hours long shift), the two flows need to be considered:

- 1 ELV dropped-off, to be removed on averaged 3 hours rate;
- 1 ELV withdrawn from the car dealers, according to a 2.6 hours rate.

Material	Lorries fulfilled
drained liquids	3.59
batteries	0.57
tyres	11.23
glasses	1.11
plastics	3.83
ferrous metals	27.70
non-ferrous metals	4.11

Table 3. Quantities of dismantled materials

The transportation fleet, for the all backwards flow, was established to include:

- haul-away cars, carrying up to six ELV (mainly, from car-dealers);
- break-down vans, mostly, for the fetching of single dropped off ELV;
- motor lorries, for the treated output, handled in containers or as wreck in bulk.

N.	Total In (ELVs)	Max (ELVs)	Now In (ELVs)	Total Out (ELVs)	Avg Size (ELVs)	Avg Time (min)
1	62	6	2	60	3.05	1419.51
2	63	1	0	63	0.41	186.46
3	63	6	3	60	2.40	1100.64
4	60	6	6	54	2.83	1360.98
5	62	1	0	62	0.24	110.38
6	60	7	0	60	2.75	1322.66
7	60	7	6	54	3.33	1601.74
8	61	1	1	60	0.49	234.07
9	63	1	1	62	0.56	258.78
10	62	7	2	60	3.69	1720.18
11	65	2	1	64	0.69	305.38
12	61	8	1	60	2.82	1337.66
13	61	8	1	60	4.07	1929.24
14	61	2	0	61	0.68	321.38
15	60	8	6	54	3.52	1695.74
16	59	2	1	58	0.33	162.07
17	62	6	2	60	2.81	1310.33
18	62	2	1	61	0.59	275.36
19	60	7	6	54	3.48	1675.43
20	61	2	1	60	0.85	404.41
21	61	7	1	60	2.94	1393.42
22	61	7	1	60	3.41	1614.04
23	62	7	7	55	3.21	1496.41
24	60	8	7	53	3.56	1715.86
25	61	6	1	60	2.25	1067.67
26	61	7	7	54	3.34	1584.10
	1594	5.08	2.50	1529	2.24	1061.69
	Tot.	Med.	Med.	Tot.	Med.	Med.

Table 4. Collection stands statistics

By simulation, several reverse logistics policies are compared. An example policy aims at concentrating in the local ATFs self-consistent recovery steps, to handle in output sets of containers, with diversified contents. Then, the reference figure addresses the number of

ELV necessary to fulfil the loading capacity of a lorry, by standard 20 feet containers, Tab. 2, for the considered kind of removed pieces, Tab. 3.
The investigation, from then on, provides quantitative figures, depending on the selected operation scenarios, for the temporary allocated resources. Considering, for instance, 20 working-days long (4 weeks) simulation runs, the total amount of ELVs treated by a local facility reaches 831 units. Based on the yearly amount of ELVs, the averaged quantities of dismantled materials listed by Tab. 4 are found, for the Liguria case (six collection stands for the dropped-off vehicles and twenty for the car-dealers withdrawals).

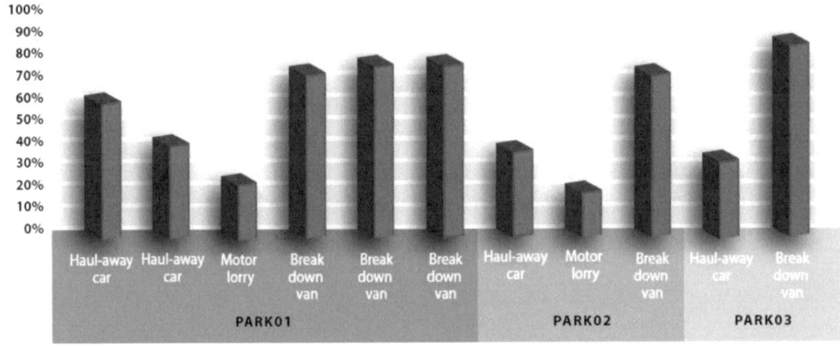

Fig. 5. Backward logistics fleet utilization ratio

The PMAR**RL**ELV code allows showing the performance figures of the engaged resources. As example results, the Fig. 5 gives of the transportation fleet: 4 haul-away cars, 5 break-down vans, and 2 motor lorries; the Fig. 6 shows the number of containers fulfilled by the two ATFs operating in Genova, with detailed specification of the carried parts or materials. The transported materials are considered shredded, assuming that the required machinery is locally available, to optimise the transfer/handling costs.

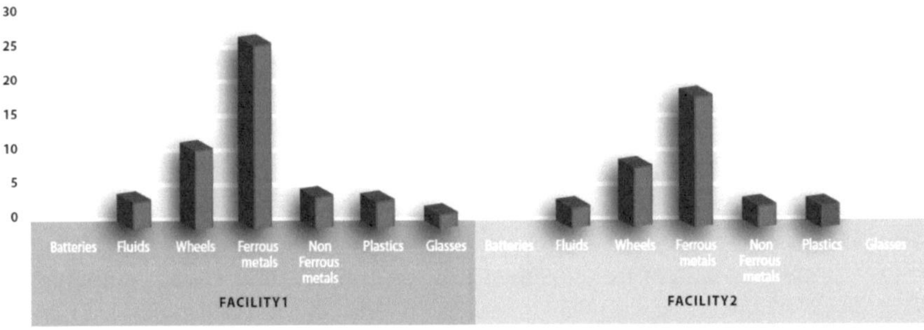

Fig. 6. Number of fulfilled lorries

The Fig. 7 displays the utilisation ratios of the said ATFs, separately specifying the pre-treatment (to reach safeness) and the dismantling (for selective withdrawal) stands. The sample results correspond to suitable performance operation conditions, with account of the unexpected occurrences (resources unavailability for break-down, traffic jamming, etc.) randomly generated by the simulator. The Liguria case investigation compared several logistic lay-outs and different resource allocations and distributions, each time providing quantitative assessments of the actually achieved performance.

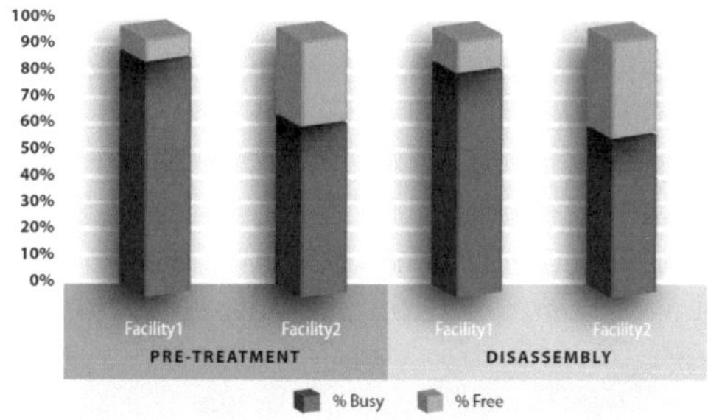

Fig. 7. Treatment facilities utilization ratio

The PMAR**RL**ELV code makes easy obtaining detailed results, such as the ones exemplified, and drawing general conclusions, based on repeated simulation runs. In this study, the attention is especially focused on the switching from the voluntary agreements approach, to the compulsory targets policy, to understand the drawbacks and advantages in terms of combined economic and ecologic burdens and fostered innovation vision. To such purpose, the simulation study allows quantitative forecasts. Explanatory hints are also summarised as concluding comments.

5. Pre-treatment and dismantling shop

Developing effective car dismantling and recycling facilities is challenge in the carmakers field, with, probably, the most demanding innovations on the automotive field to overcome the world-wide competition. Several investigation lines have been undertaken these recent years, (Paul, 2006), aiming at:

- quantitative assessment of recovery/reuse/recycle processes, under different operation plans, for existing situations (vehicles not produced with recovery mind) and alternative organisations and technologies;
- establishing appropriate recommendations and warnings to improve (by design-for-dismantling, DfD, design-for-recovering, DfR, etc., practices), the future, more eco-conservative, automotive market;
- balancing forward and backward chain operations, to optimise return on investment of the manufacture business, based on lifecycle contracts, driven by voluntary agreements and compulsory targets;
- reconsidering the reverse logistics as mandatory requirement for growth sustainability, in front of natural resources ceaseless depletion and human surroundings progressive pollution.

These points are shared by many end-of-life goods, today, massively dumped to landfills. The connection of their backward flows could, possibly, improve, by economy of scale, the logistic flows (collection, transport, storing, etc.) and given steps of recycling (shredding, dispatching, sorting, etc); the effectiveness, however, is highly dependent on the knowledge streams, and, more specifically on the information linked to the material streams, when the individual product is conceived. The fact, is most likely to increase, as the design of new items will start keeping the reverse logistics in mind: this means including the product-data

management, PDM, in the construction files, for efficient recovery/reclamation, so that oriented programming and equipment are used for enhanced effectiveness.
The investigation and performance assessment of the dismantling facilities, Fig. 8, will, thereafter, become standard routine. The well-established approach, for shop-floor selection, goes across implementing suitable software aids, to describe the equipment behaviour and simulate actual operation achievements. The process physical model shall, first, move from defining work-cycles and work-stations. Indeed: to dismantle means to take to pieces an artefact, or to strip/deprive of its outfits; while: to disassemble, means to systematically separate an artefact into its constitutive parts. Efficiency would lead to prefer the second process. Then, the disassembly process should consider different features: - manual vs. automatic (also: mixed mode operation); - partial (a subset of parts are not removed), selective (a set of parts are removed the first); - parallel (two or more parts are jointly removed), sequential (parts are removed one by one); - non destructive (unbroken parts are withdrawn) vs. destructive (parts are cut/broken during removal); - and so on.

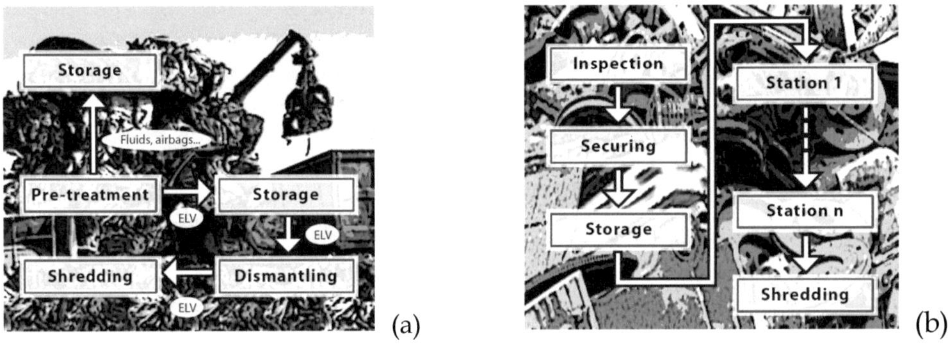

Fig. 8. Dismantling shop: operation lay-out, and dismantling process (a); operation flow (b)

Today, basic knowledge of car-wreckers, Fig. 9, comes from IDIS, International Dismantling Information System, http://www.idis2.com, a data-base of some 1 000 vehicle types of 25 carmakers, listing about 46 000 pieces. This helps displaying the part solid models and describing texts (in 21 languages), with instructions and tool/fixture requirements.
For environmental protection, the enacted regulations require special care to handle hazardous materials and to safely avoid contamination. This leads to preliminary ELV treatments, to remove potentially harmful or noxious parts (containing lead, mercury, etc.), fluids (for brakes, lubrication, conditioning, etc.), or items (air-bags, exhaust silencer, etc.), etc., which are subject of special restrictions. The subsequent steps address the disassembly-for-reuse, looking after separating pieces to be restored or remanufactured for second-hand marketing; for competitiveness, the safety and reliability figures need comply suitably high standards. At this stage only, the dismantling-for-recycle should start. The process sequencing aims at clearly separating items into homogeneous blocks as for material properties and recovery potentials, namely:

- outer outfits and glasses (windscreen, window-panes, etc.), for special purpose recovery;
- special pieces (doors, front/rear bonnet, ..) and groups (gearbox, engine, ...), for recovery;
- plastic parts, possibly, ordered according to preselected identifiers or included markers;
- internal outfits/fabrics (covers, upholstery, stuffing, ...), following scheduled plans;

- metallic parts, possibly, keeping (or re-establishing) the ordering trim of the data-base;
- residual crock-skeleton/wreck, for the subsequent compacting/shredding operations.

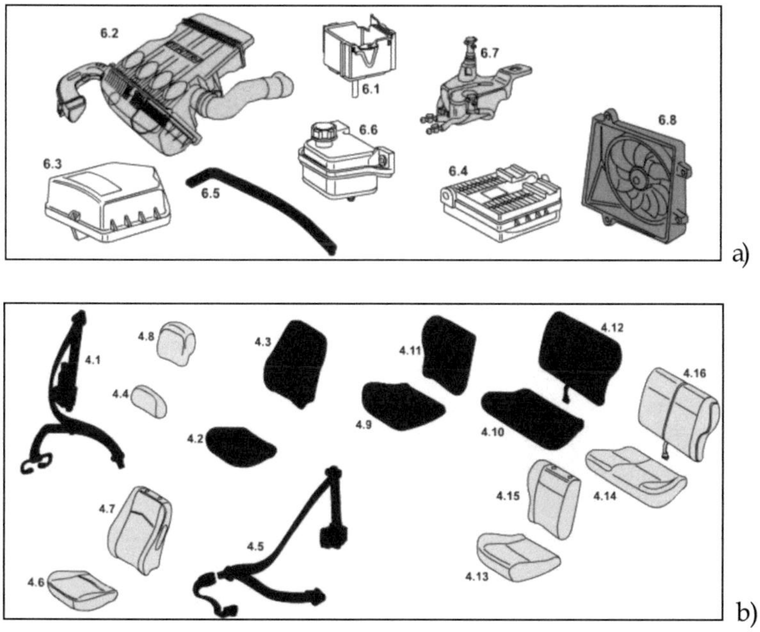

Fig. 9. IDIS db: example engine components (a); example upholstering and stuffing (b)

The detailed description of the work-cycles and accurate development of structured models are basic premise for choosing the plant and assessing the usefulness of robotic aids.
The state of the art is fast evolving, with example plants and prototypal facilities with different levels of sophistication. The Canadian AADCO line, http://www.aadco.ca/, for instance, is useful choice, when productivity is special request, or the German ADEMA system, http://www.lsd-gmbh.com, is valuable support, when leanness and flexibility are primary objectives. Basically, the on-progress trends look after modularity, with series of automatic units (fluids draining, wheels removal, rim/tyre separation, ELV lifting or overturn, gearbox/engine pulling out, etc.), and general purpose handling and transport equipment, between the work-stands. This, quite commonly, leads to mixed-mode flows, with interposed human operators and robotic devices, as, typically, subsets of duties require careful decision-making (e.g., selective handling of hazardous materials, quality figures of reusable components, etc.) and automatic processing would result unreliable, at least, at the present state of the art. The functional modelling of the disassemble/ dismantle line, thereafter, ought to deal with hybrid algorithmic/procedural knowledge frames, which include causal blocks, to duplicate the physical transformations, and heuristic blocks, to emulate the behavioural counterparts. The obtained models directly yield to expert simulation, providing powerful means to experiment on virtual plants, during the facility design, or to compare virtual process-plans, for the on-duty operation, Fig. 8.
The modelling and simulation studies can be undertaken at different deepness of details, from the bird-eye view of the preliminary assessments, to actual feasibility checks of the

overall reverse logistics schemes and the selection of the individual Authorised Treatment Facilities arrangements.

For the automotive domain, the investigation lines start by the quantitative assessment of the recover/reuse/recycle processes, to comply the mandatory thresholds of the directives. The market size is impressive, with 225 million vehicles (185 million cars) circulating, in 2001, in the original 15 EU Countries and, each year, 10 million cars, moved to landfills. The regulations affect national Governments, and fair transpositions are required, to not bias the common market. Thus, national, regional and local set-outs should be devised, properly tailored to current needs and entrepreneurship qualification.

The Italian case shall face, for instance, some 2 million ELV per year. Notably, around 20 000 ELV each year, are processed in Liguria. The eco-bylaws are ruled on the regional scale, but, of course, other collection/processing settings could develop, should be achieved higher return on investment. Today, the car-wreckers represent quite distributed realities, with tiny processing abilities, scarcely complying the eco-protection requests. At the same time, overall inverse logistics networks are far to have reached fully operational deployment, as for carmakers side, as for official monitoring. The law, DL 24.06.2003, suitably transposes the 2000/53/CE directive, but factual specifications still lack, with, e.g., the free-take-back even burdened by severe de-registration fees and loose carmakers interpretations. Last, but not least, the regional and local authorities, most of the time, seem to do not entirely realise the technical relevance of the overall incumbents and related business, primarily interested to bureaucratic accomplishments.

The recovery/reclamation processes, rather than academic study, are urgent necessity, with fully specified legal (directive mandatory rules) and technical (available dismantle/recycle equipment) constraints. Difficulties, due to lack of profitable markets for reverse logistics outcomes, are got over, by combining pertinent economic instruments, namely, free-take-back and visible fees management on the all artefacts lifecycle. This means: - careful effectiveness assessment of actual solutions, as decision aid for the organisational choice and setting; - full transparency of forward and backward supply chain, with optimal allocation of the visible fees, to enhance the national/regional/local competitiveness. Occurrence-driven expert-simulation provides both the scopes: as off-process tool, at the design stage; as on-process support, at lifelong operation. On these premises, the PMAR**RL**ELV environment has been considered to simulate the ELV reverse logistics (Acaccia et al., 2006a). Basically, it addresses problems in automotive systems, for withdrawal, collection and dismantling end-of-life vehicles, and for shredding, sorting and dispatching the residuals; it is based on the WITNESS language, and incorporates modules for the interactive remote-inquiry, intelligent data-vaulting, and text/graphic restitution, to insert the pertinent data describing the processed ELV, and related components details, Fig. 9.

For explanatory purpose, an example application, focused on ELV dismantling, is discussed. The Liguria case is taken in consideration, singularly and in relation to broader national set-ups. Generally, wastes (and, with full evidence ELV) are bulky, potentially dangerous and very poor materials, thus, every added cost in handling and transportation will lower the process effectiveness. This suggests to localise the dismantling shops on the territory, possibly, with reusing/recycling flows linked to decentralised end-users. Modular lay-outs, based on the ADEMA concept, are arranged, distinguishing separate stands (safety fitting, disassembly for reuse, dismantling for recycle), the transport and manipulation devices and the auxiliary storages (line-buffers and parts collectors). A reasonable setting

deals with local facilities conceived to process 10 000 ELV per years, roughly leading to five lines in Liguria (200 in Italy), according to the expected market.
The example details referred to the Liguria, especially the Genova case is retained. Looking at specific ATFs, Fig. 10, we distinguish between the two phases because the first one has mandatory constraints issued by the EU Directive, thus we have a list of operations to fulfil without optimisation possibilities. Actually, the pre-treatment needs to be done where cars, coming from the road, are collected, while the dismantling can be delayed, after transportation of the wrecks to a different location. The transfer and handling costs of heavy and bulky stuffs are quickly increasing, and the investigation is carried, combining both the functional stands in the same location. In the pre-treatment zone, the ELV are put in non-dangerous conditions (for workers and for environment); the work-stations are: inspection, drainage of fluids, removal of dangerous pieces. The withdrawn materials follow prescribed flows, to grant the safety and recovery targets. In the dismantling zone, the ELV are disassembled by selective pick-up or destructive shearing, with logics given by recovery technologies and reuse/recycle opportunities. The obtained parts follow two paths: the reuse path, after reconditioning and remanufacturing; the recycling path, through shredding, sorting, etc. processes.

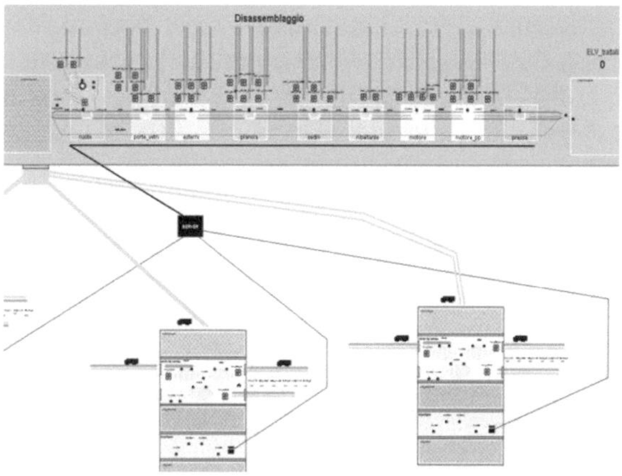

Fig. 10. Pre-treatment and disassembly plants

The ATF dismantles all what is required for safeness requirements, is convenient to recover or reuse, or shall be moved for recycling, up to reach the residual amounts for lawful landfilling. Parameters like accessibility, weight, materials have a great impact at this stage. The main transport system (for ELVs) is a trolley, one in-line, which brings the ELVs through the all the work-stands. The work-stands organize to aim at optimal material collection. Two workers, several containers and internal transports are assigned to every cell. Above all, non metallic materials (glass, plastics, etc.) and reusing components (engines, etc.) distinguish. At the end of the dismantling process, the ELV wrecks shredding or packing (according to logistic requirements) stands are located. The dismantling facility technical data cover: space requests (to store, process, etc.); material flow (internal transport, handling, etc.); process resources (technologies, workers, etc.); production agenda (ELV technical data: weighs, quantities, materials, tasks, times, etc.).

Further to the technical specifications, the legal constraints play relevant roles. In Italy, the ELVs follow a legal deregistration line (with payment of official charges), either come out from the unlawful line of dropped out vehicle wrecks. With the latter line, the fees and charges, unless the final user is found, are covered by town local bodies. Thus, the dropped aside wrecks are, generally, stored before processing at the ATFs for a considerable time, to check and to indict the end owners.
The simulation runs considered different feeding scenarios, referred to daily, weekly and monthly agendas, with due parameters setting and alternative end-users flows. The data entry exploits a suitably structured input (every parameter listed in the sheet corresponds to an attribute in the WITNESS coding). The facility operation assume work conditions on shifts base, distinguishing the warming-up and the steady-state running; the normal set-up uses a single daily shift of 8 hours; the exceptional duty could cover up to three shifts. To set the simulation, main data are: the facility data (space requirements, internal transports, etc.); data about operations to be fulfilled and available technologies; the ELVs and their components data (it is necessary to study ELV components to select the items to dismantle, with the pertinent parameters values: weigh, materials, quantities, work-cycles, etc.). The items data require careful assessments; e.g., "time schedules" are manuals with nominal maintenance times, including non destructive dismantling times: scaling factors are needed, to obtain reasonable results from simulation. A time for maintenance, as it appears in a timer manual, is called "assigned" and is the result of this expression that weigh the direct (required to complete the job) and the indirect (required to prepare ELV and fixtures for the job to be done) times; their adaptation for the dismantling tasks, requires a trimming factor, still object of assessments. By simulation, important hints are obtained on the critical nature of competing work-cycles.

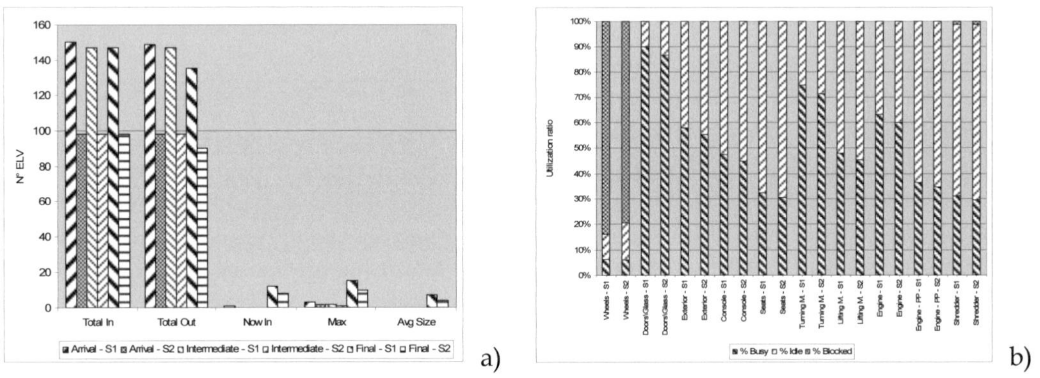

Fig. 11. Pre-treatment buffers statistics (a); disassembly stations utilization ratio (b)

The mixed mode automation is evaluated, with different labours (on-line personnel) or duty-oriented robots. The visualisation avails of animated displays, Fig. 10, where the resources bear clear graphical presentation. On-progress schedules include discontinuities (failures, supply stops, etc.) by occurrence management. The sample outputs, (Fig. 11a-b), show benefits and drawbacks of the case-investigation of decentralised lay-outs, and provide reference hints to acknowledge the main operation details of actual solutions by the WITNESS modules. The performance figures and process statistics are shown as decision aid support. The sample issues refer to simulation runs with warm-up time of about 2 000

minutes (to show how this affects the steady state performance, in the case of interrupted duties): the figure is due to the simulation start time (which is at 12 p.m., on a 3 shifts/day base, possibly, only partially enabled), thus, in the pre-treatment zones, this correspond to more than a 1 week time (with 9 ELV/hour entering the simulation, after 2000 minutes we have 84 ELV entered). The example diagram of the Fig. 11a shows a typical steady state flow giving the stand input/output, with timely work-in-progress and statistical figures; in the Fig. 11b, the utilisation ratio of the processing units are plotted, distinguishing the type of the withdrawal in the dismantling stand, each time giving the busy (on an ELV), the idle (no ELV) and the block (for queuing or other external reason) state.
The concept, behind spreading on the territory local dismantling shops, leads to establish synergies in the reverse logistics of the different durables/consumables covered by the EU mandatory take-back policy. The study shows the sample ATF settlement, highly dependent on the case example, where the carmakers' responsibility is still too much thwarted by car-recycling aids, offered by governments to support the carmakers.

6. Example remarks

The role of the manufacturers is fundamental to support reverse logistics by product-data management aids for enhanced dismantling and selective recycling, and turns to be critical, in the short time, to enable design-for-recycling paradigms (e.g., modularity and material segregation, disassembly pre-setting, etc.) and to profit of sustainable manufacture (high resort to recovered or recycled provisions, etc.) and maintenance (proactive up-keeping, re-integration, etc.) options. Besides, governmental authorities need to analyse the whole supply chains, which distinguish one producer from another, suitably defining pertinent taxing rule. The costing will be ascribed to the consumers side, with tax collection duty, mainly, put in charge by the goods sellers, at the point-of-sale. The availability of local multi-task dismantling shops, capable of taking charge of the different backward chains and feeding the subsequent shredding, sorting and dispatching flows, becomes opportunity for enhanced eco-conservativeness.
The connection between backward chains has relevant falls-out. The complexity of problems needs not hinder the obligation that sustainability shall be put directly in charge to the parties having benefits, and not poured on unrelated peoples, if the impact on the environment ought to be kept under acceptable limits. The present EU policy is, certainly, at a very early stage; the enacted bylaws, however, already aim at:

- acting on the consumers (producers+users) side, to foster a thrifty society, instead of a throw-away economy;
- re-orienting the supplier side, to offer functions, instead of goods, for satisfying current needs, without individual ownership;
- establishing positive acts (not series of vetoes that simply give rise to hidden bargains), to empower service economy by fair trade rules, respectful of welfare ecologic side;
- stimulating the jobs for the reuse of tangibles (reverse logistic: to collect, disassemble, recover, sort, sell, etc., second-hand materials);
- supporting knowledge-driven infrastructures, while discouraging the processes with intensive tangibles spoilage;
- fostering common practices the common market over, to look after world-wide covering.

The effectiveness assessment and operation transparency are, once again, shared incentive: these allow checks of return on investment and on eco-targets achievement. The simulation

environments are powerful means, to study useful synergies, suggesting actually enabling options. The end-of-life vehicle ELV case has simple knowledge transparency The waste electrical and electronic equipment WEEE case, already in force by mid 2005, is partially different, as it deals with non-registered goods. Without giving details, producers/dealers, again, are required for items call-back, collection and reclaiming. The recovery and recycle targets apply, depending on appliances size and lighting rigs. The *visible* fees are collected when new devices are sold. The EU prescriptions are differently transferred into national acts, and some country is considering transient alternatives for some legal (data registration and vaulting, etc.) and technical (withdrawal, dismantling, recycling, dumping, etc.) duties.
The two chosen EU cases deal with (chiefly, high quality) durables. The *visible* fees collection aims at linking the forward and backward tracks, uniformly spreading the extra costs, with balanced effects, and unbiased market deployment, because of economic instruments giving apt support to the chosen EU environmental policy.
These economic instruments attract increasing research attention. Industrial innovation is main answer; still, how the specific measures affect the changes, mostly, address "induced off-springs" and "evolutionary up-grading", while eco-sustainability requests complete paradigm shifts in the growth methods. By now, many projects consider technologic and organisation issues linked to given areas (automotive, electrical/electronic equipment, etc.) once regulations are enacted, and the enterprises' strategies follow the black-box approach, acknowledging the input-output flows and experiencing sample on-the-path adjustments. This way, typically, exploits flexibility and leanness by pace-wise betterments, leaving aside the method innovation, which only will lead to competitive divide in business paradigms. Then, to move a step onward, the black-box research projects ought to operate an integrated approach, joining technical and legal drivers into balanced promotions, with properly wide-ranging actions. These paths shall encompass (Michelini& Razzoli, 2000), (Michelini & Razzoli, 2005):

- process innovation: resource-recovery path, with higher value in part-reuse and material-recycling; thermo-enhancement path, by energy recovery from waste; full-substitution path, by modified material choice and items design for high recovering; etc.;
- method innovation: extended artefact path, through commodities and utilities joint delivery; extended enterprise path, through efficient supporting nets; information value-added path, to replace materials by intangible equivalent-functions; etc.

The choice of the dominant innovation path is questionable subject. The process innovation follows smooth up-grading, due to cumulated knowledge from R&D projects or empirical tests. The method innovation moves from dissimilar national contexts (some countries have carmakers, some not; sometimes shredding facilities are combined with steel production plants; chemical factories can foster plastic recycling; etc.); etc.; moreover, the expected cost/benefit ratios do not depend only on technical choices; they include wide amount of bureaucracy and governmental biases, forcing the pursuit of one or more tracks, not steered by consistent rules. This means that, in front of the same recovery/remediation compulsory targets in the EU area, largely different cost/benefit issues appear, penalising less efficient structures, with high local charges or low work productivity. The EU will, possibly, not suffer as a whole; the final outcome being to transfer industrial and economic activities from one country to another one, as, in the average, the expected eco-conservativeness will be achieved, with, of course, outcomes in wealth distribution across the common market, (Morin, 1999), (Suhas, 2001).

The PMAR**RL**ELV code helps providing visibility of the conditioning knowledge bases, addressing noteworthy aspects. Example issues are:

- for process innovation: the logistics costs (handling and transport of very poor items) as compared with recovery (reuse, recycle) processing; this knowledge helps to localise the dismantling sites and to establish treatment chains, selectively addressing given goods (WEEE, ELV, etc.), either mixing material refuses, for scale economy;
- for method innovation: the value chain of service engineering supply, covering, out of the mandatory take-back, the whole eco-consistent operation life, to exploit synergic value-added options; this knowledge will help organising the materials and information flows, setting transparency requisites, in view of balancing return on investment and (law-driven) fair-trade constraints (and costs).

Indeed, eco-innovation follows alternative/complementary paths, with interrelated links, exploring technical and legislation drivers to achieve demanding targets and economical profit, with visible outcomes within the different EU partners, as shown by the noteworthy aspects. Other example issues could be mentioned, and the ability of progressing through modelling and simulation is winning opportunity to get over the simple black-box approach, and to aim at systemic innovation.

Moreover, the focus on the reverse logistics dramatically appeared in the recent years. The method innovation, on the contrary, will become permanent requirement. Indeed, the eco-conservativeness is imperative demand, if quality of life continuation is dealt with. This results in sets of accomplishments, with, mainly, two purposes (Michelini, 2010):

- to expand the value chain intangible additions, exploiting ICT means for wealth creation;
- to lower consumption, acting on dumping and pollution, by mandatory recovery.

It shall not be forgot, however, that the EU regulation aims at recovery/reclamation goals, since the European counties are highly inhabited regions, and landfill problems are critical. The enacted bylaws are not specially conservative in terms of energy balance, because of the mandatory targets do not leave alternatives on exhaustive treatments. The point is object of present discussions, entailing the technical specifications. The method innovation, anyway, looks at the efficiency of the extended enterprise, exploiting fully structured corporations, in lieu of the virtual enterprise, limited to co-operating focused net-concerns (Michelini, 2010), (Michelini & Razzoli, 2009), (Michelini & Razzoli, 2010). Of course, such an entrepreneurial achievement effectiveness is highly conditioned by the bureaucratic helpfulness (or lack of efficiency) of each national context (and the recalled ELV case offers significant motivations to rethink the all deregistration course, notably too expensive in Italy).

7. Conclusions

To draw conclusions from discussing the topics in sustainable engineering management, the compulsory targets are recognised to establish characterising facts, driven by economic instruments (Hang, 2006), (Knight, 1965):

- the producers responsibility principle, as it surfaces from the EU directives, with regards of the dismissal/ dismantling/recovery requirements;
- the law frame, given by the recover (reuse/recycle) compulsory targets, as economic instruments for process effectiveness with return on investment;
- the example regulation enacted for ELV and WEEE, by free-take-back, grounded on recycling visible-fees and design-for-dismantling/recovering rules;

- the operation set-ups, leading to enhanced usability and reverse logistics achievements, for environment protection and eco-sustainability.

The economic instruments are, moreover, starting aids for method innovation promoting knowledge-driven entrepreneurship. In that context, the ambient intelligence as noteworthy option to enrich the product-service delivery, (Michelini & Razzoli, 2008), (Michelini & Razzoli, 2008b), supported by extended enterprise organisations, explicitly warranting the producers' responsibility principle, expanded to cover on-duty and end-of-life operations, including eco-footprint control and conformance-to-use checks. The ambient intelligence provides ubiquitous computing and communication aids, to fulfil the monitoring and vaulting duties, already, required by the EU environmental policy by compulsory recovery and reclamation targets, fixed for mass-product durables, such as, ELV or WEEE.
The same class of ICT aids are winning opportunity, for restructuring the supply chain by information intensive deliveries, to avoid or, at least, drastically lower polluting emissions and wreck dumping, and to provide adequate recording of resource consumption. On these grounds, ambient intelligence tools acquire quite special flavour, since they are invoked to face very demanding incumbents, with resort to the frameworks of the reverse logistics in the knowledge society issues. The suitable choice of fitting economic instruments is critical premise, to permit efficient opening out of the reverse logistics treatment from the today limited cases of durables, to the more pervasive situations of the disposables. The question is totally open, but the eco-policy cannot reach balanced achievements, unless the totality of the tangible goods undergo suited remediation.

8. References

Abe, J.M.; Dempsey, P.E. & Basset, D.A. (1998). *Business ecology: giving your organisation the natural edge*, Butterworth-Heinemann, London.

Acaccia, G.M.; Michelini, R.C. & Qualich, N. (2005). End-of-life vehicles collection and disassembly: modelling and simulation, *Joint ESM-MESM Conf., EUROSIS 05*, pp. 34-40, Porto, Oct. 24-26.

Acaccia, G.M.; Michelini, R.C.; Penzo, L. & Qualich, N. (2006a). Modelling and simulation of car dismantling facilities, *Joint ECEC & FUBUTEC Intl. Conf.*, pp. 70-75, Athens, Apr. 17-19, ISBN 90 77381 24 4.

Acaccia, G.M.; Michelini, R.C. & Qualich, N. (2006b). End-of-life vehicles models with recycling in mind, *Joint ECEC & FUBUTEC Intl. Conf.*, pp. 76-82, Athens, Apr. 17-19, ISBN 90 77381 24 4.

ARN (2008). *ARN Sustainability Report 2008*, Auto Recycling Nederland, www.arn.nl

Blumberg, D.F. (2004). *Introduction to management of reverse logistics and closed loop supply chain processes*, D.F. Blumberg Associates, CRC Press, p. 296.

BMW Group (2004). *Innovation, efficiency, responsibility: sustainable value report 2003/2004*, Brand: BMW, Rolls-Royce Motor Cars Limited, MINI.

CEN/TC 273 WG4 (1999). *Logistics performance measures requirements and measuring methods*, Report BT N 5976, 19 November 1999.

Dekker, R.; Fleischmann, M.; Inderfurth, K. & van Wassenhove, L.N., Eds. (2004). *Reverse logistics: quantitative models for closed loop supply chains*, Springer, p. 436.

Dyckhoff, H.; Lackes, R. & Reese, J., Eds. (2004). *'Supply chain management and reverse logistics*, Springer, p. 426.

European Commission, (2006): http://ec.europa.eu/environment/waste/index.htm.
Freedman, M. & Jaggi, B., Eds. (2006). *Advances in environmental accounting*, Emerald Book, London.
Hang, W. (2006). Chances and limits of design-for-recycling: view on current developments, *6th Intl. Automobile Recycling Congress*, Amsterdam, March 15-17.
Kahraman, E. & Baig, A., Eds. (2009). *Environmentalism: environmental strategies and environment sustainability*, Nova Sci. Pub., New York.
Knight, G.B. (1965). *Basic concepts of ecology*, Macmillan, New York.
Lapide, L., (2005). *Proceeding of the supply chain 2020 project's industry advisory council*, March 17, MIT Centre for Transportation and Logistics.
Larson, B.A., Ed. (2009). *Sustainable development research advances*, Nova Sci. Pub., New York.
Leavis, F.R. & Thompson, D. (1993). *Culture and environment: the training of critical awareness*, Chatto & Windus, London.
Loeffe, C.V., Ed. (2009). *Conservation and recycling of resources: new research*, Nova Sci. Pub., New York.
Meijer, D. & DeJong, F., Eds. (2009). *Environmental regulation, evaluation, compliance and economic impact*, Nova Sci. Pub., New York.
Michelini, R.C. (2009). *Robot age knowledge changeover*, Nova Sci. Pub., New York.
Michelini, R.C. (2010). *Knowledge society engineering: the sustainable growth pledge*, Nova Sci. Pub., New York.
Michelini, R.C.; Acaccia, G.M. & Molfino, R.M. (2002) Simulation and intelligent automation: activity at the industrial robot design research laboratory, *Modeling & Simulation Magazine*, Vol. 1, No. 2, pp. 6-7.
Michelini, R.C.; Acaccia, G.M.; Callegari, M.; Molfino, R.M. & Razzoli, R.P. (2001). Computer integrated assembly for cost effective development, In: *C.T. Leondes Ed.: Computer Integrated Manufacturing*, Vol. II, CRC Press LLC, Boca Raton (FL), pp. 2.01-2.68.
Michelini, R.C.; Acaccia, G.M.; Callegari, M.; Molfino, R.M. & Razzoli R.P. (1997). Shop controller-and-manager for intelligent manufacturing, In: *S. Tzafestas Ed.: Management and Control of Manufacturing Systems*, Springer, London, pp. 219-254.
Michelini, R.C. & Coiffet, P. (2010). *Essai sur les capitaux assurant la fortune de l'humanité*, Académie de France des Technologies, Paris, Librairie: http://www.academie-technologies.fr.
Michelini, R.C. & Kovàcs, G.L. (2002). Integrated design for sustainability: intelligence for eco-consistent products-and-services, *The Estonian Business School Review*, Tallin, Winter 2002-3 issue, No. 15, Dec., pp. 81-95.
Michelini, R.C. & Razzoli, R.P. (2000). *Affidabilità e sicurezza del manufatto industriale: progetto per lo sviluppo sostenibile*, Tecniche Nuove, Milano, p. 300, ISBN 88-481-1085 I.
Michelini, R.C. & Razzoli, R.P. (2004). Product-service for environmental safeguard: a metric to sustainability, *Intl. J. Resources, Conservation and Recycling*, Vol. 42, No. 1, August, pp. 83-98.
Michelini, R.C. & Razzoli, R.P. (2004b). Product-service eco-design: knowledge-based infrastructures, *Intl. J. Cleaner Production*, Elsevier, Vol. 12, No. 4, May, pp. 415-428.
Michelini, R.C. & Razzoli, R.P. (2005). Collaborative networked organisations for eco-consistent supply-chains, In: *Virtual Enterprise Integration: Technological and Organisational Perspectives*, G.D. Putnik, M.M. Cunha (Eds.), IDEA Group, IGI Press, Hershey, PA, pp. 45-77.

Michelini, R.C. & Razzoli, R.P. (2008). Innovation for sustainability in product lifecycle design, In: *Computer-Aided Innovation*, G. Cascini (Ed.), Springer, Boston, pp. 217-228, ISBN 978-0-387-09696-4.

Michelini, R.C. & Razzoli, R.P. (2008b). Ubiquitous computing & communication for product monitoring, In: M. Khosrow-Pour, Ed., *Encyclopaedia of Information Science & Technology*, 2nd Ed., IDEA Group Inc., 2008, pp. 3851-3857, ISBN 978-1-60566-026-4.

Michelini, R.C. & Razzoli, R.P. (2009). The service net facility integration appraisal, *Intl. J. Services, Economics and Management*, No. 4, pp. 371-392, ISSN: 1753-0822.

Michelini, R.C. & Razzoli, R.P. (2010). Environment-enterprise integration: networked entrepreneurial opportunities, In: F. Teuteberg & J.M. Gomez, Eds., *Corporate Environmental Management Information Systems*, IDEA Group Inc., Hershey (PA).

Mihailovich, D.T. & Lalic, B. Eds. (2009). *Advances in environmental modelling and measurements*, Nova Sci. Pub., New York.

Morin, P.J. (1999). *Community ecology*, Blackwell Scientific, New York.

Muñoz, S.I., Ed. (2009). *Ecology research progress*, Nova Sci. Pub., New York.

Naess, A. (1989). *Ecology, community and lifestyle: an eco-sophy outline*, Cambridge Univ. Press, Cambridge.

O'Neill, J. (2001). *Ecology, policy and politics*, Cambridge Univ. Press, London.

Paul, R.T. (2006). Recyclability of selected vehicles in North America, *6th Intl. Automobile Recycling Congress*, Amsterdam, March 15-17.

Pertsova, C.C., Ed. (2008). *Ecological economics research trends*, Nova Sci. Pub., New York.

Popov, F. & DeSimone, F.D. (1997). *Eco-efficiency: the business link to sustainable development*, The MIT Press, Cambridge.

Sakao, T. & Lindhal, M. (2009). *Introduction to product-service systems design*, Springer Verlag, Berlin, ISSN 978-1-84882-908-4.

Scarpa, R. & Alberini, A.A. (2005). *Application of simulation in environment and resource economics*, Springer, London.

Schoensleben, P. (2004). *Integral logistics management: planning and control of comprehensive supply chains*, 2 ed., CRC Press, Boca Raton.

Schmidt, M.; Joao, E. & Albrecht, E., Eds. (2005). *Implementing strategic environment assessment*, Springer, London.

Sperling, D. (2009). *Two billions of cars*, Oxford Uni. Press, Oxford.

Stark, J. (2005). *Product lifecycle management*, Springer, London.

Suhas, H.K. (2001). *From quality to virtual enterprise: an integrated approach*, CRC Press, Boca Raton.

Uchitelle, L. (2006). *The disposable America: layoffs and their consequences*, Knopf, New York.

Veleva, V. & Ellenbecker, M. (1996). *Ecological design*, Inland Press, Washington.

Wackernagel, M. & Rees, W. (1995). *Our ecological footprint: reducing human impact on the earth*, New Society Pub., Gabriola Inland.

Weizsäcker, E.V.; Lovins, A.B. & Lovins, L.H. (1997). *Factor four: doubling wealth, halving resource use*, The new Report to the Club of Rome, Earthscan Pub. Ltd., London.

8

Simulating service systems

Raid Al-Aomar, PhD
Industrial Engineering Department
Jordan University of Science & Technology
Irbid 22110, JORDAN

1. Introduction and Overview

During the last two decades, the service sector has shown a remarkable growth in different aspects of both national and international economies. Service companies such as banking, hospitality, restaurants, health systems, telecommunication, transportation, and insurance industry play a major role in today's market. As a result, many engineering techniques, analytical methods, and software tools were developed to help designing service systems, solving problems in their operation, and optimizing their performance. In such context, simulation is a key engineering tool that is widely used for the analysis of service systems.

Simulation modeling is an engineering tool that has been widely used in both service and manufacturing systems applications. Simulation has been utilized to model banks, fast food restaurants, computer systems, telecommunication networks, health clinics, traffic and transportation, logistics, airports, post offices, and many other service systems. Simulation has been also used in modeling business operations such as product development processes, manpower planning, financial transactions, data processing, and information flow.

Similar to manufacturing systems, service systems provide one or more service/processing to flowing entities (for example, customers) through system resources and operations. Entities are routed through a sequence of processing operations/stations at which system resources such as employee or automatic processing machines provide the required service. The resemblance between service and manufacturing should not preclude the analyst from recognizing and taking into consideration the unique characteristics of service systems. Unlike physical products, services are often intangible, difficult to be put in storage, their outputs are hard to measure and quantify, and highly impacted by human behavior.

With the flexibility of simulation software, however, many of service systems characteristics can be captured in a computer model that behaves almost similar to a real-world service system. As a result, simulation modeling has become a popular management Decision Support System (DSS) tool for planning, improvement, and problem-solving. In the context of service systems, simulation is used to study the service system behavior, quantify the provided service, compare proposed alternatives for providing services, improve service level, better utilize resources, reduce service time and cost, and setup/configure the service system to provide the best performance possible within given business constraints.

Example of industries who can benefit from service system simulation:
- Healthcare and hospital management
- Hospitality and hotel management
- Banking and finance
- Supply chain and logistics
- Warehousing and storage systems
- Airports and aviation
- Traffic and transportation systems
- Restaurants and food services
- Postal services
- IT systems, communication networks, and data flow

Examples of objectives or benefits of simulating service systems:
- Optimize asset management
- Increase productivity
- Analyze and optimize supply chain and logistics
- Forecast demand and predict performance
- Increase upstream profitability
- Design, plan, and manage operations
- Optimize resource reallocations
- Identify and resolve bottlenecks
- Analyze alternative work processes
- Test the effect of alternative layouts
- Facilitate and support decision making
- Address risks and vulnerabilities

Examples of performance measures used to assess the performance of service systems:
- Throughout
- Utilization and efficiency
- Waiting time and overall lead time
- Consistency
- Waste, errors, and rework
- Cost and profit

This chapter presents the basics of service system simulation with application case studies. It first identifies and defines the main elements of service systems. It discusses the modeling techniques used in developing Discrete Event Simulation (DES) models of service systems. It also presents the Key Performance Indicators (KPIs) that can be used to measure and assess the performance of service systems. Finally, example case studies are presented.

2. Basics of Service Systems

This section provides the readers with the basic information necessary to understand the nature and functionalities of service systems.

2.1 Elements of Service Systems

Several elements commonly form a service system in various sectors of service industry. Such elements include wide range varieties in types and applications. Understanding such elements is essential to building simulation models that represent service systems. Most service systems involve a process for receiving customers and/or their requests. This process often includes activities such as receiving, registering at the reception, preparation of documents or material, and waiting for service. Service providers take care of customers and their requests by processing orders, serving customers, treating customers, and so on. Other business functions involved in providing services include sales, cashier, data entry, payments, etc. Services also develop and implement a process for service/facility departure. Departure process provides means for checking service/product quality, packaging, shipping, etc. Figure 1 depicts the main elements of a service system:

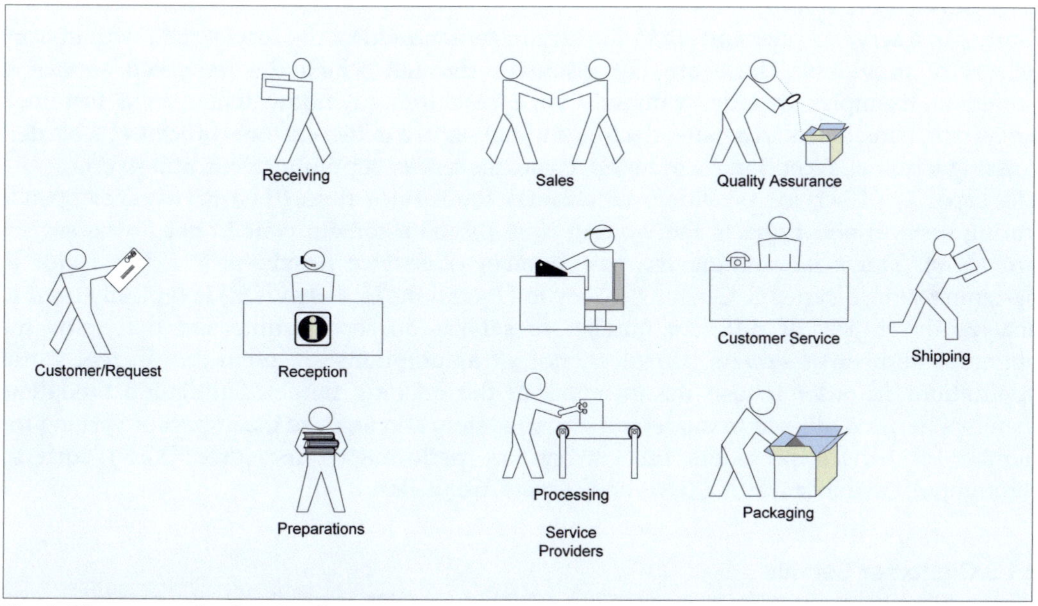

Fig. 1. Elements of a Service System

Other elements may exist in the service system based on its nature and business functions. For examples, a healthcare clinic often involves medical resources (doctors and nurses, X-ray facility, dental care equipment, etc.). A bank often involves tellers, ATM machines, loan officers, and so on. In general, basic building blocks in any service system often include the following:

2.1.1 System Entities

Customers (humans) represent the main entity that flows through various types of service systems. Customers arrive to the service system, request the service, receive the service, and departure the service system. For example, customers arrive to a bank and select/request the kind of service they wish to do such as making deposits, withdrawals, money transfers, and so on. Customers often wait for bank services in queues when the bank tellers are not available. Once a customer gets to the server (bank teller), he/she receives the service (the transaction) and then departs the bank. Other similar examples include patients at a clinic, customers at a fast food restaurant, a checkpoint, a post office, and so on.

In addition to customers, there could be other types of entities in a service system. Such entities are usually initiated by customers such as paperwork in a governmental office, insurance claims in an insurance company, calls in a calling center, and information bytes in a computer network. While the word "service" may not be of a direct meaning with such entities, these entities are processed in order to provide a certain service to the end customers. Such entities are moved in a certain sequence between service areas/stations, where value is added to such entities through processing. Value in such context may refer to percent of completion or benefit obtained from processing stations.

2.1.2 Service Providers

Entities in a service system arrive to the service center, request the service, and wait in front of service providers. Those are the resources through which the requested service is provided. Examples include waitresses in a restaurant, window tellers in a fast food restaurant, bank tellers in a bank, doctors and nurses in a clinic, customs officers at a border-crossing terminal, receptionists in hotels, customer service representatives, and so on.
The capacity of service providers determines the service time (time a customer spends during service) and impacts the waiting time (time customers wait to get to the service providers). Thus, determining the best number of service providers is a key factor in designing service systems. Queuing theory in Operations Research (OR) is typically used to analyze the impact of different number of servers on service time and determine the optimum number of servers. However, not all assumptions are often met in real world applications in order to use the formulas of the queuing model. Simulation modeling, therefore, is often utilized to model the service system and analyze the impact of varying the number of service providers on key system performance measures (KPIs) such as throughput, customer waiting time, and servers' utilization.

2.1.3 Customer Service

Most service systems include a mean for customer service through which complaints and feedback from customers are received and analyzed. Free of charge telephone numbers, centers of customer service, and though website customer feedback, are common forms of customer service in service systems. In retail stores, customer service allows shoppers to return or replace merchandise, help customer find merchandise, and allows for reporting concerns directly to store management.
The role of customer service is crucial to provide high quality products and services to customers, establish a direct/indirect relationship with customers, retain customers, and gain their trust. A service system with no customer service is similar to an open-loop control system where no feedback signal is fed back into the system controller to adjust its operation. As a result, valuable customer notes and complaints are wasted, service operations are not enhanced to meet customers' expectations, and consequently some unsatisfied customers will eventually look for service at another place, typically the competition.

2.1.4 Staff and Human Resources

Staff, business managers, and customer service associates are key building block that can greatly contribute to the success or failure of a service system. Most service systems rely on humans for providing services. For example, no matter how sophisticated and powerful hospital equipment get, hospital doctors and nurses will play the major role in providing medical services. Similarly, we can understand the role of bank tellers, calling officers, and receptionists. Some of those are direct service providers in the front office and some work in the back office.

2.1.5 Service Facility

The layout and the physical structure of the service facility have a special importance in service systems. Designing the facility layout in an effective manner that assists both service providers and customers is often critical to the performance of the service system. Certain safety and operational requirements and construction codes are essential to be met when designing the service facility. Examples include the parking lot, handicapped parking, waiting areas, location of reception and help desks, layout and structure of service areas/station, male and female rest rooms space and capacity, and facility environment such as illumination, air condition, insulation, and heat.

Building codes and standards that are compliant to regulations of cities and provinces provide the specific requirements of service facilities. Such requirements vary based on the service nature. For example, what is required for a gas station and oil change facilities is different from that of banks and restaurants. The interior design of the facility (each area's capacity and features), the organization of the place layout (interdepartmental relationships) and the physical structure of the facility (material and flow of service in the facility) is a combination of art and design, regulations, and business needs.

2.1.6 Operating Policy

Operating policies are also critical component in any service systems. Operation pattern (opening and closing hours), routing customers, flow of each service, queue and service discipline, and departure rules are examples of operating policies. This also extends to what is allowed and not allowed within the facility or during the service, dress code, and accessibility.

2.2 Characteristics of Service Systems

There are several business characteristics that are unique to service systems. One key characteristic of service systems is dealing directly/indirectly with customers. As mentioned earlier, service systems entities are mostly humans or human requests. This requires that the service system to be flexible and agile in order to accommodate varying customer demands and desires. Consequently, service systems are characterized by being highly impacted with customer behavior and the level of customer service. In addition, service operations often involve high variability due to varying customer needs and requests. Providing the service may also require making complex decisions that balance customer service and business interest.

Comparing services to tangible products can help in understanding the nature of service systems. Unlike manufacturing facilities where customers are not directly involved in the process, service systems involve direct interaction with customers to provide them with intangible services or to sell customers tangible products. The performance of systems offering customers intangible services/products can be expressed in terms of effectiveness, presentation, reliability, and cost. For tangible products we often ask questions about the following:

- Effectiveness: Does the product do its job well?
- Presentation: Does the product look good?
- Reliability: Is the product trouble free?
- Cost: Is the product reasonably priced?

Services are, on the other hand, are slightly different from physical products. For services, we often ask questions differently but on the same quality aspects:

- Effectiveness: Am I getting the right service?
- Presentation: Am I getting the service in a way that appeals to me?
- Reliability: Am I getting the service on time or within acceptable time?
- Cost: Are the service fees reasonable?

In general, the key aspects of service quality often include the following:

- Tangibles: Facility, location, office, etc.
- Convenience: Proximity, parking, services, etc.
- Reliability: Availability, trust, safety, etc.
- Flexibility: Responsiveness, operating pattern, order fulfillment, etc.
- Time: Waiting, processing, schedule, etc.
- Assurance: System, feedback, control, etc.
- Courtesy: Friendliness, smile, experience, etc.

In terms of the process, the flow of services may not be structured such as the case in a manufacturing process. The service specifications may not be also quantified and consistent such as the case in products. This reflects on developing the sequence and the logic of service industry as well as on selecting the Key Performance Indicators (KPIs) to assess and improve the performance of service systems. The amount of variability involved in service operations is higher than that of manufacturing processes. Human performance and effectiveness is different from those of machines and automated assembly lines.

3. Modeling Service Systems

"How to model a service system?" is a question that is frequently asked by simulation analysts. This concern often results from the difficulties modelers have in structuring a service system and in developing a model that accurately resembles the defined structure and logic. This section presents the basic techniques that can be utilized to model service systems.

A generic step-by-step simulation processes such as the one discussed in earlier chapters can be used to simulate service systems as well as other systems. However, experience in modeling service systems often lead to certain modeling considerations that are particularly important to capture the unique characteristics of service systems. Given the discussed elements of service systems, certain set of modeling elements can be used to model service systems. Along with that, and by analyzing the structure of the underlined service system, certain set of model control factors and performance measures can be defined and used to design experiments and optimize the settings of service systems.

3.1 Modeling Considerations

Because of the unique characteristics of service systems, it is typically difficult to prescribe a specific modeling technique to simulate service systems. Instead, the simulation process is adapted to the specifics of the underlying service system. In general, it is recommended to model the service system as a manufacturing system that involves complex manual operations of high variability. Special attention is paid to the sequence and the content of each service process within the system. Certain modeling assumptions are then made to approximate the functionality of these service operations. A generic model of a service system is shown in Figure 2. Similar to queuing models, a model of a service system often involves an arriving process, a waiting discipline, a service process, and a departure process.

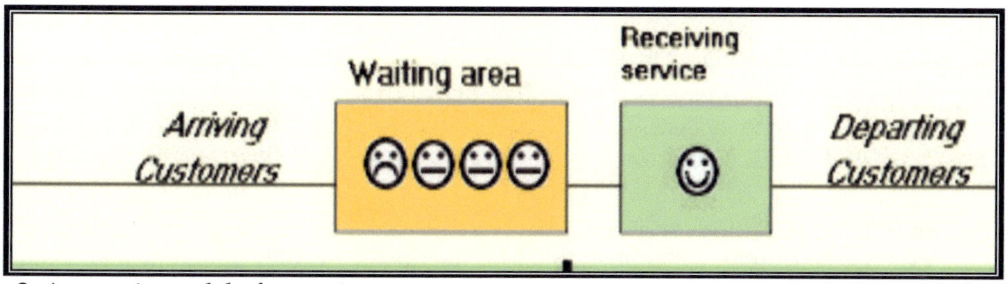

Fig. 2. A generic model of a service system

The following set of modeling considerations can help in simulating service systems:

1- Entities arrival to service system is random which can be considered a Poisson process. This does not apply to scheduled services such as doctor appointment and legal consultations. With the Poisson process assumption, entities inter-arrival time (t) is considered to be exponentially distributed with a Mean Time Between Arrival (MTBA) of $1/\lambda$ where λ is the arrival rate of entities (for example, customers per unit time). The number of entities who arrive within the specified time interval is a random variable that follows Poisson distribution with mean arrival rate of λ = 1/MTBA. In the simulation study, the entities' arrival process is observed and collected data (inter-arrival times) is used to estimate the distribution parameter (i.e., MTBA). Other standard and empirical probability distributions can be fit to collected data. However, based on experience, the random arrival of customers to many service systems such as banks, clinics, and restaurants follows the Poisson process is a good approximation. In some cases, certain limit can be put on the number of entities arriving to the system such as in paperwork processing and in orders made to copying centers.

2- Customer waiting time before reaching the service provider is collected from the model. Modeler needs to specify each queue's size and discipline. Model logic can be used to route customers, control their waiting pattern, and provide priority rules for processing. The size of waiting lines is determined based on facility features such as number of available seats, number of vehicles that can fit in drive-thru lane, and so on. With systems of limited capacity, the number of customers who left without service need to be recorded. In some cases, infinite system capacity can be assumed to focus the study on the performance of the service system.

3- Based on the nature of the service provided, service time is typically random. Data is collected on processing time using automatic or manual means. Since human-based services are mostly manual, motion and time studies can be used to record observations and estimate the service time considering human allowances. Observed service time can be approximated using standard probability distributions. In queuing system, an exponential distribution of service time with a Mean Service Time (MST) is assumed in order to apply the formulas of the queuing model. The service rate (μ) is then defined as $\mu = 1/MST$. In simulation, there is no need to be restricted to exponential distribution. The number of servers (s) and the service strategy highly impact the service and waiting times. The model logic can be used to implement service rules and the structure servers (serial or parallel, for example).
4- The flow of entities and customers between different types of services (if applicable) is implemented using the logical design of the business process in the modeled service system. Complex or simple decisions are often made during the flow of entities. For example, the process of applying for a loan at a mortgage company may include several steps before deciding to approve or decline the loan approved. Similarly, when a patient is admitted to a hospital, he/she may be exposed to different diagnostics before the doctor decides on the proper treatment of the patient.
5- The departure of customers or entities from the system may require some processing such as when a patient is released from a hospital or a clinic. Such rules also need to be considered in modeling the service system.

3.2 Model Elements

The structural components of a service system discrete-event simulation model typically include:

- Model entities: customers, requests, and orders.
- Model activities: Steps for processing customers and their orders/requests.
- Model resources: Service providers, labor, machines, etc.
- Model layout: Service departments, locations, areas, etc.

Other non-structural elements include model logic, a Random Number Generator (RNG), run controls, model data, variables (system state variables and global variables), statistics collectors, and a schedule/ a calendar. Once the components are known one could construct a model easily.

In general, elements of a service system model often include the following:

1- The structure of the service system including facility layout, departments, and locations of servers and waiting areas.
2- Entities/customer's arrival process. Empirical distribution or standard probability distribution can be used to model the arrival process.
3- One or more waiting lines in front of service providers. Queues size, discipline, and routing logic are modeled.
4- A service providing method that can be manual or automatic. Labor resources and/or automated operations can/ be used to model the service. Empirical distribution or standard probability distribution can be used to model the service time.

5- Logical design of flow between multiple servers along with decision-making process at decision points within the flow.
6- A departure process along with departure rules.
7- Statistics collections methods using counters, tallies, and customized code.

3.3 Model logic

Model logic controls the flow of entities through model activities, enforces the service rules and policies, and specifies the nature of services provided to customers. For example, the logic of a healthcare clinic model should capture the rules for classifying, scheduling, and admitting different types of patients. It also specifies policies such as overbooking, accepting walk-in patients, and cancellation. The logic also controls the flow of patients through clinic activities/departments from admission to release and specifies treatment rules, times, and resources.

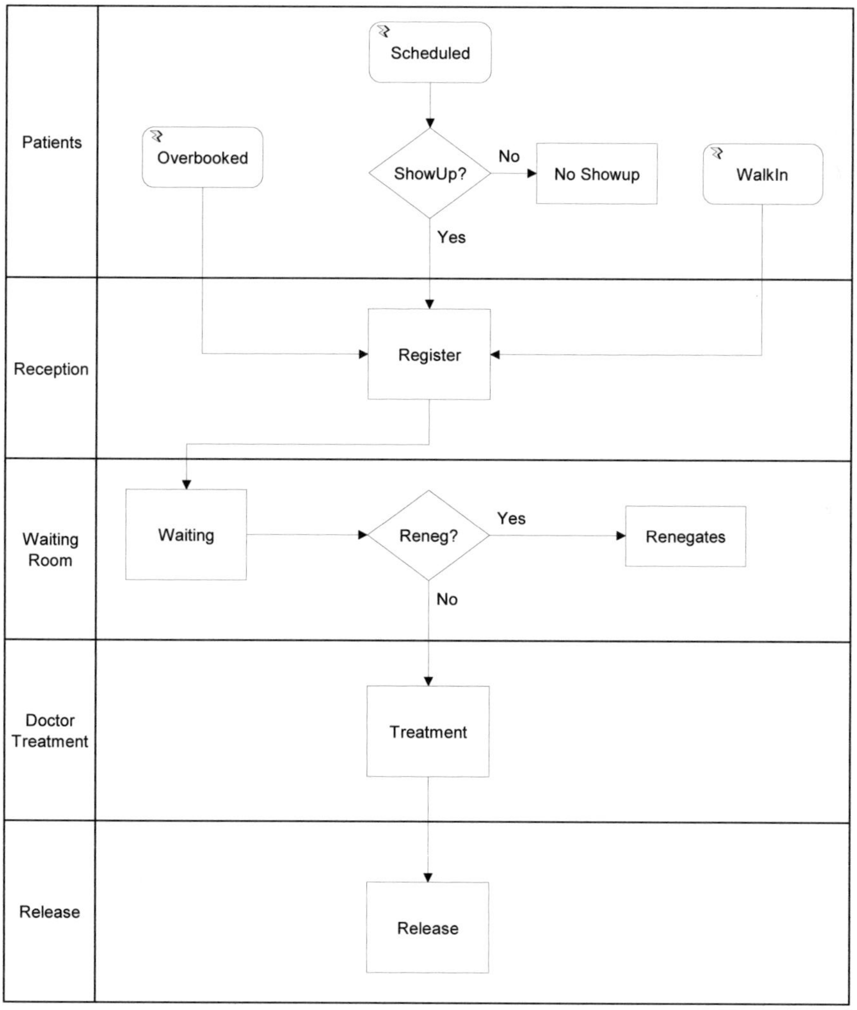

Fig. 3. An example of a healthcare clinic logic flow chart

Process maps, block diagrams, and flow charts are typically used to develop a conceptual model of the logic. Figure 3 shows an example flow chart that depicts the logic of a healthcare clinic model. The flow chart shows service phases (swim lanes), service inputs/outputs, start/finish, service sequence and flow, and decision points. Once ready, the flow chart is used to develop the clinic simulation model.

3.4 Model Data

Service systems such as banks, clinics, and restaurants require data on customer arrival, availability of resources, service times, size of waiting rooms, and so on. Examples of data requirements for a healthcare clinic simulation model can be, but not limited to:

- Patients schedule
- Patients admission and release time
- Size of waiting room
- Treatment time
- Allocation of nurses and doctors
- Operation time and reliability of X-Ray machines
- Clinic working hours

As discussed earlier, a key skill of model building is data collection where the analyst determines model data requirements and collects data. The following are proposed guidelines to properly determine model data requirements:

- Be clear on simulation objectives and deliverables.
- Understand the details of the service process.
- Specify the model measures of performance (KPIs)
- Develop a representative conceptual model
- Review similar/benchmark models
- Explore available data
- Be familiar with the specific requirements of the simulation software

3.4.1 Collecting inter-arrival and service times

Arrival and service rates are critical to model service systems such as banks, call centers, and restaurants. Arrival rates and service rates are essential to calculate system performance measures such as average waiting time, utilization, and average time in system. A simple table (Table 1) can be used to collect the arrival and service rates. For example, for customers arriving at a service center, the following form (showing the data for 20 customers only) can be used:

Customer number	Arrival time	Time since last arrival (TBA)	Service start time	Service end time	Service time (ST)
001	8:05	5 min	8:05	8:12	7 min
002	8:07	2 min	8:12	8:25	13 min
...					
020					
Sum	---	500 min	---	---	420 min

Table 1. A form for collecting inter-arrival and service times

For each customer, we record the times of arrival, service start, and service end (departure time). Using these times, we can calculate Time Between Arrivals (TBA) and service time (ST). The third and sixth columns are then averaged out to determine Mean Time Between Arrivals (MTBA) and Mean Service Time (MST), respectively. In this example, these values are calculated as follows:

MTBA = 500/20 = 25 min. and Arrival rate = 2.40 customers/hr
MST = 420/20 = 21 min. and Service rate = 2.86 customer/min

The entities arrivals can be modeled using distributions with mean values of MTBA and MST.

3.4.2 Collecting data for a call center

In cases where data collection is time consuming and costly, the data collection form should be designed to collect only relevant data at lowest cost and effort possible. For example, the "call time" is a key element when collecting data to model a customer service call center. Call centers typically receive calls for different purposes and at different times. These calls are answered by associates of different level of experience. For example, if a call center receives 4 types of calls (Complaint, Service, Payment, and Information). These calls are answered by operators of a 3-level experience ("A" less than three months, "B" three months to a year, and "C" more than one year) working three shifts (Morning, Afternoon, and Evening). This setup results in 4x3x3=36 combinations. If a sample size of 10 is used at each combination, a total of 360 call times is collected. A simple form (Table 2) can be used for collecting calls time.

Call No.	Call Type	Call Time	Operator Level	Call duration (sec)
1	Complaint	AM	B	163
2	Service	PM	A	120
...	Payment	AM	B	215
360	Information	EV	C	55

Table 2. A form for collecting data for a call center

3.5 Model parameters and decision variables

Model control factors include the parameters that can be set and changed by the service system designer in order to enhance the system performance. In general the service system design is in control of the entities acceptance/admission to system, entities waiting and classification rules, the service providing process, the logic of entities flow between servers, and the rules of system departure. Entities arrival rate to the system is typically not within the control of system designers. Adjusting such processes may be translated into providing settings of key model control factors such as:

1- Percent or rate of admitted entities to the service system.
2- Capacity of waiting area or line.
3- Waiting discipline and rules of selecting customers to receive service. First Come First Served (FCFS) is the most common waiting discipline in service systems. A preemptive method can be also used to expedite or select customers to service.

4- Number of servers in the service system and their configuration.
5- Service time at each server.
6- Percentages used to route entities flow among servers.
7- Rules of system departure (if applicable).

Other model control factors include the set of decision variables that needs to be optimized in order to enhance the system performance. These include service prices, inventory levels, staffing level, and so on.

3.6 Model performance measures

A set of measures can be used to assess the performance of a service system as well as to compare performance of several system designs. Quantified performance measures should be used to assess the service system performance. Such measures can be estimated from model accumulated statistics or special code may be necessary to compute the measures values. Examples of services performance measures include:
1- Average waiting time per customer.
2- Number of customers left without receiving the service (in case no capacity or the waiting time was too long).
3- Time-in-system: The total time a customer spends in the service system (this includes waiting time, transfer time, and service time).
4- Average and maximum size of the queue (length of waiting line).
5- Servers utilization (percent idle and percent busy).
6- Service system throughput (number of processed entities per time unit such as number of served customers per day).
7- Service level (number of customers who finished the service without waiting or only with less than 5 minutes of waiting time).
8- Service cost
9- Percent of satisfied customers

4. Example of a Single-Server simulation

The single-server queues are, perhaps, the most commonly encountered queuing lines in service systems. Examples include business (e.g. sales clerk), industry (e.g. a production line), transport (e.g. a bus, a taxi rank, an intersection), telecommunications (e.g. Telephone line), computing (e.g. processor sharing). Even where there are multiple servers in the service system, it is possible to consider each server individually as part of the larger system (e.g. a supermarket checkout has several single-server queues that the customer can select from.) Consequently, being able to model and analyze a single-server queue is a particularly important in simulating service systems. Figure 4 shows a conceptual model of a single-server system with arrival rate (λ) and service rate (μ).

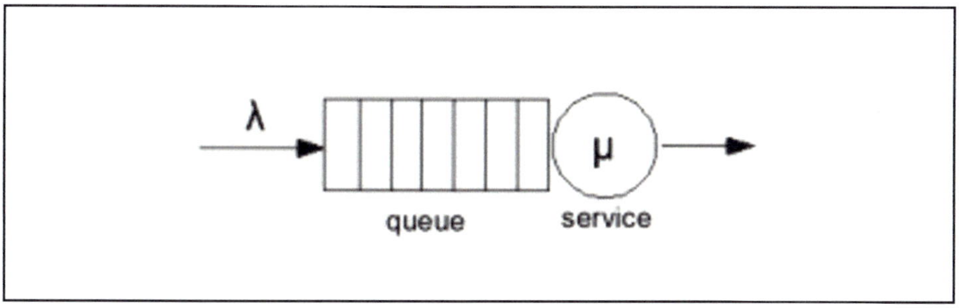

Fig. 4. A single-server model

As shown in Figure 5, the logic for a simple single server model can be presented using two flow charts; an arrival event and a departure event. The arrival event is executed based on the server status "busy or idle" and the departure event is executed based on the queue status "empty or full".

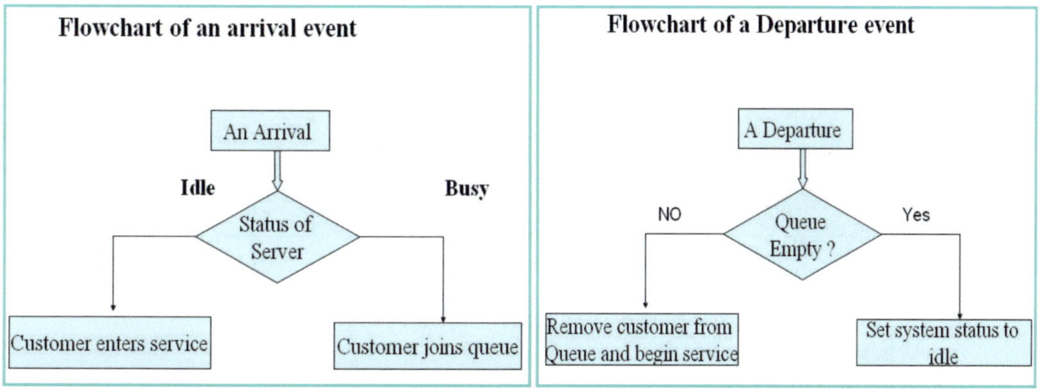

Fig. 5. The logic of a single-server model

Two data elements are required to model the single server; an arrival rate (λ) and a service rate (μ). To this end, the inter-arrival times and service times for 100 customers are collected. The mean inter-arrival time (MIAT) also known as Mean Time Between Arrivals (MTBA) for the 100 customers is found to be 3 minutes and the Mean Service Time (MST) is 2 minutes. Thus, the arrival rate (λ) and service rate (μ) are determined as follows:

$$\lambda = 1/\text{MIAT} = 1/3 \text{ customer/minute} = 20 \text{ customer/hr}$$
$$\mu = 1/\text{MST} = 1/2 \text{ customer/minute} = 30 \text{ customer/hr}$$

The simple single server simulation model can be then easily built based on the conceptual model in Figure 4, given the model logic in Figure 5, and using collected data (λ and μ values). In this example, ARENA™ simulation software is used to build the model. ARENA is one of the world's leading simulation software has been used successfully by organizations the world over to advance the efficiency and productivity of their business. Arena is designed to provide the power required for successful simulation within an easy-to-use modeling environment. With an animated Arena simulation model, we can design a new service facility or make changes to an existing one, and try different service scenarios

before we commit capital and resources. We can also compare operational strategies based on performance and confidently select the best one for implementation. Simulation results can be communicate to all parties concerned with the success of the project (from the management team who sign off on the decision, through to the general labor) and show all how the service system will function and specify the critical practical implications to consider in system implementation.
For our single-server model, the ARENA simulation model is show in Figure 6. As discussed earlier, the model comprises three main processes; an arrival process, a service process, and a departure process. The model is set to run for 8 hours per day as an example of terminating simulation.

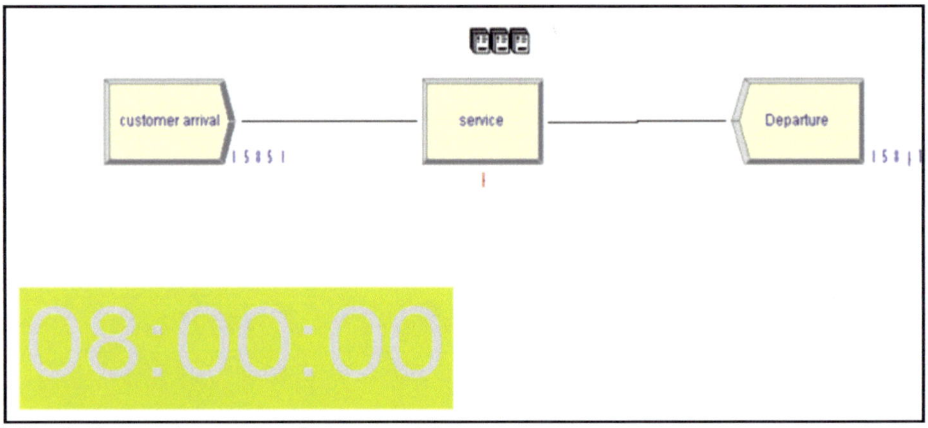

Fig. 6. Single Server Arena simulation model

Five KPIs are used to assess the performance of the single server model:
- Avg. waiting time (Wq)
- Avg. time in service system (W)
- Avg. number of customers in queue (Lq)
- Avg. number of customers in system (L)
- Server utilization (U)

Due to simplicity, these KPIs can be determined using queuing formulas. The single-server (M/M/1) queuing model formulas for the five KPIs are as follows:

$$L = \frac{\lambda}{\mu - \lambda} \qquad W = \frac{1}{\mu - \lambda},$$

$$Lq = \frac{\lambda^2}{\mu[\mu - \lambda]} \qquad W_q = \frac{\lambda}{\mu[\mu - \lambda]} \qquad U = \lambda/\mu$$

The following are the results of applying the queuing formulas to our single-server example:
- Avg. waiting time (Wq) = 0.067 hr = 4 minutes
- Avg. time in system (W) = 0.010 hr = 6 minutes
- Avg. number of customers in queue (Lq) = 1.333 customers
- Avg. number of customers in system (L) = 2 customers
- Server utilization (U) = 0.667

The simulation results for the 5 KPIs are as follows:

- Average waiting time in the queue = 4.07 min
- Average spent in service system = 6.08 min
- Avg. number of customers in queue = 1.28 customers
- Avg. number of customers in system = 2.02 customers
- Utilization = 0.66 or 66%

5. Simulation applications in Service Systems

Wide range of simulation applications can be used in service systems. These applications range from the design of new service facility to solving performance problems in existing service systems. Section 6 provides some case studies of applying simulation in modeling typical service systems. Some of those applications include. Examples of industry sectors that benefit from simulations studies in service systems include shipping companies, transportation, aviation, fast food, telecommunication, banking, and so on.

Planning the Service Facility

Simulation studies can be used to plan the facility of the service system. This includes designing the facility system, designing the layout of the service facility, and designing flow within the service facility. Different design alternatives can be evaluated using simulation based on the design implications on system performance.

Designing the Business Process

Modeling the business process in a service system includes modeling the way in which the service system receives orders, interacts with supplies, provides services, assures quality, receives payments from customers, and so on. Modeling the business process of service systems has become typically in the latest years especially with the applications of Business Process reengineering (BPR) methods.

Performance Improvement

Improving the performance of service systems is another key simulation application in this regard. Service systems may suffer from declining service levels, throughput, and utilizations of resources. They may also suffer from long waiting time and waiting lines and increasing loss in business opportunity. Simulation studies have been widely used to model the underlying system, analyze its performance, determining root causes of performance troubles, and propose solutions to the problems.

Decision Support

Because of the type of complex decisions that are often involved in business process of service systems, simulations studies are also used to act as a decision support system. Decision-makers can highly benefit from the model in making decisions. Model provides animation and statistics that can help decision makers draw inferences on model performance, compare alternatives, and select best-performing operating strategies.

Staffing and Scheduling
Since service systems are often operated by human, staffing human resource and scheduling their operating pattern is another simulation application in service systems. Examples include scheduling the work of nurses in hospital and deciding on best staffing level or chasing strategy. Staffing and scheduling is directly related to customer needs and demands.
Logistics and Supply Chain
Modeling the supply chain of a service system is also a typical simulation application. Supply Chain Management (SCM) in general includes scheduling supplies so that the service system needs are met and customer satisfaction is increased.

The following section presents three examples of simulating service systems. The objective is to show how our understanding of the nature of service system, the elements of service systems, and the service data and logic can be utilized in developing models that help in measuring performance, outlining problems, analyzing results, and improving performance.

5.1 Bank simulation example

The type of queuing system a business uses is an important factor in determining the business efficiency. This section presents an example of using simulation to assess the performance of a bank with multiple-channel queues. This type of queuing systems is commonly seen in banks and fast food restaurants. The bank model is used to simulate the queues and predict key statistics of queue length, waiting time, throughput, and time in system.
Main objectives of the bank simulation study include:

- Collecting data needed for building accurate model that is useful for taking improvement decisions.
- Using the model to analyze the behaviors of the existing system and predict its performance at various levels of input parameters (i.e., the arrival rate and service rate).
- Using the model to conduct "What-if" analysis and enhance performance

The bank receives customers and provides banking services between 8:00 AM - 5:00 PM five days a week. Each customer takes a numbered card upon arrival and waits for his/her number to be displayed on a digital screen. There are up to eleven servers in this bank (eight operate under normal conditions and three are utilized in peak times). Figure 7 shows the bank facility layout, the servers and service areas, and the queues at various types of banking services. As shown in Figure 7, the services provided to customer by the eight bank tellers in normal conditions are classified into four types:

- Service A: Cash (entrusting, checking, exchanging, etc.). Due to heavy demand for service A, 5 tellers are A-dedicated in normal conditions.
- Service B: Foreign currency (single server).
- Service C: Export exchanges (single server).
- Service D: Checkbooks and other services (single server).

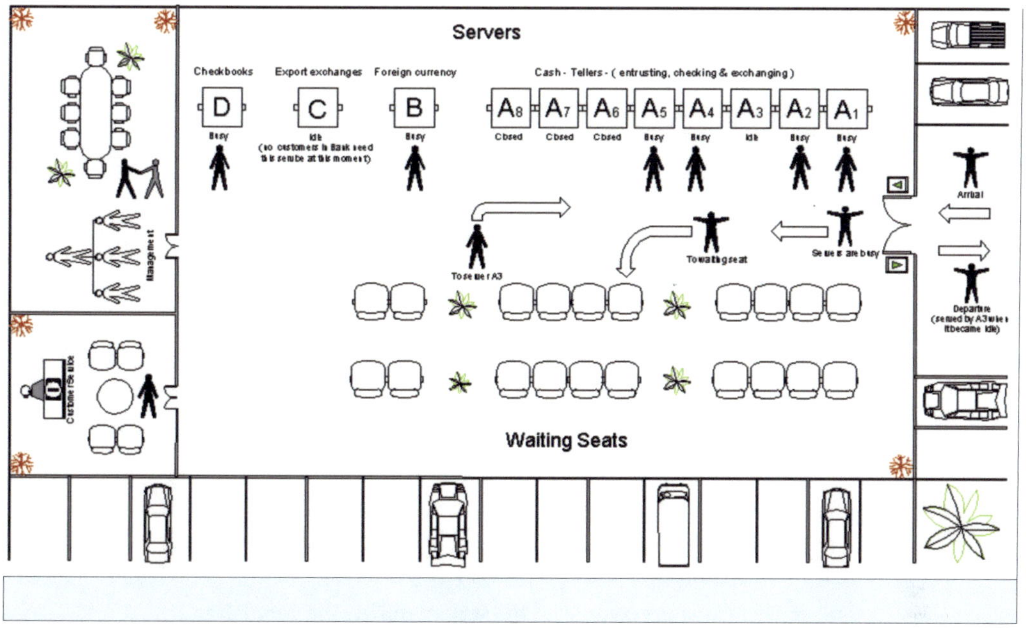

Fig. 7. Layout of the bank simulation example

The following assumptions are made in the development of the example DES bank model:

- Normal distribution of service time (the empirical data approximately satisfy the required conditions for this distribution).
- Exponential distribution of inter-arrival time (the empirical data approximately satisfy the required conditions for this distribution).
- No queue at the self-serve waiting card machine
- The model is focused on four customer stages: arriving, waiting at queue (if the required server is busy), receiving the service, and departure.
- No restriction on departure process or rerouting customers. Customers exit the bank immediately after completing their transactions.
- No warm-up period is used for the bank terminating simulation.
- Run time is 40 hours with 5 replications

The model data is collected and standard probability distributions are fitted to collected data. Table 3 shows the distributions and parameters used in the model in terms of MTBA and the parameters of the normal distributions of service times at each type of bank service.

Type	**Exponential Arrival process**	**Normal Service process**
Service A	MTBA =1.262 min	(μ = 4.983 min, σ = 0.980)
Service B	MTBA =11.190 min	(μ = 4.857 min, σ = 0.970)
Service C	MTBA =8.667 min	(μ = 5.185 min, σ = 0.862)
Service D	MTBA =18.000 min	(μ = 5.308 min, σ = 0.910)

Table 3. Standard distribution fitted to collected bank data

The following simulation elements are used in the example bank model:

- Entity: customers.
- Attribute: balance of customers checking accounts.
- Activity: making deposits or entrusting.
- State variables: number of busy servers, the number of customers being served or waiting in line.
- Exogenous event: the arrival of a customer.
- Endogenous event: completion of service of a customer.
- Queue: waiting lines or waiting seats.

Figure 8 summarizes the performance measures determined from the collected simulation statistics at each type of service provided by the bank example. The results indicate that most of customer demand is focused on service type A and an improvement plan is essential to be focused at service A in order to increase the number of served customers, reduce time in system, and increase customer satisfaction.

Service A

- A total of 724 customers requested the service per day.
- A total of **478** customers completed the service during the simulation.
- The average time a customer spends to get the service is **16.04 min**.
- The average number of customers requesting the service is 120.94.
- Average server utilization is 99.5% (4 servers)

Service B

- A total of 48 customers requested the service per day.
- A total of **48** customers completed the service during the simulation.
- The average time a customer spends to get the service is **7.88 min**.
- The average number of customers requesting the service is 0.79.
- Average server utilization is 47.6% (1 server)

Service C

- A total of 58 customers requested the service per day.
- A total of **57** customers completed the service during the simulation.
- The average time a customer spends to get the service is **9.77 min**.
- The average number of customers requesting the service is 1.14.
- Average server utilization is 61.2% (1 server)

Service D

- A total of 27 customers requested the service per day.
- A total of **27** customers completed the service during the simulation.
- The average time a customer spends to get the service is **6.02 min**.
- The average number of customers requesting the service is 0.34.
- Average server utilization is 29.3% (1 server)

Fig. 8. Summary of performance measure at different bank services

Model output analysis can highly benefit from the numerous statistics generated from simulation. Several scenarios and what-if-analysis can be tested and compared using the generated statistics.

6.2 Clinic simulation example

In this example, simulation is utilized to build a clinic model to assess proposed operational alternatives for maximizing the number of served patients while minimizing the patient's time-in-system. The example describes how DES mechanics are utilized to represent clinic elements and patients' flow and generate simulation data from relevant sampling distributions. A sample of model output analysis will be presented to demonstrate how the model provides answers to key questions relevant to clinic operation.

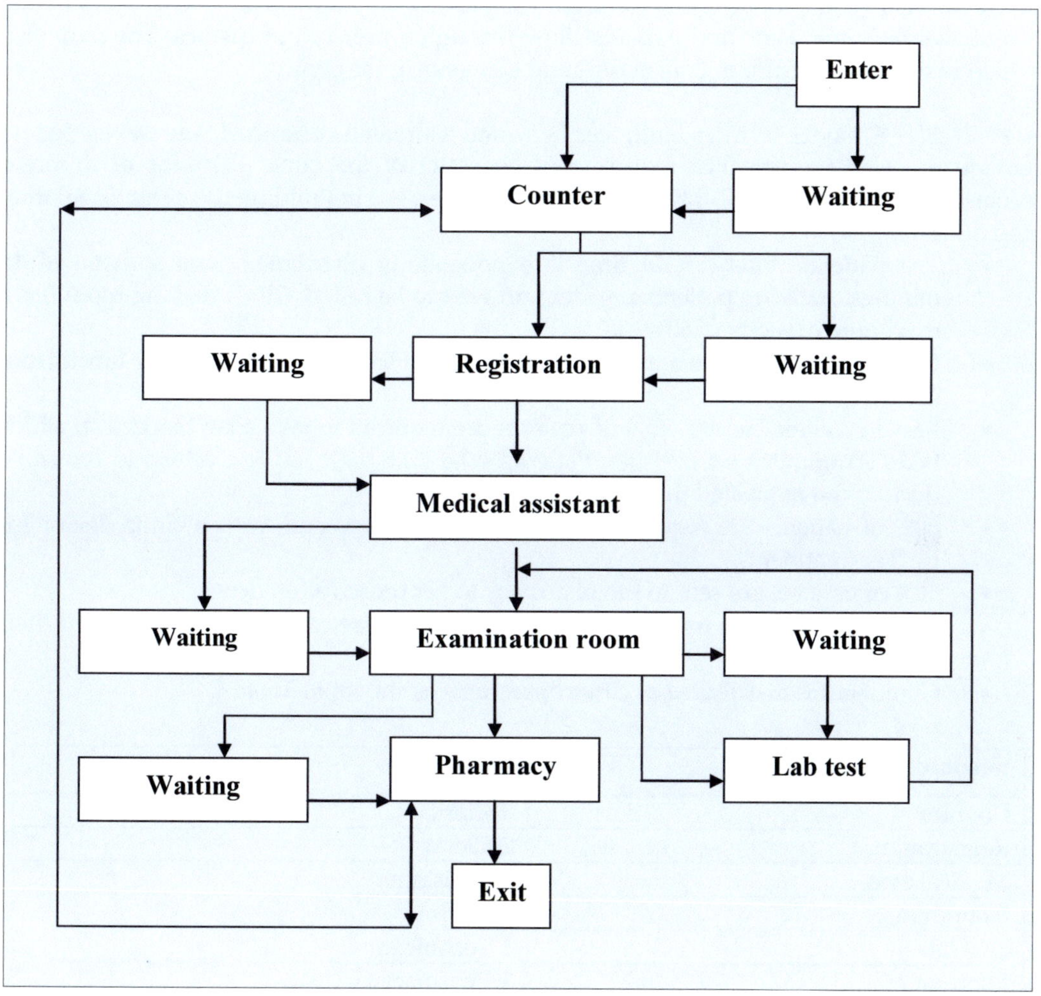

Fig. 9. A Process map of patients flow in the clinic example

The clinic consists of urgent care and acute care. Typically, most patients require acute care. Most of the urgent care patients are assessed by clinic doctors and sent to hospital. The clinic admits two types of patients; new patients (i.e. walk-ins) and returning patients (i.e. patients with appointments). Patients first arrive to the clinic's registration counter. If busy, they wait until its available, register, and wait for the medical assistant to admit them to the clinic. The medical assistant admits patients for initial checkup (blood pressure, temperature, etc.) and asks questions to assess each patient's case before they enter the examination room. The two physicians in the examination rooms diagnose patients, release them or direct them to lab test and pharmacy. If the patient is sent to the lab, he/she returns with lab results to the examination room to see the same doctor. Released patients leave the clinic through the registration counter.
Figure 9 shows a process map of the patients flow in the clinic. Patients' potential waiting points are also included in the process map. The process map represents a conceptual model that shows the clinic logic and patients' flow through a network of queues. The map also helped in collecting pertinent data at different elements in the clinic.

A WITNESS™ model is then built, verified, and validated. The model is developed to provide a set of performance metrics that characterize the clinic behavior at different scenarios of operation. The following assumptions are used in building the clinic simulation model:

- The patients' inter-arrival time is exponentially distributed with a mean of 15 minutes. Arriving patients register and wait to be called. Clinic waiting room has a maximum capacity of 50 seats.
- Clinic opens five days a week from 8:00 AM to 5:00 PM with one hour lunch from 12:00-1:00 PM.
- Based on clinic history, 25% of patients are required to take a lab blood test, which takes 25 minutes on average. Patients who take their lab test return to the same doctor who requested the lab test.
- 60% of patients are required to reschedule appointments with a clinic doctor for further treatment.
- 50% of patients are sent to the pharmacy to get prescription drugs.
- 15% of patients are treated by a clinic doctor and released from the clinic in their first visit.
- Clinic staff is distributed at clinic operations as shown in Table 4.

Resource	**Staff**
Counter	1 Clerk
Registration	2 Clerks
Medical care	2 Assistants
Examination	2 Doctors
Test lab	1 Technician
Pharmacy	1 Pharmacist

Table 4. Distribution of clinic staff

In order to model the variable times of clinic operations, standard distributions are fitted to collected simulation data. Table 5 summarizes the sampling distributions used in the clinic model.

Process	Patient type	Distribution
Arrival	All patients	Exponential (15 min)
Counter	Just entering clinic To be released from clinic	Uniform (0.6,1.2) min Exponential (4 min)
Registration	New and walk-ins Returning	Uniform (1.5,3.5) min Uniform (0.5,2.0) min
Medical assistant	Taking blood pressure Checking temperature Questionnaire	Normal (60, 5) sec Normal (60, 5) sec Triangular (2,4,10) min
Examination	All patients Returning from lab test	Triangular (10,15,40) min Triangular (4,6,10) min
Lab test	Performing blood test	Normal (25, 3) min
pharmacy	First time Returning	Triangular (1.6, 4, 8) min Triangular (1, 3, 5) min

Table 5. Sampling distributions in the clinic example

The clinic model involves a process for creating and directing the flow of two types of patients (Walk-Ins and Scheduled). Queues and Resources are then used to construct the clinic model. Syntax is written to direct patient flow and control the interactions among clinic operations.

Model Statistics and Confidence Interval:

The clinic model is an example of terminating simulation. The model is set to run 5 replications each of 5 days run length (8 hours/day) with no warm-up or initial conditions. Averages of the following clinic performance measures are generated from the model:

Average time patients spend in the clinic = **84.62 min**
Average treatment time (initial checkup and examination) = **56.1 min**
Average waiting time (at all stages) = **28.52 min**
Number of patients treated daily = **27 patients**

For each clinic performance measure, a set of descriptive statistics are also produced along with the half-width (*hw*) confidence intervals of 95% level of confidence. For example, if the waiting time in the clinic is a major concern to patients, the following statistics are collected:

Average	Std. Deviation	Min	Max	*hw*
28.52	3.81	14.50	42.00	±4.71

Model outputs indicate that the patient's waiting time can range from 14.5 min to 42.0 min with an average of 28.52 min. If we collect more samples and record the waiting time for the patients population, we can be 95% sure that the population mean is within 23.80 min to 33.34 min. This interval estimate can be more meaningful than the 28.52 min point estimate. For example, if the mean of the actual waiting time is turned to be 30 min, model results are still valid since this mean is within the established confidence interval.

Model Validation:

If records of these clinic performance measures are available, that data can be also used to statistically validate the simulation model. To this end, hypothesis testing can be used to test if the mean of any model-reported clinic performance measure matches that of the real-world historical mean. The collected sample of the 5 simulation replications can be used to reject or fail to reject the selected null hypothesis. For example, to test if the model produces a mean of 25 for the daily treated patients, the null hypothesis is set to H_0: $\mu = 25$ and the alternative hypothesis is set to H_a: $\mu \neq 25$. If we fail to reject the null hypothesis, then there is no enough evidence to believe that model is invalid. Similarly, if the actual mean waiting time is 30 min, H_0: $\mu = 30$ min, H_a: $\mu \neq 30$ min, $t_0 = -0.87$, and $t_{0.025, 4} = 2.77$. Since $|t_0| < t_{\alpha/2, n-1}$, we cannot reject the null hypothesis and we conclude that there is no sufficient evidence to believe that the model is invalid.

Comparing Simulation Scenarios:

Based on the model-reported results, the patient examination process was found to contribute to the major delay in the clinic. Examination process takes on average 42.90 min (i.e., waiting time of 20.97 minutes and treatment time of 21.93 minutes). The two clinic examination physicians are utilized as follows: 93.6% and 89.5%. This relatively high utilization explains why patients frequently complain of doctors pressured to complete treatment quickly.

The model is, therefore, used to reduce patients' waiting time and to increase treatment time without reducing the number of daily treated patients. To this end, a what-if scenario is suggested to remove one of the registration clerks due to reduced utilization and to add one examination physician due to the relatively high utilization. The analyst used the WITNESS Experiment module to set the two situations (scenarios) for the current (baseline scenario 1) and the proposed changes in clinic resources (scenario 2). Table 6 summarizes the results obtained from running the model experiments at the two scenarios of clinic operation. Results are expressed in terms of the four defined performance measures:

Performance measure	**Scenario1**	**Scenario2**
Average time in clinic	84.62 min	74.30
Average treatment time	56.10 min	60.12
Average waiting time	28.52 min	14.18
Number of daily patients	27	32

Table 6. Comparison of two clinic scenarios

It's clear from the results that Scenario 2 is better than Scenario 1 at all aspects. The proposed clinic changes have reduced the average of time spent in the clinic and increased treatment time. The reduction is mainly achieved in waiting time not in treatment time. This allows physicians to spend more time with patients without compromising the schedule. Increasing the physicians also allowed the clinic to admit more walk-in patients which resulted in increasing the total number of patients treated daily to an average of 32. The average utilization of the three physicians is reduced to an average of 75% (i.e., 74.8%, 75.5%, and 73.4%). The proposed clinic changes are validated with subject matter experts and recommended for implementation. Improvement was also justified with a cost-benefit analysis.

To compare scenarios based on waiting time, the following statistics are collected for waiting time at Scenario 2:

Average	Std. Deviation	Min	Max	*hw*
14.16	1.75	10.65	18.05	±2.17

It can be concluded from the results that Scenario 2 is better than Scenario 1 since it leads to lower average waiting time with less variability in terms of lower Std. Dev. and narrower confidence interval. Comparison analysis can be similarly conducted between the two scenarios at all clinic performance measures using the numeric and graphical descriptive statistics discussed earlier. To establish statistical evidence that Scenario 2 is superior compared to Scenario 1, we can test several hypothesis on the means and standard deviations of the four performance measures in Table 9.9. Using the procedure discussed earlier for the waiting time, null hypotheses can be set to indicate that means of waiting time at the two scenarios are equal (H_0: $\mu_1 = \mu_2$) and the alternative hypothesis to H_0: $\mu_1 > \mu_2$. The test statistic is $t_0 = 7.63$ and the critical value is $t_{0.05, 8} = 1.86$. Since $t_0 > t_{\alpha,v}$, we reject the null hypothesis and conclude that there is sufficient evidence to believe that Scenario 2 has less mean of waiting time.

7. References

Introduction to Operations Research, 9th edition, Hillier, F.S., McGraw-Hill Higher Education (2009).

Computer Simulation in Management Science, 5th edition, Pidd, M., Wiley (2005).

System Modeling and Simulation: An Introduction, Severance, F.L., Wiley (2001).

Principles of Modeling and Simulation: A Multidisciplinary Approach, Sokolowski, J.A. and Banks, C.M., Wiley (2009).

Simulation Modeling and Analysis (4th edition), Law, A., McGraw-Hill College (2006).

Discrete-Event System Simulation (3rd edition). Nelson, B.L., Banks, J., Carson, J.S., and Nicol, D.M., Prentice Hal (2006).

Business Modeling and Simulation, Oaksholt, L., Pitman Publishing, London (1997).

Towards Service oriented Simulations, Gustavsson, P. M., Björk, Å., Brax, C., and Planstedt, P., FallSIW 04, Orlando, Florida, 2004.

Simulation Modelling for Business, Andrew Greasley, Ashgate Publishing Limited; illustrated edition (2003).

Simulation: Modeling Manufacturing and Service Systems, Institute of Industrial Engineers (1988).

Using Process Mapping and Business Process Simulation to Support a Process-Based Approach to change in a Public Sector Organization, Greasley, A., *Technovation*, 26: 95-103 (2006).

Simulation-Animation: Improving service Systems, Villarreal, D., Annual Quality Congress, 49(0); 661-666, ASQC (1995).

Simulation modeling: A powerful tool for process improvement, Boxerman, S.B., *Best Practices and Benchmarking in Healthcare*, 1:109–117 (1996).

Handbook of Simulation; Principles, Methodology, Advances, Applications, and Practice, Banks, J. (editor), Wiley (1998).

Application of discrete-event simulation in health care clinics: A survey, Jun, J., Jacobson, S. and Swisher, J., *Journal of the Operational Research Society*, 50: 109–123 (1999).
Simulation-Based Lean Six-Sigma and Design for Six-Sigma, El-Haik, B. and Al-Aomar, R., Wiley (2006).
Simulation with Arena with CD, 4th edition, Kelton, W., McGraw-Hill Series in Industrial Engineering and Management (2006).
Modeling Emergency Service Centers with Simulation and System Dynamics, Ying Su, Xiaodong Huang, Zhanming Jin, 11th International Conference on Computer Modelling and Simulation, 305-310, UKSim (2009).
ARENA simulation software (http://www.rockwell.com). Rockwell (2009).
WITNESS simulation software (http://www.lanner.com). Lanner Group (2008).

9

Evaluation of methods for scheduling clinic appointments in surgical service: a statecharts-based simulation study

Boris G. Sobolev[1], PhD, Victor Sanchez[2], MSc and Lisa Kuramoto[2], MSc
[1]*School of Population and Public Health, The University of British Columbia*
[2]*Centre for Clinical Epidemiology and Evaluation, Vancouver Coastal Health Research Institute*
Vancouver, Canada

1. Introduction

The management of outpatient consultations constitutes an important aspect of planning activities in surgical services (Vissers, 1979). The scheduling process used for clinic appointments determines the appointment date for any patient referred for consultation about an operation (Jun et al., 1999). Within a regional network of hospitals, a variety of methods may be used for scheduling surgical consultations, but a better understanding is needed of the implications of these different methods for access to elective surgery (Naylor, 1991).

Walshe and Rundall have argued that the paradigm of evidence-based medicine should be applied to health care management so that decisions about organizing, structuring, and delivering health services are based on practices that are known to be effective (Walshe & Rundall, 2001). Increasingly, health services research seeks to evaluate proposed changes in health systems. When feasible, intervention studies are used to compare existing and proposed approaches to management and policy (Ham et al., 2003). However, when organizational interventions are not feasible for ethical, economic, or other reasons, computer simulation provides an alternative method of quantifying the effects of proposed changes in the organization and management of health care delivery (Fone et al., 2003).

Previous studies have used analytical and simulation models to explore in detail the scheduling of appointments for outpatient services, and a comprehensive review of this literature has been published elsewhere (Cayirli & Veral, 2003). Applications of the simulation approach have included assessing the impact of alternative appointment schedules on waiting times in a specialty department (Harper & Gamlin, 2003), examining the capacity needed to reduce access times in outpatient departments (Elkhuizen et al., 2007), evaluating scheduling rules in terms of physicians' idle time when the type of patient requesting an appointment at a later time is unknown (Klassen & Rohleder, 1996; Klassen & Rohleder, 2004), comparing appointment systems for patients with different needs in a multifacility internal medicine department (Wijewickrama & Takakuwa, 2008), and assessing the impact of operating conditions on the performance of rules for scheduling appointments (Ho & Lau, 1999). Other authors have described the use of computer simulation to support decision-making in outpatient clinics (Erdem et al., 2002), to improve utilization of resources, and to reduce physicians' overtime (Westeneng, 2007).

Other investigators have established that the length of time a patient has to wait between referral and consultation depends not only on the method for scheduling appointments and the number and type of referrals, but also on the availability of surgeons for appointments, as these physicians may have administrative, educational, or research commitments in addition to their clinical practices (Harper & Gamlin, 2003; Meredith et al., 1999). Our previous analysis suggested that the clinic appointment system may influence the time between consultation and surgery; for example, pooling referrals, i.e., placing all patients on one appointment list and scheduling appointments with the first available surgeon, seemed to reduce the time to consultation but increased the time to surgery for patients with non-urgent needs (Vasilakis et al., 2007).

In surgical services where patients may see any one of a group of surgeons, directing patients to the shortest queue has long been considered a suitable alternative to the single-queue system of appointments (Edwards et al., 1994). Both of these systems differ in one important respect from the scheduling of appointments with specific surgeons as named in the referrals: any particular patient may have to see a surgeon other than the one who was recommended by the referring specialist. Similar to the argument that Murray and Berwick developed for the primary care setting (Murray & Berwick, 2003), adopting this appointment system in the surgical services setting would present the patient with a trade-off between the value of consulting with the surgeon recommended by the referring physician and the value of early consultation, which might not be with the surgeon originally recommended.

The purpose of this simulation study was to estimate the impact of methods for scheduling appointments for surgical consultation on the flow of patients from referral to consultation and from consultation to surgery in the context of cardiac surgical services. We compared three appointment systems (assigning patients to a pooled list, to individual lists for specific surgeons, and to the shortest list) in terms of the following performance measures: clearance time for appointment lists (Cottrell, 1980), time to clinic appointment for individual patients (Sobolev et al., 2008) and time to surgery (Sobolev & Kuramoto, 2008). In particular, we were interested in whether the shortest-queue system would reduce the average clearance time, whether it would increase the proportion of patients having appointments each week and whether it would increase the proportion of patients undergoing an operation from wait lists each week. We chose to focus on cardiac surgical care because this type of health care is well structured in terms of the activities involved and is thus amenable to study and improvement (Cohn & Edmunds, 2003).

In this study, we applied the results of a previous study in which we mapped the process of cardiac surgical care at a teaching hospital in British Columbia, Canada, where 650 open-heart surgeries were being performed annually (Sobolev et al., 2006). Three cardiac surgeons had admitting privileges at this hospital and used a shared clinic for outpatient consultations. In this setting, the availability of the surgeons for operations depended on their schedules for consultations, planned operations, on-call duties, and vacations. Sixteen consultation appointments, seven operating room slots for planned operations and eight for urgent cases were available each week; and emergency cases might cause the cancellation of planned operations.

To emphasize the designed nature of this simulation experiment, throughout the paper we have used the terminology suggested by Law, whereby experimental variables are called "experimental factors" and performance variables are called "experimental responses" (Law, 2007). We used performance measures derived from the experimental responses to assess the results of the simulation experiment.

2. Methods

2.1 Modeled activities of surgical care

We simulated the delivery of surgical care using a discrete-event model, which has been described elsewhere (Sobolev et al., 2008). Patient-level models are commonly used to simulate steps in service delivery and response pathways for individual patients (Jun et al., 1999; O'Hagan et al., 2007). Compared with analytical models, simulation models allow the investigator to take into account variations in demand on different weekdays and a realistic schedule for doctors' multiple activities (Elkhuizen et al., 2007). The use of simulations for evaluating health care policy is based on two premises: first, that simulated individual care paths represent the delivery of health services to a patient population and second, that simulation produces care paths that are likely under the policy in question (Sobolev & Kuramoto, 2005). Davies and Davies argued that discrete-event simulation is appropriate when patient entities pass through a series of managerial and clinical activities, and take part in multiple activities (Davies & Davies, 1995). As such, discrete-event models can avoid the unrealistic assumptions of analytical models (Harper & Gamlin, 2003; Sobolev et al., 2008).

In this study, the modeled processes encompassed the continuum of clinical and managerial activities in cardiac surgical care. The diagram in Figure 1 shows activities at preoperative, operative, and postoperative stages included in the simulation model. Table 1 provides further explanation of the modeled activities. Using the Statecharts language, we described the progress of individual patients through surgical care as a series of asynchronous updates in patient records. The updates were produced in response to events generated by parallel finite state machines representing concurrent clinical and managerial activities (Gruer et al., 1998). The Statecharts specifications of these activities were based on the process of cardiac surgical care at a tertiary care hospital in British Columbia, Canada (Vasilakis et al., 2007). The Appendix provides a more detailed description of the simulation approach, its underlying assumptions, and the values of the model parameters.

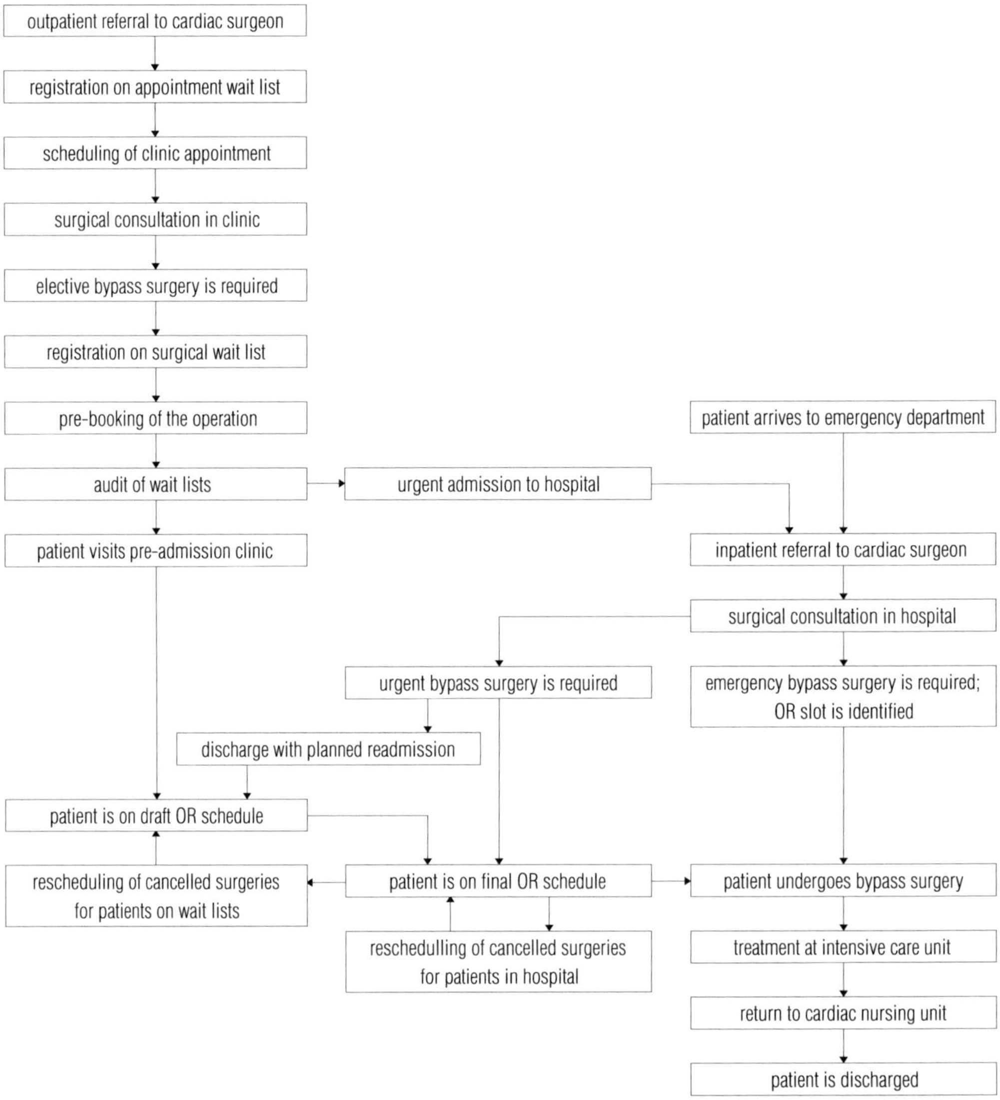

Fig. 1. Flow diagram of clinical and managerial activities included in the simulation model, modified from Sobolev & Kuramoto, 2008 [page 19]

We modeled three care paths that patients with established coronary artery disease are likely to experience, according to initial presentation and subsequent decisions leading to surgery: elective, inpatient, and emergency; these paths have been described in detail elsewhere (Sobolev et al., 2006). The elective path applies to patients for whom surgical consultation and subsequent operation can be safely delayed. The inpatient path applies to patients admitted to hospital from the catheterization laboratory when surgical assessment is urgently needed. The emergency path applies to patients requiring immediate surgical intervention.

Activity	Description
Referral of patients needing elective surgery for outpatient assessment	Patients presenting with symptoms are sent for consultation with surgeon in outpatient clinic
Registration of patients needing elective surgery on appointment list	Sex, age, coronary anatomy, and comorbidity of referred patients are recorded
Scheduling of patients needing elective surgery for consultation appointment	Dates of appointments are determined
Outpatient appointments for elective patients	Surgeon assesses indication for the procedure
Registration of patients needing elective surgery on surgical wait list	Details of patients who require and decide to undergo the operation are recorded
Prebooking of patients needing elective surgery for their operations	Committed dates of surgery within the upcoming 36-week period are determined
Referral of patients requiring urgent surgical consultation	Cardiologist refers patients for after assessment in hospital
In-hospital assessment of patients requiring urgent assessment	On-call surgeon determines patients' suitability for admission to hospital as inpatients
Registration of inpatients in surgical queue	Details are recorded for patients who must undergo the operation and who are admitted directly to hospital
Scheduling of operating time	Inpatients and patients awaiting elective surgery are identified, and hospital resources are reserved
Updating of operating room time	Final schedule for operating room is created
Arrival of emergency patients	Patients requiring emergency operation are sent for procedure
Cancellation of scheduled operations by emergency arrivals	Emergency patients requiring immediate operation replace previously scheduled patients in the operating room schedule
Cancellation of scheduled operations by inpatients	Inpatients requiring surgery replace previously scheduled patients in the operating room schedule
Rescheduling of cancelled procedures	Patients who are still waiting for operation after surgery was canceled are identified, and hospital resources are reserved
Surgical procedures	Operation is performed, during which time patients have access to operating room resources
Recovery in the cardiac surgery intensive care unit (CS-ICU)	Patients recover in the CS-ICU or in another hospital ICU if required
Discharge from hospital	Patients are prepared for postoperative care at home or in rehabilitation or community facilities
Audit of wait lists	Names of patients who die, became inpatients, or are admitted on an emergency basis while waiting for the operation are removed from surgical waiting lists
Unplanned emergency admissions	Patients whose condition deteriorates while waiting for the operation are admitted to hospital as emergency patients or inpatients
Allocation of appointment and theatre slots to surgeons	Appointment and theatre slots are allocated to surgeons according to duty rotation and vacation schedule for upcoming 18-week period

Table 1. Clinical and managerial activities included in the model

In our model, patients referred for consultation with a surgeon were kept on the appointment list with a designated priority (high or low) until an opening for a clinic appointment became available. In the case of individual appointment lists, consultations were scheduled with the surgeon named in the referral. This method ensured that the surgeon chosen by the referring physician assessed each patient. In the case of pooled appointment lists, consultations were scheduled with the first available surgeon (Vasilakis et al., 2007). In the case of the shortest appointment list, patients were placed on the appointment list of the surgeon with the fewest patients waiting. This method maintains an even distribution of patients among surgeons, while giving each surgeon an individual list of specific patients (Edwards et al., 1994).

After the consultation, the office of the consulting surgeon registered on his or her wait list patients who required coronary revascularization, designating the required procedure as high, medium, or low priority according to the affected coronary anatomy and the patient's symptoms. The hospital's booking office assigned patients to the operating room slots that had been allocated to the consulting surgeon according to their priority and date of registration on the wait list. As discussed elsewhere, we considered a situation in which the hospital's booking office prebooked each patient for the next available operating room slot allocated to the consulting surgeon for the upcoming 36-week period (Sobolev et al., 2008). In addition, we allowed patients who were prebooked for surgery to be admitted to the hospital as inpatients or emergency patients if their condition deteriorated before they underwent elective surgery (Sobolev et al., 2003).

A draft schedule for the operating rooms, listing procedures for planned procedures, was generated every Friday. The schedule was finalized the following Monday and could be subsequently changed to reflect the arrival of inpatients and emergency patients, as well as the availability of beds in the intensive care unit (ICU). The latter is an important constraint, because patients recover in the ICU after the operation, and the duration of stay in the ICU may vary among patients.

The availability of the three surgeons for operations and consultations was coordinated through their weekly schedules such that, in any given week, one surgeon was on call (assessing inpatients and performing urgent operations), one performed planned operations, and one conducted outpatient consultations. During weeks in which one surgeon was on vacation, the two remaining surgeons alternated on-call and planned duties, and no consultations were scheduled.

2.2 Experimental design

Rationale for study design

In the evaluation of health care services, there is recognition that hospital-level factors and policies may make the outcomes of patients served in the same hospital relatively similar (Ukoumunne et al., 1999). For the purpose of our study we were concerned that patient-level responses in a given simulation run might be correlated, because scheduling appointments involves complex decision-making at the level of the hospital. To address this concern, we used a cluster randomized design (Donner & Klar, 1994), according to which the simulation runs, rather than the simulated patient entities, were randomly assigned to the three study groups according to appointment system, as described elsewhere (Sobolev & Kuramoto, 2005).

Experimental factors

The experiment consisted of runs of the discrete-event simulation model with different algorithms for scheduling clinic appointments and different combinations of four additional hospital-level experimental factors likely to influence hospital operations: method of allocating operating room slots and the size of the queues for outpatient consultation, elective surgery, and inpatient surgery at the start of the simulation (Table 2). In addition, at entry into the simulation, patient entities were assigned patient-level factors that would influence their progress through the process of care: age, sex, coronary anatomy, comorbidity (i.e., coexisting medical conditions), and priority of elective referral (Davies & Davies, 1995). These patient-level factors were not controlled by the simulation design but rather were assigned randomly according to their frequency in the population of patients undergoing isolated coronary artery bypass surgery.

Experimental responses

Each run generated a group, or cluster, of patients served in a modeled hospital, the cluster size being determined by arrival and service rates and by simulation time. During each run of the simulation, the software recorded output data for the occurrence and timing of simulated events in the patient population, such as referrals, appointments, registrations, cancellations, and the operation itself, as well as unexpected emergency surgery and preoperative death, if such occurred (Table 2). In addition, the simulation records contained the following patient-level experimental responses: time on the appointment list, time on the surgical wait list, priority of registration for operation, and size of the surgical wait list at registration. The experimental response at the hospital level was the number of patients on the appointment list. The full list of output data produced in the simulation experiment is available from the authors on request.

Performance measures

Although ultimately intended to improve patient care, changes in the delivery of hospital care are generally implemented at the hospital level. Management alternatives, however, may be evaluated at either the hospital or the patient level. Hospital-level evaluations are used to compare the performance of hospitals in the study groups. Patient-level evaluations are used to compare the proportions of patients in the study groups with certain outcomes, for example, to determine whether pooling referrals increases the proportion of patients having a consultation each week.

Performance measures in our study were computed from experimental responses generated by the simulation runs. At the hospital level, the performance measure was clearance time for appointment lists, defined as the ratio of the appointment list census to clinic capacity (Cottrell, 1980). As such, the clearance time referred to a hypothetical time within which the list could be cleared if there were no new arrivals. The appointment list census was a count of patients on the appointment list at the end of a 6-week cycle. The clinic capacity was the weekly number of available appointments for that in the cycle. At the patient level, the performance measure was the weekly rate of clinic appointments and the weekly rate of surgery (Sobolev et al., 2008).

Study variables	Possible values
Experimental factors	
Method of scheduling clinic appointment	1 – assignment of patients to individual surgeons' lists
	2 – assignment of patients to one pooled list
	3 – assignment of patients to shortest list
Method of allocating operating room slots	1 – daily split between elective and urgent procedures
	2 – weekly split between elective and urgent procedures
Initial size of queue for outpatient consultation	16, 32, or 48 patients on appointment list
Initial size of queue for elective surgery	21, 28, 35, or 42 patients on surgical wait list
Initial size of queue for inpatient surgery	0, 8, or 16 patients awaiting surgery in hospital cardiac ward
Simulation output data[a]	
Referral date	date
Date of removal from appointment list	date
Reason for removal from appointment list	1 – received appointment
	2 – did not attend
Registration date for surgical list	date
Date of removal from surgical list	date
Reason for removal from surgical list	1 – underwent surgery
	2 – died
	3 – removed for other reason
	4 – cancelled from final operating room list
	5 – unplanned emergency admission
	6 – became inpatient
Experimental responses	
Appointment list census	number of patients on the appointment list at the end of the week
Time on appointment list	number of weeks from referral to removal from appointment list
Time on surgical wait list	number of weeks from registration to removal from surgical wait list
Performance measures	
Hospital clearance time	ratio of appointment list census to clinic capacity (weeks)
Weekly rate of clinic appointments	number of appointments per 100 patient-weeks
Weekly rate of elective surgery	number of procedures per 100 patient-weeks

[a] The full list of output data produced in the simulation experiment is available from the authors on request.

Table 2. Experimental and performance variables

Simulation time

To increase variation in the experimental responses, we simulated hospital operations over six 18-week cycles of allocation of clinic and operating time to three surgeons. In practice, hospitals are evaluated annually, so the performance measures of our experiment could be regarded as representing averages over two years.

Sample-size calculation

We compared performance measures across the three appointment systems such that a difference between two systems could be interpreted as the effect of switching from one system to the other. To determine how many simulation runs would be required we set the sample size to detect the anticipated effects of the appointment systems with high probability. For analyses at the hospital level, we estimated that five runs (i.e., five modeled hospitals) per scheduling method would yield 90% power to detect a one-week difference in the clearance time for clinic appointments in a two-sided 5% significance test (Cohen, 1977).

For analyses at the patient level, dependence between experimental responses in each hospital necessitated adjustment for within-hospital correlation (Sobolev & Kuramoto, 2010). We assumed an average of 3,188 patient-weeks per simulation run and a coefficient of variation of 0.04 (Hayes & Bennett, 1999). We estimated that 5 runs per scheduling method would yield 90% power to detect a 10% difference in the weekly appointment rate between groups of patients in a two-sided 5% significance test (Donner & Klar, 2000).

For the purpose of regression analysis, we increased the number of runs to generate an adequate number of observations per regression variable. Our primary experimental factor was represented by two indicator variables for the three appointment scheduling methods. In addition, two variables represented three initial sizes of the outpatient queue, three variables represented four sizes of the initial queue for elective surgery, two variables represented three sizes of the queue for inpatient surgery, and one indicator variable for method of allocating operating room slots. Therefore, with a total of 10 variables, we estimated that 36 runs per scheduling method were needed, allowing for 10 observations per independent variable (Harrel et al., 1985).

The sample size for assessment of all main effects required 108 runs (36 runs for each scheduling method). This number of runs was less than the 216 runs that would have been required for a full factorial design (Law, 2007). Therefore, we used the Fedorov algorithm (Fedorov, 1972) to ensure an optimal distribution of the experimental factors across the runs. The initial allocation was chosen by randomly selecting design points (individual combinations of the experimental factors) from the full factorial design. The algorithm then switched pairs of design points from the initial design and the remainder of the design space to maximize the determinant of the information matrix for the design output (Atkinson & Donev, 1992).

Coincidently, the number of runs and the number of weeks for evaluation of system performance were the same.

2.3 Statistical analysis

We compared the performance of the scheduling methods at the level of the hospital, with application of linear regression methods to clearance times for appointment lists, and at the level of the patient, with application of discrete-time survival regression methods to waiting times. Linear regression methods model the relation between the average clearance time and experimental factors. Discrete-time survival regression methods model the relation between the time to an event and experimental factors, when many events could occur at the same time (Sobolev et al., 2008). In all of the regression analyses, we used two indicator variables to represent the three methods of scheduling clinic appointments. The reference group (pooled list method) was represented by values of zero for both of the indicator variables.

The coefficients derived from linear regression measured the effects of using the individual list and shortest list methods on the average clearance times for appointment lists, relative to scheduling with pooled lists (Vittinghoff et al., 2007). The average clearance time was estimated as the average of observed clearance times over 18 cycles for each run. The effects of scheduling by the individual list and shortest list methods were compared with an F test (Chatterjee & Hadi, 2006). We used multivariable models to adjust for four experimental hospital-level factors: method of allocating operating room slots and initial size of the queues for outpatient consultations, elective procedures, and inpatient procedures (Table 2).

The odds ratios derived from discrete-time survival regressions measured the effects of using the individual list and shortest list methods on the weekly proportion of patients on the appointment lists who received their appointments and who underwent the operation, relative to what occurred with the pooled list method (Sobolev et al., 2008). In the model for appointment waiting times, we adjusted for the hospital-level factors mentioned above and for five patient-level factors, namely sex, age group, coronary anatomy, comorbidity, and priority of elective referral. In the model for surgical waiting times, we adjusted for the hospital- and patient-level factors, replacing referral priority with priority of registration on the surgical wait list, size of the surgical wait list at registration, and weekly number of inpatient and emergency admissions (Sobolev et al., 2004).

We reported results and constructed tables according to published guidelines for reporting statistics in medicine (Lang & Secic, 2006).

3. Results

3.1 Simulated patients

The 108 simulation runs generated a total of 81,569 referrals for elective procedures, 80,294 urgent cases, and 5,827 emergency cases over six 18-week cycles of allocation of clinic and operating time starting on the arbitrarily chosen day of September 1, 2008. On average, the simulation generated 363 elective referrals, 357 urgent cases, and 26 emergency arrivals per modeled hospital in one year. The modeled surgical services performed 658 procedures per year on average.

3.2 Distribution of hospitals and patients by hospital-level factors

By design, the distribution of simulation runs by hospital-level factors was identical across the three methods of scheduling clinic appointments. More specifically, one-third of the runs were allocated to each of the three levels of initial size of the queue for outpatient consultations, one-quarter to each of the four levels of initial size of the queue for elective procedures, one-third to each of the three levels of initial size of the queue for inpatient procedures, and one-half to each of the two levels of method of allocating operating room slots. As a result, the distribution of outpatient referrals by hospital-level factors was similar across scheduling methods as well.

3.3 Distribution of patients by patient-level factors

The distribution of referrals by patient-level factors was also similar across scheduling methods as shown in Table 3. The majority of referrals were men (about 83%) and about 38% of patients were 60 to 69 years old. Most patients had multivessel disease (about 74%) and either major or minor concurrent conditions (about 50%).

	Scheduling method; no. (%) of referrals		
Characteristic	Individual lists (n=27,268)	Shortest list (n=27,236)	Pooled list (n=27,065)
Age group (years)			
<50	1,901 (7)	1,874 (7)	1,939 (7)
50–59	6,266 (23)	6,148 (23)	6,152 (23)
60–69	10,296 (38)	10,405 (38)	10,133 (37)
70–79	7,953 (29)	7,921 (29)	7,984 (30)
≥80	852 (3)	888 (3)	857 (3)
Sex			
Men	22,574 (83)	22,760 (84)	22,604 (84)
Women	4,694 (17)	4,476 (16)	4,461 (16)
Coronary anatomy			
Left main	4,574 (16)	4,610 (17)	4,472 (16)
Multi-vessel[a]	20,087 (74)	20,049 (74)	19,999 (74)
Limited[b]	2,607 (10)	2,577 (9)	2,594 (10)
Comorbidity			
Major conditions[c]	6,071 (22)	6,109 (22)	5,964 (22)
Other conditions[d]	7,453 (27)	7,355 (27)	7,488 (28)
None	13,744 (51)	13,772 (51)	13,613 (50)
Priority of elective referral			
High	1,892 (7)	1,885 (7)	1,979 (7)
Low	25,376 (93)	25,351 (93)	25,086 (93)

[a] Two- or three-vessel disease with stenosis of the proximal left anterior descending (PLAD) artery

[b] Two-vessel disease with no stenosis of the PLAD artery or one-vessel disease with stenosis of the PLAD artery

[c] Congestive heart failure, diabetes mellitus, chronic obstructive pulmonary disease, rheumatoid arthritis, or cancer

[d] Peripheral vascular disease, cerebrovascular disease, dementia, peptic ulcer disease, hemiplegia, renal disease, or liver disease

Table 3. Simulated referrals for clinic appointments by patient characteristics and scheduling methods

At the time of referral, 93% of the patients had low priority for the consultation. Regardless of the method of scheduling appointments, most of the referred patients had a surgical consultation by the end of the simulation (94% for individual list method, 94% for shortest list method, and 96% for pooled list method). The rest of the patients were still awaiting an appointment because their referral times were close to the end of the simulation period.

At the time of registration on a surgical wait list, about 71% of the cases had medium priority for the operation. The waiting time for elective surgery was 1 week or less for 69% of the patients scheduled through the individual list or the shortest list method; however, the proportion with waiting time of 1 week or less was only 56% for those scheduled via the pooled list method. Of all the patients who were registered on a surgical wait list, 78% underwent the planned procedure. The reasons for removal from the lists without surgery were similar across scheduling methods: 10% of planned procedures were cancelled because no beds were available in the intensive care unit for recovery after surgery and 9% of planned procedures were cancelled because an inpatient was admitted for surgery. Another 3% of patients were removed from the list for other reasons or they remained on the wait list at the end of the simulation (Sobolev & Kuramoto, 2008).

3.4 Clearance times for appointment lists

The average clearance time for appointment lists was similar when patients were scheduled to individual surgeons' lists (5.2 weeks) and when they were assigned to the surgeon with the shortest list (5.3 weeks); however, clearance time was much shorter when a pooled list was used (3.6 weeks) (Table 4). After adjustment for hospital-level factors, the average clearance time was more than 1.5 weeks longer for the individual list or the shortest list method than for the pooled list method (Table 4). There was no difference in clearance times between services using the individual list and shortest list methods (F test statistic = 5.7 for 1 and 97 degrees of freedom, $p = 0.26$).

Performance measure	**Scheduling method**		
	Individual lists	Shortest list	Pooled list
Hospital level			
Average clearance time (standard deviation), weeks	5.2 (0.7)	5.3 (0.2)	3.6 (0.2)
Difference (95% confidence interval)[a], weeks	1.6 (1.4–1.8)[b]	1.7 (1.5–1.9)[b]	reference group
Patient level			
Appointment rate (95% confidence interval)[c]	19.7 (19.5–20.0)	19.5 (19.3–19.7)	33.9 (33.5–34.3)
Odds ratio (95% confidence interval)[d]	0.22 (0.21–0.22)	0.22 (0.22–0.23)	reference group

[a] Difference relative to the pooled list method, adjusted for initial queue size at clinic appointment, for initial size of queues at registration for elective and urgent surgery, and for method of allocating operating room slots

[b] No difference between individual list and shortest list methods ($p = 0.26$)

[c] Weekly appointment rate was calculated as the number of appointments divided by the sum of wait times (and is expressed per 100 patient-weeks)

[d] Ratio relative to the pooled list method, adjusted for initial queue size at clinic appointment, for initial size of queues at registration for elective and urgent surgery, and for method of allocating operating room slots, and also for age, sex, anatomy, comorbidity, priority at referral, and week from referral

Table 4. Relation between scheduling methods and average clearance times (in weeks), and relation between scheduling methods and weekly rate of clinic appointment

3.5 Weekly rate of clinic appointment

The average weekly number of appointments was similar with the individual list and shortest list methods (about 20 per 100 patients remaining on the appointment list), but was much greater with the pooled list method (about 34 per 100 patients remaining on the list) (Table 4). Patients whose appointments were scheduled by the individual list and shortest list methods had longer waiting times (about one-half had their appointments within 5 weeks) than those scheduled by the pooled list method (about one-half had their appointments within 3 weeks) (Figure 2). After adjustment for hospital-level and patient-level factors, which were described in the Statistical analysis section, the weekly odds that a patient on the wait list would have his or her appointment were 78% lower for both the individual list and shortest list methods relative to the pooled list method (Table 4).

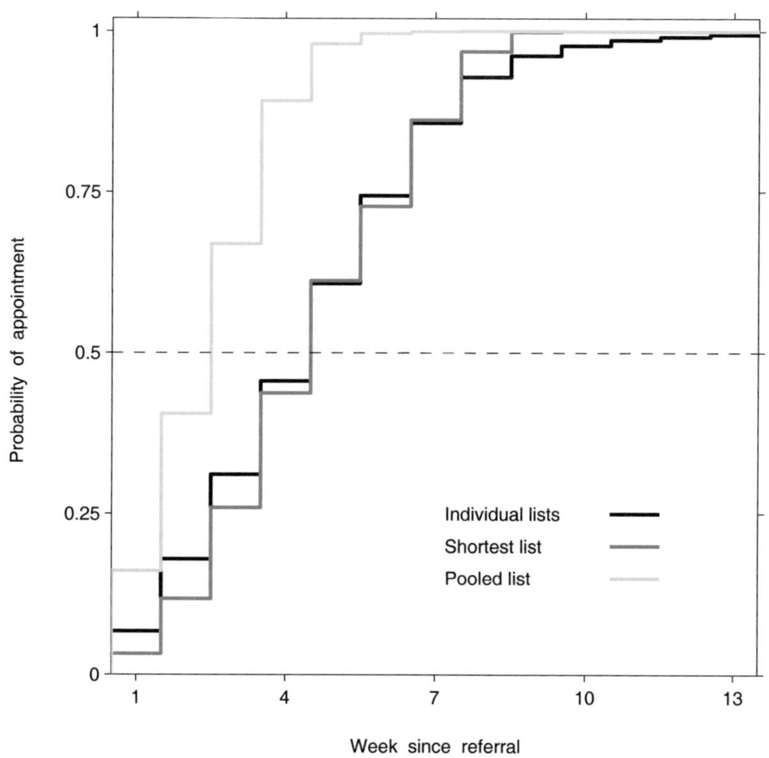

Fig. 2. Estimated probability of patient getting a clinic appointment within a certain waiting time, by scheduling method

3.6 Weekly rate of surgery

Once patients were registered on a surgical wait list, the average weekly number of operations was similar, regardless of the method of scheduling the consultation appointment (34 procedures for every 100 patients remaining on wait lists generated by the individual list and shortest list methods and 32 procedures for every 100 patients remaining on wait lists generated by the pooled list method). The effect of scheduling method on the odds of undergoing an operation was adjusted for a variety of hospital-level and patient-level factors, as described in the Statistical analysis section. After adjustment, and using the pooled list method as the reference group, the weekly odds that a patient on the wait list would undergo the operation were more than 10% with the individual list method (adjusted odds ratio = 1.13, 95% confidence interval 1.10–1.16) and the shortest list method (adjusted odds ratio = 1.12, 95% confidence interval 1.09–1.15). For every eight additional operations (the average weekly number of procedures) that were performed for emergency and urgent inpatient cases, the weekly odds that a patient who was registered on a surgical wait list would undergo the planned operation were reduced by 50% (adjusted odds ratio = 0.50, 95% confidence interval 0.48–0.51).

4. Discussion

We conducted a series of simulation experiments to test for differences between three methods of scheduling clinic appointments in a surgical service. The three methods were placing patients on the appointment list of the surgeon named in the referral (the individual list method), placing patients on the appointment list of the surgeon with the fewest patients waiting (the shortest list method), and placing all patients on one appointment list and scheduling appointments with the first available surgeon (the pooled list method).

We simulated the entire process of surgical care, beginning with the referral and incorporating appointment scheduling, consultation, registration for surgery, pre-surgical assessment, the operation itself, intensive care treatment and discharge from the hospital, accounting for interactions between the appointment and booking systems. Using the Statecharts specifications for the continuum of clinical and managerial activities, a discrete-event simulation model, and a cluster randomized experimental design, for each scheduling method we generated 36 runs, each representing a surgical service with three surgeons who rotated clinic and operating time. The runs differed in terms of the method of allocating slots between urgent and elective procedures and the initial size of queues for outpatient consultation, elective procedures, and inpatient surgery. The delivery of surgical services was simulated over six cycles of allocation of clinic and operating time, to increase variation in the experimental responses.

To estimate the impact of scheduling methods on patient flow, we focused on two common performance measures: clearance time for the appointment list (at the hospital level of analysis) and time to appointment (at the patient level of analysis). Comparisons at the hospital level were used to determine which method of scheduling clinic appointments would reduce the clearance times. Comparisons at the patient level were used to determine which scheduling method would reduce patients' waiting times.

We found that clearance times for appointment lists were more than 1.5 weeks longer for surgical services that used the individual list and shortest list methods than for services that used the pooled list method. After adjustment for hospital and patient factors, the weekly likelihood that patients on an appointment list would have had a consultation with a specialist was 78% lower for services using the individual list and shortest list methods than for those using the pooled list methods. One explanation for these longer clearance times and lower appointment rates can be derived from the observation that in hospitals using the individual list and shortest list methods for scheduling appointments with a specialist, the appointments were scheduled only in time slots assigned to a specific surgeon. If, by chance, the number of patients waiting on an individual appointment list was higher, or the schedule made the surgeon unavailable for appointments during the week following registration on the list, then both the clearance time and the waiting time would be prolonged.

We also observed that the variance in clearance times was similar in services using the pooled list and shortest list methods. It was also substantially smaller as compared with the individual list method. This may be attributed to more predictable patient flow, due to more even distribution of patients among surgeons in the service than was the case for the individual list method. As expected, the scheduling method affected patient flow after the consultation appointment. For example, higher appointment rates for hospitals using the pooled list method resulted in more patients waiting for subsequent care steps, such as surgery. Given that the number of operations done weekly was the same, the weekly rate for elective surgery became higher with scheduling via the individual list and shortest list methods than with scheduling via the pooled list method.

The most important contribution of our simulation study is the assessment of alternative appointment systems that account for interaction between specialists' and hospitals' schedules. Using the Statecharts language, we were able to incorporate the complex pattern of weekly availability of surgeons for operations that depended on their schedules for consultations, planned operations, on-call duties and vacations. We were also able to use information on patient-level factors that influenced the simulated experimental responses, such as referrals, appointments, wait-list registrations, planned and unplanned emergency surgery, cancellations, and preoperative deaths.

We evaluated the appointment systems using specifications for activities that constitute the process of cardiac surgical care. Because these managerial and clinical activities are generic across surgical services, the results of our evaluation may be applicable to other settings where appointments and wait lists are used to manage access to surgical procedures. Indeed, by varying other factors that are likely to influence service performance, such as the method of allocating operating room slots, we were able to delineate the independent effect of methods for scheduling clinic appointments.

However, our model also had several limitations. First, although we were able to account for the availability of surgeons for operations, we lacked information about shortages of other hospital staff, so our model did not consider fluctuations in their availability. A second limitation related to the size of the modeled surgical service. Coordinating clinic and operating room schedules for surgeons might have a different effect in a larger service. Whether the effect of the shortest list system depends on the number of surgeons who share these duties requires further investigation. Third, we did not control the distribution of patient-level factors through the design of experiment but instead assigned these factors randomly according to their frequency in the patient population in British Columbia. The case mix of patients needing elective operations could be different in other regions of the world. For example, women consistently accounted for 20% of patients undergoing isolated coronary artery bypass surgery in the United Kingdom, Norway, France, Italy, and Japan in the period 2000–2005 (Keogh & Kinsman, 2004; Motomura et al., 2008). Conversely, patients who undergo this procedure in the United States are slightly older, with greater proportions of women, diabetic patients, smokers and patients with lung disease. Reasons offered for the lower rates of coronary artery bypass grafting among women include greater comorbidity, which augments the operative risk, and smaller size of the coronary arteries, which presents greater technical challenges and increases the potential for incomplete revascularization (Guru et al., 2004). Determining whether the effect of the appointment system is independent of the case mix requires further investigation.

The results of our simulation experiments may have implications for policies on managing access to elective surgery in a regional network of hospitals. If the size of the appointment list and the weekly number of referrals vary significantly from one hospital to another, policy makers may consider redistributing the cases across surgical services, which would require a centrally managed appointment system. Our findings suggest that compared to other alternatives, pooling referrals will substantially reduce access time for appointment at the expense of a slight delay in the timing of elective operations. However, adopting this appointment system in the surgical services setting would present the patient with the choice of waiting to schedule an appointment with the surgeon named in the referral or seeing another surgeon. Further research is required to explore the impact of patient preferences on the performance of various appointment systems.

5. Appendix

5.1 Simulation approach

We used the Statecharts language to define detailed functional and behavioral specifications of states and transitions within each activity of the delivery of care (Sobolev et al., 2008). This approach allowed us to include realistic features of the processes of scheduling consultations and booking admissions, which made the simulation results applicable to other surgical services.

For example, using Statecharts notions of parallelism and event broadcasting, we represented the availability of surgeons for consultations, scheduled operations and on-call duties by developing one statechart for describing the rotation of duties and vacation schedules and another for describing the allocation of clinic and operating room slots to surgeons according to their weekly availability.

5.2 Underlying assumptions

In constructing the simulation model, we made the following simplifying assumptions.

For each simulation week, the random numbers of referrals for consultations, of emergency patients, and of inpatients were drawn from Poisson distributions, to allow for fluctuations in demand for service.

Patients differed by sex, age group, coronary anatomy, and comorbidity. The distribution of referrals by patient factors was based on historical data obtained from the British Columbia Cardiac Services for the period 1991 through 2000 (Sobolev et al., 2006).

Referred patients could have high or low priority for surgical consultation: patients with high priority were scheduled before those with low priority, and patients with the same priority were scheduled by their respective referral times.

Sixteen consultation appointments were available each week, and all patients attended their appointments.

Seven operating room slots for elective surgery and eight for urgent procedures were available each week. Two methods for allocating operating room slots over weekdays were studied: weekly or daily split between elective and urgent procedures.

Elective cases with high and medium priority were eligible for scheduling in both elective and urgent slots, and those with low priority could be scheduled only in elective slots available to the consulting surgeon.

Emergency and urgent inpatient cases were placed on a current operating room schedule immediately. They were scheduled in urgent slots, if such were available; otherwise, previously scheduled operations could be cancelled to accommodate these cases.

Inpatients whose need for surgery was less urgent were placed on the current schedule if urgent slots were available; otherwise, they were scheduled in available urgent slots the next week.

After surgery, patients recovered in the cardiac surgery intensive care unit (CS-ICU), for an average of one day.

Four beds were available in the CS-ICU. Two additional beds from the main hospital ICU could be used for emergency patients if no CS-ICU beds were available.

If no CS-ICU beds were available for recovery from a planned operation, the operation was cancelled.

When scheduled operations were cancelled, patients with high or medium priority for elective surgery became inpatients, and those with low priority joined a separate queue.

The surgeons' service and vacation schedules were planned according to an 18-week cycle, with a booking horizon of 36 weeks.

The outcomes of decision-making that determined the progress of patients from consultation priority groups to surgical priority groups were governed by binomial (branching) probabilities.

Adverse events, such as deaths or unplanned emergency admissions, that determined whether patients would progress from registration to elective surgery or to removal from the list without surgery were governed by binomial (branching) probabilities. These probabilities were dependent on sex, age, coronary anatomy, and comorbidity.

Table A1 shows the values of the model parameters that were used in all simulation runs, including the number of priority groups, arrival rates, branching probabilities, and surgical capacities.

Priority groups	
Outpatient referral for consultation	high, low
Operation	high, medium, low
Referral rates, patients per week	
High priority for consultation	0.5
Low priority for consultation	6.5
Inpatients	5.8
Emergency	0.5
Probability of progression to next care step	
Patients needing elective surgery, with high consultation priority	
Outpatient assessment to high surgical priority	1
Patients needing elective surgery, with low consultation priority	
Outpatient assessment to medium surgical priority	0.76
Outpatient assessment to low surgical priority	0.24
Inpatients	
Inpatient assessment to inpatient surgical queue	0.5
Inpatient assessment to discharge from hospital	0.5
Probability of leaving intensive care unit, per day	
Elective patients	0.25
Inpatients	0.25
Capacity	
Number of surgeons	3
Weekly number of outpatient consultations	16 (8 on Monday and 8 on Tuesday)
Weekly number of elective slots	7
Weekly number of urgent slots	8
Number of beds for elective patients in cardiac surgery intensive care unit	4
Number of beds for emergency patients in main intensive care unit	2

Table A1. Simulation parameters

6. References

Atkinson, A.C. & Donev, A.N. (1992). Criteria of optimality. In: *Optimum Experimental Designs*, 106-115, Oxford Science Publications

Cayirli, T. & Veral, E. (2003). Outpatient scheduling in health care: A review of literature. *Production & Operations Management*, 12, 4, 519-549, 10591478

Chatterjee, S. & Hadi, A.S. (2006). *Regression Analysis by Example*, Wiley-Interscience, New Jersey

Cohen, J. (1977). Statistical Power Analysis for the Behavioral Sciences, Academic Press, New York

Cohn, L.H. & Edmunds, L.H.J. (2003). *Cardiac Surgery in the Adult,* McGraw-Hill, New York

Cottrell, K.M. (1980). Waiting lists: some problems of definition and a relative measure of waiting time. *Hospital and Health Services Review,* 76, 265-269

Davies, H.T. & Davies, R. (1995). Simulating health systems: modelling problems and software solutions. *European Journal of Operation Research,* 87, 35-44

Donner, A. & Klar, N. (2000). Design and Analysis of Cluster Randomization Trials in Health Research, Arnold Publishing Co., New York

Donner, A. & Klar, N. (1994). Cluster randomization trials in epidemiology: theory and application. *Journal of Statistical Planning and Inference,* 42, 37-56

Edwards, R.H.; Clague, J.E.; Barlow, J.; Clarke, M.; Reed, P.G. & Rada, R. (1994). Operations research survey and computer simulation of waiting times in two medical outpatient clinic structures. *Health Care Analysis,* 2, 164-169

Elkhuizen, S.G.; Das, S.F.; Bakker, P.J. & Hontelez, J.A. (2007). Using computer simulation to reduce access time for outpatient departments. *Quality and Safety in Health Care,* 16, 5, 382-386

Erdem, H.I.; Demirel, T. & Onut, S. (2002). An efficient appointment system design for outpatient clinic using computer simulation. *The Proceedings of the 2002 Summer Computer Simulation Conference,* pp. 299-304.

Fedorov, V.V. (1972). *Theory of Optimal Experiments,* Academic Press, New York

Fone, D.; Hollinghurst, S.; Temple, M.; Round, A.; Lester, N.; Weightman, A.; Roberts, K.; Coyle, E.; Bevan, G. & Palmer, S. (2003). Systematic review of the use and value of computer simulation modelling in population health and health care delivery. *Journal of Public Health and Medicine,* 25, 4, 325-335

Gruer, P.; Koukam, A. & Mazigh, R. (1998). Modelling and quantitative analysis of discrete event systems: a statecharts based approach. *Simulation Practice and Theory,* 6, 397-411

Guru, V.; Fremes, S.E. & Tu, J.V. (2004). Time-related mortality for women after coronary artery bypass graft surgery: a population-based study. *Journal of Thoracic and Cardiovascular Surgery,* 127, 4, 1158-1165

Ham, C.; Kipping, R. & McLeod, H. (2003). Redesigning work processes in health care: lessons from the National Health Service. *Milbank Quarterly,* 81, 3, 415-439

Harper, P.R. & Gamlin, H.M. (2003). Reduced outpatient waiting times with improved appointment scheduling: a simulation modelling approach. *OR Spektrum,* 25, 2, 207-222

Harrel, F.E.; Lee, K.L.; Matchar, D.B. & Reichert, T.A. (1985). Regression models for prognostic prediction: Advantages, problems and suggested solutions. *Cancer Treatment Reports,* 69, 1071-1077

Hayes, R.J. & Bennett, S. (1999). Simple sample size calculation for cluster-randomized trials. *International Journal of Epidemiology,* 28, 319-326

Ho, C.J. & Lau, H.S. (1999). Evaluating the impact of operating conditions on the performance of appointment scheduling rules in service systems. *European Journal of Operational Research,* 112, 3, 542-553, 0377-2217

Jun, J.B.; Jacobson, S.H. & Swisher, J.R. (1999). Application of discrete-event simulation in health care clinics: a survey. *Journal of the Operational Research Society*, 50, 109-123, 0160-5682

Keogh, B. & Kinsman, R. (2004). Fifth national adult cardiac surgical database report 2003: Improving outcomes for patients. Dendrite Clinical Systems, Reading, MA

Klassen, K.J. & Rohleder, T.R. (1996). Scheduling outpatient appointments in a dynamic environment. *Journal of Operations Management*, 14, 2, 83-101, 02726963

Klassen, K.J. & Rohleder, T.R. (2004). Outpatient appointment scheduling with urgent clients in a dynamic, multi-period environment. *International Journal of Service Industry Management*, 15, 167-186, 0956-4233

Lang, T.A. & Secic, M. (2006). *How to report statistics in medicine,* American College of Physicians, Philadelphia

Law, A.M. (2007). *Simulation Modeling & Analysis,* McGraw-Hill, New York

Meredith, P.; Ham, C. & Kipping, R. (1999). Modernising the NHS: booking patients for hospital care. Health Services Management Centre, University of Birmingham, Birmingham

Motomura, N.; Miyata, H.; Tsukihara, H.; Okada, M. & Takamoto, S. (2008). First report on 30-day and operative mortality in risk model of isolated coronary artery bypass grafting in Japan. *Annals of Thoracic Surgery*, 86, 6, 1866-1872

Murray, M. & Berwick, D.M. (2003). Advanced access: reducing waiting and delays in primary care. *Journal of the American Medical Association*, 289, 8, 1035-1040

Naylor, C.D. (1991). A different view of queues in Ontario. *Health Affairs*, 10, 3, 110-128

O'Hagan, A.; Stevenson, M. & Madan, J. (2007). Monte Carlo probabilistic sensitivity analysis for patient level simulation models: Efficient estimation of mean and variance using ANOVA. *Health Economics*, 16, 10, 1009-1023, 1057-9230

Sobolev, B.; Brown, P.; Zelt, D. & Kuramoto, L. (2004). Waiting time in relation to wait-list size at registration: statistical analysis of a waiting-list registry. *Clinical and Investigative Medicine*, 27, 298-305

Sobolev, B.; Harel, D.; Vasilakis, C. & Levy, A.L. (2008). Using the statecharts paradigm for simulation of patient flow in surgical care. *Health Care Manag Sci*, 11, 79-86

Sobolev, B. & Kuramoto, L. (2005). Policy analysis using patient flow simulations: conceptual framework and study design. *Clinical and Investigative Medicine*, 28, 359-363

Sobolev, B. & Kuramoto, L. (2008). Analysis of Waiting-time Data in Health Services Research, Springer, New York

Sobolev, B. & Kuramoto, L. (2010). Cluster-randomized design for simulation-based evaluation of complex healthcare interventions. *Journal of Simulation*, 4, 24-33

Sobolev, B.; Levy, A.; Hayden, R. & Kuramoto, L. (2006). Does wait-list size at registration influence time to surgery? Analysis of a population-based cardiac surgery registry. *Health Services Research*, 41, 23-39

Sobolev, B.; Mercer, D.; Brown, P.; FitzGerald, M.; Jalink, D. & Shaw, R. (2003). Risk of emergency admission while awaiting elective cholecystectomy. *Canadian Medical Association Journal*, 169, 7, 662-665

Sobolev, B.; Sanchez, V.; Kuramoto, L.; Levy, A.; Schechter, M. & FitzGerald, M. (2008). Evaluation of booking systems for elective surgery using simulation experiments. *Healthcare Policy*, 3, 4, 113-124

Ukoumunne, O.C.; Gulliford, M.C.; Chinn, S.; Sterne, J.A.; Burney, P.G. & Donner, A. (1999). Methods in health Service research. Evaluation of health interventions at area and organisation level. *British Medical Journal*, 319, 376-379

Vasilakis, C.; Sobolev, B.; Kuramoto, L. & Levy, A. (2007). A simulation study of scheduling clinic appointments in surgical care: individual surgeon versus pooled lists. *Journal of the Operational Research Society*, 58, 202-211

Vissers, J. (1979). Selecting a suitable appointment system in an outpatient setting. *Medical Care*, 17, 1207-1220

Vittinghoff, E.; Glidden, D.V.; Shiboski, S.C. & McCulloch, C.E. (2007). Regression Methods in Biostatistics: Linear, Logistic, Survival, and Repeated Measures Models, Springer, New York

Walshe, K. & Rundall, T. (2001). Evidence-based management: from theory to practice in health care. *Milbank Quarterly*, 79, 3, 429-457

Westeneng, J.B. (2007). Outpatient appointment scheduling: An evaluation of alternative appointment systems to reduce waiting times and underutilization in an ENT outpatient clinic. Dissertation, University of Twente.

Wijewickrama, A. & Takakuwa, S. (2008). Outpatient appointment scheduling in a multi facility system. *Proceedings of the 2008 Winter Simulation Conference*, pp. 1563-1571.

10

Condition based maintenance optimization of multi-equipment manufacturing systems by combining discrete event simulation and multiobjective evolutionary algorithms

Aitor Goti[1] and Alvaro Garcia[2]
[1]*University of Mondragon – Mondragon Unibertsitatea*
[2]*Polytechnic University of Madrid*
[1,2]*Spain*

Abstract

Modern industrial engineers are continually faced with the challenge of meeting increasing demands for high quality products while using a reduced amount of resources. Since systems used in the production of goods and deliveries of services constitute the vast portion of capital in most industries, maintenance of such systems is crucial (Oyarbide-Zubillaga, Goti, & Sánchez 2008). Several studies compiled by Mjema (2002) show that maintenance costs represent from 3 to 40 % out of the total product cost (with an average value of a 28%).

Within maintenance, the Condition-Based Maintenance (CBM) techniques are very important. Nevertheless, and comparing it to the Preventive Maintenance (PM) optimization problem, relatively few papers related to CBM have been developed: According to Aven (1996), one of the reasons to justify this fact is that CBM models are usually by its nature rather sophisticated compared to the more traditional replacement models. Within this maintenance strategy, Das & Sarkar (1999) distinguish two CBM subtypes, On-Condition Maintenance (OCM) and Condition Monitoring (CMT). OCM is based on periodic inspections, while CMT performs a continuous monitoring on the hardware through instrumentation.

Considering the described context, this paper focuses on the problem of CMT optimisation in a manufacturing environment, with the objective of determining the optimal CMT deterioration levels beyond which PM activities should be applied under cost and profit criteria in a multi-equipment system. The initiative considers the interaction of production, work in process material, quality and maintenance aspects. In this work the suitability of discrete event simulation to model or modify complex system models is combined with the aptitude that multiobjective evolutionary algorithms have shown to deal with multiobjective problems to develop a maintenance management and optimisation approach. An application case where the activities applied on a system that produces hubcaps for the car maker industry is performed, showing the quantitative benefits of adopting the detailed approach.

Keywords
Maintenance, Optimization, Discrete Event Simulation, Multi-objective Evolutionary Algorithm.

1. Introduction

Industrial plant management, especially maintenance optimization, is usually characterized by the need to consider multiple non-commensurable and often conflicting objectives (see i.e. (Bader & Guesneux 2007;Goti & Sánchez 2006)). Equipment can be over maintained increasing preventive maintenance (PM) expenditures or under maintained increasing catastrophic failures. In these situations, and considering that maintenance requirements depend on many facts (whether the maintained equipment is a productive bottleneck, if it has a crucial impact in manufactured products' quality, etc.), it is very difficult to determine the optimal maintenance strategy that maximizes the profitability of the studied equipment considering different criteria.

In the latest years, many works have been presented devoted to find an optimal maintenance policy focused on different points of view, mainly oriented to the optimization of single deteriorating equipment and without taking into account the configuration of the productive system which contains the equipments to be maintained. Single equipment optimization approaches may be especially interesting when productive bottlenecks or continuous processes (such as foundries, rolling mills, etc.) are analyzed. Nevertheless, these initiatives might be less useful in manufacturing machines which work in multi-equipment systems, as they usually do not take into account the influence that the whole system has in each of the studied machines. Maintenance requirements related to a single machine of a multi-equipment system depend strongly the amount of semi-elaborated products' stock related to the machine, whether it is a bottleneck or not, etc. For instance, if the studied machine is a bottleneck its availability will be crucial for the profitability of the company, whereas if not the impact of its failure will not be so important for the whole system (depending on stock levels and repair times (Li & Zuo 2007)). However, and although maintenance applied on equipment depends on the configuration of the system where the equipment is, little research can be found in the literature where a system composed by several equipments is optimized (Fiori de Castro & Lucchesi Cavalca 2006;Gharbi & Kenné 2005;Goyal & Kusy 1985;Grigoriev, van de Klunder, & Spieksma 2006;Kenne, Boukas, & Gharbi 2003;Yao 2005).

This paper provides a solution for the joint optimization of CBM strategies applied on several equipments. Precisely, the research is focused on the problem of CMT optimization in a manufacturing environment with the objective of determining the optimal age or deterioration levels when a Preventive Maintenance (PM) action should be performed for multi-equipment systems under cost and profit criteria. The approach developed takes into account the interaction of production, work in process material, quality and maintenance aspects. For this purpose, a model that considers maintenance, productive speed loss and non-quality costs along with productive profit has been developed.

The model has been implemented using Discrete Event Simulation (DES) and optimized using a Multiobjective Evolutionary Algorithm (MOEA). Thus, the suitability of DES to model or modify complex system models is combined with the aptitude that MOEAs have shown to deal with multiobjective problems.

This paper is organized as follows: the problem to be optimized is shown in section 2 whereas the age or deterioration model and the developed DES model are presented in section 3 and 4, respectively. The optimization MOEA is detailed in section 5 while problem formulation is shown in section 6. Finally, optimization results and concluding remarks are stated in section 7.

2. Optimization problem

2.1 System definition

The approach shown in this paper is applied to the optimization problem of PM activities of a simplified hub cap production system installed in a company of the Mondragón Corporación Cooperativa (MCC) Corporation (the third largest company in Spain). The system consists of three identical plastic injection machines and a painting station, as it is described in Fig. 1:

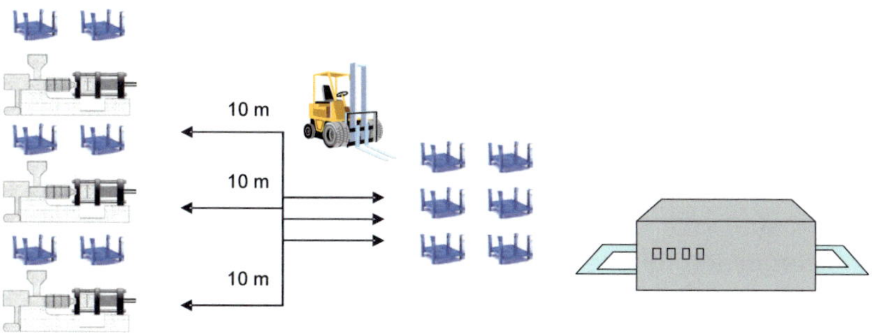

Fig. 1. Configuration of the simplified plastic injection system

The studied production system produces plastic made hub caps for car-maker companies. The production starts in the injection machine, where the plastic is injected, compressed concurrently, dwelled and cooled, to finally open the mould and extract the product. Then, the injected product is located next to the injection machine buffer (composed by two pallets of 100 hubcaps each). Once a pallet is filled with hub caps, a lift truck transports the pallet from the injection machine buffer to the painting station buffer (which has an area for storing up to 10 pallets). Then the products are loaded onto a conveyor that feeds the painting station. In the painting station the products are painted to be sent to a warehouse afterwards.

Each machine of the model consists of three subsystems (which are modelled as components) organized in serial configuration, and one maintenance activity is executed over each subsystem in order to control its aging: M1, M2 and M3 are respectively applied over sub-systems S1, S2 and S3 of the injection machines while M4, M5 and M6 are respectively executed on sub-systems S4, S5 and S6 of the painting station. The influence of each subsystem on the performance of each machine is defined in Table 1: for the injection machine, S1's deterioration influences only unavailability, S2's deterioration affects unavailability and productive speed loss and, S3's deterioration has an effect on unavailability and quality. Similarly, considering the painting station, S4's deterioration influences only unavailability, S5's deterioration affects unavailability and productive speed loss and, S6's deterioration has an effect on unavailability and quality.

Maintained equipment	Name of the PM activity executed when the age of its corresponding subsystem achieves an age	Subsystem	Influences on
Injection machines	M1	S1	Unavailability
	M2	S2	Unavailability and Productive speed loss
	M3	S3	Unavailability and Quality
Painting station	M4	S4	Unavailability
	M5	S5	Unavailability and Productive speed loss
	M6	S6	Unavailability and Quality

Table 1. System components, PM activities and their influences on productive parameters

The equipments failure process is modeled by using a two-parameter (λ_1, γ_1) Weibull failure rate. Additionally, it is considered that the production process can be subject to a process deterioration that shifts the system from an under-control state to an out-of-control state. This process deterioration follows also a Weibull distribution of parameters λ_2, γ_2. Table 2 shows the Weibull reliability data for the studied problem.

Group	$\lambda_1(10^{-2}hrs^{-1})$	γ_1	$\lambda_2(10^{-2}hrs^{-1})$	γ_2
S1	5	2		
S2	2	2.9		
S3	4	2	4	2
S4	6.6	2		
S5	7.7	3		
S6	10	3	10	3

Table 2. Weibull data of the studied subsystems

3. Deterioration or reliability model

3.1 Deterioration model

Traditionally, the effect of the maintenance activities on the state of a equipment is based on three situations: a) perfect maintenance activity which assumes that the state of the component after the maintenance is "As Good as New" (GAN), b) minimal maintenance which supposes that activity leaves the equipment in "As Bad as Old" (BAO) situation, and c) imperfect maintenance which assumes that the activity improves the state of the equipment by some degree depending on its effectiveness. Last situation is closer to many real situations.

There exist several models developed to simulate imperfect maintenance (Chan & Shaw 1993;Malik 1979;Shin, Lim, & Lie 1996). In this paper, an age reduction preventive maintenance model, named Proportional Age-Set Back (PAS), proposed by Martorell et al. (1999) is used to model the effect of the maintenance activities on the equipment.
In the PAS approach, each maintenance activity is assumed to shift the origin of time from which the age of the component is evaluated. PAS model in Ref. (Martorell, Sánchez, & Serradell 1998) considers that the maintenance activity reduces proportionally, in a factor of ε, the age that the component has immediately before it enters maintenance, where ε ranges in the interval [0,1]. If $\varepsilon = 0$, the PAS model simply reduces to a BAO situation, while if $\varepsilon = 1$ it is reduced to a GAN situation. Thus, this model is a natural generalization of both GAN and BAO models in order to account for imperfect maintenance. Based on Ref (Martorell et al. 1999), the age of the component immediately after the (m-1)-maintenance activity (w^{+}_{m-1}) is given by:

$$w^{+}_{m-1} = (t_{m-1} - \sum_{k=0}^{m-2} (1-\varepsilon)^{k} \cdot \varepsilon \cdot t_{m-k-1}) \tag{1}$$

where t_{m-1} is the time in which the component undertakes the m-1 maintenance activity

As Sherif & Smith (1981) state, if it is assumed that a probability distribution of the time to failure is available, risk can be measured. Risks associated to degradation in monitoring equipment consider poor quality and performance, productive breakdowns related to Corrective Maintenance (CM), etc. The following paragraphs go deep into the modelling of such risks.
Considering a CMT strategy, PM is performed when the component gets a determined critical age or deterioration level (w_c). It is worth to remember that PAS model considers that the maintenance reduces proportionally, in a ε factor, the age that the component has immediately before it enters maintenance. Considering these conditions, maintenance always will be applied to a component when it has the same age, and as effectiveness is assumed to be constant the age of the component will always be the same after performing a PM action. This means that w^{-}_{m} and w^{+}_{m}, which represent respectively the age of the component just before and after the mth PM intervention, will always get the same values:

$$w^{-}_{m} = w_c \tag{2}$$

$$w^{+}_{m} = (1-\varepsilon) \cdot w_c \tag{3}$$

As a consequence, the time interval M between two PM activities will have this value:

$$M = w_c \cdot \varepsilon \tag{4}$$

3.2 Reliability model

Using Equations 2-4, it is possible to obtain an age-dependent reliability model in which the induced or conditional failure rate, in the period m, after the maintenance number m, given by:

$$h_m(w_m(t,\varepsilon)) = h(w_m(t,\varepsilon)) + h_0 \tag{5}$$

where h_0 represents the initial failure rate of the component, that is, the one that equipment has when it installed. Considering the age of the component after maintenance m given by Equation 1, and adopting a Weibull model for the failure rate, the expression for the induced failure rate after the maintenance number m can be written as:

$$h_m(w_m(t,\varepsilon)) = \left\{\lambda^\gamma \cdot \gamma \cdot \left[w_m(t,\varepsilon)\right]^{\gamma-1}\right\} + h_0 \tag{6}$$

where λ is the scale parameter, γ is known as the shape parameter. The behaviour of $h_m(w_m(t,\varepsilon))$ function fluctuates between two values as was observed for the age of the component and its maximum and minimum values are given by:

$$h_m^- = \lambda^\gamma \cdot \gamma \cdot \left(w_m^-\right)^{\gamma-1} + h_0 \tag{7}$$

$$h_m^+ = \lambda^\gamma \cdot \gamma \cdot \left(w_m^+\right)^{\gamma-1} + h_0 \tag{8}$$

Then, in order to introduce the effect of maintenance activities into the cost and profit models, to be presented in the following section, it is derived an averaged standby failure rate over the component's life based on a double averaging process. First, it is formulated h_m^* the average failure rate over the period between two consecutive maintenance activities, m and m+1. Next, it is formulated the average failure rate, h^*, over the analysis period, L, which is practically equal to h_m^*. Thus is:

$$\begin{aligned} h^* \approx h_m^* &= \frac{1}{t_{m+1}^- - t_m^+} \int_{t_m^+}^{t_{m+1}^-} h_m(t).dt \\ &= (M)^{\gamma-1} \cdot \left(\frac{\lambda}{\varepsilon}\right)^\gamma \cdot \left[1 - (1-\varepsilon)^\gamma\right] + h_0 \end{aligned} \tag{9}$$

3.3 Availability model

As a consequence of what it is explained in the previous subsection, and based on Ref. (Martorell, Serradell, & Samanta 1995), $u_r(\mathbf{x})$, the time-dependent unreliability for discontinuous equipment can be calculated as:

$$u_r(\mathbf{x}) = \rho + (1-\rho).\left(1 - e^{-h^*.M}\right) \quad (10)$$

where ρ is the probability of failure on demand, and h^* is evaluated using Equation 10. Then $U(\mathbf{x})$ is the total unavailability of the studied system evaluated using the system fault tree and the single component unavailability contributions. These contributions are $u_{cm}(\mathbf{x})$ which is the unavailability due to CM given by:

$$u_{cm}(\mathbf{x}) = \frac{1}{M} \cdot u_r(x, M) \cdot d_{cm} \quad (11)$$

Where d_{cm} is the mean time for CM; and $u_{pm}(\mathbf{x})$ that represents the unavailability associated to the PM interventions launched due to CMT monitoring in the L period. Considering the periodicity of the PM activities explained in Equation 4, $u_{pm}(\mathbf{x})$ is given by:

$$u_{pm}(\mathbf{x}) = \frac{1}{M} \cdot d_{pm} \quad (12)$$

Where d_{pm} the mean time for PM; Finally, the total availability of the studied system $A(\mathbf{x})$ is evaluated as:

$$A(\mathbf{x}) = 1 - U(\mathbf{x}) \quad (13)$$

being $U(\mathbf{x})$ the system unavailability to be evaluated using the system fault tree and the single component corrective and preventive maintenance unavailability contributions.

4. Discrete event simulation model

DES concerns the modeling of a system as it evolves over time by a representation in which variable states change suddenly at separate points in time, as it is detailed in the other chapter of this book authored by the same author. These changes happened in the system are considered events. Systems do not change between events, so DES considers that it is not necessary to analyze what happens in a system in periods taken place between two events.
The main advantages of DES are two: i) standard DES-based tools provide capabilities of modeling or modifying complex system models easily, and ii) DES is closely related to stochastic systems so they are appropriate when simulating real-world phenomena, since there are few situations where the actions of the entities within the system under study can be completely predicted in advance. In order to generate stochastic events, simulation packages generate pseudo-random numbers to select a particular value for a given distribution. Similarly, equations related to analytical models (i.e. breakdown models) can also be implemented due to the generation of these pseudo-random numbers. Thus, using pseudo-random numbers it is possible to implement the stochastic nature of real models in DES models.

The DES model simulates the injection machines, the painting station, the lift, the product buffers and its pallets. The implementation of each of these components is detailed in the following subsections.

4.1 Equipment modeling

The behavior pattern of the machines represented in the DES model bases on an analytical model. This model is presented in (2006). In that work a single equipment model is detailed. The paper models maintenance, quality and production speed loss costs jointly with the benefit related to the production of non-defective products. All of these terms depend on the PM activities performed, which act as decision variables (**x**) and are optimized under cost and profit criteria.

That equipment model was developed considering the following assumptions: 1) the effect of the maintenance activities is modeled by using an imperfect maintenance model. In this case a Proportional Age Set-Back (Martorell, Sánchez, & Serradell 1999) is assumed, 2) the failure process and deterioration process are independent, 3) the system only produces non-conforming items, with a rate constant (α), while the process is out-of-control, 4) Preventive maintenance and process inspection are performed simultaneously, 5) inspections are error free and 6) the process is restored to under control state when the preventive maintenance is realized, 7) productive speed is assumed to fall from its initial speed (V_0) to another speed value ($V^*(\mathbf{x})$) which depends on the PM frequency, 8) as in (Li & Pham 2005), we assume that all the deterioration processes of the three studied components are independent, and 9) it is assumed that the process produces a single product type, so setup times of reference changes are not simulated.

The relevant productive parameters of the described equipment model include: i) direct maintenance parameters, ii) quality parameters and iii) productive speed loss parameters. These parameters can be evaluated as:

$$V^*(\mathbf{x}) = V_0 - \left[\tau \cdot M \cdot \left(\frac{2\text{-}\varepsilon}{2\varepsilon}\right)\right] \tag{14}$$

$$\kappa^*(x) = \frac{1}{M}\int_0^M t \cdot f_m(w(t,\varepsilon))dw \approx \frac{1}{2} \cdot h^* \cdot e^{-h^*(x) \cdot M} \tag{15}$$

Where; $V^*(\mathbf{x})$ the mean production speed of the equipment during the L period; and $\kappa^*(\mathbf{x})$ the mean fraction of time where the process is under control. In addition, the following notation is used: V_0 the initial (e.g. as per design) production speed; τ the speed loss coefficient; ρ the cyclic or per-demand failure probability; and $f_m(w(t,\varepsilon))$ the density function obtained using the conditional hazard function.

In this research, analytical formulation corresponding to each machine of the productive system is implemented within the equipment to generate stochastic events that make equipment work as it is defined in the analytical model. This integration is performed in two steps: first the components of the decision vector related to the studied machines are evaluated analytically, obtaining the working parameters $U_{cm}(\mathbf{x})$, $U_{pm}(\mathbf{x})$, $V^*(\mathbf{x})$ and $\kappa^*(\mathbf{x})$ of the corresponding PM frequencies (where $U_{cm}(\mathbf{x})$ and $U_{pm}(\mathbf{x})$ are respectively the unavailability of a machine due to CM and PM, evaluated using the system fault tree and the single component $u_{cm}(\mathbf{x})$ and $u_{pm}(\mathbf{x})$ contributions). In a second step, the generated working parameters are introduced as inputs in the DES modelled machines to execute then a simulation where the results to be optimised are obtained.

The implementation of values obtained in the analytical evaluation executed in the DES model derives in the generation of planned PM, unplanned CM, speed reduction and defective product actions and events during the simulation. As a consequence, at the end of the simulation machines generate the same values of $U_{cm}(\mathbf{x})$, $U_{pm}(\mathbf{x})$ and $\kappa^*(\mathbf{x})$ defined by the analytical model to produce items in a $V^*(\mathbf{x})$ productive speed. Fig. 2 shows the generation of unavailability, speed loss and quality events for an equipment during a simulation:

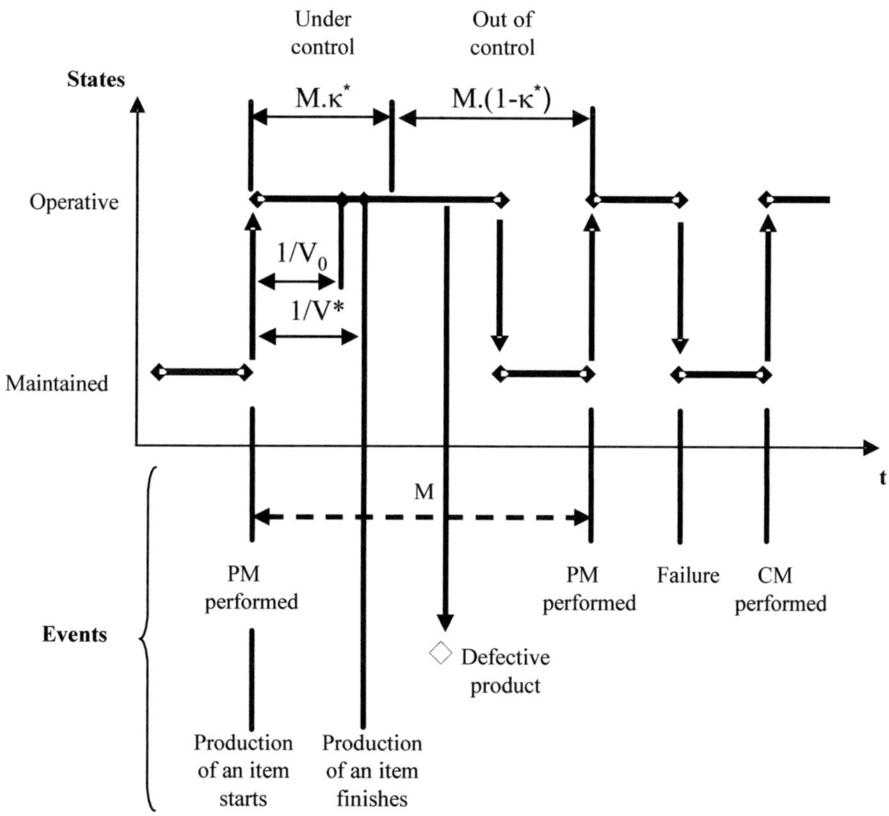

Fig. 2. Generation of events related to maintenance, productive speed and quality

As it can be seen in Fig. 2 events related to PM are generated with a determined periodicity (M) and each product needs a $1/V^*$ cycle time to be produced. Failures are generated randomly to obtain an unavailability related to CM which is equal to $U_{cm}(\mathbf{x})$. Referred to quality, there are no defective products during the first $\kappa^*(\mathbf{x})$ fraction between two PM activities, while there is a α defective fraction during the following $(1-\kappa^*(\mathbf{x}))$ fraction. Thus, thanks to the interaction between analytical evaluation and DES modelling simulation equipments work as it is defined in analytical models shown in Eqns. (14 – 15). Additionally,

and thanks to the capability of combining different machines in a system, the DES model not only models the features of a single machine, but the interaction among several machines.
The generation of each one of the above mentioned events is related to a specific inefficiency so their costs have to be taken into account. Costs are quantified considering CM, PM, speed loss, quality and CMT terms. In order to do that, individual cost counters related each one of these terms ($c_{cm}(\mathbf{x})$, $c_{pm}(\mathbf{x})$, $c_{sl}(\mathbf{x})$, $c_q(\mathbf{x})$ and $c_{cmt}(\mathbf{x})$, respectively) are defined; these counters are initialized to zero at the beginning of the simulation and increased every time an event related to them is generated by the simulation using Eqns. (16 - 20):

$$c_{cm}(\mathbf{x}) = c_{cm}(\mathbf{x}) + d_{cm} \cdot c_{hcm} \tag{16}$$

$$c_{pm}(\mathbf{x}) = c_{pm}(\mathbf{x}) + d_{pm} \cdot c_{hpm} \tag{17}$$

$$c_{sl}(\mathbf{x}) = c_{sl}(\mathbf{x}) + \left[\left(1 / V^*(\mathbf{x})\right) - \left(1 / V_0\right)\right] \cdot c_{hsl} \tag{18}$$

$$c_q(\mathbf{x}) = c_q(\mathbf{x}) + c_\alpha \tag{19}$$

$$c_{cmt}(X) = c_{hcmt} \cdot L \tag{20}$$

where c_{hcm}, c_{hpm}, c_{hsl} and c_{hcmt} represent respectively the hourly cost related to the CM, the PM, the reduced speed and the CMT, while c_α represents the cost of manufacturing a defective product. Finally, P($\mathbf{x}$) characterizes the profit function obtained as a result of selling non-defective products, which can be evaluated as:

$$P(\mathbf{x}) = n(\mathbf{x}) \cdot \psi \tag{21}$$

where n($\mathbf{x}$) represents the amount of non-defective products obtained during the analysis period (L), and ψ is the estimated margin of a single product.

4.2 Buffer and transportation modeling

System buffers have a determined maximum capacity. The model assumes that if a buffer is full it will not receive any products until it has free pallets to store them (so the transportation events will not be executed). This means also that a machine will stop producing products in case it does not have any place to leave them. The painting station is fed by a buffer of ten pallets, being each one capable of storing 100 products, whereas each injection machine feeds a buffer of two pallets of 100 each.
Referred to transportation modeling, only semi-elaborated product movements have been modeled, considering movements between: i) a machine and a buffer location, ii) two machines, iii) a buffer location and a machine, and iv) two buffer locations. It is worth to note that for transportation types i), ii) and iii) products are moved one by one, whereas for movements between two buffer locations products are transported in pallets. All of these movements are modeled by introducing a delay in the system. Thus, in instant t the element is at the initial point, to be at the destination point in instant t+delay. For sake of simplicity transportation types i), ii) and iii) are not modeled (delay=0), whereas injection machines are fed with empty pallets and empty pallets of the painting station are removed from the

system automatically and instantaneously. The lift truck transport is modeled using a delay which has a uniform distribution range between 14.4 and 28.8 s.

4.3 Simulation values of the productive system

Data collected for the simulation model is shown in the next 4 tables. Tables 3 and 4 show parameters related to PM and CM, whereas Tables 5 and 6 detail respectively information about inputs related to CM, unavailability, speed, quality and cost for the injection machines and the painting station.

Preventive maintenance activity	ε	d_{pm} (hrs)
M1	0.9	0.5
M2	0.9	1
M3	0.9	1
M4	0.9	2
M5	0.9	1
M6	0.9	3

Table 3. PM data related to the productive system

Corrective breakdown of sub-system	d_{cm} (hrs)
S1	0.5
S2	1
S3	2
S4	0.5
S5	1
S6	2

Table 4. CM data related to the productive system

C_{α} (€/u[1])	τ (u/h^2)	C_{hsl} (€/hr)	ρ (10^{-3})	α	h_0 (fail/hr)	V_0 (u/hr)	C_{hcm} (€/hr)	C_{hpm} (€/hr)	C_{hcmt} (€/hr)
6	0.0017	25	1	0.03	0	180	45	30	1

Table 5. Productive and cost parameters for the injection machines

C_{α} (€/u)	τ (u/h^2)	C_{hsl} (€/hr)	ρ (10^{-3})	α	h_0 (fail/hr)	V_0 (u/hr)	C_{hcm} (€/hr)	C_{hpm} (€/hr)	C_{hcmt} (€/hr)
6	0.02	150	1	0.04	0	900	175	160	1

Table 6. Productive and cost parameters for the painting station

[1] Where u represents a product unit

Additionally, the net profit value of a non-defective product (ψ) is 0.2 €/unit and the simulation time L is 62400 working hours, which corresponds to 10 years of production working 5 days a week and 24 hours a day.

Finally, the time required to execute a simulation in DES increases in an exponential way compared to the complexity of the studied model (Oyarbide-Zubillaga, Baines, & Kay 2003). For this reason and in order to reduce the time which the simulation is being executed products are elaborated in batches of 100 units.

5. The NSGA-II multiobjective evolutionary algorithm

In this approach the Non-dominated Sorting Genetic Algorithm (NSGA-II) proposed by Deb et al. (2002) has been implemented. The NSGA-II is the most recent and improved version of the NSGA which incorporates: a) a faster non-dominated sorting approach, b) an elitist strategy i.e. the best non-dominated individuals are preserved from one generation to another by using a crowding measurement, and c) no niching parameter. This algorithm is capable of performing a joint optimization under several criteria offering non-dominated solutions. The non-dominated results are situated in a Pareto optimal front, where each of the solutions is better than any other solution of the front at least in one of the studied optimization criterion.
The working procedure of the NSGA-II is shown in Fig. 3 and detailed in the following steps:

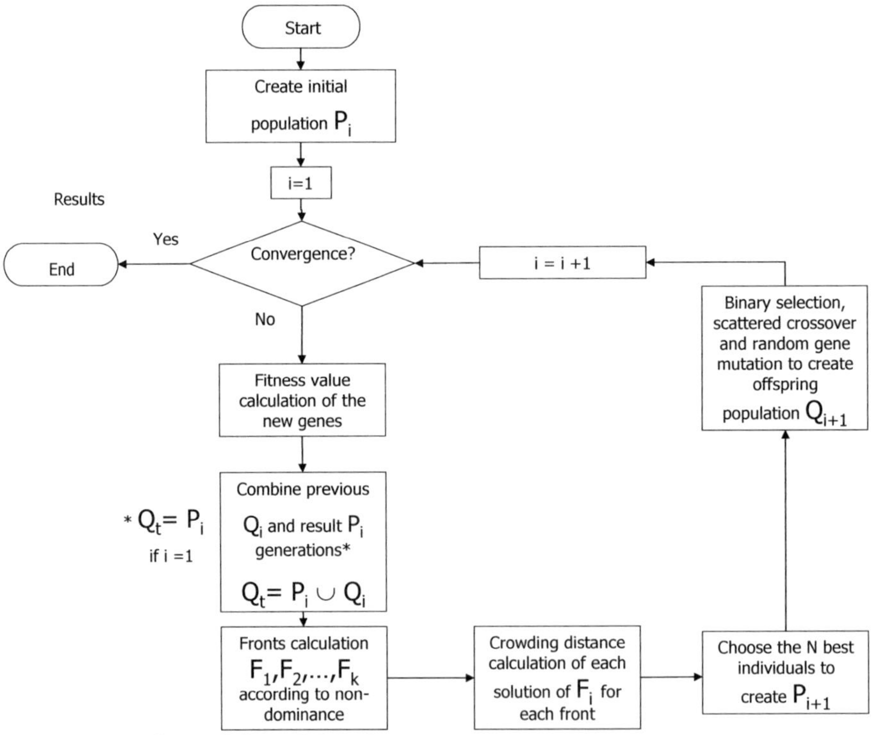

Fig. 3. Working procedure of the NSGA-II

Step 1. Fix N, i=1, and i_{max}.

- N = population size
- i = number of generations
- i_{max} = maximum number of interactions of the genetic algorithm

Step 2. Create and evaluate a random parent population P_i of size N.
Step 3. If $i=i_{maxGA}$ return P_i else:
Step 4. Form a combined population of size 2N as $T_i= P_i \cup Q_i$.

- Q_i = offspring population
- T_i size N and equal to P_i in the first interaction

Step 5. Ranking (according to restriction violations).
Step 6. Identify non dominated fronts F_1, F_2, ..., F_k. Thus an each solution is assigned a fitness equal to its non-domination level.
Step 7. Create P_{i+1} as the N best individuals from P_i.
Step 8. Select randomly N couples from P_{i+1} using a binary tournament selection.
Step 9. Create offspring population Q_{i+1} applying crossover and mutation (size N).
Step 10. Evaluate the offspring population.
Step 11. Do i=i+1.
Step 12. Go to step 4.

Following the procedure detailed above the algorithm evaluates the $\mathbf{x_1}, \mathbf{x_2}, \ldots, \mathbf{x_N}$ genes of each generation. In this case, to obtain the respective $f(\mathbf{x_1}), f(\mathbf{x_2}), \ldots, f(\mathbf{x_N})$ fitness values of the evaluation, the DES model performs a simulation where PM frequencies act as decision variables to obtain economic parameters.

6. Problem formulation

The optimization of preventive maintenance activities based on cost and benefit criteria can be formulated as a multi-objective optimization problem (MOP). A general MOP includes a set of parameters (decision variables), a set of objective functions, and a set of constraints. Objective functions and constraints are defined in terms of the decision variables using the models presented in the previous section. The optimization goal can be formulated to optimize a vector of functions of the form (Martorell et al. 2004):

$$\mathbf{y} = f(\mathbf{x}) = (f_1(\mathbf{x}), f_2(\mathbf{x}), \ldots, f_n(\mathbf{x})) \tag{22}$$

subject to the vector of constraints

$$g(\mathbf{x}) = (g_1(\mathbf{x}), g_2(\mathbf{x}), \ldots, g_n(\mathbf{x})) \tag{23}$$

where

$$\mathbf{x} = \{\mathbf{x}_1, \mathbf{x}_2, \ldots, \mathbf{x}_n\} \in \mathbf{X} \tag{24}$$

$$\mathbf{y} = \{\mathbf{y}_1, \mathbf{y}_2, \ldots, \mathbf{y}_n\} \in \mathbf{Y} \tag{25}$$

and **x** is the decision vector (vector of decision variables), **y** the objective vector, **X** the decision space and **Y** is the objective space, that is to say **Y**=f(**X**).
The optimization of PM activities proposed in this paper considers the productive costs and profit as optimization criteria. Both cost and profit models depend on maintenance intervals, which act as decision variables and are encoded in the decision vector, **x**. So, the vector of bi-objective function, f(**x**), is defined as:

$$f(\mathbf{x}) = \{C(\mathbf{x}), P(\mathbf{x})\} \tag{26}$$

where the objective is to minimize the function C(**x**) and maximize a profit function P(**x**). C(**x**) is the cost system which is evaluated as sum of the maintenance, production speed lost and quality costs for each of the m machines of the system which are evaluated using Eqns. (16 - 20).

$$C(\mathbf{x}) = \sum_{i=1}^{m} \left(c_{cm_i}(\mathbf{x}) + c_{pm_i}(\mathbf{x}) + c_{sl_i}(\mathbf{x}) + c_{q_i}(\mathbf{x}) \right) \tag{27}$$

and P(**x**) is the profit function obtained as a result of selling non-defective products, evaluated as it is detailed in Eq. (9).

In this case there are no constraints defined in terms of the vector of constraints. Nevertheless, constraints are imposed directly over the values the decision variables can take, which must get typified values, representing each one a day, two days, etc.
This maintenance optimization MOP can be solved using a MOEA. A MOEA is a multi-objective search method based on Darwin's evolutionary theory applied to a population of possible solutions which evolves and tends to converge to an optimal solution set.
The MOEA, in this case the NSGA-II, evolves the population which is evaluated executing simulations by using the developed model. The scheme of the optimization approach is shown in Fig. 4:

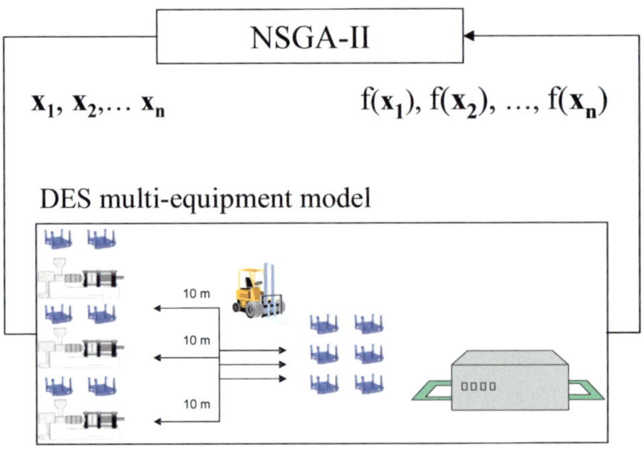

Fig. 4. Optimization approach

As it can be seen in Fig. 4, the NSGA-II creates a population of n decision vectors ($\mathbf{x}_1$, $\mathbf{x}_2$,... $\mathbf{x}_n$) which are evaluated executing simulations. The model returns the fitness values of each one of these vectors (f($\mathbf{x}_1$), f($\mathbf{x}_2$), ..., f($\mathbf{x}_n$)) which are processed in the NSGA-II to generate new populations. These evolutions tend to achieve solutions which are located in a Pareto optimal front, where it cannot be determined that a solution obtained is better than another without considering additional information.

7. Results

Fig. 5 represents a cost plot of results found by the NSGA-II. The results shown were calculated using a Pentium 4 3.2 GHz 1 GB RAM running the MOEA evolving a population of size 50 individuals for 200 generations with a selection rate of 0.25, crossover rate of 0.5 and mutation rate of 0.75. The DES model was using Witness PwE 1.00 by Lanner while the NSGA-II was implemented in Matlab R2010a by The Mathworks 2010.

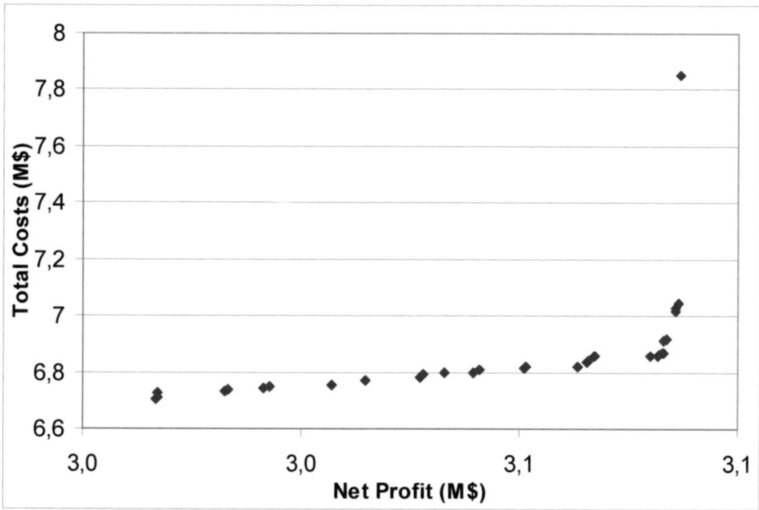

Fig. 5. Pareto front obtained in the optimization process

Additionally, Table 7 details the periodicities and cost-profit values of the PM activities shown in Fig. 5:

Wc1	Wc2	Wc3	Wc4	Wc5	Wc6	Net Profit (€)	Total Cost (€)
57	24	217	287	101	49	5073840	11569746,08
259	203	276	287	36	254	4958660	11391119,09
259	220	284	287	36	137	4944400	11376236,31
259	234	284	287	36	128	4934460	11363711,18
261	21	49	287	36	170	5069720	11557158,79
261	21	282	283	36	244	5072660	11558294,87
261	24	120	287	36	137	5078500	11824125,91
261	24	120	287	36	170	5078700	11819128,42
261	24	168	283	36	74	5079760	11864908,78
261	24	217	287	36	49	5074500	11577481,48
261	24	217	287	36	231	5073900	11570285,34
261	24	217	287	36	254	5073840	11569746,08
261	24	276	287	36	74	5075560	11658237,44
261	24	276	287	36	102	5080300	13330001,56
261	24	276	287	36	102	5073260	11551843,41
261	24	276	287	36	137	5078820	11839544,71
261	24	276	287	57	143	5080480	13209311,2
261	24	276	287	36	186	5078780	13088264,73
261	24	276	287	36	254	5075040	11644593,44
261	24	284	287	36	137	5074240	11575248,3
261	24	284	287	36	143	5072840	11561591,77
261	72	217	287	36	231	5049060	11529753,47
261	72	282	287	36	231	5050680	11557092,2
261	74	217	283	36	49	5048160	11520395,78
261	77	217	287	36	214	5045100	11494831,02
261	88	276	287	36	137	5038940	11503122,02
261	104	120	287	36	214	5027520	11491780,06
261	107	217	287	36	143	5026920	11484713,39
261	128	271	287	57	196	5011400	11474116,47
261	129	120	287	36	170	5009660	11458363,92
261	143	168	287	36	74	4999720	11453174,76
261	156	168	287	36	137	4992060	11442624,64
261	156	168	287	36	254	4991260	11423301,86
261	156	217	287	36	143	4992340	11441827,68
261	156	217	287	36	170	4991340	11429164,3
261	182	271	287	36	170	4972380	11407934,91
261	182	276	287	36	280	4973340	11402901,84
261	199	271	287	36	128	4960780	11378041,99
261	229	272	287	36	163	4939140	11369356,24
261	231	282	283	36	170	4937080	11361320,55
261	249	168	283	36	254	4924000	11340232,17
261	249	217	283	36	254	4924860	11351080,1
261	249	271	283	36	196	4925160	11354773,53
261	249	276	287	36	102	4924580	11339726,48
261	249	276	287	36	254	4924500	11337625,08
261	249	284	287	36	58	4924680	11343427,54
261	282	120	287	36	170	4900260	11297333,11
261	282	237	287	36	170	4900680	11305358,67
261	282	276	287	36	170	4902120	11337373,85
261	282	276	287	36	254	4900700	11306826,13

Table 7. PM periodicities and objective values of the obtained Pareto front

As it was stated previously, the developed MOP offers solutions which are situated in a Pareto optimal front. Thus, the analyst can select externally the best maintenance strategy, since it has to be considered simultaneously possible additional restrictions imposed over the solutions after having them. Hence, they can analyze afterwards how every solution of each Pareto set score in cost and profit criteria. Additionally, the Pareto front generated satisfies the constraint imposed to the problem. Each one of the elements calculated in the Front is related to critical age or deterioration levels when a preventive activity must be executed. So, the decision maker can select a solution of the Pareto front in accordance with his preferences knowing that the elected solution will accomplish all the imposed constraints.

Acknowledgments

We want to thank people of Mondragon Cooperación Cooperativa, for the valuable confidence and help provided to this research.
This project has been funded by the following projects and funding programs:

DEMAGILE TOOLS: Development of decision making tools for the implementation of principles related to the 'Leagile production'. Project funded by the Basque Government (Basic and Applied Research Project, PI2009-24 code).

AVAILAFACTURING: Development of a tool for the management of technical assistance service networks for the availability maximization of Manufacturing equipment and/or products (European transnational project MANUNET-2009-BC-006).

RCMTOOLS: Development of a simplified RCM tool. Project funded by the Basque Government (University-Industry Research Project, UE2010-03 code).

IMBOEE: Development of a continuous improvement program based on the Money Based OEE. Project funded by the Basque Government (University-Industry Research Project, UE09+/120 code).

8. References

Bader, J. M. & Guesneux, S. 2007, "Use real-time optimization for low-sulfur gasoline production", *Hydrocarbon Processing* no. February, pp. 97-103.

Chan, J. & Shaw, L. 1993, "Modeling repairable systems with failure rates that depend on age and maintenance", *IEEE Transactions on Reliability*, vol. 42, no. 4, pp. 566-571.

Deb, K., Pratap, A., Agarwal, S., & Meyarivan, T. 2002, "A fast and elitiste multiobjective genetic algorithm: NSGA-II", *IEEE Transactions on Evolutionary Computation*, vol. 6, no. 2, pp. 182-197.

Fiori de Castro, H. & Lucchesi Cavalca, K. 2006, "Maintenance resources optimization applied to a manufacturing system", *Reliability Engineering and System Safety*, vol. 91, pp. 413-420.

Gharbi, A. & Kenné, J. P. 2005, "Maintenance scheduling and production control of multiple-machine manufacturing systems", *Computers and Industrial Engineering*, vol. 48, pp. 693-702.

Goti, A. & Sánchez, A. 2006, "Multi-objective genetic algorithms optimize industrial maintenance", *Hydrocarbon Processing*, vol. 85, no. 12, pp. 106-108.

Goyal, S. K. & Kusy, M. I. 1985, "Determining economic maintenance frequency for a family of machines", *Joumal of the Operations Research Society*, vol. 36, no. 12, pp. 1125-1128.

Grigoriev, A., van de Klunder, J., & Spieksma, F. C. R. 2006, "Modeling and solving the periodic maintenance problem", *European Journal of Operational Research*, vol. 72, pp. 783-797.

Kenne, J. P., Boukas, E. K., & Gharbi, A. 2003, "Control of production and corrective maintenance rates in a multiple-machine, multiple-product manufacturing system", *Mathematical and Computer Modelling*, vol. 38, pp. 351-365.

Li, W. & Pham, H. 2005, "An inspection-maintenance model for systems with multiple competing processes", *IEEE Transactions on Reliability*, vol. 54, no. 2, pp. 318-327.

Li, W. & Zuo, M. J. 2007, "Joint Optimization of Inventory Control and Maintenance Policy, in "*2007 Proc.Ann.Reliability & Maintainability Symp.*"", in *Reliability and Maintainability in the New Frontier*, IEEE, Piscataway, New Jersey, pp. 321-326.

Malik, M. A. K. 1979, "Reliable preventive maintenance scheduling, ", *AIIE Transactions*, vol. 11, pp. 221-228.

Martorell, S., Sánchez , A., Carlos, S., & Serradell, V. 2004, "Alternatives and challenges in optimizing industrial safety using genetic algorithms", *Reliability Engineering and System Safety*, vol. 86, no. 1, pp. 25-38.

Martorell, S., Sánchez, A., & Serradell, V. 1998, "Residual life management of safety-related equipment considering maintenance and working conditions", in *ESREL'98*, Trondheirn, pp. 889-896.

Martorell, S., Sánchez, A., & Serradell, V. 1999, "Age-dependent reliability model considering effects of maintenance and working conditions", *Reliability Engineering and Systems Safety*, vol. 64, pp. 19-31.

Martorell, S., Serradell, V., & Samanta, P. K. 1995, "Improving allowed outage time and surveillance test interval requirements: a study of their interactions using probabilistic methods", *Reliability Engineering and System Safety*, vol. 47, no. 2, pp. 119-129.

Oyarbide-Zubillaga, A., Baines, T. S., & Kay, J. M. 2003, "Manufacturing Systems modelling using system dynamics: Forming a dedicated modelling tool", *Journal of Advanced Manufacturing Systems*, vol. 2, no. 1, pp. 71-87.

Sánchez, A. & Goti, A. 2006, "Preventive maintenance optimization under cost and profit criteria for manufacturing equipment, in "*Proceedings of ESREL 2006*"", in *Proceedings of ESREL 2006: Safety and Reliability for Managing Risk*, C. Guedes Soares & E. Zio, eds., Taylor & Francis Group, London, UK, pp. 607-612.

Sherif, Y. S. & Smith, M. L. 1981, "Optimal maintenance models for systems subject to failure", *Naval Research Logistics Quarterly*, vol. 28, no. 1, pp. 47-74.

Shin, Y., Lim, T. J., & Lie, C. H. 1996, "Estimating parameters of intensity function and maintenance effect for repairable unit", *Reliability Engineering and System Safety*, vol. 54, pp. 1-10.

Yao, M.-J. 2005, "On determining the optimal maintenance frequency for a family of machines", *Journal of the Chinese Institute of Industrial Engineers*, vol. 22, no. 3, pp. 199-209.

11

Advanced discrete event simulation methods with application to importance measure estimation in reliability

Arne Huseby, Bent Natvig and Jørund Gåsemyr
University of Oslo
Norway

Kristina Skutlaberg
FFI
Norway

Stefan Isaksen
DNV Energy
Norway

1. Introduction

Discrete event models are typically used in simulation studies to model and analyze pure jump processes. For an extensive introduction to discrete event models we refer to Glasserman & Yao (1994). A discrete event model can be viewed as a system consisting of a collection of stochastic processes, where the states of the individual processes change as results of various kinds of *events* occurring at random points of time. Between these events the states of the processes are considered to be constant. We refer to the processes included in the collection, as the *elementary processes* of the system. In our context we always assume that each event only affects *one* of the elementary processes.

More formally we consider a pure jump process S, and let $S(t)$ denote the state of the process at time $t \geq 0$. Moreover, we let $T_1 < T_2 < \cdots$ denote the points of time of the events affecting the process, and let $T_0 = 0$. In our context a pure jump process is a process where the state function, $S(t)$, can be written in the following form:

$$S(t) = S(0) + \sum_{j=1}^{\infty} I(T_j \leq t) J_j, \qquad t \geq 0, \tag{1}$$

where $I(\cdot)$ denotes the indicator function, and J_j denotes the change in the state of the process at time T_j. The representation (1) implies that the state function $S(t)$ is piecewise constant and right-continuous in t, with jumps at $T_1 < T_2 < \cdots$. In particular, for $j = 0, 1, \ldots$, we have $S(t) = S(T_j)$ for all $t \in [T_j, T_{j+1})$, implying that $\lim_{t \to T_j^+} S(t) = S(T_j)$.

The fact that a pure jump process is right-continuous and piecewise constant in t is convenient during simulations. Hence, in order to keep track of how the process evolves and to update

the value of the state function, only the points of time where the events happen need to be considered.
The infinite sum in (1) indicates that the number of events occurring in the interval $[0, t]$ is unbounded. The possibility of having an infinite number of events in $[0, t]$, however, may cause various technical difficulties. In particular, this may cause simulations to break down since an infinite number of events need to be generated and handled. See Glasserman (2004) for a further discussion of this issue. To avoid these difficulties, we always assume that the number of events occurring in any finite interval is finite with probability one. A pure jump process satisfying this assumption is said to be *regular*. Some basic results on regularity are included in the appendix. See also Klebaner (2005).

Stationary statistical properties of a system, can easily be estimated by running a *single* discrete event simulation on the system over a sufficiently long time horizon, or by working directly on the stationary probability distributions of the elementary processes. Sometimes, however, one needs to estimate how the statistical properties of the system evolve over time. In such cases it is necessary to run many simulations to obtain stable results. Moreover, one must store much more information from each simulation. A *crude* approach to this problem is to sample the system state at fixed intervals of time, and then use the mean values of the states at these points as estimates of the corresponding statistical properties. Using a sufficiently high sampling rate, i.e., short intervals between sampling points, a satisfactory estimate of the full curve can be obtained. Still, all information about the process between the sampling points is thrown away. Thus, we propose an alternative sampling procedure where we utilize process data between the sampling points as well.
In order to illustrate the main ideas we use discrete events in order to analyze a *multicomponent binary monotone system* of repairable components. In Natvig et al. (2009) the simulation methods developed in the present chapter, are used to estimate the Natvig measures of component importance in repairable binary systems of binary components and applied to an offshore oil and gas production system. For nonrepairable systems the Natvig measure is treated in Natvig (1979), Natvig (1982) and Natvig (1985).

2. Basic reliability theory

We start out by briefly reviewing basic concepts of reliability theory. See Barlow & Proschan (1981). A *binary monotone system* is an ordered pair (C, ϕ) where $C = \{1, \ldots, n\}$ is a nonempty finite set, and ϕ is a binary function. The elements of C are interpreted as components of some technological system. Each component, as well as the system itself can be either functioning or failed. We denote the state of component i at time $t \geq 0$ by $X_i(t)$, where $X_i(t) = 1$ if i is functioning at time t, and zero otherwise, $i = 1, \ldots, n$. We also introduce the component state vector $\boldsymbol{X}(t) = (X_1(t), \ldots, X_n(t))$. The function ϕ is called the *structure function* of the system, and expresses the state of the system as a function of the component state vector, and is assumed to be non-decreasing in each argument. Thus, $\phi = \phi(\boldsymbol{X}(t)) = 1$ if the system is functioning at time t and zero otherwise.
In the present chapter we consider systems with repairable components. Thus, for $i = 1, \ldots, n$ and $j = 1, 2, \ldots$ let:

$$U_{ij} = \text{The } j\text{th lifetime of the } i\text{th component.}$$

$$D_{ij} = \text{The } j\text{th repair time of the } i\text{th component.}$$

We assume that U_{ij} has an absolutely continuous distribution with a positive mean value $\mu_i < \infty$, while D_{ij} has an absolutely continuous distribution with a positive mean value $\nu_i < \infty$, $i = 1, \ldots, n$, $j = 1, 2, \ldots$. All lifetimes and repair times are assumed to be independent. Thus, in particular the component processes $X_1, \ldots, X_n$ are independent of each other.
Let $A_i(t)$ be the availability of the ith component at time t, i.e., the probability that the component is functioning at time t. That is, for $i = 1, \ldots, n$ we have:

$$A_i(t) = \Pr(X_i(t) = 1) = E[X_i(t)].$$

The corresponding stationary availabilities are given by:

$$A_i = \lim_{t \to \infty} A_i(t) = \frac{\mu_i}{\mu_i + \nu_i}, \qquad i = 1, \ldots, n. \tag{2}$$

Introduce $\boldsymbol{A}(t) = (A_1(t), \ldots, A_n(t))$ and $\boldsymbol{A} = (A_1, \ldots, A_n)$. The system availability at time t is given by:

$$A_\phi(t) = \Pr(\phi(\boldsymbol{X}(t)) = 1) = E[\phi(\boldsymbol{X}(t))] = h(\boldsymbol{A}(t)),$$

where h is the system's reliability function. The corresponding stationary availability is given by:

$$A_\phi = \lim_{t \to \infty} A_\phi(t) = h(\boldsymbol{A}). \tag{3}$$

The component i is said to be *critical* at time t if $\psi_i(\boldsymbol{X}(t)) = \phi(1_i, \boldsymbol{X}(t)) - \phi(0_i, \boldsymbol{X}(t)) = 1$. We will refer to $\psi_i(\boldsymbol{X}(t))$ as the *criticality state* of component i at time t. The Birnbaum measure of importance of component i at time t, is defined as the probability that component i is critical at time t, and denoted $I_B^{(i)}(t)$. See Birnbaum (1969). Thus,

$$\begin{aligned} I_B^{(i)}(t) &= \Pr(\psi_i(\boldsymbol{X}(t)) = 1) = E[\psi_i(\boldsymbol{X}(t))] \\ &= h(1_i, \boldsymbol{A}(t)) - h(0_i, \boldsymbol{A}(t)). \end{aligned} \tag{4}$$

The corresponding stationary measure is given by:

$$I_B^{(i)} = \lim_{t \to \infty} I_B^{(i)}(t) = h(1_i, \boldsymbol{A}) - h(0_i, \boldsymbol{A}). \tag{5}$$

3. Discrete event simulation

Let (C, ϕ) be a binary monotone system with component state processes $X_1, \ldots, X_n$. For $i = 1, \ldots, n$ we denote the events affecting the process X_i by $E_{i1}, E_{i2}, \ldots$, listed in chronological order. Since we assumed that all lifetimes and repair times have absolutely continuous distributions, all these events happen at distinct points of time almost surely. We let $T_{i1} < T_{i2}, \ldots$ be the corresponding points of time for these events. We also let $T_{i0} = 0$, $i = 1, \ldots, n$. As in (1) the component state processes can then be expressed as:

$$X_i(t) = X_i(0) + \sum_{j=1}^{\infty} I(T_{ij} \leq t) J_{ij}, \qquad t \geq 0, \; i = 1, \ldots, n, \tag{6}$$

where the jumps J_{ij} are either -1 if E_{ij} is a failure event, or $+1$ if E_{ij} is a repair event. We assume that all components start out by being functioning. Thus, we have $X_i(0) = 1$, and

$J_{ij} = (-1)^j$, for $i = 1, \ldots, n$ and $j = 1, 2, \ldots$. Finally, for $i = 1, \ldots, n$ we introduce the times between the events defined as:

$$\Delta_{ij} = T_{ij} - T_{ij-1}, \qquad i = 1, \ldots, n, \; j = 1, 2, \ldots. \tag{7}$$

Then for $i = 1, \ldots, n$ we have:

$$\Delta_{i1} = U_{i1}, \quad \Delta_{i2} = D_{i1}, \quad \Delta_{i3} = U_{i2}, \quad \ldots \tag{8}$$

Since $U_{i1}, U_{i2}, \ldots$ are independent and identically distributed with positive mean value μ_i, it follows by Proposition A.1 that X_i is a regular pure jump process, $i = 1, \ldots, n$. Hence, by Proposition A.4 the system state $\phi = \phi(\boldsymbol{X})$ as well as the criticality states $\psi_1(\boldsymbol{X}), \ldots, \psi_n(\boldsymbol{X})$ are regular pure jump processes.
At the system level the event set is the *union* of all the component event sets. Note that since we assumed that all lifetimes and repair times have absolutely continuous distributions, each system event corresponds almost surely to a unique component event.

In order to simulate such a system, we use an *object oriented approach* where the components as well as the system are represented as *objects*. The component objects are equipped with methods for generating failure and repair events according to their respective life- and repair time distributions. The system object determines the state of the system as a function of the component states. To keep track of the events and process them in the correct order, they are organized in a dynamic queue sorted with respect to the points of time of the events. The component processes place their upcoming events into the queue where they stay until they are processed.
More specifically, at time zero each component starts out by being functioning, and places its first failure event into the queue. As soon as all these failure events have been placed into the queue, the first event in the queue is processed. That is, the *system time* is set to the time of the first event, and the event is taken out of the queue and passed on to the component responsible for handling this event. The component then updates its state, generates a new event, in this case a repair event, which is placed into queue, and notifies the system about its new state so that the system state can be updated as well. Then the next event in the queue is processed in the same fashion, and so forth until the system time reaches a certain predefined point of time. Note that since the component events are generated as part of the event processing, the number of events in the queue stays constant.

3.1 Sampling events

Although the system state and component states stay constant between events, it may still be of interest to log the state values at predefined points of time. In order to facilitate this, we introduce yet another type of event, called a *sampling event*. Such sampling events will typically be spread out evenly on the timeline. Thus, if $e_1, e_2, \ldots$ denote the sampling events, and $t_1 < t_2 < \cdots$ are the corresponding points of time, we would typically have $t_j = j \cdot \Delta$ for some suitable number $\Delta > 0$.
The sampling events will be placed into the queue in the same way as for the ordinary events. As a sampling event is processed, the next sampling event will be placed into the queue. Thus, at any time only one sampling event needs to be in the queue.

3.2 Updating system and criticality states

In principle one must update the system state every time there is a change in the component states. For large complex systems, these updates may slow down the simulations considerably. Thus, whenever possible one should avoid computing the system state. Fortunately, since the structure function of a binary monotone system is non-decreasing in each argument, it is possible to reduce the updating to a minimum. To explain this in detail, we consider the event E_{ij} affecting component i. Let T_{ij} be the corresponding point of time, and let $\boldsymbol{X}(T_{ij}^-)$ denote the value of the component state vector immediately before E_{ij} occurs, i.e.,

$$\boldsymbol{X}(T_{ij}^-) = \lim_{t \to T_{ij}^-} \boldsymbol{X}(t).$$

Note that by Proposition A.2 these limits exist since the component state processes are regular. If E_{ij} is a failure event of component i, i.e., $X_i(T_{ij}^-) = 1$ and $X_i(T_{ij}) = 0$, then the event cannot change the system state if the system is already failed, i.e., $\phi(\boldsymbol{X}(T_{ij}^-)) = 0$. Similarly, if E_{ij} is a repair event of component i, i.e., $X_i(T_{ij}^-) = 0$ and $X_i(T_{ij}) = 1$, this event cannot change the system state if the system is already functioning, i.e., $\phi(\boldsymbol{X}(T_{ij}^-)) = 1$. Thus, we see that we only need to recalculate the system state whenever:

$$\phi(\boldsymbol{X}(T_{ij}^-)) \neq X_i(T_{ij}). \tag{9}$$

Hence, the number of times we need to recalculate the system state is drastically reduced.
In cases where we keep track of the criticality state of each of the components, we can simplify the calculations even further by noting that the system state is changed as a result of the event E_{ij} if and only if component i is critical at the time of the event. Moreover, if i is critical, and E_{ij} is a failure event, it follows that the system fails as a result of this event, i.e., $\phi(\boldsymbol{X}(T_{ij})) = 0$. If on the other hand i is critical, and E_{ij} is a repair event, it follows that the system becomes functioning as a result of this event, i.e., $\phi(\boldsymbol{X}(T_{ij})) = 1$. Thus, we see that all the calculations we need to carry out, are related to the updating of the criticality states.
A similar technique can be used when updating the criticality states of the components. Thus, we consider the event E_{ij} affecting the state of component i. We first note that the criticality state function of component i, $\psi_i(\boldsymbol{X}(t)) = \phi(1_i, \boldsymbol{X}(t)) - \phi(0_i, \boldsymbol{X}(t))$ does not depend on the state of component i. Thus, the event E_{ij} does not have any impact on the criticality state of i. However, E_{ij} may still change the criticality state of other components in the system even when the system state remains unchanged. Thus, let $k \neq i$ be another component, and consider its criticality state function $\psi_k(\boldsymbol{X}(T_{ij}))$.
If $X_k(T_{ij}) = 1$ and $\phi(\boldsymbol{X}(T_{ij})) = 0$, it follows that $\phi(1_k, \boldsymbol{X}(T_{ij})) = \phi(0_k, \boldsymbol{X}(T_{ij})) = 0$. Thus, in this case we must have $\psi_k(\boldsymbol{X}(T_{ij})) = 0$. On the other hand, if $X_k(T_{ij}) = 0$ and $\phi(\boldsymbol{X}(T_{ij})) = 1$, it follows that $\phi(1_k, \boldsymbol{X}(T_{ij})) = \phi(0_k, \boldsymbol{X}(T_{ij})) = 1$. Thus, we must have $\psi_k(\boldsymbol{X}(T_{ij})) = 0$ in this case as well. Hence, we see that a necessary condition for component k to be critical at time T_{ij} is that:

$$\phi(\boldsymbol{X}(T_{ij})) = X_k(T_{ij}). \tag{10}$$

Utilizing these observations reduces the need to recalculate the criticality states.

3.3 Estimating availability and importance

Stationary availability and importance measures are typically easy to derive. If the system under consideration is not too complex, these quantities can be calculated analytically using (2), (3) and (5). For larger complex systems one may estimate the availability and importance using Monte Carlo simulations. A fast simulation algorithm for this is provided in Huseby & Naustdal (2003). Alternatively, estimates can be obtained by running a *single* discrete event simulation on the system over a sufficiently long time horizon

Here, however, we focus on the problem of estimating the system availability $A_\phi(t)$ and the component importance measures $I_B^{(1)}(t), \ldots, I_B^{(n)}(t)$ as functions of t for all $t \in [0, t_{\max}]$. For practical purposes, however, we have to limit the estimation to a finite evenly spaced set of points. More specifically, we will estimate $A_\phi(t)$ for $t \in \{t_1, \ldots, t_N\}$, where $t_j = j \cdot \Delta$, $j = 1, \ldots, N$, and $t_N = N \cdot \Delta = t_{\max}$.

A simple approach to this problem is to run M simulations on the system, where each simulation covers the time interval $[0, t_{\max}]$. In each simulation we sample the values of ϕ and $\psi_1, \ldots, \psi_n$ at each sampling point $t_1, \ldots, t_N$. We denote the sth simulated value of the component state vector process at time $t \geq 0$ by $\boldsymbol{X}_s(t)$, $s = 1, \ldots, M$, and obtain the following estimates for $j = 1, \ldots, N$:

$$\hat{A}_\phi(t_j) = \frac{1}{M} \sum_{s=1}^{M} \phi(\boldsymbol{X}_s(t_j)), \tag{11}$$

$$\hat{I}_B^{(i)}(t_j) = \frac{1}{M} \sum_{s=1}^{M} \psi_i(\boldsymbol{X}_s(t_j)). \tag{12}$$

We will refer to these estimates as *pointwise estimates*. It is easy to see that for $j = 1, \ldots, N$, $\hat{A}_\phi(t_j)$ and $\hat{I}_B^{(i)}(t_j)$ are unbiased and strongly consistent estimates of $A_\phi(t_j)$ and $I_B^{(i)}(t_j)$ respectively. In order to estimate $A_\phi(t)$ and $I_B^{(i)}(t)$ between the sampling points, one may use interpolation. Using a sufficiently high sampling rate, i.e., a high value of N or equivalently a small value of Δ, a satisfactory estimate of the full curve can be obtained. Still, all information about the process between the sampling points is thrown away.

We now present an alternative approach where we utilize process data between the sampling points as well. As above we assume that the system is simulated M times over the interval $[0, t_{\max}]$, and let $\boldsymbol{X}_s(t)$ denote the sth simulated value of the component state vector process at time $t \geq 0$, $s = 1, \ldots, M$. Then let $E_s^{(1)}, E_s^{(2)}, \ldots$ denote the events in the interval $[0, t_{\max}]$ in the sth simulation, *including* sampling events at times $t_1, \ldots, t_N$, and let $T_s^{(1)} < T_s^{(2)} < \cdots$ be the corresponding points of time, $s = 1, \ldots, M$. In this case we also include an extra sampling event in each simulation at time $t_0 = 0$, denoted $E_s^{(0)}$, and let $T_s^{(0)} = 0$, $s = 1, \ldots, M$.

The idea now is to use average simulated availability and criticalities from each interval $[t_{j-1}, t_j)$, $j = 1, \ldots, N$ as respective estimates for the availability and criticalities at the midpoints of these intervals. By using Proposition A.3, we obtain the following estimates for

$j = 1, \ldots, N$:

$$\tilde{A}_\phi(\bar{t}_j) = \frac{1}{M}\sum_{s=1}^{M}\frac{1}{\Delta}\int_{t_{j-1}}^{t_j}\phi(\boldsymbol{X}_s(t))dt$$
$$= \frac{1}{M\Delta}\sum_{s=1}^{M}\sum_{k\in\mathcal{E}_s^{(j)}}\phi(\boldsymbol{X}_s(T_s^{(k)}))(T_s^{(k+1)} - T_s^{(k)}), \quad (13)$$

$$\tilde{I}_B^{(i)}(\bar{t}_j) = \frac{1}{M}\sum_{s=1}^{M}\frac{1}{\Delta}\int_{t_{j-1}}^{t_j}\psi_i(\boldsymbol{X}_s(t))dt$$
$$= \frac{1}{M\Delta}\sum_{s=1}^{M}\sum_{k\in\mathcal{E}_s^{(j)}}\psi_i(\boldsymbol{X}_s(T_s^{(k)}))(T_s^{(k+1)} - T_s^{(k)}), \quad (14)$$

where $\mathcal{E}_s^{(j)}$ denotes the index set of the events in $[t_{j-1}, t_j)$ in the sth simulation, and where we have introduced the interval midpoints $\bar{t}_j = (t_{j-1} + t_j)/2, j = 1, \ldots, N$. We will refer to these estimates as *interval estimates*.

By using the right-continuity of the component state processes, it is easy to see that for $j = 1, \ldots, N$, $\tilde{A}_\phi(\bar{t}_j)$ and $\tilde{I}_B^{(i)}(\bar{t}_j)$ are unbiased and strongly consistent estimates of the corresponding average availability and criticality in the intervals $[t_{j-1}, t_j)$ respectively. By choosing Δ so that the availabilities and criticalities are relatively stable within each interval, the interval estimates are approximately unbiased estimates for $A_\phi(\bar{t}_j)$ and $I_B^{(i)}(\bar{t}_j)$ as well. In fact the resulting interval estimates tend to stabilize much faster than the pointwise estimates. In order to estimate $A_\phi(t)$ and $I_B^{(i)}(t)$ between the interval midpoints, one may again use interpolation. Note that since all process information is used in the estimates, satisfactory curve estimates can be obtained for a much higher value of Δ than the one needed for the pointwise estimates. In the next section we will demonstrate this on some examples.

4. Numerical results

In order to illustrate the methods presented in Section 3 we consider a simple bridge system shown in Figure 1. The components of this system are the five edges in the graph, labeled 1,...,5. The system is functioning if the source node s can communicate with the terminal node t through the graph. All the components in the system have exponential lifetime and repair time distributions with mean values 1 time unit. The objective of the simulation is to estimate $A_\phi(t)$ and $I_B^{(1)}(t), \ldots, I_B^{(5)}(t)$ for $t \in [0, t_{\max}]$, where $t_{\max} = 1000$.

All the simulations were carried out using a program called *Eventcue*[1]. This program has an intuitive graphical user interface, and can be used to estimate availability and criticality of any undirected network system.

Since all the lifetimes and repair times are exponentially distributed with the *same mean*, it is easy to derive explicit analytical expressions for the component availabilities. To see this, we consider the ith component at a given point of time t and introduce $N_i(t)$ as the number of failure and repair events affecting component i in $[0, t]$. With times between events being

[1] Eventcue is a java program developed at the Department of Mathematics, University of Oslo. The program is freely available at http://www.riscue.org/eventcue/.

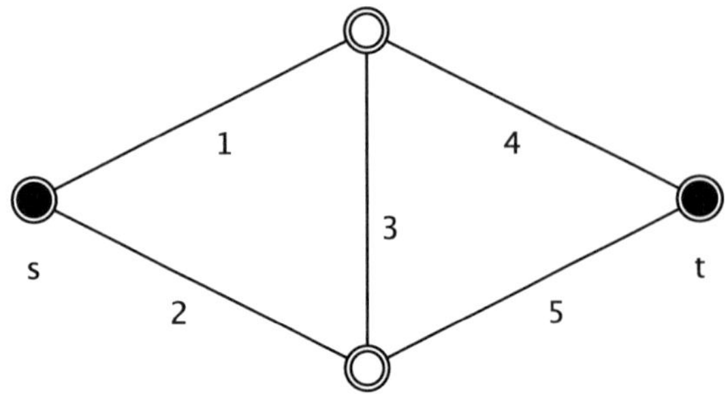

Fig. 1. A bridge system.

independent and exponentially distributed with mean 1 it follows that $N_i(t)$ has a Poisson distribution with mean t. Moreover, component i is functioning at time t if and only if $N_i(t)$ is even. Thus, the ith component availability at time t is given by:

$$A_i(t) = \sum_{k=0}^{\infty} \Pr(N_i(t) = 2k) = \sum_{k=0}^{\infty} \frac{t^{2k}}{(2k)!} e^{-t}. \quad (15)$$

Using (15) one can verify numerically that all the component availabilities converge very fast towards their common stationary value, 0.5. As a result of this the system availability, $A_\phi(t)$, converges very fast towards its stationary value, 0.5, as well. In fact, for $t > 20$, numerical calculations show that $|A_\phi(t) - 0.5| < 10^{-15}$. Similarly, the Birnbaum measures of importance converges so that for $t > 20$, $|I_B^{(i)}(t) - 0.375| < 10^{-15}$, $i = 1, 2, 4, 5$, while $|I_B^{(3)}(t) - 0.125| < 10^{-15}$. Thus, for $t > 20$ the true values of all the curves are approximately constant. This makes it easy to evaluate and compare the quality of the different Monte Carlo estimates in this particular case.

Figure 2 and Figure 3 show respectively the system availability curve and the criticality curve of component 1. The black curves are obtained using the interval estimates, while the gray curves show the corresponding pointwise estimate curves. In all cases we have used $M = 1000$ simulations and $N = 100$ sample points.

The plots clearly show the difference between the two methods. The black interval estimate curves are much more stable, and thus much closer to the true curve values, compared to the gray pointwise estimates.

One may think that increasing the number of sampling points would make the pointwise curve estimate better as more information is sampled. However, it turns out that the main effect of this is that the curve jumps more and more up and down. In fact with shorter intervals between sampling points the interval estimate becomes more unstable as well, and in the limit where the interval lengths go to zero, the two methods become equivalent. The only effective way of stabilizing the results for the pointwise curve estimate is to increase the number of simulations, i.e., M.

In Table 1 we have listed estimated standard deviations for pointwise curve estimates of the system availability curve for different values of M. We see that the standard deviation shows

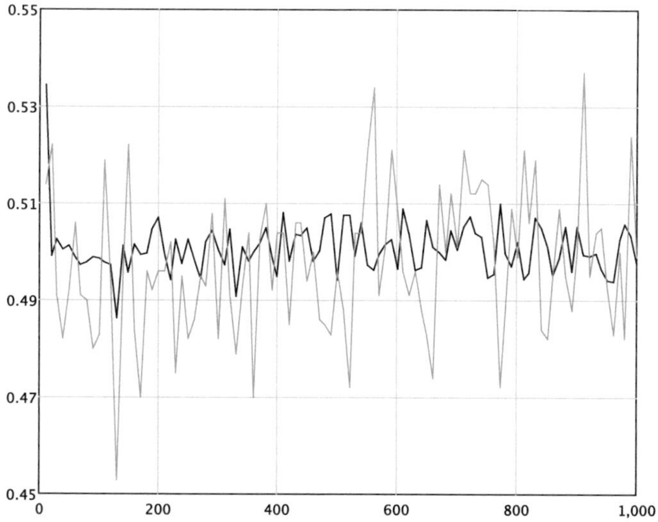

Fig. 2. Interval estimate (black curve) and pointwise estimate (gray curve) of the system availability curve.

M	2000	4000	6000	8000
St.dev.	0.0121	0.0076	0.0062	0.0054

Table 1. Standard deviations for the pointwise curve estimates of the system availability curve.

a steady decline as M increases. The corresponding numbers for $M = 1000$ are 0.0055 for the interval curve estimate and 0.0148 for the pointwise estimate. Thus, in this particular case we see that to obtain a pointwise curve estimate with a comparable stability to the interval curve estimate, one needs about eight times as many simulations.

For the interval curve estimate it is possible to obtain an even smoother curve simply by increasing Δ. Still, in general Δ should not be made too large, as this could produce a curve where important effects are obscured. Thus, in order to obtain optimal results, one should try out different values for Δ, and balance smoothness against the need of capturing significant oscillation properties of the curve.

Now, if smoothness is important, it is of course possible to apply some standard smoothing technique, such as moving averages or exponential smoothing, to the pointwise curve estimate. While such post-smoothing would clearly make the curve smoother, this technique does not add any new information to the estimate. The main advantage with the interval curve estimates is that such estimates actually use information about all events. Especially in cases where events occur at a very high rate, this turns out to be a great advantage.

5. Applications to importance measure estimation

In this section we shall explain how the sampling methods developed in Section 3 can be used to estimate the more advanced importance measures introduced in Barlow & Proschan (1975) and Natvig & Gåsemyr (2009).

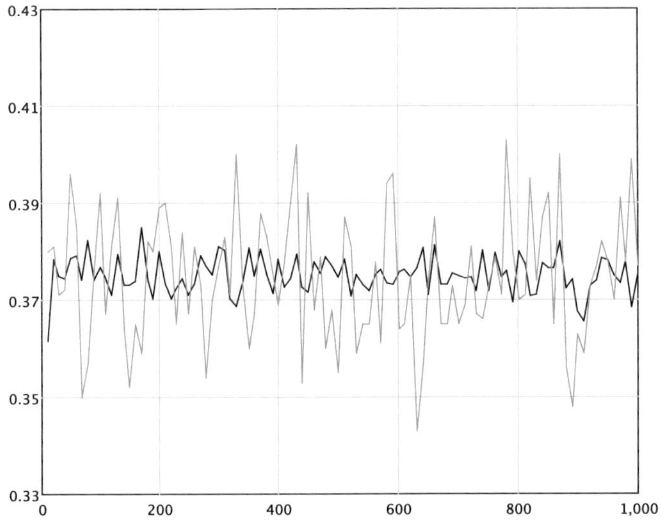

Fig. 3. Interval estimate (black curve) and pointwise estimate (gray curve) of the importance curve of component 1.

5.1 Barlow-Proschan importance measure estimation

Let (C, ϕ) be a binary monotone system where $C = \{1, \ldots, n\}$, and introduce the following pure jump processes for $i = 1, \ldots, n$ and $t > 0$:

$$K_i(t) = \text{The number of failures of the } i\text{th component in } [0, t], \tag{16}$$

$$L_i(t) = \text{The number of system failures caused by the } i\text{th component in } [0, t]. \tag{17}$$

We also introduce the mean value functions of the K_i- and L_i-processes. That is, for $i = 1, \ldots, n$ and $t > 0$ we let:

$$\kappa_i(t) = E[K_i(t)], \tag{18}$$

$$\lambda_i(t) = E[L_i(t)]. \tag{19}$$

In Barlow & Proschan (1975) it is proved heuristically that for $i = 1, \ldots, n$ and $t > 0$:

$$\lambda_i(t) = \int_0^t I_B^{(i)}(u) d\kappa_i(u). \tag{20}$$

The Barlow-Proschan importance measure is based on the quantity $\lambda_i(t)$. According to this measure a component which often causes system failure is considered to be important.
Now, for $i = 1, \ldots, n$ and $t > 0$ it is very easy to estimate $\lambda_i(t)$ directly by simply running M simulations of the system over the time interval $[0, t]$, and counting the number of times component i causes system failures. Thus, if $L_{is}(t)$ denotes the number of system failures caused by the ith component in $[0, t]$ in the sth simulation, we get the following strongly consistent estimate of $\lambda_i(t)$:

$$\bar{\lambda}_i(t) = \frac{1}{M} \sum_{s=1}^{M} L_{is}(t). \tag{21}$$

However, in order to better understand the interaction between the criticality function ψ_i and the K_i-process, it can sometimes be of interest to estimate $\lambda_i(t)$ using (20) instead. In order to accomplish this, we use the curve estimates for $I_B^{(i)}$ obtained in the previous sections in combination with curve estimates for κ_i.

Pointwise estimates for κ_i over a suitable time interval $[0, t_{\max}]$ are obtained by running M simulations of component i and sampling the state of the K_i-process at evenly spaced points $t_1, t_2, \ldots, t_N$, where as before $t_N = t_{\max}$. Thus, if $K_{is}(t)$ denotes the number of failures of component i in $[0, t]$ in the sth simulation, we get the following strongly consistent estimate of $\kappa_i(t_j)$, for $i = 1, \ldots, n$ and $j = 1, \ldots, N$:

$$\hat{\kappa}_i(t_j) = \frac{1}{M} \sum_{s=1}^{M} K_{is}(t_j). \tag{22}$$

Furthermore, interval estimates for κ_i over the time interval $[0, t_{\max}]$ are obtained by running M simulations of component i and calculating the average values of the K_i-process over the intervals $[t_{j-1}, t_j)$, $j = 1, \ldots, N$ and where $t_0 = 0$.

We assume as before that each of these intervals has length Δ. Then for $i = 1, \ldots, n$, we let $E_{is}^{(1)}, E_{is}^{(2)}, \ldots$ denote the events affecting the process K_i in the interval $[0, t_{\max}]$ in the sth simulation, *including* the sampling events, and let $T_{is}^{(1)} < T_{is}^{(2)} < \cdots$ be the corresponding points of time, $s = 1, \ldots, M$. As before we also include an extra sampling event in each simulation at time $t_0 = 0$, denoted $E_{is}^{(0)}$, and let $T_{is}^{(0)} = 0$, $s = 1, \ldots, M$. By using Proposition A.3 we then get the following interval estimates for $i = 1, \ldots, n$ and $j = 1, \ldots, N$:

$$\begin{aligned} \tilde{\kappa}_i(\bar{t}_j) &= \frac{1}{M} \sum_{s=1}^{M} \frac{1}{\Delta} \int_{t_{j-1}}^{t_j} K_i(t) dt \\ &= \frac{1}{M\Delta} \sum_{s=1}^{M} \sum_{k \in \mathcal{E}_{is}^{(j)}} K_{is}(T_{is}^{(k)})(T_{is}^{(k+1)} - T_{is}^{(k)}), \end{aligned} \tag{23}$$

where $\mathcal{E}_{is}^{(j)}$ denotes the index set of the events affecting the process K_i in $[t_{j-1}, t_j)$ in the sth simulation, and where the interval midpoints are $\bar{t}_j = (t_{j-1} + t_j)/2$, $j = 1, \ldots, N$.

By combining pointwise curve estimates or interval estimates with the respective estimates for $I_B^{(i)}$ we get the following estimates for $\lambda_i(t)$, $i = 1, \ldots, n$ and $t > 0$:

$$\hat{\lambda}_i(t) = \int_0^t \hat{I}_B^{(i)}(u) d\hat{\kappa}_i(u), \tag{24}$$

$$\tilde{\lambda}_i(t) = \int_0^t \tilde{I}_B^{(i)}(u) d\tilde{\kappa}_i(u), \tag{25}$$

where the integrals are easily calculated numerically.

5.2 Natvig importance measure estimation

In order to explain the ideas behind the Natvig importance measures introduced in Natvig & Gåsemyr (2009), we consider once again a binary monotone system (C, ϕ). Moreover, let $i \in C$ be a component in the system, and let $E_{i1}, E_{i2}, \ldots$ be the events affecting this component occurring respectively at $T_{i1} < T_{i2} < \cdots$. For each of these events we then introduce new *fictive* events $E'_{i1}, E'_{i2}, \ldots$ occurring respectively at $T'_{i1}, T'_{i2}, \cdots$. We assume that the fictive events always occur after their respective *real* events. That is, $T_{ij} < T'_{ij}$, $j = 1, 2, \ldots$. The fictive events could represent the results of some sort of fictive action altering how the state of the component interacts with the system throughout the interval between the real event and the corresponding fictive event. If E_{ij} is a failure event, then E'_{ij} could e.g., be a fictive failure event occurring as a result of the component undergoing a fictive minimal repair at T_{ij} and then functioning until T'_{ij}. Similarly, if E_{ij} is a repair event, one may consider fictive actions, such as e.g., a fictive minimal failure at T_{ij} that extends the repair interval until T'_{ij}, where a fictive repair event occurs. For a precise definition of the concept of minimal repairs and failures, we refer to Natvig & Gåsemyr (2009). The effect on the system of such fictive actions typically says something about the importance of the component. In any case, however, unless the component is critical at some point during the interval $[T_{ij}, T'_{ij})$, the system will not be affected by the fictive action. This motivates the definition of the following pure jump processes ($i = 1, \ldots, n$):

$$Z_i(t) = \int_0^t \sum_{j=1}^{\infty} c_{ij} \cdot I(T_{ij} \leq u < T'_{ij}) \psi_i(\boldsymbol{X}(u)) du, \tag{26}$$

where $c_{ij} = c_F$ if E_{ij} is a failure event, and $c_{ij} = c_R$ if E_{ij} is a repair event, and where c_F and c_R are suitable known constants, typically 0 or 1. Note that if $c_F = 1$, all the fictive minimal repairs occurring in $[0, t]$ will be included as contributions to $Z_i(t)$, while if $c_F = 0$, these fictive actions will be ignored. Similarly, if $c_R = 1$, all the fictive minimal failures occurring in $[0, t]$ will be included as contributions to $Z_i(t)$, while if $c_R = 0$, these fictive actions will be ignored. We also introduce the mean value functions of the Z_i-processes. That is, for $i = 1, \ldots, n$ and $t > 0$ we let:

$$\zeta_i(t) = E[Z_i(t)]. \tag{27}$$

The mean value functions $\zeta_1(t), \ldots, \zeta_n(t)$ now serve as a basis for an importance measure. In particular, it can be shown that the importance measures introduced in Natvig & Gåsemyr (2009) can be derived from these functions. The so-called extended Natvig measure is e.g., obtained by setting $c_F = c_R = 1$.

Since the process $Z_i(t)$ involves both real and fictive events, estimating its mean value function using standard discrete event simulation can be a complex task. While the real events represent a single possible sequence of changes in the states of the system and its components, each of the fictive events introduces an alternative sequence of state changes. Note in particular that it may happen that a fictive event, E'_{ij}, occurs after the *next* real event, E_{ij+1}, in which case the intervals $[T_{ij}, T'_{ij})$ and $[T_{ij+1}, T'_{ij+1})$ overlap. Hence, keeping track of all the different parallel sequences of events is indeed a challenge. Armed with the methods introduced in the previous section, however, the problem can easily be solved. In order to study this in further detail we first note that since the component processes are assumed to be independent, we have:

$$\begin{aligned}\zeta_i(t) &= \int_0^t [\sum_{j=1}^{\infty} c_{ij} \Pr(T_{ij} \leq u < T'_{ij})] I_B^{(i)}(u) du \\ &= \int_0^{t_N} \omega_i(u) I_B^{(i)}(u) du,\end{aligned} \tag{28}$$

where we have introduced the weight function:

$$\omega_i(u) = E[\sum_{j=1}^{\infty} c_{ij} I(T_{ij} \leq u < T'_{ij})] = \sum_{j=1}^{\infty} c_{ij} \Pr(T_{ij} \leq u < T'_{ij}). \tag{29}$$

Now, by running a separate discrete event simulation for each of the components the weight functions, $\omega_1, \ldots, \omega_n$, can easily be estimated using similar techniques as the ones discussed in the previous sections. More specifically, we introduce the processes $W_1(t), \ldots, W_n(t)$ defined by:

$$W_i(t) = \sum_{j=1}^{\infty} c_{ij} I(T_{ij} \leq t < T'_{ij}), \quad t \geq 0, i = 1, \ldots, n. \tag{30}$$

To simplify the expressions it is convenient to introduce a common notation for *all* events, real or fictive, affecting the process $W_i(t)$, $i = 1, \ldots, n$. We sort these events in chronological order and denote them by $E_i^{(1)}, E_i^{(2)}, \ldots$. Moreover, we let $T_i^{(1)} < T_i^{(2)} < \cdots$ be the points of time corresponding to these events.
Since we have assumed that the fictive events always occur after their respective real events, it is easy to see that the processes $W_1(t), \ldots, W_n(t)$ are regular pure jump processes that can be written as:

$$W_i(t) = W_i(0) + \sum_{j=1}^{\infty} I(T_i^{(j)} \leq t) J_i^{(j)}, \quad t \geq 0, i = 1, \ldots, n, \tag{31}$$

where $W_1(0) = \cdots = W_n(0) = 0$, and where the jumps are given by:

$$J_i^{(j)} = \begin{cases} +c_F & \text{if } E_i^{(j)} \text{ is a real failure event} \\ -c_F & \text{if } E_i^{(j)} \text{ is a fictive failure event} \\ +c_R & \text{if } E_i^{(j)} \text{ is a real repair event} \\ -c_R & \text{if } E_i^{(j)} \text{ is a fictive repair event} \end{cases} \qquad i = 1, \ldots, n, \; j = 1, 2, \ldots. \tag{32}$$

From (29) and (30) we have $E[W_i(t)] = \omega_i(t), t \geq 0, i = 1, \ldots, n$. Thus, in order to estimate the weight functions $\omega_1(t), \ldots, \omega_n(t)$ over a suitable time interval $[0, t_{\max}]$, we run M simulations for each of the processes $W_1, \ldots, W_n$ over this interval, and sample the processes at the evenly spaced points $t_1, t_2, \ldots, t_N$, where $t_N = t_{\max}$. Unbiased and strongly consistent pointwise estimates of the weight functions are then obtained using the following formula:

$$\hat{\omega}_i(t_j) = \frac{1}{M} \sum_{s=1}^{M} W_{is}(t_j), \quad j = 1, \ldots, N, \; i = 1, \ldots, n, \tag{33}$$

where $W_{is}(t)$ denotes the value of $W_i(t)$ at time $t \geq 0$ in the sth simulation, $s = 1, \ldots, M$, $i = 1, \ldots, n$.

Alternatively, we can obtain interval estimates of the weight functions in the same way as we did in the previous subsection. As above we assume that the processes $W_1, \ldots, W_n$ are simulated M times over the interval $[0, t_{\max}]$, and let $W_{is}(t)$ denote the value of $W_i(t)$ at time $t \geq 0$ in the sth simulation, $s = 1, \ldots, M$, $i = 1, \ldots, n$. Then for $i = 1, \ldots, n$, we let $E_{is}^{(1)}, E_{is}^{(2)}, \ldots$ denote the events affecting the process W_i in the interval $[0, t_{\max}]$ in the sth simulation, *including* the sampling events, and let $T_{is}^{(1)} < T_{is}^{(2)} < \cdots$ be the corresponding points of time,

$s = 1, \ldots, M$. As for the previous interval estimates we also include an extra sampling event in each simulation at time $t_0 = 0$, denoted $E_{is}^{(0)}$, and let $T_{is}^{(0)} = 0$, $s = 1, \ldots, M$.
The interval estimates for the weight functions are then obtained by using average simulated values of the processes $W_1, \ldots, W_n$ from each interval $[t_{j-1}, t_j)$, $j = 1, \ldots, N$ as estimates for the respective weight functions at the midpoints of these intervals. By using Proposition A.3 we obtain the following estimates for $i = 1, \ldots, n$ and $j = 1, \ldots, N$:

$$\begin{aligned} \tilde{\omega}_i(\bar{t}_j) &= \frac{1}{M} \sum_{s=1}^{M} \frac{1}{\Delta} \int_{t_{j-1}}^{t_j} W_{is}(t) dt \\ &= \frac{1}{M\Delta} \sum_{s=1}^{M} \sum_{k \in \mathcal{E}_{is}^{(j)}} W_{is}(T_{is}^{(k)})(T_{is}^{(k+1)} - T_{is}^{(k)}), \end{aligned} \tag{34}$$

where once again $\mathcal{E}_{is}^{(j)}$ denotes the index set of the events affecting the process W_i in $[t_{j-1}, t_j)$ in the sth simulation, and where the interval midpoints are $\bar{t}_j = (t_{j-1} + t_j)/2$, $j = 1, \ldots, N$.
By combining pointwise curve estimates or interval estimates with the respective estimates for $I_B^{(i)}$ we get the following estimates for $\zeta_i(t)$, $i = 1, \ldots, n$ and $t > 0$:

$$\hat{\zeta}_i(t) = \int_0^t \hat{\omega}_i(u) \hat{I}_B^{(i)}(u) du, \tag{35}$$

$$\tilde{\zeta}_i(t) = \int_0^t \tilde{\omega}_i(u) \tilde{I}_B^{(i)}(u) du, \tag{36}$$

where the integrals are easily calculated numerically.

Note that in cases where several different importance measures are used, each with its own weight function, the proposed methodology allows us to reuse the curve estimate for $I_B^{(i)}$ when calculating each of the measures. This makes it easier and faster to compare the different measures like e.g., the Barlow-Proschan importance measure and the Natvig importance measure.

5.3 Estimating importance in the bridge structure

We close this section by applying the proposed methods to the example considered in Section 4. That is, we consider once again the bridge system shown in Figure 1, and focus on component 1. Our first goal is to estimate the weight function $\omega_1(t)$ given in (29) for $t \in [0, t_{\max}]$, where $t_{\max} = 1000$.
In this particular case we let $c_F = 1.0$ while $c_R = 0.0$. Thus, only effects of the fictive failure events are included. Moreover, if E_{1j} is a (real) failure event occurring at time T_{1j} then the corresponding fictive failure event, denoted E'_{1j} occurring at time T'_{1j} is a result of component 1 being minimally repaired at T_{1j} and then functioning until T'_{1j}. The time between the real and fictive events is easily generated using a standard rejection method.
In order to obtain an estimate of $\omega_1(t)$, we run $M = 1000$ simulations of the process W_1 defined in (30) with $N = 100$ sample points. The resulting curve estimates are shown in Figure 4. As before, the black curve is obtained using the interval estimates, while the gray curve shows the corresponding pointwise estimate curve. As for the availability and criticality curve estimates, the interval method produces more stable results.

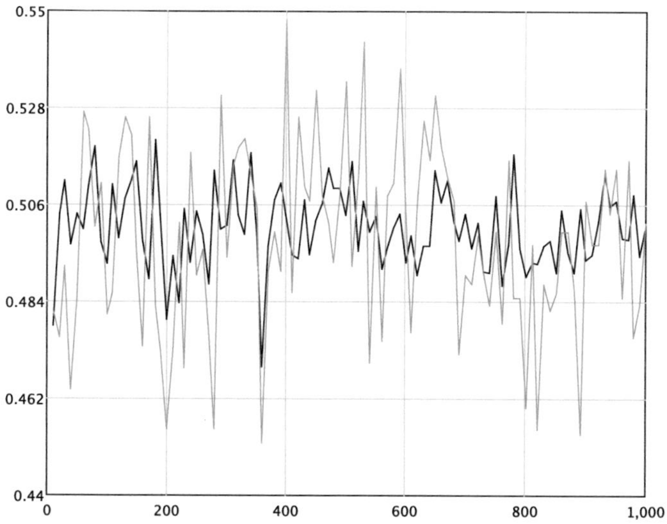

Fig. 4. Interval estimate (black curve) and pointwise estimate (gray curve) of the weight function $\omega_1(t)$

Having estimates for both $\omega_1(t)$ and $I_B(t)$ we can then proceed to estimating $\zeta_i(t)$ as defined in (28). This is done by calculating numerically the integrals (35) and (36). Since, however, $\zeta_i(t)$ typically is an unbounded function of t it is often more convenient to work with a normalized version of the form $\zeta_i(t)/t$. In Figure 5 we have plotted the resulting normalized estimates as functions of t. The black curve is derived using the interval estimates, while the gray curve is obtained using pointwise estimates. We observe that in this case the two methods produce almost identical results, although the interval estimates are slightly more stable, especially for small values of t. The reason for this is that the integrals tend to smoothen the curve estimates considerably. This effect makes the increased precision obtained by using interval estimates less significant. For more examples of the use of this technique see Natvig et al. (2009).

6. Conclusions

In the present chapter we have discussed two different approaches to curve estimation in discrete event simulations. In particular, we have indicated that using interval estimates may produce more stable curve estimates compared to pointwise estimates. The proposed methods are particularly useful in relation to importance measure estimation, especially when several different importance measures are calculated and compared.

An important parameter used in the curve estimates is the distance between the sampling points, i.e., Δ. Finding a suitable value for this parameter, may be challenging as it depends on how fast the underlying processes converge to a stationary state. Note, however, that it is not necessary to use the same distance between the sampling points throughout the sampling period. Instead it is possible to use shorter distances between the sampling points in the early stage, where the processes have not converged, and then use longer distances as soon as all the processes have entered an approximate stationary state. By studying this issue further, we think that the proposed methods can be improved considerably.

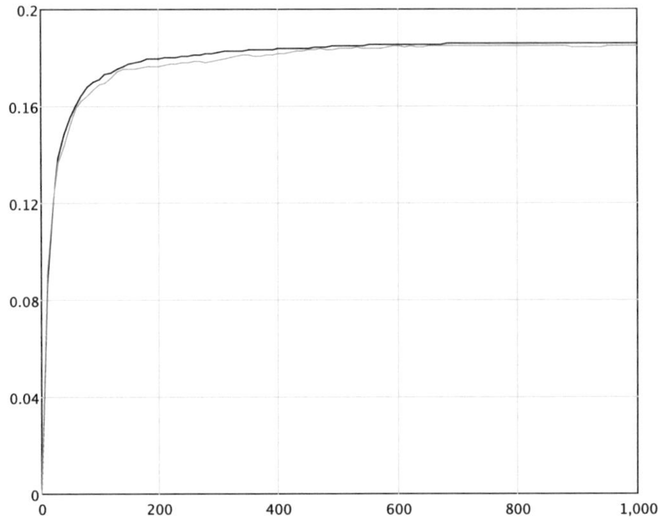

Fig. 5. Interval estimate (black curve) and pointwise estimate (gray curve) of $\zeta_i(t)/t$ for different values of t.

7. References

R. E. Barlow and F. Proschan. Importance of system components and fault tree events. *Stochastic Process. Appl.*, (3): 153–173, 1975.

R. E. Barlow and F. Proschan. *Statistical Theory of Reliability and Life Testing.* To Begin With – Silver Spring MD, 1981.

Z. W. Birnbaum. On the importance of different components in a multicomponent system. In P. R. Krishnaia, editor *Multivariate Analysis - II*, pp. 581–592, 1969.

P. Glasserman and D. D. Yao. *Monotone Structure in Discrete-event Systems.* John Wiley and Sons, Inc., 1994.

P. Glasserman. *Monte Carlo Methods in Financial Engineering.* Springer Verlag, 2004.

A. B. Huseby and M. Naustdal. Improved Simulation Methods for System Reliability Evaluation. In *Mathematical and Statistical Methods in Reliability.*, pp. 105–121. World Scientific Publishing Co. Pte. Ltd., 2003.

F. C. Klebaner. *Introduction to stochastic calculus with applications.* Imperial College Press, 2005.

B. Natvig. A suggestion of a new measure of importance of system components. *Stochastic Process. Appl.*, (9): 319–330, 1979.

B. Natvig. On the reduction in remaining system lifetime due to the failure of a specific component. *J. Appl. Prob.*, (19): 642–652, 1982. Correction *J. Appl. Prob.*, (20): 713, 1983.

B. Natvig. New light on measures of importance of system components. *Scand. J. Statist.*, (12): 43–54, 1985.

B. Natvig and K. A. Eide and J. Gåsemyr and A. B. Huseby and S. L. Isaksen. Simulation based analysis and an application to an offshore oil and gas production system of the Natvig measures of component importance in repairable systems. *Reliability Engineering & System Safety*, (94): 1629-1638, 2009.

B. Natvig and J. Gåsemyr. New results on the Barlow-Proschan and Natvig measures of component importance in nonrepairable and repairable systems. *Methodol. Comput. Appl. Prob.*, (11): 603-620, 2009.

A. Regular pure jump processes

In this appendix we present a few basic results on pure jump processes needed in the present chapter. We consider a pure jump process S with jumps at $T_1 < T_2 < \cdots$. We also let $T_0 = 0$ and introduce the times between the events defined as:

$$\Delta_j = T_j - T_{j-1}, \qquad j = 1, 2, \ldots. \tag{37}$$

Using these quantities the event times can be expressed as:

$$T_k = \sum_{j=1}^{k} \Delta_j, \qquad k = 1, 2, \ldots. \tag{38}$$

Obviously, the process S is regular if and only if $T_\infty = \infty$ almost surely. Thus, it follows that a necessary and sufficient criterion for regularity is that the series $\sum_{j=1}^{\infty} \Delta_j$ is *divergent* with probability one. This condition can often be verified using the following simple result:

Proposition A.1. *Let S be a pure jump process with jumps at $T_1 < T_2 < \cdots$. Assume then that the sequence $\{\Delta_j\}$ defined in* (37) *contains an infinite subsequence $\{\Delta_{k_j}\}$ of independent, identically distributed random variables such that $E[\Delta_{k_j}] = d > 0$. Then S is regular.*

Proof: By the strong law of large numbers it follows that:

$$P(\lim_{n\to\infty} n^{-1} \sum_{j=1}^{n} \Delta_{k_j} = d) = 1.$$

This implies that the series $\sum_{j=1}^{\infty} \Delta_{k_j}$ is divergent with probability one. Hence, since obviously $\sum_{j=1}^{\infty} \Delta_{k_j} \leq \sum_{j=1}^{\infty} \Delta_j$, the result follows. ■

The regularity property implies that the set of points where the process jumps does not have any accumulation points. The following result utilizes this to show the existence of left limits of the state function of a regular pure jump process.

Proposition A.2. *Let S be a regular pure jump process with jumps at $T_1 < T_2 < \cdots$. Then $\lim_{t\to s^-} S(t)$ exists for every $s > 0$ with probability one.*

Proof: Let $0 \leq t < s < \infty$. We then consider the set $\mathcal{T} = \{T_j : t \leq T_j < s\} \cup \{t\}$. Since S is assumed to be regular, the number of elements in $\mathcal{T}$ is finite with probability one. Moreover, $\mathcal{T}$ is non-empty since $t \in \mathcal{T}$. Thus, this set contains a maximal element, which we denote by t'. Moreover, since every element in $\mathcal{T}$ is less than s, then so is t'. From this it follows that the interval (t', s) is nonempty. At the same time (t', s) does not contain any jumps, so $S(t)$ is constant throughout this interval. Hence, $\lim_{t\to s^-} S(t)$ exists. Since s was arbitrarily chosen, this holds for any $s > 0$. ■

Regularity is also of importance when considering the integral of a pure jump process:

Proposition A.3. *Let S be a regular pure jump process with jumps at $T_1 < T_2 < \cdots$, and let $0 \leq u < v < \infty$. Assume that $\{T_j : u < T_j < v\} = \{T^{(1)}, \ldots, T^{(k)}\}$, where $T^{(1)} < \cdots < T^{(k)}$. Moreover, we let $T^{(0)} = u$ and $T^{(k+1)} = v$. Then we have:*

$$\int_u^v S(t)dt = \sum_{j=0}^{k} S(T^{(j)})(T^{(j+1)} - T^{(j)}).$$

Proof: We first note that since S is assumed to be regular, the number of elements in the set $\{T_j : u < T_j < v\}$ is finite with probability one. Thus, this set can almost surely be written in the form $\{T^{(1)}, \ldots, T^{(k)}\}$, for some suitable $k < \infty$. Since S is right-continuous and piecewise constant, it follows that $S(t) = S(T^{(j)})$ for all $t \in [T^{(j)}, T^{(j+1)})$, $j = 0, 1, \ldots, k$. Thus, we have:

$$\int_{T^{(j)}}^{T^{(j+1)}} S(t)dt = S(T^{(j)})(T^{(j+1)} - T^{(j)}), \quad j = 0, 1, \ldots, k.$$

The result then follows by adding up the contributions to the integral from each of the $k+1$ intervals $[T^{(0)}, T^{(1)}), \ldots, [T^{(k)}, T^{(k+1)})$. ■

We then consider a system consisting of a collection of n regular pure jump processes, $S_1, \ldots, S_n$. The state of the system is then typically expressed as a function of the states of the elementary processes. It is easy to see that the system state also evolves as a regular pure jump process. That is, we have:

Proposition A.4. *Let $\boldsymbol{S} = (S_1, \ldots, S_n)$ denote a vector of regular pure jump processes, and let H be a process such that $H = H(\boldsymbol{S})$. Then H is a regular pure jump process as well. That is, $H(t) = H(\boldsymbol{S}(t))$ is piecewise constant and right-continuous in t, and the number of jumps in any finite interval is finite with probability one.*

Proof: Let $\mathcal{T}_i$ be the set of time points corresponding to the jumps of the process S_i, $i = 1, \ldots, n$, and let $\mathcal{T}$ be the set of time points corresponding to the jumps of the process H. Since the state value of H cannot change unless there is a change in the state value of at least one of the elementary processes, it follows that $\mathcal{T} \subseteq (\mathcal{T}_1 \cup \cdots \cup \mathcal{T}_n)$. Thus, $H(t)$ is piecewise constant and right-continuous in t. Moreover, for any finite interval $[t, s]$ we also have:

$$\mathcal{T} \cap [t, s] \subseteq [(\mathcal{T}_1 \cap [t, s]) \cup \cdots \cup (\mathcal{T}_n \cap [t, s])].$$

Since by regularity $(\mathcal{T}_i \cap [t, s])$ is finite with probability one for $i = 1, \ldots, n$, it follows that $\mathcal{T} \cap [t, s]$ is finite with probability one as well. Hence, we conclude that H is regular. ■

12

Agent-based modelling and simulation of network cyber-attacks and cooperative defence mechanisms

Igor Kotenko
St.-Petersburg Institute for Informatics and Automation of Russian Academy of Sciences
39, 14th Liniya, St. Petersburg, 199178
Russia

1. Introduction

The important *problem in network security* which solution is urgently needed is the investigation of counteraction between malefactors and defence systems in computer networks, including the Internet, and the creation of effective cyber-defence systems.
It is important to underline that experienced malefactors realize *sophisticated strategies of cyber-attacks*. These strategies can include:

- Information gathering about the computer system under attack, detecting its vulnerabilities and defence mechanisms;
- Determining the ways of overcoming defence mechanisms (for example, by simulating these mechanisms);
- Suppression, detour or deceit of protection components (for example, by using slow ("stretched" in time) stealthy probes, separate coordinated operations (attacks) from several sources formed complex multiphase attack, etc.);
- Getting access to resources, escalating privilege, and implementation of thread intended (violation of confidentiality, integrity, availability, etc.) using the vulnerabilities detected;
- Covering tracks of malefactors' presence and creating back doors.

Defence mechanisms should support real-time fulfilment of the following operations:

- Implementing the protection mechanisms appropriated to the security policy (including proactive intrusion prevention and attack blocking, misinformation, concealment, camouflage, etc.);
- Vulnerability assessment, gathering data and analysis of the current status of the computer system defended;
- Intrusion detection and prediction of the malefactors' intentions and actions;
- Direct incident response, including deception of the malefactors, their decoy with the purpose of disclosure and more precise determining the malefactors' purposes, and reinforcement of critical protection mechanisms;
- Elimination of intrusion consequences and detected vulnerabilities, adaptation of the information assurance system to the next intrusions.

The design and implementation of effective cyber-defence system is a very complicated problem. According to contemporary view the *prospective network cyber-defence systems* have to be fully integrated and multi-echeloned ones. To effectively detect computer attacks or unauthorized operations and to flexibly react on them, it is needed to carry out the continuous control of network functioning, analyze possible risks, collect knowledge about counteraction, detection and reaction methods and use them for defence reinforcement.

Besides, the effective cyber-defence should include the mechanisms of attack prevention, detection, source tracing and protection as well as can only be achieved by the cooperation of different distributed components ((Kotenko, 2005), (Kotenko & Ulanov, 2005)).

For example, detection of Distributed Denial of Service (DDoS) flooding attack ((Chen & Song 2005), (Ioannidis&Bellovin, 2002), (Keromytis et al., 2002), (Mirkovic et al., 2002), (Mirkovic et al., 2004), (Mirkovic et al., 2005), (Papadopoulos et al., 2003)] is most accurate close to the victim, but separation of legitimate is most successful close to the sources, therefore the security sub-systems (or teams) have to be located at different network places and tightly cooperate.

The cyber-defence systems have to be adaptive and evolve dynamically with the change of network conditions.

To realize these possibilities in prospective cyber-defence system, one must implement the dynamic behaviour, autonomy and adaptation of particular components, the use of methods based on negotiations and cooperation that lie in the basis of multi-agent systems and (or) autonomic computing.

Furthermore, the prospective cyber-defence system has to provide at least *three levels of cyber-security.*

First level contains *"traditional" static cyber-defence mechanisms* implementing identification and authentication, cryptographic protection, access control, auditing, network filtering, etc.

Second level includes *proactive cyber-defence mechanisms* that provide information collection, security assessment, network state monitoring, attack detection and counteraction, malefactor deception, etc.

Third level corresponds to *cyber-defence management* that fulfils the integral evaluation of network state, the choice of adequate or optimal defence mechanisms and their adaptation. This level is built on top of various non-adaptive security mechanisms, which makes it applicable for a wide range of cyber defences.

The issues of modeling and simulation of network security have been actively researched for more than thirty years. The various formal and informal models of particular protection mechanisms were developed, but practically there are not enough works formalizing complex antagonistic character of network security. Understanding of network security as uniform holistic system is extremely hampered. It depends on great many interactions between different cyber warfare processes and is determined by dynamic character of these processes and different components of computer systems. Especially it is fair in conditions of *the Internet evolution to a free decentralized distributed environment* in which a huge number of cooperating and antagonistic software components (agents) interchange among themselves and with people by large information contents and services. Modeling and simulation of these aspects is supposed to put as a basis of our research. This will allow developing an integrated approach to construction of network security systems which can operate in aggressive antagonistic environment.

Our long-term research goal is to develop a powerful simulation framework and software-hardware environment which can help investigate the Internet attacks and defense mechanisms and elaborate well-grounded recommendations to choose efficient defense mechanisms and develop effective cyber-defence systems.

In our previous papers ((Kotenko, 2005), (Kotenko & Ulanov, 2005), (Kotenko, 2007)) we have examined the common approach to agent-based simulation of network defense mechanisms, types of team-based cooperative defense, and various adaptation schemas.

This paper considers and advances the approach to agent-based simulation of cyber-attacks (Distributed Denial of Service, network worms, botnets, etc.) and distributed cooperative multi-level cyber-defence for the exploration of prospective intelligent cyber-defence systems.

The approach is based on the agent-based simulation of cyber-attacks and cyber-protection mechanisms which combines discrete-event simulation, multi-agent approach and packet-level simulation of network protocols.

We analyze various methods of counteraction against cyber-attacks by representing attack and defence components as agent teams using the simulation environment developed. Various teams of defence agents are able to cooperate as the defence system components of different organizations and Internet service providers (ISPs).

Thus, the paper represents the conceptual framework for modelling and simulation, the implementation peculiarities of the simulation environment as well as the experiments aimed on the investigation of distributed network attacks and defence mechanisms.

The rest of the paper is structured as follows. *Section 2* outlines the common multi-agent modelling and simulation framework suggested and relates work. The classes of agents, used for network attack and defence simulation, and their cooperation schemes are considered in *section 3*. *Section 4* describes the implementation peculiarities of the simulation environment under development. *Section 4* demonstrates the examples of experiments provided with the simulation environment. Conclusion surveys the main results of the paper.

2. Simulation Framework

The *multi-agent approach to simulation* supposes that the cyber-counteraction is represented as the interaction of different teams of software agents ((Kotenko, 2005), (Kotenko & Ulanov, 2005)). The aggregated system behaviour becomes apparent by means of local interactions of particular agents in dynamic environment that is defined by the model of computer network.

Agents of different teams can be in indifference ratio, cooperate or compete up till explicit counteraction. Agents are supposed to collect information from various sources, operate incomplete knowledge, forecast the intentions and actions of other agents, try to deceive the agents of competing teams, react to actions of other agents. Every team member might have different information about actions done by other team members.

Therefore, the model of agent behaviour must be able to represent the incompleteness of information and the possibility of accidental factors. Besides, the agent behaviour depends on information that the team has and on its distribution on the set of particular agents. The models of agent functioning are to foresee, what each agent knows, what task has to be solved and to which agent it must address its request to receive such information, if it is outside of its competence.

The **general conceptual model of cybernetic agents' counteraction and cooperation** includes (Fig. 1) ((Gorodetski & Kotenko, 2005), (Kotenko & Ulanov, 2006)):

- Ontology of application domain containing application notions and relations between them (we differentiate the problem ontology, the shared application ontology, the application ontology of particular team and particular agent);
- Protocols of teamwork for the agents of different teams;
- Models of scenario behaviour of agents for team, group and individual levels;
- Libraries of agent basic functions;
- Communication platform and components for agent message exchange;
- Models of functioning environment, including topological, functional and other components;
- Models that provide the interaction of teams (antagonistic and non-antagonistic competing or various kinds of cooperation).

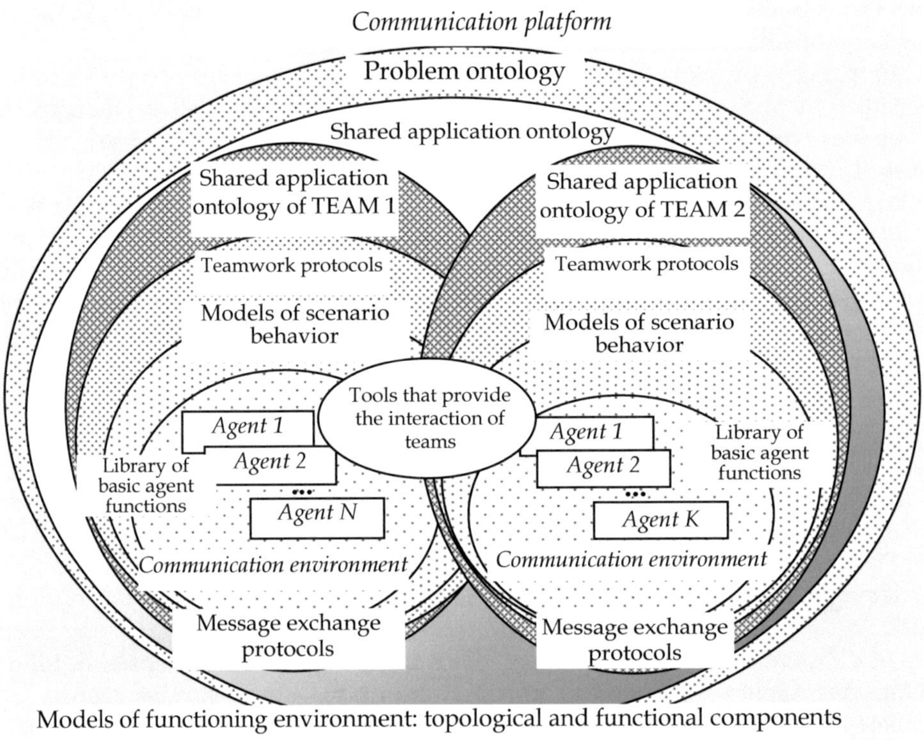

Fig. 1. Abstract model of team interaction

The following **main simulation components** are represented on the basis of this approach:

- Models of agent teams;
- Models of team interactions;
- Interaction environment model.

Models of agent teams are intended for the representation of investigated processes. They include: particular team ontologies, agent basic functions, agent classes, agent interaction protocols, behaviour scenarios.

Team ontologies are based on the subject domain ontology and include the notions and relations used by agents of this team.

The list of *agent basic functions* includes the following functions: initialization; shutdown; access to the agent ontology; management of active agents list; basic work with transport-level modules (connection establishing, message sending, connection closing).

The needed *agent classes* are defined for the teams. The amount of agents of predefined classes is set in each team.

Agent interaction protocols are represented as the sequence of instructions with specific parameters. The type of instruction defines how to use these parameters. The conditions of protocol initialization provide communication selectivity for agents. Agent interaction protocols are based on the transport layer that is provided by the communication environment. For example, the developed protocol for agent team establishing is based on dividing agents into "clients" and "servers". The first send the messages about their existence to "server". Server contains the list of agents in the team. Periodically it checks the agents in this list to actualize it and to know which of agents are active. Agent team establishing protocol is the part of procedures for monitoring and recovery of agent functionality.

Behaviour scenarios represent various stages of team actions. Adaptation procedures are implemented in scenarios to act depending on other team actions and environment reaction. Agent teams' behaviour scenarios ensure action consistency maintenance.

Models of team interactions include the models of antagonistic competing, team cooperation and adaptation.

Model of antagonistic competing lies in the basis of competing teams' interaction. This model defines the goals, subgoals, intentions and actions of competing teams that are aimed on the interaction environment or (and) the opponent team.

Cooperative interaction happens between teams that pursue the same goal. The proposed model of cooperation is based on the exchange of information between teams. Such exchange is made to raise the effectiveness of reaching the common goal and occurs on several different levels with the use of agents of various classes. For example, in the task of cooperative network defence simulation it is possible to exchange attack signatures, network traffic data, filtering requests, etc.

Adaptation is in reacting to the actions of other teams and environment changes by modifying the scenarios of team behaviour.

Model of environment for agent teams' interaction allows determining such interaction environments that are characterized by various representation granularity that depends on the requirements for simulation fidelity and scalability.

As for every application domain the *ontology* represents the partially normalized set of notions that are to be used by other agents. The ontology defines the subset of notions that various agents use for cooperative solving of stated tasks. Each agent uses a certain part of application domain ontology.

Each agent specialization is represented by the subset of ontology nodes. Some of ontology nodes can be shared by the pair or more of agents. Usually only one of these agents has the detailed description of this node. Exactly this agent is the owner of the corresponding knowledge base fragment. At the same time some part of ontological knowledge base is shared for all agents. This part is the fragment that is to be the shared context (shared knowledge). The structure of agent team is described in terms of group and individual roles hierarchy. The mechanisms of agent interaction and coordination are based on the following procedures: action consistency maintenance; monitoring and the recovery of agent functionality; and communication selectivity ensuring. The specification of action plans hierarchy is made for every role.

The *main basis for the research is the agent teamwork approaches*: joint intentions theory (Cohen & Levesque, 1991), shared plans theory (Grosz & Kraus, 1996) and the hybrid approaches (Tambe, 1997).

It is supposed to use the combination of *methods and models* to form agent teams, to make agent decisions and to coordinate actions between teams and particular agents (Paruchuri et al., 2006):

(1) traditional *BDI-models* which are defined by schemes of agents functioning determined by subject domain dependencies;

(2) methods of distributed optimization on the basis of constraints that use local interactions while searching local or global optimum (*Distributed Constraint Optimization*, DCOP);

(3) methods of distributed decision making on the basis of partly-observable Markov chains that allow to implement the teamwork coordination in the presence of uncertainty in actions and observations (*distributed Partially Observable Markov Decision Problems*, POMDPs);

(4) *game-theoretical models and auction models* focusing on coordination between various agent teams that use market-based decision making mechanisms.

In our approach it is offered that the *agents' teamwork* is organized by the group (team) plan of the agents' actions. In result, a team has a mechanism of decision-making about who will execute particular operations. As in the joint intention theory, the basic elements, allowing the agents' team to fulfil a common task, are common (group) intentions, but its structuring is carried out in the same way as the plans are structured in the shared plans theory. The common (group, individual) intention and commitment are associated with each node of a general hierarchical plan. These intention and commitment manage execution of a general plan, providing necessary flexibility. During functioning each agent should possess the group beliefs concerning other team-mates. For achievement of the common beliefs at formation and disbandment of the common intentions the agents should communicate. All agents' communications are managed by means of common commitments built in the common intentions. For this purpose it is supposed to use the special mechanism for reasoning of agents on communications. Besides it is supposed, that agents communicate only when there can be an inconsistency of their actions. It is important for reaction to unexpected changes of network environment, redistributing roles of the agents which failed or unable to execute the general plan, and also at occurrence of not planned actions.

The *mechanisms of the agents' interaction and coordination* are based on three groups of procedures:

(1) *Coordination of the agents' actions* (for implementation of the coordinated initialization and termination of the common scenario actions);

(2) *Monitoring and restoring the agents' functionality;*

(3) *Communication selectivity support* (for choice of the most "useful" communications).

The specification of the plan hierarchy is carried out for each role. The following elements of the plan should be described: initial conditions, when the plan is offered for fulfilment; conditions for finishing the plan execution (these conditions can be as follows: plan is fulfilled, plan is impracticable or plan is irrelevant); actions fulfilled at the team level as a part of the common plan. For the group plans it is necessary to express joint activity. To cope with the information heterogeneity and distribution of intrusion sources and agents used we apply ontology-based approach and special protocols for specification of shared consistent terminology.
Another fundamental component of the research is represented by the studies on *reasoning systems about opponent intentions and plans* ((Charniak & Goldman, 1993), (Gorodetski & Kotenko, 2005), (Vilain, 1990), (Wellman & Pynadath, 1997)). The important components in this research are the methods of reflexive processes theory (Lefevre, 2003), game theory and control in conflict situations (Druzhinin et al., 1989).
The agents are supposed to implement the mechanisms of *self-adaptation* and to evolve during functioning. The team of agents-malefactors evolves due to generation of new instances and types of attacks and to scenarios of their realization to overcome the defence subsystem. The team of defence agents adapts to malefactors actions due to changing the executed security policy, forming of new defence mechanisms and profiles instances. Therefore it is important to take into account the present studies in the area of adaptation (Silva et al., 2000), agent learning ((Back et al., 2000), (Gamer et al., 2006), (Gu &Yang, 2004), (Zou, et al., 2006)), autonomic computing ((Horn, 2001), (Keromytis et al., 2002), (Want et al., 2003)), and combining artificial immune systems with different computational intelligence methods, such as fuzzy systems, neural networks, etc. ((Ishida, 2004), (Negoita et al., 2005)).

3. Specialised Classes of Agents and their Cooperation Schemes

Let us consider the main classes of teams and agents we currently use in our simulation framework.
There are at least three different *classes of agent teams* (Kotenko & Ulanov, 2006):
- Teams of agents-malefactors,
- Teams of defence agents,
- Teams of agents-users.

Attack agents are subdivided at least into two classes:
- "Demons" and
- "Masters".

Daemons and masters are deployed on compromised hosts in the Internet on a preliminary stage. The class of attacks is defined by intensity of packet sending, IP address spoofing technique (no spoofing, constant, random, and random with real IP addresses), etc.

To simulate distributed cooperative defence, the *security agents* belong to the following classes:
- Information processing ("samplers");
- Attack detection ("detectors");
- Filtering and balancing ("filters");
- Traceback and investigation ("investigators");
- Traffic limiting ("limiters").

Samplers collect and process network data for anomaly and misuse detection. *Detectors* coordinate the team, correlate data from samplers, and detect attacks. *Filters* are responsible for traffic filtering using the rules provided by detector. *Investigator* tries to defeat attack agents. *Limiter* is intended to implement cooperative defence. Its local goal is to limit the traffic according to the team goal. It lowers the traffic to the attack target and allows other agents to counteract the attack more efficiently.

There are three *types of limiting*:

- By the *IP address of attack target*. When detector reveals an attack, it sends to limiter the attack target address. Limiter begins to drop the packets destined to the attack target with the given probability.
- By the *IP addresses of attack sources*. When detector reveals an attack, it sends to limiter the attack source addresses (if detector manages to trace them). Limiter begins to drop the packets from these sources with the given probability.
- According to the *packet marking*. Filter adds to the legitimate-classified packets the mark (it uses one of the packet fields). If limiter sees such mark it does not drop that packet.

Different defence teams can jointly implement investigated defence mechanisms. Defence teams can interact using various schemes. In the one of them that detector acts which team is under attack (when attack is detected). It sends the request to agent-samplers of other teams to receive the information that might be relevant to the mentioned attack. The samplers of other teams reply on the request by sending the requested data. If attack is detected the detector from the victim network sends the information about attack agent addresses to the detector of team in which network this agent might be. Then this team tries to deactivate attack agent. Detector uses the protocol "limiting by the IP address of attack target" to let limiter start or stop the traffic limiting. One of the goals of filter is to add the mark in packets that passed through the filtering table.

The main attention in *cooperative mechanisms* is given to the methods of distributed filtering and rate-limiting. These methods are to trace the attack sources and drop the malicious traffic as far from attack target as possible. The teams of defence agents are able to cooperate as the defence system components of different organizations and Internet service providers.

In the paper we investigate *three cooperative defence mechanisms*:

- DefCOM (Defensive Cooperative Overlay Mesh) (Mirkovic et al., 2005);
- COSSACK (coordinated suppression of simultaneous attacks) (Papadopoulos et al., 2003);
- full cooperation of defence components (suggested in the paper).

The following agent classes are proposed to introduce in compliance with *DefCOM architecture*:

- "Alert generator" - detects an attack and warns about it other hosts in the DefCOM network; attack is detected if the traffic exceeds some threshold;
- "Rate limiter" - limits the traffic that is destined to the attack target;
- "Classifier" - provides selective traffic limiting, tries to classify attack and legitimate packets and to drop the former.

"*Alert generator*" agent is based on "detector" agent. It gathers traffic data from "sampler", detects the IP-addresses of hosts that generate the greatest traffic. If it exceeds the given threshold the alert is generated.

Agent "*Rate limiter*" is based on "limiter" agent. It can drop the packets destined to the attack target providing some volume of traffic.

Agent "*Classifier*" is based on "filter" agent that receives filtering data from detector. This agent is able to filter the disclosed attack packets. It also marks the legitimate packets to let "limiter" pass them. DefCOM "Classifier" receives data from DDoS source network detection system D-Ward) (Mirkovic et al., 2002).
When "Alert generator" detects the attack it sends the attack messages to other agents. Then "Rate limiter" agents start to limit the traffic destined to the attack target. "Classifier" agents start to classify and drop the attack packets and to mark legitimate packets.

COSSACK architecture consists of the following agent classes:

- "Snort" prepares the statistics on the transmitted packets for different traffic flows; the flows are grouped by the address prefix. If one of the flows exceeds the given threshold then its signature is transmitted to "watchdog";
- "Watchdog" receives traffic data from "snort" and applies the filtering rules on the routers.

Agent "*snort*" is based on the agent "sampler". It processes the network packets and creates the model of normal traffic for this network (in the learning mode). Then, in the normal mode, it compares the network traffic with the model and detects the malefactor's IP addresses which it sends to "watchdog".
Agent "*watchdog*" is based on the agent "detector". It makes the decision about attack due to data from "snort".
Agent "filter" is used to simulate filter on the router. It is deployed on router and performs traffic filtering using data from detector.
Detector-level cooperation is used to simulate "watchdog" cooperation. Detectors of different teams are able to transmit the filtering rules to one another due to "filter" agents deployed on routers. Cooperation is in the following: when a "watchdog" detects the attack it composes the attack signature; this "watchdog" sends it to the other known "watchdogs"; "watchdogs" try to trace in their subnets the attack agents that send attack packets; when they detect them the countermeasures are applied.

Full cooperation architecture stipulates for the following classes of defence agents: "samplers", "detectors", "filters", and "investigators".
In common, agent teams are able to interact using various *cooperation schemes*:

- *No cooperation*: all teams work on their own;
- *Filter-level cooperation*: team which network is the attack victim can apply the filtering rules on filters of other teams;
- *Sampler-level cooperation*: team which network is the attack victim can receive traffic data from the samplers of other teams;
- *Poor cooperation*: teams can receive traffic data from the samplers of some other teams and apply the filtering rules on filters of some other teams. Each team "knows" some other teams depending on cooperation degree;
- *Full cooperation*: the team which network is an attack victim can receive traffic data from the samplers of other teams and apply the filtering rules on the filters of other teams.

4. Simulation Environment

A multi-level software environment was supposed to be developed to implement the proposed approach. It differs from the known tools for agent-oriented simulation, as the basis for simulation the tools should be used which provide adequate simulation of network processes.

The spectrum of possible approaches to modelling and simulation are differentiated from analytical to scaled-down and full-scale (see Fig. 2) (Perumalla & Sundaragopalan, 2004).

The choice of model depends on the needed fidelity and scalability of simulation.

The scalability is defined as number of network host (client hosts and routers) which can be simulated using the given method.

The fidelity is defined as a degree of network and hosts destabilization used.

Analytical models allow simulating large-scale Internet processes (including DDoS attacks and worms epidemics) but these models describe the processes only on abstract level.

Packet-level simulation allows enough adequate rendering of such processes. The defence and attack actions are represented as the exchange of packets. This allows the high-fidelity simulation of datalink, network, transport and application layers.

The highest fidelity is reached on the hardware testbeds, but the size of simulated network is restricted enough.

We have chosen the packet-based approach as it provides acceptable scalability and fidelity. In Fig. 2, various program simulators, which can be used for simulation, are depicted: NS2, OMNeT++ INET Framework, SSF Net, J-Sim, etc.

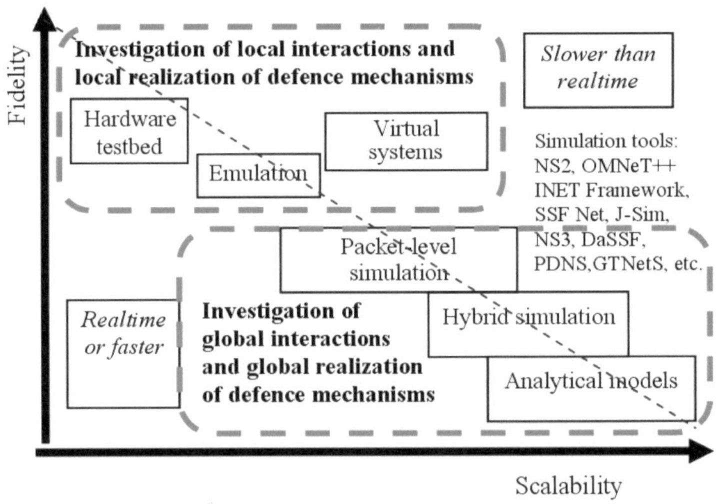

Fig. 2. Variety of used models

We take into account the following *main requirements to the simulation environment* (Kotenko & Ulanov, 2005):

- The detailed implementation of the protocols that are engaged in DDoS attacks. It is necessary at least to simulate the present DDoS attacks.
- The ability of writing and plugging in the personal modules. It is necessary to implement the agent approach.

- The ability of changing parameters during the simulation.
- Implementation for OS Windows and Linux (or platform-independency).
- Advanced graphical interface.
- Free for use in research and educational purposes.

To choose the necessary tool we fulfilled the detailed analysis of these simulation environments, and OMNeT++ INET Framework was chosen (OMNeT++, 2010).

The simulation environment architecture suggested includes the following components (Fig. 3):

- Simulation Framework (discrete event simulator),
- Internet Simulation Framework (modular simulation suite with a realistic simulation of Internet nodes and protocols),
- Multi-agent Simulation Framework (modules representing the intelligent agents implemented as application),
- Subject Domain Library (attack and defence modules).

Simulation framework is a discrete event simulator. Other components are expansions or models for Simulation Framework.

Internet Simulation Framework is a modular simulation suite with a realistic simulation of Internet nodes and protocols. The highest IP simulation abstraction level is the network itself, consisting of IP nodes. IP node corresponds to the computer representation of Internet Protocol. IP node can represent router or host. IP node in Internet Simulation Framework corresponds to the computer representation of Internet Protocol. The modules of IP node are organized as operating system process IP datagram. The module that is responsible for the network layer (implementing IP processing) and the "network interface" modules are mandatory. In addition one can plug the modules that implement higher layer protocols.

Multi-agent Simulation Framework allows realizing agent-based simulation. It consists of modules representing the intelligent agents implemented as applications. There were used the elements of abstract FIPA architecture during agent modules design and implementation. Agent communication language is implemented for the agent interactions. The message transmission occurs above the TCP protocol (transport layer) implemented in Internet Simulation Framework. Agent directory is mandatory only for agent that coordinates other agents in its team. Agent can control the other modules due to messages.

Subject Domain Library is the library used for imitation of processes from subject domain and containing modules that extend functionality of IP-host: filtering table and packet analyzer.

This architecture was implemented for multi-agent simulation DDoS attack and defence mechanisms with the use of OMNeT++ INET Framework and software models developed in C++.

Agent models implemented in *Multi-agent Simulation Framework* are represented with generic agent, attack and defence agents.

Subject Domain Library contains various models of hosts, e.g. attacking host, firewall etc., and also the application models (attack and defence mechanisms, packet analyzer, filtering table).

Fig. 4 shows the multi-window user interface of the simulation environment.

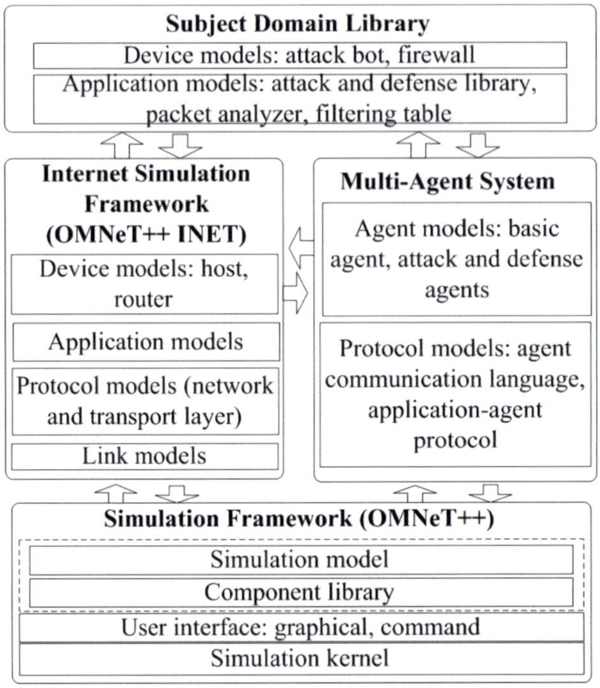

Fig. 3. Simulation environment architecture

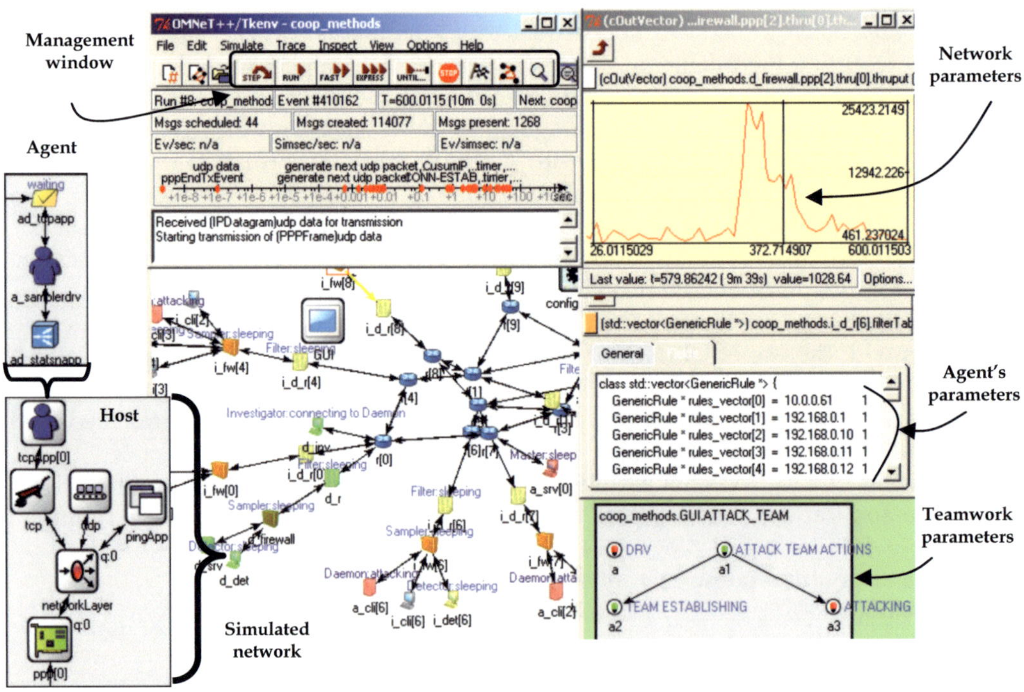

Fig. 4. Multi-window user interface of environment

The management window has the time axis with the system events: opening or closing the TCP connection, attack signals, defence acts, etc.

The simulated network window depicts the network hosts and channels. Hosts can fulfil different functionality depending on their parameters or a set of internal modules. Internal modules are responsible for functioning of protocols and applications at various levels of OSI model. Hosts are connected by channels which parameters can be changed. Applications (including agents) are established on hosts. Applications are connected to corresponding modules of protocols.

The structure of generic host is depicted on the bottom left. The deployed agent is represented as the blue symbol of human in the frame.

The environment allows to examine the different information describing the simulation functioning. For example, the diagram that shows the change in network parameters is depicted at the top right.

The networks used for simulation consist of various subnets that are, for instance, the regions of responsibility of various ISPs.

For example, one can mark out the defence subnet where the attack victim is located, the intermediate subnets where the standard hosts generate generic network traffic, and attack subnets where the attack agents are located.

The networks are built with the methods of generating topologies that are close to the real Internet (Mahadevan et al., 2005).

There are the following *specification elements to define the investigated network models, attack and defence mechanisms*:

- Network topology: quantity and types of hosts, channels between them and their types. The possibility to deploy certain type of application (or agent) depends on host type.
- Defence team parameters: quantity of daemons; master's address and port used for interactions; daemon's port used to send attack packets; victim's address and port; time of attack; attack intensity; address spoofing technique.
- Attack realization parameters: victim type (application, host or network; one must define the IP-address and port of victim); type of attack (brute force (UDP/ICMP flood, smurf/fraggle, etc.) or semantic (TCP SYN, incorrect pack-ets, hard requests, etc.)); attack rate dynamics (can be constant or variable); adaptation scheme depending on attack severity, etc.
- Defence team parameters: address of defended host; detector's address and port for interactions; server's reply size and delay time; adaptation scheme (changing of defence mechanisms) depending on attack severity, etc.
- Defence mechanisms parameters: deployment location (source, intermediate or defended subnets); the stages the defence method can implement (attack prevention, attack detection, tracing the attack source, attack counteraction); attack detection technique (misuse and anomaly detection; one chooses one particular detection method or the set of methods), etc.
- User team parameters: quantity of users; server's address and port; time to start; quantity of requests to server, interval between them and their size; interval between connections.
- Defence team cooperation parameters: scheme of cooperation.
- Simulation parameters: simulation duration; quantity of experiments; initialization of random number generator.

5. Experiments

The developed simulation environment allows carrying various experiments aimed to investigate attacks and prospective defence strategies. One can vary network topology and configuration, structure and configuration of attack and defence teams, attack and defence mechanisms, team cooperation parameters etc. The evaluations of various effectiveness parameters of defence mechanisms are done on the basis of experiments results. The analysis of applying conditions is also fulfilled for these parameters.

The attack parameters used in the experiments are as follows: Victim type - host (server that provides some service); Attack type - brute-force; Impact on the victim - disruptive; Attack rate dynamics - constant, variable; Agents' set permanency - constant, variable; Possibility of exposure - discoverable filterable attack; Source addresses validity - valid (real), spoofed: random, subnet; Degree of automation - semi-automatic with direct communication.

In the experiments we have used three defence methods: Hop counts Filtering (HCF) (Jin et al.,2003), Source IP address monitoring (SIPM) (Peng et al., 2003) и Bit Per Second (BPS). HCF consists in building the tables of subnets and amount of hops till them in the learning mode. Attack is found out on the basis of amount of hops differing from received in learning mode. SIPM uses the assumption that during attack a lot of new IP addresses appear. BPS allows detecting the attacker due to exceeding the normal traffic threshold.

The other defence parameters are as follows: Deployment location - intermediate, defended subnets; Covered defence stages - attack prevention, attack detection, attack source detection, attack counteraction; Attack source detection technique - can detect when source address is not spoofed; Attack prevention technique - packet filtering; Technique for gathering of model data - learning; Determination of deviation from model data: thresholds (HCF, BPS), determination of fluctuation in probabilistic traffic parameter (SIPM).

Let us consider three examples of experiments fulfilled where we analyzed different modes of DDoS attacks and defence: (1) experiment 1 - investigation of simple adaptation of attack and defence teams; (2) experiment 2 - investigation of different, suggested in the paper, cooperation modes between defence teams; (3) experiment 3 - investigation of cooperative defence mechanisms DefCOM, COSSACK and full cooperation.

Let us consider the values of the main parameters that define the computer network models, attack and defence mechanisms that are used for the experiments.

To create a topology for testing, we used the generator of networks that are close to the real Internet networks. The following basic network topology parameters were set: minimum amount of connection is 2, the amount of routes in simulated networks is 10, the probabilistic value $\gamma = 2.25$ (Mahadevan et al., 2005)]. Routers are connected with the fiber-glass data channels, propagation delay is 1 microsec; datarate is 2488 Mbit. Other hosts are connected by Ethernet data channels, propagation delay is 0.1 microsec; datarate is 100 Mbit. Clients are randomly connected to the routers of the basic network. The amount of clients is an input parameter for experiments (its initial value is 10). The defended server is d_srv. The basic parameters of network clients are as follows: server address "d_srv"; server port - 80; start time is a random value with the exponential probability distribution function (PDF) and mean 5 sec; one request per session is used; request length is a random value with normal PDF with mean 350 and dispersion 20 bits; reply length is a random value with exponential PDF and mean 2000 bits; Think time is a random value with normal PDF with mean 2 and dispersion 3 sec; Idle interval is a random value with normal PDF with mean 36 and dispersion 12 sec; Reconnect interval is 30 sec.

Let us consider below the results of experiments fulfilled.

5.1 Investigation of simple adaptation of attack and defense teams

The fragment of the network which was used in the first experiment is depicted in Fig. 5.
The fragment of decision making and acting sequence is as follows (Fig. 6):

- Normal work of users (interval 0 - 300 seconds).
- Defence team: formation of the team; the team start using BPS method.
- Attack team: formation of the team; after 300 seconds the team begins the attack actions (intensity of attack for every daemon - 0.5, no IP spoofing).
- Defence team: data processing, attack detecting (using BPS) and reacting (interval 300 - 350 seconds); blocking the attack, destroying some attack agents (interval 300 - 600 seconds).
- Attack team: after 600 seconds the automatic adaptation is fulfilled (redistributing the intensity of attack (0.83), changing the method of IP spoofing (Random)).
- Defence team: data processing, failing to detect the attack (using BPS method) - Detector sees that the input channel throughput has noticeably lowered, but does not receive any anomaly report from sampler because BPS does not work.
- Defence team: Changing defence method on SIPM (automatic adaptation); Data processing, attack detecting (using SIPM method) and reacting - (interval 600 - 700 seconds).

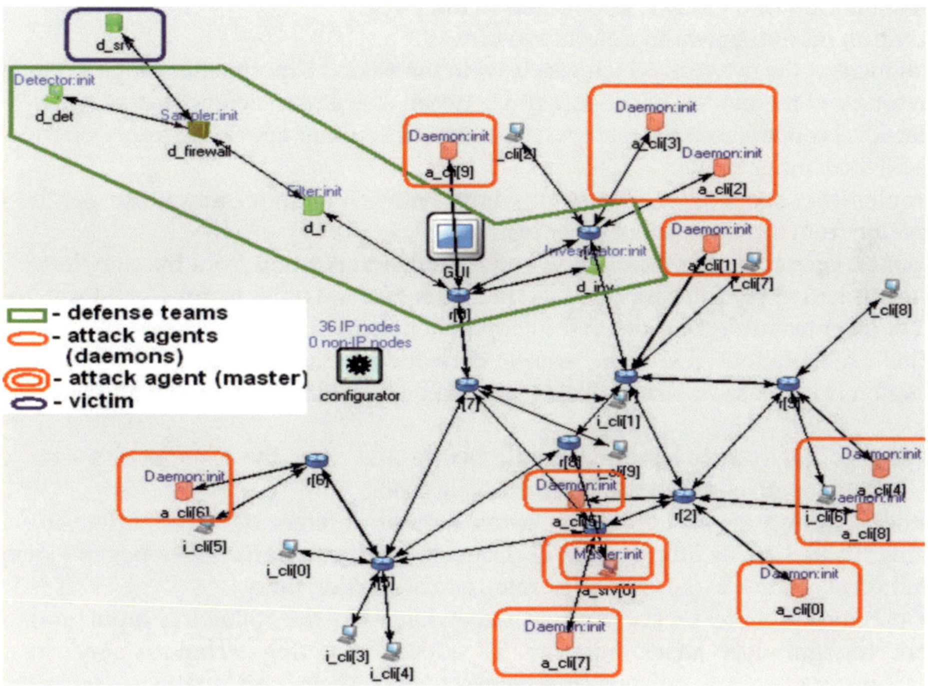

Fig. 5. Experiment 1: the Internet fragment and agent teams

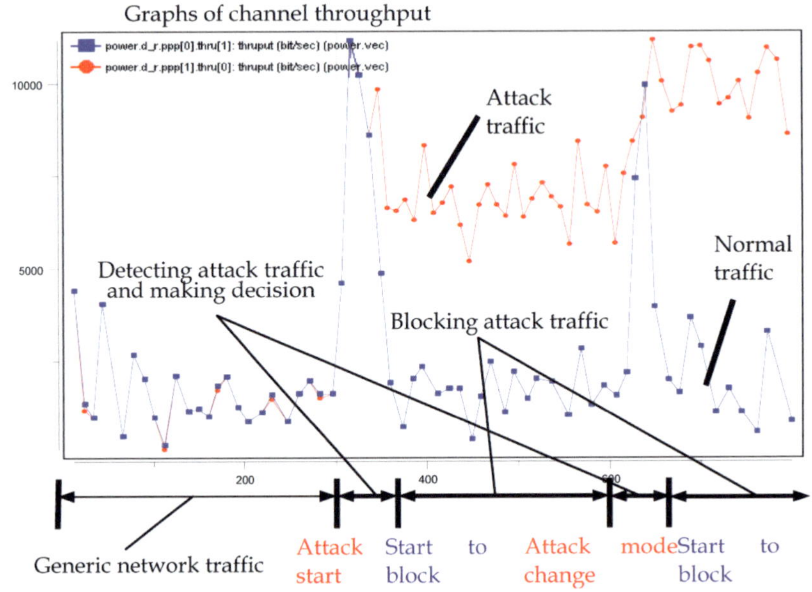

Fig. 6. Scheme of teams' acting

5.2 Investigation of different, suggested in the paper, cooperation modes between defense teams

The fragment of the network which was used in the second experiment is depicted in Fig. 7. We investigated the models of cooperation between distributed defence teams:

(1) filter-level cooperation: the team whose network is under attack can apply filtering rules on the filters of other teams;

(2) sampler-level cooperation: the team whose network is under attack can get the traffic information from the samplers of other teams;

(3) "poor" cooperation: the teams can get the traffic information from the samplers of some other teams and apply filtering rules on the filters of some other teams (each team knows a subset of other teams depending on the cooperation degree);

(4) "full" cooperation: the team whose network is under attack can get the traffic information from all samplers of other teams and apply filtering rules on all filters of other teams.

Fig. 8 depicts the volume of input traffic before and after the filter of the team which network is under attack when the BPS method is used.

The other effectiveness and efficiency parameters of different defence mechanisms which were investigated are as follows: rate of dropped legitimate traffic (false positive rate); rate of admitted attack traffic (false positive rate); attack reaction time.

These parameters were investigated in dependence on the following input parameters: network configuration; attack intensity; IP address spoofing technique used in attack; internal parameters of defence mechanisms and their combinations; quantity and distribution of defence teams, etc.

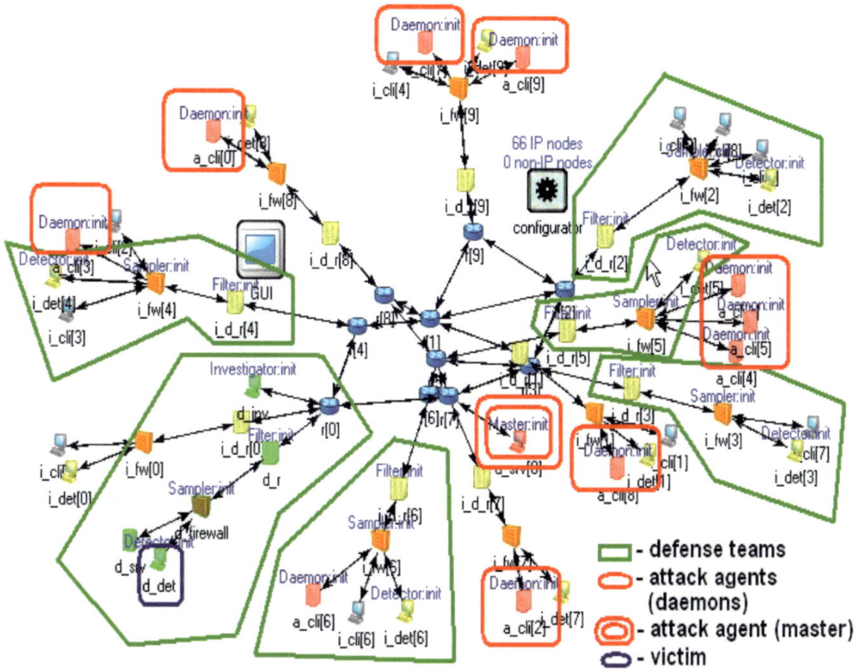

Fig. 7. Experiment 2: the Internet fragment and agent teams

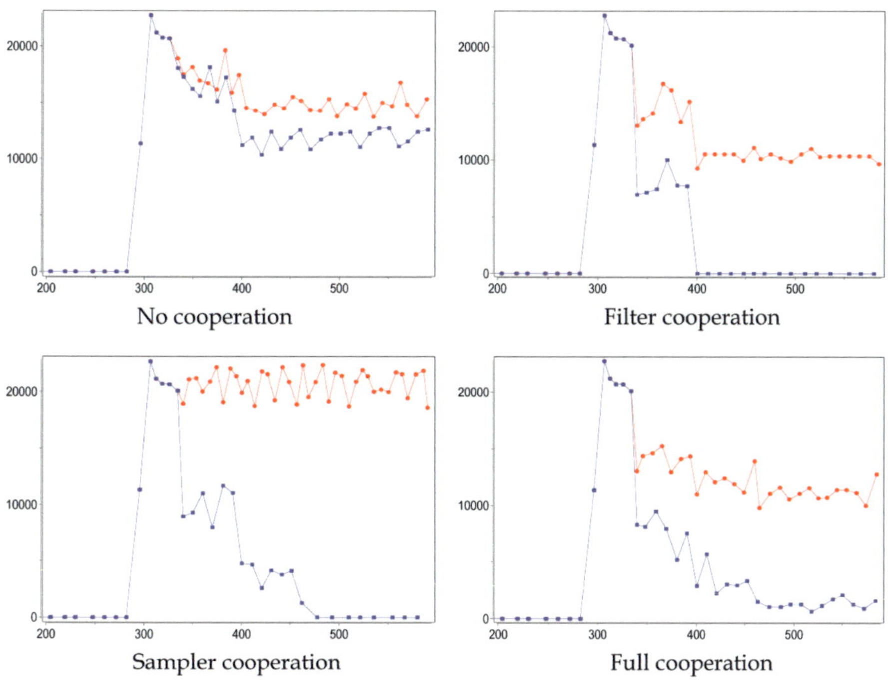

Fig. 8. Volume of input traffic before and after the filter

The best cooperative schema on the basis of output parameters is "full cooperation". Samplers-agents cooperation played the crucial role in defence. It causes the permanent traffic data exchange between various defence teams.

5.3 Investigation of cooperative defense mechanisms DefCOM, COSSACK and full cooperation

Fig. 9 shows the example of DefCOM agents' configuration in the tool developed. Agents "Filter" play the role of "Classifier", "Limiter" - "Rate limiter" and "Sampler" with "Detector" - "Alert generator". Defence team of d_srv host has the following configuration: detector is deployed on the host d_det (in the defended subnet), sampler - d_firewall (on the entrance to the defended subnet), two agents "filter" - on the hosts i_d_r[0] and i_d_r[1] (in the source subnets), limiter - r[0] (router that provides the connection to the defended subnet). Other basic parameters are as follows: detectors port for team interaction - 2000; interval for SIPM and BPS - 5 seconds; time shift for SIPM and BPS - 5 seconds.

Fig. 10 shows the example of COSSACK agents configuration in the tool developed. Defence network consists of three agents "watchdog" that are simulated by the defence agent teams. Defence team of d_srv host has the following configuration: detector is deployed on the host d_det (in the defended subnet), sampler - d_firewall (on the entrance to the defended subnet), agent "filter" - on the hosts d_r (on the entrance to the defended subnet, before sampler), limiter - r[0] (router that provides the connection to the defended subnet). Two other teams consist of detector and filter in the source subnets (hosts i_cli[1] and i_cli[2], and i_d_r[0] and i_d_r[1] accordingly).

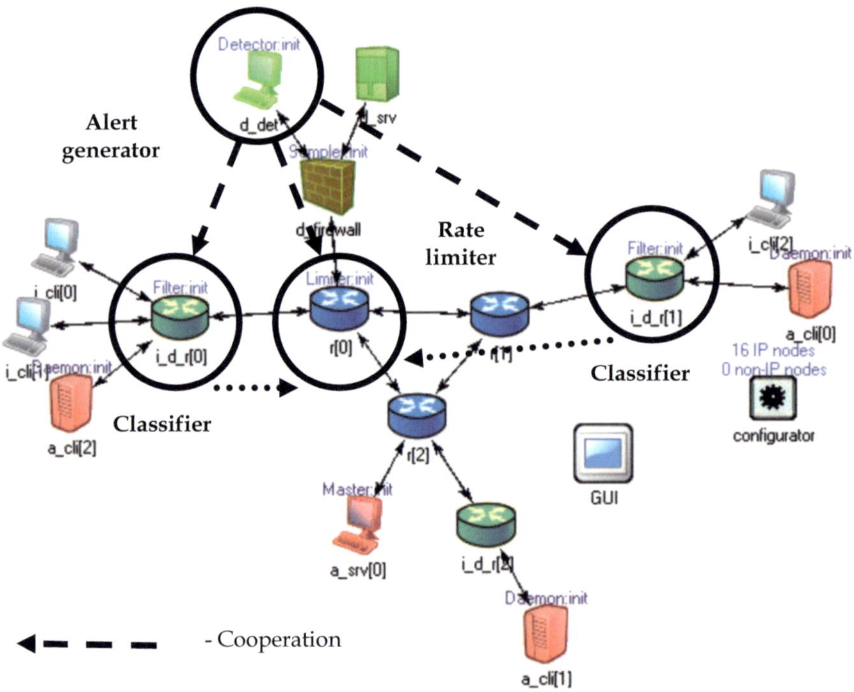

Fig. 9. Configuration of DefCOM agents

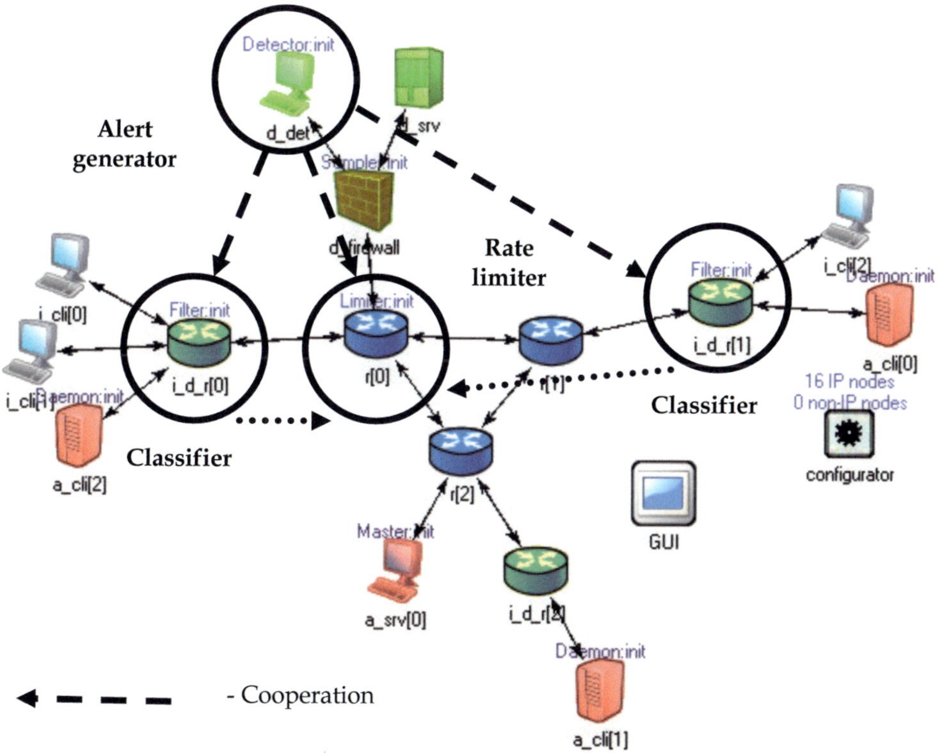

Fig. 10. Configuration of COSSACK agents

Fig. 11 shows the example of Full cooperation defence system proposed by the authors. This defence network consists of defence teams that are able to cooperate to reach the mutual goal.

Each team has the following configuration: detector is deployed on the host d_det[i] (in the defended subnet), sampler - d_firewall (on the entrance to the defended subnet), agent "filter" - on the hosts d_r[i] (on the entrance to the defended subnet, before sampler), investigator is deployed out of defended subnet ("i" is the subnet number).

The following cooperation schemes have been investigated in a set of experiments:

- DefCOM: when an attack is detected "Alert generator" sends the attack messages to the other agents. "Rate limiter" agents start to limit the traffic destined to the attack target. Agents "Classifier" classifies, drops the attack packets, and marks the legitimate packets.
- COSSACK (or filter-level cooperation): the team which network is the attack victim can apply the filtering rules on filters of other teams. When "watchdog" detects the attack it creates attack signature and sends it to the other known "watchdogs"; they try to trace in their subnets the attack agents that send attack packets; when they detect them the packet filtering rules are applied as close as possible to the attack source.
- full cooperation: the team which network is the attack victim can receive traffic data from the samplers of other teams and apply the filtering rules on filters of other teams; this scheme has the best effectiveness comparing with the other proposed.

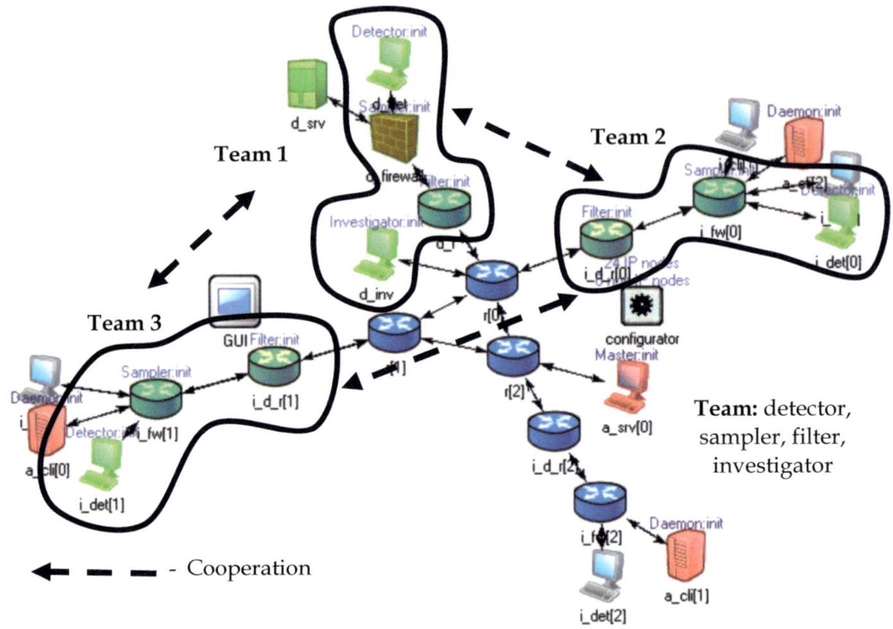

Fig. 11. Configuration of full cooperation defence system

The investigation has been done on the basis of analysis of two main classes of parameters:

- the amount of incoming attack traffic before and after filter of team which network is the attack victim;
- false positive and false negative rates of defence team which network is the attack victim.

Fig. 12 shows the examples of attack traffic inside the attacked subnet for the COSSACK (triangles), DefCOM (dots) and full cooperation schema (crosses). Attack starts at 300 seconds. The random real IP spoofing technique is applied as the most complicated for detection (the addresses for spoofing are taken from the same network). SIPM is used as the defence method.

Attack traffic for COSSACK is measured on the entrance to the defended subnet on filter. The significant traffic increase is noticed in the beginning of attack. But in the area of 350 seconds the defence system detects the attack. Filtering rules are applied and the traffic inside the subnet is reduced (after 350 seconds). Attack signature is sent to the other defence components. They apply filtering rules in their subnets. The traffic on the entrance to the defended subnet is decreased due to their actions.

The attack traffic inside the attacked subnet for DefCOM is represented with the dots in Fig. 12. The traffic was measured at the entrance to the subnet, since the last component in the subnet that changes the traffic is the limiter. It is deployed on the router that has four interfaces and the incoming attack traffic was summarized into one graph. In the area of 350 seconds the defence system detects the attack and traffic is being limited before the defended subnet and being filtered in the source subnets. Rate limiter proceeds to limit the traffic because of the high attack traffic volume. But this cooperation schema succeeds to keep the traffic on the acceptable level due to limiting and to applying of filtering rules.

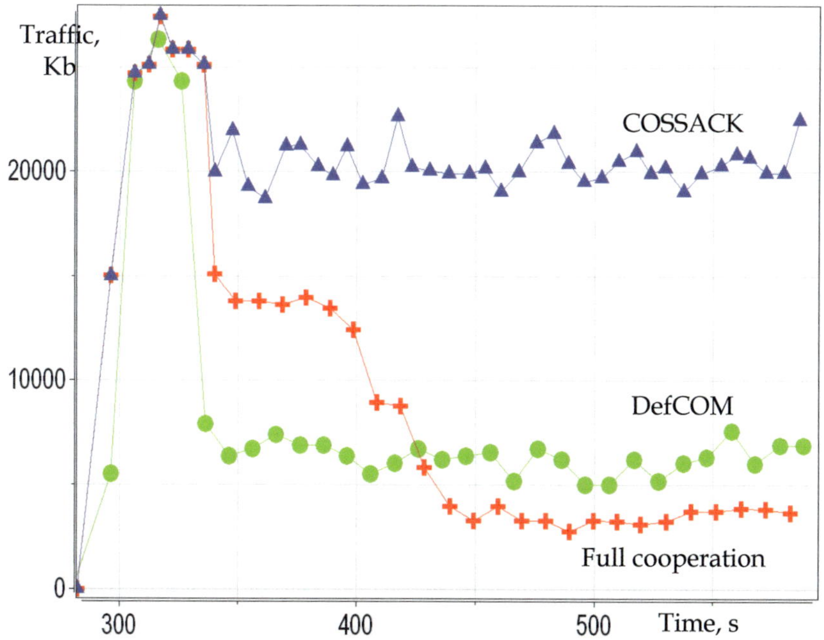

Fig. 12. Attack traffic inside the attacked subnet for COSSACK, DefCOM and full cooperation

The attack traffic inside the attacked subnet for the full cooperation schema is represented with the crosses in Fig. 12. Traffic is measured on the entrance to the defended subnet on filter. The significant traffic increase is noticed in the beginning of attack. But in the area of 350 seconds the main defence team detects the attack requesting the traffic data not only from its sampler but from the samplers of other teams. Filtering rules are applied and traffic inside the defended subnet is significantly decreased (around 350 seconds). Attack signature is sent to the other cooperating teams. They apply the filtering rules in their subnets. The traffic on the entrance to the defended subnet is decreased due to their actions (after 350 seconds). System succeeds to decrease the traffic much more due to permanent attack signatures renewing (400–450 seconds).

The experiments implemented demonstrated that full cooperation shows the best results on blocking the attack traffic. It uses several defence teams with cooperation on the level of filters and samplers.

DefCOM comes after full cooperation. Its advantage is in using the rate limiter before the defended network. It allows lowering the traffic during attack and letting the defended system work properly.

COSSACK is the third. It is one of the examples of peer-to-peer defence network. It uses attack signatures transmission between agents to apply the filtering rules near the source. The communication overhead for cooperative defence is restricted by the communication selectivity procedures. The agent protocols can be executed only periodically or in the strict sequence. Therefore their influence on the joint traffic is low.

6. Conclusion

This paper considered the approach to investigation of distributed cooperative cyber-defence mechanisms against network attacks. The approach is based on the simulation of network cyber-attacks (Distributed Denial of Service, network worms, botnets, etc.) and cyber-protection mechanisms which combines discrete-event simulation, multi-agent approach and packet-level simulation of network protocols.

The environment developed is written in C++ and OMNeT++. It allows imitating a wide spectrum of real life infrastructure attacks and defence mechanisms.

A lot of different experiments were carried. They were aimed to investigate dependence of defence effectiveness parameters from network topology and configuration, structure and configuration of attack and defence teams, attack and defence mechanisms and defence teams' cooperation.

Experiments showed that team cooperation leads to the essential defence effectiveness improvement. The multitude of experiments we implemented demonstrated that full cooperation shows the best results on blocking the attack traffic. It uses several defence teams with cooperation on the level of filters and samplers.

Future work is related with more thorough investigation of effectiveness of cooperation mechanisms for different teams and inter-team interaction of agents, implementation of self-adaptation and self-learning of agents. We are planning to expand the attacks and defences library, elaborate particular components functionalities.

One of the main tasks of our current and future research is to improve the scalability and fidelity of the simulation. We now in the process of designing and experimenting with the parallel versions of our simulation environment and developing a simulation tesbed combining a hierarchy of macro and micro level models of attack and defence (analytical, packet-based, emulation-based), and real small-sized networks.

7. Acknowledgement

This research is being supported by grant of Russian Foundation of Basic Research (Project No. 10-01-00826-a), program of fundamental research of the Department for Informational Technologies and Computation Systems of the Russian Academy of Sciences (contract No. 3.2), Russian Science Support Foundation and partly funded by the EU as part of the MASSIF project (contract No. 257475). Author thanks Aleksey Alekseev, Alexey Konovalov, Alexander Ulanov, and Andrey Shorov for software development and testing.

8. References

Back, T.; Fogel, D.B. & Michalewicz, Z. (2000). *Evolutionary computation*. Vol. 1. Basic algorithms and operators, Institute of Physics Publishing.

Charniak, E. & Goldman, R.P. (1993). A Bayesian Model of Plan recognition. *Artificial Intelligence*, Vol. 64, No. 1.

Chen, S. & Song, Q. (2005). Perimeter-Based Defence against High Bandwidth DDoS Attacks. *IEEE Transactions on Parallel and Distributed Systems*, Vol. 16, No. 7.

Cohen, P. & Levesque, H.J. (1991). Teamwork. *Nous*, No. 35.

Druzhinin, V.V.; Kontorov, D.S. & Kontorov, M.D. (1989). *Introduction into conflict theory. Moscow*, Radio i svyas' (in Russian).

Gamer, T.; Scholler, M. & Bless, R. (2006). A Granularity-adaptive System for in-Network Attack Detection, *Proceedings of the IEEE/IST Workshop on Monitoring, Attack Detection and Mitigation*.

Geib, C.W. & Goldman, R.P. (2001). Plan recognition in intrusion detection systems, *DARPA Information Survivability Conference and Exposition, DARPA and the IEEE Computer Society*.

Gorodetski, V. & Kotenko, I. (2005). Conceptual foundations of stochastic simulation in the Internet. *Proceedings of system analysis institute of RAS*, Vol.9, Moscow, URSS (in Russian).

Grosz, B. & Kraus, S. (1996). Collaborative Plans for Complex Group Actions. *Artificial Intelligence*, Vol. 86.

Gu, D. & Yang, E. (2004). Multiagent Reinforcement Learning for Multi-Robot Systems: A Survey, *Technical Report of the Department of Computer Science*, University of Essex, CSM-404.

Horn, P. (2001). *Autonomic Computing: IBM's Perspective on the State of Information Technology*, Technical Report, IBM Corporation.

Ioannidis, J. & Bellovin, S.M. (2002). Implementing Pushback: Router-Based Defence Against DDoS Attacks, *Proceedings of Symposium of Network and Distributed Systems Security (NDSS)*, California.

Ishida, Y. (2004). *Immunity-Based Systems A Design Perspective*. Springer Verlag.

Jin, C., Wang, H. & Shin, K.G. (2003). Hop-count filtering: An effective defence against spoofed DDoS traffic, *Proceedings of ACM Conference on Computer and Communications Security*.

Kephart, J.O. & Chess, D.M. (2003). The Vision of Autonomic Computing. *IEEE Computer Magazine*, No. 1.

Keromytis, A.; Misra, V. & Rubenstein, D. (2002). SOS: Secure Overlay Services, *Proceedings of ACM SIGCOMM'02*, Pittsburgh, PA.

Kotenko, I.V. (2005). Agent-Based Modeling and Simulation of Cyber-Warfare between Malefactors and Security Agents in Internet, *Proceedings of 19th European Simulation Multiconference "Simulation in wider Europe"*.

Kotenko, I.V. & Ulanov, A.V. (2005). Agent-based simulation of DDOS attacks and defence mechanisms. *Journal of Computing*, Vol.4, Issue 2.

Kotenko, I.V. & Ulanov, A.V. (2006). Agent Teams in Cyberspace: Security Guards in the Global Internet, *Proceedings of CYBERWORLDS'2006*.

Kotenko, I. (2007). Multi-agent Modelling and Simulation of Cyber-Attacks and Cyber-Defence for Homeland Security, *Proceedings of IDAACS'2007*. Dortmund, Germany.

Lefevre, V.A. (2003). *Reflexion*. Moscow, "Kognito-Center" (in Russian).

Mahadevan, P.; Krioukov, D.; Fomenkov, M.; Huffaker, B.; Dimitropoulos, X.; Claffy, K. & Vahdat, A. (2005). *Lessons from Three Views of the Internet Topology*. Technical Report, CAIDA.

Mirkovic, J.; Prier, G. & Reiher, P. (2002). Attacking DDoS at the Source, *Proceedings of ICNP*, Paris, France, 2002.

Mirkovic, J.; Dietrich, S.; Dittrich, D. & Reiher, P. (2004). *Internet Denial of Service: Attack and Defence Mechanisms*. Prentice Hall PTR.

Mirkovic, J.; Robinson, M.; Reiher, P. & Oikonomou, G. (2005). Distributed Defence Against DDOS Attacks, *Technical Report CIS-TR-2005-02*. University of Delaware. CIS Department.

Negoita, M.; Neagu, D. & Palade, V. (2005). *Computational Intelligence Engineering of Hybrid Systems*. Springer Verlag.

OMNeT++ (2010). http://www.omnetpp.org/

Papadopoulos, C.; Lindell, R.; Mehringer, I.; Hussain, A. & Govindan, R. (2003). Cossack: Coordinated suppression of simultaneous attacks, *Proceedings of DISCEX III*.

Paruchuri, P.; Bowring, E.; Nair, R.; etc. (2006). Mutiagent Teamwork: Hybrid Approaches. *Computer society of India Communications*.

Peng, T.; Christopher, L. & Kotagiri, R. (2003). Protection from Distributed Denial of Service Attack Using History-based IP Filtering, IEEE Conference on Communications.

Perumalla, K.S. & Sundaragopalan, S. (2004). High-Fidelity Modeling of Computer Network Worm, *Proceedings of 20th Annual Computer Security Applications Conference (ACSAC'04)*.

Silva, F.; Endler, M.; Kon, F.; Campbell, R.H. & Mickunas, M.D. (2000). Modeling Dynamic Adaptation of Distributed Systems, *Technical Report UIUCDCS-R-2000-2196*, University of Illinois at Urbana-Champaign.

Tambe, M. (1997). Towards flexible teamwork. Journal of AI Research, Vol. 7.

Vilain, M. (1990). Getting Serious about Parsing Plans: A Grammatical Analysis of Plan Recognition, *Proceedings of the Eighth National Conference on Artificial Intelligence*, Cambridge, MA,

Want, R.; Pering, T. & Tennenhouse, D. (2003). Comparing autonomic and proactive computing. *IBM Systems Journal*, Vol.42, No.1.

Wellman, M.P. & Pynadath, D.V. (1997). *Plan Recognition under Uncertainty*, Unpublished web paper.

Zou, C.C.; Duffield, N.; Towsley, D. & Gong, W. (2006). Adaptive Defence against Various Network Attacks. *IEEE Journal on Selected Areas in Communications*: High-Speed Network Security (J-SAC), Vol. 24, No. 10.

13

Wireless sensor networks: modeling and simulation

Sajjad A. Madani
COMSATS Institute of Information Technology, Abbottabad [*]
Pakistan

Jawad Kazmi
COMSATS Institute of Information Technology, Abbottabad [†]
Pakistan

Stefan Mahlknecht
Vienna University of Technology, Vienna [‡]
Austria

Abstract

Although different modeling techniques have been proposed during the last 300 years, the differential equation formalism proposed by Newton and Leibniz has been the tool of choice for modeling and problem solving Taylor (1996); Wainer (2009). Differential equations provide a formal mathematical method (sometimes also called an analytical method) for studying the entity of interest.

Computational methods based on differential equations could not be easily applied in studying human-made dynamic systems (e.g., traffic controllers, robotic arms, automated factories, production plants, computer networks, VLSI circuits). These systems are usually referred to as *discrete event systems* because their states do not change continuously but, rather, because of the occurrence of events. This makes them asynchronous, inherently concurrent, and highly nonlinear, rendering their modeling and simulation different from that used in traditional approaches. In order to improve the model definition for this class of systems, a number of techniques were introduced, including Petri Nets, Finite State Machines, min-max algebra, Timed Automata, etc. Banks & Nicol. (2005); Cassandras (1993); Cellier & Kofman. (2006); Fishwick (1995); Law & Kelton (2000); Toffoli & Margolus. (1987).

Wireless Sensor Network (WSN) is a *discrete event system* which consists of a network of sensor nodes equipped with sensing, computing, power, and communication modules to monitor certain phenomenon such as environmental data or object tracking Zhao & Guibas (2004). Emerging applications of wireless sensor networks are comprised of asset and warehouse

[*] madani@ciit.net.pk
[†] jawhaikaz@ciit.net.pk
[‡] mahlknecht@ict.tuwien.ac.at

management, automotive, home and building automation, civil infrastructure monitoring, healthcare, industrial process control, military battlefield awareness, and security and surveillance Cerpa et al. (2001).
As discussed earlier, modeling and simulation is a mean to verify the working and to measure the effectiveness of the different techniques proposed for WSNs. Analytical modeling provides quick insight for the techniques developed for WSNs but fail to give realistic results because of WSN specific constraints like limited energy and sheer number of sensor nodes Chen et al. (2006). Real world implementation and test beds are the most accurate method to verify the concepts but are restricted by costs, effort, and time factors as well as repeating environmental conditions is also not possible Zeigler (1976). Simulations provide a good approximation to verify different schemes and applications developed for WSNs at low cost and in less time. To have credible results through simulation, the choice of models and the simulation environment is important.
There is always a tradeoff between credible simulation results and the time required to get these simulation results. The results always depend upon the level of abstraction of the models. The more detailed is the model, the better the accuracy of results but higher the amount of time required for simulation.
The models used for simulation can have a significant impact on the overall simulation study. In this chapter, we will present a brief overview of the models available for different modules of sensor network simulation study in addition to the general-purpose simulation frameworks and tools that can be used to study WSNs. Such tools include *NS-2, OMNeT ++, SenSim, NesCT, GlomoSim, OPNET Modeler, SENSE, Ptolemy II, VisualSense* and *J-Sim*. Additionally, some WSNs specific simulators frameworks/emulators are also covered including *TOSSIM, EmStar, ATEMU* and *PAWiS*.

1. Introduction

Recent advances in MEMS and distributed computing has enabled WSNs powered diverse applications ranging from military to kindergartens. WSN is a network of sensor nodes equipped with sensing, computing, power, and communication modules to monitor certain phenomenon such as environmental data or object tracking Raghavendra et al. (2004). In current scenarios, the number of sensor nodes may be 20 to 30 but in future it may consist of nth power more sensor and actuator systems Dietrich et al. (2001). The position of the sensor nodes may not be pre-determined and require sensor nodes to be equipped with self organizing protocols Akyildiz et al. (2002).Generally, sensor nodes observe and sense the phenomenon with a sensing module, process the data with a computing module, and send the data to a required destination via wireless link with a communication module.

2. Wireless Sensor Network Applications

Emerging applications of wireless sensor networks are comprised of asset and warehouse management, automotives, home and building automation, civil infrastructure monitoring, healthcare, industrial process control, military battlefield awareness, and security and surveillance Zhao & Guibas (2004). Some examples of these application like robotic navigation Fu et al. (2009), aircraft corrosion monitoring Demo et al. (2010) , direct load control in residential areas Molina-Garcia et al. (2007), personal mobile physiological monitoring and management system for chronic disease Toh et al. (2008), Wildfire detection Antoine-Santoni et al. (2006), in-service motor monitoring and energy management Hu (2008), application in petrochemical industry Ke et al. (2008), application for critical infrastructure risk analysis of fossil fuelled power stations Isreb (2006) and tactical military applications Lee et al. (2009) can be found in the litrature.

3. Historical Perspective

History of wireless communication used in the field can be traced back to late 1890's to Anglo-Boer war in Namibia, the then German Southwest Africa, and was declared by IEEE as electrical engineering milestone in which Marconi's system was used for wireless communication Sarkar et al. (2006). In 1921, the US Department of Defense initiated a radiotelegraphic network, which resulted in 125 stations network by 1925 Callaway et al. (2002). The Aloha system Abramson (1970) developed at the University of Hawaii is considered the first successful data network, which connected different campuses of the University of Hawaii. The Packet Radio Network Jubin & Tornow (1987), comprising of 138 network devices was developed in 1972. In 1997, IEEE 802 LAN/MAN Standard Committee released the first Wireless LAN standard. The development of Wireless Personal Area Networks began in 1997, with the formation of Home RF Working Group and with the formation of Bluetooth Special Interest Group in 1998 Callaway et al. (2002). Like other wireless networks, the sensor networks also has a long history with can be traced back to 1978 DARPA -sponsored Distributed Sensor Nets Workshop. Wireless Integrated Network Sensors (WINS)[1] project was initiated in 1993 by University of California at Los Angeles. The University of California at Berkeley started PicoRadio[2] project in 1999. AMPS [3] project started in MIT, to develop a complete architecture for low power wireless sensor networks. LonWorks Dietrich et al. (2001) in 2001 and EIB: Installation Bus System Sauter et al. (2002) in 2002 was a big step towards building automation. Wireless Self Sustaining Sensor Network Project [4](WSSN) at institute of computer technology, Vienna University of technology aimed to establish sensor networks for building automation which are low power and self sufficient in energy.

4. Discret Event Modeling and Simulation Methodologies

Modeling techniques for discrete event driven systems (including WSNs) are relatively recent. In this section, we present a non-comprehensive list of some of the formal modeling techniques created for modeling these systems.

4.1 Automaton

An automaton is defined as a graph representing system states and the transitions between them. The automaton receives a string of symbols as input, and it recognizes/rejects the inputs by advancing through the transitions. The input is read one symbol at a time; depending on the ending state, the automaton will accept or reject the input Cassandras (1993).

4.2 Timed automata

Timed automata, in particular, use clocks to describe the model's timing behavior Alur & Dill (1994). The automaton is defined as a graph of states associated with clocks that determine

[1] www.janet.ucla.edu
[2] bwrc.eecs.berkeley.edu
[3] www-mtl.mit.edu
[4] http://www.ict.tuwien.ac.at/wireless

the passage of time since the occurrence of an event. Every link is associated with a timing constraint that will define when the transition can be triggered. Whenever a transition executes, the associated clocks are reset. Timing constraints can also be associated with the model states, defining the duration of each of the states.

4.3 Finite state machines

Finite state machines (FSMs) can be represented as a graph in which the system's behavior is defined as a finite set of nodes (the model's states) and links between them (transitions between states). A given state reflects the evolution of the model, and transitions are associated with a given logical condition to enable the execution of the transition. When entering a state, an entry action can be executed (and an exit action can be executed when leaving it). Likewise, an input action can be triggered based on the current state and an input Cassandras (1993). An FSM is formally defined as

$$FSM = (S, X, Y, f, g) \tag{1}$$

Where
X= finite input set
Y= finite output set
S = finite state set

4.4 Markove chain

A Markov chain is a discrete-time stochastic model described using a graph. Models' states are defined as nodes in the graph, and transitions between states are represented by links. One important property of Markov chains is that they are memoryless; thus, no state has a cause–effect relationship with the previous state. Therefore, knowledge of previous states is irrelevant for predicting the probability of the future states.

4.5 Generalized Semi-Markovian Process

A Generalized Semi-Markovian Process (GSMP) is a stochastic process (i.e., a collection of random variables over a probability space indexed by time). A GSMP is based on the notion of a state that makes a transition when an event associated with the current state occurs, and the state space is generated by a stochastic timed automaton Glynn (1989). Several possible events can compete to trigger the next transition, and each of these events has its own probabilistic distribution for determining the next state.

4.6 Petri nets

Petri nets Peterson (1981) define the structure of concurrent systems using a bipartite graph. One type of the graph's nodes, the places, represents the system states, and the second kind, the transitions, represents the net evolution Adi Mallikarjuna et al. (2007).

4.7 Queuing networks

Queuing networks are based on a customer–server paradigm, in which customers make service requests to the servers and these requests are queued at the server until they can be serviced. The arrival time for customers and the service time at a server are described as stochastic models. By defining the number of servers and the buffering capacity on each of them, we can determine performance metrics (including the number of customers in line, throughput–number of customers serviced per time unit, turnaround times, etc.). Different policies can be used (priorities; preemption; first in, first out; etc.) Li & Li (2003).

4.8 Calculus of communicating systems

The formal language of calculus of communicating systems (CCS) provides primitives for concurrency and parallelism, based on synchronous communications between exactly two components. The language expressions are interpreted as a labeled transition system, and bi-simulation can be used to prove equivalence of models Hansson & Jonsson (1990).

4.9 Temporal logic

Temporal logic is a system of rules and symbols used for representing propositions that can include the timing properties of the system Manna & Pnueli (1992). It consists of a logic set of propositions that view time as a sequence of states and that can be true or false according to their state and their time of occurrence. Temporal logic has been used to verify formally timed automata. The idea is to check predictability of certain conditions according to the time that they occur, conditions that might eventually arise, or others that are guaranteed not to occur.

4.10 Communicating sequential processes

Communicating sequential processes (CSP) is a formal language based on process algebra that has been widely used to model concurrent systems Hoare (1985). Models are described using independent processes that interact with each other through message-passing representing the occurrence of events Wainer (2009).

4.11 Specification and Description Language

Specification and Description Language (SDL) was created to specify in a nonambiguous way the behavior of real-time applications. It was originally focused on communication systems, by providing a graphical and textual representation with equivalent semantics. A system is defined as a set of extended FSMs that can be interconnected Belina & Hogrefe (1989).

4.12 Event graphs

Event graphs are oriented graphs that represent the organization of the events of a discrete event system Schruben et al. (2003). Events constitute nodes of the graph; that is, the vertices represent the state transition functions, and the links between nodes capture the scheduling of such events. Each link starts at the node performing the scheduling operation (which represents an event), and it ends at the node representing the event to be scheduled. Each scheduling relationship has an associated delay and condition (a Boolean function of the state), and an event is scheduled only when the condition is true Wainer (2009).

4.13 Systems theory

Systems-theoretical approaches derive from systems theory von Bertalanffy (1969). Systems theory represents every entity under study using the concept of system, which is seen as a collection of objects and their interactions. In systems theory, the system's global behavior is seen as a composition of the individual behavior of the components, and we can find emergent behavior that is not explicitly defined in the parts of the system. Systems theory is based on the idea that every phenomenon can be viewed as a mathematical relationship among a set of entities in the system. The theory is generic and tries to find common behavior and properties in different fields of study (for instance, hydraulics, economy, biology, or social sciences), thus providing a unified view of science and engineering.

4.14 Discrete-Event Systems Specifications

Discrete-Event Systems Specifications (DESS) formalism Zeigler (1976; 1990) is a mathematical modeling technique derived from systems theory that allows the construction of hierarchical and modular models, providing a well-defined coupling of components. Given its hierarchical nature, DEVS allows the coupling of existing models modularly, allowing us to build complex systems from simple ones. DEVS theory provides a rigorous methodology for representing models, and it presents an abstract way of thinking about the world independently of the simulation mechanisms Wainer (2009).

5. Phases in a Simulation Study

There have been different kinds of life cycles proposed for studies in modeling and simulation. In this section, we summarize the basic steps that should be considered in doing a simulation study. The life cycle does not have to be interpreted as strictly sequential; it is iterative by nature, and sometimes transitions in opposite directions can appear. Likewise, some of the steps can be skipped, according to the complexity of the application. It is highly recommended to use a spiral cycle with incremental development for steps 2–8 (Section 5.2 through Section 5.8), which can cause a revision to earlier phases. Each phase in the spiral cycle should end with a working prototype including more functionality than the previous cycle:

5.1 Problem formulation

The simulation process begins with a practical problem that requires solving or understanding. It might be the case of a cargo company trying to develop a new strategy for truck dispatching or an astronomer trying to understand how a nebula is formed. At this stage, we must understand the behavior of the system of interest (which can be a natural or artificial system, existing or not), organizing the system's operation as objects and activities within the experimental framework of interest. Then we need to analyze different alternatives of solutions by investigating other previously existing results for similar problems. The most acceptable solution should be chosen (omitting this stage could cause the selection of an expensive or wrong solution). We also must identify the input/ output variables and classify them into decision variables (controllable) or parameters (non-controllable). If the problem involves performance analysis, this is the point at which we can also define performance metrics (based on the output variables) and an objective function (i.e., a combination of some of the metrics). At this stage, we can also do risk analysis and decide whether to follow or discard the project.

5.2 The Conceptual Model

This step consists of building a high-level description of the structure and behavior of the system and identifying all the objects with their attributes and interfaces. We also must define what the state variables are, how they are related, and which ones are important for the study. In this step, key aspects of the requirements are expressed (if possible, using a formalism, which introduces a higher degree of precision). During the definition of the conceptual model, we need to reveal features that are of critical significance (e.g., possibility of instability, deadlock, or starvation). We must also document nonfunctional information–for instance, possible future changes, nonintuitive (or non-formal) behavior, and the relation with the environment.

5.3 The collection and analysis of input/output data phase

In this phase, we must study the system to obtain input/output data. To do so, we must observe and collect the attributes chosen in the previous phase. When the system entities are studied, we try to associate them with a timing value. Another important issue during this phase is the selection of a sample size that is statistically valid and a data format that can be processed with a computer. Finally, we must decide which attributes are stochastic and which are deterministic. In some cases, there are no data sources to collect (for instance, for non-existing systems). In those cases, we need to try to obtain data sets from similar systems (if available). Another option is to use a stochastic approach to provide the data needed through random number generation.

5.4 Modeling phase

In the modeling phase, we must build a detailed representation of the system based on the conceptual model and the I/O data collected. The model is built by defining objects, attributes, and methods using a chosen paradigm. At this point, a specification model is created, including the set of equations defining its behavior and structure. After finishing this definition, we must try to build a preliminary structure of the model (possibly relating the system variables and performance metrics), carefully describing any assumptions and simplifications and collecting them into the model's EF.

5.5 Simulation phase

During the simulation stage, we must choose a mechanism to implement the model (in most cases using a computer and adequate programming languages and tools), and a simulation model is constructed. During this step, it might be necessary to define simulation algorithms and to translate them into a computer program. In this phase, we also must build a model of the EF for the simulation.

5.6 Verification and validation

During the previous steps, three different models are built: the conceptual model (specification), the system's model (design), and the simulation model (executable program). We need to verify and validate these models. Verification is related to the internal consistency among the three models (is the model correctly implemented?). Validation is focused on the correspondence between model and reality: are the simulation results consistent with the system being analyzed? Did we build the right model? Based on the results obtained during this phase, the model and its implementation might need refinement. As we will discuss in the next section, the V&V process does not constitute a particular phase of the life cycle, but it is an integral part of it. This process must be formal and must be documented correctly because later versions of the model will require another round of V&V, which is, in fact, one of the most expensive phases in the cycle.

5.7 Experimentation

We must execute the simulation model, following the goals stated in the conceptual model. During this phase, we must evaluate the outputs of the simulator, using statistical correlation to determine a precision level for the performance metrics. This phase starts with the design of the experiments, using different techniques. Some of these techniques include sensitivity analysis, optimization, variance reduction (to optimize the results from a statistical point of view), and ranking and selection (comparison with alternative systems).

5.8 Output analysis phase

In the output analysis phase, the simulation outputs are analyzed in order to understand the system behavior. These outputs are used to obtain responses about the behavior of the original system. At this stage, visualization tools can be used to help with the process. The goal of visualization is to provide a deeper understanding of the real systems being investigated and to help in exploring the large set of numerical data produced by the simulation.

6. M&S Tools and Environments for WSNs

Different schemes developed for Wireless Sensor Networks (WSNs) are verified by analytical techniques, simulations, and test bedsCinque et al. (2007); Lopez et al. (2005). Analytical modeling may provide quick insight but fail to give realistic results for reasons like limited energy, memory, and processing power, and sheer number, unattended operation, harsh environments of sensor nodes Chen et al. (2006). Real world implementation and test beds are the most accurate ways to study WSNs but such methods requires huge effort, time and money. Simulations provide a good approximation to verify different schemes and applications developed for WSNs at low cost and in less time. To have credible results through simulations, correct modeling and the selection of simulation tool plays a vital role. In the following sections, we present brief description of different models as well as simulation tools available to study WSNs.

6.1 Simulation Tools and Environments

6.1.1 NS-2

NS-2[5] is a discrete event, object oriented, general purpose network simulator written in C++. It is the most widely used simulator Kurkowski et al. (2005). Its main focus is IP networks. To simulate WSNs with more or less 100 nodes, NS-2 can be a good choice because of its large community but for 100+ nodes, it is no more scalable Naoumov & Gross (2003). *"One of the problems of ns2 is its object-oriented design that introduces much unnecessary inter-dependence between modules. Such interdependence sometimes makes the addition of new protocol models extremely difficult, which can only be mastered by those who have intimate familiarity with the simulator."*Chen et al. (2006). SensorSim Park et al. (2000) is a NS-2 based simulator for modeling sensor networks. Some WSN specific features are included but because of the *"unfinished nature of the software"*[6], the simulator is no longer available.

6.1.2 OMNeT++

OMNeT ++ Varga (2001) is a discrete event, component based, general purpose, public source, modular simulation framework written in C++. It provides a strong GUI support for animation and debugging. Mobility framework (MF) Drytkiewicz et al. (2003) for OMNet++ is specific purpose add-on to simulate ad-hoc networks. The lack of a WSN specific module library Lopez et al. (2006) may be a problem currently but many research groups are working to add WSN specific additional modules. SenSim Mallanda et al. (2005) is OMNeT based simulation framework for WSN. It provides the basic implementation of different hardware (e.g., basic radio, and CPU) and software (simple routing schemes) modules for WSN. It provides a template with basic implementation or empty body which can help anyone to jump start simulating WSNs Egea-Lopez et al. (2006).

---

[5] www.isi.edu/nsnam/ns

[6] nesl.ee.ucla.edu/projects/sensorsim

6.1.3 NesCT

NesCT[7] is an add-on for OMNeT++ which allows simulation of TinyOS based sensor networks in OMNeT (language translator between OMNeT and TinyOS implementations).

6.1.4 PAWiS

PAWiS[8] simulation framework is OMNeT plus plus based discrete event simulation framework. It provides a rich library of modules and supports mobility and environmental dynamics. It also provides a simulation template for users to quick start simulation study Madani et al. (2008); Weber et al. (2007).

6.1.5 GlomoSim

Global Mobile Information System Simulator (GlomoSim) Zeng et al. (1998) is a library based general purpose, parallel simulator written in Parsec[9]. It can simulate up to 10,000 nodes Lopez et al. (2005) and can be very useful in studying large scale WSNs. . GlomoSim is superseded by QualNet[10], a commercial network simulator. sQualNet Varshney et al. (2007), an evaluation framework for sensor networks, based on QualNet is released recently.

6.1.6 OPNET

OPNET Modeler[11] is general purpose, object oriented, C-based discrete event simulation environment. It's commercial and therefore not used widely. It comes with a version for academic use but with limited capabilities. OPNET is a large and powerful software with a wide variety of possibilities. OPNET can be used as a research tool and also as a network design/analysis tool. OPNET was originally built for the simulation of fixed networks, and therefore, it contains extensive libraries of accurate models from commercially available fixed network hardware and protocols Cai & Jia (2009); Hammoodi et al. (2009); Hasan et al. (2009); Zhuo et al. (2007).

6.1.7 SENSE

SENSE Chen et al. (2006) is a sensor network specific, component based simulator written in C++ built on the top of COST Chen & Szymanski (2002). Parallel simulation can be done to study large scale WSNs. It provides basic implementations like AODV and DSR as well as oversimplified models for batter and energy consumption.

6.1.8 Ptolemy II and J-Sim

Ptolemy II Liu et al. (2001) and J-Sim Miller et al. (1997); Sobeih et al. (2005; 2006) are general purpose, component based simulation frameworks written Java. Both simulation frameworks provide a rich support for WSNs.

6.1.9 Cell-DEVS

The Cell-DEVS formalism allows defining cellular models based on the discrete-event system specification. Cell-DEVS allows defining asynchronous cell spaces with explicit timing definition. This approach is still based on the formal specifications of DEVS, but it allows the user to

[7] www.omnetpp.org
[8] www.ict.tuwien.ac.at/pawis
[9] pcl.cs.ucla.edu/projects/parsec
[10] www.scalable-networks.com
[11] www.opnet.com

focus on the problem to be solved by using simple rules for modeling (like with CA). Explicit timing delay constructions can be used to define precise timing in each cell. This approach allows enhancing the modeling experience in different aspects. In terms of performance, only active cells execute their local computing function, and the execution results are spread out after a predefined delay (only if a state change has occurred). The delay function provides a natural mechanism for defining timing information.
The modeling technique permits keeping the ability of CA to describe complex systems using very simple rules, while also permitting us to bridge the gap between a discrete time and a discrete event description like DEVS. The use of DEVS as the basic formal specification mechanism enables us to define interactions with models defined in other formalisms. Individual cells can provide data to those models; integration between them could enable defining of complex hybrid systems and multimodels developed with different techniques and integrated through a DEVS interface. This approach provides "evolvability" of the models through a technique that is easy to understand and to map into other existing techniques, while having the potential of evolving into complex models Qela et al. (2009).

6.1.10 GTNetS

The "Georgia Tech Network Simulator," (GTNetS) [12] developed and maintained by the Department of Electrical and Computer Engineering at Georgia Tech is an object-oriented design written completely in C++. The design of GTNetS matches closely the design of actual network protocol stacks and other network elements. Further, GTNetS was designed from the beginning to run a distributed environment, leading to better scalability Cheng et al. (2006); Riley (2003); Zhang & Riley (2004).

6.1.11 SystemC

SystemC is a C++ based modeling platform supporting design abstractions at the register-transfer, behavioral, and system levels. The SystemC classes add the necessary constructs to C++ for modeling systems and hardware at various levels of abstraction-from the abstract untimed models to cycle-accurate RTL models. The power of SystemC is that it can be used as a common language by system designers, software engineers, and hardware designers Rafiee et al. (2009); Vasilevski et al. (2007).

6.1.12 Prowler

Prowler [13] is an event-driven wireless network simulator designed to run in Matlab environment. The simulator, written originally to simulate Berkeley MICA motes, is extendable also for more general platforms. Prowler is implemented in Matlab language (m-file) which makes direct simulation code, e.g., routing protocol or application, interchange between simulator and sensor platforms impossible. Benefits gained from Matlab environment are easy prototyping of applications, integration of different optimization algorithms, GUI interface and good visualization capabilities.

6.1.13 NCTUns2.0

NCTUns2.0 [14] is a discrete event simulator whose engine is embedded in the kernel of a UNIX machine. The actual network layer packets are tunnelled through virtual interfaces that simu-

[12] http://www.ece.gatech.edu/research/labs/MANIACS/GTNetS/
[13] http://www.isis.vanderbilt.edu/projects/nest/prowler
[14] http://nsl.csie.nctu.edu.tw

late lower layers and physical devices. This notable feature allows simulations to be fed with real program data sources. A useful GUI is available in addition to a high number of protocols and network devices, including wireless LAN. Unfortunately, no specific designs for WSN are included.

6.1.14 JiST/SWANS

JiST/SWANS [15] is a discrete event simulation framework that embeds the simulation engine in the Java bytecode. Models are implemented in Java and compiled. Then, bytecodes are rewritten to introduce simulation semantics. Afterwards, they are executed on a standard JVM. This implementation allows the use of unmodified existing Java software in the simulation, as occurs with NCTUns2.0 and UNIX programs.

6.1.15 SSFNet

SSFNet [16] is a set of Java network models built over the Scalable Simulation Framework (SSF). SSF is a specification of a common API for simulation, that assures portability between compliant simulators. There are multiple Java and C++ implementations of SSF. DartmouthSSF (DaSSF) [30], for instance, is a C++ implementation of SSF oriented to (parallel) simulation of very large scale communication networks.

6.1.16 Ptolemy II

Ptolemy II [17] is a set of Java packages that support different models of simulation paradigms (e.g. continuos time, dataflow, discrete-event). It also addresses the modeling, simulation and design of concurrent, real-time and embedded systems.

6.2 Emulation Tools

In addition to the above cited simulation tools/environments for WSNs, there are number of emulation tools/environments as well. Some of the these are TOSSIM Levis et al. (2003), EmStar Girod et al. (2004), and ATEMU Polley et al. (2004). Such tools come with inherent advantage. Whatever code is used for simulation/emulation, the same code is used on the real sensor node with slight modifications. It also provides detailed information about resource utilization. The main problem with such frameworks is *"the user is tied to a single platform either software or hardware (typically MICA motes), and to a single programming Language (typically TinyOS/NesC)"*Lopez et al. (2005).

6.3 Other Tools

There are many tools which do not fall into either simulation or emulation catagories like TEPAWSN Man et al. (2009) which is a tool environment for Wireless Sensor Networks.

7. Summary

Wireless Sensor Netwroks is an emerging field with many apllication in almost all walk of life. Researchers are actively involved in the development of new and improving the existing techiques and technologies for making the life more easier. Each of these developed and/or improved techniques need to be extensively testes and varified before it can be used in the

[15] http://jist.ece.cornell.edu/
[16] http://www.ssfnet.org
[17] http://ptolemy.berkeley.edu/ptolemyII/

actual production. Most accurate and reliable method is, of-course, the real-world implementation and test-beds. But these are sometimes not possible or even harder. In that case the method of the choice is the modeling and simulation.
In this chapter we presented a partial list of available models and simulation/emulation tools for the wireless sensor networks, available. The chapter started with an introduction and the historical perspective to the field of WSN and some of its applications. We then briefly discussed the different discrete event modeling and simulation methodologies after which the major steps/phases in a M&S study are outlines with the identification of major milestone. The chapter concludes with a list of different models, simulation and emulation tools.

8. References

Abramson, N. (1970). The ALOHA System-Another alternative for computer communications, *Fall Joint Computing Conf*, pp. 281–285.

Adi Mallikarjuna, R. V., Kumar, A. V. U. & Janakiram, D. (2007). e-petri net model for programming integrated network of wireless sensor networks and grids, *Proc. 7th IEEE Int. Conf. Computer and Information Technology CIT 2007*, pp. 1038–1043.

Akyildiz, I., Su, W., Sankarasubramaniam, Y. & Cayirci, E. (2002). A survey on sensor networks, *IEEE Communications Magazine* **40**(8): 102–114.

Alur, R. & Dill, D. L. (1994). A theory of timed automata, *Theor. Comput. Sci.* **126**(2): 183–235.

Antoine-Santoni, T., Santucci, J. F., de Gentili, E. & Costa, B. (2006). Using wireless sensor network for wildfire detection. a discrete event approach of environmental monitoring tool, *Proc. First international Symp. Environment Identities and Mediterranean Area ISEIMA '06*, pp. 115–120.

Banks, J., J. S. C. B. L. N. & Nicol., D. (2005). *Discrete-event system simulation, 4th ed.*, Upper Saddle River, NJ: Prentice Hall.

Belina, F. & Hogrefe, D. (1989). The ccitt-specification and description language sdl, *Comput. Netw. ISDN Syst.* **16**(4): 311–341.

Cai, J. & Jia, B. (2009). Network simulation based on opnte and application, *Proc. First Int. Workshop Education Technology and Computer Science ETCS '09*, Vol. 1, pp. 199–202.

Callaway, E., Paul Gorday, L. H., Guiterrez, J. A., M. Naeve, B. H. & Bahl, V. (2002). Home Networking with IEEE802.15.4: A Developing Standard for Low-Rate Wireless Personal Area Networks, *IEEE Communication Magazine* **40**(8).

Cassandras, C. G. (1993). *Discrete event systems: Modeling and performance analysis*, Homewood, IL:Aksen: Irwin.

Cellier, F. E. & Kofman., E. (2006). *Continuous system simulation*, Springer Science+Business Media.

Cerpa, A., Elson, J., Estrin, D., Girod, L., Hamilton, M. & Zhao, J. (2001). Habitat monitoring: Application driver for wireless communications technology, *In Proceedings of the 2001 ACM SIGCOMM Workshop on Data Communications in Latin America and the Caribbean.*

Chen, G., Branch, J., Pflug, M., Zhu, L. & Szymanski2, B. (2006). *Advances in Pervasive Computing and Networking*, Springer US, chapter Sense: A Wireless Sensor Network Simulator, pp. 249–267.

Chen, G. & Szymanski, B. (2002). COST: a component-oriented discrete event simulator, *Proceedings of the Winter Simulation Conference.*

Cheng, L., Zhang, X. & Bourgeois, A. G. (2006). Ieee 802.15.4 simulation module in network simulator gtnets, *Proc. VTC 2006-Spring Vehicular Technology Conf. IEEE 63rd*, Vol. 3, pp. 1308–1312.

Cinque, M., Cotroneo, D., Di Martinio, C. & Russo, S. (2007). Modeling and assessing the dependability ofwireless sensor networks, *Proc. 26th IEEE Int. Symp. Reliable Distributed Systems SRDS 2007*, pp. 33–44.

Colitti, W., Steenhaut, K., Lemmens, B. & Borms, J. (2009). Simulation tool for wireless sensor network constellations in space, *Proc. Int. Conf. Ultra Modern Telecommunications & Workshops ICUMT '09*, pp. 1–5.

Demo, J., Steiner, A., Friedersdorf, F. & Putic, M. (2010). Development of a wireless miniaturized smart sensor network for aircraft corrosion monitoring, *Proc. IEEE Aerospace Conf*, pp. 1–9.

Dietrich, D., Loy, D. & Schweinzer, H. (2001). Open Control Networks LonWorks/EIA 709 Technology. Kluwer Academic Publishers.

Drytkiewicz, W., Sroka, S., Handziski, V., Koepke, A. & Karl, H. (2003). A Mobility Framework for OMNeT++, *3rd International OMNeT++ Workshop*.

Egea-Lopez, E., Ponce-Marin, F. & Vales-Alonso, J. (2006). Obiwan: wireless sensor networks with omnet++, *Proc. IEEE Mediterranean Electrotechnical Conf. MELECON 2006*, pp. 777–780.

Fishwick, P. A. (1995). *Simulation model design and execution: Building digital worlds*, Englewood Cliffs, NJ: Prentice Hall.

Fu, S., Hou, Z.-G. & Yang, G. (2009). An indoor navigation system for autonomous mobile robot using wireless sensor network, *Proc. Int. Conf. Networking, Sensing and Control ICNSC '09*, pp. 227–232.

Girod, L., Stathopoulos, T., Ramanathan, N., Elson, J., Estrin, D., Osterweil, E. & Schoellhammer, T. (2004). A system for simulation, emulation, and deployment of heterogeneous sensor networks, *2nd international Conference on Embedded Networked Sensor Systems*.

Glynn, P. (1989). A gsmp formalism for discrete event systems, *Proceedings of the IEEE* **77**(1): 14 –23.

Hammoodi, I. S., Stewart, B. G., Kocian, A. & McMeekin, S. G. (2009). A comprehensive performance study of opnet modeler for zigbee wireless sensor networks, *Proc. Third Int. Conf. Next Generation Mobile Applications, Services and Technologies NGMAST '09*, pp. 357–362.

Hansson, H. & Jonsson, B. (1990). A calculus for communicating systems with time and probabilities, *Proc. th Real-Time Systems Symp.*, pp. 278–287.

Hasan, M. S., Yu, H., Carrington, A. & Yang, T. C. (2009). Co-simulation of wireless networked control systems over mobile ad hoc network using simulink and opnet, *IET Communications* **3**(8): 1297–1310.

Hoare, C. A. R. (1985). *Communicating sequential processes*, Englewood Cliffs, NJ: Prentice Hall International.

Hu, J. (2008). The application of wireless sensor networks to in-service motor monitoring and energy management, *Proc. First Int. Conf. Intelligent Networks and Intelligent Systems ICINIS '08*, pp. 165–169.

Isreb, M. (2006). Parallel distributed wireless sensor network application for critical infrastructure risk analysis of fossil fuelled power stations, *Proc. IEEE Int Information Acquisition Conf*, pp. 301–305.

Jubin, J. & Tornow, J. D. (1987). The DARPA Packet Radio Network Protocols, *Proceedings of the IEEE*, Vol. 75, pp. 21–32.

Ke, Z., Yang, L., Wang-hui, X. & Heejong, S. (2008). The application of a wireless sensor network design based on zigbee in petrochemical industry field, *Proc. First Int. Conf. Intelligent Networks and Intelligent Systems ICINIS '08*, pp. 284–287.

Kurkowski, S., Camp, T. & Colagrosso, M. (2005). MANET simulation studies: the incredibles, *Mobile Computing and Communications Review* **9**(4): 50–61.

Law, A. M. & Kelton, W. D. (2000). *Simulation modeling and analysis, 3rd ed*, Boston: McGraw Hill.

Lee, S. H., Lee, S., Song, H. & Lee, H. S. (2009). Wireless sensor network design for tactical military applications : Remote large-scale environments, *Proc. IEEE Military Communications Conf. MILCOM 2009*, pp. 1–7.

Levis, P., N.Lee, Welsh, M. & D.Culler (2003). TOSSIM: accurate and scalable simulation of entire tinyOS applications, *1st international Conference on Embedded Networked Sensor Systems*, pp. 126–137.
URL: *http://www.cs.berkeley.edu/p̃al/pubs/nido.pdf*

Li, G.-L. & Li, V. O. K. (2003). Networks of queues: myth and reality, *Proc. IEEE 18th Annual Workshop Computer Communications CCW 2003*, pp. 154–158.

Liu, H., Liu, X. & Lee, E. (2001). Modeling distributed hybrid systems in Ptolemy II, *American Control Conference*, Vol. 6.

Lopez, E., Alonso, V., Sala, M., Mario, P. & Haro, G. (2006). Simulation scalability issues in wireless sensor networks, *IEEE Communications Magazine* **44**(7): 64–73.

Lopez, E. E., Alonso, J. V., Sala, A. M., Marino, P. P. & Haro, J. G. (2005). Simulation tools for wireless sensor networks, *International Symposium on Performance Evaluation of Computer and Telecommunication Systems (SPECTS05)*, Philadelphia, USA.
URL: *http://ait.upct.es/ẽegea/*

Madani, S. A., Weber, D. & Mahlknecht, S. (2008). Tpr: Dead end aware table less position based routing scheme for low power data-centric wireless sensor networks, *Proc. Int. Symp. Industrial Embedded Systems SIES 2008*, pp. 149–154.

Mallanda, C., Suri, A., Kunchakarra, V., Iyengar, S., Kannan, R. & Durresi, A. (2005). Simulating Wireless Sensor Networks with Omnet++, [submitted to IEEE Computers].
URL: *http://csc.lsu.edu/ĩyengar/final-papers/SensorSimulator-IEEE-Computers.pdf*

Man, K. L., Vallee, T., Leung, H. L., Mercaldi, M., van der Wulp, J., Donno, M. & Pastrnak, M. (2009). Tepawsn - a tool environment for wireless sensor networks, *Proc. 4th IEEE Conf. Industrial Electronics and Applications ICIEA 2009*, pp. 730–733.

Manna, Z. & Pnueli, A. (1992). *The temporal logic of reactive and concurrent systems*, New York:Springer Verlag.

Miller, J., Nair, R., Zhang, Z. & Zhao, H. (1997). JSIM: A Java-based simulation and animation environment, *30th Annual Simulation Symposium*, pp. 31–42.

Molina-Garcia, A., Fuentes, J. A., Gomez-Lazaro, E., Bonastre, A., Campelo, J. C. & Serrano, J. J. (2007). Application of wireless sensor network to direct load control in residential areas, *Proc. IEEE Int. Symp. Industrial Electronics ISIE 2007*, pp. 1974–1979.

Naoumov, V. & Gross, T. (2003). Simulation of large ad hoc networks, *6th ACM international Workshop on Modeling Analysis and Simulation of Wireless and Mobile Systems*, San Diego, CA, USA.
URL: *http://citeseer.ist.psu.edu/naoumov03simulation.html*

Park, S., Savvides, A. & Srivastava, M. B. (2000). SensorSim: a simulation framework for sensor networks, *International Workshop on Modeling Analysis and Simulation of Wireless*

and Mobile Systems.
URL: *http://portal.acm.org/citation.cfm?id=346870*

Peterson, J. L. (1981). *Petri net theory and the modeling of systems*, Englewood Cliffs, NJ: Prentice Hall.

Polley, J., Blazakis, D., McGee, J., Rusk, D. & Baras, J. (2004). ATEMU: a fine-grained sensor network simulator, *First Annual IEEE Communications Society Conference on Sensor and Ad Hoc Communications and Networks (SECON)*, pp. 145–152.

Qela, B., Wainer, G. & Mouftah, H. (2009). Simulation of large wireless sensor networks using cell-devs, *Proc. Winter Simulation Conf. (WSC) the 2009*, pp. 3189–3200.

Rafiee, M., Ghaznavi-Ghoushchi, M. B., Kheiri, S. & Seyfe, B. (2009). Modeling and simulation of wireless sensor network (wsn) with specc and systemc, *Proc. Int. Conf. Computer Engineering and Technology ICCET '08*, Vol. 1, pp. 515–519.

Raghavendra, C., Sivalingam, K. M. & Znati, T. (2004). Wireless Sensor Networks, Kluwer Academic Publishers.

Riley, G. F. (2003). Large-scale network simulations with gtnets, *Proc. Winter Simulation Conf*, Vol. 1, pp. 676–684.

Sarkar, T. K., Oliner, M. R., A., A., Salazar-Palma, Magdalena, Sengupta & L., D. (2006). *History of Wireless*, Vol. 1, 1 edn, Wiley Series in Microwave and Optical Engineering, chapter 7, pp. 451–452.

Sauter, T., Dietrich, D. & Kastner, W. (2002). *EIB: Installation Bus System*, Wiley-VCH.

Schruben, L. W., Roeder, T. M., Chan, W. K., Hyden, P. & Freimer, M. (2003). Advanced event scheduling methodology: advanced event scheduling methodology, *WSC '03: Proceedings of the 35th conference on Winter simulation*, Winter Simulation Conference, pp. 159–165.

Sobeih, A., Chen, W.-P., Hou, J. C., Kung, L.-C., Li, N., Lim, H., Tyan, H.-Y. & Zhang, H. (2005). J-sim: a simulation environment for wireless sensor networks, *Proc. 38th Annual Simulation Symp*, pp. 175–187.

Sobeih, A., Hou, J. C., Kung, L.-C., Li, N., Zhang, H., Chen, W.-P., Tyan, H.-Y. & Lim, H. (2006). J-sim: a simulation and emulation environment for wireless sensor networks, **13**(4): 104–119.

Taylor, M. (1996). *Partial differential equations: Basic theory*, Springer Verlag.

Toffoli, T. & Margolus., N. (1987). *Cellular automata machines: A new environment for modeling*, Cambridge, MA: MIT Press.

Toh, S.-H., Lee, S.-C. & Chung, W.-Y. (2008). Wsn based personal mobile physiological monitoring and management system for chronic disease, *Proc. Third Int. Conf. Convergence and Hybrid Information Technology ICCIT '08*, Vol. 1, pp. 467–472.

Varga, A. (2001). 'The OMNeT++ Discrete Event Simulation System, *In the Proceedings of the European Simulation Multiconference.*
URL: *http://www.omnetpp.org/links.php?category=Publications*

Varshney, M., Xu, D., Srivastava, M. B. & Bagrodia, R. L. (2007). sQualNet: An Accurate and Scalable Evaluation Framework for Sensor Networks, *International Conference on Information Processing in Sensor Networks.*
URL: *http://pcl.cs.ucla.edu/papers/files/spots07-varshney.pdf*

Vasilevski, M., Pecheux, F., Aboushady, H. & de Lamarre, L. (2007). Modeling heterogeneous systems using systemc-ams case study: A wireless sensor network node, *Proc. IEEE Int. Behavioral Modeling and Simulation Workshop BMAS 2007*, pp. 11–16.

von Bertalanffy, L. (1969). *General system theory: Foundations, development, applications*, New York: G. Braziller.

Wainer, G. A. (2009). *Discrete-Event Modeling and Simulation A Practitioner's Approach*, CRC Press.

Weber, D., Glaser, J. & Mahlknecht, S. (2007). Discrete event simulation framework for power aware wireless sensor networks, *Proc. 5th IEEE Int Industrial Informatics Conf*, Vol. 1, pp. 335–340.

Zeigler, B. P. (1976). *Theory of modeling and simulation*, New York: Wiley Interscience.

Zeigler, B. P. (1990). *Object-oriented simulation with hierarchical, modular models: Intelligent agents and endomorphic systems*, Boston: Academic Press.

Zeng, X., Bagrodia, R. & Gerla, M. (1998). GloMoSim: a library for parallel simulation of large-scale wireless networks, *Twelfth Workshop on Parallel and Distributed Simulation*. **URL:** *http://qualnet.com/pdf/glomosim.pdf*

Zhang, X. & Riley, G. F. (2004). Bluetooth simulations for wireless sensor networks using gtnets, *Proc. IEEE Computer Society's 12th Annual Int. Symp. Modeling, Analysis, and Simulation of Computer and Telecommunications Systems (MASCOTS 2004)*, pp. 375–382.

Zhao, F. & Guibas, L. (2004). *Wireless Sensor Networks, an information processing approach*, Morgan Kaufmann. 294-300.

Zhuo, Z., Donglei, X., Qianli, L. & Maopei, L. (2007). Wireless modeling of hf networks in opnet, *Proc. Int Microwave, Antenna, Propagation and EMC Technologies for Wireless Communications Symp*, pp. 285–288.

14

Discrete event simulation of wireless cellular networks

Enrica Zola, Israel Martín-Escalona and Francisco Barceló-Arroyo
Universitat Politècnica de Catalunya (UPC)
Spain

1. Introduction

The design of telecommunication networks usually comprises three major phases. First, mathematical analysis is carried out and numerical results obtained. During this phase, simple models are used to facilitate calculations. These simple models involve hypotheses that are not realistic, leading to rough performance figures that are valid only as a first approach to the feasibility of the proposed network. Simulation is the second step in the design process before performance can be monitored and measured in the true network. In contrast to the simple models necessary for the mathematical analysis, models used in simulations permit the relaxation of strict adherence to most of the hypotheses assumed in those models. The results obtained by simulation are much closer to the true world than those obtained by analysis. The simulation of wireless cellular networks raises a set of specific problems that are not encountered in the simulation of other networks. The aim of this chapter is to state those issues and to present several ways to cope with them.

Two types of simulation, Montecarlo and discrete event, are most commonly used in cellular networks to cope with two different problems. Montecarlo simulation has been shown to be appropriate for determining the coverage of base stations (BSs), the radiation patterns of antennas and other related problems. The main goal after these simulations is to fit the BSs at their possible emplacements using a geographic information system (GIS). Given the parameters of the equipment at the BS and receiving devices and the probabilistic models employed for propagation in the specific environment, the probability of a certain device at a certain point being covered can be determined. This is computed by averaging snapshots of the coverage in the desired area. On the other hand, most researchers and network designers make use of discrete event simulation for addressing issues related to the cellular features, mobility, handovers between neighbouring cells and traffic.

The simulation of traffic-related issues in cellular networks is based on the arrival of traffic events (e.g., voice or data calls, packets, messages, etc.) to the network. The goal is to compute the probability of traffic being carried by the network given a certain network capacity (e.g., number of BSs, channels, bandwidth, etc.). A key issue is the intuitive fact that increasing the mobility leads to lower performance: i.e., when devices move faster, they need more handovers of their session between different BSs, increasing the probability of interruption. In fact, mobility not only depends on speed, but also smaller cells lead to more handovers for the same speed; even the cell shape has an impact on the handover rate. These layout and mobility issues are dealt with in Section 2. Propagation issues are presented in Section 3. The models presented are common to the Montecarlo simulation of radio coverage, but they are used in a different manner when applied to the discrete event simulation of traffic and mobility. Section 4 deals with other issues, such as the cell wrapping needed to improve the efficiency of the simulation to achieve statistically reliable results, the features of different traffic classes and the various methods used to obtain statistical results.

2. Layout and Mobility

When simulating a cellular network, a layout for the BSs to which the mobile devices are connected must be assumed. There are several well established patterns, including hexagonal (typical for suburban areas), Manhattan (urban) and linear (highways). The possibility of having several connection layers must also be considered, e.g., microcells as the first choice and macrocells as umbrellas for overflowing traffic. In real cellular networks, the designer can plan BSs at any point, and therefore, the simulation should allow any position for the BSs. The problem of the cell borders is related to the layout. For simplicity, it is possible to simulate a network in which devices are covered by the BS closest to them. This kind of simulation is simple and allows direct conclusions from the results; however, it is not realistic. When the radiation patterns and random nature of the radio channel are taken into account (see Section 3), the borders are not regular shapes and may change with time. This increases the complexity of the simulation significantly; however, it offers realistic results, although they are more difficult to interpret. Section 2.1 addresses the above-mentioned issues, showing how each kind of layout must be programmed and the way in which results must be interpreted.

The mobile behaviour of devices within the cellular network can be characterised and simulated in a variety of ways, with each of them corresponding to a different scenario and environment. Experimental research has been conducted during the last two decades to determine the statistical properties of each representative user class, e.g., public networks, local area networks (LANs), indoors, outdoors, cars, pedestrians, etc. According to the network technology, geographical area and type of user, it is possible to feed the simulation with certain parameters such that the resulting movement will be similar to the real one. The Random Waypoint and Gauss-Markov models are the most relevant, but other useful models are also available. Section 2.2 addresses the way in which every model must be programmed and the different properties found with every movement. It also shows the simulation results acquired by the authors about the residence time in cells belonging to a wireless LAN (WLAN) when different models are applied.

2.1 Layout

The first issue is to select the area of the network that should be simulated. Depending on the environment (e.g., suburban, dense urban, indoors, etc.) and on the technology under study (e.g., GSM, UMTS, WiMax, WiFi, Bluetooth, etc.), the simulation area may encompass square kilometres (e.g., big city) or square meters (e.g., a single building). This area may be covered by a single high transmission power antenna or by many low power transmitters, with each providing coverage to a small portion of the whole simulation area. The second solution is the basis for cellular systems; the area covered by a single antenna (i.e., one BS) corresponds to the cell area. Different layouts can be obtained by positioning BSs according to different patterns. The selection of the best pattern to use can be driven by simple observations of the geometry of the area under study. As an example, linear patterns can be used to provide coverage on highways; BSs will be positioned along the path at regular distances.

A regular pattern can also be applied when modelling symmetrical layouts in large suburban areas. The common technique used to position antennas to obtain a network of non-overlapping cells is by following the **hexagonal pattern** displayed in Fig. 1. Each cell is allocated a subset of the total radio channels assigned to the system. The cells are grouped into clusters, wherein the available channels are not allowed to be reused, to prevent interference among users of different cells. The number of cells per cluster represents the cluster size (*N*). According to (Rappaport, 1996), *N* can only have values that satisfy the following equation

$$N = i^2 + i \cdot j + j^2 , \tag{1}$$

where *i* and *j* are non-negative integers. *N* is equal to 7 in Fig. 1.

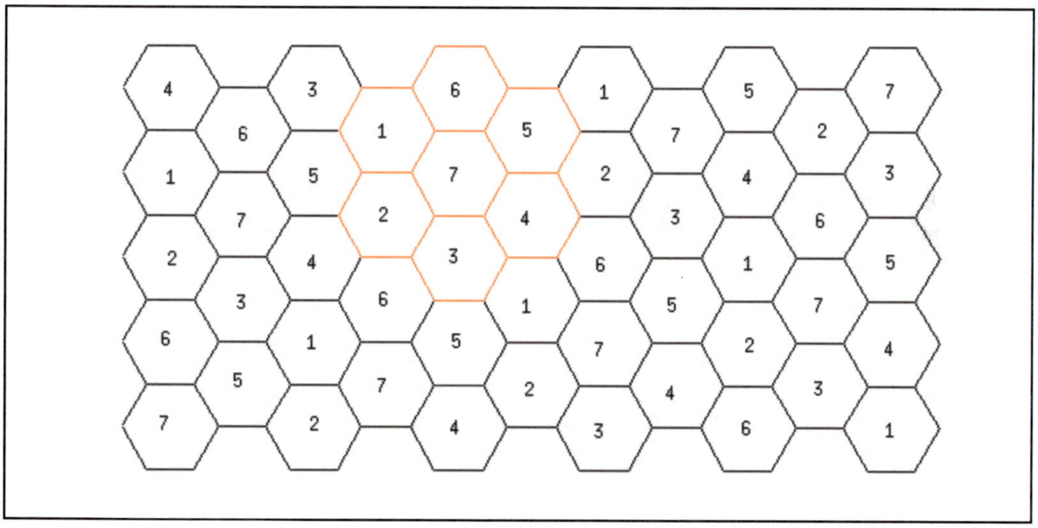

Fig. 1. Hexagonal layout with a cluster size of 7 (in red).

In dense urban environments with regular patterns, the **Manhattan model** is preferred because it follows the geometry of the streets, thus providing coverage both outside and inside the buildings. It considers a regular pattern of buildings, which are represented by regular squares, and a regular network of horizontal and vertical streets between the blocks. Antennas should be placed at every street crossing, and the cell size is assumed to be half a block in all directions. The cluster size for this layout can be computed using the equation from (Rappaport, 1996)

$$N = i^2 + j^2 , \tag{2}$$

where *i* and *j* are non-negative integers.

Multi-layer layouts may be needed for capacity constraints (i.e., hotspots). A regular macrocell pattern (e.g., hexagonal or Manhattan) representing the first layer of coverage, which provides continuity in the service, is superimposed, like an umbrella, onto a microcell pattern, which guarantees service for the overcrowded areas. Of course, different radio channels should be assigned to the two layers.

Once the layout has been selected, the following problem is to find the number of BSs needed to cover the whole simulation area. For this purpose, the area covered by a single cell must be known. The cell boundaries can be evaluated according to the antennas' parameters (e.g., transmission power, the radiation diagram, the antenna gain, the antenna height, etc.) and the radiation pattern of the environment under study. In a first approximation, the cell boundaries can be estimated according to the free space model, for which the transmission power decays with the power of distance. Different radiation patterns can be selected to represent a more realistic scenario in which the cell boundaries are not regular shapes and may change over time (see Section 3.2). The theoretical boundaries may be verified with specific simulation tools.

Besides the BSs needed for **coverage constraints**, the number of antennas may also be tuned to meet the specific **capacity requirements**. The number of channels that a single BS may support limits the number of simultaneous users that can be connected to that BS. In dense urban areas, where a higher concentration of users is forecasted, it is better to position more BSs than the minimum number specified by coverage constraints. An example of tuning the cell boundaries can be found in (Zola & Barceló, 2006). Their work relies on an analytical study, known as link budget, from which it is possible to estimate the coverage range of a single-cell in different environments for a given system capacity. Many issues affect the system performance (i.e., propagation conditions, traffic density, user profiles, interference conditions, cell breathing, etc.), making the network designer's task quite complex. Software planning tools can assist greatly in managing complex situations. Starting from simulation analysis in a single-cell environment in which analytical results have been tested, a first layout of the BSs in the city of Barcelona is provided in (Zola & Barceló, 2006). In this multiple-cell asset, the intercell interference, the cell breathing, and the capacity requirements due to soft-handover generate new problems that do not appear in the single-cell scenario (i.e., noise rise, BS power limits, etc.). With the final purpose of providing good coverage, the authors investigate how to improve this first layout by changing the configuration of any BSs (e.g., tilt and height) and, eventually, changing their locations (see Fig. 2). Optimal planning requires a long process of trial and error, from which one has to adjust the parameters to finally achieve a good provision of service.

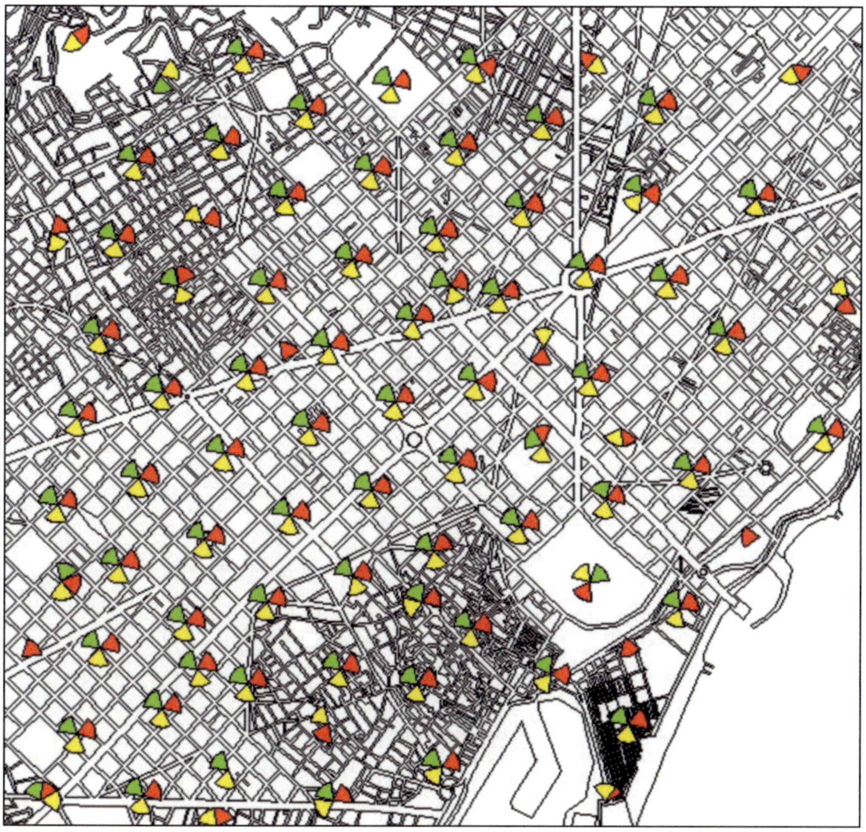

Fig. 2. BS layout in the city of Barcelona.

2.2. Mobility patterns

The purpose of a wireless network is to provide coverage to moving users. Knowledge about the pattern followed by mobile stations (MSs) in a given scenario may help network planning to guarantee service along the pathway followed by each user. The mobility pattern should mimic the movements of real MSs. Both **trace-based models** and synthetic models, based on theoretical algorithms, which describe the movement of a node statistically, can be used. The former can be derived from the observation of real movements; to achieve this, user's log traces should be collected during a period long enough to capture periodical behaviours. An executable mobility model is described in (Tuduce & Gross, 2005). This model uses parameters extracted from the real-life mobility of WLAN users and generates mobility scenarios based on these parameters. In that study, spatial parameters and temporal parameters are independent from each other; however, a strong correlation between the space and time dimensions has been proven to exist. This aspect is overcome in (Kim et al., 2006). The authors specified a method for extracting users' mobility tracks from real WLAN traces and applied it to a large set of traces of wireless users from Dartmouth College. Despite the ability of trace-based models to reflect real movements, they may be too specific for the environment from which they have been extracted.

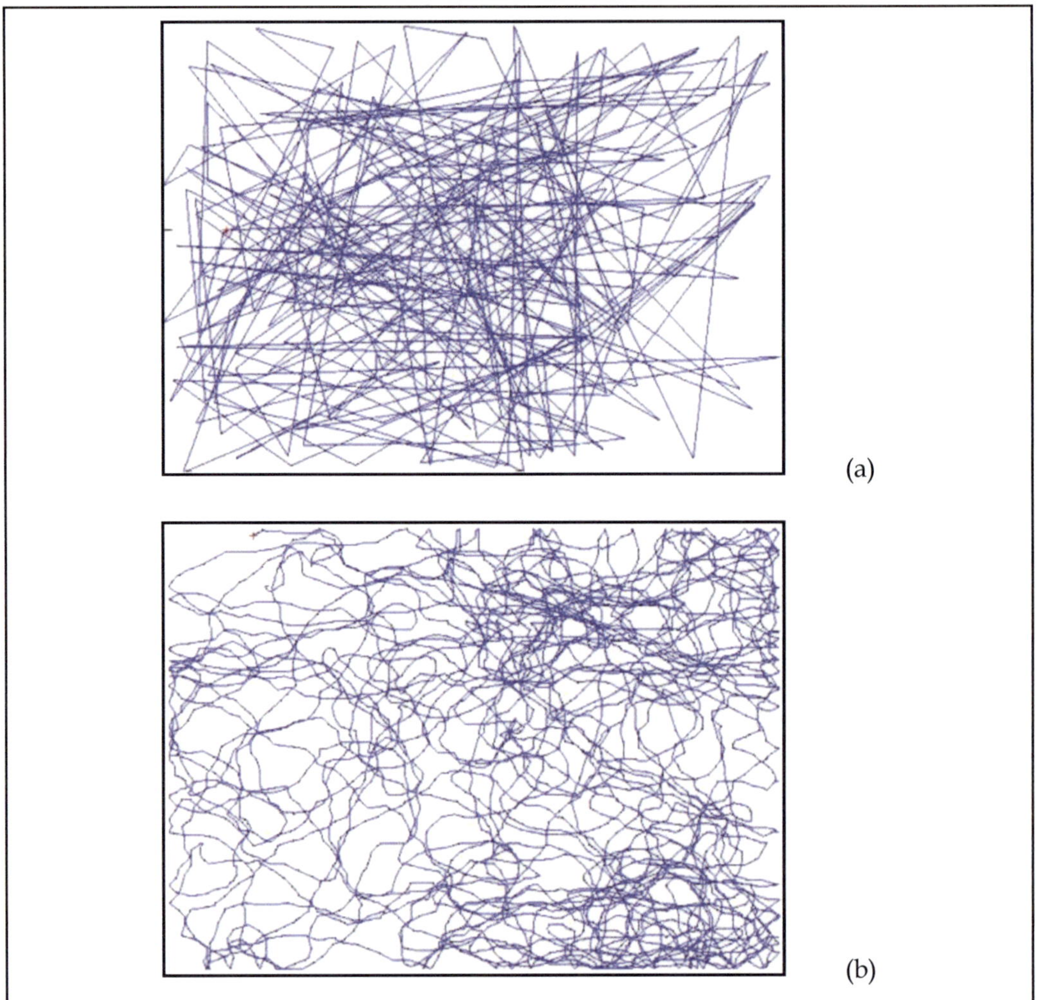

Fig. 3. Movement patterns following the Random Waypoint (a) or Gauss-Markov (b) mobility model. Simulation has been performed with *ns-2* (NS-2).

On the other hand, **synthetic models** attempt to realistically represent the behaviours of MSs over time while providing a simplified algorithm that describes their movements. Speed, direction and pause times are the main parameters needed to define how users move inside the simulation area. Despite the simplified and less realistic movement pattern generated, they capture enough of the key characteristics of human mobility to make protocol evaluation meaningful and easier. The Random Waypoint model and its variants have been widely used, as they are designed to emulate the movement of MSs in a simplified fashion. More realistic mobility models (e.g., Manhattan grid, Gauss-Markov, etc.) have been developed, which can capture some of the important characteristics of human movement patterns, such as regularity, the temporal dependence of velocity, the spatial dependence of velocity and geographic restrictions. In addition to **individual models**, in which each MS is allowed to move independently from the others, **group mobility models** have been developed to represent situations in which a cluster of MSs follow the same pattern while moving. We refer the interested reader to (Camp et al., 2002) for a comprehensive survey of the existing synthetic mobility patterns. Here, we only provide details of the Random Waypoint and the Gauss-Markov mobility models.

The *Random Waypoint* mobility model was originally proposed in (Johnson & Maltz, 1996). In this model, each node is assigned an initial location (p_0), a destination (p_1) and a speed; both p_0 and p_1 are chosen independently and uniformly on the region in which the nodes move. The speed is chosen uniformly (or according to any other distribution) on an interval (v_{min} to v_{max}) independently of both the initial location and the destination. After reaching p_1, a new destination and a new speed are chosen according to their distributions and independently of all previous destinations and speeds. The node may also remain still for a random pause time before starting its movement towards the next destination. With the pause time set to zero, the movement pattern obtained is very similar to that of the Random Walk mobility model. Fig. 3(a) depicts the resulting pattern with the pause time set to one. Due to the random fashion of the Random Waypoint model, it can generate unrealistic movements, such as sudden stops and sharp turns.

The *Gauss-Markov* mobility model (Liang & Haas, 1999) introduces the concept of drift in the node's movement. Initially, each node is assigned a current speed and direction. At fixed intervals of time (Δt), movements occur by updating the speed and direction of each node. The next location is computed based on the current location, speed and direction of movement, according to the following equations

$$s_i = \alpha\, s_{i-1} + (1-\alpha)\mu_s + \sqrt{(1-\alpha^2)} \cdot x_{i-1}, \tag{3}$$

$$d_i = \alpha\, d_{i-1} + (1-\alpha)\mu_d + \sqrt{(1-\alpha^2)} \cdot y_{i-1}, \tag{4}$$

where s_i and d_i are the new speed and direction of the node at time interval i; a ($0 \le a \le 1$) is the tuning parameter used to vary the degree of randomness in the mobility pattern; μ_s and μ_d are constants representing the asymptotic mean value of the speed and direction as $i \to \infty$; and x_{i-1} and y_{i-1} are independent, uncorrelated, and stationary Gaussian processes with a mean of zero and a standard deviation equal to the asymptotic standard deviation of the speed and direction as $i \to \infty$. By varying a, it is possible to model different mobility patterns: for example, as a approaches zero, a drifting Random Walk is obtained, whereas with a=1, a linear motion is generated. At time interval i, the MS's position is given by the equations

$$x_i = x_{i-1} + \Delta t \cdot s_{i-1} \cos d_{i-1}, \tag{5}$$

$$y_i = y_{i-1} + \Delta t \cdot s_{i-1} \sin d_{i-1}, \tag{6}$$

where (x_i, y_i) are the x and y coordinates of the MS's position at the i_{th} time interval, s_i and d_i are the old speed and direction, and Δt is the fixed time interval of a leg. Fig. 3(b) depicts the resulting pattern according to the Gauss-Markov model. From Fig. 3, it is evident that the

Random Waypoint model tends to concentrate a node's movements in the centre of the area, while the Gauss-Markov model does not. Moreover, the Gauss-Markov model eliminates the sudden stops and sharp turns of the Random Waypoint model because the next movement depends on the current one.

The above-mentioned models can be applied when simulating a free surface in which the MS is allowed to move in any direction. Other environments should account for limitations in the paths followed by a given MS. For example, in urban environments, in which a regular pattern of horizontal and vertical streets is considered, MSs are allowed to move following one direction (e.g., horizontally) until the intersection with a vertical street is reached; then, the MS can turn left or right (90 degrees), or it follow the previous street. This is the basis of the *Manhattan grid* mobility model. Another example is given by vehicles driving on a highway. MSs follow the lane on the highway and their speed can be tuned according to the density of the traffic on the highway. This is known as the *Freeway* mobility model.

In general, any network simulator should integrate a **mobility tool** in which a given mobility pattern can be generated according to a specific synthetic model. Once the mobility data have been generated, the MSs move inside the simulation area following that pattern. As an example, *ns-2* (NS-2) integrates the *setdest* tool, by which the Random Walk or Random Waypoint mobility models can be simulated. Because of the limitations in the set of mobility models implemented by the network simulators, many research groups have been developing independent mobility tools (Bai et al., 2003; BONNMOTION), which provide mobility traces according to different synthetic models and to different formats; this last issue enables the integration of mobility data in different simulators.

The impact of different mobility models on network parameters has been studied in recent years. In (Bai et al., 2003), the authors provide a framework to evaluate the impact of the mobility models on the routing protocols in ad-hoc networks. In contrast to other studies, in which only random mobility was taken into account, the authors pick scenarios that span a larger set of mobility characteristics than only the change of maximum velocity and pause time. Their results show that the protocol performance may vary drastically across mobility models and that performance rankings of protocols may vary with the mobility models used. The effect may be explained by the interaction of the mobility characteristics with the connectivity graph properties.

In recent years, researchers have been interested in the distribution of node locations and in its effect on different network parameters (e.g., cell residence time, arrival rate at a cell, number of neighbours, etc.). In (Zola & Barcelo-Arroyo, 2009), the authors analyse the time that an MS remains under the coverage of the same AP (cell residence time) in a WLAN of medium size designed for pedestrians. The study is carried out by running simulations for different AP layouts and mobility models with *Omnet++* (OMNET++). Different layouts have been implemented: 4 APs for minimal full coverage; 8 APs for reasonable coverage, and 16 APs for high capacity coverage. The effects that the use of different mobility patterns for pedestrians may have on the cell residence time and on the handover (HO) process have been studied. As shown in Table 1, the average number of HOs per hour at each AP decreases as the number of APs increases; moreover, the HO behaviour of the Gauss-Markov model is very stable compared to that observed with the Random Waypoint model.

Name	Mobility model Speed distribution	Pause time	4APs	Layout 8APs	16APs
Random Waypoint	Uniform	0	10.96	6.34	4.92
Random Waypoint	Uniform	100	7.13	3.89	2.85
Random Waypoint	Normal	0	10.60	6.73	5.16
Random Waypoint	Normal	100	6.68	3.71	2.81
Gauss-Markov	Uniform	0	7.05	6.79	7.37
Gauss-Markov	Normal	0	7.03	6.72	7.82

Table 1. Average number of handovers per hour and AP.

3. The radio channel

First, it must be stated that it is possible to simulate the cellular network without taking radio propagation into account. This is sometimes done to avoid the cumbersome programming of all the radio channel features when obtaining the first rough results or with the purpose of drawing mathematical conclusions. However, when fine tuning the network, it is absolutely necessary to take into account as many factors as possible. Most detailed models for radio channels share the same template, which can be written as

$$P_{rx}(dBm) = P_{tx}(dBm) - \sum_{i=1}^{N} f_i\,(dB), \tag{7}$$

where P_{rx} and P_{tx} are the received and transmitted power and f_i is the ith factor impacting the radio transmission. The main factors related to the radio path that mainly affects the results are detailed in the next sections.

3.1. Path loss

This factor is usually represented by the slope in a logarithmic scale and, together with the radiated power, provides an idea of the range of the signal (i.e., coverage span). The nature of this factor is deterministic for a specific area; i.e., it is assumed that its value does not change with time as long as the scenario remains the same. Path loss models, also known as propagation models, are mainly considered in the network planning stage; consequently, they are used in the simulation field to assess the radio network planning or to study any other teletraffic variable that can be impacted by the radio channel features. There are several approaches for path loss modelling, depending on the application and the scenario in which the network is to be deployed. Most of these approaches have been proposed (and even adopted) by standard bodies, such as the International Telecommunications Union (ITU) or the Federal Communications Commission (FCC), but others have been developed by private organisations and public institutions. All of these models are based on a large amount of empirical data that are collected to characterise the propagation of radio signals in one or a few specific scenarios. Accordingly, no single model is able to fit all of the applications and scenarios. Consequently, it is likely that several independent models must be used to bind the expected results in terms of propagation.

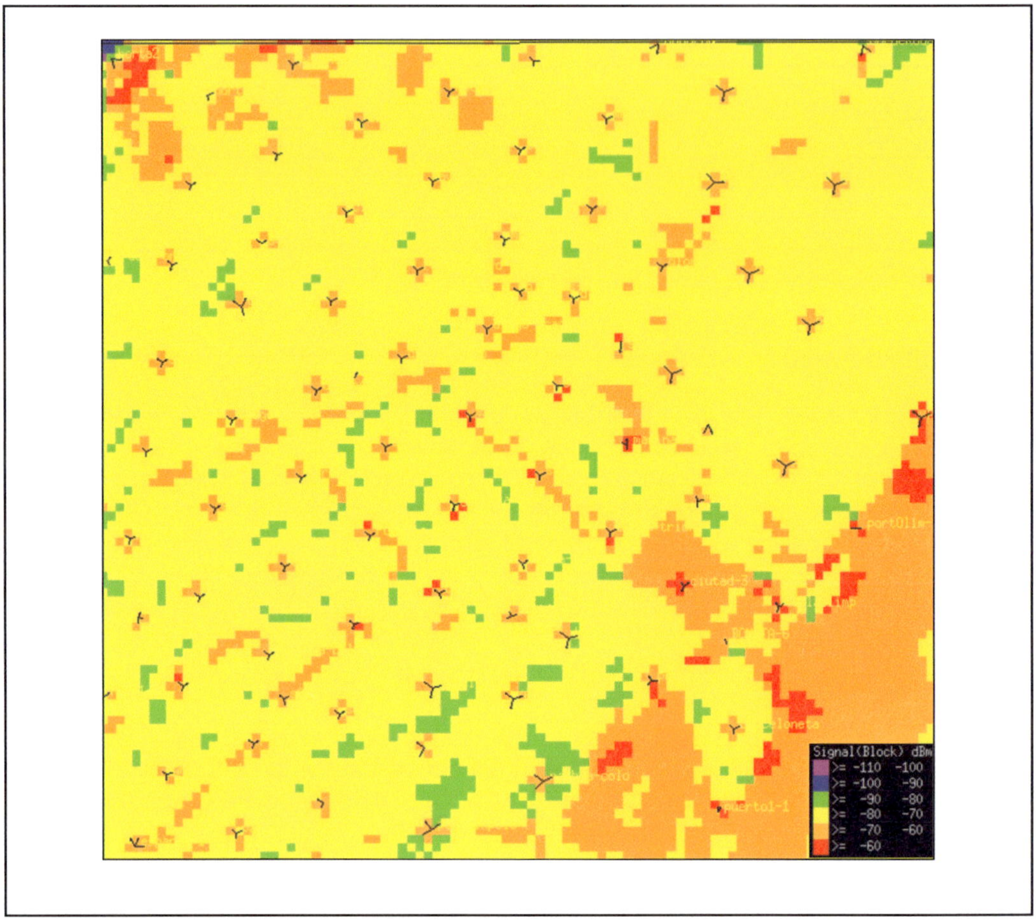

Fig. 4. BS coverage map in the city of Barcelona according to the layout shown in Fig. 2. for the UMTS system.

Propagation models can be classified according to several parameters. From the point of view of formulation, models are usually classified as empirical or semi-empirical. The difference between them is that semi-empirical models are analytical models with parameters that have been fitted using empirical data, whereas empirical models are based solely on data and have no underlying analytical model. Another common classification for models comes from the usage scenario: models are classified as either outdoor or indoor. A detailed survey on propagation models can be found in (Sarkar et al., 2003), but the most commonly used models are detailed below.

- *Okumura-Hata.* This model is an empirical model addressed to the outdoors. It was built from measurements collected in Tokyo in 1960 (Okumura et al., 1968). Those measurements were used to determine the median field strength and several correction factors (e.g., degree of urbanisation, BS and MS heights, etc). Hata improved the Okumura proposal, adapting the model according to the scenario: urban, suburban and open areas. The Okumura-Hata model is especially applicable in networks operating in the band under 1500 MHz and in medium to large urban areas.

- *COST-231.* The Cost Action 231 (COST 231) proposed two models for signal propagation in urban areas in the band from 900 to 1800 MHz: the Hata model and the Walfisch-Ikegami model. The former is a semi-empirical model addressed to the urban outdoors. The Walfisch-Ikegami model is based on the theoretical Walfisch-Bertoni model. The Walfisch-Ikegami and Okumura-Hata models are commonly used for path-loss modelling in wireless networks simulations (e.g., GSM, UMTS, etc.).
- *Young.* This model was built on the data collected in New York City in 1952 (Seybold, 2005). It is a simpler model compared with those mentioned above and, hence, is less used but still suitable for first approaches. It is addressed to applications from 150 MHz to 3.7 GHz, and it has been used for radio modelling in technologies such as IEEE 802.11.
- *Dual-Slope Model.* This model is based on a two-ray model (Feuerstein et al., 1994), accounting for the reflection of signals from the ground in addition to the direct path. It is mainly addressed to line-of-sight propagation (e.g., WiMax links).

Most of the radio channel models presented above can be computed as proposed in (Martin-Escalona & Barceló, 2004)

$$A_{PL}\,(dB) = A_1\,(dB) + 10\,\mathrm{A_s}\mathrm{Log}(d), \quad (8)$$

where A_1 is the power lost at one-meter, A_s stands for the path-loss slope and d is the distance between network nodes (usually a base station and a mobile station).
Table 2 shows the parameters proposed for featuring the propagation in UMTS (e.g., public land mobile networks (PLMNs)) and in IEEE 802.11 networks (e.g., WLAN) according to (Holma & Toskala, 2000) and (Martin-Escalona & Barcelo-Arroyo, 2008), respectively. Furthermore, (ETSI TR 101 112) provides figures for these parameters in several environments typically used for radio-channel planning in PLMN. It has been observed that completely different radio channels can be characterised by the same propagation model as long as the parameters can be suited to the technology studied.

Parameter	UMTS	WLAN
A1	23 dB	40 dB
AS	4	3.5

Table 2. Parameters of Equation (8) according to two network technologies.

An example of a coverage study for the UMTS system is described in (Zola & Barceló, 2006). The Okumura-Hata propagation model is used, in which the propagation losses in urban scenario can be computed as

$$A_{PL} = 133.76 + 34.79\mathrm{Log}(d), \quad (9)$$

where d is the distance in kilometres. The coverage map for the BS layout in Barcelona shown in Fig. 2 is displayed in Fig. 4. Colours from red to yellow represent good coverage. The green areas represent weaker signal strength, and in those areas, users may not be allowed to connect to the system (or the service may be interrupted) due to coverage constraints.

3.2. Slow fading

The path loss suffers from fading that randomly depends on time and space. This phenomenon can be included in the simulation and alters the borders of the cell. In addition, the shape and coverage of the cell depends on time. Hence, slow fading is related to the mobility patterns because the same mobility pattern will provide different handover rates for different fading patterns.

The slow fading (or shadowing) is generally modelled using the **lognormal distribution**, with a mean of zero and a specific standard deviation that depends on the scenario simulated. Typical values for such deviations range from 6 dB up to 12 dB (ETSI TR 101 112). The lognormal shadowing model is the simplest approach for modelling the slow fading and, hence, does not account for several aspects that may distort the results of the simulation. The most important of these aspects are presented below.

- *Decorrelation distance.* It is reasonable to think that a pedestrian user moving slowly involves slowly changing shadowing (i.e., near positions that involve similar fading). Conversely, mobile stations in vehicles moving at high speeds involve noticeably changing shadowing. Thus, the decorrelation distance addresses the question of how far a mobile station has to move for the shadowing conditions to change, i.e., the correlation of shadowing values according to the terminal displacements.
- *Correlation between base stations.* This issue addresses the scenario in which one MS receives signals from two different BSs. Because the two links are partially determined by the placement of the MS, it is expected that the shadowing impacting the two links are similar (to some degree).

Accordingly, correlated models are necessary for actual radio-channel modelling. **Auto-correlated models**, which address the decorrelation distance issue, are the most common approach for slow fading simulations. One of the most popular auto-correlated models was proposed in (Gudmundson, 1991). According to (ETSI TR 101 112), the Gudmundson normalised autocorrelation function can be computed as

$$R(\Delta x) = e^{-\left(\frac{|\Delta x|}{d_x}\right) ln(2)}, \tag{10}$$

where A_x accounts for the displacement and d_x stands for the decorrelation length, which is dependent on the scenario being simulated. For instance, a decorrelation length of 20 meters is proposed in vehicular scenarios, whereas 5 meters is preferred in pedestrian environments. Further information on these values are provided in (ETSI TR 101 112). Autocorrelation models are used as follows:

1. Compute the lognormal shadow at time t_1, using a zero-mean Gaussian random variable with a variance of σ^2 dB. Hereafter, it will be known as S_1.
2. Compute the distance travelled between times t_1 to t_2, i.e., Δx.

3. Evaluate the normalised autocorrelation function at Δx, i.e., $R(\Delta x)$.
4. The lognormal shadow at t_2 (i.e., S_2) is computed as a Gaussian random variable (in dB) with an average of $R(\Delta x) \cdot S1$ and a variance of $(1-R(\Delta x)) \cdot \sigma^2$.

3.3. Channel featuring

Several parameters have to be accounted for in comprehensive channel featuring. These parameters might not be directly involved in the path loss computation or the shadowing, but they can affect other simulated processes related to the radio link. An example of these parameters can be found in simulations modelling power control algorithms or connection admission control procedures. The data in Table 3, extracted from (Martin-Escalona & Barcelo-Arroyo, 2007; Martin-Escalona & Barcelo-Arroyo, 2008), are proposed as a framework for the main parameters required by these algorithms when simulating wireless networks.

Parameter	UMTS	WLAN
Minimum Signal to Noise Ratio (SIR)	-9 dB	-9 dB
Sensitivity of the stations	-109.2 dBm	-65 dBm
Maximum MS transmission power	21 dBm	17 dBm
Minimum MS transmission power	-44 dBm	0 dBm
BS transmission power	43 dBm	17 dBm
Handoff threshold for received power	-106.2 dBm	-62 dBm
Handoff threshold for SIR at reception	-6 dB	-6 dB

Table 3. Additional parameters used for radio channel characterisation.

Users can currently choose from a wide range of free and commercial simulation tools, such as *ns-2*, *Opnet*, *Omnet++*, *NetSim*, *CPSim*, *J-Sim*, *Packet*, *Tracer*, *Swans*, etc. According to the literature, the three former tools are the ones that concentrate most of the simulation market. They provide a large amount of ready-to-use and highly configurable propagation models. Table 4 summarises the propagation models supported by the main current simulators.

Simulator	Radio channel models
Omnet++	Deterministic (based on predefined boundaries), Rayleigh, Rice and Nakagami
Opnet	CCIR, Free Space, Hata, Longley-Rice, TIREM, Walfish-Ikegami, Rayleigh, Ricean and Two-Ray
ns-2	Free-space (A_s = 2), dual-slope and lognormal shadowing

Table 4. Propagation models supported by the most popular simulators.

4. Simulation issues

4.1. Cell wrapping

Telecommunications is an area in which simulation is especially relevant, mainly due to the huge investment that network deployment or upgrades can represent. Operators have developed simulators to plan and manage all the features and services provided by their networks. The first simulators were highly constrained by the limitations of the hardware they used, which led to simulations that were very time-consuming. Technology has evolved to the point that relatively complex models can be handled in acceptable execution times. However, cellular networks raise new issues that must be dealt with by simulation tools.

Cellular networks divide coverage area into cells. Though planners are often interested in obtaining performance metrics for an area that is ideal, continuous and unlimited, an infinite area is impossible to simulate. If the simulated area is finite, there is a major difference between core cells (i.e., in the middle of the simulated layout) and boundary cells (i.e., at the edge of the layout). Core cells receive more traffic and interference than boundary cells. Because core cells are surrounded by other cells, performance metrics obtained in them are less impacted by the edge effect, and they can be considered to be representative of the ideal infinite layout. This fact raises an issue: because metrics and statistics are only obtained from centre cells, the simulation will consume much more time than is strictly necessary to obtain results. In addition, simulators have to set specific procedures to deal with users reaching the boundaries of the simulation area. These issues are collectively known as the **edge or boundary effect** (Zander & Kim, 2001).

Several proposals address mitigating the edge effect in cellular network simulators. Overcoming the edge effect involves addressing two issues: mobility and the propagation model. Mobility wrapping aims to stop the mobile station from determining the limits of the simulated area. On the other hand, propagation wrapping assures that all of the cells show the same propagation features without accounting for their position inside the simulated area. Several proposals are explained below.

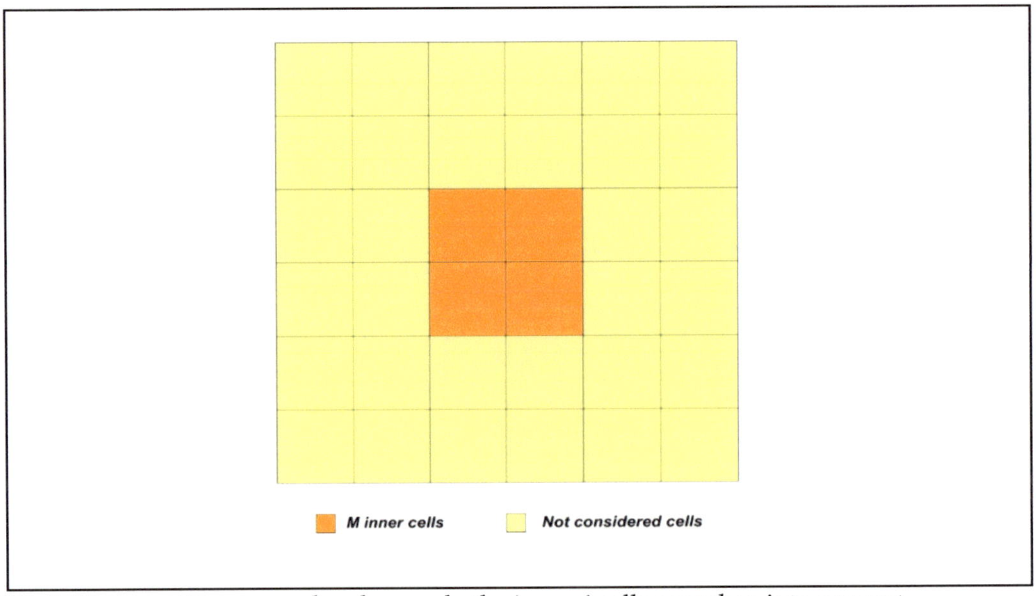

Fig. 5. Ring-erasing approach, where only the inner 4 cells are taken into account.

The simplest approach for addressing the edge effect is the **ring-erasing technique** (Zander & Kim, 2001). This approach is based on simulating a set of N cells; however, only the results that come from the M inner cells are considered. Using this technique reduces the edge effect but does not remove it completely (i.e., the simulation area is not actually unbounded). The lower the M/N ratio, the more accurate are the results, but a low M/N ratio involves a more time-consuming simulation. Fig. 5 illustrates this technique, where N and M are set to 36 and 4, respectively.

A more efficient method for reducing the edge effect is **mirroring**, which forces the mobile stations to return to the simulation area when they reach the boundaries. This means that every time an MS exits the simulation area, another one will enter; this method assumes a homogeneous system in long-term equilibrium. In this technique, all of the cells receive the same amount of traffic. However, the edge effect is not removed in its entirety, as only the mobility issue of the edge effect is overcome and the propagation constraints are not dealt with (e.g., mobile and base stations in the boundary-cells are affected by fewer sources of interference). Moreover, as this approach affects the mobility pattern of mobile stations, it may not be suitable for all simulation scenarios. There are several implementations of this approach available, depending on the new position, direction and speed set for the MS after the simulation boundary is reached. The author in (Guerin, 1987) proposes mirroring the trajectory of the MS whenever it reaches the layout limits, as can be seen in Fig. 6. The authors in (Zonoozi & Dassanayake, 1997) propose a method for repositioning an MS within the cell whenever the MS reaches the cell boundaries. This means that the simulation can be carried out using only one cell, and therefore, the mobility edge effect is removed.

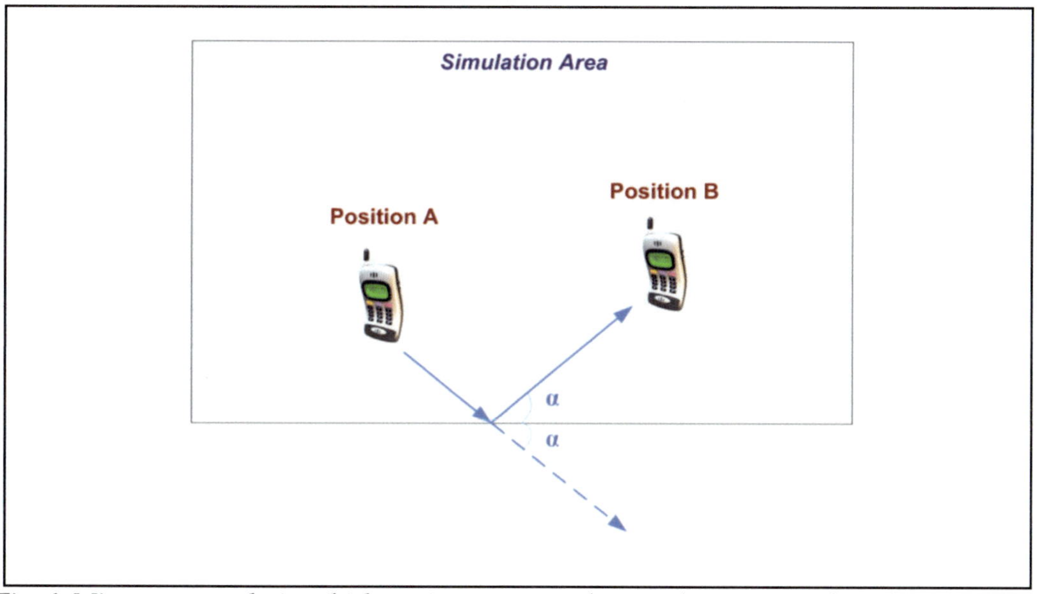

Fig. 6. Mirror approach, in which stations re-enter the simulation area when they reach the boundaries.

The most efficient method for allaying the edge effect is **cell-wrapping**. It is based on projecting the simulation area inside a torus, thus converting a finite area into an unbounded surface (Zander & Kim, 2001). Wrapping can apply to mobility (Domingo, 1996;

Saitoh et al., 2001) and propagation (Orozco Lugo et al., 2001). Fig. 7 illustrates the procedure followed in mobility wrapping when an MS reaches the simulation boundaries. This figure shows an MS moving from *Position A* toward the bottom of the simulation area. The simulator updates the position of the MS until it reaches the lower limit of the simulation area at a point labelled *A*. The MS is then moved from point *A* to point *B*; these points are actually the same point, as the simulation area has become a torus. Finally, the MS moves on until it covers the forecasted distance. This wrapping has no influence on the mobility pattern set in the simulation. It only supplies the simulation with a way to remove the boundaries of the simulation area and, therefore, the edge effect on mobility. This approach is in accordance with simulations carried out in (Domingo, 1996; Saitoh et al., 2001).

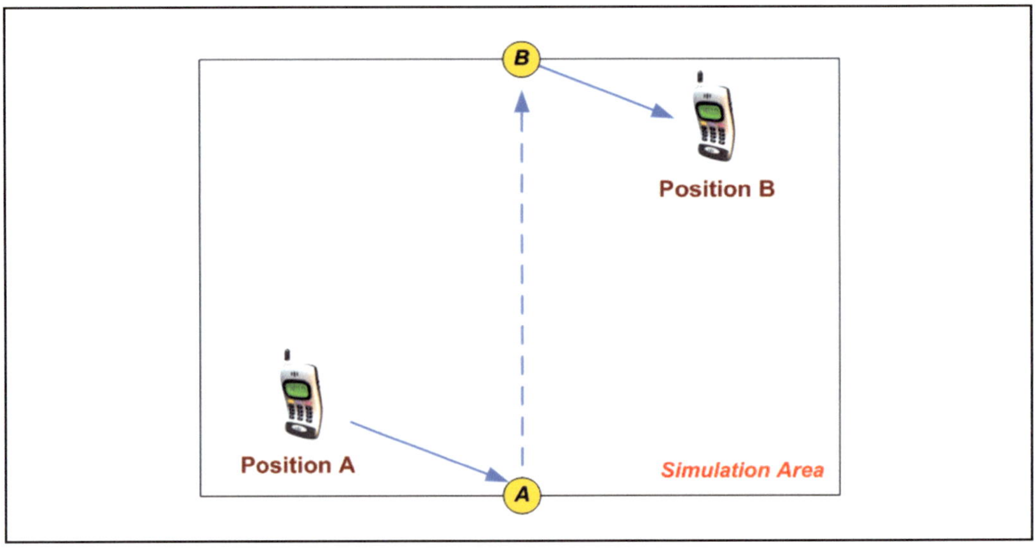

Fig. 7. Mobility wrapping.

A cross-shaped layout (e.g., Manhattan or similar) in which each cell is linked to four neighbouring cells is shown in (Orozco Lugo et al., 2001). As this approach considers both mobility and propagation wrapping, the edge effect is largely mitigated. However, its use is limited to cross-shaped layouts, because each cell is only connected to four neighbours.

Double wrapping is a combination of mobility and propagation wrapping used by authors in several simulation studies (Martin-Escalona & Barcelo-Arroyo, 2007; Martin-Escalona & Barcelo-Arroyo, 2008). It is based on projecting a rectangular simulation area onto a toroidal surface. This means linking the top and bottom boundaries and the left and right boundaries. Although it is possible to use several shapes, a rectangular area was selected because this shape has been widely used and it entails low complexity upon implementation. Mobility wrapping is achieved by means of the algorithm described in Fig. 7. Double wrapping uses this algorithm together with a new approach for removing the edge effect in the propagation. The explanation of this approach is based on the scenario shown in Fig. 8 in which two stations (*TX* and *RX*) act as a transmitter and a receiver, respectively.

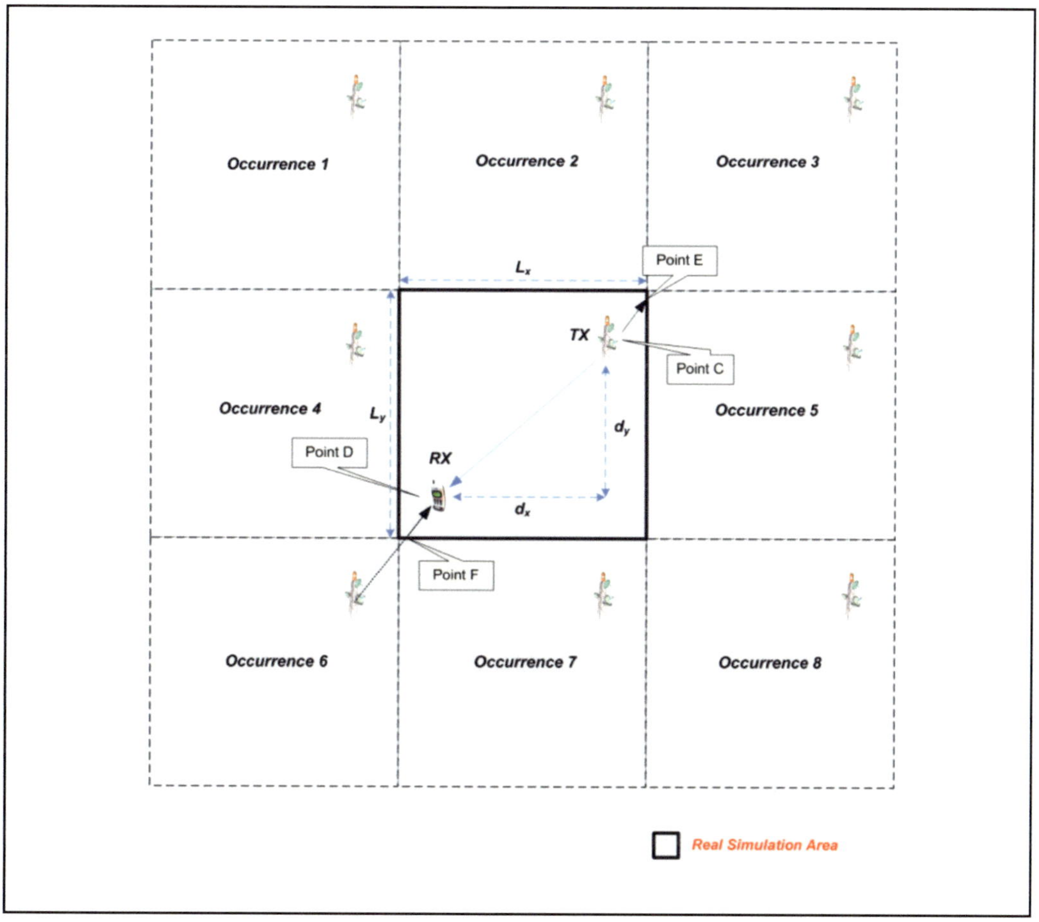

Fig. 8. Cell-wrapping at the propagation level.

Propagation wrapping must emulate an infinite surface (virtual surface) on the actual simulation area. A preliminary method for achieving this consists of replicating the actual simulation area of *N* cells in the eight possible directions (i.e., top, bottom, left, right, and the four combinations.). This means that all of the cells and stations in the simulation area have multiple occurrences. Thus, a station inside the actual simulation area receives signals from all occurrences of the other stations. Hence, we must calculate as many propagation paths as there are occurrences taken into account. Note that the number of occurrences remains undefined, which can lead to highly time-demanding simulations. The complexity of this approach can be reduced by applying two simple assumptions: the first is to consider distance as having the greatest impact on propagation; this is the most common assumption; the second involves considering only the eight closest occurrences in the propagation pattern. Notice that this second assumption hardly constrains the system, because simulation areas are considered to be sufficiently large (i.e., they include several cells). According to these hypotheses, only the closest occurrence is relevant. Therefore, the path between two stations is established by checking two paths, i.e., the direct and inverse paths. The direct path is the path between the two stations inside the actual simulation area. The inverse path accounts for wrapping and is defined as the shortest path between any occurrence of the transmitter station outside the real simulation area and the receiver station. For example, in Fig. 8, the direct path goes from point *C* to *D*, but the inverse path involves *Occurrence* 6 (the closest one). This means that the inverse path goes from point C to *E* and then from point *F* to *D*.

The path selected for propagation purposes is the shortest path between the direct and inverse paths. The distance associated with this path can be computed as

$$d_{sp} = \sqrt{ds_x^2 + ds_y^2} = \sqrt{\left(min(|d_x|, |L_x - d_x|)\right)^2 + \left(min(|d_y|, |L_y - d_y|)\right)^2}, \qquad (11)$$

where ds_x and ds_y indicate the distance of the shortest path in the x and y axes, respectively. Additionally, the path direction can be easily obtained using the following expression

$$\alpha_{sp} = arctg\left(\frac{sign(L_y - 2d_y)ds_y}{sign(L_x - 2d_x)ds_x}\right), \qquad (12)$$

where a_{sp} is the angle of the path if the position of the transmitter is considered as the origin of the coordinate system. Accordingly, the propagation path is completely defined by Equations (11) and (12). Note that this approach can be used together with any propagation model because it only removes the edge effect and does not interfere with the application propagation model.

4.2. Traffic issues

Each kind of traffic is characterised and modelled with different features that must be accounted for in the simulation. This includes the bandwidth required, time use, mobility, etc. In this way, it is unlikely that a worker using a laptop in a WLAN moves at a high speed, whereas voice traffic can be provided to devices in cars on a highway. On the other hand, the arrival of connections to the network and the time connected must be simulated in a different way depending on the service. Whereas a Poisson arrival process, which is easy to implement in the simulation, is suitable for voice, video or data connections must be simulated by other distributions that introduce further complexity. In the case of voice and low bit-rate data services, call duration is often modelled as a lognormal variable instead of the classic (and less complex) exponential assumption. This latter fact tends to favour lower service durations, whilst the lognormal assumption provides more realistic durations.

The impact of the service duration model in certain teletraffic variables is studied in (Spedalieri et al., 2005). Specifically, channel holding time (i.e., the time that a channel of a cell remains busy due to the call), the time between handoff arrivals (i.e., the handoff traffic) and the handoff duration in UMTS networks are studied. In the case of the channel holding time, the exponential assumption involves lower average values compared with those of the lognormal case. Furthermore, the exponential call duration involves channel holding times that are not particularly sensitive to the load (in average), whilst the lognormal assumption produces more realistic figures, i.e., the higher the load, the lower is the mean channel holding time.

Table 5 shows the average value under both assumptions and different network loads. The results show that even though shape and scale factors are different, the channel holding time is fit by the same candidate functions independently of whether the service duration is exponential or lognormal.

Load	Average(Log)	Average(EXP)
50 %	8.36 s	8.60 s
70 %	8.32 s	8.39 s
90 %	7.83 s	8.68 s

Table 5. Channel holding time according to service duration: lognormal (log) and exponential (exp).

The time between two consecutive handoffs to the same cell (i.e., sector in a BS) is studied in (Spedalieri et al., 2005) from a twofold point of view: including and neglecting simultaneous handoffs requests. It must be noted that the higher the user mobility, the more likely are simultaneous handoffs. Thus, in vehicle simulation, simultaneous handoffs occur frequently. The probability density function is then expected to show a peak at the origin due to the presence of the simultaneous handoffs. Table 6 shows the results achieved in (Spedalieri et al., 2005), where P_0 provides the probability that the time between consecutive handoffs is zero. As in the case of the channel holding time, results under the lognormal assumption are more sensitive to the load, especially when the load is very high. The results obtained for exponential service durations also depend on the system load, but the evolution is smoother. In both cases, simulations without accounting for the simultaneous handoffs do not seem to be sensitive to the load (on average). Furthermore, the model for the service duration also impacts the handoff traffic model, which is best fit by means of different random variables according to the approach followed to characterise the service duration.

Load	P_0 (%)		With all handoffs		Without simultaneous handoffs	
	Log	Exp	Average (Log)	Average (Exp)	Average (Log)	Average (Exp)
50 %	62.73	64.20	0.43 s	0.41 s	1.18 s	1.16 s
70 %	69.43	69.50	0.34 s	0.33 s	1.10 s	1.09 s
90 %	81.97	72.23	0.18 s	0.29 s	1.16 s	1.06 s

Table 6. Results for the time between consecutive handoff requests.

4.3. Gathering simulation results

Collecting data is one of the main tasks of the simulation tools. The procedure followed to gather the information resulting from simulation has to be set up when modelling the system, because it can constrain the whole simulation process. Simulation tools usually allow three types of sampling: deterministic, event-driven and probabilistic. The former sets a **deterministic** rate and collects samples accordingly. This approach is the simplest and is generally followed in continuous simulations (e.g., electrical models). The main difficulty in this approach is setting the sampling frequency. High sampling frequencies involve more precise data but also entails a longer runtime (i.e., time spent until the simulation finishes). Conversely, low sampling frequencies provide faster simulations but less precise data. Setting a suitable sampling frequency can be hard work, and it is often based on experience, which usually involves running the simulation several times. **Event-driven** sampling is proposed to overcome the drawbacks of deterministic sampling. It is used in discrete event simulations, which is the common case in the network field. Event-driven sampling consists of collecting one sample per event in the system. Hence, it is a comprehensive approach, as is deterministic sampling, but it only obtains a sample when something in the system happens. Although it requires lighter constraints in terms of computer resources, event-driven sampling can represent a noticeable part of the simulation in complex systems where events are very frequent. The achievement of results can sometimes be simplified if the characteristics of the processes involved are considered. This is the main purpose of **probabilistic** sampling, which aims to reduce the complexity and improve the scalability of the sampling procedure. In this way, because of the PASTA property (Poisson arrivals see time averages), if the traffic is Poisson, the time statistics will be the same as the per connection statistics, and therefore, only one of them is needed. For other simple distributions, it is possible to obtain time results from connections, or vice versa, by simple calculations, simplifying the simulation needs.

5. Concluding remarks

This chapter offers an overview of discrete event simulation applied to wireless cellular networks. The layout and mobility patterns selected in the simulation are more realistic than are those assumed in the mathematical calculation. However, the specific model for a given network must be selected with care because the differences in the results obtained with different models are not negligible. The propagation models applied are common to Montecarlo simulations of radio coverage, but due to the different simulation principles, they are applied in a different manner. In addition, different simulated propagation models have an impact on the obtained traffic performance. The number of operations to be carried out in the discrete event simulation of wireless networks is high, raising the need for other techniques, such as cell wrapping. This technique performs best when applied to both the mobility and the propagation.

6. References

Bai, F.; Sadagopan, N.; Helmy, A. (2003). The IMPORTANT framework for analyzing the Impact of Mobility on Performance Of RouTing protocols for Adhoc NeTworks, *Ad Hoc Networks*, Vol. 1, No. 4, (November 2003) 383-403, ISSN 1570-8705.

BONNMOTION. *http://net.cs.uni-bonn.de/wg/cs/applications/bonnmotion/.* Last access: April 2010.

Camp, T.; Boleng, J.; Davies, V. (2002). A survey of mobility models for ad hoc network research, *Wireless Communication and Mobile Computing: Special Issue on Mobile Ad Hoc Networking*, Vol. 2, No. 5, (August 2002) 483-502.

COST 231 TD (90). (1991). Urban transmission loss models for mobile radio in the 900 and 1800 MHz bands (rev. 2), 119, Rev. 2, Den Haag, 1991.

Domingo, L.R. (1996). Influence of the Handoff Process on the Channel Holding Time Distribution for Cellular Systems, *Proceedings of IEEE International Conference on Personal Wireless Communications*, pp. 149-152, ISBN 0-7803-3177-X, New Delhi (India), February 1996.

ETSI Technical Report TR 101 112. Universal Mobile Telecommunications System (UMTS); Selection procedures for the choice of radio transmission technologies of the UMTS, *UMTS 30.03, version. 3.2.0.*

Feuerstein, M. J.; Blackard, K. L.; Rappaport, T. S.; Seidel, S. Y.; Xia, H. H. (1994). Path Loss, Delay Spread, and Outage Models as Functions of Antenna Height for Macrocellular System Design, *IEEE Transactions on Vehicular Technology*, vol. VT-43, No. 3, (August 1994) 487-498, ISSN 0018-9545.

Gudmundson, M. (1991). Correlation Model for Shadow Fading in Mobile Radio Systems, *Electronics Letters*, vol. 27, No 23, (November 1991) 2145-2146, ISSN 0013-5194.

Guerin, R.A. (1987). Channel occupancy time distribution in a cellular radio system, *IEEE Transactions on Vehicular Technology*, Vol. 35, No. 3, (August 1987) 89-99, ISSN 0018-954.

Holma, H.; Toskala, A. (2000). *WCDMA for UMTS*, John Wiley & Sons, ISBN 0471720518.

Johnson, D. B.; Maltz, D. A. (1996). Dynamic Source Routing in Ad Hoc Wireless Networks, *Mobile Computing*, Vol. 353, (1996) 153-181.

Kim, M.; Kotz, D.; Kim, S. (2006). Extracting a mobility model from real user traces, *Proceedings of the 25th Annual Joint Conference of the IEEE Computer and Communications Societies (INFOCOM)*, pp. 1-13, ISBN 1-4244-0221-2, Barcelona (Spain), April 2006.

Liang, B.; Haas, Z. (1999). Predictive distance-based mobility management for PCS networks, *Proceedings of Joint Conference of the IEEE Computer and Communications Societies (INFOCOM)*, pp. 1377-1384 vol.3, New York (NY, USA), March 1999.

Martin-Escalona, I.; Barceló, F. (2004). Characterization of teletraffic and QoS variables in urban FCA cellular networks: A simulation approach, *Proceedings of International Conference on Next Generation Teletraffic and Wired/Wireless Advanced Networking (New2an'04)*, pp. 260-265, St. Petersburg, Russia, February 2004.

Martin-Escalona, I.; Barcelo-Arroyo, F. (2007). Performance evaluation of middleware for provisioning LBS in cellular networks, *Proceedings of IEEE International Conference on Communications (ICC)*, pp. 5537-5544, ISBN 1-4244-0353-7, Glasgow (UK), June 2007.

Martin-Escalona, I.; Barcelo-Arroyo, F. (2008). An approach to increase the scalability of location systems in WLAN networks, *Proceedings of the 1st international conference on MOBILe Wireless MiddleWARE, Operating Systems, and Applications (MOBILWARE)*, pp. 1-6, Vol. 278, ISBN 978-1-59593-984-5, Innsbruck (Austria), 2008.

NS-2. *http://isi.edu/nsnam/ns//*. Last access: April 2010.

Okumura, Y.; Ohmori, E.; Kawano, T.; Fukuda, K. (1968). Field Strength and Its Variability in VHF and UHF Land-Mobile Radio Service, *Review of the Electrical Communication Laboratory*, Vol. 16, No. 9-10, (September 1968) 825-873.

OMNET++. *http://www.omnetpp.org/*. Last access: April 2010.

Orozco Lugo, A.G.; Cruz Prez, F.A.; Hernandez Valdez, G. (2001). Investigating the Boundary Effect of a Multimedia TDMA Personal Mobile Communication Network Simulation, *Proceedings of Vehicular Technology Conference (IEEE VTC 2001 Fall)*, pp. 2740-2744, Vol. 4, ISBN 0-7803-7005-8, Atlantic City (NJ, USA), October 2001.

Prabhakaran, P.; Sankar, R. (2006). Impact of Realistic Mobility Models on Wireless Networks Performance, *Proceedings of IEEE International Conference on Wireless and Mobile Computing, Networking and Communications (WiMob'2006)*, pp. 329-334, ISBN 1-4244-0494-0, Montreal (Canada), June 2006.

Rappaport, T. S. (1996). *Wireless Communications. Principles and Practice,* Prentice Hall PTR, ISBN 0-13-375536-3, Upper Saddle River, New Jersey 07458.
Saitoh, K.; Hidaka H.; Shinagawa N.; Kobayashi T. (2001). Vehicle motion in large and small cities and teletraffic characterization in cellular communication systems, *IEICE Transactions on Communication*, Vol. E84-B, No. 4, (April 2001) 805-813, ISSN 0916-8516.
Sarkar, T. K.; Zhong, J.; Kyungjung, K.; Medouri, A.; Salazar-Palma, M. (2003). A survey of various propagation models for mobile communication, *IEEE Antennas and Propagation Magazine*, Vol. 45, No. 3, (January 2003) 51-82, ISSN 1045-9243.
Seybold, J. S. (2005). *Introduction to RF Propagation*, John Wiley & Sons, ISBN 978-0-471-65596-1, New Jersey.
Spedalieri, A.; Martin-Escalona, I.; Barcelo, F. (2005). Simulation of Teletraffic Variables in UMTS Networks: Impact of Lognormal Distributed Call Duration, *Proceedings of IEEE Wireless Communications and Networking Conference (WCNC05)*, pp. 2381–2386, Vol. 4, ISBN 0-7803-8966-2, New Orleans (USA), March 2005.
Tuduce, C.; Gross, T. (2005). A Mobility Model Based on WLAN Traces and its Validation, *Proceedings of the 24th Annual Joint Conference of the IEEE Computer and Communications Societies (INFOCOM 2005)*, pp. 664-674, Vol. 1, ISBN 0780389689, Miami (Florida, USA), March 2005.
Zander, J.; Kim, S.L. (2001). Radio Resource Management for Wireless Networks, Artech House, ISBN 1580531466, Norwood (MA, USA).
Zola, E.; Barcelo-Arroyo, F. (2009). Impact of Mobility Models on the Cell Residence Time in WLAN Networks, *Proceedings of IEEE Sarnoff Symposium*, pp. 1-5, ISBN 978-1-4244-3381-0, Princeton (NJ, USA), March 2009.
Zola, E.; Barceló, F. (2006). About the location of Base Stations for a UMTS System: analytical study and simulations. *Journal of Communications and Networks*, Vol. 8, No. 1, (March 2006), pp. 49-58, ISSN 1229-2370.
Zonoozi, M.M.; Dassanayake, P. (1997). User Mobility Modeling and Characterization of Mobility patterns, *IEEE Journal on Selected Areas in Communications*, Vol. 15, No. 7, (September 1997) 1239-1232, ISSN 0733-8716.

Acronyms

BS	Base Station
FCC	Federal Communications Commission
GIS	Geographic Information System
GSM	Global System for Mobile communications
HO	Handover
ITU	International Telecommunications Union
LAN	Local Area Network
MS	Mobile Station
PLMN	Public Land Mobile Network
UMTS	Universal Mobile Telecommunications System
WiFi	Wireless Fidelity
WiMax	Worldwide Interoperability for Microwave Access
WLAN	Wireless LAN

15

Discrete-Event Supervisory Control for Under-Load Tap-changing Transformers (ULTC): from synthesis to PLC implementation

Ali A. Afzalian[1], S. M. Noorbakhsh[2] and W. M. Wonham[3]
[1]*Department of Electrical Engineering, Abbaspour University of Technology, Tehran, Iran*
[2]*Department of Electrical Engineering, Islamic Azad University-Boroujen Branch, Iran*
[3]*Department of Electrical and Computer Engineering, University of Toronto, Toronto, ON, Canada*

1. Introduction

Discrete-event systems (DES) can be found as essential integrated subsystems in many complex systems, e.g. electrical power systems. Under-load tap-changing (ULTC) transformers, which obviously have discrete-event behaviour, are widely used in transmission systems to take care of instantaneous variations in the load conditions in substations. In this chapter, the voltage control problem in ULTC is solved in different modes of operation, using DES-based solutions. These solutions include: DES supervisory control, timed DES supervisory control and a hierarchical structure for the control system. It is shown that the specifications are controllable and the closed loop control system is non-blocking. A heuristic method has been used for easier implementation of the supervisor on a Programmable-Logic-Controller (PLC), to overcome the general implementation problems, as well as the implementation problem caused by the Auto/Manual mode of ULTC operation. A step-by-step procedure is developed to generate a ladder diagram code which implements the DES supervisor on a PLC.

A discrete-event system (DES) is a dynamic system that evolves in accordance with the sudden occurrence of physical events at possibly unknown irregular intervals (Ramadge & Wonham, 1989). The supervisory control technique is an effective analytical tool for automation and control of DES (Ramadge & Wonham, 1987). Discrete-event models are generally used to describe systems where coordination and control are required to ensure the orderly flow of events, and/or to prevent the occurrence of undesired chains of events. DES can be employed to describe a wide variety of behaviors in industrial and physical systems. These include control and scheduling of electrical power systems, manufacturing systems, queuing systems, communication protocols, and database management systems. The behavior of electrical power systems can be characterized by interactions between continuous dynamics and discrete-event dynamics.

In the last two decades, discrete-event systems have been studied by researchers from different fields, with respect to modeling, analysis and control. Several models have been proposed and investigated. These models can be classified as *untimed* DES models and *timed* DES models. In an untimed model, when considering the state evolution, only the sequence of states visited is of concern. That is, only the logical behavior is of interest. In a timed model, both logical behavior and timing information are considered. (Brandin & Wonham, 1994) adjoined to the structure of untimed DES (Ramadge & Wonham, 1989) the timing features of timed transition models. The BW framework, which is used in this chapter, retains the concept of maximally permissive supervision introduced in (Brandin & Wonham, 1994), allows the timed modeling of DES, admits subsystem composition, and admits forcing and disablement as means of control. Different synthesis methods have been developed and implemented as the software TCT (for untimed models) and TTCT (for timed models) (Wonham, 2009) to compute controllers that are optimal in the sense that the controlled system not only satisfies the specifications but is also as permissive as possible. TCT and TTCT are used in this study for synthesizing the supervisory controllers.

There are good reasons for organizing the control of large systems in a distributed hierarchy structure. Among these are: deeper understanding facilitated by the hierarchical structure, reduction in complexity of communication and computation, modularity and adaptability to change, robustness, and generalization. The supervisory control of discrete-event systems can be designed to be hierarchically structured. In the present chapter, implementation of this approach to a control problem in electrical power systems is also discussed.

A power system, in its simplest representation, comprises a set of lines intersecting at nodes (buses). Energy is injected at buses by generators, and loads can be considered as negative injections. The flow of power along lines to and from buses is a phenomenon of primary interest in power system operation and control. Transformers with tap-changing facilities constitute an important means of controlling voltage throughout electrical power systems at all voltage levels. Transformers with off-load tap-changing facilities can help to maintain satisfactory voltage profiles. Under-load tap-changing transformers (ULTC) can be used to take care of daily, hourly, and minute-by-minute variations in system conditions. ULTC may be controlled either automatically or manually (Kundur, 1994). Many dynamic subsystems in a power system exhibit discrete-event behavior. Typically, the continuous dynamics relate to components that obey physical laws. Event-driven discrete behavior results from logical rules that govern the system. The continuous trajectory of the system state can be interrupted by discrete control actions and uncontrolled disturbances, which may be frequent or infrequent. The time scale for these events changes from milliseconds, through seconds and minutes, to hours, days, and weeks or longer (Fink, 1999).

Discrete-event systems theory has been applied to problems in electrical power systems (Prosser, 1995, Selinsky et al., 1995; Lee & Lim, 2004; Lin et al., 2004; Afzalian et al., 2006, Afzalian & Noorbakhsh, 2008; Afzalian & Wonham, 2006 & 2009; Noorbakhsh & Afzalian, 2007a&b & 2009). These applications include: supervisory control, modeling and analysis, and monitoring and diagnosis. The synthesis of a DES-based supervisory control for ULTC was introduced in (Afzalian et al., 2006), where the ULTC along with different specifications (control logics) were modeled as automata. The automatic voltage controller of a tap-changer transformer can be regarded as a discrete–event system. The processes associated with this system may be regarded as asynchronous and discrete in time and/or state space. A DES generating a formal language can be considered as a representation of this tap-changer transformer (plant).

Though supervisory control (SC) theory has received substantial attention for over a decade in academia, industrial applications are scarce. The main reason for this seems to be a discrepancy between the abstract supervisor and its physical implementation. Typically, finite-state automata describe the plant, specification and supervisor. But the step to a physical implementation is not necessarily straightforward. In the special case of industrial systems, where PLC-control is of great importance, the gap between the event-based asynchronous automata world and the synchronous signal based PLC-world has to be bridged. The asynchronous event-driven nature of the supervisor is not straightforwardly implemented in the synchronous signal-based PLC. The first attempt to implement a DES supervisory control on a PLC was made by Leduc (Leduc & Wonham, 1995, Leduc, 1996). PLC implementation of DES supervisory control was discussed in (Leduc & Wonham, 1995; Fabian & Hellgren, 1998; Dietrich et al., 2001; Hellgren et al., 2002; Jiang & Darabi, 2002; Gasper 2002, Max et al. 2002, Vieira et al. 2006, Noorbakhsh & Afzalian 2007a&b, Manesis & Akantziotis, 2005; Noorbakhsh, 2008; Afzalian & Noorbakhsh, 2008; André et al., 2009).
After a brief review of DES supervisory approaches, this chapter deals with the modeling of ULTC as an automaton. Control specifications in each mode of operation are also modeled as finite automata. As a first solution, supervisory controllers are designed for the ULTC in Automatic and Auto/Manual modes of operation. The second solution employs the timed DES approach to design a supervisory control for the ULTC. A hierarchical structure for the supervisory control of the problem is also investigated as the third solution to the ULTC control problem. A two-level hierarchy structure has been used to control the ULTC. A manager has been introduced in the high-level to shut down the system in certain contingencies. The manager deals with an abstract model of the plant in the high-level, and so can apply the control requirements easily. It is shown that a high-level manager can easily supervise the plant using this abstract model of the low-level subsystem, i.e. the low level closed loop control system of ULTC. A step-by-step transformation procedure transferring the automaton of the designed supervisor into a ladder diagram for PLC is presented in Section 7.
The contributions of the chapter are summarized as follows:

1- Discrete-event system modeling of an under-load tap-changing transformer and its control specification.
2- Evaluation of the required properties for the supervisory control system, i.e. controllability, non-blocking, and freedom from conflict.
3- The synthesis of a DES-based supervisory control in the monolithic, modular and hierarchical structures.
4- Systematic approaches for the implementation of supervisory control solutions.

2. Supervisory Control of DES

The supervisory control problem for a discrete-event system is formulated by modeling the plant as well as its control logic (specifications) as finite automata. To solve the supervisory control problem, it is necessary to show that a controller which forces the specification to be met exists and is constructible (Wonham, 2009).

2.1 Discrete-Event Models

A DES model is specified by: the set of states (including an initial state, and marker states which in some applications can be desired or target states), the set of events, and the state transition function of the system. Formally, a DES is represented by an automaton G = (Q, Σ, δ, q_0, Q_m) in which Q is a finite set of states, with $q_0 \in Q$ as the initial state and $Q_m \subseteq Q$ being the desired (marker) states; Σ is a finite set of events (σ) which is referred to as an alphabet; and finally δ is a transition mapping δ: Q×Σ →Q, δ(q, σ)= q' which gives the next state q' after an event σ occurs when G is in the state q. In general δ is only *partially* defined on Q×Σ. G plays the role of the plant and, together with its states, events and transition operator (mapping) models a physical process. G is called a generator, as it generates a set of strings (sequences of events). In other words it generates a language L(G), consisting of strings of events which are physically possible in the plant.

Let Σ^* denote the set of all finite strings of symbols in Σ, including the empty string, denoted ε . A *prefix* of a string *s* is an initial subsequence of *s*, i.e. if *r* and s are strings in Σ*, *u* is a prefix of *s* if *ur=s*. A set which contains all the prefixes of each of its elements is said to be *prefix closed*. Clearly, Σ^* is a prefix closed set. As some sets of strings may not contain all of their prefixes, the *prefix closure* of a set *A*, denoted by $\overline{A}$, is defined which contains all the prefixes of each element of *A*. If *A*= $\overline{A}$, then the set A is prefix-closed. If *A* is not prefix-closed, then $A \subset \overline{A}$. The language *L*(G) is the set of all event sequences which are physically possible in the plant. *L*(G)={$s \mid s \in \Sigma^*, \delta(q_0, s)$ is defined}. Clearly, *L*(G) is a subset of Σ^*, and *L*(G) is also prefix-closed, because no event sequence in the plant can occur without its prefix occurring first. Those strings which can be extended to a marker state are of particular importance. The *marked* behavior, denoted by $L_m(G)$, is the sublanguage of *L(G)* consisting of all strings which reach some marker state. L_m(G) is a subset of *L*(G) and can be formally given as: $L_m(G)=\{s \in L(G) \mid \delta(q_0, s) \in Q_m\}$.

A discrete-event system is said to be *non-blocking* if $\overline{L_m(G)} = L(G)$. This means that there always exists a sequence of events which takes the plant from any (reachable) state to a desired (marker) state. In some applications of DES models, it is necessary to consider several independent and asynchronous processes simultaneously. There is a procedure called *synchronous product* which combines two DES (G_1 and G_2) into a single, more complex DES, i.e. $G_3 = G_1 \mid\mid G_2$. The synchronous product defines new states for G_3 as ordered pairs of states from G_1 and G_2. The event set for G_3 is the union of event sets for G_1 and G_2. The initial and marker states of G_3 are defined similarly.

2.2 Controllable Specifications and Non-blocking Supervisor

A discrete-event plant must be controlled based on certain specifications (required behavior logic). By adjoining controller structure to the plant, it is possible to vary the language generated by the closed loop system within certain limits. The desired performance of such a controlled plant will be specified by stating that its generated language must be contained in some specification language. It is often possible to meet these specifications in a minimally restrictive way, called optimal supervision in the DES literature.

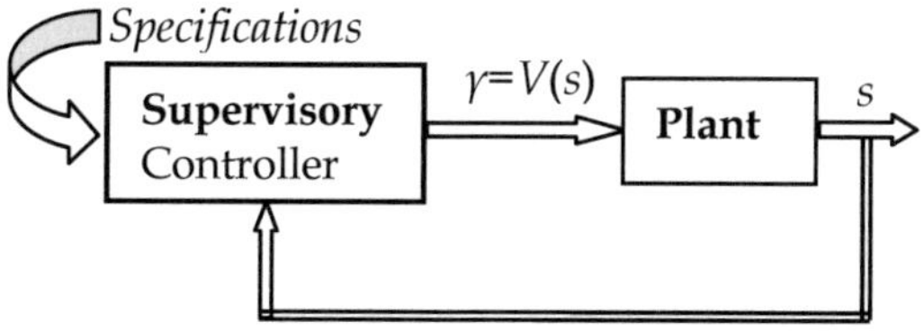

Fig. 1. Block diagram of a supervisory control system.

Suppose $G=(Q, \Sigma, \delta, q_0, Q_m)$, is a nonempty DES representing the plant which must be controlled. $\Sigma = \Sigma_c \cup \Sigma_u$ is the set of controllable and uncontrollable events in the plant. Σ_c is the set of controllable events; these can be enabled or disabled by an external agent (supervisor). A possible set of enabled events which includes some controllable events and all uncontrollable events is called a *control pattern* (γ). Uncontrollable events (Σ_u) are always enabled by their nature. Then it is clearly true that $\Sigma \supseteq \gamma \supseteq \Sigma_u$. The set of all control patterns, which is actually a family of sets, is defined as: $\Gamma = \{\gamma \in Pwr(\Sigma) \mid \gamma \supseteq \Sigma_u\}$. A supervisory control for the plant G is any function $V: L(G) \rightarrow \Gamma$. The pair (G, V) is written V/G, to suggest the concept of "G under the supervision of V ".
The plant along with the supervisor forms a closed loop system (Fig. 1). The Plant G, generates strings of events $s \in L(G)$ and sends them to the supervisor as a feedback signal. The supervisory controller, which has been designed based on a required behavior of the plant (specifications), first determines implicitly in which state the system is working and then sends a list of events which are allowed to be enabled in that particular state, as a control signal to the plant. The supervisory controller is actually a DES synthesized using specifications in such a way as to guarantee the required behavior of the plant. The *closed behavior* of the system is defined to be the language $L(V/G) \subseteq L(G)$ described as follows:

- $\varepsilon \in L(V/G)$
- If $s \in L(V/G)$, $\sigma \in V(s)$, *and* $s\sigma \in L(G)$, then $s\sigma \in L(V/G)$
- No other strings belong to $L(V/G)$

In other words, the closed loop system only generates either the "empty" string or a string of the plant which is concatenated immediately by an event declared by the supervisor as allowed. Clearly $L(V/G)$ is nonempty and closed. The marked behavior of V/G is: $L_m(V/G)=L(V/G) \cap L_m(G)$. In other words, the strings reaching marker states in V/G are exactly the strings of $L_m(G)$ that survive under supervision by V. It is always true that $\emptyset \subseteq L_m(V/G) \subseteq L_m(G)$. The supervisor V is said to be *non-blocking (for G)* if $\overline{L}_m(V/G)=L(V/G)$. A language K representing some specification of a plant G is said to be *controllable (with respect to G)* if its prefix-closure $\overline{K}$ doesn't change under the occurrence of uncontrollable events in G. In other words, K is controllable if and only if $\overline{K}\Sigma_u \cap L(G) \subseteq \overline{K}$, where $\overline{K}\Sigma_u=\{s\sigma \mid s \in \overline{K},\ \sigma \in \Sigma_u\}$. Therefore the controllability condition on specification K only constrains $\overline{K} \cap L(G)$. Based on this definition, to test the controllability of K, one only needs to test its closure $\overline{K}$. The existence of an optimal (marking) non-blocking supervisory controller is proved in (Wonham, 2009). Let $K \subseteq L_m(G)$, $K \neq \emptyset$. Then there exists a supervisory controller V such that $L_m(V/G)=K$ if and only if K is controllable. The supervisory control of a discrete-event system enforces the controllable and non-blocking behavior of the plant that is admissible under the given specification. The optimal solution to the supervisory control problem is the supremal controllable sublanguage (of the specification language). The DES representing the supremal supervisor typically has a large state size. Its state size is of order the product of state sizes of the plant and specification (plant control logic) DES models. Actually, the supremal supervisor contains redundant information about transition constraints which are already enforced by the plant itself. Therefore, the state size of the supremal supervisor can be reduced without affecting controlled behavior of the closed-loop system (Su & Wonham, 2004). A reduced supervisor has the following advantages:

- Easier implementation.
- The simpler structure may provide the designer with better understanding of the supervisor's control actions.
- The supervisor reduction is useful in the design of modular controls, where optimal local modular supervisors may admit quite small reduced versions that are simple and practical to implement.

It is shown in (Su & Wonham, 2004) that, finding a supervisor of minimal size is an NP-hard problem. Usually, a supervisor is looked for which is smaller than supremal supervisor (S) that does the job. The TCT procedure, *supreduce* (Plant, Supervisor, *condat*(·)) procedure calculates a small equivalent implementation of the supervisor (S_r) such that the following conditions are satisfied: $L(G) \cap L(S_r) = L(S)$ and $L_m(G) \cap L_m(S_r) = L_m(S)$.

The following steps can be done to design and implement a supervisory controller for a given plant (G) and given specifications:

1) Model the plant (components) as automata.
2) Model the specifications as DES and construct one DES, called *EDES*, representing all the specifications together. This can be done by the "*meet*" operation in TCT.
3) Find the non-blocking supervisory controller using the "*supcon*" operation in TCT i.e. *SUPER*=supcon(*G*, *EDES*).
4) There are some redundant constraints in *SUPER*, as the latter embodies a controller with a larger than necessary number of states and/or number of transitions. To simplify the supervisor the command "*supreduce*" in TCT can be used. In this procedure certain (automated) heuristics are employed to reduce the supervisor. The reduced supervisor has exactly the same control action as the original, but is structurally more economical.

This was a quick review of DES supervisory control. The TDES model is briefly reviewed in next subsection.

2.3 Timed Discrete-Event Systems

This section briefly reviews the *TDES* model proposed by (Brandin & Wonham, 1994). First, a finite automaton $G_{act} = (A, \Sigma_{act}, \delta_{act}, a_0, A_m)$ is introduced, which is called an *activity transition graph* (ATG) to describe the untimed behavior of the system. In G_{act}, A is a finite set of *activities*, Σ_{act} is the finite set of *events*, a partial function $\delta_{act} : A \times \Sigma_{act} \rightarrow A$ is the activity *transition* function, $a_0 \in A$ is the *initial* activity, and $A_m \subset A$ is the subset of *marked* activities. In order to construct a TDES model, timing information is introduced into G_{act}. Let N denote the nonnegative integers. In Σ_{act}, each event σ will be equipped with a *lower time bound* $l_\sigma \in N$ and an *upper time bound* $u_\sigma \in N \cup \{\infty\}$ such that $l_\sigma \le u_\sigma$. Then the set of events is decomposed into two subsets, the *prospective* events $\Sigma_{spe} = \{\sigma \in \Sigma_{act} | u_\sigma \in N\}$ and the *remote* events $\Sigma_{rem} = \{\sigma \in \Sigma_{act} | u_\sigma = \infty\}$. For a detailed discussion and interpretation see (Wonham, 2009). The lower time bound would typically represent a delay, while an upper time bound is a hard deadline.

For each $\sigma \in \Sigma_{act}$, the timer interval T_σ is defined as $T_\sigma = \begin{cases} [0, u_\sigma] & if \sigma \in \Sigma_{spe} \\ [0, l_\sigma] & if \sigma \in \Sigma_{rem} \end{cases}$. The TDES defined by (Brandin & Wonham, 1994) is a finite automaton $G = (Q, \Sigma, \delta, q_0, Q_m)$ which can be displayed by its *timed transition graph* (*TTG*). The state set Q is defined as $Q = A \times \prod\{T_\sigma | \sigma \in \Sigma_{act}\}$. A state $q \in Q$ is of the form $q = (a, \{t_\sigma | \sigma \in \Sigma_{act}\})$, where $a \in A$ and $t_\sigma \in T_\sigma$. The initial state $q_0 \in Q$ is defined as $q_0 = (a_0, \{t_{\sigma,0} | \sigma \in \Sigma_{act}\})$, where $t_{\sigma,0} = \begin{cases} u_\sigma & if \sigma \in \Sigma_{spe} \\ l_\sigma & if \sigma \in \Sigma_{rem} \end{cases}$.

The set $Q_m \subseteq Q$ is given by a subset of $A_m \times \prod\{T_\sigma | \sigma \in \Sigma_{act}\}$. The event set Σ is defined as $\Sigma = \Sigma_{act} \cup \{tick\}$, where the additional event *tick* represents the passage of one time unit. The state transition function $\delta : Q \times \Sigma \to Q$ is defined as follows. For any $\sigma \in \Sigma$ and any $q = (a, \{t_\tau | \tau \in \Sigma_{act}\}) \in Q, \delta(q, \sigma)$ is defined, written $\delta(q, \sigma)!$, if and only if one of the following conditions holds:

- $\sigma = tick$ and $\forall \tau \in \Sigma_{spe}; \delta_{act}(a, \tau)! \Rightarrow t_\tau > 0$
- $\sigma \in \Sigma_{spe}$ and $\delta_{act}(a, \sigma)!$ and $0 \le t_\sigma \le u_\sigma - l_\sigma$
- $\sigma \in \Sigma_{rem}$ and $\delta_{act}(a, \sigma)!$ and $t_\sigma = 0$

When $\delta(q, \sigma)!, q' = \delta(q, \sigma) = (a', \{t'_\tau | \tau \in \Sigma_{act}\})$ is defined as follows:

- if $\sigma = tick$ then $a' = a$ and for all $\tau \in \Sigma_{act}, t'_\tau := \begin{cases} t_\tau - 1, & if \ \delta_{act}(a, \tau)! \wedge t_\tau > 0 \\ t_\tau, & otherwise \end{cases}$
- if $\sigma \in \Sigma_{act}$ then $a' = \delta_{act}(a, \sigma), t'_\sigma = t_{\sigma,0}$, and for $\tau \in \Sigma_{act}$ if $\tau \ne \sigma$ then
$$t'_\tau := \begin{cases} t_\tau & if \ \delta_{act}(a', \tau)! \\ t_{\tau,0} & otherwise \end{cases}$$

The function δ is extended to $\delta : Q \times \Sigma^* \to Q$ in the natural way.

The *closed* behavior, the strings that are generated by G, and *marked* behavior, the strings that are generated by G and lead to a marker state, of the TDES G are defined by $L(G) = \{s \in \Sigma^* | \delta(q_0, s)!\}$ and $L_m(G) = \{s \in \Sigma^* | \delta(q_0, s) \in Q_m\}$, respectively. G is called *non-blocking* if $\overline{L_m(G)} = L(G)$. As in untimed supervisory control, the set Σ_{act} is partitioned into two subsets Σ_c and Σ_u of controllable and uncontrollable events. An event δ that can preempt the event *tick* is called a *forcible* event. The set of forcible events is denoted by Σ_{for}. A forcible event can be either controllable or uncontrollable. By forcing an enabled event in Σ_{for} to occur, the event *tick* can be disabled. In this framework a supervisor repeatedly decides to disable or enable each event in $\Sigma_c \cup \{tick\}$.

The simplest way to visualize the behavior of a TDES *G* under supervision is first to consider the infinite reachability tree of *G* before any control is operative (Wonham, 2006). Each node of the tree corresponds to a unique string *s* of *L*(*G*). At each node of the tree the subset of *eligible* events can be defined by $Elig_G(s) := \{\sigma \in \Sigma | s\sigma \in L(G)\}$. In order to define the notion of *controllability* a language $K \subseteq L(G)$ is considered to define: $Elig_K(s) := \{\sigma \in \Sigma | s\sigma \in \overline{K}\}$. K is *controllable* with respect to *G* if, for all $s \in K$, $Elig_K(s) \supseteq \begin{cases} Elig_G(s) \cap (\Sigma_u \cup \{tick\}), & Elig_K(s) \cap \Sigma_{for} = \phi \\ Elig_G(s) \cap \Sigma_u, & Elig_K(s) \cap \Sigma_{for} \neq \phi \end{cases}$.

The control objective is, for the given plant language $L(G_p)$ and the specification language $L(G_s)$, to find a supervisor such that the closed loop language is, in the sense of set inclusion, the largest sublanguage of $L_m(G_p) \cap L_m(G_s)$ which is controllable w.r.t G_p and also non-blocking, written $\sup C(L_m(G_p), L_m(G_s))$.

2.4 Hierarchical Control Structure

A brief overview of hierarchical supervisory control for DES is given in this section. The reader is referred to (Wonham, 2009) for a detailed discussion. Roughly speaking, a complex system is one made of a large number of parts that interact in a non-simple way (Simon, 1962). In such systems, the whole is more than the sum of the parts. In other words, given the properties of the parts and the laws of their interaction, it is not trivial to infer the properties of the whole. Often, complexity takes the form of hierarchy. Hierarchical structure is a common feature of control solutions of complex dynamic systems. A complex system is composed of subsystems which, in turn have their own subsystems until some lowest level of elementary subsystems is reached. The scope of a control action is defined by the breadth of its temporal horizon and/or by the depth of its logical dependence in a task breakdown. The broader the temporal horizon of control subtasks, or the deeper its logical dependency on other controls, the higher it is said to reside in the hierarchy. Hierarchical systems possess some general features that are independent of their specific application (Zhong & Wonham, 1990).

The DES supervisory control can be designed to be hierarchically structured. Fig. 2 shows a two-level hierarchy consisting of a low level plant and controller, e.g. as field level, and a high-level plant and controller, e.g. as management level [7, 9]. The actual plant, for example a tap-changing transformer, is controlled in the real world by the operator; while the high-level plant is an abstract and simplified model of the actual plant that is employed for decision-making in the ideal world by the manager, e.g., the substation manager in an electrical power system. The high-level plant model is refreshed or updated every so often via the report channel from the actual plant. Alternatively, this report channel can be interpreted as carrying information sent by the operator to the manager, in terms of significant events. The information channel from the plant to the low-level controller provides the conventional feedback path. The low-level controller applies conventional control to the plant through the "control law" channel.

How is the hierarchical loop closed? The function of the "command" channel is to convey the high-level manager's command to the operator, which in turn must translate (compile) these commands into corresponding low-level control signals which will actuate the plant. State changes in the plant will eventually be conveyed in summary and abstract form to the management level via the report channel. The high level plant is updated accordingly and then provides appropriate feedback to the manager through the "advice" channel. The command centre of a complex system, such as an electric power distribution system or a micro-grid, can be considered as the site of the "high-level plant" where a high-level decision maker (manager) is in command. The external (real) world and those (operators) coping with it are embodied in the low-level plant and controller.

The problem to be addressed concerns the relationship between the required or expected behavior of the high-level model (G_h) by the manager, and the actual behavior implemented in the plant (G_l) by the operator. It will turn out that a relationship of *hierarchical consistency* constrains the report channel from the low to the high level. In other words, it is necessary to refine the information conveyed by this channel, before a consistent hierarchical control structure can be achieved. The information sent up by the operator to the manager must be timely, and sufficiently detailed for various critical low level situations to be distinguished.

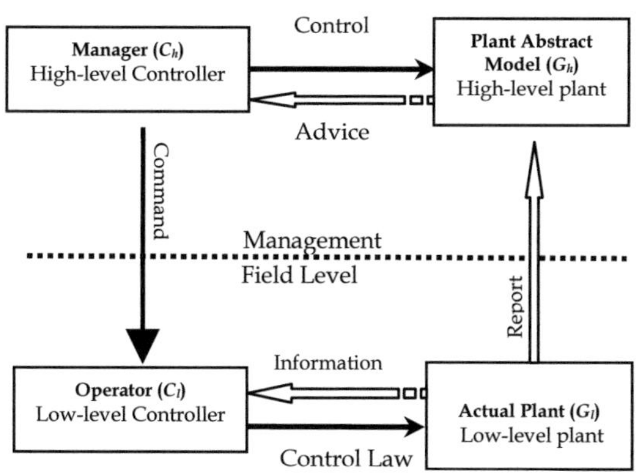

Fig. 2. A two-level hierarchy control system

2.5 Hierarchical Control Action in a Two-Level Controlled DES

Suppose the actual plant is modeled by an automaton $G_l=(Q, \Sigma, \delta, q_0, Q_m)$ that generates a language $L_l := L(G_l) \subseteq \Sigma^*$ as its uncontrolled behavior. Σ^* is the set of finite strings s, for which the extended transition map $\delta : Q \times \Sigma^* \rightarrow Q$ is defined.

Recall from DES supervisory control (section 2) that to every specification represented by a closed language E_l, there corresponds a supervisor as the (closed) supremal controllable sublanguage sup $C(E_l \cap L(G_l))$. The following notation is used for this supervisor: $M\uparrow :=$ sup $C(M)$. The refined information flow through the "report" channel consists of strings of significant events, represented by symbols in a high-level alphabet T. Thus the "report" can be modeled as a causal map $\theta : L_l \to T^*$ with the following properties: $\theta(\varepsilon)=\varepsilon$, $\theta(s\sigma)=$ either $\theta(s)$ or $\theta(s)\tau$ for some $\tau \in T$, where $s \in L_l$ and $\sigma \in \Sigma$.

An abstract model for the plant in the high level can be given as an automaton G_h that generates the language $L_h := \theta(L_l) \subseteq T^*$. The high-level controller C_h that observes only the strings of L_h must be able to make meaningful control decision. The following steps and related TCT procedures were proposed to formulate the suitable control structure (Wonham, 2009): Adopt the usual supervisory structure having the same type as in G_l **(Supcon(.,.))**

1) Refine the state structure of G_l **(Recode(.))**
2) Extend the high-level event alphabet T **(Vocalize(.,.))**
3) Find the corresponding structure for G_h **(Higen(G$_l$))**
4) Partition this extension into controllable and uncontrollable subsets to provide the manager with the ability to set up specifications in terms of controllable events. This is achieved by converting the G_l to a new DES called "output-control-consistent" in which each output event is unambiguously controllable or uncontrollable. **(Outconsis(G$_l$))**
5) Design a high-level supervisory control using a given specification (E_h) for G_h **(Supcon(.,.))**

The behavior E_h expected by the manager in G_h may be larger than what the operator can actually realize. In other words the manager may be over-optimistic in respect to the effectiveness of the command-control process. But if E_h is not larger than what the operator can realize at the low level, i.e. the equation $\theta((\theta^{-1}(E_h))^{\uparrow})=E_h$ holds for every closed and controllable language $E_h \subseteq L_h$ then, the pair (G_l, G_h) is said to possess hierarchical consistency. Achieving this equality in the hierarchical control system requires a further refinement of the transition structure of the DES model of the low-level plant, in other words, enhancement of the information sent up to the high-level. Such enhancement might or might not be feasible in an application. In TCT, hierarchical consistency can be achieved by running the **Hiconsis(G$_l$)** procedure.

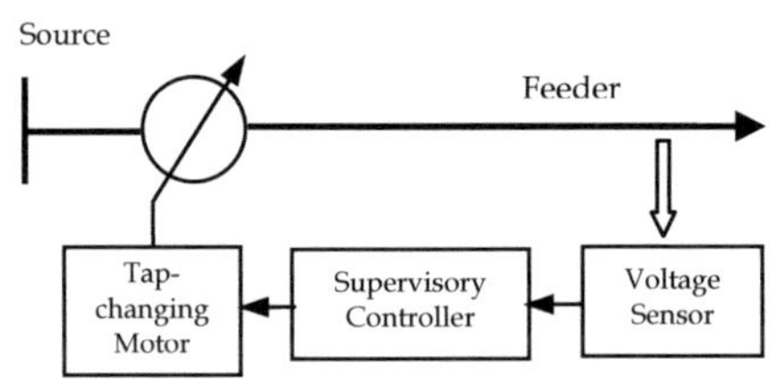

Fig. 3. Block diagram of control system for automatic changing of transformer taps

The two-level hierarchy discussed here can be extended to any number of levels. Once hierarchical consistency has been achieved for the bottom level and first level up, the construction may be repeated on assigning state outputs in the first level and bringing in the next higher level.

3. Tap-Changing Transformer

Transformers with tap-changing facilities constitute an important means of controlling voltage throughout electrical power systems at all voltage levels. Transformers with ULTC are widely used in transmission systems. For example, Ontario Hydro provided ULTC facilities on most 500/230 kV autotransformers and on all "area supply" transformers stepping down from 230 kV or 115 kV to 44 kV, 27.6 kV, or 13.8 kV (Kundur, 1994).

Whereas many articles considered ULTC as a nonlinear element in the power system models for voltage stability studies, a Petri net based model for tap-changer has been used in a framework of differential, switched algebraic and state-reset equations (Hiskens & Sokolowski, 2001). The control logic for tap-changer transformers can be found in the literature (Ohtsuki et al., 1991; Kundur, 1994; Otomega et al., 2003) as well as in manufacturers' catalogues (e.g. (GE Consumer Industrial, 2005)) in varying detail. When the voltage is not "normal" (i.e. is outside a desired limit) then after a time delay the controller changes the tap ratio to restore the voltage, i.e. bring it back into its dead-band. The delay is used to prevent unnecessary tap changes in response to transient voltage variations and to introduce the desired time delay before a tap movement. Fig. 3 shows the block diagram of a ULTC.

The timing behavior of the ULTC suggests a TDES approach to the supervisory control solution. To synthesize a supervisory control for the ULTC, the designer needs to be equipped with DES (TDES) models of the plant and the control specifications which are given in section 4. In sections 4, 5, and 6, DES, hierarchical structure, and TDES approaches are employed respectively to implement the supervisory control for the ULTC.

4. DES Supervisory Control for ULTC

In this section, the DES models of the plant and the control logic governing the ULTC are discussed. The models will be used later to study implementation of the supervisory controller.

4.1 DES Modelling of the Plant

As shown in Fig. 3, a ULTC (plant) consists of three components: Voltmeter, Timer, and Tap-changer. Each component is modeled as a DES. Then DES models of plant components are synchronized to form the plant model.

Voltmeter: The (measured) load voltage (V_l) must be within a dead-band ($V_o \pm$ ID), where: V_o is the set point, $\Delta V := V_o - V_l$, is the Voltage Deviation and ID: Insensitivity Degree, which is defined as the maximum admissible variation of the voltage before originating a command to change the tap. Voltmeter reports the following events associated with the load voltage: (Fig. 4):

- Voltmeter Initialized (ev11)
- Report $| \Delta V | >$ ID and ΔV is Negative (ev10)
- Report $| \Delta V | <$ ID (Voltage Recovered) (ev12)
- Report $| \Delta V | >$ ID and ΔV is Positive (ev14)
- Report Voltage exceeds V_{max} (ev16)

Timer: The timer times out after a certain delay *Operating Time* (OT). The following events are associated with the timer (Fig. 4):

- Timer Starts (ev21)
- Timer Blocks and Resets (ev25)
- Timer Times out (ev27)
- Timer Resets (ev23)

Tap-changer: The transformer tap-changer controls the transformer ratio "manually" or "automatically" in order to keep the power supply voltage practically constant, independently of the load. If the tap increase (decrease) is successful, the system returns to a state and waits for another command. If the tap increase (decrease) operation fails, the controller changes to the Manual mode, and waits for another command.

It is assumed here that the tap-changer has 5 steps. Events associated with the TAP-CHANGER are (Fig. 4):

- Tap down command (ev31)
- Tap down successful (ev32)
- Tap up command (ev33)
- Tap up successful (ev34)
- Tap up/down failed (ev30)

DES models of three plant components will be synchronized in order to get an automaton for the plant.

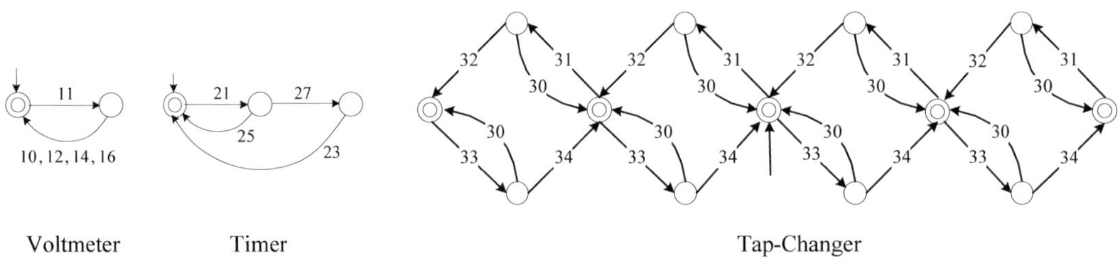

Fig. 4. DES models of different components of the ULTC

4. 2 Control Specifications

The control logic for an under-load tap-changing transformer is normally provided by the manufacturer and/or by the designer. A control logic which is given in (GE Consumer Industrial, 2005) by the GE company is employed in this chapter. The control logic is modeled by suitable automata, which will be described in this section.

The coordination control of the ULTC transformer and other FACTS (Flexible AC Transmission Systems) devices can be achieved by defining appropriate specifications (Thukaram et al., 2004; Kim & Lee, 2005). DES models of these specifications can be used to design modular supervisors. In a hierarchical control structure, the coordination control can be considered as higher level control logic.

There are two modes of operation: "Automatic" and "Manual".

I. Automatic Mode

The tap-changer works in Automatic mode according to the following logic (control specifications):

a. If the voltage deviation | ΔV | > ID and ΔV is Negative (ev10) then the timer will start and when it "times out", i.e. reaches its maximum (ev27) then a "tap increase command" (ev33) will be made and the timer will be "reset" (ev23).

b. If the voltage deviation | ΔV | > ID and ΔV is Positive (ev14) then the timer will start and when it "times out" i.e. reaches its maximum (e27) then a "tap decrease command" (ev31) will be made and the timer will be "reset" (ev23).

c. If the voltage returns to the dead-band (ev12), because of smooth system dynamics or a tap-changer or some other system events, then the timer is blocked and reset (ev25).

d. If the voltage exceeds the value set for "Quick Lowering" (ev16), then the timer OT becomes 0 seconds and therefore the lowering tap command (ev31) happens instantaneously.

Fig. 5 shows the DES model of the control specification in the Automatic mode. It actually implements all above logics in a single automaton. The automatic voltage controller of a tap-changer transformer can be regarded as a discrete-event system. The processes associated with this system may be thought of as asynchronous and discrete in time and/or state space. A DES generating a formal language can be considered as a representation of this tap-changer transformer (plant).

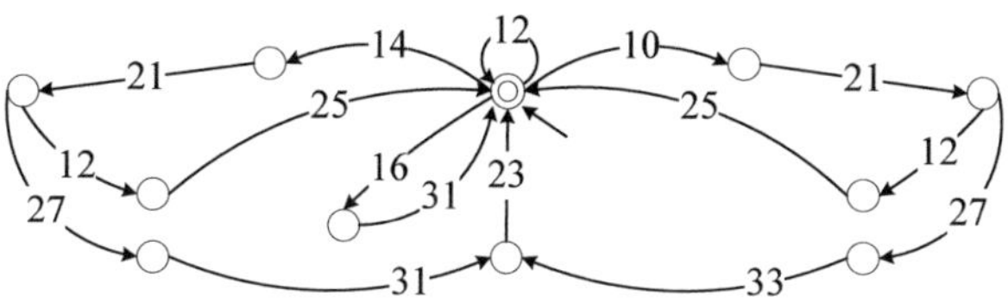

Fig. 5. DES model of the control logic (specification) for ULTC in Automatic mode.

II. Incorporating Operator Override (Auto/Manual mode)

If a fault in tap increase or decrease happens (ev30), or the operator forces the system from Automatic to Manual mode at any time (ev43), the system moves to the Manual state and waits for the operator. In the Manual mode of operation, a model for the operator action is needed to switch the modes and to override in abnormal situations.

OPERATOR: Events associated with the OPERATOR are (Fig. 6-a):

- Enter "Automatic" Mode (ev41)
- Enter "Manual" Mode (ev43)

The operator can force the system from Automatic to Manual mode at any time (ev43). System switches to Manual mode from Automatic mode by the following events:

- A "Manual" command from the operator (ev43).
- An abnormal situation such as, failed tap up/tap down (ev30).

In Manual mode the system is waiting for "Tap-up", "Tap-down", "Automatic", or "Stop" commands. When returning to Automatic mode the controller is reinitialized at "state 0" of the Automatic mode specification. A specification for the Auto/Manual mode (SPEC2) can be achieved by inserting some transitions after the occurrence of ev31 and ev33 and also by adding a new state as the "Manual-operation" state. "Manual" command (ev43) takes the system from any state (*) to the Manual-operation state. Then ev41 takes this state back to the initial state. Fig. 6-b shows the DES model for control specification in the Auto/Manual mode.

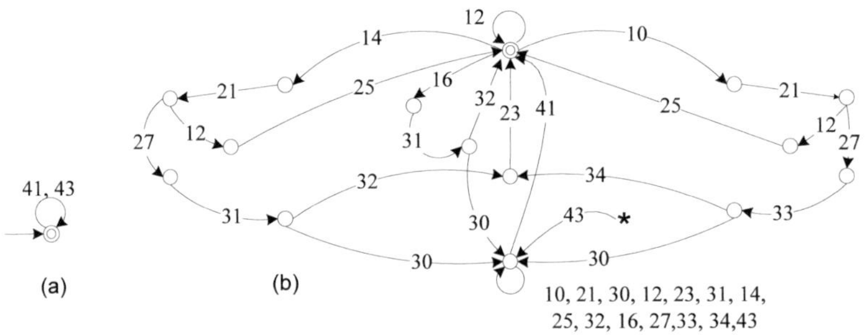

Fig. 6. a) An automaton for the operator, b) DES model for control specification in the Auto/Manual mode. The transition 43 from * represents the similar transition from all states to the "Manual operation"

4. 3 Design of the DES Supervisor

The plant and the specification DES models are implemented in the TCT software. Brief descriptions of the TCT procedures which are used in this chapter are given in the Appendix. The supervisory control and its reduced mode have been designed separately for the Automatic and Auto/Manual modes of operation.

I. Automatic Mode

The supervisor and the control data for the ULTC in the Automatic mode are calculated using TCT.

SUPER1 = Supcon(PLANT1,SPEC1) (78,171)
CONDAT1 = Condat(PLANT1,SUPER1) Controllable.
SIMSUP1 = Supreduce(PLANT1,SUPER1,CONDAT1) (22,92;slb=20)

SIMSUP1 is the reduced order supervisor with 22 states and 92 transitions.

II. Auto/Manual mode

The operator override is incorporated in the model by the control specification shown in Fig. 6-b. Using this specification and the new plant model which is synchronized by the "Operator" automata, the supervisory control is synthesized.

SUPER2 = Supcon(PLANT2,SPEC2) (198,831)
CONDAT2 = Condat(PLANT2,SUPER2) Controllable.
SIMSUP2 = Supreduce(PLANT2,SUPER2,CONDAT2) (12,54;slb=11)
SIMCD2 = Condat(PLANT2,SIMSUP2) Controllable.
MPS = Sync(PLANT2,SIMSUP2) (198,831) Blocked_events = None
true = Isomorph(MPS,SUPER2;identity)

As can be seen, the supervisor state-transition size has been reduced significantly from (198, 831) to (12, 54). The reduced order supervisory control in Auto/Manual mode (SIMSUP2) is shown in Fig. 7.

4.4 Verification of the Results

It is guaranteed by the theorems and procedures of supervisory control (Wonham, 2009) that are employed in this chapter, that the supervisor is non-blocking and meets the control specification in an 'optimal', that is, minimally restrictive fashion. It is shown in section 4.3 that such a controller which forces the specifications of ULTC to be met, exists and is constructible. In this section, the proposed supervisor is verified by inspecting its behavior when an increase in the voltage is reported.

Suppose that ev14 has occurred. Therefore a tap decrease is required until the voltmeter reports that the load voltage is restored, i.e. $|\Delta V| < ID$ (ev12). The event sequence applied by the proposed supervisory control is specified in the DES shown in Fig. 7. The trajectory includes states 0, 3, 7, 10, 11, 6 and finally 0, which is a marker state (the dotted path in Fig. 7). At state (0), events 21, 31, and 33 are disabled. This means that all components of the plant are disabled except for the voltmeter. If the voltmeter reads ev14, the closed loop system will be sent to state (3) by the supervisor. At state (3), the timer starts. When it "times out", i.e. reaches its maximum (ev27) the system goes to state (10). At state (10), the tap-up command (ev33) is disabled by the supervisor, and thus the transformer can only receive a tap-down command, i.e. (ev31). The ev31 takes the system to state (11). At state (11), if the tap-down is successful (ev32), the supervisor sends the plant to state (6), where first the timer will be reset (ev23), and then the system goes to state (0). State (0) is a marker state where the voltmeter is activated to read new voltages. If the voltmeter reads ev12 i.e., the voltage is restored, then the system stays in this state, unless the voltmeter reads ev10 or ev14. If ev10 occurs, the trajectory would go through states 2, 6, 9, 8, 6, and 0.
Similarly, one can follow the supervisor actions on this trajectory.

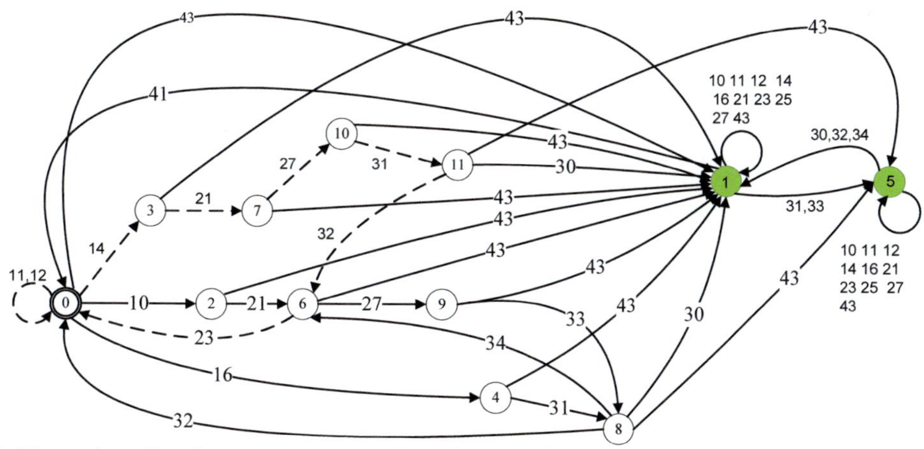

Fig. 7. The reduced order supervisor in Auto/Manual mode.

5. Hierarchical Solution

High level management executes a "Stop" command only after the occurrence of abnormal behavior in the plant, such as a specific number of tap-up/down failures, to shut down the regulation mechanism of the tap-changer. As described in section 2.5, the following steps are taken to synthesize a hierarchical supervisory structure.
1) A supervisor has been synthesized for the Automatic mode of the ULTC (SUPER1) and is considered as the low level plant.
2) Using vocalization, an abstract model for the supervisor in the Automatic mode (SUPER1) is developed, with the objective of letting a high-level manager execute a system Shutdown (ev61 in Fig. 8-a). The shutdown specification (SP_STOP) will require that both tap-up (ev31) and tap-down (ev33) commands along with the Timer (ev21) specification be disabled (Fig. 8-b). A supervisory control is synthesized again after adding the DES models for the manager and the shut-down logic to the plant (SUPER3).

SUPER3 = Supcon(PLANT3,SPEC3) (100,228)
CONDAT3 = Condat(PLANT3,SUPER3) Controllable.
SIMSUP3 = Supreduce(PLANT3,SUPER3,CONDAT3) (29,123;slb=28)

Significant events corresponding to tap-up/down failure (ev30) and the shutdown (ev61) are vocalized.

MINSUP3 = Minstate(SUPER3) (82,201)
VMSUP3 = Vocalize(MINSUP3,[[*,61,61],[*,30,30]) (118,252)
RVSUP = Recode(VMSUP3) (118,252)
RVSUP_H = Higen(RVSUP) (3,3)

Reasonably, a small abstraction model (Fig. 9-a) of the low-level controlled behavior is achieved (3 states vs. 29 states).

3) The specification shown in Fig. 9-b, is used to shut the system down after 3 occurrences of tap-up/down failure (ev300). Event labels 300 and 611 are new labels for vocalized events in the high-level.

4) The high level supervisor has been synthesized after finding a hierarchical and output consistent version of the high-level plant. The reduced order version of the high-level supervisor is shown in Fig. 9-c.

OC_P = Outconsis(RVSUP) (119,252)
HC_P = Hiconsis(RVSUP) (123,268)
false = Isomorph(HC_P,OC_P)
X = Hiconsis(OC_P) (123,268)
true =Isomorph(HC_P,X;[[101,102],[102,103],[103,104],[104,105],[105,106],[106,107],
[107,108],[108,109],[109,110],[110,112],[111,113],[112,114],[113,115],[114,116],[115,117],
[116,118], [117,101],[118,111]])
SUPER_H = Supcon(PLANT_H,SPEC_H) (103,330)
CONDAT_H = Condat(PLANT_H,SUPER_H) Controllable.
SIMSUP_H = Supreduce(PLANT_H,SUPER_H,CONDAT_H) (4,96;slb=4)

As shown in Fig. 9-c, the top manager can easily control the plant using a simple automaton which generates the required performance for the closed loop system.
Devices such as timers, transformers, etc. in the field-level may be provided by different vendors, and hence may have different specifications, i.e. control logic. Obviously, the hierarchical structure for the supervisory control is the appropriate solution in such cases. The DES models of the plant and the control logic can be achieved using the given technical

specifications from the vendors. While technical specifications can differ from one vendor to another, the differences can easily be accounted for in the DES models.

The hierarchical control structure can also be employed to synthesize coordination control of ULTC transformer and some FACTS devices.

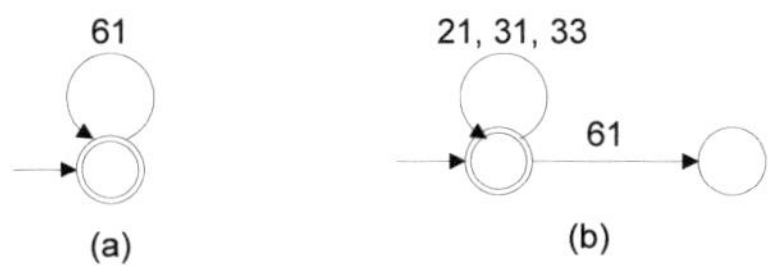

Fig. 8. DES models a) Manager, b) System Shut-down specification

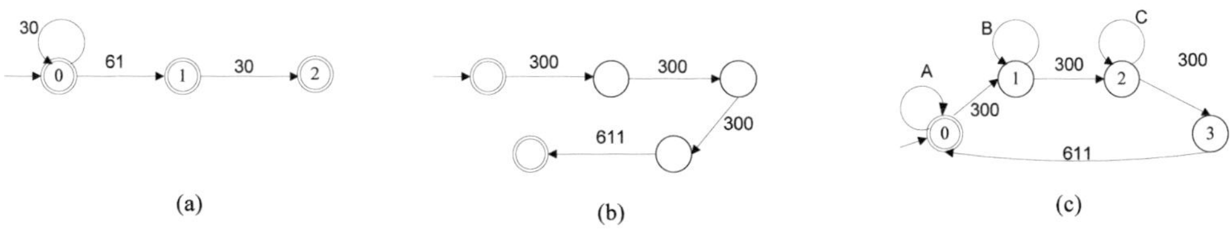

Fig. 9. DES models in the high level a) an abstract model of the low level plant, b) the control logic, c) The reduced order of the high level supervisor control for ULTC, where A, B, and C are lists of some events.

6. TDES supervisory control for ULTC

In this section the timed DES approach is employed to solve the supervisory control problem of the ULTC. First the plant and control logic are modeled as TDES, and then the supervisory control is designed in the different modes of operation.

6.1 TDES representation of the Plant

As discussed in Section 2, the system components are modeled by the corresponding ATGs for their untimed behavior first. When adding timing features, the time bounds (lower and upper) for the events of the system are defined. The plant consists of two main components:

Voltmeter: The voltmeter reports events associated with the load voltage using these events:

- Initialize Voltmeter (ev11 , [0,inf])
- Report $|\Delta V| >$ ID and $\Delta V > 0$ (ev14 , [0,inf])
- Report $|\Delta V| <$ ID and $\Delta V < 0$ (ev10 , [0,inf])
- Report $|\Delta V| <$ ID – i.e. Voltage Recovered (ev12 , [0,inf])
- Report Voltage exceeds V_{max} (ev16 , [0,inf])

Tap-Changer: The transformer tap-changer controls the transformer ratio "manually" or "automatically" in order to keep the power supply voltage practically constant, independently of the load. If the tap increase (decrease) is successful, the system returns to a state and waits for another command. If the tap increase (decrease) operation fails, the controller changes to the Manual mode, and waits for another command. It is assumed here that the tap-changer has 5 steps. Events associated with the Tap-Changer are:

- Tap up command (ev33 [5, inf]),
- Tap up successful (ev34 [0, inf]),
- Tap up/down failed (ev30 [0, inf]),
- Tap down command with 5s delay (ev31 [5, inf]),
- Tap down command without delay (ev35 [0, inf]),
- Tap down successful (ev32 [0, inf]),

The ATGs for the voltmeter and tap-changer are shown in Fig. 10. In order to find the whole system's model, the composition (analogous to synchronous product in untimed DES) of the ATGs of the system is found first, and then the TTG of the plant is worked out by converting the ATG to TTG.

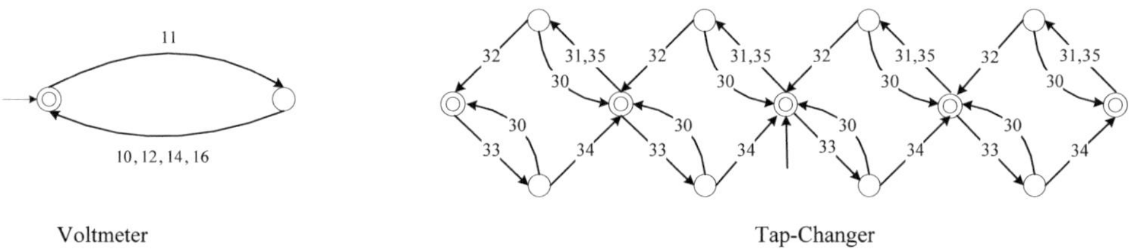

Fig. 10. ATGs for (a) Voltmeter (b) Tap-Changer.

6.2 TDES representation of Control Specifications

There are two modes of operation: "Automatic" and "Manual".

I. Automatic Mode

The tap-changer works in Automatic mode according to the following logic (control specifications):

If the voltage deviation $|\Delta V|$ > ID and ΔV is Negative (ev10) then the timer will start and when it times out, i.e. the time delay in occurrence of ev31 elapses, then a "tap increase " event (ev33) will occur and the timer will reset.

a) If the voltage deviation $|\Delta V|$ > ID and ΔV is Positive (ev14) then the timer will start and when it times out then a "tap decrease" (ev31) will occur and the timer will reset.

b) If the voltage returns to the dead-band (ev12), because of smooth system dynamics or a tap change or some other system events, then no tap change will occur.

c) If the voltage exceeds the value set for "Quick Lowering" (ev16), then the lowering tap command without delay (ev35) happens instantaneously.

Fig. 11 shows the TDES model of the control specification in the Automatic mode. It actually implements all the above logic in a single TDES. Notice that because the events tap-up/down command (31, 33, 35) are needed to preempt *tick* in some states of the above specifications, these events should be defined as "forcible" events (Section 2).

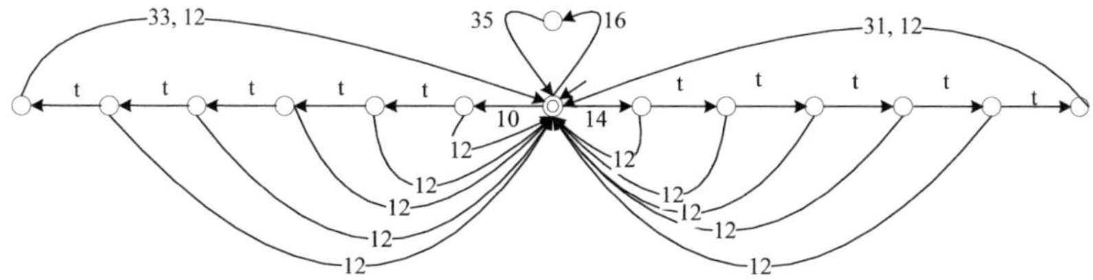

Fig. 11. TTG of the control specifications in Automatic Mode

II. Auto/Manual mode

In this mode of operation, the operator action is modeled to switch the modes and to override in abnormal situations. Events 41 and 43 are defined for operator actions:

- Enter "Automatic" Mode (ev41, [0,inf]),
- Enter "Manual" Mode (ev43, [0,inf])

The operator can force the system from Automatic to Manual mode at any time (ev43). System switches to Manual mode from Automatic mode by a "Manual" command from operator (ev43), or an abnormal situation such as, failed tap-up/tap down. In Manual mode the system is waiting for "Tap-up", "Tap-down" or "Automatic" commands. On returning to Automatic mode the controller is reinitialized at state 0 of the Automatic specification. A specification for the Auto/Manual mode (SPEC2) can be achieved by inserting suitable transitions after the occurrence of ev31 and ev33 and also by adding a new state as the "Manual-operation" state. The "Manual" command (ev43) takes the system from any state (*) to the Manual-operation state. Then ev41 takes this state back to the initial state. Fig. 12 shows the TDES model (TTG) for the control specification in Auto/Manual mode.

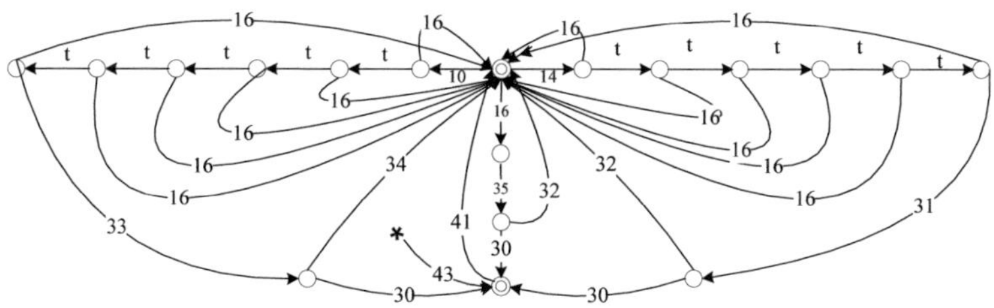

Fig. 12. TTG of the control specifications in Auto/Manual mode. The transition 43 from * represents similar transitions from all states to the "Manual operation" state

6.3 Design of TDES Supervisors

The plant and the specification TDES models are implemented in the TTCT software. The supervisory controller has been designed for the Automatic and Auto/Manual modes of operation separately. The supervisor and the control data for the ULTC in the Automatic mode are calculated using TTCT.

SUPER1 = Supcon(PLANT1,SPEC1) (198,300)
MINSUPER1 = Minstate(SUPER1) (52,79)

So a supervisory controller has been found for the Automatic mode of operation with 52 states and 79 transitions. In the Auto/Manual mode, the operator override is incorporated in the model by the control specification shown in Fig. 12. Using this specification and the new plant model which is composed by the "Operator" ATG (which has one state and two transitions i.e. 41 and 43), the supervisory control is synthesized:

SUPER2 = Supcon(PLANT2,SPEC2) (231,543)
MINSUPER2 = Minstate(SUPER2) (56,130)
PMINSUP = Project(MINSUPER2, 'tick') (26,53)

As can be seen, the supervisor state-transition size is (56,130) after applying the "Minstate" operation. By projecting out *tick* from the supervisor, its transition structure can be displayed as the *timed activity transition graph* (TATG). While the TATG suppresses *tick*, it does incorporate the constraints on ordering of activities induced by time bounds. The TATG of the supervisor for Auto/Manual mode is shown in Fig. 13.

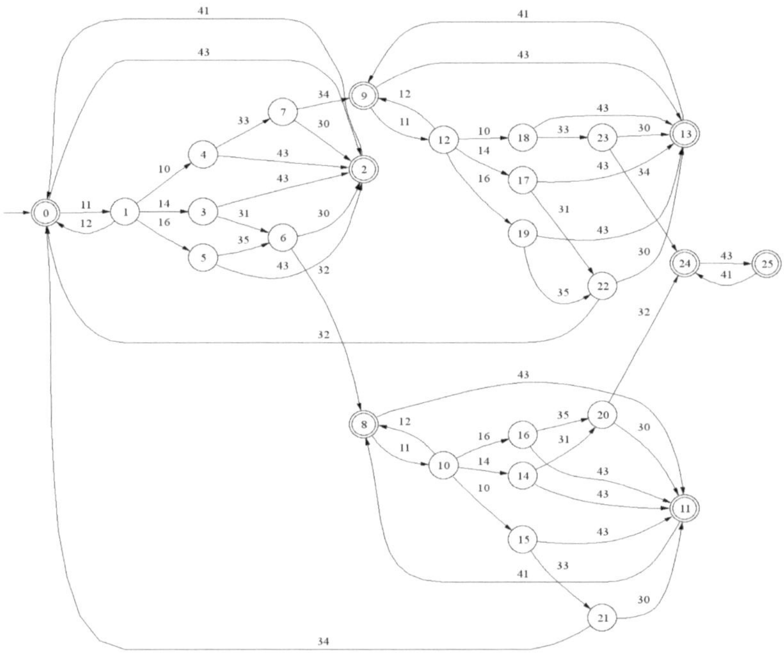

Fig. 13. TATG of the supervisory controller for Auto/Manual mode of operation

7. PLC Implementation of the Auto/Manual ULTC Supervisor

Though supervisory control theory has for over a decade received substantial attention in academia, industrial applications are scarce. Typically, finite-state automata describe the plant, specification and supervisor, and the step to a physical implementation is not necessarily straightforward. In the special case of industrial systems, where PLC-control is of great importance, the gap between the event-based asynchronous automata world and the synchronous signal based PLC-world has to be bridged (Fabian & Hellgren, 1998). The supervisor implementation is a matter of making the PLC behave as an automaton. However, there are a number of problems associated with the implementation in practice, and at the time of writing few guidelines for this can be found. Some generic problems are reported in (Fabian & Hellgren, 1998; Noorbakhsh & Afzalian, 2007a&b; Afzalian & Noorbakhsh 2008; Noorbakhsh, 2008).

One of the most important problems in the PLC-Implementation of a DES supervisory control system concern with the size of the automaton describing the behavior of the closed-loop system. Here, implementation of the untimed ULTC supervisor SUPER2 has been considered. Because of the large size of SUPER2, we have to use its reduced-order version (Fig. 7). There are some limitations in the algorithm applied to reduce the order of a supervisor in TCT software that need attention in developing the PLC ladder diagram. The reduced version of a supervisor generates all possible strings in the original model of the supervisor plus some "superfluous" strings; the latter cannot be eliminated without paying a possibly undesirable price in state size. In any case the new DES model may generate some strings that cannot be generated in the original model. Therefore, it is possible that some of these strings have no particular physical interpretation. For example, consider the following string in the reduced supervisor SIMSUP2 (Fig. 7): *s1: 11, 14, 21, 27, 31, 32, 27, 33, 34, 23*. The string *t:11, 14 ,21, 27, 31, 32* means that after an over voltage (ev14) and after a delay in the timer (ev27), the tap ratio of the transformer is decremented successfully (ev32). The event 27 after the string "t" in the string "s1" hasn't any meaning in the real system. Therefore from a physical point of view, the string "s1" can never occur in the real-world.
By inspecting all possible strings which can be generated in the DES model Fig. 7, we concluded that this problem can be solved by dividing each of the states 6 and 8 into two new states. The modified supervisor is shown in Fig. 14.
The limitation in the tap steps (Fig. 4 .c) is considered in the reduced supervisor (Fig. 14) in the state 9 and state 10 which can be reached by a string such as: *s2:11, 10, 21, 27, 33, 34, 23, 11, 10, 21, 27, 33, 34, 23, 11, 10, 21 ,27*. After this string the supervisor guides the system in Manual operation mode anyway.

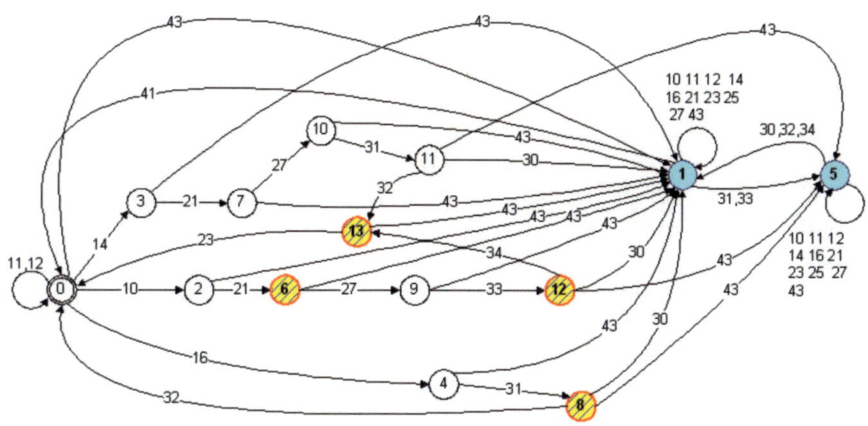

Fig. 14. The modified automaton of the reduced supervisor

The Manual mode should be performed by the operator. State 1 and state 5 in Fig. 14 correspond to Manual operation mode. Indeed when the plant operates in one of the states 1 or 5 the operator is responsible for controlling the required behavior of the plant. Therefore before finding the PLC ladder diagram for the supervisor, we need to extract the automatic part of the supervisor by deleting state 1 and state 5 along with the corresponding transitions in Fig. 14. The extracted automaton is shown in Fig. 15. Finally, the automaton in Fig. 15 is used to implement the ULTC supervisor on a PLC as a ladder diagram.

A straightforward way to implement an automaton on a ladder diagram is to represent each state and each event as an internal Boolean variable, and let the transitions be represented by a Boolean AND between the state variable and the event variable. When a transition occurs the next state is set and the previous state is reset (Fabian & Hellgren, 1998). Following this straightforward approach, a ladder diagram is developed to represent the ULTC supervisor shown in Fig. 16. The ladder code can be downloaded directly into the memory of a PLC. Now the PLC guarantees the required behavior (control specifications) of the plant in Automatic mode of operations. When a fault in tap increase or decrease occurs (ev30), or the operator forces the system from Automatic to Manual mode at any time (ev43), the system moves to the Manual state and waits for the operator commands. Indeed in this situation PLC does nothing. If the system has been switched to Manual mode, then whenever the operator changes the operation mode of ULTC from Manual to Automatic (ev41), the PLC will be reinitialized at "state 0" (Fig. 15).

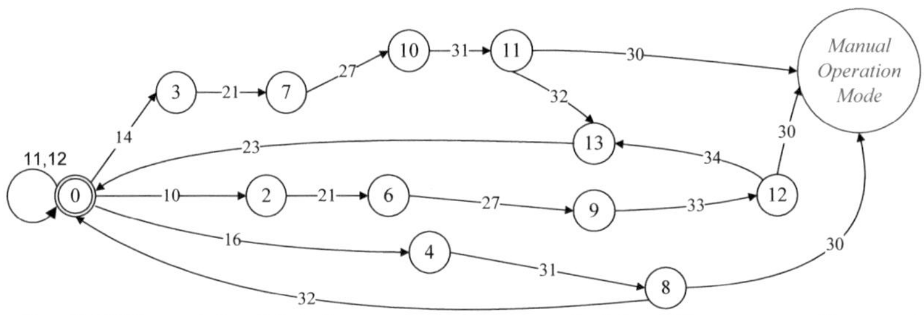

Fig. 15. The final DES model which is converted into a ladder diagram as the controller

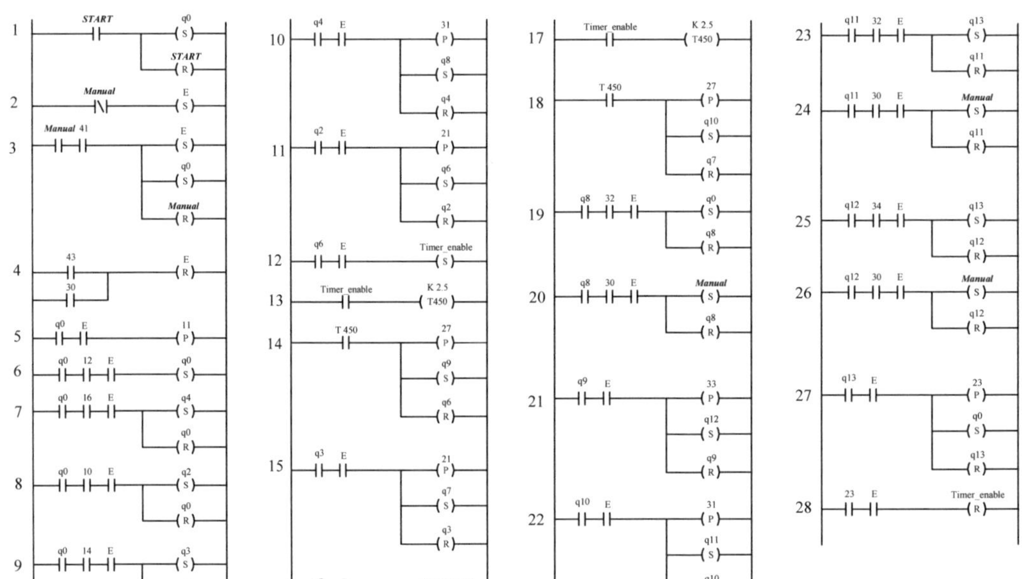

Fig. 16. Converted ladder diagram of the automaton shown in Fig. 15.

8. Conclusions

In this chapter, different solutions based on supervisory control of DES have been proposed and implemented for a control problem in electrical power systems. The problem of voltage regulation by ULTC was first modeled in terms of plant components and control specification. Controllability of the specification was evaluated and, by use of the TCT software, supervisory controllers were designed in different modes of operation including a two-level hierarchical structure. It is guaranteed by the synthesis procedure that the designed supervisors are optimal and non-blocking. The state size of the supervisory controllers was reduced for easier implementation. In the hierarchical supervisory control structure, the abstracted plant model in the high level was controlled by another supervisor, or manager, to handle the ULTC in failure situations.

The synthesis study shows that hierarchical supervisory control structure can be applied as a solution to the control problem in electrical power substations. Designers of protective systems for electrical power systems can use the proposed solutions to design appropriate supervisory control systems and to verify their control logic for ULTC. The hierarchical control structure can also be employed to synthesize the coordination control of ULTC transformers and certain FACTS devices, where DES models are available.

The designed supervisory controllers can be implemented by programmable logic controllers (PLC) to be used in real world. Generalizing this design approach to an electrical grid where many ULTCs and other switches are integrated is considered for future research work. Using a step-by-step procedure, a ladder diagram was developed for implementation of the designed Auto/Manual untimed ULTC supervisor that can be directly downloaded into a PLC. The generated PLC codes can be used in the real-time control of electrical power systems.

Appendix

A quick review of the TCT commands used in this chapter:

DES3= **supcon** (DES1, DES2)
for a controlled generator DES1, forms a trim recognizer for the supremal controllable sublanguage of the marked ("legal") language generated by DES2 to create DES3. This structure provides a proper supervisor for DES1.

DAT3= **condat** (DES1, DES2) returns control data DAT3 for the supervisor DES2 of the controlled system DES1. If DES2 represents a controllable language (with respect to DES1), as when DES2 has been previously computed with supcon, then *condat* will display the events that are to be disabled at each state of DES2. In general condat can be used to test whether a given language DES2 is controllable: just check that the disabled events tabled by *condat* are themselves controllable (have odd-numbered labels).

DES3= **supreduce** (DES1, DES2, DAT2) is a reduced supervisor for plant DES1 which is control-equivalent to DES2, where DES2 and control data DAT2 were previously computed using Supcon and Condat. Also returned is an estimated lower bound slb for the state size of a strictly state-minimal reduced supervisor. DES3 is strictly minimal if its reported state size happens to equal the *slb*.

DES2= **minstate**(DES1) reduces DES1 to a minimal state transition structure DES2 that generates the same closed and marked languages, and the same string mapping induced by vocalization (if any). DES2 is reachable but not necessarily coreachable.
DES2= **project** (DES1, NULL/IMAGE EVENTS) is a generator of the projected closed and marked languages of DES1, under the natural projection specified by the listed Null or Image events.
DES2=**vocalize** (DES1,[STATE-OUTPUT PAIRS]) has the same closed and marked behaviors as DES1, but with state outputs corresponding to selected state/event input pairs.
DES2= **outconsis** (DES1) has the same closed and marked behaviors as DES1, but is output-consistent in the sense that nonzero state outputs are unambiguously controllable or uncontrollable. A vocal state with output V in the range 10...99 may be split into siblings with outputs V1 or V0 in the range 100…991.
DES2= **hiconsis** (DES1) has the same closed and marked behaviors as DES1 but is hierarchically consistent in the sense that high-level controllable events may be disabled without side effects. This may require additional vocalization together with change in the control status of existing state outputs. **hiconsis** incorporates and extends **outconsis**.
True/False= **isomorph** (DES1, DES2) tests whether DES1 and DES2 are identical up to renumbering of states; if so, their state correspondence is displayed.
DES2= **higen** (DES1) is defined over the state-output alphabet of (vocalized) DES1, and represents the closed and marked state-output (or 'high-level') behaviors of DES1.

9. References

Afzalian, A.; Saadatpoor, A. & Wonham, W.M. (2006). Discrete-event system modeling and supervisory control for under-load tap-changing transformers, *Proceedings of 2006 IEEE International conference on Control Applications (CCA'06)*, pp.1867-1872, 2006, Munich, Germany.

Afzalian, A. & Wonham, W. M. (2006). Discrete-event system supervisory controller design for an electrical power transmission Network, *14th Iranian Conference on Electrical Engineering (ICEE'06)*, 2006, Tehran, Iran.

Afzalian, A. & Noorbakhsh, M. (2008). PLC implementation of decentralized supervisory control for dynamic flow controller. *2008 IEEE International Conference on Control Applications (CCA'08)*, pp. 522-527, September 3-5, 2008, San Antonio, Texas (USA).

Brandin, B.A. & Wonham, W.M. (1994). Supervisory control of timed discrete-event systems, *IEEE Transactions on Automatic Control*, Vol. 39, No. 2, pp. 329-342.

Dietrich, P.; Malik, R.; Wonham, W.M. & Brandin, B.A. (2001). Implementation considerations in supervisory control. In B. Caillaud, P. Darondeau, L. Lavagno, X. Xie, editors, *Synthesis and Control of Discrete Event Systems*. Kluwer Academic Publishers. 2001, pp. 185-201.

Fink, L.H. (1999). Discrete events in power systems, *Discrete Event Dynamic Systems,* Vol. 9, No. 4, pp. 319-330.

Fabian, M. & Hellgren, A. (1998). PLC-based implementation of supervisory control for discrete event systems, *Proceedings of the 37th IEEE conference on Decision & Control,* pp. 3305-3310, 1998, Tampa, Florida, USA.

GE Consumer Industrial, M. (2005). DTR - Digital Tap Changer Controller Instruction Manual GEK-106305A: 7-12.

Hellgren, A.; Lennartson, B. & Fabian, A. (2002). Modeling and PLC-based implementation of modular supervisory control, *Proceedings of the 6th International Workshop on Discrete Event System (WODES'02)*, pp. 371-376.

Hiskens, I.A. & Sokolowski, P.J. (2001). Systematic modeling and symbolically assisted simulation of power systems, *IEEE Transactions on Power Systems*, Vol. 16, No. 2, pp. 229-234.

Kim, G.W. & Lee, K.Y. (2005). Coordination control of ULTC transformer and STATCOM based on an artificial neural network, *IEEE Transactions on Power Systems*, Vol. 20, No. 2, pp. 580 - 586.

Kundur, P. (1994). *Power System Stability and Control*, McGraw-Hill.

Leal, A..; Cruz, D. & Hounsell, M. (2009). Supervisory control implementation into programmable logic controllers, *Proceedings of the 14th IEEE international conference on Emerging technologies & factory automation*, Palma de Mallorca, Spain, pp. 899-905.

Leduc, R.J. & Wonham W.M. (1995). PLC implementation of a DES supervisor for a manufacturing test bed. *Proceeding of Thirty-Third Annual Allerton Conference on Communication, Control and Computing*, pp. 519-528, University of Illinois.

Leduc, R.J. (1996). *PLC Implementation of a DES Supervisor for a Manufacturing Test bed: an Implementation Perspective*. M.A.Sc Thesis, Dept. of Electl. & Cmptr. Engrg., Univ. of Toronto, January 1996.

Lee, M.S. & Lim, J.T. (2004). Restoration strategy for power distribution networks using optimal supervisory control, *IEE Proceedings Generation, Transmission and Distribution*, Vol. 151, No. 3, pp. 367-372.

Liu, J. & Darabi, H. (2002). Ladder logic implementation of Ramadge-Wonham supervisory controller, *Proceedings of the 6th International Workshop on Discrete Event System (WODES'02)*, pp. 383-389.

Lin, S.Y.; Ho, Y.C. & Lin, C.H. (2004). An ordinal optimization theory-based algorithm for solving the optimal power flow problem with discrete control variables, *IEEE Transactions on Power Systems*, Vol. 19, No 1, pp. 276-286.

Manesis, S. & Akantziotis, K. (2005). Automated synthesis of ladder automation circuits based on state-diagrams. *Advances in Engineering Software*, 36, pp .225–233.

Music, G. & Matko, D. (2002). Discrete event control theory applied to PLC Programming, *Automatica*, Vol 43, 1–2, pp. 21–28.

Noorbakhsh, M. & Afzalian, A. (2007a). Implementation of supervisory control of DES using PLC. *15th Iranian Conf. on Electrical Engineering (ICEE'07)*, (in Farsi), Tehran, Iran.

Noorbakhsh, M. & Afzalian, A. (2007b). Design and PLC Based Implementation of Supervisory Controller for Under-load Tap-Changer. *Proc. of the 2007 IEEE Int. Conf. on Control, Automation and Systems (ICCAS'07)*, pp. 901-906, Seoul, Korea.

Noorbakhsh, M. (2008). *DES Supervisory Control for Coordination of Under-Load Tap-Changing Transformer (ULTC) and a Static VAR Compensator (SVC)*. M.A.Sc Thesis, Dept. of Elect. & Cmptr. Eng., Shahid Abbaspour University of Technology, (in Farsi), Tehran, 2008.

Noorbakhsh, M. & Afzalian, A. (2009). Modeling and synthesis of DES supervisory control for coordinating ULTC and SVC. *2009 American Control Conf. (ACC' 09)*, pp. 4759-4764, Saint Louis, Missouri USA.

Ohtsuki, H.; Yokoyama, A. & Sekine, Y. (1991). Reverse action of on-load tap changer in association with voltage collapse, *IEEE Transactions on Power Systems*, Vol. 6, No. 1, pp. 300-306.

Otomega, B.; Sermanson, V. & Cutsem, T.V. (2003). Reverse-logic control of load tap changers in emergency voltage conditions, *IEEE Power Tech Conference Proceedings*, Vol. 1, Bologna.

Prosser, J.; Selinsky, J.; Kwatny, H. & Kam, M. (1995). Supervisory control of electric power transmission networks, *IEEE Transactions on Power Systems*, Vol. 10, No. 2, pp. 1104-1110.

Queiroz, M. & Cury, J. (2002). Synthesis and implementation of local modular supervisory control for a manufacturing cell, Proceedings of the *6th International Workshop on Discrete Event System (WODES'02)*, pp. 377-382.

Ramadge, P. J. G. & Wonham, W. M. (1987). Supervisory control of a class of discrete event processes, *SIAM Journal on Control and Optimization*, Vol. 25, No. 1, pp. 206 - 230.

Ramadge, P.J.G. & Wonham, W.M. (1989). The control of discrete event systems, *Proceedings of the IEEE*, Vol. 77, No. 1, pp. 81-98.

Simon, H. A. (1962), The architecture of complexity, *Proceedings of the American Philosophical Society*, Vol. 106, No. 6, pp. 467-482.

Su, R.; Wonham, W. M. (2004). Supervisor reduction for discrete-event systems, *Discrete Event Dynamic Systems*, Vol. 14, No. 1, pp. 31-53.

Thukaram, D.; Jenkins, L.; Khincha, H.P.; Yesuratnam, G. & Kumar, B.R. (2004). Monitoring the effects of on-load tap changing transformers on voltage stability, *International Conference on Power System Technology*, Vol. 1, pp. 419–424.

Vieira, A.D., Cury, J.E.R. & Queiroz, M. (2006). A model for PLC implementation of supervisory control of discrete event systems, *IEEE Conference on Emerging Technologies and Factory Automation, ETFA '06.*, pp. 225 - 232.

Wonham, W. M. (2009). *Supervisory Control of Discrete-Event Systems*, The University of Toronto, available from: _http://www.control.utoronto.ca/DES.

Zhong, H. & Wonham, W.M. (1990). On the consistency of hierarchical supervision in discrete-event systems, *IEEE Transactions on Automatic Control*, Vol. 35, No. 10, pp. 1125-1134.

16

Stability analysis of 2-d linear discrete feedback control systems with state delays on the basis of lagrange solutions

Guido Izuta
Department of Social Information
Yonezawa Women's College
Yonezawa City
992-0025 Yamagata
Japan

1. Introduction

Researches on the two dimensional (2d) systems back to 1950s, when the main concern was the study of stability conditions for analog networked circuits (Levenstein, 1958; Ozaki & Kasami, 1960). Then, with the advent of new technologies and developments in the digital systems engineering as well as advances in the mathematical fields, this paradigm has evolved over the last decades into a major shift to discrete systems, addressing in addition to stability issues the control systems theory problems, which have ever since called the attention of mathematicians, digital signal processing community, control systems theorists and computer scientists among others.

These investigations on the stability and control of 2d systems can be gathered into basically two approaches: the multidimensional z-transform framework (Bose, 1982; Lim, 1990) and the energy method (see for example (Du & Xie, 2002) and references therein). The z-transform formalism has contributed greatly to the stability analysis of systems expressed in terms of the transfer function representation by providing a variety of stability methods as the well known Shanks stability criteria. Due to the fact that these techniques are useful instruments to checking the bounded input bounded output (BIBO) stability of system (Lim, 1990), this philosophy has been applied to systems described by their state space model representations, and as a result many stability conditions have been established in terms of the characteristic equations and eigenvalues (Fornasini & Marchesini, 1978), which have provided helpful tools for people in the systems engineering to establish control systems design methodologies (Kaczorek, 1985). On the other hand, unlike the z-transform, the energy method consists essentially in finding a Lyapunov function that expresses the energy of the system, and then showing that this energy vanishes as the equations indices increase. Thus, since the success of this method relies fundamentally in one's ability to formulate an adequate energy function, the role and the influence of the eigenvalues of the state space matrices are in many cases left uncovered. Incidentally, the discovering of a suitable function is also inherent in the stability and design procedures based on the linear matrix inequalities (LMI) approach, which is essentially a branch of the energy method (Boyd et al., 1994). Despite this point, LMI's based

techniques have led to hands on control design tools in a 'black box' fashion; and due to this fact, they have been intensively studied in the last decades.
Nevertheless there are quite a large number of published materials on these subjects, the kind of systems concerned there are primarily systems whose state space descriptions are partial difference equations depending only on the actual values, which means that none of the equations variables are functions of variables with indices less than the current values. These kinds of systems including past indices are called systems with delays or delayed systems, and unfortunately, due to the mathematical characteristics of their partial difference equations, which define the state space models, a generalization of the theories and techniques so far to this more general case is neither straightforward nor easy. The few recent reports focusing on these systems with delays and carried out on the grounds of the LMI formalism (Izuta, 2; 1; Pazke et al., 2004) have suggested interesting procedures focusing mainly on the control design issues.
Motivated by the facts described above, this paper is concerned with the stability analysis of 2-d discrete linear feedback control systems with delays. Thus, the state space model is composed by a matrix with current indices variables and another one with past indices variables. Moreover, the main goal here is to understand the conditions for this control system to be stable. In fact, to accomplish it, a feedback scheme is applied on the original discrete systems to yield a feedback control system with at least one of the matrices diagonal. Furthermore, rather than the resulting control system with a diagonal matrix of any values, two other systems are studied here. The first one is the system with the diagonal matrix of any values replaced by another diagonal matrix, but with all entries set to the maximum value in the original diagonal matrix. Similarly, the diagonal matrix of the other system that is considered has all entries set to the minimum value. These two systems are used to draw conclusions on whether the original system is asymptotically stable or not. For this, the similarity transformation is applied on these systems in order to transform the other non-diagonal matrix composing the system into either a diagonal or a Jordan type matrix. Once done, the Lagrange method comes into play here to render solutions to the set of partial difference equations expressing the systems transformed by means of the similarity transformation, and these solutions are used to study the stability conditions of the feedback control systems
The remainder of this paper is organized as follows. In section 2, the 2-d discrete linear systems with delay terms in the state space model, the controller used to turn one of the matrices of the model into a diagonal matrix, and the definitions are presented. The basic framework for solving the problem is introduced in section 3; and the results are given in section 4, which is split into four parts. Section 4.1 handles the case in which both system matrices are diagonal, and sections 4.2 through 4.3 are concerned with the systems with matrices of dimension 2×2 whereas section 4.4 presents the stability conditions for general systems. Examples to illustrate how the suggested procedures work are given in section 5 and a few remarks are given in the last section, 6.

2. Problem Formulation

In this section, the problem statement is formalized following the definition of 2-d control systems with delays terms in their state space models, and the concept of asymptotic stability which is closely related to the Lagrange solutions fulfilling the partial difference equations describing the state space models.

Definition 1. *2-d control systems with state delays are systems in which the state space models are described by the set of partial difference equations*

$$\begin{bmatrix} x_h(i+1,j) \\ x_v(i,j+1) \end{bmatrix} = \begin{bmatrix} A_{11} & A_{12} \\ A_{21} & A_{22} \end{bmatrix} \begin{bmatrix} x_h(i,j) \\ x_v(i,j) \end{bmatrix} + \begin{bmatrix} \bar{A}_{11} & \bar{A}_{12} \\ \bar{A}_{21} & \bar{A}_{22} \end{bmatrix} \begin{bmatrix} x_h(i-\theta,j) \\ x_v(i,j-\phi) \end{bmatrix}$$
$$+ \begin{bmatrix} B_{11} & B_{12} \\ B_{21} & B_{22} \end{bmatrix} \begin{bmatrix} u_h(i,j) \\ u_v(i,j) \end{bmatrix}, \tag{1}$$
$$\begin{bmatrix} y_h(i,j) \\ y_v(i,j) \end{bmatrix} = \begin{bmatrix} C_{11} & C_{12} \\ C_{21} & C_{22} \end{bmatrix} \begin{bmatrix} x_h(i,j) \\ x_v(i,j) \end{bmatrix},$$

where the states vectors $x_h \in \Re^{n_h}, x_v \in \Re^{n_v}$ are such that the entries $x_h's$, $x_v's : \Re \times \Re \to \Re$; the inputs vectors $u_h \in \Re^{m_h}, u_v \in \Re^{m_v}$ have entries $u_h's$, $u_v's : \Re \times \Re \to \Re$, and the outputs vectors $y_h \in \Re^{l_h}$, $y_v \in \Re^{l_v}$ are composed by $y_h's$, $y_v's : \Re \times \Re \to \Re$. Moreover, A_{pq}, $\bar{A}_{pq}$, B_{pq} and C_{pq}, $\forall p, q$, are real valued matrices of adequate dimensions.

Remark 1. *Nevertheless in 2-d systems the meaning of the word 'delays' referring to the components θ and ϕ is not necessarily related to the concept of time in the common sense, this terminology is adopted here in order to be consistent with the jargon used in the ordinary 1-d control systems theory.*

In order to simplify the notations, the vectors and matrices are compactly written accordingly to the following definition.

Definition 2. *Compact representations for the vectors and matrices are the notations*

$$\begin{aligned} x(i\pm\hat{i},j\pm\hat{j}) &= \begin{bmatrix} x_h(i\pm\hat{i},j) \\ x_v(i,j\pm\hat{j}) \end{bmatrix}, & &\begin{cases} \hat{i} = 1,0,\theta \\ \hat{j} = 1,0,\phi \end{cases} \\ u(i,j) &= \begin{bmatrix} u_h(i,j) \\ u_v(i,j) \end{bmatrix}, & y(i,j) &= \begin{bmatrix} y_h(i,j) \\ y_v(i,j) \end{bmatrix}, \\ A &= \begin{bmatrix} A_{11} & A_{12} \\ A_{21} & A_{22} \end{bmatrix}, & A_d &= \begin{bmatrix} \bar{A}_{11} & \bar{A}_{12} \\ \bar{A}_{21} & \bar{A}_{22} \end{bmatrix}, \\ B &= \begin{bmatrix} B_{11} & B_{12} \\ B_{21} & B_{22} \end{bmatrix}, & C &= \begin{bmatrix} C_{11} & C_{12} \\ C_{21} & C_{22} \end{bmatrix}. \end{aligned} \tag{2}$$

Remark 2. *In the sequel, when it is clear from the context and no confusion arises, the vectors and matrices will sometimes be expressed by not only their compact notations but also both the compact and the original ones will be used in a mixed fashion.*

As far as the feedback control laws are concerned, the following schemes will be objects of study in this work.

Definition 3. *A closed loop system is a feedback control system composed by (1) and the feedback law*

$$u(i,j) = Kx(i,j) + K_d x(i-\theta, j-\phi), \tag{3}$$

which renders

$$x(i+1,j+1) = (A+BK)x(i,j) + (A_d + BK_d)x(i-\theta,j-\phi). \tag{4}$$

For the state feedback law

$$u(i,j) = Kx(i,j) + K_d x(i-\theta, j-\phi), \tag{5}$$

the system reads

$$x(i+1,j+1) = (A+BKC)x(i,j) + (A_d + BKC_d)x(i-\theta,j-\phi). \tag{6}$$

Remark 3. *It is worth pointing out that, in practice, measurement limitations and restricted data storage capacity may force matrices K or K_d be null.*

Next, the following concept of asymptotic stability, which relies on the solutions given by the Lagrange method, is adopted here.

Definition 4. *A feedback control system is said to be asymptotically stable if the real valued Lagrange solutions x(i,j) given by the Lagrange method vanish as i, j tend to infinity (Jerri, 1996).*

Taking these into account, the problem to be discussed is the following:

Problem 1. *Let system (1) be such that its matrices have eigenvalues assigned at any desired points by means of the pole assignment techniques developed for 1-d control systems theory. Then, the question to be investigate here is "what are the conditions that the assigned eigenvalues have to fulfill in order to guarantee the asymptotic stability of the feedback control systems?".*

The purpose here is to carry out a stability analysis by pursuing the Lagrange solutions of the partial difference equations defining the feedback control system. Hence, the controller design is basically settled by means of the assumption that pole assignment procedures can be used to place the eigenvalues of the feedback control system matrices at any points. Finally, pole assignment procedures developed for 1-d systems can be found for example in (Bachelier et al., 2006; Chen, 1999; Kailath, 1980; Syrmos et al., 1997).

3. Preliminaries

In this section, the basic framework for handling the problem is presented. Basically, the feedback control system is linearly transformed twice by means of the similarity transformations into a system with either diagonal matrices or a diagonal and Jordan matrices in its state space model description. The stability conditions are discussed on the basis of the Lagrange solutions of the transformed systems. Thus, the similarity transformation that is used in the sequel is provided in the following statement.

Definition 5. *Consider system (4)-(6) and let $J = \bar{T}T\bar{A}T^{-1}\bar{T}^{-1}$ ($\bar{A} = A - BF$ or $\bar{A} = A - BFC$), and $y_{max}(i,j)$, $y_{min}(i,j) = \bar{T}Tx(i,j)$, in which T and $\bar{T}$ are matrices composed by the eigenvectors of $\bar{A}_d$ ($\bar{A} = A - BF$ or $\bar{A} = A - BFC$), and $T\bar{A}T^{-1}$, respectively. Furthermore, let $\Lambda_{max} = diag\{\lambda_{max}, \cdots, \lambda_{max}\}$ and $\Lambda_{min} = diag\{\lambda_{min}, \cdots, \lambda_{min}\}$ be diagonal matrices with maximum and minimum eigenvalues of $\bar{A}_d$ as entries. Then, the systems obtained are the maximum and minimum doubly transformed systems and are given by*

$$y(i+1,j+1) = J_y y(i,j) + \Lambda_{max} y(i-\theta, j-\phi) \tag{7}$$

and

$$y(i+1,j+1) = \bar{J}_y y(i,j) + \Lambda_{min} y(i-\theta, j-\phi), \tag{8}$$

where the J's are Jordan matrices. Analogously, interchanging the roles of the matrices $\bar{A}$ and $\bar{A}_d$, one arrives at

$$z(i+1,j+1) = \bar{\Lambda}_{max} z(i,j) + J_z z(i-\theta, j-\phi) \tag{9}$$

and

$$z(i+1,j+1) = \bar{\Lambda}_{min} z(i,j) + \bar{J}_z z(i-\theta, j-\phi). \tag{10}$$

Clearly if there are no constraints on the values of the assigned eigenvalues for at least one of the matrices of (4)-(6) , then just set the all the eigenvalues of this matrix to the same value, and the stability conditions for the system can be established without being aware of the maximum and minimum eigenvalues cases. However, if it is necessary to assign eigenvalues of different values, then the asymptotic stability conditions are established by considering only these cases. To see that this procedure is in fact reasonable, focus, without loss of generality, on the simply similarity transformation of (4), which is given by

$$w(i+1,j+1) = \bar{A}w(i,j) + \Lambda w(i-\theta, j-\phi), \tag{11}$$

where Λ is a diagonal matrix composed by the eigenvalues of $\bar{A}_d$. It is easy to see that each single equation in (11) can be expressed as

$$w_1(i,j) = \textstyle\sum_{k=1}^{k} a_{1k} w_k(i-1,j) + \lambda_1 w_1(i-\theta-1, j-\phi) \tag{12}$$

in which λ_1 is an eigenvalue of $\bar{A}_d$.
Now, let us see what happens to $w_1(i,j)$ if one replaces λ_1 by λ_{max} or λ_{min} in (12) for the same values of $w_k(i-1,j)$ and $w_1(i-\theta-1, j-\phi)$. On carrying out these operations, the following set of equations

$$\begin{aligned} w_1(i,j) &= (\text{constant value}) + \breve{}_{1}\mathrm{w}_1(\mathrm{i} - \grave{} - 1, \mathrm{j} - \text{Œ}), \\ \hat{w}_1(i,j) &= (\text{constant value}) + \breve{}_{\mathrm{max}}\mathrm{w}_1(\mathrm{i} - \grave{} - 1, \mathrm{j} - \text{Œ}), \\ \check{w}_1(i,j) &= (\text{constant value}) + \breve{}_{\mathrm{min}}\mathrm{w}_1(\mathrm{i} - \grave{} - 1, \mathrm{j} - \text{Œ}), \end{aligned} \tag{13}$$

are yielded.
Clearly, these equations mean that the values of $w_1(i,j)$ are in-between the ones of $\hat{w}_1(i,j)$ and $\check{w}_1(i,j)$. In addition, the fact that the definition 2 of asymptotic stability adopted here is concerned only with the values of the solutions as the indices increase allows us to examine the behavior of (12) by using only the maximum and minimum eigenvalues.
Thus, due to the fact that the theory on the similarity transformation of systems (Gantmatcher, 1959; Kawamata & Higuchi, 1995) guarantees that the original feedback control system in terms of the vector $x(i,j)$ is stable if and only if either the simply similarity transformed system in terms of $w(i,j)$ or doubly similarity transformed system $y(i,j)$'s ($z(i,j)$'s) is also stable, hereafter the subscripts *max* and *min* are dropped. The variable without the subscripts will implicitly mean that it is referred to both cases treated separately each time.
It is worth noting that in some cases, a singular similarity transformation will be enough to analyze the stability of the system. In what follows, no matter whether the systems are doubly or simply transformed, the feedback system in terms of the variables $z(i,j)$'s mean transformed systems.
In the sequel, in order to keep track of the overall picture of the work, the Lagrange solutions are determined only for the transformed systems. To see what the solutions for the original feedback control systems look like, for example in the doubly similarity transformation case, simply compute $x(i,j)$ from the relation $z(i,j) = \bar{T}Tx(i,j)$.
Finally, a very useful notation from the combinatory mathematics is written down here for future use.

Definition 6. *Let $C_\theta(p,q)$ be a set of selections of q elements from the set $\{\theta_1, \cdots, \theta_p\}$ (for example, $C_\theta(n,n) = \{\theta_1\theta_2\cdots\theta_n\}$). Then, $S(p,q)$ is defined to be a set with same cardinality as $C_\theta(p,q)$ equipped with elements that are the sum of the θ's constituting the elements of $C_\theta(p,q)$ (for example, $S_\theta(n,n) = \{\theta_1 + \theta_2 + \cdots + \theta_n\}$). Moreover, $S_{\theta i}(p,q)$ stands for an element in $S_\theta(p,q)$.*

4. Results

For the sake of clarity, the results are divided into four parts. The stability conditions for systems with both diagonal matrices of any dimensions in the state space representation are dealt with in the first section. These very simple and ideal systems allow us to figure out the basic computations procedures to pursue the results for general systems as well as to shed some light onto the relationships between the matrices eigenvalues and the stability of the systems. The following two sections present stability conditions in a more general framework in the sense that these basic ideas are extended to systems with 2×2 matrices. In the last section, the previous results are further generalized to systems with matrices of any sizes.

4.1 State space models with both $n \times n$ matrices diagonal

This section gives the results for systems equipped with both matrices diagonal, which can be of any size greater than dimension 2×2. Let us firstly focus on the doubly similarity transformation of (4)-(6) yielding diagonal matrices, for which the following claim holds.

Theorem 1. *Let the doubly similarity transformation of (4)-(6) be*

$$\begin{bmatrix} z_h(i+1,j) \\ z_v(i,j+1) \end{bmatrix} = \begin{bmatrix} \lambda_1 & 0 \\ 0 & \lambda_2 \end{bmatrix} \begin{bmatrix} z_h(i,j) \\ z_v(i,j) \end{bmatrix} + \begin{bmatrix} \lambda_\theta & 0 \\ 0 & \lambda_\phi \end{bmatrix} \begin{bmatrix} z_h(i-\theta,j) \\ z_v(i,j-\phi) \end{bmatrix}, \tag{14}$$

for some given scalars $\lambda_1, \lambda_2, \lambda_\theta, \lambda_\phi$. Furthermore, let the Lagrange solutions to (14) be the expressions

$$\begin{aligned} z_h(i,j) &= \alpha^i, \ \ \alpha \neq 0, \\ z_v(i,j) &= \beta^j, \ \ \beta \neq 0. \end{aligned} \tag{15}$$

Then the asymptotic stability is guaranteed with α's, $|\alpha| < 1$, and β's, $|\beta| < 1$, fulfilling the characteristic equations of the system described by

$$\begin{cases} \alpha^{\theta+1} - \lambda_1 \alpha^\theta - \lambda_\theta = 0 \\ \beta^{\phi+1} - \lambda_2 \beta^\phi - \lambda_\phi = 0 \end{cases} \tag{16}$$

Proof. Since (14) is a set of partial difference equations, in which the first one is a function of only index i whereas the second one depends only on j, it is natural to expect that the Lagrange solutions $z_h(i,j)$ and $z_v(i,j)$ are such that $z_h(i,j) = z_h(i)$ and $z_v(i,j) = z_v(j)$, respectively. Thus, (15) are in fact candidate solutions to the transformed system (14).
Now, the substitution of (15) into (14) yields the set of partial difference equations described by

$$\begin{cases} \alpha^i(\alpha^{\theta+1} - \lambda_1 \alpha^\theta - \lambda_\theta) = 0, \\ \beta^j(\beta^{\phi+1} - \lambda_2 \beta^\phi - \lambda_\phi) = 0, \end{cases} \tag{17}$$

which means that the candidate solutions are indeed Lagrange solutions (14) if (16) is satisfied. On the other hand, it is not difficult to verify from (15) that, for given λ_1, λ_2, λ_θ and λ_ϕ, the asymptotic stability conditions for the feedback control system translate into the existences of α with $|\alpha| < 1$, and β with $|\beta| < 1$ as claimed. □

Remark 4. *The system (15) is in general reached only in special cases. Nevertheless, as pointed out in the previous section, the similarity transformation leads to (15) with either $\lambda_1 = \lambda_2$ or $\lambda_\theta = \lambda_\phi$. Here* *these values are taken as different numbers in order to include all the cases. Thus, if* $\lambda_\theta = \lambda_\phi$ *for given* $\lambda_1, \lambda_2, \lambda_\theta$ *and* λ_ϕ*, then from (16), the equality*

$$\alpha^{\theta+1} - \lambda_1 \alpha^{\theta} = \beta^{\phi+1} - \lambda_2 \beta^{\phi}, \tag{18}$$

holds. Thus, the solutions α'*s and* β'*s to the characteristic equations are related by means of (18), which means that* β'*s are determined by* α'*s, and vice-versa.*

The above result means that the matrices of the feedback control system must be such that the eigenvalues $\lambda_1, \lambda_2, \lambda_\theta$ and λ_ϕ lead to characteristic equations (16) provided with real and norm less than unit polynomial roots.
It is also interesting to recall that researches on the 2-d systems with delays on the grounds of the Lyapunov methods (Izuta, 2) tend to handle these systems by separating into delay dependent and independent cases; each one with its specific methods for analyzing the stability. Here, since the 'delay terms' θ and ϕ turn to be the order of the characteristic polynomials, the splitting into delay dependent and independent cases is not a concern.

Remark 5. *Note that since the Lagrange solutions are composed by the solutions of the characteristic equations, the number of solutions in terms of, for example,* α *is equal to the degree of the polynomial representing the characteristic equation; however, for the sake of simplicity, equations in (16) refer loosely to only a single solution. Hence, when solving them one has to be aware that* $z_h(i,j)$ *and* $z_v(i,j)$ *are linear combinations of the solutions* α'*s and* β'*s, respectively.*

Remark 6. *Although the initial values and boundary conditions problems play key roles in the studies of the solutions to the partial difference equations, this work concentrates only on the system stability problem and leave these issues to be discussed elsewhere.*

Now, before making it clear the $\lambda_1, \lambda_2\ \lambda_\theta, \lambda_\phi$ that solve the problem, another way to interpret the solutions of (14) is introduced at this point in order to help us to understand the roles of λ's in the characteristic equations.

Theorem 2. *Consider the characteristic equation described by*

$$\alpha^{\theta+1} - \lambda_1 \alpha^{\theta} - \lambda_\theta = 0, \tag{19}$$

and let the functions $f(x_\alpha)$ *and* $g(x_\alpha)$ *be expressed as*

$$\begin{aligned} f(x_\alpha) &= -\lambda_1 - x_\alpha, \\ g(x_\alpha) &= \frac{(-1)^\theta \lambda_\theta}{x_\alpha^\theta}, \end{aligned} \tag{20}$$

with a finite number of points fulfilling the equality $f(x_\alpha) = g(x_\alpha)$*. Then, these points with opposite signals provide the set of solutions to (19).*

Proof. Firstly, note that from basic polynomial algebra, equation (19) can be written as

$$(\alpha - \alpha_1) \cdots (\alpha - \alpha_{\theta+1}) = 0. \tag{21}$$

On the other hand, the combinatorial notation as stated in definition 6, allows one to express the coefficients of (19) with respect to the terms $\alpha_i's$ as

$$\begin{cases} \alpha_1 + \sum_{p=2}^{\theta+1} \alpha_p = -\lambda_1 \\ \alpha_1 \sum_{p=2}^{\theta+1} \alpha_p + C^2_{\{\alpha_2,\cdots,\alpha_{\theta+1}\}} = 0 \\ \alpha_1 C^2_{\{\alpha_2,\cdots,\alpha_{\theta+1}\}} + C^3_{\{\alpha_2,\cdots,\alpha_{\theta+1}\}} = 0 \\ \vdots \\ \alpha_1 C^{\theta-1}_{\{\alpha_2,\cdots,\alpha_{\theta+1}\}} + C^{\theta}_{\{\alpha_2,\cdots,\alpha_{\theta+1}\}} = 0 \\ \alpha_1 C^{\theta}_{\{\alpha_2,\cdots,\alpha_{\theta+1}\}} = -\lambda_\theta \end{cases} . \tag{22}$$

From the last equation in (22), $C^{\theta}_{\{\alpha_2,\cdots,\alpha_{\theta+1}\}}$ can be determined in terms of λ_θ and α_1. Taking this value and substituting into the upper equation and continuing this computation process up to the second equation in (22), the following equations are obtained.

$$\begin{cases} \sum_{p=2}^{\theta+1} \alpha_p = -\lambda_1 - \alpha_1, \\ \sum_{p=2}^{\theta+1} \alpha_p = \frac{(-1)^\theta \lambda_\theta}{\alpha_1^\theta}, \end{cases} \tag{23}$$

which mean that the set of solution to the problem, when exists, is composed by $\theta + 1$ points that fulfill both the polynomials in (20) simultaneously. In addition, once α_1 is computed, the computation steps above are carried out θ times to establish the remaining α's. However, due to the pattern of the polynomials, it turns out that the $(\theta + 1)$'s α_1 computed at the very beginning are the solutions to (19) unless the signal. □

Remark 7. *Similar result can be established for the characteristic equation expressed in terms of β's and, throughout the text, their solutions are written x_β to distinguish from the solutions x_α's relative to α's. However, as far as the stability of the system is concerned, the solutions to both characteristic equations (16) play indistinctly the same role, and must be analyzed individually.*

Hence, taken into account these standpoints, theorem 1 can alternatively be rewritten making explicit requirements on λ_θ and λ_ϕ.

Theorem 3. *The stability of the feedback control is guaranteed if and only if there exist λ_1, λ_2, λ_θ ($|\lambda_\theta| < 1$) and λ_ϕ ($|\lambda_\phi| < 1$) yielding solvable $f(x_\alpha) = g(x_\alpha)$ and $f(x_\beta) = g(x_\beta)$ as in (20), for which the solutions x_α's and x_β's have non null absolute values less than unit.*

Proof. Firstly, it is clear from (21) that asymptotic stability implies x_α's and x_β's with non null absolute values less than unit. Hence, by means of the proof to theorem 2, the claim holds. On the other hand, beginning with non null and absolute values less than unit x_α's and x_β's, the arguments of the same proof straightforwardly yield an asymptotically stable system. □

Remark 8. *If the feedback control systems are such that they are devoided of delay components; i.e., $\theta = 0$ and $\phi = 0$ then $\lambda_\theta = 0$, $\lambda_\phi = 0$. Furthermore, the equation (17) becomes*

$$\alpha^\theta(\alpha - \lambda_1) = 0, \tag{24}$$

which means that λ_1 and λ_2 have to be less than unit to assure the asymptotic stability of the feedback control system.

Thus, to establish the values of λ_θ, λ_ϕ, λ_1 and λ_2 that provide a feasible solution to the problem, start out by setting λ_θ ($|\lambda_\theta| < 1$) and λ_ϕ ($|\lambda_\phi| < 1$) and then seek for λ_1 and λ_2 that leads to $f(x_\alpha) = g(x_\alpha)$ and $f(x_\beta) = g(x_\beta)$ with all the solutions with non null absolute values less than unit. Once, a solution is settled, apply the feedback laws in order to generate matrices with the above eigenvalues characteristics, and finally establish an asymptotically stable feedback control system.
Note that theorem 3 makes explicit allusion only to the possible values constraints that λ_θ and λ_ϕ have to bound, and there is no reference related to the values of λ_1 and λ_2 as far as they exist. Thus, it is interesting to characterize λ_1 (λ_2) in terms of λ_θ (λ_ϕ) and some kind of constraints as $|\lambda_1| < c$ ($|\lambda_2| < c$) for a given constant positive number c.

Proposition 1. *Let the feedback control system be as in theorem 2. Then $|\lambda_1| < c$ for $c \in \Re > 0$ if*

$$|\lambda_\theta| < c(|x^\theta| - |x^{\theta+1}|). \tag{25}$$

Proof. Equation (25) can be arranged as

$$\frac{|\lambda_\theta|}{|x^\theta|} + |x| < c. \tag{26}$$

On applying the inequalities rules

$$\frac{|\lambda_\theta|}{|x^\theta|} + |x| \geq \left| \frac{\lambda_\theta}{x^\theta} + x \right| \tag{27}$$

holds. Consequently, the following inequality is valid.

$$\left| \frac{\lambda_\theta}{x^\theta} + x \right| < c. \tag{28}$$

On recalling equation (20), the expression

$$|-\lambda_1| = \left| \frac{(-1)^\theta \lambda_\theta}{x^\theta} + x \right| \tag{29}$$

comes up. Hence, comparing (29) with (28) and back tracking the calculations up to (26), the hypothesis is reached. □

4.2 State space models with a single 2×2 diagonal matrix - case 1

In what follows, transformed systems with only one 2×2 diagonal matrix are studied. Since the non diagonal matrix can be of any type, in general, the transformed system is likely to be the result of a single transformation.

Lemma 1. *Let the system transformed via similarity transformation be*

$$\begin{bmatrix} z_h(i+1,j) \\ z_v(i,j+1) \end{bmatrix} = \begin{bmatrix} t_{11} & t_{12} \\ t_{21} & t_{22} \end{bmatrix} \begin{bmatrix} z_h(i,j) \\ z_v(i,j) \end{bmatrix} + \begin{bmatrix} \lambda_\theta & 0 \\ 0 & \lambda_\phi \end{bmatrix} \begin{bmatrix} z_h(i-\theta,j) \\ z_v(i,j-\phi) \end{bmatrix} \tag{30}$$

and its Lagrange candidate solutions be expressed by

$$\begin{array}{l} z_h(i,j) = \alpha^i \beta^j, \\ z_v(i,j) = \gamma^i \delta^j, \\ \alpha,\ \beta,\ \gamma,\ \delta \neq 0. \end{array} \tag{31}$$

Then (31) are solutions of (30) if

$$\beta^{\phi+1} - \lambda_\beta(\alpha)\beta^\phi - \lambda_\phi = 0 \tag{32}$$

is satisfied. Here $\lambda_\beta(\alpha)$ is a polynomial in terms of variable α given by

$$\begin{array}{l} \lambda_\beta(\alpha) = t_{22}\frac{\lambda_n(\alpha)}{\lambda_d(\alpha)}, \\ \lambda_n(\alpha) = \alpha^{\theta+1} - \frac{det(T)}{t_{22}}\alpha^\theta - \lambda_\theta, \\ \lambda_d(\alpha) = \alpha^{\theta+1} - t_{11}\alpha^\theta - \lambda_\theta, \\ \det(\mathrm{T}) = \begin{vmatrix} t_{11} & t_{12} \\ t_{21} & t_{22} \end{vmatrix}. \end{array} \tag{33}$$

Proof. On substituting (31) into (30), the following system of partial difference equations is yielded.

$$\begin{cases} \alpha^{i+1}\beta^j - t_{11}\alpha^i\beta^j - \lambda_\theta\alpha^{i-\theta}\beta^j = t_{12}\gamma^i\delta^j \\ \gamma^i\delta^{j+1} - t_{22}\gamma^i\delta^j - \lambda_\phi\gamma^i\delta^{j-\phi} = t_{21}\alpha^i\beta^j. \end{cases} \tag{34}$$

Thus, from the first equation in (34)

$$\gamma^i\delta^j = \frac{\alpha^{i+1}\beta^j - t_{11}\alpha^i\beta^j - \lambda_\theta\alpha^{i-\theta}\beta^j}{t_{12}} \tag{35}$$

is computed. Now, plugging (35) into the second equation in (34) produces

$$\beta^{\phi+1} - \lambda_\beta(\alpha)\beta^\phi - \lambda_\phi = 0, \tag{36}$$

in which $\lambda_\beta(\alpha)$ is the fractional polynomial defined in (33). Hence, (31) are the solutions to the partial difference equations defining the transformed feedback control system as claimed. □

Remark 9. *Note that (33) allows one to write (35) as*

$$\gamma^i\delta^j = \frac{\lambda_n(\alpha)}{t_{12}}\alpha^{i+\theta}\beta^j, \tag{37}$$

which says that the solutions (31) are basically a function of the solutions α's and β's. In addition, if $\lambda_n(\alpha)$ is written as

$$\lambda_n(\alpha) = \lambda_d(\alpha) + \frac{t_{12}t_{21}}{t_{22}}\alpha^\theta \tag{38}$$

the roots of the polynomials $\lambda_n(\alpha)$ and $\lambda_d(\alpha)$ are distinct from each other as far as the roots are non null and the off diagonal entries of the matrix are non null.

On gathering all the details discussed so far, the following asymptotic stability conditions for systems with only one diagonal matrix are settled.

Theorem 4. *Let the feedback control system transformed by means of the similarity transformation be as in lemma 1, and let $\alpha_1, \cdots, \alpha_{\theta+1}$ be the roots of the polynomial $\lambda_n(\alpha)$ in (33). Then the system is asymptotically stable at α_i $(i, \cdots, \theta+1)$ and β's fulfilling*

$$\begin{aligned} \beta^{\phi+1} &= \lambda_\phi, \\ |\lambda_\phi| &< 1. \end{aligned} \tag{39}$$

if there exists λ_θ with $|\lambda_\theta| < 1$ such that the absolute values of the roots of $\lambda_n(\alpha)$ are all non null and less then unit.

Proof. The hypothesis implies that $\lambda_\beta(\alpha) = 0$. Hence, (33) reduces to (39), which is endowed with $(\phi+1)$ roots at λ_ϕ. By imposing λ_ϕ to assume values $|\lambda_\phi| < 1$, the solutions $z_h(i,j)$ in (31) of the partial difference equations will vanish as the indices increase. On the other hand, (39) assures that $z_v(i,j)$ in (31) decreases as the indices tend to infinity. Finally, the second equation in (33) and the last equation in (22) imply that a condition to have α less than unit is the constraint $|\lambda_\theta| < 1$. □

Remark 10. *If the non-diagonal matrix is triangular, then the solutions are quite much simpler. In fact, since $\lambda_\beta(\alpha) = t_{22}$ holds, the solutions are functions of elements as described by $z_h(i,j) = z_h(i,j,\beta)$, $z_v(i,j) = z_v(i,j,\gamma,\delta)$ for lower triangular matrix case, and $z_h(i,j) = z_h(i,j,\alpha,\beta)$, $z_v(i,j) = z_v(i,j,\delta)$ for upper triangular matrix case.*

If the non diagonal matrix of the transformed system is non singular, then from (33), the stability condition depends only on λ_θ and λ_ϕ.
Finally, it is interesting to note that the value of $det(T)$ is restricted by the values of α_i $(i = 1, \cdots, \theta+1)$, λ_θ and t_{22} as stated next.

Corollary 1. *Let the system be as in theorem 4. Then*

$$|det(T)| \geq |t_{22}| \frac{|\alpha_i^{\theta+1}| - |\lambda_\theta|}{|\alpha_i^\theta|}, \quad \forall i, \tag{40}$$

holds.

Proof. It is settled straightforwardly by just applying the inequality rules on $\lambda_n(\alpha_i)$ in (33). □

4.3 State space models with a single 2×2 diagonal matrix - case 2

This section parallels the previous one. The difference is that here the first matrix in (4)-(6) is a 2×2 diagonal matrix, and the second one can be anything else. Thus, since the analogous reasoning applies here, the details are left out.

Lemma 2. *Let the similarity transformed system be*

$$\begin{bmatrix} z_h(i+1,j) \\ z_v(i,j+1) \end{bmatrix} = \begin{bmatrix} \lambda_1 & 0 \\ 0 & \lambda_2 \end{bmatrix} \begin{bmatrix} z_h(i,j) \\ z_v(i,j) \end{bmatrix} + \begin{bmatrix} \bar{t}_{11} & \bar{t}_{12} \\ \bar{t}_{21} & \bar{t}_{22} \end{bmatrix} \begin{bmatrix} z_h(i-\theta,j) \\ z_v(i,j-\phi) \end{bmatrix}. \tag{41}$$

and its Lagrange candidate solutions be expressed by

$$\begin{aligned} z_h(i,j) &= \alpha^i \beta^j, \\ z_v(i,j) &= \gamma^i \delta^j, \\ \alpha, \beta, \gamma, \delta &\neq 0. \end{aligned} \tag{42}$$

Then (42) are solutions of (41) if

$$\beta^{\phi+1} - \lambda_2\beta^{\phi} - \lambda_\theta(\alpha) = 0 \tag{43}$$

is satisfied. Here $\lambda_\theta(\alpha)$ is a polynomial in terms of variable α given by

$$\begin{aligned}
\lambda_\theta(\alpha) &= \bar{t}_{22}\frac{\lambda_n(\alpha)}{\lambda_d(\alpha)},\\
\lambda_n(\alpha) &= \alpha^{\theta+1} - \lambda_1\alpha^{\theta} + \frac{det(\bar{T})}{\bar{t}_{22}},\\
\lambda_d(\alpha) &= \alpha^{\theta+1} - \lambda_1\alpha^{\theta} - \bar{t}_{11},\\
\det(\bar{T}) &= \begin{vmatrix} \bar{t}_{11} & \bar{t}_{12} \\ \bar{t}_{21} & \bar{t}_{22} \end{vmatrix}.
\end{aligned} \tag{44}$$

Proof. Note that the following system of partial difference equations are yielded by substituting (42) into (41).

$$\begin{cases} \alpha^{i+1}\beta^j = \lambda_1\alpha^i\beta^j + \bar{t}_{11}\alpha^{i-\theta}\beta^j + \bar{t}_{12}\gamma^i\delta^{j-\phi} \\ \gamma^i\delta^{j+1} = \lambda_2\gamma^i\delta^j + \bar{t}_{21}\alpha^{i-\theta}\beta^j + \bar{t}_{22}\gamma^i\delta^{j-\phi}. \end{cases} \tag{45}$$

Thus, by using the first equation in (41) and substituting $\gamma^i\delta^j$ into the second equation renders

$$\beta^{\phi+1} - \lambda_2\beta^{\phi} - \lambda_\theta(\alpha) = 0, \tag{46}$$

where $\lambda_\theta(\alpha)$ is the fractional polynomial as defined in (44). Hence the claim follows. □

Now, the asymptotic stability conditions are as in the following theorem.

Theorem 5. *Consider the similarity transformed system as in lemma 2 and let $\alpha_1, \cdots, \alpha_{\theta+1}$ be the roots of $\lambda_n(\alpha)$. Then the asymptotic stability at the points α_i $(i, \cdots, \theta+1)$ for all λ_2 $(|\lambda_2| < 1)$ is guaranteed as far as $\frac{det(\bar{A})}{\bar{a}_{22}} < 1$ and there exists λ_1 such that the absolute values of the roots of $\lambda_n(\alpha)$ are all non null and less then unit.*

Proof. It basically parallels the reasoning of the proof to theorem 4. □

Theorem 5 can be stated without making it explicit the condition $\frac{det(\bar{A})}{\bar{a}_{22}} < 1$ as in the following paragraph.

Theorem 6. *Consider the similarity transformed system as in lemma 2 and let α_p, $(p = 1 \cdots, \theta+1)$ be the roots of $\lambda_n(\alpha)$, and $\beta_q (q = 1 \cdots, \phi+1)$ the roots of (46). Then the asymptotic stability at the points α_p and β_q (for $\forall p, q$) is guaranteed if there exist λ_1 and λ_2 such that the absolute values of the roots of $\lambda_n(\alpha)$ are all non null and less then unit.*

4.4 State space models with a single $n \times n$ diagonal matrix

Let us begin by looking at the Lagrange solutions for a set of equations. As a matter of fact, these equations are sub-structures of the first type of systems transformed by means of similarity transformation that shall be considered hereafter.

Lemma 3. *Consider the set of equations given by*

$$\left\{\begin{array}{lcl} w_1(i+1,j) & = & \lambda_1 w_1(i,j) + w_2(i,j) + \lambda w_1(i-\theta_1,j) \\ & \vdots & \\ w_{n-1}(i+1,j) & = & \lambda_1 w_{n-1}(i,j) + w_n(i,j) + \lambda w_{n-1}(i-\theta_{n-1},j) \\ w_n(i+1,j) & = & \lambda_1 w_n(i,j) + \lambda w_n(i-\theta_n,j) \end{array}\right. \tag{47}$$

or

$$\left\{\begin{array}{lcl} w_1(i+1,j) & = & \lambda w_1(i,j) + \lambda_1 w_1(i-\theta_1,j) + w_2(i-\theta_2,j) \\ & \vdots & \\ w_{n-1}(i+1,j) & = & \lambda w_{n-1}(i,j) + \lambda_1 w_{n-1}(i-\theta_{n-1},j) + w_n(i-\theta_n,j) \\ w_n(i+1,j) & = & \lambda_1 w_n(i,j) + \lambda w_n(i-\theta_n,j). \end{array}\right. \tag{48}$$

Then, for given λ and λ_1, the Lagrange solutions

$$\begin{array}{lll} w_1(i,j) = \alpha_1^i, & \cdots, & w_n(i,j) = \alpha_n^i, \\ \alpha_i \neq 0, & |\alpha_i| < 1 & \end{array} \tag{49}$$

to (47) or (48) satisfy

$$\begin{array}{l} (-1)^{n+1}(\alpha_1 - \lambda_1)^n (\alpha_1^{S_{\theta 1}(n,n)})+ \\ (-1)^n \lambda (\alpha_1 - \lambda_1)^{n-1} (\sum_{over\ i} \alpha_1^{S_{\theta i}(n,n-1)})+ \\ \vdots \\ (-1)^2 \lambda^{n-1} (\alpha_1 - \lambda_1)(\sum_{over\ i} \alpha_1^{S_{\theta i}(n,1)})+ \\ (-1)^1 \lambda^n \\ = 0. \end{array} \tag{50}$$

Proof. The claim is shown by means of the mathematical induction on n. Due to the lengthy computations required to get the final result for large n, it is here presented only an outline of the operations. Firstly, consider the set of equations (47) with $n = 2$. Thus

$$\begin{array}{l} \alpha_1^{i+1} = \lambda_1 \alpha_1^i + \alpha_2 + \lambda \alpha_1^{i-\theta_1} \\ \alpha_2^{i+1} = \lambda_1 \alpha_2^i + \lambda \alpha_2^{i-\theta_2} \end{array} \tag{51}$$

hold. Now, substituting the first equation in (51) into the second one leads to

$$\begin{array}{l} \lambda_1(\alpha_1^{i+1} - \lambda_1 \alpha_1^i - \lambda \alpha_1^{i-\theta_1}) + \lambda \alpha_1^{i+1+\theta_2} - \lambda_1 \lambda \alpha_1^{i-\theta_2} \\ -\lambda^2 \alpha_1^{i-\theta_1-\theta_2} - \alpha_1^{i+2} + \lambda_1 \alpha^{i+1} + \lambda \alpha_1^{i-\theta_1+1} = 0 \end{array} \tag{52}$$

and hence

$$-(\alpha_1 - \lambda_1)^2 \alpha_1^{\theta_1+\theta_2} + \lambda(\alpha_1 - \lambda)\alpha_1^{\theta_1-\theta_2)} - \lambda^2 = 0, \tag{53}$$

which is in accordance with (50).
For the case $n = 3$, the following set of equations are obtained.

$$\begin{array}{l} \alpha_2^i = \alpha_1^{i+1} - \lambda_1 \alpha_1^i - \lambda \alpha_1^{i-\theta_1} \\ \alpha_3^i = \alpha_2^{i+1} - \lambda_1 \alpha_2^i - \lambda \alpha_2^{i-\theta_2} \\ \lambda_1 \alpha_3^i + \lambda \alpha_3^{i-\theta_3} - \alpha_3^{i+1} = 0. \end{array} \tag{54}$$

Now, on substituting the first equation in (54) into the second one and further substituting this result into the third equation give

$$\begin{aligned}&(\alpha-\lambda_1)^3\alpha^{\theta_1+\theta_2+\theta_3}-\lambda(\alpha-\lambda_1)^2(\alpha^{\theta_1+\theta_2}+\alpha^{\theta_1+\theta_3}+\alpha^{\theta_2+\theta_3})\\&+\lambda^2(\alpha-\lambda_1)(\alpha^{\theta_1}+\alpha^{\theta_2}+\alpha^{\theta_3})-\lambda^3=0.\end{aligned} \tag{55}$$

Finally, continuing this process mechanically for higher values of n, clearly one establishes the claim of the theorem. □

Remark 11. *Once α_1 is determined by means of (53), α_2 is computed by inserting α_1 into the first equation in (51); and this is the procedure to completely solve the set of difference equations.*

In fact, the results collected in the following claim.

Theorem 7. *Consider the system*

$$\begin{bmatrix} w(i+1,j) \\ v(i,j+1) \end{bmatrix} = \begin{bmatrix} J_{11} & 0 \\ 0 & J_{22} \end{bmatrix} \begin{bmatrix} w(i,j) \\ v(i,j) \end{bmatrix} + \begin{bmatrix} \Lambda & 0 \\ 0 & \Lambda \end{bmatrix} \begin{bmatrix} w(i-\theta,j) \\ v(i,j-\phi) \end{bmatrix}, \tag{56}$$

or

$$\begin{bmatrix} w(i+1,j) \\ v(i,j+1) \end{bmatrix} = \begin{bmatrix} \Lambda & 0 \\ 0 & \Lambda \end{bmatrix} \begin{bmatrix} w(i,j) \\ v(i,j) \end{bmatrix} + \begin{bmatrix} J_{11} & 0 \\ 0 & J_{22} \end{bmatrix} \begin{bmatrix} w(i-\theta,j) \\ v(i,j-\phi) \end{bmatrix} \tag{57}$$

with Jordan matrices J_{11} and J_{22} such that the vectors $w(i,j)$ and $v(i,j)$ are composed by equations as in (47) (or (48)). Then system (56) (or (57)) is asymptotically stable if and only if there exist Lagrange solutions

$$\begin{aligned} &w_s(i,j)=\alpha_s^i, && v_t(i,j)=\beta_t^i, && \forall s,t. \\ &0<|\alpha|<1, && 0<|\beta|<1, && \forall \alpha,\beta. \end{aligned} \tag{58}$$

to the set of equations

$$\begin{aligned}&(-1)^{n+1}(\alpha_1-\lambda_1)^n(\Sigma_{over\ i}\,\alpha_1^{S_{\theta i}(n,n)})+\\&\qquad+\cdots+\\&(-1)^2\lambda^{n-1}(\alpha_1-\lambda_1)(\Sigma_{over\ i}\,\alpha_1^{S_{\theta i}(n,1)})+\\&(-1)^1\lambda^n\\&=0\end{aligned} \tag{59}$$

and

$$\begin{aligned}&(-1)^{n+1}(\beta_1-\lambda_1)^n(\Sigma_{over\ i}\,\beta_1^{S_{\phi i}(n,n)})+\\&\qquad+\cdots+\\&(-1)^2\lambda^{n-1}(\beta_1-\lambda_1)(\Sigma_{over\ i}\,\beta_1^{S_{\phi i}(n,1)})+\\&(-1)^1\lambda^n\\&=0\end{aligned} \tag{60}$$

for given λ_1, λ_2 and λ

Proof. It follows from lemma 3. □

Now, let us investigate a more general type of state space models, which have sub-structures of the following type.

Lemma 4. *Consider the set of equations described by*

$$\left\{\begin{array}{lcl} w_1(i+1,j) & = & \lambda_1 w_1(i,j) + w_2(i,j) + \lambda w_1(i-\theta_1,j) \\ & \vdots & \\ w_n(i+1,j) & = & \lambda_1 w_n(i,j) + v_1(i,j) + \lambda w_n(i-\theta_2,j) \\ v_1(i,j+1) & = & \lambda_1 v_1(i,j) + v_2(i,j) + \lambda v_1(i,j-\phi_1) \\ & \vdots & \\ v_m(i,j+1) & = & \lambda_1 v_m(i,j) + \lambda v_m(i,j-\phi_2) \end{array}\right. \tag{61}$$

or

$$\left\{\begin{array}{lcl} w_1(i+1,j) & = & \lambda w_1(i,j) + \lambda_1 w_1(i-\theta_1,j) + w_2(i-\theta_2,j) \\ & \vdots & \\ w_n(i+1,j) & = & \lambda w_n(i,j) + \lambda_1 w_n(i-\theta_n,j) + v_1(i,j-\phi_1) \\ v_1(i,j+1) & = & \lambda v_1(i,j) + \lambda_1 v_1(i,j-\phi_1) + v_2(i,j-\phi_2) \\ & \vdots & \\ v_m(i,j+1) & = & \lambda v_m(i,j) + \lambda_1 v_m(i,j-\phi_m). \end{array}\right. \tag{62}$$

Then the Lagrange solutions

$$\begin{array}{ll} w_1(i,j) = \alpha_1^i \beta_1^j, & w_2(i,j) = \alpha_2^i \beta_2^j, \\ v_1(i,j) = \gamma_1^i \delta_1^i, & v_2(i,j) = \gamma_2^i \delta_2^i. \end{array} \tag{63}$$

to either (61) or (63) satisfy

$$\begin{array}{l} \mathcal{A}(\alpha,\lambda,\lambda_1) = \\ \qquad (-1)^n(\alpha_1-\lambda_1)^n(\sum_{over\ i}\alpha_1^{S_{\theta i}(n,n)})+ \\ \qquad \vdots \\ \qquad (-1)^1\lambda^{n-1}(\alpha_1-\lambda_1)(\sum_{over\ i}\alpha_1^{S_{\theta i}(n,1)})+ \\ \qquad (-1)\lambda^n \\ = 0, \text{ for } \ n>1 \end{array} \tag{64}$$

$$\mathcal{A}(\alpha,\lambda,\lambda_1) = 1, \quad \text{for } n>1$$

and

$$\begin{array}{l} \mathcal{B}(\beta,\lambda,\lambda_1) = \\ \qquad (-1)^m(\beta_1-\lambda_1)^m(\sum_{over\ i}\beta_1^{S_{\phi i}(m,m)})+ \\ \qquad \vdots \\ \qquad (-1)^1\lambda^{m-1}(\beta_1-\lambda_1)(\sum_{over\ i}\beta_1^{S_{\phi i}(m,1)})+ \\ \qquad (-1)\lambda^m \\ = 0 \end{array} \tag{65}$$

which yield α_1's and β_1's, and from which the other solutions are derived.

Proof. The result is obtained by means of the mathematical induction. As in the previous case, only a rough sketch of the computations is presented here.
Thus, in the very simple case for (61) with $n = m = 1$, the following system of difference equations

$$\begin{cases} \alpha^{i+1}\beta^j - \lambda_1\alpha^i\beta^j - \lambda\alpha^{i-\theta}\beta^j = \gamma^i\delta^j \\ \gamma^i\delta^{j+1} - \lambda_1\gamma^i\delta^j - \lambda\gamma^i\delta^{j-\phi} = 0 \end{cases} \tag{66}$$

render

$$\gamma^i\delta^j = \alpha^{i+1}\beta^j - \lambda_1\alpha^i\beta^j - \lambda\alpha^{i-\theta}\beta^j \tag{67}$$

and

$$\beta^{\phi+1} - \lambda_1\beta^{\phi} - \lambda = 0, \tag{68}$$

which give the assertion of the theorem.
Furthermore, for the case $n = m = 2$, the following set of equations holds.

$$\begin{array}{l} \alpha_2^i\beta_2^j = \alpha_1^{i+1}\beta_1^j - \lambda_1\alpha_1^i\beta_1^j - \lambda\alpha_1^{i-\theta_1}\beta_1^j, \\ \gamma_1^i\delta_1^j = \alpha_2^{i+1}\beta_2^j - \lambda_1\alpha_2^i\beta_2^j - \lambda\alpha_2^{i-\theta_2}\beta_2^j, \\ \gamma_2^i\delta_2^j = \gamma_1^i\delta_1^{j+1} - \lambda_1\gamma_1^i\delta_1^j - \lambda\gamma_1^i\delta_1^{j-\phi_1}, \\ \lambda_1\gamma_2^i\delta_2^j + \lambda\gamma_2^i\delta_2^{j-\phi_2} - \gamma_2^i\delta_2^{j+1} = 0. \end{array} \tag{69}$$

Thus, the first two equations in (69) yield

$$\begin{array}{rl} \gamma_1^i\delta_1^j = & \alpha_2^{i+2}\beta_2^j - (\lambda+\lambda_1)\alpha_2^{i+1}\beta_2^j - \lambda\alpha_2^{i-\theta_1+1}\beta_2^j \\ & +\lambda_1^2\alpha_2^i\beta_2^j + \lambda_1\lambda\alpha_2^{i-\theta_1}\beta_2^j - \lambda\alpha_2^{i-\theta_2+1}\beta_2^j \\ & +\lambda\lambda_1\alpha_2^{i-\theta_2}\beta_2^j + \lambda^2\alpha_2^{i-\theta_1-\theta_2}\beta_2^j. \end{array} \tag{70}$$

Hence, on substituting this into the third equation in (69), and this result into the fourth equation in (69) produce

$$\begin{array}{l} \alpha_1^{\theta_1+\theta_1+2}\mathcal{B}(\beta_1,\lambda,\lambda_1) - \alpha_1^{\theta_1+\theta_2+1}\{\lambda\mathcal{B}(\beta_1,\lambda,\lambda_1) - \lambda_1\mathcal{B}(\beta_1,\lambda,\lambda_1)\} \\ +\alpha_1^{\theta_1+\theta_2}\lambda_1^2\mathcal{B}(\beta_1,\lambda,\lambda_1) - \alpha_1^{\theta_1+1}\lambda\mathcal{B}(\beta_1,\lambda,\lambda_1) + \alpha_1^{\theta_1}\lambda\mathcal{B}(\beta_1,\lambda,\lambda_1) \\ -\alpha_1^{\theta_2+1}\lambda\mathcal{B}(\beta_1,\lambda,\lambda_1) + \alpha_1^{\theta_2}\lambda\mathcal{B}(\beta_1,\lambda,\lambda_1) + \lambda^2\mathcal{B}(\beta_1,\lambda,\lambda_1) \\ = 0, \end{array} \tag{71}$$

which reduces to

$$\mathcal{A}(\alpha_1,\lambda,\lambda_1)\mathcal{B}(\beta_1,\lambda,\lambda_1) = 0, \tag{72}$$

with $\mathcal{A}(\alpha_1,\lambda,\lambda_1)$ and $\mathcal{B}(\beta_1,\lambda,\lambda_1)$ as stated in (64). □

Finally, on putting all the results so far together gives.

Theorem 8. *Consider the system*

$$\begin{bmatrix} w(i+1,j) \\ z(i+1,j+1) \\ v(i,j+1) \end{bmatrix} = \begin{bmatrix} J_1 & 0 & 0 \\ 0 & J_{12} & 0 \\ 0 & 0 & J_2 \end{bmatrix} \begin{bmatrix} w(i,j) \\ z(i,j) \\ v(i,j) \end{bmatrix} + \begin{bmatrix} \Lambda & 0 & 0 \\ 0 & \Lambda & 0 \\ 0 & 0 & \Lambda \end{bmatrix} \begin{bmatrix} w(i-\theta_w,j) \\ u(i-\theta_u,j-\phi_u) \\ v(i,j-\phi_v) \end{bmatrix}, \tag{73}$$

or

$$\begin{bmatrix} w(i+1,j) \\ z(i+1,j+1) \\ v(i,j+1) \end{bmatrix} = \begin{bmatrix} \Lambda & 0 & 0 \\ 0 & \Lambda & 0 \\ 0 & 0 & \Lambda \end{bmatrix} \begin{bmatrix} w(i,j) \\ z(i,j) \\ v(i,j) \end{bmatrix} + \begin{bmatrix} J_1 & 0 & 0 \\ 0 & J_{12} & 0 \\ 0 & 0 & J_2 \end{bmatrix} \begin{bmatrix} w(i-\theta_w,j) \\ u(i-\theta_u,j-\phi_u) \\ v(i,j-\phi_v) \end{bmatrix}, \tag{74}$$

where $w(i,j)$, $z(i,j)$, $v(i,j)$ are subsystems as in lemma 3 and 4; J_1, J_{12} and J_2 are Jordan matrices with eigenvalues λ_1, λ_{12} and λ_2 respectively, and Λ is a diagonal matrix. Then the system is asymptotically stable if and only if there exist non-null $\lambda_\star$ $(\forall\star)$, λ $(|\lambda| < 1)$, and α's $(|\alpha| < 1)$ such that the solutions to (64) and (65) are Lagrange solutions vanishing as the indices increase.

5. Illustrative Example

In this section, a simple example is presented to show how the procedure described so far works. For this purpose, consider the system model described by the following system of difference equations

$$\begin{bmatrix} x_1(i+1,j) \\ x_2(i+1,j) \\ x_3(i,j+1) \end{bmatrix} = \begin{bmatrix} 0.825 & 0.222 & 0.623 \\ -1.850 & -0.207 & -1.455 \\ 0.050 & -0.102 & 0.082 \end{bmatrix} \begin{bmatrix} x_1(i,j) \\ x_2(i,j) \\ x_3(i,j) \end{bmatrix} + \begin{bmatrix} 0.181 & -0.014 & -0.041 \\ -0.489 & 0.147 & 0.118 \\ 0.170 & 0.049 & 0.273 \end{bmatrix} \begin{bmatrix} x_1(i-1,j) \\ x_2(i-1,j) \\ x_3(i,j-1) \end{bmatrix}, \tag{75}$$

which is assumed, in order to focus only on the essence of the work, to be the feedback control system originated by the means of pole assignment method.

Thus, hereafter the aim is to check whether the feedback control system is asymptotically stable.

For this, note that that a matrix composed by the eigenvectors of the second matrix on the right hand side of (75) is given by

$$T = \begin{bmatrix} 1.000 & 0.100 & 0.400 \\ 1.000 & 0.200 & 0.100 \\ 0.200 & 0.300 & 1.000 \end{bmatrix}. \tag{76}$$

Thus, the similarity transformation of (75) by means of (76) leads to

$$\begin{bmatrix} y_1(i+1,j) \\ y_2(i+1,j) \\ y_3(i,j+1) \end{bmatrix} = \begin{bmatrix} 0.500 & 0.100 & 0.300 \\ 0.000 & 0.400 & 0.300 \\ 0.000 & -0.300 & -0.200 \end{bmatrix} \begin{bmatrix} y_1(i,j) \\ y_2(i,j) \\ y_3(i,j) \end{bmatrix} + \begin{bmatrix} 0.200 & 0.000 & 0.000 \\ 0.000 & 0.100 & 0.000 \\ 0.000 & 0.000 & 0.300 \end{bmatrix} \begin{bmatrix} y_1(i-1,j) \\ y_2(i-1,j) \\ y_3(i,j-1) \end{bmatrix}. \tag{77}$$

Now, since a matrix composed by the eigenvectors of the first matrix on the right hand side of (77) is given by

$$\bar{T} = \begin{bmatrix} 1.000 & 0.500 & 0.833 \\ 0.000 & 1.000 & 3.333 \\ 0.000 & -1.000 & 0.000 \end{bmatrix}, \tag{78}$$

apply the similarity transformation on (77), but considering the entries of the second matrix set all to the maximum singular values. Thus, the system turns into

$$\begin{bmatrix} z_1(i+1,j) \\ z_2(i+1,j) \\ z_3(i,j+1) \end{bmatrix} = \begin{bmatrix} 0.500 & 0.000 & 0.000 \\ 0.000 & 0.100 & 1.000 \\ 0.000 & 0.000 & 0.100 \end{bmatrix} \begin{bmatrix} z_1(i,j) \\ z_2(i,j) \\ z_3(i,j) \end{bmatrix} + \begin{bmatrix} 0.300 & 0.000 & 0.000 \\ 0.000 & 0.300 & 0.000 \\ 0.000 & 0.000 & 0.300 \end{bmatrix} \begin{bmatrix} z_1(i-1,j) \\ z_2(i-1,j) \\ z_3(i,j-1) \end{bmatrix}. \tag{79}$$

Thus, the first difference equation

$$z_1(i+1,j) - 0.5z_1(i,j) - 0.3z_1(i-1,j) = 0, \tag{80}$$

gives

$$z_1(i,j) \in \{(0.852)^i, (-0.352)^i\}. \tag{81}$$

On the other hand, the second and third vector terms in (79)

$$\begin{aligned} z_3(i,j) &= z_2(i+1,j) - 0.1z_1(i,j) - 0.3z_1(i-1,j), \\ z_3(i,j+1) &- 0.1z_3(i,j) - 0.3z_3(i,j-1) = 0 \end{aligned} \tag{82}$$

yield

$$\begin{aligned} z_2(i,j) \in \{&(-0.500)^i(-0.500)^j, (-0.500)^i(0.600)^j, \\ &(0.600)^i(-0.500)^j, (0.600)^i(0.600)^j\}, \end{aligned} \tag{83}$$

from which the solutions $z_3(i,j)$ can be easily computed by using the first equation in (82). Finally, to complete the stability analysis, one should repeat the computations so far for system (79) with the first diagonal matrix replaced by a matrix with minimum value. However, due to the fact that the all diagonal entries are less than unit, let us to conclude that the system (75) is asymptotically stable.

6. Final Remarks

This work investigated indirectly the conditions for 2-d discrete control systems with delays to be asymptotically stable when interconnected by feedback control laws. The point key point is the stability analysis is accomplish on the basis of the doubly similarity approach. Moreover, unlike the related investigations so far, the analysis procedure is not split into delay dependent and independent cases, because the delay elements appear naturally as the degrees of the polynomials that one has to solve in order to obtain the solutions to the doubly transformed systems. Finally, an example was presented to show the procedures obtained.

7. References

Bachelier O., Bosche J. & Mehdi D. (2006). On pole placement via eigenstructure assignment approach. *IEEE TAC*, Vol. 51, No. 9, 2006, -1554 – -1558

Bose N. K. (1982). *Applied multdimensional systems theory*, Van Nostradand Reinhold Co., England.

Boyd S., Ghaoui L. E., Feron E. & V. Balakrishnan (1994). *Linear Matrix Inequalities in System and Control Theory*, Society for Industrial and Applied Mathematics (SIAM)-V.15 of Studies in Applied Mathematics, Philadelphia, USA.

Chen C.T. (1999). *Linear systems theory and design*, Oxford University Press, New York.

Du C.& Xie L. (2002). *H-infinity control and filtering of two-dimensional systems*, Springer Verlag, Berlin.

Fornasini E. & Marchesini G. (1978). Doubly indexed dynamical systems: State space models and structural properties. *Math. Syst. Th.*, Vol. 12, 1978, -59 – -72

Gantmatcher F.R. (1959). *The Theory of matrices*, Chelsea, New York.

Givone D.D. & Roesser R.P. (1997). Multidimensional linear iterative circuits - General properties. *IEEE Trans. Comp.*, Vol. C, No. 21, 1972, -1067 – -1073

Izuta G. (2007). Stability and disturbance attenuation of 2-d discrete delayed systems via memory state feedback controller. *Int. J. Gen. Systems*, Vol. 36, No. 3, 2007, -263 – -280

Izuta G. (2007). 2-d Discrete Linear Control Systems with Multiple Delays in the Inputs and Outputs on the Basis of Observer Controllers. *WSEAS trans. systems*, Vol. 16, No. 1, 2007, -9 – -17

Jerri A.J. (1996). *Linear difference equations with discrete transform methods*, Kluwer Acad. Pub., Netherlands.

Kaczorek T. (1985). *Two-dimensional linear systems*, Springer Verlag, Berlin.

Kailath T. (1980). *Linear Systems*, Prentice Hall, New York.

Kawamata M. & Higuchi T. (1995). *Multidimensional Digital Signal Processing (in Japanese)*, Asakura Shoten, Tokyo.

Kodama S.& Suda N. (1978). *Matrix Theory for Control Systems (in Japanese)*, SICE, Tokyo.

Levenstein H. (1958). Theory of networks of linearly variable resistences. *Proceedings of IRE*, Vol. 46, 1958-Feb, -486 – -493

Lim J.S. (1990). *Two-dimensional linear signal and image processing*, Prentice Hall, New Jersey.

Ozaki H. & Kasami T. (1960). Positive real functions of several variables and their applications to variable networks. *Proceedings of IRE*, Vol. 7, 1960, -251 – -260

Pazke W., Lam J., Galkowski K. & S. Xu (2004). Robust stability and stabilisation of 2D discrete state-delayed systems. *Systems and Control Letters*, Vol. 51, No. 3 – 4, 2004, -277 – -291

Syrmos V.L., Abdallah C.T., Dorato P. & Grigoriadis K. (1997). Static output feedback - a survey. *Automatica*, Vol. 33, No. 2, 1997, -125 – -137